Your Money or Your Life

Your Money
[or]
Your Life

THE TYRANNY OF GLOBAL FINANCE

UPDATED EDITION

Eric Toussaint

Translated by Vicki Briault Manus
In collaboration with Raghu Krishnan and Gabrielle Roche

CHICAGO, ILLINOIS

First published in French by the CADTM (Belgium), CETIM (Switzerland), Editions Luc Pire (Belgium), and Editions Syllepse (France), in 1998,
as *La bourse ou la vie : La finance contre les peuples*

First English language edition published in 1999 by Pluto Press

This updated edition published in 2005 by Haymarket Books
PO Box 180165, Chicago IL 60618
www.haymarketbooks.org

Cover design by Eric Ruder
Inside design by David Whitehouse; help with figures from Sarah Macaraeg

Library of Congress Cataloging-in-Publication Data
Toussaint, Eric.
[Bourse ou la vie. English]
Your money or your life : the tyranny of global finance / Eric Toussaint ;
translated by Vicki Briault Manus, in collaboration with Raghu Krishnan.--
3rd ed.
    p. cm.
Includes bibliographical references and index.
ISBN-13: 978-1-931859-18-9 (13 digit)
ISBN-10: 1-931859-18-3 (10 digit)
1. Debts, External--Developing countries. 2. International Monetary
Fund--Developing countries. I. Title.
HJ8899.T6813 2005
336.3'435'091724--dc22

                                    2005015963

Printed in Canada

Contents

Dedication

This work is dedicated to my parents, José Toussaint (1920–1997) and Rose Clermont Toussaint (1923–2002); to Ernest Mandel (1923–1995), Marxist activist in word and deed; to the admirable struggle for public goods of the Bolivian people; to Sémira Adamu, murdered by the Belgian police, which had been ordered to deport her by force when she was seeking asylum in Belgium; to Yaguine and Fodé, the two Guinean adolescent castaways who froze to death in an airplane's landing-carriage while trying to reach Europe, where they hoped to study; to all those men and women fighting for their emancipation.

Acknowledgements

My heartfelt thanks to Denise Comanne and Damien Millet without whom this work would not have been possible.

I also wish to thank the following people for their help, their criticism and their encouragement, understanding and patience: Danielle Alvernhe and Pierre Caron (ATTAC Sud Lubéron and CADTM), Jacques Bournay (INSEE), Yannick Bovy (CADTM Brussels), Vicki Briault Manus (CADTM-Isère, University of Grenoble), Pierre Cours-Saliès (University of Paris VIII), Martin Erpicum, Jean-Marie Haribey (Montesquieu University at Bordeaux), Michel Husson (IRES), Bruno and Nadji Linhares (Brazil), Dalhia Luksenburg, Christine Pagnoulle (University of Liège), Hugo Ruiz Diaz (CADTM Liège), Bernard Teissier (CADTM Lyons), Juan Tortosa (CADTM Geneva), Tristan and Ivan Toussaint, Arnaud Zacharie (CNCD), the friends of the CADTM's international network in Niger, Mali, Senegal, Congo-Brazzaville, Democratic Republic of Congo, Burkina Faso, Ivory Coast, Tunisia, Algeria, Morocco, Colombia,…and the whole CADTM team.

Translator's acknowledgements

This translation was done free of charge as an act of solidarity with the populations struggling under the burden of debt. As well as Raghu Krishnan for his translation of the first edition and Gabrielle Roche who patiently compared the English and French texts from beginning to end, I would also like to thank the people who kindly agreed to put their competence to the service of rereading a chapter or two: Colin Anderson, Elizabeth Anne, Madhu Benoît, Susan Blattès, Alex Briault, Claire Briault, Anita Budisa, Dan Hirst, Richard Trim, Christine Vandamme, David Voas, Sheila and Philip Whittick, James Underhill, Jonathan Upjohn. Neither they nor I are responsible for modifications subsequently made to the British text by the publishers in adapting it for American readers.

Vicki Briault Manus, translator.

Preface to the 2005 edition

From 2001 to 2005, policies decided in Washington and Peking dominated the world economy. Authorities in Washington combated the economic crisis in the United States by instituting policies to boost the economy: a radical drop in interest rates (to negative levels in real terms, which allowed American households to continue to accumulate debt in order to maintain consumption levels, and allowed businesses to get out of debt), fiscal reform that favored consumption and the accumulation of wealth, a drastic increase in the state deficit, and the invasion of Afghanistan and Iraq to bolster the military-industrial complex. China's entry into the World Trade Organization (WTO) in 2001 and its opening to foreign investments reinforced its role as a large capitalist workshop exploiting an abundant labor force that was underpaid, disciplined, and educated. China did not engage in international competition by dropping all barriers, however: its currency is unconvertible and tied to a dollar whose value is dropping (which increases China's competitive edge in foreign markets), it maintains control over the movement of capital in and out of its borders, its domestic market enjoys continued protection, and foreign investors cannot take control of any and all sectors (the Chinese banking sector remains public and Chinese).

Washington's decision to lower interest rates addressed domestic policy problems. This decision had international ramifications: it lightened the load with regard to debt repayment for developing countries with access to financial markets (approximately twenty-five countries, including China, Russia, Brazil, Mexico, Venezuela, Southeast Asian countries, South Korea, and South Africa). While the risk premiums (the spread) paid by developing countries for access to private capital in the form of loans were unusually high between 1998 and 2000, they began to fall beginning in 2001. From 2004 to 2005, they reached a record low.

Various factors that I will not analyze here brought about a sharp increase in oil prices in 2003–04. China's sustained growth was like a breath of fresh air for a suffocating world market: the price of most raw materials (iron, copper, nickel, combustibles) and semi-finished goods (steel) climbed sharply in 2003, 2004, and 2005. China won considerable shares of the market on a world scale (going from 2.5 percent in 2000 to 5.4 percent in 2004). The foreign exchange reserves of 101 developing countries increased greatly. The combination of low interest rates, lowered risk premiums, and rising raw material prices produced a sharp increase in the foreign exchange reserves of developing countries, which rose to $1.6 trillion at the end of 2004—a level never reached before and greater than the total external public debt of all developing countries![1]

The increase in the main developing countries' solvency (more than $200 billion in new debt between 2002 and 2004) allowed them to increase their indebtedness by issuing public and private bonds on financial markets in the North. Although some developing countries partially reduced their external debt (Russia and Venezuela, for example), others continue to increase their debt greatly (Brazil, Mexico, and Argentina after the conclusion of negotiations with its creditors). All or nearly all are increasing their internal public debt.

The current situation presents an unusual opportunity for the governments of developing countries to modify their situation substantially or even radically. It is possible to get out of debt. China alone, with $600 billion of foreign exchange reserves could change the international situation in favor of developing countries, if its autocratic government wanted to. What if there existed a united Chinese-Russian front against the governments of the major industrialized nations? These two countries could stack the deck on the world scale if they had an alternative project in common. The governments of a considerable number of developing countries spread over four continents (Asia, Latin America, Africa, and Eastern Europe—if you include Russia, as the IMF and World Bank do) temporarily hold the key to change. On a global level, they are net creditors to the main world superpower and private banks of the North. Theoretically, they could completely do without the IMF by repaying what they still owe. They could create a support fund for those developing countries that have less hard currency than they do (beginning with the fifty least developed countries), enabling them to rapidly get out of debt (the total amount necessary to eliminate their debt is quite low).

Never before has the situation been as advantageous for the periphery from a financial standpoint. Yet, no one is talking about changing the rules. The governments of China, Russia, and the main developing countries (India, Brazil,

Nigeria, Indonesia, Mexico, South Africa…) do not express any intention of changing the world situation in practice in favor of the people. Yet, politically, if they wanted to, these governments could constitute a powerful movement capable of imposing fundamental democratic reforms on the entire multilateral system, fifty years after Bandung. They could adopt moderate policies—a planned repayment of debts with a below par rating—or radical policies—repudiate the debt and institute a series of policies that break with neoliberalism. The international situation is in their favor because the main world superpower is bogged down in the war in Iraq and the occupation of Afghanistan, and is confronted by strong resistance in Latin America that is leading to bitter defeats (in Venezuela, Cuba, Ecuador…) or to an impasse (in Colombia).

I am persuaded, however, that this will not materialize; neither the moderate nor the radical scenario will be put in place in the short term. The overwhelming majority of the current leaders of the developing countries are totally caught up in the neoliberal model. In the majority of cases, they are completely tied to the interests of local ruling classes that have no perspective for distancing themselves concretely from (not to mention breaking with) the policies followed by the major industrial powers. Capitalists in the South confine themselves to a rentier behavior and when they do not, they try at most to capture market shares. This is the case with Brazilian, South Korean, Russian, South African, Indian, and other capitalists, who ask that their governments exact this or that concession from the most industrialized nations in the context of bilateral or multilateral commercial negotiations. In addition, competition and conflicts between developing countries' governments are real and can get worse. The commercial aggression of Chinese, Russian, and Brazilian capitalists with regard to their competitors in the South is causing tenacious divisions.

Only the irruption of the people on the stage of history could change the course of things, but there is as yet no solid indication pointing in this direction. There has been a succession of radical struggles in the developing countries in recent years: Ecuador and Bolivia in 2000, Argentina in 2001–02, Venezuela in 2002–03, Bolivia in 2003, China in 2004, South Korea in 2003–04, Bolivia in 2005, Nigeria in 2004–05, Niger in 2005, not to mention liberation struggles and resistance to occupation from Palestine to Afghanistan to Iraq. Those participating in these struggles have demonstrated extraordinary courage. Some of their struggles have been partly successful (Ecuador, Bolivia, Argentina, Venezuela, Niger…), but they have not gone beyond local or national boundaries. Although the antiglobalization and antiwar movements, the World Social Forum, continental social forums, the campaigns for debt cancellation and against the WTO continue to grow, they are unfortunately not (yet?) in a position to unite these struggles and put forward an offensive strategy for doing away with neoliberalism.

Besides, the current situation, temporarily favorable to developing countries, is at risk of changing in 2006–07. Two basic factors can intervene in a globally unfavorable way: first, a continuation of the rise in interest rates started by the United States in June 2004; second, a decrease in demand in the United States that would have repercussions in China and, from there, in the rest of the world (assuming no boost in European or Japanese demand), leading to a drop in the price of raw materials. A rise in interest rates combined with a drop in the price of raw materials occurred between 1979 and 1982, and triggered the debt crisis of 1982. If the rise in interest rates is sharp, if the price of raw materials begins to drop, and if a number of deeply indebted developing countries such as Brazil, Turkey, Mexico, Argentina (once more), and Nigeria experience difficulties in paying, it is not impossible to see a new crisis erupt in a synchronized way.

The current, unusual situation illustrates the impasse that the neoliberal model represents for people of the South. According to the dominant economic theory, development of the South has been delayed due to insufficient domestic capital (insufficient local savings). Also according to this theory, countries wishing to undertake or accelerate development must appeal to external capital in three ways: first, by taking on external debt; second, by attracting foreign investments; third, by increasing exports in order to procure the hard currency necessary to buy foreign goods that facilitate growth. The poorest countries are also supposed to behave themselves, like good students of the developed countries, to attract grants. However, reality contradicts theory: developing countries supply capital to the most industrialized nations, to the US economy in particular. The World Bank does not deny this: "Developing countries, in aggregate, were net lenders to developed countries" (World Bank 2003a, 13), and "Developing countries are now capital exporters to the rest of the world" (World Bank 2005, 56).

It is not true that developing countries only have recourse to debt to finance their development. Today, recourse to loans essentially serves to ensure the continuation of repayments. In spite of the existence of significant foreign exchange reserves, governments and local ruling classes in the South are not increasing investment and social expenditures—with one exception: the government of Venezuela that is in opposition to local ruling classes and to US and European Union imperialism. Sooner or later, the people will free themselves from debt slavery and from the oppression carried out by the ruling classes in the North and the South. Through their struggles, they will win the implementation of policies that redistribute wealth and put an end to the productivist model that is destroying nature. Then, public powers will be forced to give absolute priority to the satisfaction of fundamental human rights.

Eric Toussaint
Liege, Belgium
June 7, 2005
(translated by Sophie Hand)

---

1   *Source*: World Bank, *Global Development Finance 2005*, p. 165. At the end of 2004, developing countries had approximately $1.6 trillion at their disposal in the form of foreign exchange reserves ($1.591 trillion)—more than the total of their external public debt ($1.555 trillion, see p. 161). China, Malaysia, Thailand, India, and South Korea have foreign exchange reserves greater than their external public debt. As a whole, developing countries in Asia have foreign exchange reserves that are more than double the amount of their external public debt (or 30 percent more than the sum total of their public and private external debt—see tables on pp. 161 and 165). China's reserves alone constitute more than seven times its external public debt. For North Africa and East Asia, the foreign exchange reserves are as high as $141 billion while the external public debt is up to $127 billion. Algeria's reserves are as high as $41 billion against an external public debt of $27 billion.

Foreword

Contemporary history can be described as the conquest of the world by an ever-smaller number of huge conglomerates organized into multinational corporations. These corporations are engaged in a permanent war with one another to control markets with the shared aim of subordinating all human endeavor to the logic of private profit.

While the processes of capital accumulation and concentration have long been with us, in recent times they have been dramatically accelerated due to a number of technological upheavals. Thanks to the transformation of data storage, processing, and transmission techniques—computing, robotics, telecommunications—for the first time in the history of human civilization it is possible to pursue planetary strategies in real time. In other words, it is possible from a given location to track and evaluate continuously the application of decisions anywhere else on the planet—and to adapt the content, location, operating conditions, and outputs of any type of activity accordingly.

The effect of this technological revolution has been amplified by two other upheavals, of a political nature.

The first is the challenge by multinational companies—in the name of "freedom"—to the sovereignty of governments and their regulatory role. This is especially the case in the fields of the economy (currency, exchange, customs, interest rates, capital flows, monetary policy, taxation and fiscal policy, the public sector) and social policy (social programs and labor laws, from the minimum wage to family benefits, and also trade-union rights, pension plans, health care, and education). This challenge has been legitimized by a particularly aggressive brand of liberal ideology, and backed by the full weight of those who hold the reins of economic and cultural power. No effort is spared to promote the idea that private initiative is superior to public intervention, contrasting the efficiency and profitability of the former to the incompetence and wastefulness of the latter. Or the idea that humans naturally prefer private initiative over collective solidarity. Or the need to limit the state and government to the sole task of upholding law and order, social control and the defense of personal safety and private property. While this ideological campaign never tires of insisting that a free country is one in which there is freedom to do business, it remains curiously silent about the permanent collusion between the state apparatus and big business lobbies. It has, however, led to the implementation of policies of systematic deregulation that seek to fulfill two wide-ranging objectives.

First, there is the objective of progressively establishing—sector by sector—a global space, or rather a world market, in which the only law is that laid down by multinationals to regulate the competition between them, a kind of chivalrous code for economic warfare. The task of drawing up and overseeing such a code, for example, has been devolved to the World Trade Organization (WTO)—a gargantuan organization that renders null and void the legitimacy of national states and governments.

The second objective is providing the best possible opportunity for those with the requisite astronomical wealth—that is to say, the multinational corporations—to take full advantage of the potential created by new technologies. This is especially so in the financial sector—where the split-second transmission of capital and the mushrooming of exchanges, brokerage houses, financial products, and speculative instruments have created a massive financial bubble out of all proportion to economic realities. Between $1.2 trillion and $1.5 trillion are traded each day on the markets, the equivalent of one week of US GNP and sixty times the funds needed to settle actual international transactions in goods and services. This bubble could burst at any time and do irreparable damage, as has already been the case in Mexico and, more recently, in Southeast Asia. This financial bubble is the scene of the hottest investments and the most risky speculative operations; it is also the destination of choice for a significant proportion of the savings deposited in mutual and pension funds, and for the liquid assets of banks and companies.

The second political upheaval was the fall of the Berlin Wall in December 1989, an event symbolic of the collapse through implosion of the bloc of socialist countries led by the Soviet Union. It was also symbolic of the disappearance of an economic and political system that put itself forward as the historic alternative to an increasingly unpopular capitalism. The socialist sphere of influence put up no resistance and displayed a kind of greed-induced naïveté; it was quickly conquered by the Western free-market democracy model. This has not been the case for a handful of countries in the process of rapid transformation (such as Vietnam) or reduced to decrepit museums of a long-gone era (such as North Korea). Nor has it been the case for China, which intends to retain its political autonomy behind a wall of market socialism in which there is a great deal more market than socialism. The triumph of capitalism resulting from the disintegration of its archrival put an end to the East-West conflict, which had overdetermined international relations and the fate of peoples and nations for some fifty years. This triumph also put an end to the "Third World," a term used to describe the often risky attempt by countries of the South as a whole to use the superpower conflict as a means to protect their economic and political independence. Above all else, this capitalist triumph over the Soviet Bloc has confirmed the historic defeat of the working classes and the world proletariat. Henceforth, they will be condemned to limitless exploitation by a brutal and arrogant capitalism that, at long last, has been delivered from its age-old fear of world revolution.

This is the state of affairs as we embark upon an era in which the world's new masters seek to establish a universal totalitarianism. Indeed, this is the only possible way for the handful of all-powerful economic warlords, who will soon own most of the planet, to perpetuate their domination over many billions of victims. The progressive establishment of this new order is being carried out in three main areas.

In the first place, there is the near-monopoly of the ideology of the ruling classes and of the neoliberal discourse that legitimizes their rule. Whether the printed press, radio and TV, publishing, academic institutions, think tanks, or talks and seminars, little in the field of the production and dissemination of mainstream ideas is not directly or indirectly controlled by those in positions of wealth and power. The scope for manipulation provided by the mass media, their potential for "manufacturing consent" and adapting their message to each audience, gives them unlimited possibilities for subjecting ever-greater sectors of the population to their influence, especially those most likely to become their victims. Fewer and fewer people have the wherewithal to extricate themselves from the dominant discourse. An overwhelming majority of intellectuals has been won to the new dominant ideology. Before, the intelligentsia were mobilized in opposition to the Establishment; now they have become its well-paid guard dogs. A veritable caste of arrogant and cynical intellectuals has emerged to defend the liberal faith, to declare the "end of history," to hunt down and burn at the stake all those who dare contest the new doctrine. They monopolize the written and spoken word, recite the free-market mantra, and pull economic "miracles" out of thin air. These new theologians and dedicated scientists of the liberal faith do not hesitate to falsify history to erase anything that might contradict their regurgitated "truths," nor do they balk at manipulating statistics to give their pontificating a scientific gloss. In this, they have continued a proud tradition of totalitarian practices that began with the nationalist bourgeoisies and was perpetuated by fascist and socialist regimes. From a very young age, children are enrolled in the economic war, put forward as the unavoidable choice between life and death—both at school and in their sporting activities, where each is pitted against all and where victors and the powerful are praised and losers and the weak are contemptuously dismissed. For all this, however, no attempt is made to pinpoint the exact purpose of this indefinite and perpetual war of the kind described by George Orwell in *1984*. The war's objectives, one's allies, and one's conquests are ephemeral, in a constant state of flux.

Second, there is the attempt to submit the whole of human activity to the market order and the rule of profit. No sphere can escape this process, neither the protection of privacy, nor the right to breathe unpolluted air, nor the use of human genes. Everything can become a commodity, including spirituality, and enter the circuits of capital in order to be made profitable. The goal is that of granting capital totalitarian control over human and biological life and development. This shameful pillage of humanity's collective inheritance has necessarily been accompanied by wide-ranging and growing criminalization. While the old order has been destroyed and the rules governing relations between states and between states and multinationals are no longer effective, the resulting vacuum has not been filled by a new set of rules and corresponding sanctions for the new order. Brutal competition between the various economic warlords has, instead, been greased by generalized corruption. Not a single country, not a single market, remains untouched. Not a single oil contract, public works project or arms deal, not a single significant market study or supply of goods or services, nothing takes place without payment of commission along a complex and variable set of guidelines in which all concerned parties become enmeshed. A chain of offshore tax havens encircles the globe, in close proximity to the major North American, European, and Asian powers. Their banks provide the logistical backup and launder misappropriated sums totaling hundreds of billions of dollars. The same network serves to finance the underground economy, in particular drug trafficking. The banking sector is directly involved and makes a handsome profit through this permanent symbiosis between organized crime and the business world—whose natural affinities are legion.

Politics is the third area in which the new order is asserting itself. The obligatory political model has become that of market democracy, in which the legitimacy of government obtained through universal suffrage is subordinate to the sovereignty of markets, always at the ready to punish elected governments. As spaces for the peaceful resolution of social conflicts, political institutions have been reduced to shells of their former selves. They are mere window dressing, keeping up the democratic illusion in governments that are less and less so. Behind this façade of virtual democracy, ever more sophisticated techniques of surveillance and social control are developed and tumble into the hands of those holding the reins of capitalist power. Unbeknownst to most citizens, networks of computerized files, accessible to all for a price, encircle their personal and professional lives. There has been a multiplication and growing specialization of public and private police services of all kinds. Cameras monitor public and private venues; computers permanently track people's activities and movements; specialized personnel (social workers, police) monitor and control neighborhood life, communities, and age groups considered to be dangerous or at risk. One day soon they will be electronically (genetically?) tagged and tracked, as is already the case in the world of prisons and crime prevention. Wherever social control seems to be a waste of effort and too costly, vast rural and urban zones and their populations are abandoned to the barbarism of those patchwork and disparate zones of the planet where even the heartless standards of "globalization" do not hold sway.

There is, however, nothing inevitable about this process of globalization and the establishment of a totalitarian universe. The destruction and hairraising increase in social inequality that result from this process have provoked a large number of pockets of resistance scattered across the globe. Nowhere is it written that the peoples of the planet are somehow predestined to a new form of slavery. Through the course of human history, the aspiration of peoples to freedom and justice has never failed. Of course, no resistance will have long-lasting effects without an awareness of the ways in which the capitalist system operates in the era of globalization and a sound understanding of its sophisticated techniques of domination.

Eric Toussaint has done a commendable job of contributing to the development of just such an awareness and understanding. He has helped us to understand the question of debt, one of the main ways in which the peoples of the world are exploited by those who hold the reins of capitalist power. With the pedagogic approach of someone unflinchingly dedicated to overcoming this exploitation, he places the problem in its proper historical and geopolitical context. In so doing, he has fulfilled his objective of contributing to the emancipation of the oppressed, wheresoever on the planet they may be.

Christian de Brie
Editorial staff member at
Le Monde diplomatique

Introduction

The most urgent task is not to deliver up the poor to the appetites of the wealthy, as do the World Bank and the IMF at the moment, but to preserve for the long term hard-won social and environmental guarantees. Those guarantees should then be spread to all the inhabitants of the planet.

—Albert Jacquard, *J'accuse l'économie triomphante*

A growing number of the planet's inhabitants have access to little more than the strict minimum necessary for survival. Cut off from knowledge and excluded from social life, they are denied the most basic human dignity. Consequently, they lack self-confidence and self-respect, and have little confidence in and respect for others. Such things are difficult to capture statistically, but it is no exaggeration to say that more than a billion people live in such a state—a state that destroys all hope, a subhuman state, an unacceptable state of affairs.

I am haunted by the memory of street children in Cartagena de las Indias in Colombia. At dawn, dressed in rags, after sleeping on the bare ground wrapped in nothing but bits of cardboard, they began their daily search for glue to sniff. They were between the ages of seven and eleven. That was in 1992. These children had no right to food, to decent clothing, to a roof over their heads, to health care, to education, to affection. No rights. They, and thousands like them, had sunk to sniffing glue in order to quell their hunger pangs day and night.

When I bought them something to eat from a stand at the Cartagena docks, they swallowed slowly and with difficulty. Their bodies were used to glue fumes, not food, fumes that both relieve and destroy them. What is the average life expectancy of these children? Twenty years? Twenty-five years? They are known as *desechables* to many in Colombia, a term that usually refers to disposable products. These desechables, these "disposable children," are murdered by the army and police forces of Colombia, Brazil, and the Philippines in order to "clean up" the cities. According to the 1997 report of the United Nations Development Program (UNDP), 200,000 street children live in Brazil. In recent years, police have killed hundreds in the name of "law and order." Moreover, the International Labor Organization calculates that about 250 million children between the ages of five and fourteen worldwide are forced to work to survive (*Le Soir*, November 13, 1996, and February 27, 1997). A significant number of these children become bonded laborers to repay debt (see Bonnet 1996). In the countries of the South and North alike, networks for the sexual abuse of children are regularly uncovered.

No self-respecting human being can remain unmoved by such injustice. We are moved to unite with others to do what we can to put an end to this intolerable situation as quickly as possible.

Barbarism now reigns over a large part of humankind. That does not mean that those who live in such conditions have no desire for a better life. They are not barbarians. Hundreds of millions of people are engaged in daily struggles and have organized themselves in movements to fight for a better world. This book is dedicated to them. Their creativity and their experiences in struggle have strengthened my conviction that emancipation is possible.

Karl Marx declared long ago that the emancipation of the oppressed could be achieved only by the oppressed themselves. Our fundamental objective, wherever we live on the planet, must be to contribute relentlessly to this emancipation.

The book's layout

Below are forty-eight contentions that summarize the bulk of this book. Due to space limitations, the parts devoted to neoliberal ideology, alternatives, and counterinitiatives are not summarized here. A glossary has been included to assist with unfamiliar words, expressions, acronyms, and abbreviations. The works cited in the text or consulted during its writing appear in the bibliography. In the text, whenever material is quoted or reference is made to a work, the author's name, the year the work was published, and, where relevant, the page numbers are given in parentheses. A chronology of the relations between the World Bank/International Monetary Fund (IMF) duo and the Third World also appears.

Any comments, suggestions, or criticisms intended to make the work easier to understand, correct oversights, or rectify errors that escaped the author's attention are welcome.

The contentions of this book

▶ **1.** Since the 1980s, a process of massive impoverishment has occurred worldwide, resulting from a series of deliberate policies collectively referred to as "neoliberalism." This assertion, central to the book, rests on the critical analysis of statistics provided by the UNDP (see glossary) and the World Bank, among others, and observations made by the author during multiple study trips to the Third World, Eastern and Western Europe, and North America (chapter 1).

▶ **2.** Globalization (see glossary) is inseparable from the deregulation of capital markets implemented by the governments of the major economic powers and the multilateral financial institutions at their service (World Bank, IMF, BIS; see glossary) (chapter 1).

▶ **3.** Globalization entails increased financialization (see glossary) of every nation's economy, to the extent that some authors write of the "tyranny" of the financial markets, which significantly reduce the freedom of governments to determine their policies (chapter 4). However, this does not mean that the point of no return has been reached; the financial markets could be brought under control if the political powers so decided.

▶ **4.** Globalization is not a purely economic process. The policies pursued by a growing number of governments, following in the footsteps laid down by Reagan and Thatcher in the early 1980s, have greatly accelerated it. Political leaders have deliberately curtailed possibilities for their governments to intervene (chapters 1 and 5).

▶ **5.** A clear change of direction is needed, where fulfilling human needs is central to government policies. To reach this goal, restrictive measures must be taken against capital holders. The oppressed can become agents for revolutionary change. Corporate-driven globalization is not inescapable, and those who claim otherwise must realize that they, too, can be circumvented (chapters 19 and 20).

▶ **6.** In twenty years of neoliberal policies, economic growth has not attained the levels of the three decades that followed the Second World War. Not only has development slowed, but the neoliberal project depends on increased inequality, both within countries and between the countries of the center and the periphery (chapters 1–4).

▶ **7.** Globalization in its present form entails recentering investments, production, and trade on the three main poles for industry, finance, commerce, and the military, i.e., the Triad of North America, Western Europe, and Japan (chapter 3).

▶ **8.** The Third World and the former Soviet Bloc have been marginalized, with a few exceptions (chapter 3). Within these two regions, where 85 percent of the world population lives, marginalization of the majority of the population is growing, concentrated in the most deprived regions.

▶ **9.** In the countries of the North, a growing minority is excluded from production and resorts to public welfare systems (social security), won through the struggles of the oppressed in the twentieth century, or lives by its wits (chapter 1).

▶ **10.** Globalization in its present phase means opening borders to capital flows and closing the borders of the highly industrialized countries to people from the Third World and the Eastern Bloc (chapters 9 and 13).

▶ **11.** Wealth is produced by human labor and nature. Capital holders are diverting a growing proportion of the surplus produced by human labor to the financial sphere, while the fraction of the surplus they invest in the productive sphere is diminishing. This process cannot continue indefinitely; however, without pressure from below, it could last for some time and cause more frequent and far-reaching financial crashes (chapters 3, 4, and 17).

▶ **12.** Globalization is part of a global offensive of capital against the labor of workers and small producers (chapter 1).

▶ **13.** Globalization accelerates the concentration of capital in the hands of a few hundred companies. Multinational corporations (MNCs) become more powerful, and a state of oligopoly (see glossary) results (chapters 2 and 3). Nevertheless, this process should not be exaggerated. Competition between MNCs is intense and none is in a position to have a global monopoly. Furthermore, MNCs have not shaken themselves free of national states, a clear indication of their limitations. As a rule, they continue to rely on the state of their country of origin, where they make more than half of their total sales (UNCTAD 2000a). Foreign direct investment (FDI; see glossary) increased in volume from $200 billion to $1.1 trillion between 1990 and 2000 . After the sharp slowdown in growth that began in 2001, FDI plummeted. FDI to the periphery is spread unevenly, with five to eight countries receiving more than 50 percent of it each year, while the forty-nine least developed countries (LDC; see glossary) together receive only 0.5 percent. On a global scale, the greater part of FDI (more than 70 percent in 1999 and 2000) was used to buy existing companies in order to strengthen the impact of the MNCs concerned. Acquisitions are often followed by job cuts, factory closures, and the discontinuation of services.

▶ **14.** Unemployment in the North is not due to massive transfers of production from the North to the South or Eastern Europe (chapter 3). The unequivocal results published in two comprehensive National Bureau of Economic Research (NBER) working papers are interesting in this regard. The papers were based on a large sample of US MNCs and their subsidiaries over the ten-year period from 1983–92. In only a marginal number of cases were jobs from the headquarters of companies in industrialized countries replaced by jobs in their Third World subsidiaries. At the same time, substantial movement occurred between the various subsidiary branches. The papers also note that "the rise of investment in countries like Brazil poses a much smaller threat to employment at company headquarters in the USA than it does to employment in the subsidiaries of developing countries in Asia." NBER's meticulous econometricians then compare the different subsidiaries and conclude that "the activities of subsidiaries in developing countries are complementary to, and do not substitute for, the activities of subsidiaries in the developed countries" (Brainard and Riker 1997). Therefore, even between subsidiaries, workers are placed in competition with one another, but only when the subsidiaries are in countries with comparable skill and productivity levels.

▶ **15.** The crisis that shook Southeast Asia—specifically Thailand, Indonesia, the Philippines, and Malaysia—beginning in summer 1997, shows the limitations of a "development" model based on low wages, an open economy, and export-oriented growth that relegates the domestic market. This model goes hand in hand with a tendency to add continually to the trade deficit. As in the 1994 Mexican crisis, the problem is rooted in a fundamental imbalance: imports increase faster than exports due to the imposed relationship of dependency that leads countries to import investment and consumer goods from the rich countries. Exports grow only if wages are kept down to an "attractive" level, because of the competition with subsidiaries in other countries. Growth may be strong, but it is based on an unstable, breakneck race that entails continual distortion of the socioeconomic structure. The total liberalization of capital inflow and outflow puts these economies at the mercy of a sudden massive withdrawal of a large quantity of capital in search of quick profits or a safe haven. Such a capital outflow leaves the governments and companies of the countries involved with an immediate need for liquid assets, and debt rises quickly (chapter 17).

▶ **16.** Beginning in the sixteenth century, the development of international lending has gone hand in hand with the international expansion of European capitalism (chapter 6).

▶ **17.** At the end of the nineteenth and in the early part of the twentieth centuries, external debt played a fundamental role as an instrument of domination and destruction in the policies of the major capitalist powers toward some secondary powers that might have become powerful capitalists, for example, China and the Ottoman Empire (chapter 7).

▶ **18.** During the Latin American external debt crisis in the 1930s, fourteen countries unilaterally decided to suspend debt payments, which contributed to their economic success. Fourteen governments of different political leanings reacted simultaneously to implement policies more favorable to the domestic market. During the debt crisis of the 1980s, the United States and other major capitalist powers imposed country-by-country negotiations and came out on top (chapters 7 and 8).

▶ **19.** The debt crisis of the Third World (and the former Soviet Bloc) is closely intertwined with the first stages of deregulation of the financial markets in the latter half of the 1960s (chapters 6 and 8).

▶ **20.** Third World debt climbed steeply from the second half of the 1960s until the late 1970s. Private banks, the World Bank, and the governments of the North (with export credits, in particular) pursued a policy of low-interest, or even negative interest, loans. Therefore, it was a good time for the countries of the South to borrow, especially as export revenues were growing due to an increase in the prices of products exported from the South. The governments in the North encouraged debt in the South in order to provide an outlet for Northern products. Private banks, for their part, held a considerable volume of capital on deposit and were looking for investments, even high-risk ones (chapters 6, 8, 10, 11, 15, and 17).

▶ **21.** The Third World debt crisis, which broke in 1982, was due to the combined effects of the sudden interest rate increase decided by the US Federal Reserve at the end of 1979; the fall in export revenues, which created a trade deficit for countries in the South; and the suspension of bank loans (chapter 8).

▶ **22.** The governments of the North and South, the multilateral financial institutions (the World Bank and the IMF), and the big private banks managed the debt crisis in such a way as to draw into a cycle of increased dependency Third World and former Soviet Bloc countries that had achieved real industrial, even financial, power. The Southeast Asian crisis produced the same result (chapter 17). The least developed countries of the Third World that had not reached a cumulative process of industrialization became more deeply subordinated to the interests of the major industrialized countries (chapters 11, 12, 15, and 16).

▶ **23.** The international lenders—the IMF; the World Bank; the Paris Club, which brings together the governments of the North as creditors; and the London Club, which brings together the private banks of the North (see glossary)—dictate their conditions to debtor nations (chapters 10–12 and 15–18).

▶ **24.** Structural adjustment plans (SAPs) serve as instruments to rein in the countries of the Third World and former Soviet Bloc (chapters 11–13 and 15–18). The underlying logic of SAPs has been exported to the North, whose populations are also subjected to austerity plans (chapter 13).

▶ **25.** The effects of SAPs are generally disastrous. In some cases, they have aggravated dramatic social crises, leading to renewed outbreaks of so-called ethnic or so-called religious conflicts and even to the breakup of states. Somalia, Yugoslavia, Algeria, and Rwanda are cases in point. Although SAPs were not the decisive factor in these crises, they were certainly powerful catalysts (chapters 12 and 16).

▶ **26.** Repayment of internal and external debts has proved a formidable mechanism for transferring to the center the surplus wealth created by workers and small producers in the countries of the periphery and the former Soviet Bloc— indeed, for transferring the wealth created by labor to capital the world over (chapter 9). This is not a simple matter of the center draining wealth from the periphery. Rather, a class analysis clearly shows that this transfer of wealth is part of the aforementioned generalized offensive of capital against labor.

▶ **27.** Debt is one of several mechanisms for subordinating the peoples and states of the periphery to the center, symbolized by the Group of Seven (G7). Other mechanisms include unfair trade, with less favorable terms for the countries of the South; control of world trade by MNCs and the industrialized nations; military domination by the powers of the North; repatriation of profits by MNCs of the North implanted in the South; the "brain drain" from the South to the North; environmental depredation; depredation of natural resources; protectionist barriers raised by the North against goods from the South; and restrictions on the movement and settlement of citizens of the South in the North (chapter 9).

▶ **28.** Repayment of the public debt by the industrialized states is analogous to Third World repayment of external debt. However, the context is slightly different, as this is mainly debt contracted within the same country. Public debt bonds are primarily bought by capital holders. The debt is repaid by the state, which devotes an increasing share of taxes, paid mainly by workers, to this purpose. This is another mechanism for transferring the surplus (see glossary) from workers to capital holders (chapter 9).

▶ **29.** The internal public debt of the states of the South is growing fast, especially in Latin America and Asia. Here, too, repayment acts as a mechanism for transferring part of the surplus wealth to capital holders (chapters 15 and 16).

▶ **30.** The main powers of the capitalist center control the World Bank and the IMF, which intervene daily in the political life of debtor countries to decide the main orientation of their governmental policies (chapters 9, 11, 12, and 14–16). Since 1995, when it was created, the World Trade Organization (WTO; see glossary) has formed a trio with the two Bretton Woods institutions (chapter 18).

▶ **31.** These institutions have a highly efficient means of blackmail. If governments do not repay their debts as stipulated in the conditions dictated by the IMF, the World Bank, and the Paris and London Clubs, their lines of credit will be cut off. If that happens, all sources of external funding may dry up (chapters 11, 12, and 16).

▶ **32.** Much of the debt contracted is illegitimate and odious (chapters 15, 16, and 19).

▶ **33.** The peoples of the periphery have largely repaid the debt contracted prior to the interest rate hike in the early 1980s, for which they were in no way responsible. Between 1980 and 2002, the periphery repaid more than $4.6 trillion ($4,600,000,000,000), eight times what was owed in 1980 (chapters 8, 9, 15, 19). The amount paid is equivalent to more than fifty Marshall Plans (see glossary).

▶ **34.** The Third World is four times more indebted now than it was in 1980, because it was forced to take out new loans in order to pay higher interest rates (chapter 9).

▶ **35.** Real export revenues of Third World countries have fallen, though the volume of exports has increased. Trading terms between the countries of the periphery and those of the center have evolved to the detriment of the former (chapters 8, 9, 13, 15).

▶ **36.** In the 1980s, the biggest Third World debtors were Mexico, Brazil, and Argentina. The character of their external debt has since been modified to benefit the private banks of the North with the complicity of those governments concerned. This required the joint intervention of the US government (the Baker and Brady Plans), the cartel of private lender banks (the London Club), the IMF, and the World Bank. The banks significantly reduced the weight of these debts in their portfolios, and they have found ways to protect themselves from bad debts. In most of the countries of the North, they can qualify for tax exemption or reduction by providing a bad debts reserve. Since the early 1990s, the North's private banks make only short-term, high-interest loans. Moreover, following the example of other financial players (pension funds, mutual funds, insurance companies, etc.), they mainly buy debt paper or bonds issued by some of the biggest debtor countries (Mexico, Argentina, Brazil, Turkey) and guaranteed by the state. This debt "securitization" (see glossary) enables private financial players to part with debt paper the moment risk appears or whenever they decide that it would be more profitable to invest in another sector or country (chapters 6, 15, and 17). This fluidity is synonymous with instability, because capital can be moved fast and in vast amounts. This was what happened in 1997–98: the Southeast Asian crisis, the international stock market crisis, the Russian and the Brazilian crises followed one after the other in quick succession, as there was nothing to prevent them from spreading. Moreover, after the Southeast and East Asian crises, the big private financiers and the IMF forced those governments to nationalize the debts of their private companies and issue state debt bonds on the international financial markets. This would ensure the repayment of emergency loans made by the big lenders, under the auspices of the IMF. Broadly speaking, the handling of the Asian crisis mirrored that of the Latin American crisis. The idea of "securitization" gained ground, and the adjustment imposed on the populations and economies of East and Southeast Asia was as brutal as the Latin American adjustment.

▶ **37.** This overall evolution makes debtor countries more fragile, as the debt paper or bonds they issue can be sold easily. Overnight, these countries may find themselves unable to raise the large sums needed for debt servicing or to ensure their balance of payments. A string of crises illustrates this fragility: Mexico in December 1994, Southeast and East Asia in 1997 and 1998, Russia in August 1998, Brazil from December 1998 to January 1999, Argentina and Turkey from 2000 to 2003, and Brazil in 2002.

▶ **38.** As in the 1994 Mexican crisis, the IMF intervenes to try to limit the damage. However, the IMF is tightfisted: it makes loans with a risk premium, increasing the external debt burden for borrower countries. This gives the IMF an even tighter stranglehold over those countries.

▶ **39.** Since 2000, the flows of loans and investments to the periphery, with the exception of China, have been sharply reduced. The World Bank had to acknowledge that "the developing countries are still net exporters of capital" (World Bank 2003a, cited in chapter 9).

▶ **40.** There has also been a change in the form of debt in the heavily indebted poor countries (HIPC; see glossary). Private banks are no longer interested in them (unless, like Angola, they have immense natural resources). The governments of the North (bilateral debt) and the international financial institutions (multilateral debt held by the IMF, the World Bank, and its continental colleagues—the African Development Bank, the Inter-American Development Bank, and the Asian Development Bank) are the main lenders. Most debt payments made by the HIPC go to the international financial institutions. These indebted countries are obliged to devote an increasing share of the Official Development Assistance (ODA; see glossary) they receive to repaying their bilateral and multilateral debts. The crowning irony is that a portion of the loans granted by the International Development Association (IDA, a division of the World Bank) is immediately used to repay the International Bank for Reconstruction and Development (IBRD, the main division of the World Bank) and the IMF. The money from one till at the World Bank—ostensibly earmarked to improve the living conditions of people in debtor countries—returns to the World Bank via another till as external debt repayment. It is as if the money never leaves Washington, where the IDA, the IBRD, and the IMF all have their main offices (chapter 14). There is more: in 2000, the forty-two HIPC repaid $2.3 billion more than they received. Moreover, contrary to commitments made by the industrialized countries at the Rio Summit in 1992, ODA is plummeting (chapters 9 and 19).

▶ **41.** Facing heavy criticism from sections of the social movements of North and South, the World Bank decided to improve its image by granting loans for health, education, sanitation, and water purification projects. Increasingly, these loans, which only make up a small part of World Bank operations, go to local authorities and nongovernmental organizations (NGOs). In 1996, the World Bank and the IMF launched a program of debt reduction for the HIPC (42 of 180 periphery countries), which received a great deal of media coverage. The goal was to make debt servicing "sustainable" (chapter 11). Over five years, from 1996–2000, the amount of money actually deposited into the trust fund used to finance debt reduction by the IMF was less than the amount required to pay its 2,300 employees in the year 2000 alone. As another comparison, the amount spent by the IMF over five years to finance the debt reduction of all of the HIPC came to less than 2 percent of the sum it committed to bailing out the creditors of the Southeast Asian countries, Brazil, Argentina, and Russia over the same period. The World Bank disbursed less than its annual profits of about $1.5 billion. The total amount disbursed by all of the contributors to the HIPC Debt Initiative between 1996 and 2003 is equal to or less than the cost to the US Treasury of only one month of occupation in Iraq in 2003. Also, the money disbursed by the IMF and the World Bank comes back to them in the form of repayments, for neither institution ever renounces a debt. The IMF and the World Bank are really pursuing two objectives: first, to ensure that indebted countries can maintain regular debt payments, and, second, to keep these countries under their control. In spite of the scandalous hypocrisy of the HIPC Debt Initiative, it garnered approval from some NGOs in the North and the South, the governments of the countries concerned, and the media. Yet, as noted by UNCTAD in 2000, the various measures have brought no worthwhile solution to problems of indebtedness and the drastic austerity imposed on the countries concerned: "Current expectations regarding the implementation of the enhanced HIPC Initiative are unrealistic. The scale of debt relief will prove insufficient to ensure debt sustainability in the medium term...moreover, the magnitude of debt relief, and its manner of delivery, will not have major direct effects on poverty reduction" (UNCTAD 2000c).

▶ **42.** Since 1997–98, the World Bank and the IMF have undergone the worse legitimacy crisis in their histories. Innumerable demonstrations of opposition have taken place, both in the countries that are subjected to their policies and in the industrialized countries of the North. Since 1999, powerful and radical counterdemonstrations have dogged every one of their two annual meetings (one in April, the other in September). The institutions are also riven by internal crises: the resignation in 1999–2000 of Joseph Stiglitz, senior vice president and chief economist of the World Bank, and Ravi Kanbur, director of the World Bank's annual *World Development Report*, both of whom wanted reform within the World Bank. Finally, in the United States, the majority of congressional Republicans and some Democrats have criticized these institutions severely (chapter 11). (See the report by the International Financial Institutions Advisory Commission, headed by Republican Allan Meltzer. The Meltzer Commission's conclusions were made public in February 2000.) The WTO has not escaped the crisis, with the foundering of the Millennium Round in Seattle in 1999, then, after the respite afforded by Doha in 2001, the debacle of the interministerial conference in Cancún in September 2003. Disagreements among the major trading powers (with the United States and the European Union in the fore) and between them and the countries of the periphery are at the root of the failure. Add to this widespread social protest and the antiglobalization movement, which has gone from strength to strength (chapter 20).

▶ **43.** In an attempt to counteract the effects of their legitimacy crisis while continuing with their project to implement more neoliberal measures, the Bretton Woods institutions in 1999 undertook an initiative known as the poverty reduction strategy. They ask the governments of HIPC that wish to obtain debt relief to draw up a Poverty Reduction Strategy Paper (PRSP; see glossary). The idea is to give a human face to structural adjustment by increasing health and education spending for the lower classes, and by implementing policies that target the very poor. However, under no circumstances may the paper evade the pursuit of structural adjustment measures: accelerating privatization of services (water, electricity, telecommunications, public transport); privatizing or shutting down public industrial companies; ending subsidies on basic products such as bread or other staples; increasing taxation of the poor through generalization of the value added tax (at a single rate of 18 percent in the West African Economic and Monetary Union); lifting tariff barriers (which places local producers in competition with MNCs); liberalizing capital inflow and outflow (which generally results in massive capital flight); privatizing land; and implementing cost-recovery policies in health and education. The IMF, the World Bank, and the Paris Club make acceptance of these policies by the HIPC a precondition for future debt reduction and fresh adjustment loans. Furthermore, the IMF estimates that approximately ninety countries will qualify for structural adjustment loans—renamed Poverty Reduction and Growth Facility (PRGF) since 1999. These policies are no more likely to succeed in reducing poverty than did their predecessors. The Bretton Woods institutions are like arsonists, lighting new social fires, then waiting for the NGOs and local communities to play firefighter (chapter 11).

▶ **44.** The acts and declarations of the Bretton Woods institutions over the last two years indicate that they do not intend to change course (chapter 18).

▶ **45.** Globalization in its present form increases environmental degradation, despite decisions made in the world summits held in Rio (1992) and Kyoto (1997) on the theme of environmental protection (chapters 1 and 9–11).

▶ **46.** From the start, the facts have systematically contradicted the basic tenets of liberal ideology; however, the economic and social crisis of the 1970s and 1980s opened the way for a forceful return of this ideology, entailing a global offensive of capital against labor (chapter 14). However, does it not seem that the neoliberal wave is reaching its limits?

▶ **47.** Alternatives are urgently needed with the guarantee of fundamental rights and the fulfillment of basic human needs as their starting point. These are the priorities for most of the world's population (chapter 19).

▶ **48.** To bring these alternatives into effect, the various social movements need to come together in a new internationalism and plan how to throw off the shackles of corporate-driven global finance (chapter 20).

1
Globalization and the neoliberal offensive

Deterioration in the living conditions of populations: Employment and wages

During the 1970s, the world economy began a long wave of slow growth. This stood in stark contrast to the nearly thirty years of rapid postwar economic growth immediately preceding it (Mandel 1975b, 1982, 1995; Husson 1996; Montes 1996; Went 1996).

This long, slow wave of growth is still unfurling. Businesses have seen their profits slump, the stock market bubble has burst, the myth of the "new economy" has collapsed, exchange rates are unstable, resounding bankruptcies abound. In the countries of the periphery, there has been a succession of economic and financial crises. The result of more than twenty years of neoliberalism is a fiasco in terms of growth and stability, let alone in terms of human and environmental consequences. A heavy increase in arms spending and military aggression added to that results in complete mayhem.

Since the beginning of the crisis in the 1970s, the world has experienced a series of major changes that have progressively eroded living conditions for a majority of the inhabitants of the planet. Mass unemployment has settled in, the unequal distribution of wealth has intensified, and workers' wages have fallen sharply. In addition, there are the disastrous consequences of closing the borders of industrialized countries to migrants, increasing recourse to violence in case of conflict, destroying the environment (the greenhouse effect, pollution, massive deforestation, etc.), and deregulating food production. Also, imperialist wars have reasserted themselves during the first years of the third millennium.

Mass unemployment

The industrialized capitalist countries

Considering only those countries that already belonged in 1993 to the Organization for Economic Cooperation and Development (OECD; see glossary), in 1996, there were officially 37 million unemployed. This is three times the figure of the early 1970s, in a population with a near-zero growth rate. The average unemployment rate in these countries more than doubled, from 3.2 percent in 1960–73, to 7.3 percent in 1980–94.

After a short period of economic recovery in 1998–2000, during which unemployment fell, a great wave of mass layoffs in all countries ensued, including 2.5 million job cuts in the United States alone between March 2001 and March 2003.

Such figures always underestimate the true situation because they do not consider a number of different categories of unemployed. The deregulation of the labor market is one way to shift from "declared" to "disguised" forms of unemployment through the creation of poorly paid and unproductive jobs.

The former Eastern Bloc countries

Unemployment has skyrocketed since the beginning of the 1990s. World Bank officials prescribe a necessary unemployment rate of 20 percent for these countries. Indeed, at an April 1992 seminar held in Turin on the Eastern European adjustment, one of the two World Bank representatives suggested, "[Perhaps we should] judge our success in achieving adjustments in Central and Eastern Europe by the extent to which unemployment rises rather than by the extent to which we [are] able to keep unemployment down" (George and Sabelli 1994).

According to the (generally moderate) estimates produced by the International Labor Organization (ILO) in early 2001, unemployment reached 13 percent in the Russia Federation. Only two unemployed persons in one hundred were paid any unemployment benefit. If hidden forms of unemployment, such as incomplete working weeks or enforced holidays, were included, the number of unemployed would be far higher. In Poland, unemployment reached 20 percent in 2002. It would seem that our World Bank representative could claim success....

The Third World

Official figures systematically understate the reality of unemployment. Our calculations reveal that at least one billion jobs would have to be created to ensure properly paid work for all. The implementation of structural adjustment programs has led to a steep increase in unemployment for a number of reasons. First, there have been mass dismissals in the public sector. Second, the domestic market has been sharply cut back, leading to bankruptcy for many companies.

Third, export-oriented policies in agriculture have hit subsistence farming hard, accelerating the exodus of huge numbers of rural unemployed to the cities.

According to ILO estimates, the Southeast Asian crisis that began in 1997 and the ensuing structural adjustment policies resulted in the loss of 23 million jobs in the region in 1998–99. In Mexico in 2001, after the recession that hit the United States, 500,000 jobs were lost. As many jobs were lost in Argentina during 2002.

Growing inequality in the distribution of wealth and a drop in wages

The unequal distribution of wealth has been greatly accentuated. There has been a pronounced drop in revenue for those who are dependent on waged work, those who work the land, and those condemned to unemployment. Those who live off revenues from capital, on the other hand, amass an ever-growing share of new wealth. In the thirty years from 1960 to 1990, the ratio of inequality in the way wealth was shared out between the richest and poorest sectors of the world's population doubled. In 2001, the wealthiest 5 percent of the planet's inhabitants earned more than 114 times the income of the poorest 5 percent (UNDP 2003, 39).

According to the United Nations Development Program *Human Development Report 2003*, citing a 2001 study by Giovanni Andrea Cornia and Sampsa Kiiski,

> Between the 1980s and the mid- to late 1990s, inequality increased in 42 of the 73 countries with complete and comparable data. Only 6 of the 33 developing countries (excluding transition countries) in the sample saw inequality decline, while 17 saw it increase. In other words, within national boundaries control over assets and resources is increasingly concentrated in the hands of a few people.

The report goes on to highlight the link between increased inequality and the eruption of the debt crisis:

> Though not the case for all these countries, in many inequality began increasing during the debt crisis of the early 1980s (Kanbur and Lustig 1999). Since then, inequality has soared, particularly in the Commonwealth of Independent States (CIS) and in south-eastern Europe. And in many Latin American countries inequality remains extremely high.

The increase in the incomes of CEOs is astonishing. According to *Business Week*, the ten best-paid CEOs in the United States in 1981 were earning between $2.3 million and $5.7 million a year. Twenty years later, their annual incomes had jumped to between $64 million and $706 million (Eric Leser in *Le*

Monde, July 9, 2002). A little lower down the scale, the incomes of European company directors have followed the same pattern. Emilio Botín, director of the second-largest Spanish bank, Santander Central Hispano, was paid 3.5 million euros, while Rolf Breuer, president of the Deutsche Bank, received 8 million euros. We have calculated that Breuer earns an amount equivalent to the salaries of 10,000 secondary school teachers in West Africa or 2,200 university teachers in the same region. Yet, Breuer envies his colleague, Richard S. Fuld, director of Lehman Brothers, who earns 125.5 million euros (*El Pais*, June 25, 2002). This is equivalent to the annual salaries of 156,000 secondary school teachers or 35,000 university teachers in West Africa—though it is doubtful that the region has 35,000 university teachers.

There is also a gulf between the revenues of CEOs and workers in the North. The French weekly *Le Nouvel Observateur* reported June 27, 2002, that "the package picked up in 2000 by former General Electric boss Jack Welch was equivalent to the salary of 21,578 French workers earning minimum wage or 9,061 on the average salary." In 2002, because of the fall of the stock exchange, top salaries could not be maintained at such levels. According to Mercer Human Resource Consulting and the *Wall Street Journal*, the best-paid managing director was Jeffrey C. Barbakow, the CEO of Tenet Healthcare, who earned more than $116 million. However, in a sample of 350 big companies, "total direct pay (on average) had progressed by 15 percent to $3.02 million" (*Les Echos*, April 18, 2003).

In 1995, the cumulated fortunes of the 358 richest individuals on the planet came to a total of $760 billion. When this figure was published by *Forbes* and widely publicized by the UNDP it made media headlines. Six years later, membership in the highly exclusive club of those whose cumulated wealth totaled one trillion dollars was significantly reduced: to 147. Indeed, the 147 individuals who topped the 2002 *Forbes* "World's Richest People" list had a total cumulated wealth equal to the total annual income of about three billion of the planet's inhabitants, or half the world's population. The comparison here is between estate and income, but if it were possible to compare estate only, the result would be even more astounding. The estate of poor people is generally far inferior to their revenues.

What else does the 2002 *Forbes* list teach us? Of 497 billionaires, 240 obtained their wealth through inheritance. In 2001, there were eighty-three fewer billionaires in the world than in 2000. The bursting of the stock market speculation bubble and the collapse of the "new economy" had a hand in that. Bill Gates was still the richest person. Half the world's billionaires were North

American; two were Chinese.

What about millionaires? Since 1997, investment bank Merrill Lynch and fortune consultant Cap Gemini Ernst & Young have published an annual *World Wealth Report* for the very wealthy to whom they offer their services. According to their 2003 report, the number of millionaires had risen to 7.3 million (i.e., a little more than a thousandth of the world population). Their total assets came to $27.2 trillion.[1]

The assets of the richest thousandth (0.1 percent) of the global population represent about 25 times the annual income of half the global population (3.1 billion inhabitants).While the economic situation of the majority of the population stagnated or deteriorated, the assets of millionaires rose by 18 percent in 1999, 6 percent in 2000, 3 percent in 2001, and 3.6 percent in 2002.[2]

These millionaires constitute the "global" capitalist class, composed mainly of rich residents of the North, but where the rich of the South occupy a non-negligible position. In 2000, 2001, and 2002, the millionaires of Latin America held a 13 percent slice of the cake. Why do these facts never make the headlines? Why do World Bank reports not give them the emphasis they deserve? One wonders whether the absence of information is not a deliberate ploy to fog over the issue. It is much easier to place the emphasis on the opposition between the North as a whole, presented as a homogenous entity living in comfort, and the South as a whole, eking out a meager living. Once this image has been presented a hundred times over, the opposition between social classes that divides all the capitalists of the planet from all those who toil for a living fades into the background. The world's capitalists, whether from the highly industrialized countries or the periphery, live on their wealth, while most men and women—whether blue-collar or white-collar workers, small farmers or artisans, working or unemployed—basically depend on their own labor to live. The gaping abyss between North and South (or between the center and the periphery) cannot suffice to explain the complexity of social forces on a global scale. The contradictions between social classes, between men and women or concerning issues of gender must also be taken into account (see the section on the feminization of poverty below).

The developing countries

According to the World Bank, about 1.2 billion people were living on less than one dollar per day, i.e., below the absolute poverty line, in 2002. If the World Bank, which arbitrarily fixes the poverty line at one dollar per day for the developing countries, raised the threshold in line with the actual cost of living, how would the statistics be affected? For example, if the sum were fixed at two, three, or four dollars per day, it would be apparent that the majority of the population of Third World countries lives in extreme hardship.

Indeed, with the rising cost of basic goods and services in the Third World and the former Soviet Bloc, three or four dollars a day are not enough for decent food and lodging, let alone access to education, health care, and culture. By setting the figure at one dollar per day, the World Bank deliberately underestimates the number of those who live in absolute poverty. This creates the impression that absolute poverty is marginal in the Third World and former Soviet Bloc, whereas, in fact, it affects the majority of the population in these countries.

Setting the absolute poverty line at one dollar per day yields completely different results from those obtained by fixing the bar at two dollars per day. Table 1.1 illustrates that, in most cases, the population living below the absolute poverty line shifts from the minority to the majority when two dollars per day is used.

Treating poverty as a marginal phenomenon is part of denying the ruinous failure of the structural adjustment policies of the IMF and World Bank. It also enables them to deny the urgent need for fundamental changes toward the egalitarian redistribution of wealth, the sine qua non for any genuine development.

TABLE 1.1. ABSOLUTE POVERTY LINE

	Year of survey	Population in absolute poverty (percent)	
		< $1 per day	< $2 per day
India	1999–2000	35	80
Indonesia	2000	7	55
Laos	1997–98	26	73
Nigeria	1997	70	90
Pakistan	1998	13	66
Philippines	2000	15	46
Senegal	1995	26	68
Tanzania	1993	20	60
Vietnam	1998	18	64
Russia	2000	6	24
Ghana	1998	45	78
Egypt	2000	3	44
China	2000	16	47
Bangladesh	2000	36	83

Source: World Bank 2003b.

UNDP casts doubt on World Bank criteria for world poverty assessment

The United Nation Development Program (UNDP) *Global Human Development Report 2003* notes that the criteria adopted by the World Bank and the results of its surveys increasingly raise questions.

...The World Bank uses an extreme poverty line of about $1 a day (measured in purchasing power parity terms). Behind this approach is the assumption— based on national poverty lines from a sample of developing countries—that after adjusting for cost of living differences, $1 a day is the average minimum consumption required for subsistence in the developing world. But this approach has been assailed as being conceptually and methodologically inaccurate in capturing minimum subsistence levels across developing countries....

One of the main problems with $1 a day poverty data derives from underlying adjustments of international price differences. Assuming that $1 a day is the correct average price of the subsistence consumption bundle in developing countries—a major assumption—the price of this bundle needs to be translated into national currencies. The World Bank does this using purchasing power parity (PPP) rates: price indices that compare the price of a bundle of goods in one country with the price in another.

But the process for obtaining these rates is not entirely transparent. Moreover, they produce inaccurate poverty lines because many of the prices they are based on are for goods that poor people do not consume (Reddy and Pogge 2002; Deaton 2003). Making matters worse, these conversions do not take into account the considerable price differences between countries' urban and rural areas. Moreover, poor people have to pay higher unit prices for many goods and services because they cannot afford to buy in bulk (Ward 2003)....

Because of these concerns, more efforts should be made internationally and nationally to improve the price collection efforts behind purchasing power parities (the World Bank is currently engaged in such an effort and expects to release new rates in 2005), to harmonize design and collection methods for income and consumption surveys and to agree on local bundles of minimum capabilities on which to base poverty figures, for which feedback and guidance from countries and communities are crucial.

The World Bank and the IMF identify poverty as a central problem only for a limited number of countries, including the forty-nine least developed countries (LDC). Even with the LDC, the experts of the two institutions do not hesitate to disguise the figures to reduce the amount of poverty.

In June 2002, in a report on poverty in the LDC, the United Nations Conference on Trade and Development (UNCTAD) directly questioned World Bank estimates. According to UNCTAD, when measuring poverty, the World Bank makes do with samples of local populations used for its surveys, extrapolating the global figures from these limited studies. "Thus, the World

Bank claims that in 1994 Tanzanians had an annual income of $814. Yet, UNCTAD finds less than $300. Again, according to the World Bank, 41.7 percent of the population of Niger survived on less than one dollar per day in 1992, while UNCTAD shows more than 75 percent for that year" (Vittorio de Filippis, *Libération*, June 19, 2002). The same UNCTAD study found that poverty had doubled in the LDC over the last thirty years. Using two dollars per day as the poverty line, 87.5 percent of the inhabitants of the African LDC live below that line (Sixtine Leon-Dufour, *Le Figaro*, June 19, 2002).

Perspectives on the evolution of absolute poverty in developing countries

During the period 1945–80, at different speeds and to varying degrees, the populations of what are now classified "developing countries" (DC) experienced a gradual progression of their financial incomes and living conditions: generalized use of medicines, reduced mortality, sweeping vaccination campaigns, development of basic health-care infrastructures, expansion of primary education, etc. After 1982, eruption of the debt crisis and generalization of structural adjustment policies (to be analyzed in detail in chapters 12 and 13) brought on the degradation of living conditions. This first affected Latin American countries, Africa, and the former Soviet Bloc, then East Asia (except China). As mentioned above, it is difficult to assess the evolution of poverty accurately, especially since the criterion of purchasing power alone is wholly inadequate (see discussions of the gender factor and the human poverty index below). However, there is little doubt that the absolute number of people living in subhuman, or at least extremely precarious, conditions has increased in most regions that have undergone structural adjustment.

The World Bank tries to present a glorified version of reality. Various World Bank documents explain that the number of "absolute" poor (those who survive on less than one dollar per day) dropped worldwide by about 100 million at the end of the 1990s. The World Bank admits that between 1990 and 1999, the number of destitute increased by about 100 million, combining figures from sub-Saharan Africa (74 million), Latin America (9 million), and the former Soviet Bloc (20 million). However, it claims that the overall result globally is positive. As evidence, it cites figures provided by the Chinese government that claim a decrease of about 200 million in the number of Chinese who live below the absolute poverty line (World Bank 2002b, 2003b; UNDP 2003). It also claims a reduction in the number of destitute in India.

The World Bank's version of reality induces several observations. First, as mentioned above, the criterion of one dollar per day is questionable and challenged. Second, recent studies carried out by UNCTAD show that the World Bank's poverty statistics for Africa have been considerably low (see above). Third, the figures provided by China, the World Bank's joker, are extremely difficult to verify. Without the 200 million fewer poor reported by China, the World Bank would have to admit a clear global increase in the number of destitute people. The Chinese joker has allowed the World Bank to save face. Fourth, while the World Bank claims that the number of destitute in the former Soviet Bloc grew from 6 million in 1990, to 26 million in 1999 (an increase of 400 percent), the UNDP reckons that the number of destitute rose from 31 million to 97 million during the same period. The UNDP (2003, table 2.3) considers it more appropriate to adopt two dollars per day as the baseline for poverty, which yields 71 million more poor in 1999 than the World Bank's figure. Fifth, the figures provided by the World Bank for North Africa and the Middle East appear to be unfounded. The World Bank claims that only 2 percent of the population in this region survive on less than one dollar per day. In absolute figures, the World Bank considers there were 5 million destitute in 1990, and 6 million in 1999. Can Morocco (29 million inhabitants), Algeria (31million), Egypt (65 million), and Iraq (25 million), to name only a few countries in the region, have fewer than 6 million destitute between them? Absurd!

The World Bank's figures arouse suspicion. The data seem to be manipulated to back World Bank claims that the number of absolute poor in the world is decreasing. With the proclaimed mission to "reduce global poverty" as its top priority, the World Bank is prepared to fiddle the figures to prevent them from giving the lie to its story.

Without departing from the reservations mentioned above, the World Bank's data could also lead to the following observation: The regions of the world that have most assiduously applied the policies recommended by the World Bank register a rise in absolute poverty. The regions concerned are Latin America and the Caribbean, sub-Saharan Africa, and the former Soviet Bloc. Each of these three big areas has been subjected to at least ten years of continuous structural adjustment, and all have witnessed a rise in absolute poverty.

On the other hand, the two most populous countries on the planet, China and India, which according to the World Bank and the IMF have not yet fully entered into globalization, have seen a significant drop in their numbers of destitute—even according to the World Bank. Interestingly, neither country has signed any structural adjustment agreements with the World Bank and the IMF. China's currency remains nonconvertible and the government keeps a check on investments and capital movement, hesitates to launch a vast privatization program, and maintains protectionist policies. India has gone much further to meet the World Bank, but not far enough to satisfy it.

Is it not reasonable to suppose that if China and India were to follow World Bank and IMF recommendations, the same things that have happened to other countries would happen to them?

In Eastern European countries

According to the UNDP, 90 percent of Bulgarians were living below the poverty line in 1997 (*Le Monde*, March 5, 1997). In Central and Eastern Europe and the Commonwealth of Independent States (CIS), per capita income fell by 2.4 percent per annum in the decade beginning in 1990 (UNDP 2002). In the Russian Federation, workers' real wages had fallen to 70 percent of 1991 levels. The ratio of inequality between the 15 million "wealthiest" and the 15 million "poorest" Russians was 9.05 in 1993; one year later, it had risen to 16!

Plunged into poverty by structural adjustment led by the World Bank and the IMF, then by the massive transfer of wealth abroad by the new local capitalists (the "oligarchs"), many republics of the former Soviet Bloc are now classified as developing countries by the World Bank, along with "low-" and "middle-income" Third World countries (see World Bank annual reports since 1993). This change in classification is not merely the result of a change in the way revenue statistics are handled. Rather, it reflects the post–Cold War situation in which market-oriented reforms aim at the "Third Worldization" of Eastern Europe and the former USSR, and at concentrating wealth and well-being in a small number of "developed" market economies.

In the highly industrialized capitalist countries

Wages for the majority of people in highly industrialized countries have undeniably declined, too. US figures are quite striking in this respect. While household income rose across the board between 1950 and 1978, this tendency was rolled back radically between 1978 and 1993. The great majority of Americans have seen their wages decline, while the wealthiest social strata continue to accumulate new wealth (see table 1.2).

Under the Reagan administration, the wealthiest families (1 percent of all households) saw their average annual income rise by nearly 50 percent. According to Doug Henwood (1998), the richest 0.5 percent of US citizens owns more than do 90 percent of the US population combined. In the 1990s, the level of concentration of wealth in the United States was comparable to that of the 1920s. In 1995, the richest 1 percent of households—about 2 million adults—owned 42 percent of privately owned shares and 56 percent of bonds. The richest 10 percent owned 90 percent. The richest 1 percent of the population owns approximately one-fourth of the country's available capital, while the richest 10 percent owns half of it. At the other end of the scale, only 6 percent of African Americans and Hispanic Americans own a single share. Contrary to general belief, it is not true that most Americans own stock market shares. In 1990, only 21 percent owned any shares, only 12 percent had bought or sold any once in the year, and only 4 percent had carried out more than five transactions.

TABLE 1.2. EVOLUTION OF REAL INCOME OF U.S. HOUSEHOLDS (PERCENT)

Between 1950 and 1978:

Poorest fifth	+140
Second fifth	+98
Third fifth	+105
Fourth fifth	+110
Richest fifth	+99

Between 1978 and 1993:

Poorest fifth	-19	
Second fifth	-8	
Third fifth	-4	
Fourth fifth	+5	
Richest fifth	+18	*Source:* US News and World Report, *February 6, 1995.*

According to the European Office of Statistics (Eurostat), the share of salaries in the European GDP has fallen from 75.8 percent in the 1970s, to 69.7 percent in 2000, while the share of profits has increased proportionately. In other words, a continually growing share of European wealth is being distributed as profit and not as salaries.[3]

TABLE 1.3. SALARIES AS PERCENTAGE OF GDP

Region	1961–70	1971–80	1981–90	1991–2000
European Union	73.6	75.8	73.0	69.7
United States	69.8	70.0	68.7	67.3

Source: Eurostat.

Between 1980 and 1997, taxation of capital revenue fell 3 percent in France, while taxation of labor revenue increased 14 percent; in Germany, the respective figures are −13 percent for capital and +8 percent for labor.

US income inequality

Between 1979 and 1997, the per capita GDP in the United States rose by 38 percent, while the income of a family living on average wages increased by only 9 percent. The bulk of the increase in national revenue benefited the very rich. The income of the wealthiest 1 percent of families rose sharply by 140 percent, i.e., three times the average. In 1979, the income of the richest 1 percent of American families was ten times higher than the average; in 1997, it was twenty-three times higher.

According to a study published in 2003 by the Internal Revenue Service,* the income declared in 2000 by the 400 wealthiest taxpayers came to $70 billion, four times the amount in 1992. Their share of total taxable revenue doubled over the same period. The minimum annual revenue in this elite 400-member club came to $86.8 million. Between 1999 and 2000, the taxable income of US taxpayers taken as a whole increased by 1.8 percent, while that of the 400 wealthiest jumped 14 percent.

* IRS study quoted in *Wall Street Journal*, June 26, 2003.

UN view on declining living conditions in the world

In the Third World and Eastern Europe

According to the UNDP *Human Development Report 1997*, "Over the last 15 to 20 years, more than a hundred countries in the Third World or the former Eastern Bloc have experienced a bigger and more lasting collapse in growth and drop in the standard of living than what industrialized countries went through during the deep crisis of the 1930s."

The October 11, 1996, issue of *Le Monde*, quotes James Gustave Speth, then UNDP director, as saying, "In fact, in more than a hundred countries per capita revenue is lower today than it was 15 years ago. It is quite clear that about 1.6 billion people are worse off than they were at the beginning of the 1980s." The beginning of the 1980s coincides with the generalization of neoliberal policies across the globe.

The Third World

In the Third World, 1.2 billion people survive on less than a dollar per day, including half a billion children (UNICEF 2001, 31). Between 1995 and 2000, the number of people who survive on less than one dollar per day did not decrease, despite the fact that heads of state, the IMF, and the World

Bank pledged themselves at the 1995 World Summit for Social Development in Copenhagen to halve this number by 2015, a commitment reiterated in the Millennium Development Goals in 2000.

In the LDC, 33 percent of the population do not reach age forty (UNDP 1999, 5).

One hundred million children live or work in the streets.

In developing countries, 250 million children (140 million boys and 110 million girls) are compelled to work (UNDP 2000a, 4–5).

In the 1990s, about 2 million children were slaughtered, 6 million severely wounded or maimed for life, and 12 million left homeless (UNICEF 2001, 36).

Every day, thirty thousand children die of easily curable diseases (approximately 11 million children every year). Other easily avoidable causes of mortality: every year, 5 million people die of diarrhea, 1 million of malaria, 3 million from the consequences of air pollution (UNDP 1999, 22, 42).

In 1998–2000, 840 million people around the world went hungry every day or experienced recurrent food insecurity (FAO 2002).

In the DC, more than 1 billion people (1.1 billion, according to UNICEF 2001, 31) lack access to clean water supplies, and close to 2.4 billion people do not have access to proper sanitation facilities (UNDP 2000a, 4–5).

Fourteen African countries suffer from water shortage (less than 1,000 m^3 of water available per person per year) or drought stress (1,000–1,700 m^3 per person per year). By 2025, eleven other African countries will be similarly affected (UNEP 1999).

The chances of a woman dying due to pregnancy or childbirth are forty times higher in the developing world than in the industrialized world (UNICEF 2001, 23).

In 2002, according to UNAIDS and the World Health Organization (WHO), 42 million people worldwide had HIV/AIDS, 5 million new people were infected, and 3.1 million died of the disease.

Sub-Saharan Africa is home to 10 percent of the world's population and 70 percent of the world's HIV carriers. The same area accounts for 80 percent of AIDS mortality and 90 percent of AIDS orphans. "In four countries of Southern Africa, the prevalence of HIV has reached unimaginable heights. In Botswana, 38.8% of the population is contaminated, in Swaziland 33.4%, in Lesotho 31% and in Zimbabwe 33.7%" (*Le Figaro*, November 27, 2002). The Third World accounts for 95 percent of AIDS mortality.

In Latin America and in the Caribbean, 1.9 million were HIV positive; in Asia, 7.2 million people had contracted HIV/AIDS, including 1 million in China (UNAIDS and WHO 2002).

In countries with low human development, health and education expenses decreased from 2 percent of the GDP in 1986–90, to 1.8 percent in 1991–96. Investments in those sectors fell from 6.5 percent to 6.1 percent of public expenditure (UNDP 1999, 93).

Anna Tibaijuka, director of UN-Habitat, declared in the *Global Report on Human Settlements 2003* that in thirty years, one in three people would be living in a slum unless governments exercise some control over unprecedented urban growth. Twenty percent of the inhabitants of Africa are slum dwellers. The world's biggest ghetto is Kibera, in Nairobi, Kenya, where approximately 600,000 people live. In Latin America, slum dwellers are 14 percent of the population (a million people live in the seven hundred *favelas* of Rio de Janeiro, Brazil). However, the worst urban conditions prevail in Asia, where 550 million people live in unacceptable squalor. Two percent of the thirty richest countries lives in slums, while 80 percent of the thirty poorest countries lives in slums.

Over the next thirty years, the urban population of the DC is expected to double, reaching 4 billion, at a rate of 70 million per year. "Slums are the result of failed policies, bad governance, corruption and a lack of political will," asserts the UN-Habitat report. Its authors blame the globalization of negligence and the neoliberal economic policies imposed by international institutions such as the IMF and the WTO (*Guardian*, October 4, 2003).

The former Soviet Bloc

With the restoration of capitalism in the countries of the former Eastern Bloc, the average rate of absolute poverty based on a daily wage of four dollars (UNDP 1997, 2) has risen eightfold, from 4 percent in 1988, to 32 percent in 1994. "In 1989, only 2 percent of those living in Russia were in poverty. By late 1998, that number had soared to 23.8 percent, using the $2 a day standard. More than 40 percent of the country had less than $4 a day, according to a survey conducted by the World Bank. The statistics for children revealed an even deeper problem, with more than 50 percent living in families in poverty" (Stiglitz 2002, 153).

The weakening or even abolition of the welfare state has resulted in dramatic cuts in health and education. In seven of eighteen countries, life expectancy was lower in 1995 than in 1989 by five years. In Lithuania, registrations at kindergarten level (ages 3–6) plummeted from 64 percent in 1989, to 36 percent in 1998. In Russia, the drop is from 69 percent to 54 percent (UNDP 1999, 79). In Russia, wages were 48 percent lower, and the proportion of household income depending on wages declined from 74 percent to 55 percent. At the same time, the proportion related to rents and other intangible incomes increased more than four and a half times, from 5 percent to 23 percent. Between 1989 and 1996, the life expectancy for men was reduced more than four years, to an average of sixty, that is, two years less than the average in developing countries.

In the highly industrialized countries

In the industrialized countries, more than 100 million people live below the threshold of absolute poverty—defined as the equivalent of 50 percent of a country's mean individual disposable income (UNDP 1997, 2). In 1999, poverty affected some 65 million people within the European Union (376 million inhabitants). According to data provided by member states, 18 percent of the population were living below a "poverty line" that amounted to 60 percent of the "normal cost of living."

The main cause of exclusion and impoverishment is still unemployment; however, according to Eurostat, 12 percent of employed are still reported as poor, and 53 percent of the less well-off belong to households in which one adult has a job. In fact, Eurostat considers that 20–40 percent are close to the poverty threshold (*Le Figaro*, September 12, 2000).

In the fifteen countries that form the European Union, about 3 million people have no permanent home.

> Recent studies show inequality rising in most OECD countries during the 1980s and into the early 1990s. Of 19 countries, only one showed a slight improvement. The deterioration was worst in Sweden, the United Kingdom and the United States. In the United Kingdom the number of families below the poverty line rose by 60% in the 1980s, in the Netherlands, by nearly 40%. (UNDP 1999, 37)

According to an inquiry conducted by four British academics, the proportion of poverty-stricken households rose from 14 percent in 1983, to 24 percent in 1999. In 1999, 14.5 million British people were affected by more or less severe poverty. A quarter of the population was deprived of at least one of the three following basic requirements for a normal life: three meals a day, sufficient clothing, or heated accommodation (*Le Figaro*, September 12, 2000).

In 1971, there were 25 million poor in the United States, according to Robert McNamara (1973), then president of the World Bank. In 1995, there were 11.4 million more, bringing the total of poor in the United States to 36.4 million or about 14 percent of the population (US Bureau of the Census 1996).

In the United States in 2000, about 17 percent of children, or about 12 million, were growing up in homes where their nutritional requirements were not met (UNICEF 2001, 33).

Forty million people were not covered by health insurance, and one adult in five was illiterate (UNDP 2000a, 8).

According to US Bureau of the Census statistics, in 2001 (that is, a year after the UNDP figures were published), the number of Americans without health insurance increased 3.5 percent to 41.2 million, or one American in seven—14.6 percent of the population. Young people, ages 18–24, are the most affected age group, with 28 percent uninsured (*Le Figaro*, October 1, 2002).

In the same country, two million people are victims of violent crime every year (UNDP 1997, 34).

An innovation of the UNDP: The human poverty index

In developing countries

The team that worked on the 1997 edition of the UNDP *Human Development Report* sought to measure poverty in the Third World using criteria other than income levels. It formulated a human poverty index (HPI) that looks at more than monetary criteria. The criteria used are:

- the percentage of people at risk of dying before the age of forty;
- the adult illiteracy rate;
- services made available by the economy as a whole.

To determine the quality of these services, three factors are examined: the proportion of people who lack access to clean water supplies, of those who lack access to health care services, and of children under age five who suffer from malnutrition.

Once formulated, the UNDP team applied these criteria to a list of seventy-eight Third World countries for which they had reliable data. In spite of obvious monetary poverty, some countries are able to cushion the effects of this poverty by guaranteeing access to a number of services. "At the head of the list are Trinidad and Tobago, Cuba, Chile, Singapore and Costa Rica, in that order. These countries have managed to reduce human poverty to an HPI of less than 10%. In other words, thanks to these countries' specific efforts, less than 10% of their population suffers from human poverty" (UNDP 1997, 15, 22). According to this classification system, Cuba, in spite of the US blockade, places second, which is thirty-nine places from its ranking in a list of Third World countries evaluated according to another UNDP index, the human development index (HDI).

In the industrialized countries

In industrialized countries, the HPI focuses on the same aspects of deprivation as in developing countries, and also includes another form of deprivation: exclusion. It uses the following variables:

- the percentage of people at risk of dying before age sixty;
- the percentage of people who are illiterate;
- the percentage of people who live below the poverty line (i.e., on less than half the average disposable household income);
- the percentage of long-term unemployed (i.e., unemployed more than twelve months).

Of the eighteen industrialized countries whose HPI has been calculated, the worst off are the United States (15.8 percent of the population are under the poverty line), Ireland (15 percent), and the United Kingdom (14.6 percent). Comparing the general human development index and the HPI for 1998, the United States moves from third to eighteenth position (last place), and the United Kingdom from tenth to sixteenth (UNDP 2000a, 152).

The feminization of poverty and the oppression of women

The UNDP has estimated that women account for 70 percent of the 1.2 billion people who live below the threshold of absolute poverty. Workforce participation is indeed a key factor, but women also bear the burden of household and family well-being.

Structural adjustment programs and their array of social spending cuts hit women harder than men. Women struggle daily to make up for the difference between decreasing incomes and increasing prices. Paying for medicine, food, and school is now virtually impossible for a large number of women and their children.

Where opportunities arise in difficult economic circumstances, patriarchal reflexes kick in to restrict the access of girls, young women, and women to rights essential for development and emancipation. Boys attend school while girls help with housework or work to provide an income supplement for the family. In India, 61 percent of girls age seven and older and women are illiterate (UNDP 1997, 55).

In Nepal, twice as many girls as boys go blind due to malnutrition. In the Third World in general, more than half of all women suffer from anemia; in South Asia, anemia affects 78 percent of all women (UNDP 1997, 31). In the Zimbabwean capital Harare, the number of women who died during childbirth doubled in the two years following implementation of a structural adjustment program that cut health-care spending 33 percent (UNDP 1995, 44). Each year, more than 500,000 women die of complications related to pregnancy and childbirth (UNDP 2000a).

TABLE 1.4. LIFETIME CHANCE OF DEATH DURING PREGNANCY OR CHILDBIRTH

Sub-Saharan Africa	1 in 13
South Asia	1 in 54
Middle East and North Africa	1 in 55
Latin America and the Caribbean	1 in 157
East Asia and the Pacific	1 in 283
Central and Eastern Europe and CIS	1 in 797
OECD	1 in 4,085

Source: UNICEF, cited in UNDP 2002.

The capitalist system's tendency to reorganize the world economy in its own interest has had direct repercussions on relations between the sexes. On the one hand, the capitalist system takes full advantage of a preexisting form of oppression: patriarchy. At the same time, it accentuates the features of this oppression. Indeed, women's oppression is a weapon that capitalists use to control the workforce as a whole and even to justify their policies by shifting responsibility for social welfare from the state and collective institutions to the "privacy" of the family.

Take the example of the dowry in India. Many think that forms of gender-based violence—dowry deaths and the abortion of female fetuses—are somehow "remnants" of a "backward" society. Yet, studies by Indian feminists prove, on the contrary, that the development of capitalism in India increased and intensified these forms of violence (Shah and Srinivasan in Duggan and Dashner 1994).

Based on current wage rates, the invisible nonmonetary contribution of women is worth $11 trillion. Given that the total value of annual world production is $23 trillion, women's contribution to humankind taken as a whole is easy to understand (UNDP 1995, 6). This figure does not even account for persistent injustice in women's wage rates, where they are paid for their labor. Taking into account places where significant progress in this area has been made, not a single country in the world pays women at the same rate as men. Some industrialized countries have even fallen way back.

Predominantly female professions, such as nursing and teaching, are undervalued. As far as the social safety net is concerned (unemployment insurance, for example), women, for example "live-ins" and long-term unemployed, were the first to be excluded by austerity packages. They are herded into jobs with significantly lower wages, such as in free-market zones. In Mexico's maquiladoras, for example, women's wages have plunged from 80 percent to only 57 percent of men's wages. The fact that women work for a pittance in such zones and in the informal sector is glorified by free marketeers, starry-eyed over the absence of "paralyzing" state regulations. Official studies in the Chinese countryside carried out in 1988 and 1989 reveal that women earn 20 percent less than men. Private firms in the cities pay women on average 56 percent of a man's wage.

Women's right to work is impeded by a multitude of government measures. Women, of course, have the "option" of part-time work, which could be anything from half-time down to a "zero-hour" contract in which the worker is at the employer's beck and call to work from zero to any number of hours. This is despite the fact that every opinion poll has shown that a majority of women workers would like full-time employment.

An August 2, 2002, article in *Le Monde*, "Income gap between men and women widens," confirms the above observations:

> The income gap between men and women is widening more, throughout their careers, for the younger generations. This is particularly due to the feminization of part-time employment, according to an official survey published on Wednesday, July 31. Thus, the men who started work in 1991–92 earn 21.9 percent more than women, while the difference is only 18 percent for those who started in 1976–80. This is partly due to the high increase in part-time jobs, most often and for longer periods occupied by women.

Cutbacks in funding for services such as nurseries and day-care centers, and the privatization of other services such as retirement homes, dramatically increase the number of obstacles for women who want to work full-time. "Equality at work" has been applied negatively to bring back night shifts for women. This is unacceptable as a point of principle and extremely difficult for women in any case given their family responsibilities. In developing countries, the rate of women's economic activity is still one-third lower than that of men. In OECD countries, women devote two-thirds of their time to nonmarket activities, that is, twice as much as men (UNDP 2000a, 33).

In the Third World, the World Bank—with the help of a number of nongovernmental organizations (NGOs)—finances all sorts of women's organizations and cooperatives. It has suddenly decided that women are the key to development. Although the World Bank is clearly trying to boost its public image, it is only laying the groundwork for future misfortune. Take the example of women-run tomato cooperatives in Senegal. They did very well until an Italian multinational decided to conquer the Senegalese market, crushing the defenseless cooperatives with their competition and lower prices. The NGO involved closed up shop once "its" project was "complete," leaving the locals to deal with the nagging question of the unpaid World Bank loan.

Joseph Stiglitz recounts an experience he had when he was still senior vice president and chief economist at the World Bank:

> In 1998, I visited some poor villages in Morocco to see what impact projects being run there by the World Bank and NGOs were having on the life of the people there.... An NGO had painstakingly instructed local villagers on raising chickens, an enterprise that the village women could perform as they continued more traditional activities. Originally, the women obtained their seven-day-old chicks from a government enterprise. But when I visited the village, the new enterprise had collapsed. I discussed with the villagers and government officials what had gone wrong. The answer was simple: the government had been told by the IMF that it should not be in the business of distributing chicks, so it ceased selling them. It was simply assumed that the private sector would immediately fill the gap. Indeed, a new private supplier arrived to provide the villagers with newborn chicks. The death rate of chicks in the first two weeks is high, however, and the private firm was unwilling to provide a guarantee. The villagers simply could not bear the risk of buying chicks that might die in large numbers. Thus, a nascent industry, poised to make a difference in the lives of these poor peasants, was shut down.

The 2000 UNDP *Human Development Report* considers that in all countries the gender-related development index (GDI) is lower than the HDI. This means that once corrected with the impact of the GDI, the HDI systematically falls. In other words, inequalities between men and women are observed in all societies; if human development were shared equally among men and women, there would be no discrepancy between GDI and HDI.

Another effect of the patriarchal system is that poverty goes hand in hand with violence. Before birth, female fetuses are aborted; during childhood, there is sexual abuse; after marriage, domestic violence (in Germany, the number of battered wives is estimated at 4 million). In Canada, New Zealand, and the United Kingdom, studies show that one woman in six is raped during her lifetime. Suicide among women is higher than among men. Between 85 million and 115 million girls and women have suffered genital mutilation and endure the physiological and psychological consequences. Approximately 2 million girls are subjected to such mutilations every year (UNDP 2000a, 36). Globally, about one woman in three has experienced violence from her partner. About 1.2 million women and girls under age eighteen are transported abroad to become prostitutes (UNDP 2000a, 4). Five hundred thousand women from Eastern Europe and the CIS are brought to Western Europe against their will (UNDP 1999, 89). On a global scale, the number of "missing" women, i.e., women who were victims of infanticide, neglect, or abortion because of their sex, is as many as 100 million (UNDP 2002).

In Spain, in 1997, more than sixty women were killed by their partners. In Paris, three women die every two weeks because of violence inflicted by their partners, and half of all murdered women are killed by their partners (*Le Monde*, March 1, 2001). Women are also the victims of so-called crimes of honor: in Pakistan, the Human Rights Commission reports that more than one thousand women were murdered on such grounds in 1999 (UNDP 2000a, 36). Violence against women erupts in times of broader conflict: events in the former Yugoslavia and in Algeria provide ample evidence of this. Violence is an integral part of women's lives.

Women are underrepresented in government, as well. "While women account for half of the electorate, only 13% of seats in parliament are occupied by women; and only 7% of government posts" (UNDP 1997).

This handful of statistics, though far from exhaustive, demonstrates more than ever the need for a specific struggle by women for their emancipation. Let no one reduce this to a matter of "biology." Rather, it is a matter of the wide-ranging choices a society must make to ensure development, the only way to create genuine personal choice in a series of key areas. Women in the North have better lives than do their sisters in the South, thanks to the underlying fabric of social gains from previous decades. Women must take on the ideological, political, and economic system that erodes these gains or prevents their adoption.

Environmental damage as a factor and a consequence of poverty: Globalization of the environmental crisis[4]

"The two main causes of environmental damage are the poverty of the majority of the planet's inhabitants and the excessive consumption of the minority" (UNEP 1999).

During the 1990s, the total loss of forested areas, worldwide, was about 94 million hectares, or 2.4 percent of all forests (UNEP 2002). Almost 1 million hectares of Indonesian forest were destroyed by fires that raged for several months, from September 1997 on. In 1996, 3 million hectares of Mongolian forest burned (UNEP 1999).

Destruction of natural habitats has become a serious threat to biological diversity in the Latin American and Caribbean region, where 40 percent of the planet's animal and plant species are found. An estimated 1,244 species of vertebrates are threatened with extinction (UNEP 1999). About 24 percent (1,130) of mammalian species and 12 percent (1,183) of bird species are now considered at risk on a global scale (UNEP 2002).

Neoliberal policies are not only unsustainable because of their human cost, but also because of the serious and irreversible damage they wreak on the environment. Poor countries manifest the direst effects of the ecological crisis. They are the immediate victims of the worst environmental degradation, such as destruction of tropical forests, mineral and petroleum extraction, water pollution, and the extinction of species. The environment suffers from the direct exploitation of natural resources for global markets, with prices that never cover the ecological cost, and also from the exportation of waste from industrial countries.

TABLE 1.5. COMPARISON OF TURNOVER OF CORPORATIONS
WITH GDP OF COUNTRIES (1998)

	Billions (US dollars)	Population (in millions)
General Motors	161.3	
Poland	158.6	38
Daimler Chrysler	154.6	
Ford	144.4	
Wal-Mart	137.6	
South Africa	133.5	39
Mitsui	131.6	
Finland	123.5	5
Greece	120.7	10
Mitsubishi	118.9	
Itochu	116.8	
TotalFinaElf [a]	110.2	
Portugal	106.7	9
Colombia	102.7	40
Marubeni	102.5	
Exxon	100.7	
General Electric	100.5	
Sumitomo	95.5	
Indonesia	94.2	206
Shell	93.7	
Toyota	88.5	
Egypt	82.7	66
Ireland	81.9	3
IBM	81.7	
Volkswagen	80.5	
BP Amoco	68.3	
The Philippines	65.1	72
Pakistan	63.4	148
Honda	52.4	
Nestle´	52.2	
Sony	51.2	

Unilever	47.5	
Algeria	47.3	30
Bangladesh	42.7	124
Nigeria	41.4	106
Vivendi	33.9	
Carrefour	32.0	
ABB	30.9	
Vietnam	27.2	77
GlaxoSmithKline[a]	26.2	
Ecuador	18.4	12
7 largest corporations in table	965.3	
China	959.0	1,255
6 largest corporations in table	848.5	
Brazil	778.2	165
5 largest corporations in table	729.6	
South East Asia (incl. India)	670.5	1,364
General Motors + Daimler Chrysler + Ford	460.3	
India	430.0	982
General Motors + Daimler Chrysler	315.9	
Sub-Saharan Africa	319.8	569
Russia	276.6	147
General Motors	161.3	
48 least developed countries	145.9	581

[a] Turnover for the year 2000

Source: Drawn up by Damien Millet and Eric Toussaint, using data from UNDP 2000a, OECD 2000, and Transnationale.org.

Poor countries are undoubtedly the most vulnerable populations in the face of growing environmental risks, and especially in the face of extreme weather conditions caused by climatic change. They bear a disproportionate share of the adverse effects of "natural" disasters, conflicts, droughts, or pollution without the means for advance preparation. Since 1991, two-thirds of disaster victims have lived in "countries with a low level of human development" (UNEP 2002). In the coming decades, the rising sea level due to global warming could have catastrophic consequences for all densely populated coastal regions.

The first effects of these ecological upsets are to further worsen the living conditions of the poor and reduce possibilities for development. Situations of poverty force many men and women to eke out a living by using natural resources without the means to ensure their sustainability in a spiral of destruction. Thus, over the period 1990–95, deforestation in the thirty-three African countries classified among the most heavily indebted poor countries was 50 percent greater than deforestation in other African countries, and 140 percent greater than the global average for deforestation.

Worldwide, 1.5 billion human beings are short of firewood. Time spent each year collecting firewood has quadrupled, sometimes reaching 190 to 300 working days per year. Women are the first to suffer the consequences of this shortage. However, it would be a mistake to blame deforestation on poor populations alone. The deforestation due to governments under pressure to repay their debt (tropical wood is valuable) and the deforestation due to multinationals, always after projects and profits, certainly account for the lion's share.

The highly industrialized countries have not managed to keep environmental degradation in check in their own regions. Since 1980, waste production per inhabitant of Western Europe has increased by 35 percent. Though recycling has increased, 66 percent of waste still ends up in landfills. In many European countries, underground water supplies are being overexploited and seriously polluted with nitrates, pesticides, heavy metals, and hydrocarbons. In the North Atlantic, fish stocks off the East American coast are almost exhausted. Atlantic catches have dwindled from 2.5 million tons in 1971, to less than 500,000 tons in 1994 (UNEP 1999). In the North as in the South, the poor and workers are more exposed to ecological risks, such as urban pollution and asbestos, than the rich.

Industrialized countries have developed in such a way as to endanger the ecological balance of the planet. In the 1990s, the industrial countries produced eight times more greenhouse gases per person than the developing countries. The neoliberal offensive has led to the abandonment of the "promises" made at the Rio Summit in favor of the expansion of trading in environment and pollution (there is now a market for pollution rights).

The globalization of capital: The growth of multinationals

As part of the long wave of slow growth that began in the 1970s, a number of significant changes have occurred in the way the world economy is structured. Many economists have called this "globalization" (see glossary). Multinational corporations have played a central role in this process. They have increased their presence both in production and trade (Adda 2001; UNCTAD

1994, 1997, 2000; Andreff 1982, 1996). Today these corporations control 70 percent of international trade and 75 percent of foreign direct investment. An estimated one-third of global trade in goods and services consists of intrafirm trade between multinationals and their subsidiaries.

The UNCTAD *World Investment Report 2002* lists 65,000 multinational corporations with 850,000 subsidiaries. In 2001, delocalized subsidiaries employed some 54 million people compared with 24 million people in 1990. Among these tens of thousands of corporations, only five hundred really matter, and among these, some one hundred are really impressive in size. In 2000, the top one hundred nonfinancial multinational corporations (the Vodaphone group, General Electric, and ExxonMobil filled the top three places) accounted for more than half of the total turnover and more than half of the workforce of the delocalized subsidiaries. Their turnover largely exceeds the gross domestic product of several countries, as shown in table 1.5.

The political factor

Globalization cannot be understood merely by looking at the increase in the weight of multinationals and technological change. The political factor has also been essential. Without the active political intervention of the Reagan and Thatcher governments, and then of all the governments that chose to follow their lead, multinational corporations would not have been able so swiftly and so radically to do away with the restrictions that prevented them from acting as they please and from exploiting economic, human, and natural resources as they see fit.

This political intervention was carried out with four key objectives in mind: first, the liberalization of international capital flows and the opening of domestic markets to international competition; second, the privatization of state-owned companies and public services; third, the deregulation of the labor market and the dismantling of the social safety net; fourth, maintaining and improving competitiveness through the pursuit and achievement of the first three objectives.

Riccardo Petrella (1995) of the Lisbon Group has summed up the line of thinking that justified this political intervention:

> No matter the sector targeted (expanding or in decline, hi-tech or not), or the size, strength and level of development of the country in question, the argument has always been the same. Privatization is urgent, they say, in order to increase the competitiveness of an industrial sector, a company or an economy in the throes of globalization. In addition, all markets must be liberalized in order for local industry and companies operating on a global scale to be competitive on international markets. Finally, industrial sectors and markets have to be deregulated in order to

accelerate the privatization process, and in the process increase the competitive-ness of local companies and the national (or regional) economy as a whole.

He further adds,

Since these pressures are applied in most fields and, for the first time, in almost every single country, everyone is trying to out-compete everyone else and to be competitive the world over. In such conditions, the near-universal ascendancy of competitive cap-italism as a normative system should not come as a surprise. The bigger they are, however, the harder they fall.

Although in crisis, the neoliberal offensive pursues its course

The dominant discourse sought to obscure another battle that still rages today. The holders of capital have launched repeated attacks to reduce wages (and employer payroll taxes) and create more flexible work schedules—all in order to intensify the rate of utilization of the productive apparatus (ma-chines). They also seek to considerably reduce or even utterly destroy the mechanisms of collective solidarity that were gradually built up in the twenti-eth century as a result of bitter struggles (the distributive pension system, broad social security coverage, etc.). In spite of worker resistance, employers have scored significant victories. Mass unemployment has been created and used by the dominant classes to roll back social gains in all fields.

Thanks to this situation, the capitalists—and the institutions that serve them—have been able to force up the profitability of capital. Company profit rates increased sharply in the 1990s, especially between 1995 and 2000.

During the period from 1980 to 2000, the champions of neoliberal global-ization were flying high. Every crisis was overcome: the world recession in the early 1980s, the stock market crash of 1987, the recession of 1991–92. Even better, the dominion of capital was considerably enlarged by the implosion of the Soviet Bloc at the end of the 1980s. The dominant classes in power during the Soviet era embraced the restoration of capitalism, subtly baptized "the transition towards a market economy," and congratulated themselves on the policies recommended by the World Bank and the IMF.

Better still, thanks to the debt crisis of the so-called Third World countries and the ensuing structural adjustment policies, the highly industrialized capi-talist powers were able to strengthen their grip on the economies of the pe-riphery while imposing endless sacrifices upon the populations concerned. Apart from a few rare exceptions, the governments and the dominant classes of those countries hailed the benefits of globalization and applied, often with great docility, the policies dictated by the IMF, the World Bank, and the WTO. Massive transfers of the wealth produced by the peoples of the periphery were made in favor of the holders of capital in the highly industrialized countries, with the periphery capitalists skimming off their commissions on the way. Every crisis that struck one or several periphery countries (there have been several dozen) was resolved in such a way as to encourage continued submission to the dominant model, especially through structural adjustment.

To summarize, the neoliberal capitalist offensive has kept up its advance, both in the economies of the center (where new buzzwords were coined such as the "new economy" and the "wealth effect," while all the time the social divide widened) and in the periphery (where the countries of the so-called emerging economies were disciplined by the IMF and the "markets," and where all traces of a new world economic order were abandoned).

Since 1994–95, things have begun to deteriorate for the champions of neoliberal globalization. At the lower levels of society, both in the countries of the center and those of the periphery, the acts of resistance that had continued unceasingly, increased with renewed and unforeseen vigor. A new movement, albeit embracing a certain amount of diversity of opinion, has gradually emerged. Debates hinge on whether to be antiglobalization or for an alternative globalization. Should the World Bank and the IMF be reformed or abolished? Should debt cancellation be conditional or unconditional? Should capitalism be maintained in a regulated form or replaced by another system? These issues are the objects of wholesome and necessary debate. The important thing is the capacity to mobilize ever-increasing numbers and to engage in defining alternatives for social progress in the face of the tyranny of the (capitalist) markets. The movement is preparing not for a sprint, but a marathon.

However, from the point of view of the governments and ruling classes whose interest is to further the neoliberal offensive, the main problem is not the movement's promotion of the idea that another type of globalization is possible. In short, the champions of neoliberal globalization do not believe that the movement is capable of seriously obstructing the progress of the offensive under way since the early 1980s—at least not yet. In their view, there is a bigger, internal problem. Several factors inherent in the system itself are beginning to endanger its future: a new international economic crisis erupted in early 2001. That year saw the collapse of the "new economy," a fall in profit rates, resounding bankruptcies, a stock market crisis, increased monetary instability, and severe company and household indebtedness. However, this accumulation of problems is not sufficient to bring about a terminal crisis. The system still has its escape routes, and those at the lower levels of society are only loosely organized around a unifying alternative project. Nevertheless, after twenty years of triumph, neoliberal globalization is certainly undergoing for the first time a very marked period of turbulence from which it is unlikely to emerge unscathed.

Globalization today is not working for many of the world's poor. It is not working for much of the environment. It is not working for the stability of the global economy. The transition from communism to a market economy has been so badly managed that, with the exception of China, Vietnam and a few Eastern European countries, poverty has soared as income has plummeted.... The problem is not with globalization, but with how it has been managed. Part of the problem lies with the international economic institutions, with the IMF, World Bank and WTO, which help set the rules of the game. They have done so in ways that, all too often, have served the interests of the most advanced industrialized countries—and particularly interests within those countries—rather than those of the developing world. (Stiglitz 2002, 214)

Today the system of capitalism is at a crossroads just as it was during the Great Depression. In the 1930s, capitalism was saved by Keynes, who thought of policies to create jobs and rescue those suffering from the collapse of the global economy. Now, millions of people around the world are waiting to see whether globalization can be reformed so that its benefits can be more widely shared. (Stiglitz 2002, 249–50)

The man who wrote those words is—not insignificantly—a former top official of one of the key institutions of the apparatus for the world domination of capital and of the few major countries that impose their views on the rest. He has decided to distance himself from neoliberalism's present course and to propose a different political approach, as did J.M. Keynes.

Keynes was a British civil servant who walked out of Her Majesty's delegation during the negotiations of the Treaty of Versailles. In the ensuing years, he resolutely engaged in trying to reform capitalism and to save it, which he carried off with a certain amount of success. His proposals had a profound influence on President Roosevelt's New Deal. In 1944, Keynes was one of the main instigators of the Bretton Woods conference, where the IMF and the World Bank were founded.

Joseph Stiglitz, a Keynesian economist and high-ranking United States civil servant, has recently returned to his university professorship. A former adviser to Bill Clinton, he presided over Clinton's Council of Economic Experts before becoming senior vice president and chief economist of the World Bank in 1997. In November 1999, he resigned, pushed out by Larry Summers, the Clinton administration's secretary of the treasury.

Today, Stiglitz has embarked upon a spirited denunciation of the neoliberal policies of the United States Treasury and the IMF (largely dominated by the treasury and the big capitalist groups), and proposes, in turn, to save capitalism. He gives numerous interviews and talks and has published a book, *Globalization and Its Discontents*, which has proved a real firebrand. He makes clear references to Keynes's project. Stiglitz's arguments are not new; they have been made a great deal since 1980. The new factor in the present period is that someone of his stature should make such a terrifying diagnosis of the policies applied over the last twenty years by the governments of the main highly industrialized countries, the IMF, the World Bank, and the WTO, by the so-called developing countries, and those of the former Soviet Bloc. He knows that he can afford to be radical in his denunciation because it echoes the growing sound of discontent rising from all four corners of the planet. He knows that his words do not fall on deaf ears.

It would be idle to speculate on the future of Joseph Stiglitz. However, it is worth observing, as he does, that the human race is once again at a crossroad, a decisive moment in history, as it was between the two world wars in the last century. "History never repeats itself, it stammers." It is in such circumstances that the great debates over the choices society could make come thundering back onto the scene. Let us hope, this time, that the result will go beyond a simple remodeling of capitalism. Humankind must be able to provide itself with another system. Another world is possible.

---

1   To calculate this sum, Merrill Lynch and Cap Gemini Ernst & Young deduct residential property from the millionaires' fortunes (*World Wealth Report 2003*, 17). If an exceptional tax of 50 percent were levied on the remaining assets, that would make $13.6 trillion for the international community while the millionaires would retain half their fortunes as well as their luxury residences. The UNDP and UNICEF reckon that $800 billion over ten years ($80 billion a year) would ensure universal access to drinking water, basic health care, primary education, and proper nutrition for all. There is no reason not to envisage far more radical measures than a 50 percent tax on the handful of individuals who have accumulated such scandalous wealth.

2   It seems paradoxical that the assets of the very rich continued to grow in 2001 and 2002 while stock market capitalization fell sharply. In 2002, while world stock market capitalization fell 16.9 percent, the value of the assets of the world's millionaires grew by 3.6 percent (see above). This is because their eggs are not in one basket. Their situation is very different from the millions of salaried workers who lost their main source of revenue—their jobs. Well-informed millionaires have more than enough assets to spread across different areas. Losses in one sector can be compensated by gains in another: a few stocks and shares, public and private debt paper, cash deposits, real estate, valuable pieces of art, wine collections—the *World Wealth Report* considers the latter "an attractive investment option. A selection of wines made by Fine Wine Management made 97% higher profits than shares did over the period 2000–2002" (*WWR*, 13). According to Merrill Lynch and Cap Gemini, millionaires spread their assets as follows for 2002: 30 percent in fixed-income bonds (debt bonds); 25 percent in cash deposits; 20 percent in shares; 15 percent in real estate; and 10 percent in alternative investments (art, wine, etc.).

3   For an analysis of inequality in France, see the useful book by Alain Bihr and Roland Pfefferkorn, *Déchiffrer les Inégalités* (Deciphering Inequality), 1999, Syros-La Découverte, Paris. See also *L'économie des inégalités* (The Economics of Inequality) by Thomas Piketty, 2001, Collection Repères, La Découverte, Paris.

4   The sources for these paragraphs are UNEP's *Global Environment Outlook* reports, GEO-2 (1999) and GEO-3 (2002).

2

The concentration of capital

A wave of corporate acquisitions and mergers and the concentration of capital

During the 1990s, a large number of corporate mergers and takeovers took place the world over. This wave was helped along by the neoliberal policies described in chapter 1. Along with massive privatization was the elimination of government control over the acquisition of domestic firms by foreign capital and the development of the stock market bubble. The wave of acquisitions and mergers can best be gauged by the rapid increase in foreign direct investment (FDI).

The annual volume of the flow of foreign investments increased sixfold in ten years, going from $200 billion in 1990, to more than $1.2 trillion in 2000. The vast majority of these investments went into corporate acquisitions and mergers, and they have not served to increase productive capacity. They have involved property changing hands, leading to greater concentration of capital on an international level and favoring the companies of the main countries of the Triad (see glossary).

The value of mergers in 1999 was almost $700 billion. The six most important mergers cost $238 billion, i.e., more than the entire external debt of sub-Saharan Africa or the equivalent of the external debt of Brazil.

The crisis that erupted in the United States in 2001 had an internationally contagious effect. Investment flows fell by 56 percent in 2001 compared to 2000. In 2002, the fallback continued. The overall drop of stock market values greatly reduced the enormous liquid assets that businesses need to cover purchases. With hindsight, OECD specialists recognize a link between the enormous acquisition and merger boom in 1999–2000 and the fast-expanding stock market bubble.

A situation of oligopoly

In many economic sectors, a handful of multinational corporations controls the greater part of production (a situation of "oligopoly"; see glossary). Though oligopolies existed before, they have become much more common since the 1980s.

The authors of the 1999 UNDP *Human Development Report* ask, "In 1998, how much of the global market did the top 10 corporations in each industry control?" They answer,

> In commercial seed, 32% of a $23 billion industry; in pharmaceuticals, 35% of $297 billion; in veterinary medicine, 60% of $ 17 billion; in computers, almost 70% of $334 billion; in pesticides, 85% of $ 31 billion; and in telecommunications, more than 86% of $262 billion. The lesson is clear: privatization does not automatically lead to competition. (p. 67)

Banking, retail sales (the big chain stores), tourism, and mass media are further examples of corporate concentration in the framework of globalization.

In 1995, five advanced capitalist countries (the United States, Japan, France, Germany, and the United Kingdom) controlled 168 of the 200 biggest multinational corporations (Clairmont 1997). These 168 accounted for 85.9 percent of the overall turnover of the 200 biggest corporations. In 1998, the same five countries controlled 170, which produced 86.5 percent of the global turnover of the 200 biggest multinational corporations (Clairmont 1999).

The Third World is virtually absent from such rankings. Only China, Brazil, Venezuela, Mexico, and South Korea make a modest appearance in 1995, with one multinational each for the first four and six for South Korea. The latter was expanding fast in the first half of the 1990s, and had gained a significant position in the international division of work. Its multinationals, in their particular domains, vied with those of the highly industrialized countries, even if they only represented 2.3 percent of the turnover of the 200 biggest corporations. The ten multinationals of the Third World altogether only represented 3.3 percent.

In 1998, a year after the Southeast Asian crisis erupted, only three Korean multinationals remained instead of six, and their percentage of the overall turnover of the 200 biggest corporations had fallen from 2.3 percent to 1.1 percent. In the ensuing years, the main Korean multinationals were restructured and the main multinationals of the industrialized countries bought up whole sections. The following quotation from the first edition of this book (1998) has been borne out:

> The main multinationals of the industrialized countries are in favor of dismantling a number of South Korean industrial houses organized into chaebols. It is therefore not excluded that a number of South Korean multinationals will be cut back and lose their place in the Top 200 hit parade. (p. 32)

In 2003, only one Korean multinational figured on the list of the 200 biggest: Samsung. Of the fifty biggest multinationals (ranked by their stock market capitalization), none had its head office in a country of the periphery, and all belonged to Triad countries—thirty-three North American, two Japanese, and fifteen European (Germany, Great Britain, Finland, France, the Netherlands, Italy, and Switzerland).

TABLE 2.1. EXAMPLES OF GLOBAL CONCENTRATION

Sector
Year: Concentration

Database management
1987: Five corporations account for 65 percent of global production; ten corporations for 100 percent.

Glass automobile parts
1988: Three corporations account for 53 percent of global production.

Tires
1988: Six corporations account for 85 percent of global production.

Medical equipment
1989: Seven corporations account for 90 percent of global production.

Bananas
1994: Three corporations account for 80 percent of marketed production.

Cars
1994: Ten corporations account for 76 percent of global production; the five largest of these account for 50 percent.

Grain
1994: Five corporations account for 77 percent of marketed production.

Image banks
1994: Three corporations control 80 percent of the world market.

Instant coffee
1994: Two corporations account for 80 percent of global production.

Tobacco
1994: Four corporations account for 87 percent of marketed production.

Microprocessors
1997: One corporation (Intel) controls 60 percent of the market.

Telecommunications and related equipment
1997: Four corporations account for 70 percent of global sales.

Civilian aeronautics
1998: Two corporations (Boeing and Airbus) account for 95 percent of global production.

Audit firms
2002: Four groups control the market.

Source: Author, based on Petrella 1995 and Chesnais 1997c.

The increase in the domination of Triad multinational corporations was further accelerated by the many acquisitions and mergers in the years 1999, 2000, and 2001. Numerous companies in periphery countries were either completely bought up or sold for peanuts to Triad-country corporations. Looking at the list in the *Financial Times* supplement of May 10, 2002, of the five hundred largest firms on the planet, a clear picture emerges of the global power relationship between the companies of the Triad countries and those of the rest of the world, on the one hand, and between those within the Triad, on the other. Nearly 90 percent of the five hundred main companies have their head office in the Triad (48 percent in the United States, 30 percent in Western Europe, and 10 percent in Japan). The might of United States companies is impressive: of the top ten firms on the *Financial Times* list, nine are American; of the top twenty-five, 72 percent are American; of the top fifty, 70 percent are American; of the top one hundred, 57 percent are American. A year later, using the same criteria, the *Financial Times* (May 28, 2003) observed that firms based in the United States had maintained their position.

In 2003, six of the ten main banks had their head office in the United States (five in 2002). The same was true for six of the ten main pharmaceutical and biotech companies (same as 2002); three of the top ten telecommunications companies (four in 2002); four of the top ten oil companies (same in 2002); seven of the top ten computer software companies (nine in 2002); and eight of the top ten general retailers or chain stores (nine in 2002). In 2003, eight of ten computer hardware companies had their head office in the United States, as did five of ten insurance companies.

The "global village"

The term "globalization" is sometimes linked to the idea of a "global village," giving it a very friendly image. Accelerated concentration in the mass media sector has given a boost to this image makeover. Images we see on the television news are in fact rebroadcast by television networks the world over. A huge majority of these television images are produced, chosen, and marketed by three image banks that control 80 percent of the market (see table 2.1). In an era in which what is not shown on television simply does not exist, these image banks have tremendous power. The manner in which an event is portrayed also plays a big role, as does the spoken commentary. We have an increasingly one-dimensional and monolithic "worldview," of which CNN provides an excellent example.

The effects are staggering. African television audiences see the situation on their continent through the eyes of local networks that are fed their material by international news agencies and image banks. In other cases, television networks of the former colonial powers provide material to African stations. France's former colonies in Africa are submerged in footage from France's public networks, free of charge. Africa's public networks do not have the means to provide their own footage. A reporter from Ivory Coast once quipped that it was easier to get footage on the condition of farmers in the northeast of France than on farmers in his own country.

In this sense, the global village fosters exclusion. The globalization of news means leaving out part of the planet. In a village, everyone knows their neighbors. The global village of the media does not. Entire regions of the planet only make the news when there is some sort of catastrophe. Then, dozens of television teams all converge on one location at the same time to give viewers live coverage of the tragedy.

The genocide of Tutsis and mass murder of Hutu dissidents by the Rwandan army and the paramilitary militia of the Habyarimana regime, in which about one million people died, were not shown at the time they occurred (April–May 1994). Rwanda only really hit the screens in July–August 1994, when a section of the Rwandan population fled the country en masse toward ex-Zaire as part of the French army's Operation Turquoise. Television coverage by French networks, broadcast through much of French-speaking Africa, did not mention the support given by French officials to those responsible for the genocide before, during, and after the event. Indeed, French soldiers backed by African contingents, especially from Senegal, were portrayed as saviors.

During the second Iraq war of March–April 2003, six hundred journalists were directly embedded with British and American invading troops. Global village television viewers were fed images taken from the perspective of the invaders. There were no images from the side of the Iraqi army, and very few from the standpoint of Iraqi civilians.

Concentration in the print media and the establishment of veritable global media empires (Rupert Murdoch's News Corporation, those of Bertelsmann, Vivendi Universal, Hachette Filipacchi, O Globo in Brazil, etc.) have snuffed out a large number of quality papers, a process also under way in the former Soviet Bloc.

During the war against Iraq in spring 2003, in the three main invading countries (the United States, the UK, and Australia), Rupert Murdoch's influence on significant information media was apparent. Murdoch placed himself resolutely in the warmongers' camp and weighed heavily in a climate of divided public opinion. Indeed, in those three countries, antiwar demonstrations had received massive support. The empire of the Australian-American magnate includes a certain number of Australian newspapers (75 percent of the dailies); 40 percent of the British written press, with the *Sun* (3.6 million copies), *News of the World* (4 million), the *Times*, and the *Sunday Times*; and the New York tabloid, the *New York Post* (500,000 copies). To this, add more than a dozen television channels, including Fox News, which beat CNN for audience ratings in the United States in 2002, and the great cinema studio 20th Century Fox.

When you throw the concentration of film production and distribution companies into the mix, there is not that much left. The same big-budget movies are released almost simultaneously in all the world's main cities. The same kinds of values and ideological content flood the world with a speed and power never dreamed of in the past.

> Hollywood reaches every market, getting more than 50% of its revenues from overseas, up from just 30% in 1980. It claimed 70% of the film market in Europe in 1996, up from 56% in 1987—and 83% in Latin America and 50% in Japan. By contrast, foreign films rarely make it big in the United States, taking less than 3% of the market there. (UNDP 1999, 33)

The leading export industry in the United States is neither aeronautics nor automobiles; it is the entertainment sector. Thus, the export of Hollywood films brought in more than $30 billion in 1997. That is the equivalent of two-thirds of total Brazilian export revenues for 1996, and 30 percent more than the total export revenues of Argentina.

Those with political and economic power have always used big media to further their policies and interests, even when this involves military or repressive action. Television is fully harnessed in this respect. The landing of American soldiers in Mogadishu on December 9, 1992, was planned to coincide with prime time in the United States. A single perspective of the so-called humanitarian operation in Somalia was broadcast simultaneously across the globe.

Media coverage of the criminal attacks of September 11, 2001, and of the war launched by the United States and its allies was part of an enormous communications operation seeking to legitimate the new warmongering strategy of the Bush administration. An inquiry carried out by the French daily *Le Monde* (July 24, 2002) on the links between Hollywood and the CIA showed that a specialized CIA department successfully works at influencing certain Hollywood film scenarios in a very precise way.

The market: The new faith

Practically all political leaders—whether from the traditional Left or from the Right, from the North or the South—have a quasi-religious faith in the market, especially in the financial markets. Or rather, they are themselves the high priests of this religion. Every day in every country, anyone with a television can attend mass in honor of the market-god—in the form of stock exchange and financial market reports. The market-god sends his messages through television anchors and the financial editors of daily newspapers. Today, this not only happens in OECD countries, but most parts of the world. Whether in Moscow or Dakar, in Rio de Janeiro or Timbuktu, you can receive "market signals." Everywhere, governments have privatized and created the illusion that the population would be able to participate directly in market rituals (by buying shares) and reap the benefits in accordance with how well signals sent by the market-god are interpreted. In reality, the small part of the working population that has acquired shares has no say over market tendencies.

The reader will indulge me for a moment as I take a somewhat more humorous approach to this sad state of affairs:

> In a few centuries, the history books might say that in the 1980s and 1990s a fetishist cult prospered. The dramatic rise of this cult will perhaps be associated with two heads of state, Margaret Thatcher and Ronald Reagan. It will be noted that, from the start, this cult had the backing of governments and powerful private financial interests. Indeed, for this cult to gain ground within the population, public and private media found it necessary to pay homage to it day in and day out.
>
> The gods of this religion were the financial markets. Its temples were known as Stock Exchanges. Only the high priests and their acolytes could enter these temples. The faithful were called upon to commune with their market-god on television, in the daily papers, on the radio, and at the bank.
>
> Thanks to television and radio, even in the most remote parts of the planet, hundreds of millions of people whose right to meet their basic needs was denied were also beseeched to celebrate the market-god. In the North, in the papers read by a majority of workers, housewives, and unemployed, an "investment" section was published every day, even though the overwhelming majority of readers did not own a single share.
>
> Journalists were paid to help the faithful understand signals sent by the gods. To heighten the power of the gods in the eyes of the faithful, commentators periodically declared that the gods had sent signals to governments to express their satisfaction or discontent.
>
> The places where the gods were most likely to forcefully express their moods were Wall Street in New York; the City in London; and at the Paris, Frankfurt, and Tokyo stock exchanges. To gauge their moods, special indicators were devised: the Dow Jones in New York, the Nikkei in Tokyo, the CAC40 in France, the Footsie in London, and the Bel20 in Belgium.

To appease the gods, governments sacrificed the Welfare State to the stock markets. They also privatized public property.

Why were ordinary market operators given a religious aura? They were neither unknown nor ethereal. They had names, addresses. They were the people in charge of the 200 biggest multinationals, which controlled the world with the help of the G7 and institutions such as the IMF, the World Bank, and the World Trade Organization. Governments were no strangers to this situation; from Reagan and Thatcher onward, they relinquished the means they had of controlling financial markets.

As a result, money could cross borders with not a single cent in taxes being levied. More than $1.4 trillion raced around the planet every day. Less than 10 percent of this amount was linked to actual trade in goods and services. More than 90 percent concerned purely speculative currency trades and money laundering (for drugs, for example).

Newspapers reported on a regular basis that Wall Street had reacted favorably to the increase in unemployment and slowdowns in economic growth. It is difficult to underestimate how much this period in history contributed to the spread of a kind of ideology of death.

So much for the humorous interlude. Let us return to today's unpleasant truths, as portrayed in two examples from *Le Monde*. On October 9, 1996, a headline on page 17 reads "The Dow Jones index has temporarily crossed the 6000-point line." The story reads: "On Friday, 40,000 job losses in the USA were announced for September, while analysts had been predicting 166,000 job creations. Operators greeted the news with relief." It continues: "Since the beginning of President Clinton's mandate, the Dow Jones index has practically doubled, directly contributing to the prevailing feeling of wealth and economic well-being in the United States today."

On December 8, 1996, Eric Leser wrote in *Le Monde*, "The sixth of December was nearly a 'Black Friday' throughout the world's financial centers. Finally, damage was limited, thanks to Wall Street's resistance [*sic*] and the publication of US unemployment figures for November, judged satisfactory by analysts." What were these satisfactory figures? A little further on, Leser tells us: "A 5% rise in unemployment in the USA in November and a lower number (118,000) of job creations than forecast (175,000)."

After the succession of financial scandals and the stock market crisis in the United States and much of the rest of the world in 2001–02, some journalists have adopted a more critical tone. Leser, who has become a permanent correspondent in New York, is one example. He wrote July 9, 2002, under the headline "When capitalists become capitalism's worst enemies...":

Not a week goes by without a fresh accountancy scandal involving a big American company. Sham profits, inflated turnover figures, fiddled books, embezzlement.... The 1990s of the stock market bubble and easy money are gradually washing their dirty linen. "We knew it was a casino, but we thought that at least it was honest," wrote Barton Biggs, the main strategist at Morgan Stanley, earlier this month. Enron, WorldCom, Tyco, Adelphia, Global Crossing, Xérox…, the list of companies with rigged accounts goes on and on.

He continues, "Each time what seems like a different story turns out to be very similar to the others. Directors have deceived shareholders and employees in order to get rich. False good news keeps the stock markets rising so that stock options could be sold at huge profits." To crown it all, Leser finishes:

They have been getting away with it for years with the more or less active collusion of banks, auditors and all kinds of committees, while the inspection authorities remained blind or incompetent.

He might have added, "They did it with the kindly disposed support or the blindness of the finance editors of most of the media, not excepting the one at *Le Monde*." Nevertheless, though Leser could do with a little self-criticism, one can only approve of his newfound lucidity since he took up his post in New York.

3

Globalization and exclusion: The Third World is marginalized and the Triad gains strength

The share of the periphery countries in global flows of private capital dropped significantly in the last years of the twentieth century. This discredits the "neoclassical theory of growth which postulates that available capital in the countries with high per capita income must inevitably be directed to countries where the per capita income is low, since the productivity of capital is greater there" (Yves Mamou in *Le Monde*, April 10, 2001).

Periphery countries, in which more than 85 percent of the world's population lives, only attracted a marginal share of the capital moving around the planet during the most favorable period (1990–97) of the neoliberal era. Among the 187 countries classified by the OECD as developing countries (DC), about ten received more than half of this small sum. Between 1997 and 2000, the share of periphery countries in private capital flows shrank from 15 percent to 7.5 percent (see figure 3.1).

International flows of private capital going to the periphery are divided into four categories by the World Bank: (1) foreign direct investments (FDI), which represent most of the capital flow; (2) portfolio share investments; (3) securities and debt bonds issued by private companies or public entities of periphery countries; and (4) international bank loans.

In the period 1990–97, FDI represented about 50 percent of flows; portfolio investments and debt paper about 16 percent and 15 percent, respectively (see "Finance markets" in table 3.1); and bank loans, about 12 percent.

TABLE 3.1. COMPOSITION OF PRIVATE FLOWS TO THE DC (PERCENT OF TOTAL)

	1973–81	1990–97
Bank loans	63.9	11.7
Finance markets	3.8	31.6
FDI	16.8	50.3

Source: World Bank 2000b, 126.

Interestingly, the World Bank, the IMF, and the OECD rarely mention another flow of capital toward the periphery: the funds sent by migrant workers living in the industrialized countries to their families in the Third World. In 2002, these remittances came to $80 billion; in that same year, the net flow of bank loans to developing countries was negative (i.e., the total amount loaned came to more than the total amount repaid). The banks lent $17 billion to the DC, and the DC repaid them capital plus interest totaling $35 billion; in other words, the banks received $18 billion more than they lent. The remittances are gifts, which reach the population directly, while the loans simply add to the external debt and rarely benefit the population. Here, the solidarity of the lowly contrasts with the money grabbing of the rich.

In the late 1990s and early 2000s, bank loans fell off sharply (in fact, bank flows had become negative). Other private flows from international finance also diminished. The issue of debt paper fell by half between 1997 and 2002. Portfolio investments fell by two-thirds, and the flow of FDI also fell, although to a lesser extent. Foreign direct investment fell by about 15 percent between 1997 and 2002 (by 20 percent between 1999 and 2002).

The international financial institutions (IFIs) that for years systematically

FIGURE 3.1   **Global population distribution in 2001**

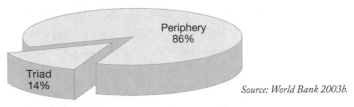

Source: World Bank 2003b.

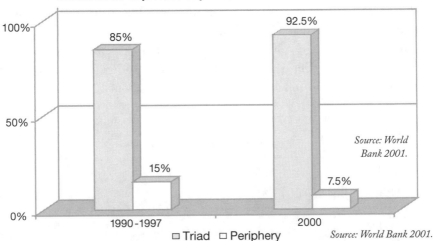

Source: World Bank 2001.

Source: World Bank 2001.

ignored the importance of migrants' remittances in private flows have made a U-turn on the issue. The World Bank *Global Development Finance* report published in April 2003 emphasized that importance, as the flows had increased by 33 percent between 1998 and 2002. Before publicly acknowledging that these remittances were significant, the World Bank had already launched programs in some Latin American and Asian countries with the aim of intervening in their management. As when it discovered that women in the DC could "manage" well in the 1980s, the World Bank, ever opportunistic, is now showing a lively interest in the activities of migrant workers and their families.

Between 1990 and 2002, migrant workers' remittances always totaled more than official development assistance (ODA) entering the DC. In 2002, migrants' remittances came to $80 billion, more than twice net ODA, which was $36.7 billion (World Bank 2003a, 201). Indeed, they came to more than total ODA (grants, concessional loans, technical assistance, and debt reduction combined), which came to $57 billion in 2002. In the rhetoric of the IFIs and governments, the IMF, World Bank, and creditor countries are called "donors," while the migrants are blatantly ignored, when not simply flown back to their home country. We will discuss migrants' remittances further in chapter 9.

Foreign direct investment

Foreign direct investment is a key element of the capital flows to the periphery. The periphery's share of the global stock of FDI continually decreased between 1960 and 1990: in 1960, it was a third; in 1980, a quarter; in 1990, a fifth. The decline is even more striking in historical perspective on the scale of

Takeover of Argentine oil company YPF by Repsol

The inflow of hard currency is usually cited among the arguments in favor of policies to attract FDI. Yet, the World Bank's *Global Development Finance 2003* illustrates that the results are not entirely satisfactory. The report cites the example of the 1999 takeover of the Argentine oil company YPF by the Spanish multinational corporation Repsol. At the time of the takeover, it was suggested that there was an inflow of capital to the tune of $15.5 billion, whereas, according to the World Bank, the net amount was only $4.6 billion. This is because $10.9 billion was paid by Repsol to foreign YPF shareholders, who immediately exported their capital elsewhere.

the entire twentieth century. In 1913, as in 1938, what was later to be called the Third World received two-thirds of FDI (see figure 3.2).

If we look at FDI flow, the share of Third World countries was considerably reduced from 38 percent to 17 percent between 1995 and 2000 (see figure 3.3).

Looking at the distribution of FDI between the 187 countries of the periphery, we see that each year, five to eight countries receive more than 50 percent. For example, in 1998, $177 billion of FDI was paid to the DC, with China ($45.5 billion), Brazil ($28.7 billion), Mexico ($10.2 billion), and Thailand ($7 billion) receiving more than half between them ($91.4 billion). Between 1990 and 2000, the main countries receiving FDI included China, Mexico, Brazil, Argentina, Thailand, South Korea, Malaysia, Hong Kong, and Singapore. In all, only about twenty countries (three or four from the former Soviet Bloc) received more than 80 percent of FDI directed toward the periphery in the 1980s.

With the exception of China, a large part of these flows is attracted by good deals to be made in taking advantage of vast privatization programs and an opening for foreign capital in the context of structural adjustment. In 1998–2000, that was the case for Argentina, Brazil, and the Southeast Asian countries. In the first half of the 1990s, Mexico and Chile led the field with the wave of massive privatizations. With the crisis in Argentina of December 2001, FDI flows (and other flows, such as bank loans, portfolio investments, and World Bank and IMF loans) were reduced. This had a contagious effect, and FDI flows to Brazil and Uruguay plummeted in 2002. Mexico continued

FIGURE 3.2

Distribution of FDI stocks

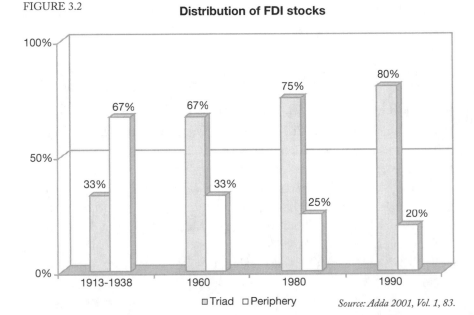

□ Triad   □ Periphery   *Source: Adda 2001, Vol. 1, 83.*

FIGURE 3.3

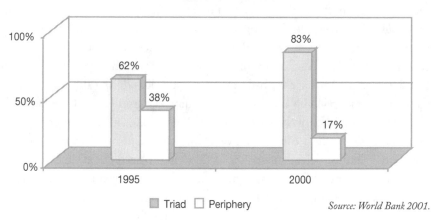

Distribution of FDI flows

Triad ☐ Periphery

Source: World Bank 2001.

to receive large flows in 2001–02, as two of its main banks, Bancomer and Banamex, were taken over by Triad firms. In 2001, the US bank Citigroup treated itself to Banamex, and in 2002, the Bilbao Vizcaya Argentaria bank won total control of Bancomer. However, flows may also dry up there unless the neoliberal government sells off the national oil company, Pemex.

While most FDI goes to a small number of countries, "For 100 countries foreign direct investment has averaged less than $100 million a year since 1990" (UNDP 1999, 31). The forty-nine least developed countries (LDC) taken together only receive an average 0.5 percent of FDI.

Intra-Triad investment

The share of Triad countries in FDI grew considerably at the end of the twentieth century. In 2000, more than 80 percent of global FDI was invested within the Triad. Most of it concerned dealings between Triad companies within a limited geographical area. It was mainly mergers and takeovers between companies to increase their ascendancy over a market sector and to become large enough that other companies would have difficulty taking them over. The consequences of these were job cuts (except in extremely rare cases), increased concentration, greater control of whole sectors of the market by just a few companies, and less innovation.

The stock market bubble in the second half of the 1990s gave companies with rising share prices enormous borrowing opportunities. They jumped at the chance to take on debts to buy up more companies. They also used borrowed money to buy up their own shares to keep prices high. This did not prevent prices from falling in 2001. At the end of that year, prices completely collapsed, and the erosion continued at a rapid pace throughout 2002–03. Many companies found themselves stripped bare. Their stock market value had collapsed, they could no longer afford to borrow, and they had enormous difficulty repaying their creditors. To free up cash to repay their debts, they began to sell the companies they had bought not long before. Desperate, they were often forced to sell very cheaply what they had bought at top prices during the stock market euphoria. Losses piled up and several resounding bankruptcies followed.

In the 1990s, US multinationals were behind a number of mergers and takeovers—in Western Europe, above all, but also in Japan. However, overall, the United States received much more FDI than it placed abroad. Over the last few years, the United States has systematically been the primary beneficiary of FDI. Between 1998 and 2000, the United States alone received more FDI annually than all periphery countries combined. In 2000, FDI flows to the main global power were three times the amount that went to the periphery.

The economic crisis that erupted in the United States in 2001–02 modified the situation. Suddenly, the United States was less attractive. The negative effects of this about-face may well weigh heavily in the balance for the future of the US economy. If US authorities opt for a weak dollar to encourage exports and maintain their policy of very low interest rates, the United States will attract far less foreign capital.

The multinationals of the different European Union (EU) countries were involved in a great many takeovers and mergers within what is now the European single market, and in North America and Japan. Starting in 1998, European firms turned increasingly to mergers and takeovers of US companies. EU multinationals invest more FDI in the other poles of the Triad than they receive from them. Since 1989–90, German multinationals have also bought a number of companies in the former Soviet Bloc, especially in countries with which Germany shares a border.

Until the early 1990s, Japanese multinationals invested in North America, Europe, and their zone of influence in Asia. Since the crisis erupted in Japan, they have considerably reduced their investments abroad. Japan's FDI output fell from $35 billion in 1988, to $24 billion in 1998 (OECD 2000, 56). Japan exports far more FDI than it receives; in 1998, it only received $3 billion of FDI from abroad. Nevertheless, from one year to the next, FDI entering Japan is increasing, also in the form of mergers and takeovers. French automobile manufacturer Renault, for example, has taken over Japanese automaker Nissan (which immediately cut 20,000 jobs). Another Japanese automaker, Mitsubishi, has been taken over by the German/US multinational Daimler-Chrysler. This was previously unheard of in Japan.

Strengthening of the Triad

In the area of global trade, the relative weight of the Triad has been increased while most of the Third World has been further marginalized.

TABLE 3.2. GLOBAL EXPORTS (PERCENT)

	1985	1998	1999
Triad	63.8	66.7	68.1
Periphery	36.2	32.3	31.9
LDC	*1.5*	*0.5*	*0.5*
Ex-Soviet Bloc	*5.0*	*4.3*	*2.0*

Sources: UNCTAD 2000c; IMF 2000a. Calculated by the author.

Are Asia's four "tigers" the exception to the rule?

Only a few Third World countries have emerged from dependence. South Korea and Taiwan are without a doubt in this category. These two countries obtained membership in the exclusive club of the developed world thanks to policies that have nothing in common with the prescriptions of the IMF and World Bank (Coutrot and Husson 1993, 125–30; Ugarteche 1997, 71–86; Stiglitz 2002). These include systematic protectionism, strong state intervention, and radical agrarian reform. However, since the 1998 crisis, South Korea has slipped into an exaggerated state of dependency for which it was not prepared. Entire sections of the South Korean industrial apparatus have been bought up for next to nothing by North American, European, or Japanese multinationals.

Hong Kong and Singapore are special cases. They are financial centers above all. Hong Kong has been returned to China, and its economic future is closely intertwined with the mainland's. In 1996, the exports of South Korea, Taiwan, Hong Kong, and Singapore accounted for more than 50 percent of total exports for the entire periphery, including the former Soviet Bloc (World Bank 1998c, 198–99).

Other Third World countries seemed to be making a leap forward, such as Argentina, Brazil, Chile, Mexico, Thailand, Malaysia, Indonesia, and the Philippines. The IMF and World Bank pointed to these countries as examples—that is, until a major crisis sent them reeling. These countries are in an extremely vulnerable position due to a combination of high external debt, a structural trade deficit and the volatility of financial inflows and outflows, privatizations, and abandonment of protectionist measures.

Malaysia has come out of it better because, in 1997–98, the Malaysian authorities refused to make any agreement with the IMF and imposed capital control measures. This choice proved successful (see chapter 17). China is also in a more enviable situation than the others, as its currency is nonconvertible and its domestic market strongly protected. China's entry into the WTO, which became effective at the WTO meeting in Doha in November 2001, is ominous. The consequences are likely to be dramatic for a large part of the population.

Increased subordination of most Third World countries to imperialist centers

Any simplistic reading of the current situation should, of course, be avoided. The Third World has not been totally brushed off by the Triad. A number of Third World countries have built up a relatively solid industrial base that is not about to disappear at the wave of a magic wand. It is nonetheless striking to observe the unprecedented degree of freedom to maneuver that multinationals from the developed capitalist countries have obtained—thanks to privatization and other neoliberal measures in the countries in question.

The external debt crisis in these countries has created a situation in which the multilateral financial institutions (IMF and World Bank) and the governments of the main industrial powers have been able to dictate a series of measures in the form of structural adjustment programs (see chapters 12 and 13). Strategic economic sectors key to the development of these countries have been handed over to the multinationals. The result has been a kind of regression, a return to pronounced dependence and subordination in a number of Third World countries that had attempted, not without success, an incipient autonomy in economic development. This applies to Mexico, India, Algeria, Brazil, Argentina, and Venezuela, among others.

Countries such as Indonesia, Thailand, and the Philippines did experience real economic growth, but it was highly dependent on the multinationals, low-cost exports, and chronic external debt. These countries are essentially suppliers of cheap labor; they are not set to develop autonomously along South Korean lines.

As for most of Africa, Central America and the Caribbean, most of South America, and South Asia, there can be no mistaking their increased marginalization.

Global commerce dominated by the industrialized countries

Not only do the highly industrialized countries help themselves to the lion's share of world trade—in 1999, the twenty-three most industrialized countries, with less than 15 percent of the global population, accounted for 68 percent of global exports—they mainly trade among themselves. More than two-thirds of trading is within the group. In recent years, the concentration has increased. Industrialized countries play an even greater role in global commerce than before. At the same time, their international trade is mainly between European countries or Europe and the United States and Japan.

J.C. Kroll notes that since 1980 trade exchanges have mainly developed between the developed countries and increasingly involve similar goods. He claims that this completely contradicts the standard theory that favors the development of exchanges of different products between countries with different characteristics (Kroll 2001, 3). An anecdote will show how absurd things have become: In 1999, Great Britain exported 111 million liters of milk and 47 million kilos of butter. In exactly the same period, it imported 173 million liters of milk and 49 million kilos of butter (Salverda 2000).

In 2000, the periphery countries combined accounted for less than a third of global trade. From a historical perspective, this is regression. Indeed, the periphery accounted for 36 percent of global exports in 1938, 41 percent in 1948, and 37 percent in 1963 (Rostow, cited in Beaud 2000, 288). In 2000, their share of global trade had dropped to 32 percent.

Taking the regions of the periphery, Latin America's share fell two-thirds between 1950 and 1999, decreasing from 12.5 percent in 1950, to 4.5 percent in 1999. The share of sub-Saharan Africa underwent a proportionate reduction. Sub-Saharan Africa's exports represented about 5 percent of global exports in 1950 and no more than 1.7 percent in 1999 (1.1 percent if South Africa is excluded). The former Soviet Bloc had 5 percent of global exports in 1948, 12 percent in 1963, 10 percent in 1971, 5 percent in 1985, and 4.3 percent in 1999. Only Asia's share (China included) increased, from about 12 percent in 1950, to 15.4 percent in 1996.

Obviously, it is important to realize that the contribution of each region to global trade is calculated using prices denominated in dollars. As will be shown further on, the volume of exports from Africa has actually increased, but its value in dollars has fallen. This is a faithful reflection of the deterioration of power relations between the countries of the periphery (except for part of Asia) and the highly industrialized capitalist countries. The beginning of this deterioration dates back to 1980–82. The industrialized countries have managed to impose ever-less favorable terms of trade on the countries of the periphery. It will become clear that industrialized countries used the debt crisis that erupted in 1982 to force down the prices of products exported by periphery countries. The reductions began in 1981–82—including reductions on oil—and came hard on the heels of a period of price increases in the 1970s.

While the industrialized countries trade mainly between themselves, the periphery countries, with a few exceptions, do so very little or not at all. Taking the periphery as a whole, trade between those countries represents less than a third of their trade; the rest is trade with the industrialized countries.

An extreme case is Congo-Brazzaville. This country's trade with other countries also in the CFA franc zone[1] only represents 1.5 percent of its inter-

The contribution of Third World countries to global wealth is hugely undervalued

The value of the global exports of the countries in the periphery is estimated using prices fixed in markets dominated by companies from the industrialized countries, in dollar equivalent.

Take the example of a pair of sneakers that costs the equivalent of $100 in the United States. If a Pakistani child was paid one dollar for the labor involved, and $14 were added to cover all other costs in Pakistan—raw materials and machines used in production, the Pakistani employer's revenue, sea or air freight to the country where the shoes will be sold (in the unlikely event that a Pakistani firm transports them, as transport companies are usually from the industrialized countries)—then the total cost of the shoes will be $15.

It is possible that $15 is the sum used to calculate Pakistan's share in global exports, whereas the shoes will be sold for $100 in the United States. The $85 difference, paid by the consumer, goes into the till of the multinational firm that sells the product under a brand-name such as Adidas or Reebok, into packaging costs, the salesperson's salary, the advertising firm that promotes the product, company profits, and dividends paid out to shareholders. Those $85 will not be counted as a contribution from the periphery to global wealth, measured in gross national product. Fifteen dollars are counted in Pakistan's GNP, while the $100 corresponding to the US sales price are counted in the GNP of the United States, where the shoes were retailed.

Let's take another example. A large portion (one-half? two-thirds?) of uncut diamonds extracted from Congolese soil leave the territory of the Democratic Republic of the Congo (DRC) illegally. This portion does not show up in DRC exports. They arrive in Antwerp, one of the world centers for diamond cutting and trade. Belgium processes and exports them. The value of the export goes into Belgium's share of global exports, while nothing (or next to nothing) is counted as DRC exports. The same happens in calculating the two countries' respective GNPs.

national trading. Most of its trade takes place with a few European countries, especially France, its former colonial ruler. Of the CFA franc zone, Mali trades the most with its colleagues; however, that still accounts only for 23.3 percent of its trade (UNCTAD 2001, 123).

Trade between East and Southeast Asian countries is much greater, ac-

If a multinational from the center "steals" the genetic code of a plant that results from centuries of cultivation by a rural community in the periphery and then patents it as a new discovery protected by the Trade-Related Aspects of Intellectual Property Rights agreement (TRIPS), cultivates the plant in the center, and finally exports the patented seed, that will be viewed as a contribution to global wealth by that multinational. The price it fetches will go into the share of global exports of the multinational's base country and into calculating its GNP. On the other hand, if the rural community in the periphery continues to cultivate that plant in a context of self-sufficiency without going through the market, even locally, its contribution will appear neither in the country's global exports (of course not, as neither the plant nor the seed were exported!), nor in its GNP, nor in global wealth as it is usually calculated.

Anything that does not enter into monetary transactions is not counted in the GNP. Thus, the immense "invisible" labor of women all over the world, but particularly in the Third World, remains absent from the economic map.

Other instruments to measure the real contribution of the periphery to global "wealth" should make it possible to correct the distorted image given by prices. If calculations were based on the qualifications and working hours needed to produce the merchandise exported by periphery countries, it should be possible to formulate estimates that reflect more closely the real contribution of periphery countries to global wealth. Environmental criteria should also be factored in. This would mean a complete change of evaluation system: the values taken into account would be different, and the trading relations between countries of the center and the periphery would also be different.

In today's capitalist system, the contribution of Third World countries to global wealth is hugely undervalued, because part of the value created in those countries is counted in the final sales price, fixed and received in the industrialized countries. (Of course, the problem has been simplified for this demonstration.)

counting for nearly 50 percent of their international trade. The countries of the Southern Cone of Latin America (with a common market, Mercosur) also have a relatively high level of trading among themselves. In the far north of Latin America, Mexico is ever more dependent on its trade with the United States (and Canada).

UNCTAD: The scramble for MNC investment

Third World and former Soviet Bloc countries abandoned policies aimed at relatively autonomous development. This resulted, on the one hand, from the external debt crisis and the disintegration of their development model and, on the other, from the increased power of multinational corporations (MNCs) and the prominence of policies dictated by the IMF, World Bank, and the WTO. Consequently, these countries were driven to fight for a share of direct investment from MNCs.

They also went to war with one another—prodded along by the IMF, World Bank, and WTO—through policies aimed at "export-oriented development." These policies have led to a generalized collapse in the prices of products exported from the Third World (see chapter 9).

The United Nations Conference on Trade and Development (UNCTAD) was created in 1964, at a time when a large number of former colonies had just gained their independence and were exerting pressure for steps toward a new global economic order. (For a historical overview of UNCTAD, see Therien 1990 and Bello 2000a.) Yet, UNCTAD itself made an about-face after the debt crisis erupted in 1982. This was accentuated in the early 1990s: as one crisis followed another, the organization's policies began to zigzag. Some of UNCTAD's reports espouse, however cautiously, the neoliberal creed, while others plead for a return to old ways.

Originally, UNCTAD was the UN's first specialist institution to take a critical, voluntarist stance on the issue of inequality between the world's nations on the North/South axis. Another particularity of this UN institution was that it consisted of groups of countries. At first, there were only four groups. Group A was composed of Africa, Asia, and Yugoslavia; group B, the developed capitalist countries; group C, Latin America and the Caribbean; group D, the former Soviet Bloc. Later, groups A and C merged to constitute the "Group of Seventy-seven" (G77, there were originally seventy-seven of them). Group B dissolved itself in 1991, and there is nothing left of group D. Today, the G77 has just over 130 members. They met in Havana in April 2000, but the G77 has lost its clout.

The first director of UNCTAD, Argentine Raùl Prebisch, already had long experience in the UN Economic Commission for Latin America and the Caribbean (ECLAC), which he had joined in 1949. There, he had contributed to drawing up a development policy that greatly irritated the capitalist countries of the center and actually went against their interests. Even so, the policy did not promote a broad program of social reforms, which would have facilitated redistribution of wealth in the periphery countries in favor of the lower classes and to the detriment of the capitalists in both the periphery and the center. The policies recommended by ECLAC and by Prebisch went against the interests of the capitalist countries of the center in that they encouraged, among other things, the creation of industries in the periphery under the control of local governments. The idea was to substitute imports from the highly industrialized countries with local industrial production, a process known as "import substitution industrialization (ISI)."

UNCTAD was going to pursue this line by providing the governments of the periphery with a single institutional framework. It was going to help strengthen the position of governments that were demanding a New International Economic Order (NIEO) by promoting new trade policies that would enable the countries of the periphery to build their own future. The high point of tension between governments of the center and those of the periphery came in 1974, when the UN General Assembly held an extraordinary session on the theme of NIEO and decided on a plan of action. Immediately afterward, on December 14, the UN General Assembly adopted the Charter of the Economic Rights and Duties of States, which gave NIEO official status. A huge majority approved the charter: 120 votes for, 6 against, and 10 abstentions. The six that voted against were the United States, Great Britain, the Federal Republic of Germany, Belgium, Luxembourg, and Denmark. The ten that abstained: France, Japan, Italy, Canada, the Netherlands, Austria, Norway, Israel, Ireland, and Spain. In other words, all the capitalist countries of the center, plus, of course, Israel.

Article 2 of the adopted text asserted the right of states to nationalize property and natural resources in the possession of foreign investors and proposed to create cartels of producers of raw materials. Thirty years later, it is easy to see how this UN vote must have caused resentment among the ruling elite of the highly industrialized countries. They were not accustomed to this kind of behavior. They were already angry that the Organization of the Petroleum Exporting Countries (OPEC) had, a year earlier, used concerted action to impose a very sharp rise in the price of oil. Many petroleum and other companies were nationalized by governments of the periphery during this time.

The eruption of the debt crisis in 1982 enabled the governments of the most industrialized countries and the MNCs whose interests they defended to get their own back.

Pressure from the governments of the center forced UNCTAD's directors to move the way the center had been going for years. The OECD, based in Paris, to which they all belonged, was one institution that explicitly and radically opposed the NIEO. In 1975, the United States, Japan, Great Britain, France, and Germany initiated the Group of Five (G5), which soon expanded to include Canada and Italy as the G7. At the informal summits between heads of state and governments of the G5, the new approach to managing the international situation and taming the UN and UNCTAD was prepared. The World Bank, completely under the thumb of the United States, also played a fundamental role in cooking up a new strategy (see chapters 10 and 11).

Whereas UNCTAD could have played a key role in global trade policies, it was finally at the older and more informal GATT (see glossary) that fundamental negotiations and discussions on trade were conducted. Approximately twelve years later, with neoliberalism in full spate, these talks resulted in the foundation of the World Trade Organization in 1995.

When UNCTAD reports of the early 1990s are compared to documents it produced between 1964 and the early 1980s, the about-face it executed is glaringly obvious. It is as though UNCTAD had put itself at the disposal of MNCs and promoted the policy of "export-oriented development." It began sending out reports to Third World governments that explained how to go about attracting investment and competing with one another. To all intents and purposes, the 1993 UNCTAD report declared, "Multinationals are the only salvation!" (Decornoy 1993).

More recently, UNCTAD has made some gestures inspired by its original objectives; its 1995 report calls for a one-off property tax and a tax on international financial transactions of the kind advanced by James Tobin (see chapter 18). However, the 1997 UNCTAD report takes a hard neoliberal line. In a September 21, 1997, press release, the institution's general secretary at the time, Rubens Ricupero, declared, "Governments must encourage liberal trade and investment policies and a culture of competition, in order to maximize their economy's potential."

When the Southeast Asian crisis broke out in 1997, UNCTAD adopted an increasingly firm critical tone toward policies dictated by the G7, the World Bank, and the IMF. In the General Overview of the 2001 *Trade and Development Report*, the same Rubens Ricupero writes (is his memory so short?): "The UNCTAD secretariat has for some time been warning that excessive financial liberalization is creating a world of systemic instability and recurrent crises.... Markets can and do get it wrong, and for developing and developed countries alike."

Further on, Ricupero defends a point of view that is closer to the institution's original approach: "Proposals for new international institutions explicitly designed to regulate and stabilize international capital flows have been summarily dismissed by critics as the work of mavericks lacking in political sense and technical judgement." His criticism of IMF and World Bank intervention in crises is clear: "The plans...shift the burden of the crisis firmly onto taxpayers in debtor countries."

Ricupero suggests that in times of crisis, indebted countries should have recourse to cessation of payments. "For some time now the UNCTAD secretariat has been advocating a temporary standstill on debt payments during crisis situations to prevent asset grabbing by creditors."

The 2002 *Trade and Development Report* places the emphasis on the limits of the apparent success of the newly industrialized countries, showing that, in most cases, they have proved incapable of really increasing their share of highly specialized production. From the introduction to the report's General Overview, UNCTAD seems to be going back to the old way:

> In his statement to the first United Nations Conference on Trade and Development in March 1964, Raúl Prebisch, its then Secretary-General, called on the industrial countries not to underestimate the basic challenge facing developing countries in the existing system.... Prebisch understood that recommending "the free play of market forces" between unequal trading partners would only punish poorer commodity exporters at the same time as it brought advantages to the rich industrial core.

These contradictions in UNCTAD's positions go back to the time in the late 1970s when governments of the periphery switched horses and most became complicit with the defenders of the neoliberal offensive. To understand UNCTAD's sporadic return to a critical approach since the Asian crisis, one needs to understand that the governments of the periphery that systematically accepted the rules of the G7, the IMF/World Bank/WTO trio, and the MNCs are now at a complete impasse. From within the impasse, the nationalist policies of a government such as Malaysia's seem to offer an alternative. In 1998, that government showed that it was possible to do better than others by establishing exchange control and control of capital flows (see chapter 17).

The future of UNCTAD will depend on the strategies that governments of the periphery decide to adopt, in particular under pressure from social movements within their countries.

MNCs take shelter from the market: Intrafirm trade

At least one-third of world trade takes place within individual multinational corporations. Consequently, world trade statistics based on trade between countries do not accurately reflect the reality of global trade.

MNCs loudly proclaim their free-market mantras in favor of unimpeded competition. This, of course, does not prevent them from protecting themselves from such competition when and wherever possible, especially as it concerns determining the price of their inputs. They organize trade between their different operations based on criteria that have little to do with free-market principles (see section devoted to South-North transfers in chapter 9). "Do as I say, not as I do."

Incredible as it may seem, those who attempt to justify these practices do not shy away from invoking the "imperfections" and "defects" of the market. One such analyst, M. Casson, author of "Transaction Costs and the Theory of the Multinational Enterprise" in A. Rugman, *New Theories of the Multinational Enterprise* (London: Croom Helm, 1982), lists the various problems MNCs can solve by placing themselves outside the ambit of the market. He explains that the market does not allow for contact between seller and buyer, that it means ignorance of one another's needs. There is no agreement on price and no confidence that the ordered goods conform to the buyer's specific needs; there are trade tariffs, taxes on profits made in the transaction, and price controls; there is no confidence that goods will be returned in case of nonpayment; and the list goes on (Chesnais 1997c).

Does Mr. Casson realize that he has in fact formulated a rather trenchant overall critique of the free-market system per se?

---

1   Fifteen African countries use the same currency, the CFA franc. They are Benin, Burkina Faso, Cameroon, the Comoro Islands, Congo, Ivory Coast, Guinea-Bissau, Equatorial Guinea, Gabon, Mali, Niger, Central African Republic, Senegal, Chad, and Togo.

4

Global finance in crisis: The financial assets of industrial MNCs increase

Multinational corporations have adapted remarkably well to the new global financial realities. No surprise, really, given their own increased involvement in financial operations that are often far removed from their largely industrial origins. A number of traditionally industrial companies now more closely resemble financial outfits, continually shifting position based on the profitability of investments made in their various subsidiaries and sectors of activity. For all intents and purposes, they are financial houses with an industrial focus.

In such a situation, even the biggest industrial concerns see their productive operations as one among many forms of return on investment. The term "global" is used to characterize the strategy of multinational corporations. In the present context, it has two complementary meanings: On the one hand, it corresponds to the planetary scope of corporate activity (even if largely concentrated in the Triad); on the other, it reflects the fact that corporate strategy is ever more clearly based on asset performance, of both a financial and industrial nature, in broadly equal parts.

Has productive investment declined as a result of this increasing company involvement in financial markets? Probably. Big companies have a growing tendency to hold significant financial assets, which has created tension between those who depend on industrial activities and those who are more concerned with the "ledger" that spells out what will be paid to shareholders in quarterly dividends.

Company accounts determine profit by adding up revenues earned on various types of capital. Profit is the measure of how far a company has been able to optimize its total capital holdings over a given period of time. However, as far as the overall reproduction of capital is concerned, things are not so simple. Indeed, revenues from various types of monetary investments are nothing more than the cream skimmed off the surplus value (see glossary) that is created in the productive sector of the economy (Serfati 1996; Husson 1996).

Loans provided by bankers and money taken in through stock and bond is-sues can clearly be seen as complements to accumulation. They allow the pro-ductive capital cycle to unfold unfettered by serious financial constraints. However, they are also pregnant with a number of conflicts over the sharing out of surplus value created in the productive process. The main quarrel concerns how much of this surplus value will, on the one hand, be kept as profit by the company and reinvested, and how much, on the other, will go toward servicing debts (i.e., making interest payments) and paying dividends on securities.

A bird's eye view of financialization and deregulation

For the last thirty years, the growth of financial markets has been fed in part by the profits that big industrial houses have declined to reinvest in production. Significant proportions of surplus value created in production have been di-verted into the financial sphere since the 1980s. We are a far cry from the pre-dictions made by Keynes (1945) that rentiers living off interest would disappear through a process of "euthanasia"! Labor and the productive cycle revolve more than ever around the need to satisfy the demands of interest-bearing capital.

After the outbreak of the Mexican crisis in December 1994, IMF head Michel Camdessus let slip, "A globalized economy without exchange controls makes the world a dangerous place" (*Le Soir Eco-Soir*, February 17, 1995). However, the IMF itself pushed for the generalized deregulation of capital flows, in particular through the elimination of exchange controls. For his part, Roland Leuschel, then head of the investment strategy division of Banque Bruxelles Lambert, declared, "We are a bit like an airline pilot who knows he is going to crash but whose computer controls no longer respond. The com-puter follows its own rules, that's what the market is like" (*Le Monde*, April 5, 1995). On several occasions in 1998–99, chair of the US Federal Reserve, Alan Greenspan, criticized the "exuberance" of the markets.

Deregulation was systematically pursued by the governments of the main industrial powers, the international financial institutions (IFIs)—the IMF, World Bank, Bank for International Settlements (BIS)—and the MNCs. Al-though the Triad governments, by and large, dictate IFI policies, this does not mean that the international institutions lack some degree of autonomy.

Currency markets are the segment of the financial markets that have regis-tered the strongest growth. Between 1970 and 1999, the volume of transac-tions increased a hundredfold from a little more than $10 billion to $1.5 trillion dollars a day). Yet the main function of currency trading is supposed to be providing currency to settle foreign trade contracts. However, the total value of actual trade transactions was not even 5 percent of the value of foreign currencies traded on exchange markets.

The table below compares the daily volume of exchange transactions to the annual volume of global exports. In 1979, the equivalent of two hundred days of activity on the currency markets was required to reach the annual volume of global exports. Two hundred working days in the exchange markets is nearly one calendar year. In 2003, four days of currency market activity was enough to reach the annual volume of global exports.

> The financial markets handle the billions and billions of dollars in capital that move from one country to another every day. As a result, they have become the policeman, judge and jury of the world economy, which is very worrying given their tendency to see events and policies through the distorting prism of fear and greed. (*Financial Times*, September 30, 1994)

TABLE 4.1. DAILY VALUE OF FINANCIAL TRANSACTIONS AND ANNUAL VALUE OF GLOBAL EXPORTS (IN BILLIONS OF DOLLARS).

Year	Daily value of financial transactions	Annual value of global exports
1979	75	1,546
1984	150	1,800
1986	300	1,998
1990	500	3,429
1994	1,200	4,269
1998	1,800	5,142
2001	1,250	6,155
2003	1,800	7,300

Source: Chesnais 1996, OECD 2000, and 2004 data from the BIS, WB, and WTO calculated by the author

Of course, the journalistic musings of the *Financial Times* do not go far enough. That such comments should appear in the flagship British financial daily, frontline defender of neoliberal orthodoxy, is significant in itself, however. It shows that the heads of the main capitalist countries (the G7 or G10) and private financial institutions—with multinational industrial houses, the IMF, World Bank, BIS, and GATT in tow—have, to a certain extent, played the role of sorcerer's apprentices. This is why the image of a pilot whose controls do not respond is so fitting.

The overaccumulation of capital has been accompanied by a real or potential (in terms of excess productive capacity) overproduction of commodities. As a result, much of the capital accumulated from new profits is not invested productively. This extra capital jumped into shares until 2000, provided the requisite liquid assets to feed into enormous merger and acquisition operations until 2001, and was going into real estate at the moment of writing (August 2003). For a few years now, there has been huge growth in speculation on currency rates, debt paper, manipulation of stocks of raw materials and agricultural produce, and transactions in various derivative products (see glossary).

Governments and financial institutions have pulled out the stops to remove all legal obstacles to the free international circulation of capital. Since the second half of the 1990s, they have begun to worry about the scale of speculative activities, which have threatened monetary stability (European Monetary System crisis in 1992), sunk major financial institutions into bankruptcy (Barings Bank in Britain and Cosmo Credit in Japan, both in 1995), and plunged entire countries into crisis (Mexico in 1994–95). Yet, they refuse to adopt measures to restrict the free circulation of capital. The BIS reiterated this refusal in its June 1995 report, as did the G7 heads of government following their June 1995 meeting in Halifax and the IMF/World Bank team during their Washington meeting in late April 1997.

The April 30, 1997, edition of the French business daily *Les Echos* ran the following completely contradictory leader:

> The Interim Committee of the IMF, the institution's highest decision-making body, gave the green light Monday evening in Washington for the IMF to *promote and organize* the liberalization of capital flows, including in developing countries. [emphasis mine]

The article in question tells us that the IMF's leading body recommended an amendment to its statutes to include the removal of obstacles to capital flows as a specific objective. This led the G24, which brings together Third World countries and non-G10 industrialized countries (see glossary), to express its concerns about the dangers of any hasty liberalization that would oblige its members to remove exchange controls and investment restrictions.

Such restrictions still existed at the time in Korea and, to a lesser degree, in Chile. In Korea's case, measures dictated by the IMF and accepted by the Korean government in December 1997 eliminated these restrictions. As for Chile, its legislation discouraging foreign investment for a period of less than one year (see Urriola 1996, 41–48) was dropped in October 1998.

Malaysia angered the IMF and the G7 by setting up exchange controls and control of capital flows in September 1998. Although the results were kept under wraps by the international press and the IMF, they were positive beyond any shadow of a doubt, proof that even a middle-sized country (25 million inhabitants) can effectively reduce the damage caused by speculative attacks (see chapter 17).

Since the Asian crisis of 1997–98, crises have broken out with increasing regularity. After Russia in 1998, Brazil in 1998–99, Argentina and Turkey in 2000–02, and Brazil in 2002, who will be next? Even the economies of the Triad countries have been affected: the United States in 2001, then Japan and the EU. Still, the Triad governments and the IFIs they control do not restore measures to control capital. They will have to eventually, but after how many more crises?

The different stages of financial deregulation

Until the end of the 1970s, financial and monetary systems were strictly regulated at the national level. Nevertheless, the birth of the eurodollar (see glossary) in the 1960s was a major event, especially given the key role of the eurodollar in the Third World debt crisis (see chapter 8). The second key event in financial internationalization began in August 1971, when US president Richard Nixon put an end to the Bretton Woods system by discontinuing the dollar's convertibility into gold. This led to the emergence of floating exchange rates, which significantly broke down the barriers between exchange markets (de Brunhoff 1996).

From 1979 on, governments in the leading industrialized countries effected measures that progressively phased out controls on capital flows abroad. In other words, they liberalized—or opened to the outside—national financial systems. This was done in three stages: (1) full opening of exchange markets; (2) opening of bond markets; (3) opening of stock markets (1986).

In the 1980s, all forms of administrative control over interest rates, credit, and capital flows were progressively eliminated. The main leaders of the industrialized world chose this course, leading to an orderly retreat of governments faced with the powerful, unfolding dynamic of financial integration. One by one, governments threw in the towel when confronted with the huge new sums of capital flooding across borders; they resigned themselves to making the best of this new reality that they had helped to create. They engaged in fierce competition to attract capital in their direction; to this end, they abandoned most taxes on capital gains.

The main players on financial markets

Who, after all, are the main players on financial markets? The heaviest hitters are a few dozen of the largely American and British private pension funds, mutual funds, and other types of investment funds; the big insurance companies; and the big multinational banks. These players are known as "institutional investors." Throw in a few dozen big multinational industrial houses and the list is complete.

Indeed, the list is quite short. A research group within the IMF carried out a confidential study to determine who had been the main players in the attacks on the European Monetary System in the summer of 1992. They found quite a small number: thirty to fifty banks and a handful of security brokerages. These control the key currency markets. During the 1992 crisis, the ten biggest banks in these two markets carried out 43 percent of transactions in London and 40 percent of transactions in New York. The findings of this IMF study were never presented at a press conference. François Chesnais writes,

> The Bank of France and the German Bundesbank closed ranks to spend 300 billion dollars in defense of the European Monetary System during the summer of 1992. But this sum was of little significance compared to the amounts that those determined to force a change in exchange rates—and pocket major profits in the process—were able to mobilize. (1994)

FIGURE 4.1

**The evolution of financial assets
by investor type from 1980 to 1988
(billions of dollars)**

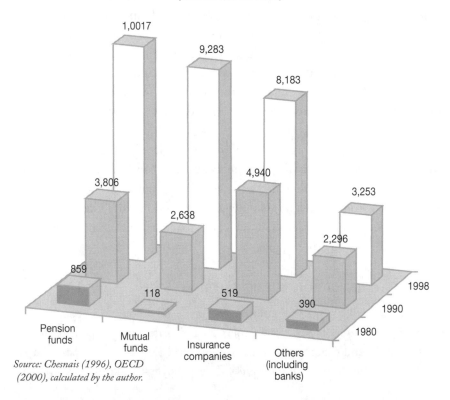

Source: Chesnais (1996), OECD (2000), calculated by the author.

In addition to speculation on exchange markets, another type of operation has emerged: derivatives. The Barings bankruptcy of spring 1995 drew public attention to this type of operation. Even if they are called "investment products," they have nothing to do with production. They are purely speculative in nature.

The changing face of financial investment by investor type

Private pension funds are among the principal players in the financial markets. Their financial assets came to $3.8 trillion in 1993. In 1999, they came to $10 trillion. All they have to do to succeed is to coalesce and place 5 percent of their assets in a concerted move against a strong currency.

To whom do pension funds belong? Do they belong to a section of the working population that, through investing its savings, has become an integral part of the capitalist class? Certainly not. Pension funds are not workers' property, but rather the property of the capitalist class.

Pension funds and other institutional investors are not oblivious to industry. A significant portion of their massive financial holdings is held in the form of company stock. The size of their share in a company's stock varies, but it is usually large enough to have definite influence over the decisions and strategies of the industrial concerns in question.

Buying up company stock on the various stock markets, institutional investors carry tremendous weight in the overwhelming majority of MNCs—to such a degree, in fact, that they can have a decisive say over what these MNCs can or cannot do. Institutional investors demand quarterly dividends that are at minimum on par with the interest rate—12 percent to 15 percent. At least, that was the case from 1990 until the stock market bubble burst in 2001. The deepening crisis of 2001–02 forced institutional investors to become less demanding. Fearful that pension funds and other institutional investors will sell off their shares, companies often decide to tone down productive investment and step up efforts aimed at obtaining short-term profit.

Not that those in charge of industrial houses are any worse for wear. The president of Elf Aquitaine, Loïc Le Floc-Prigent, for example, declared, "Share prices are a measure of a company's virtue." A few years later, this same president was under investigation by the courts and arrested for embezzlement. He apparently had his own special notion of "company virtue." In May 2001, he was sentenced to three and a half years' imprisonment by the French courts for misappropriation of funds, aiding and abetting embezzlement, and organizing large-scale corruption to obtain profitable contracts for the petroleum multinational Elf Aquitaine. The Enron bankruptcy scandal (late 2001) was followed by revelations of criminal practice on the part of company administrators in the United States, then by similar scandals in other industrialized countries (especially Spain, Belgium, Germany, the Netherlands with Ahold, Italy with Parmalat…). All this shows that capitalist management and virtue are strange bedfellows.

The case of George Soros

In general, the identity of companies and multibillionaires that speculate is a well-kept secret. This creates an aura of mystery and perpetuates the illusion that an untold mass of anonymous citizens determines what happens on the world's markets. In fact, nothing could be further from the truth.

George Soros (1995, 1998) is an exception to the secrecy rule. Soros, principal owner of Quantum Endowment ($7.2 billion in assets in June 2001) and LLC of New York ($11 billion in assets in June 2001), was one of the main players in the attack on the European Monetary System in the summer of 1992. He pocketed one billion dollars after speculating ten billion against the pound sterling. Like all gamblers, he also loses from time to time—for example, in January 1994, when he lost $600 million. In 2000, the assets of his LLC of New York fund shrank to half their size (*International Herald Tribune*, June 11, 2001). Of course, George Soros is not omnipotent; but he does sometimes play a role in crises by leading speculative attacks. He prepares the way for the big battalions made up of mutual funds, banks, insurance companies, etc.

In 1995, he published a book in which he described how he ran his operation in strict accordance with the relevant laws. In this interview-style book, which he commissioned, he raises the alarm over the dangers of unrestrained deregulation. The book is an instructive read. On the occasion of its release in France, Soros declared:

> Many people feel that markets are the best way to share out resources and create a balanced situation. I believe the opposite is true. I do not believe in market perfection. Measures have to be taken to stabilize the market, otherwise there will be dangerous developments, especially since imbalances are cumulative. I feel markets aren't sufficiently monitored and that there should be tighter regulations. Broadly speaking, market mechanisms have come to play too great a role in our societies. I am not a fan of laissez-faire. (*Le Monde*, November 2, 1996)

According to the Malaysian prime minister, such declarations did not hold Soros back from playing a leading role in attacks on various Southeast Asian currencies, the Thai baht and the Malaysian ringgit in particular. According to the Mexican daily *El Financiero*, on July 26, 1997, Malaysian prime minister Mahathir Mohammed openly accused Soros of secretly organizing speculative attacks that led to depreciation in the value of Southeast Asian currencies from July on. Soros denied any such involvement.

El Financiero relates other declarations of Mahathir's:

> He called on the international community to consider the speculative attacks on Southeast Asian currencies a crime. "This will happen again, that is why we consider it to be a crime," he said. He said that as long as the international community did not take steps against such activities, the currencies of developing countries would continue to be sabotaged and their citizens would continue to live in poverty.

In a January 1, 1998, *Financial Times* op-ed piece, Soros talks about the general implications of the Southeast Asian crisis. He makes a number of pertinent remarks:

> The international financial system is suffering from a systemic crisis but we have difficulties recognizing this. The elimination of fixed exchange rates has unleashed an uncontrollable process that has surpassed people's worst fears, including my own. The rescue packages assembled by the IMF are not producing any results.... The countries concerned have too much debt.... The private sector is incapable of allocating international credit in the right doses. It provides too much or too little. It doesn't have sufficient information for making balanced judgements. Above all, the private sector is not concerned with maintaining macroeconomic equilibriums in the borrower countries. Its goal is maximizing its own profits and minimizing risk.

After making numerous declarations to key figures regarding neoliberalism and investment in "philanthropic" foundations, Soros found favor in certain progressive circles. However, make no mistake: his position is pro-capitalist. In his book *The Crisis of Global Capitalism* (1998), Soros absolutely does not side with those who suffer from globalization, neoliberalism, and the crisis of capitalism. His is the stance of a capitalist who wants the big financial institutions to take action to prevent an even deeper crisis. He talks of a possible stock exchange or financial crash worse than those of October 1987 and October 1998. Soros has a clearly pro-capitalist, antilabor, antipopular perspective. The book title is purely a marketing ploy; in fact, the book develops the defense of global capitalism. Soros denounces market "fundamentalism" as a "disease" threatening the system and leading straight to the final crash. He adds that exaggerated deregulation is endangering the system. He is for intervention and regulation of part of the capital flows for the sake of saving global capitalism.

In September 2000, on the occasion of the annual joint assembly of the World Bank and the IMF in Prague, Czech Republic president Václav Havel (whose mandate ended in 2002) convened an unusual panel discussion to encourage debate between proponents of alternative globalization, on the one hand, and champions of the global capitalist system, on the other. Three representatives of the first group were on the panel: Walden Bello, Katrina Liskova, and Ann Pettifor. Speaking for the system were Horst Köhler (IMF managing director), James Wolfensohn (World Bank president), and George Soros (presented as a philanthropic financier). The audience was composed of nearly two hundred people, representing both sides.

Joseph Stiglitz was present, smiling blandly. Walden Bello (read his arguments in Bello 2002) and Liskova were brilliant and forceful in their criticism of globalization. Köhler and Wolfensohn were unable to find anything of consequence to say by way of argument. Soros adopted the stance of someone who wants to propose an honorable compromise based on the need to defend the existence of the World Bank and the IMF against the market fundamentalists. The fact that the two top officials of the IFIs needed Soros to plead for them shows how far advanced is the crisis of legitimacy of the two institutions.

One should not underestimate Soros's impact in certain progressive circles. He puts a lot of energy into trying to win over the movement. When he took part in the televised confrontation between representatives of the World Economic Forum in Davos, Switzerland, and the first World Social Forum in Porto Alegre, Brazil, in January 2001, Soros, who was in Davos, declared himself in favor of the Tobin Tax and said he hoped to be in Porto Alegre soon. In August 2002, he denounced the agreement imposed on Brazil by the IMF, saying that it would worsen the crisis.

In his book, *On Globalization* (2002), Soros puts forward a number of proposals aimed at reforming the system. He takes particular pains to defend the existence of the WTO, the World Bank, and the IMF. Soros is clear that if he wants to carry on playing in the field of international speculation, which is part and parcel of the capitalist system, it is no use putting his trust in the invisible hand of the market. Strong multilateral institutions are required. In this sense he is certainly consistent. He knows enough about the dangers of the chaotic dynamics of the system to defend the need for institutions to police it.

The progressive alternative to Soros's position is not to refute the need for international institutions, but to propose the need to replace the present ones by others, whose role and functioning would be based on a different logic from that of capital. We shall return to this point in the chapter on alternatives.

5

Enron and Co.: The fiasco of the new US-style economy

From the late 1990s until 2001, American capitalism was held up as the model.[1] The US president and the chair of the Federal Reserve did not hesitate to speak of the US "genius." In Europe, most journalists and politicians, including those of the Socialist and Labour Parties, followed suit.

This model spread gradually to the management of "European" multinationals (Vivendi, Vodafone, Arcelor) with the encouragement of governments—of all political hues—and the European Commission. The most frequently heard critics called for greater speed in applying the model. In France, the Jospin government, known as the "plural left," had a law passed by the National Assembly on May 2, 2001, on "new economic regulations," directly inspired by the US model still in vogue at the time.

Far from recognizing the nonreproducible and artificial nature of the growth achieved by the United States between 1995 and 2000 (the formation of the stock market bubble, credit inflation, and the enormous influx of European and Japanese capital), potential imitators around the world were mesmerized by the idea of *corporate governance*. Corporate governance was viewed as in the best interests of shareholders, most of whom were now institutional investors: pension funds, insurance companies, investment banks. It was meant to resolve the conflict between the interests of shareholders versus those of managers.

According to the proponents of corporate governance, managers seek to enhance their power and pay by taking advantage of the privileged information they are privy to through their positions. Corporate governance seeks to prevent this by reducing the "information imbalance" between shareholders and managers. The idea is to oblige managers to provide regular information to shareholders via quarterly reports. Corporate governance aims to incite managers to run the business in the interests of shareholders, doing everything possible to increase the value of shares.

To achieve this aim, managers' pay is (generally) proportionate to company profits. Stock options are a primary tool, whereby executives and managerial staff are offered the opportunity to acquire shares in the company at lower rates than those on the stock market ("buy options") and to sell them in the future when their value has increased. (Later we will see the consequences of this in the Enron case.) Stock options are therefore supposed to incite executives and managerial staff to make decisions in the interests of shareholders, i.e., to obtain a higher share value on the stock market and increase dividends.

What was presented as a new kind of capitalism has turned out to be a disastrous fiasco from the capitalist point of view and a social tragedy for wage earners. From 2001–02 on, bankruptcies on a monumental scale and repeated scandals pointing up systematic criminal practice have awakened memories of the late 1920s and the crisis of the 1930s.

The succession of scandals in 2001 and 2002 was preceded by the growth of a stock market bubble on an international scale from 1998 to 2000 (especially in North America and Europe). Share prices on the stock exchange rocketed, and the volume of stock market capitalization expanded impressively. The expanding bubble triggered a mad rush of clearly unviable mergers and acquisitions and a wave of massive investments (especially in telecommunications and information technology) quite unrelated to any real possibility of selling the products.

The bubble hid a phenomenon of great concern to capitalists: a major fall in company profits in 1997–98 (Brenner 2002). In the euphoria of exuberant markets, institutional investors closed their eyes to the completely speculative and disproportionate nature of the stock market value of companies, some of which made no profits. (This was the case for many start-up companies).

In their frenzied rush to increase prices on the stock exchange, managers (in full view of the shareholders) took their companies into high levels of debt. The debt incurred enabled the companies to buy other companies in the same sector. (One of the aims of these takeovers is to get too big to be taken over by others.) A second objective in incurring debt was for the company to buy up its own shares on the stock market to keep prices high. On the Paris Stock Exchange in 2002, 273 companies bought up their own shares at a cost of more than 11 billion euros. For example, in five years Danone bought thirty-one million of its shares, about 20 percent of its capital, for a total of 4 billion euros.

Company debt in the United States progressed phenomenally in the late 1990s (as did household debt, enabling the maintenance of a high level of consumption). The exuberance of the market, the massive indebtedness of companies and their frenzy of takeovers and mergers, the high level of investment in certain sectors (to increase production capacity), the tendency for households to consume more using more credit—all of this produced "the wealth effect." Many pro-capitalist commentators glorified it as "the new economy."

When the stock market bubble showed signs of imploding and prices began to fall (from the second semester of 2000), CEOs falsified their accounts to simulate profits and convince "the markets" to keep on buying their shares. They further increased the debt of "their" companies in order to buy even more shares to maintain share prices. Some companies pumped up their operating revenues in any way they could in order to fake continued growth.

Faced with cheating on such a scale, the US fiscal authorities—Alan Greenspan, chair of the Federal Reserve, and treasury secretary Larry Summers and his successor Paul O'Neill[2]—hypocritically pretended not to know what was going on and made a show of total confidence in the presiding genius of the markets. Yet, the practices of directors of companies such as Enron were well-known. President Bush and Vice President Cheney had themselves resorted to such practices a few years earlier (see below). Greenspan, for his part, had saved the hedge fund Long-Term Capital Management in September 1998, and knew well what erring ways had led to its bankruptcy.

The US authorities hoped that, by some miracle, the stock exchange would see prices rise again. In fact, the downward spiral of stock market prices all over the planet revealed the plight of a number of companies in the United States (and elsewhere) that had embellished their accounts. Like gamblers hoping to pick up again quickly, they took ever-greater risks and borrowed heavily in the hopes of wiping out their debts. Between March and November 2000, with the fall of stock market values and the partial deflation of the stock market bubble, more than $15 trillion worldwide went up in smoke, including about $7 trillion in the United States.

An emblematic case: The Enron scandal

The rise, the fall, and the bankruptcy of Enron will have a special place in the sordid history of capitalist globalization. When Enron went down, it was considered the biggest bankruptcy case in history. (However, it was rapidly superseded by WorldCom.) On seven occasions, *Fortune* magazine awarded the title of "Most Innovative Company" to Enron. Before declaring bankruptcy, Enron's directors helped themselves to more than $700 million from the till. The bankruptcy caused losses of $26 billion to shareholders and $31 billion to banks. Most of the employees of the parent company were made redundant, with severance pay amounting to a mere $16,500 a head. Some of them (1,200) lost 90 percent of the value of their retirement savings. In all, Enron and its eight hundred subsidiary companies employed almost twenty-five thousand staff around the world.

Enron was a brokerage firm that speculated on raw materials (oil, gas, aluminum, coal, forests for wood pulp), energy (electricity), water, and on the derivatives markets. (One of Enron's innovations was a derivative product protecting its holders from the effects of climate change!) The company had operations in forty countries, electric power stations in India, forests in Scandinavia, activities in the former Soviet republics, and, at the time of the bankruptcy, was trying to buy up the energy sector in the Czech Republic. Enron made 25 percent of its revenues outside the United States. At its height, it controlled 20 percent of the electricity market in the United States and Europe (*Wall Street Journal*, December 1, 2001).

Enron used subterfuge for systematic tax evasion in the United States and other countries where it operated. It created 874 subsidiary companies based in tax havens (Public Citizen 2001), 195 of which were in the Cayman Islands. There, profits were declared so that no income tax had to be paid to the US treasury over the last five years of its existence. Taxation was low or nonexistent in the tax havens where most of its business was registered.

Another subterfuge was to file an official tax declaration containing different information on company accounts from that presented to shareholders. To the tax collector, stock options were counted as a cost. For the shareholders, who needed to be shown proof of continued growth, stock options were not included in the balance sheet. Enron wanted to hide its losses and debts from the money markets so that its shares would remain attractive. To avoid unwanted scrutiny, Enron's financial report did not include the records of the whole of the Enron group. All of this manipulation and concealment was possible.

Enron paid for the cooperation of all those responsible for monitoring the company's financial health by sharing out the spoils with them: the auditors (Arthur Andersen), the investment banks (Merrill Lynch, Morgan Stanley), and the commercial banks (Citigroup, JPMorgan).

Enron and deregulation of the US electricity market

Enron's operating revenues took a great leap forward from the end of 1992, when it obtained exemption from government control over its speculative activities on the derivatives markets. Enron systematically paid hush money to Democratic and Republican representatives. From 1991 to 2002, Enron made gift payments into the kitties of both Democratic and Republican candidates totaling more than $5.5 million (75 percent for Republicans,

25 percent for the Democrats). This ranks Enron among the most "generous" US corporate contributors to the two capitalist parties who take turns in office. The Republican politician who received the most money from Enron was Senator Phil Gramm,[3] who, in exchange, used his influence to further Enron's objectives in deregulating the electricity market.

Wendy Gramm, the senator's wife, had served in the administrations of both Ronald Reagan and George Bush Senior. In 1992, she persuaded the Commodity Futures Trading Commission (CFTC), which she presided over at the time, to exempt Enron from its obligation to report on its operations on the derivative products markets. She pushed this decision through with unseemly haste in the last days of the Bush Senior administration. Six days later, she resigned, and five weeks later, she was hired onto Enron's board of directors. There, she headed the audit committee, where she had privileged access to a great quantity of financial information and was privy to the scale of account manipulation and criminal financial activity under way at the company. She said nothing to authorities. Between 1993 and 2001, she earned a large amount of money (more than $915,000).[4]

The deregulation of the US energy market was started in 1996, during the Clinton presidency. Numerous public companies producing and distributing electricity were privatized, which was a great boon to companies such as Enron. In 1999–2000, Enron spent $3.5 million on political lobbying to get even greater deregulation of the US energy market. Enron's donations for George W. Bush's presidential campaign were significant. In December 2000, Senator Phil Gramm got the change in legislation that Enron wanted. The company took the opportunity to create a new subsidiary, EnronOnline, which soon controlled the electricity and natural gas markets in California. After the change in legislation, California's electricity supply deteriorated rapidly, with continual electricity cuts, to the point that a state of emergency was decreed thirty-eight times during the first semester of 2001. Over the same period, Enron's revenues doubled.

How did Enron's behavior contribute to creating this crisis situation, and how did it profit? First, it is important to mention that Enron did not produce energy in California (or at least, very little). Its activity consisted in buying electricity from the producers and selling it to the state, to companies, and to households. In 2002, several inquiries, particularly some based on internal company documents and on the admissions of Timothy Belden, formerly responsible for commissioning electricity for the West Coast, were able to show that the company had deliberately caused electricity shortages by sending electricity out of state, bringing it back in, and selling it at bloated prices. This was nicknamed "Operation Ricochet" within the company.

The company used another type of operation, which was a variation on the first. The idea was to put out a rumor announcing an electricity shortage and to pretend to buy electricity from another state, allegedly for California consumers. In fact, this electricity, sold at extortionate rates, did not come from outside, but from California itself. This operation was known inside the company as "Death Star." All of this was made possible by the exemption of Enron and its subsidiaries (mainly EnronOnline) from any controls.

In 1999–2000, Enron paid $1.14 million to Bush's presidential campaign. In return, once elected president, Bush prevented Congress from acting to reinstate public control of the prices on the West Coast electricity market. Not until June 19, 2001, despite Bush and other political supporters of Enron, did a vote in Congress (where the Democrats had a slight majority) bring back price controls. The time wasted by Bush's stalling tactics cost the government and California consumers billions of extra dollars.

The decline of Enron

So far, the rise of Enron seemed irresistible. The story began in 1984, when Kenneth Lay, forty-two years old, former energy undersecretary in the Reagan administration, took over the management of Houston Natural Gas, which was to become Enron. Between 1990 and 2000, their income rose by 1,750 percent (Public Citizen 2001, 8). On December 21, 1991, Enron shares were priced at $21.50; by August 7, 2000, they had climbed to $90.00; by December 3, 2001 (the day after bankruptcy was declared), they had fallen to $1.01. Between 2000 and 2001, Enron's sales quadrupled, from $12 billion to $48 billion. In August 2001, Enron declared $401 million in profits; three months later, on October 26, it admitted to losses of $618 million.

Enron's fall was precipitated by the return to greater regulation from June 2001. However, the seeds of the crisis were sown much earlier. Stock market capitalization of the company, as for most other US companies, had shown a tendency to fall off since 2000, and real profits fell, too. To keep their shares attractive, Enron executives had artificially bloated the accounts by recording bank loans as income (especially those granted by Citigroup, the leading world bank group, and by JPMorgan) and other operations. To conceal losses, Enron executives removed them from the financial report. With the same aim of maintaining the highest possible price on the stock exchange, they had Enron buy up its own shares on a massive scale. Still in the same vein, they encouraged the pension fund of Enron's employees to increase the proportion of Enron shares in its portfolio to a level of 62 percent. In July 2001, Enron's

Kenneth Lay: Jesus was a markets guy

I believe in God and I believe in free markets. That's the fairest way to allocate and price resources. It does create more wealth and a higher standard of living for people than any other alternative. That ought to be the conclusive statement on markets.... Certainly Jesus attempted to take care of the people around him, attempted to make their lives better. He also was a freedom lover. He wanted people to have the freedom to make choices. The freer the country in terms of its market and political system, the higher the standard of living of the people.

—Kenneth Lay, son of a Baptist minister, in the *San Diego Tribune*, February 2, 2001

You must cut jobs ruthlessly by 50 percent or 60 percent. Depopulate. Get rid of people. They gum up the works.

—Jeffrey Skilling, Enron's former chief executive

Chronology

1984: Kenneth Lay takes over as CEO of Houston Natural Gas.

1985: Houston Natural Gas merges with InterNorth and becomes Enron.

1993: Enron is exempted from public control over its energy-market operations thanks to the intervention of Wendy Gramm, president of the Commodity Futures Trading Commission (CFTC). Six days later, Gramm resigns to become a director of Enron. Between 1993 and 2001, she receives from Enron, in different forms of remuneration, more than $915,000.

1996: Deregulation of the electricity market and privatization of local companies that produce and distribute electricity.

1999–2000: Enron spends $3.45 million to influence a change of legislation.

December 2000: Senator Phil Gramm, Wendy Gramm's husband, instigates in the US Congress a change in legislation in favor of more deregulation.

January 20, 2001: Start of the presidential mandate of George W. Bush.

First semester 2001: Through its subsidiary EnronOnline, Enron controls the West Coast energy market. Thirty-eight times, California authorities declare a state of emergency for energy. Electric power is suspended for hundreds of hours as a result of Enron's manipulation, designed to cause systematic cuts to force up prices (and profits).

February 22, March 7, and **April 17, 2001:** Meetings with Kenneth Lay and the Energy Commission, under the influence of US vice president Dick Cheney.

May 17: The Energy Commission reports its approval of most of Enron's proposals, including rejection of the Kyoto agreement.

June 19: Congress deregulates the electricity market once again.

August 14: Enron executive director Jeffrey K. Skilling resigns; Kenneth Lay takes on the responsibilities of CEO and vice president. *Continued, next page* ▶

▶ *Continued from previous page*

October 16: A net loss of $618 million is recorded for Enron's third term.

October 22: Enron announces that the Securities and Exchange Commission (SEC) has opened an internal enquiry into the company.

October 23: Lay reassures investors at the shareholders' meeting.

October 29: Lay approaches the federal authorities, US Secretary of Commerce, to try to hush up negative information from the brokerage firm Moody's about Enron's credit worthiness.

November 8: Lay compares Enron's situation with the finance company Long-Term Capital Management, a speculative fund that went bankrupt during the crisis of 1998 and received the full support of the Federal Reserveand the US government, forcing the big private banks, including some Swiss banks, to inject funds.

November 9: Dynegy, a rival company in the energy sector, considers taking over Enron for $9 billion.

November 28: The Dynegy/Enron merger falls through.

November 29: The SEC broadens its inquiry to include the audit company Arthur Andersen.

December 2: Enron is adjudged bankrupt; however, its shares remain on the stock market.

January 10, 2002: Arthur Andersen admits that confidential documents were destroyed September–November 2001.

June 2002: Arthur Andersen is charged with obstruction of justice.

June 2003: Federal Energy Regulatory Commission bans Enron from selling power in the United States, and the Labor Department plans to sue Enron, alleging that its actions led to huge losses in employee retirement accounts.

Stock options:

Jeffrey K. Skilling, then CEO of Enron, pocketed $62.5 million of stock options in the year 2000 alone. Kenneth Lay, between November 2000 and July 31, 2001, sold 672,000 Enron shares in small quantities. Skilling sold 500,000 shares on September 17, 2001. James Derrick, another director, sold 160,000 shares June 6–15, 2001. Lou Pai, executive director of Enron Xcelerator, sold 1.1 million shares from May 18 to June 7, 2001.

Stock option sales by Enron's directors had already been massive in 2000: "This personal enrichment was carried out to the detriment of the state. Taking advantage of existing tax laws, Enron deducted all expenses relating to the practice of stock options and their profits. Result: Instead of paying $112 million of tax on the companies in 2000, it benefited from a tax credit of $278 million" (*Le Monde*, April 6, 2002).

boss, Kenneth Lay, while inviting his employees to buy Enron shares, was secretly selling his off and pocketing a large profit margin over the price he had paid for them as stock options. (Between November 2000 and July 31, 2001, Kenneth Lay sold 672,000 Enron shares). By doing this, he accelerated the collapse of Enron share prices. At the same time, employees were forbidden from selling their shares, as the structure of the Enron pension fund was undergoing reorganization and all operations had to cease.

The Bush family and Enron

Both the Bush family and Enron are based in Texas and have their main economic interests there. The Bush family has a big interest in the oil sector. Enron and Bush Senior and Junior have constantly had interests in common. In 1988, George W. Bush used his influence on the Argentine minister of public works to get a contract in favor of Enron concerning a pipeline. Once Bush became governor of Texas, he allowed Enron to violate the state's antipollution laws. Later, Enron had no trouble persuading Bush to reject the Kyoto agreement on global warming and the emission of greenhouse gases.

Speaking of energy: What about oil?

In UNCTAD's 2001 *Trade and Development Report*, the authors note that the significant increase in the price of oil in 2000 was essentially due to speculative activities on oil reserves in the industrialized countries by brokerage firms (see also BIS 2001a). Enron, the main brokerage firm for petroleum products, was one of the companies at the origin of these speculative operations. In 2000, the rise in the price of oil was attributed by the Western press and in official Northern government discourse to the actions of OPEC. In fact, the main actors were the big companies of the North that speculated on oil reserves.

Enron: In the thick of the 2001 California electricity crisis

In the midst of the California electricity crisis in 2001, secondary players similarly were singled out for blame, i.e., private California electricity-producing companies that were accused of not investing enough in improving productivity. The charges were fair[5] but these companies were neither solely nor mainly responsible. Moreover, the Republicans, especially Bush and his treasury secretary Paul O'Neill (asked to resign in December 2002), blamed the crisis on local authorities (California's governor was a Democrat) and insisted that deregulation was beneficial.

Analysis reveals that the party most responsible for the power cuts was none other than Enron (and a few others of the same ilk), which, as explained above, deliberately caused the shortages. This is proven by the fact that the number of "Stage 3 alerts"[6] for energy jumped from a single case in 2000, to thirty-eight such cases in the first semester 2001—the period when Enron had complete freedom to manipulate the markets through its subsidiary EnronOnline. On June 19, 2001, Congress, under pressure from the small Democratic majority, abolished the deregulation measures taken at the end of 2000. In the second semester of 2001, there was not a single "Stage 3 alert."

When talking about oil, it is hard not to think of the tampering of Bush and Cheney. The SEC, which polices the markets, opened an inquiry concerning Bush in April 1991, concluding in October 1993 that there were no grounds for prosecution. One may doubt the seriousness of the inquiry, insofar as the president of the SEC at the time had been appointed by George Bush Senior.

George Bush Junior began a career as a businessman in the early 1980s at the head of a small oil company called Spectrum 7 Energy. This firm was bought out in 1986 by Harken Energy. Bush received 200,000 Harken shares, a place on the board of directors, and a consultancy contract worth $125,000 a year. Bush was criticized for using his administrative post to get a loan of $180,000 to buy, via stock options, another 105,000 shares. This is a practice that, as president, Bush put a stop to in 2002. He was also accused of selling a very large number of shares at a high price two months before Harken announced unprecedented losses of $23.2 million and share prices lost half their value. As an administrator, Bush was informed of the company's poor health. He made $848,560 from the sale of his shares—precisely the kind of behavior for which he later criticized the directors of Enron, WorldCom, etc.

Bush is not the only highly placed politician whose business practices have come under fire. The vice president, Cheney, also gave rise to a series of revelations in 2002. It is reported that in August 2000, while he was the CEO of Halliburton, world leader in petroleum research, Cheney made a profit of $18.5 million by selling more than 600,000 of his company's shares. Two months later, the company announced poor results and the share price dropped dramatically.

In 2002, revelations of Bush's insider trading and his policies in favor of big capital rattled American public opinion. A poll conducted in July 2002 for the *Washington Post* and ABC found that 54 percent of respondents considered President Bush's measures against management fraud "not severe enough." In another poll published by the *New York Times* and CBS in the same period, two-thirds of people consulted were convinced that the Bush administration preferred to defend big business rather than citizens. Fifty-seven percent thought that the president was hiding something or lying about his past management of Harken Energy. When war broke out against Iraq in March 2003, it came just at the right time to focus public opinion on other issues.

Dynegy, CMS, and others

Dynegy, headquartered 200 meters away from Enron in Houston, was a direct rival of the latter. It is controlled by the oil company ChevronTexaco. Dynegy wanted to take over Enron in November 2001, taking advantage of the stock market collapse it was going through. However, Dynegy was also spattered by scandal at this time and was unable to carry through its project. It was the transnational firm UBS Warburg that seized the opportunity to buy Enron's brokerage activities for a song.

Dynegy had a simple trick to embellish its accounts: the "round trip." It takes two players to do a round trip. The company Dynegy sells electricity to CMS Energy for a billion dollars on Day X at midday. That is the outward trip. On the same day, at the same time, CMS sells Dynegy electricity for a billion dollars. That is the return trip. No one makes any money in this game, but each has extra revenues of a billion dollars to show for it. The companies mentioned above carried out such operations several times in 2000 and 2001. Investigators of the SEC identified the same type of operation. It had taken place on November 15, 2001, for a sum of $1.7 billion, i.e., 13 percent of Dynegy's revenues for the third term of 2001 (see *Wall Street Journal*, May 10, 2002, and *Le Monde*, May 30, 2002). Dynegy and CMS intended to use this phony operation to fool the markets by increasing their companies' revenues. In the case of Dynegy, the November 15 transaction represented half of its revenue growth for that term. (Around this time, Dynegy was preparing to take over Enron, now teetering on the edge of bankruptcy.) Dynegy has other skeletons in its closet, such as a similarly phony contract to provide gas over a period of five years ("Project Alpha").

CEO Chuck Watson was forced by the scandal to resign in May 2002 and was replaced by Daniel Dienstbier, hitherto president of Northern Natural Gas, a pipeline that Dynegy had bought from Enron some time earlier. It's a small world! Dynegy's new president had been vice president of ChevronTexaco, the number two oil company in the United States. In October 2002, the CEOs continued to play musical chairs. Dienstbier was replaced by Bruce Williamson from Duke Energy, another Texan company in the same sector, which he had directed after learning the trade in the transnational Royal Dutch/Shell. These people and their origins are mentioned to show that all arrangements take place within a very narrow circle.

Furthermore, Dynegy's partner in the round trip, CMS, based in Michigan, was also the object of an SEC enquiry in 2002. The authorities reckoned that CMS had practiced enough round trips to bloat its financial report by $4.4 billion in eighteen months (in 2000–01).

WorldCom: A monumental scandal

The WorldCom scandal followed Enron. As the second-largest long distance service provider in the United States and world leader in Internet services, the company's revenues for 2000 totaled $35 billion. When it filed for protection under Chapter 11 of the Federal Bankruptcy Code, WorldCom was $41 billion in debt. WorldCom employed a workforce of 85,000 and had 20 million subscribers in 65 countries. Like Enron, it was a star, symbolizing the euphoric America of the late 1990s. The founder of the company, Bernard Ebbers, like his colleague at Enron, Kenneth Lay, was the darling of the financial world and press. Within about ten years, WorldCom went from a little start-up company to a full-blown empire, threatening AT&T, the longstanding giant of the telecommunications sector. Between 1998 and 1999, WorldCom shares on the stock market increased in value sixfold.

As with Enron, the fall was sudden and hard. Between January 1, 2002, and the declaration of bankruptcy on July 21, WorldCom shares lost 99.38 percent of their value. Like Enron, WorldCom systematically cooked its books. After the SEC inquiry was opened in March 2002, the directors admitted to having fiddled the accounts to the level of $9 billion, which led to the eviction of CEO Ebbers in April.

AOL Time Warner: The flop of the "e-economy"

The merger between AOL and Time Warner (imposed by AOL) in January 2000 saw the birth of the biggest global company from the point of view of stock market capitalization and the biggest audiovisual group in the world. (The "French" company Vivendi Universal and the German company Bertelsmann followed). AOL Time Warner was a sort of leading light in the new economy for several reasons. AOL (AOL, CompuServe, Netscape), the dazzling star of the Internet, had grown from a little start-up to a major league player in a few short years. One fine day, it took over media and entertainment behemoth Time Warner, owner of television channels, music labels, movie studios, and magazines. AOL was able to do this because its stock market capitalization at the time of the merger had reached $190 billion, while Time Warner's was "only" $129 billion. AOL boss Gerald Levin, who became boss of the newly merged company, described it as a company of the future. Thanks to the Internet, AOL would provide all the cultural and news products of traditional companies such as Time Warner to an ever-expanding audience.

A year and a half later, the stock market capitalization of AOL Time Warner had fallen to a mere sixth of its value at the time of the merger ($55 billion in July 2002, compared with $319 billion in January 2000). The $55 billion of stock market capitalization corresponded to the estimated value of Time Warner; AOL's value had fallen to near zero. Levin was fired and replaced by a director from Time Warner.

In July 2002, AOL Time Warner was under the scrutiny of the Department of Justice and the SEC for falsifying accounts. Moreover, a group of minority shareholders is prosecuting the company for "broken promises" (*El País*, July 20, 2002; *Le Monde*, August 30, 2002; *Time*, August 12, 2002).

Business banks

The main US investment banks—Merrill Lynch, Morgan Stanley, Credit Suisse First Boston (Credit Suisse Group), Smith Barney (Citigroup), Goldman Sachs—played an active role in the fraudulent practices behind all the scandals. These investment banks perform several functions. They analyze the financial health of companies to advise investors on the stock market. This includes recommending buying or selling shares in this or that company and managing very big portfolios of shares for themselves and for third parties such as pension funds, which entrust them with huge amounts to invest on the stock exchange. They deal with bringing companies onto the stock market. They issue loans when companies, states, or municipalities want to raise funds on the money markets. Some of them, such as Credit Suisse First Boston and Smith Barney, are the business-banking affiliate of a larger banking group.

The Glass-Steagall Act, repealed in 1999 under the Clinton administration, had been passed in 1933 during the Depression to avoid repeated catastrophic bankruptcies of financial institutions, which combined the collection of savings with stock market investments and with capital participation in businesses. The purpose of the law was to separate investment banks (holdings companies) and banks. In full neoliberal euphoria, with financialization of the economy proceeding apace, big financial groups such as Citibank were successful in influencing the Clinton administration to remove the obstacles to their expansion. This is how Citigroup, a major global finance group, was able to see the light of day. Citigroup arose from the merger between Citibank and Salomon Smith Barney.

Merrill Lynch, Morgan Stanley, Smith Barney (Citigroup), and Goldman Sachs were involved up to their necks in the Enron, WorldCom, and other scandals. The stock market crisis and the economic slowdown, added to the effects of their own fraudulent practices, put them into a bad position. Between January 2001 and the end of 2002, Merrill Lynch shares lost more than half of their stock market value. In 2002, all of these business banks became the objects of lawsuits on the part of the SEC and the Department of Justice. Furthermore, investors, shareholders, and employees filed complaints against them. In 2002, to put an end to the legal proceedings, about ten of these banks accepted the principle of a total penalty of $1.4 billion. Credit Suisse First Boston and Merrill Lynch paid $200 million to the treasury. Citigroup paid $400 million.

These investment banks have been accused of collusion with the directors of Enron, WorldCom, and other bankrupt companies. The authorities have plenty of evidence, made public in April 2003, that analysts from these business banks deliberately issued recommendations to buy shares in companies that they knew were in trouble. They did this because the business banks that employed them were themselves shareholders in the companies concerned. A fall in their stock market value would have gone against the interests of the business bank.

In the case of Merrill Lynch, the authorities acquired internal documents written by its leading analyst Henry Blodget, a specialist in the new economy. He privately referred to the company At Home as a "piece of crap" while, at the same time, he strongly recommended investors to buy its shares. In another internal document, Blodget explained how he and his team had taken part in fifty-two commercial transactions in violation of all ethical principles between December 1999 and November 2000. The business bank increased Blodget's salary fourfold to reward him (from $3 million to $13 million). Since these revelations, furious customers have filed dozens of class action suits against Merrill Lynch. It could cost the firm two billion dollars.

Salomon Smith Barney (Citigroup) got rid of its star analyst, Jack Grubman, in August 2002. He had been attacked by the press for having upheld positive recommendations of companies such as WorldCom. Grubman received $32 million as a golden handshake. He does not seem too depressed:

> Although I regret that, like many others, I failed to see the coming collapse of the telecom sector and I understand the disappointment and anger that investors feel due to this collapse, I am still proud of my work and of that of the other analysts who worked with me. (*Le Soir*, February 17–18, 2002)

Jack Grubman and Henry Blodget have both been forbidden from working in the securities industry and fined $15 million and $4 million, respectively (*Les Echos*, April 29, 2003).

In another directly corrupt practice, business banks gave privileged clients—like directors of companies such as WorldCom, Qwest, Metro Media, and others—packages of shares in companies that they were about to put on the stock market. The clients sold off the shares a few days after the companies launched, while the markets were still euphoric, and thus made considerable profits. By this practice, business banks sought to persuade big customers to hire them for major contracts. In September 2002, Bernard Ebbers and four other CEOs were the object of lawsuits by the attorney general of New York, Eliot Spitzer, who demanded that they repay $28 million obtained as deal sweeteners from business banks.

Rating agencies

Three firms dominate the sector of rating agencies on the global market. Two are American (Moody's, and Standard & Poor's); the other is French (Fitch). These companies evaluate the financial position of all big borrowers: states, municipalities, companies, investment funds. The ratings they assign play a decisive role in fixing the interest rates for the borrowers. In 2002, a volume of $30 trillion of debt was concerned. The rating agencies, therefore, wield considerable power. Their rates enable potential lenders to evaluate the health and the seriousness of candidates for loans. Marks go from "very safe" to "extremely risky," through "fairly safe" and "risky." "Very safe" is expressed by attributing a triple A to the borrower. Bad pupils will be rated with a C or D.

Moody's has more than 700 analysts and employs 1,500 people in 15 countries. Its ratings cover one hundred countries. Standard & Poor's employs 1,000 analysts in 21 countries, and its analyses cover about 100 countries. Fitch employs 1,200 people, including 600 analysts; it evaluates borrowers from 75 countries.

These companies have been strongly criticized for the role they played during the crises of the 1990s. They were particularly targeted during the East Asian crisis of 1997–98. Indeed, they maintained favorable judgements of private East Asian companies when those companies were borrowing massively and had been in difficulty since 1996. Once the crisis had broken in 1997, the rating agencies turned around and attributed drastically low ratings to the Asian companies and states concerned. As a result, borrowers were forced to pay several billion dollars more in interest payments. The role of rating agencies has also been criticized concerning their evaluation of the country risk for Argentina and Brazil between 1998 and 2002.

Rating agencies have also come in for heavy criticism of their role in the various scandals that broke out in the United States in 2001–02. In 2001, Moody's maintained a very high rating for Enron, just as it was hanging on the cliff edge. These rating agencies are anything but independent of the companies they rate, as the companies are the ones who pay them. In some cases, to force the clients to use their services, they give unsolicited rates, usually less favorable than if they had been paid for.

Audit firms

The Enron affair brought to light the collusion between the directors of the company and Arthur Andersen, the audit firm responsible for checking the accounts. Arthur Andersen was found guilty of obstruction of justice in June 2002. This verdict forced it out of business. Arthur Andersen had helped to disguise accounts for Enron, which had paid it $50 million in 2000 for all services rendered. To get rid of the evidence of its collusion with Enron, Arthur Andersen destroyed tens of thousands of compromising documents in October 2001, when the SEC had begun its investigation. Clearly, connivance between audit firms and the companies whose accounts they revise is widespread. Arthur Andersen no doubt rendered services comparable to those benefiting Enron to a good number of its 2,300 client companies.

Audit firms have other functions than merely checking company accounts. Their main source of income comes from the advice they proffer. For every dollar earned through auditing, they earn three more as consultants. Arthur Andersen is no exception. Indeed, the four other leading audit firms are all under SEC investigation. KPMG revised the accounts for Xerox, which admitted to bloating their revenues by $6.4 billion from 1997–2001. Deloitte Touche Tohmatsu checked the accounts of Adelphia Communications, whose resounding bankruptcy made headlines in June 2002. PricewaterhouseCoopers is involved in the Tyco scandal, where the director is accused of making fraudulent handouts totaling $96 million to fifty-one of the company's top executives. Ernst & Young is accused of exceeding its duties as an independent auditor by developing and marketing software with PeopleSoft while simultaneously auditing its accounts (*Le Monde*, June 18, 2002).

TABLE 5.1. BIG FIVE AUDIT FIRMS IN 2001

	2001 global revenues (billions of dollars)	Employees worldwide
PricewaterhouseCoopers	22.3	150,000
Deloitte Touche Tohmatsu	12.4	95,000
KPMG	11.7	100,000
Ernst & Young	9.8	84,000
Arthur Andersen	9.3	85,000

Source: Table composed by the author

Before Arthur Andersen went bankrupt, the "Big Five" audit firms had control of (almost) the entire global auditing market (see table 5.1). When Arthur Andersen went to the wall, the four other firms divvied up its customer base.

From 2002, the Bush administration and the US Justice Department tried to clean up the situation. The Enron trial was announced for December 2003. This was an opportunity to get to the bottom of all the jiggery-pokery. In 2002, twenty-five big companies and 150 CEOs or top executives (forty-five of whom intend to plead guilty) were under full investigation and/or the object of legal proceedings on behalf of the market watchdog, the SEC, and the Justice Department. Some of the charges are falsification of accounts, insider dealing, personal enrichment at the company's expense, tax evasion, association to commit offenses, and obstruction of justice. Criminal behavior has become so widespread and general that the US president had to intervene directly to threaten CEOs with prison:

> If you're a CEO and you think you can fudge the books in order to make yourself look better, we're going to find you, we're going to arrest you and we're going to hold you to account. (*Time*, August 12, 2002)

In *Le Figaro*, on July 1, 2002, he was quoted as saying, "CEOs found guilty of fraud are liable to financial sanctions, and if they have indulged in criminal behavior they will go to prison."

Alan Greenspan, in his semiannual monetary policy report to the Congress on July 16, 2002, presented things philosophically:

> [Our] market system depends critically on trust—trust in the word of our colleagues and trust in the word of those with whom we do business. Falsification and fraud are highly destructive to free-market capitalism and, more broadly, to the underpinnings of our society.

Overall, the executive and legal authorities have stopped at mere intimidation. No sitting CEO was locked up in 2002. Only Dennis Kozlowski, former head of Tyco, actually went to prison—but after the company sacked him. Some top executives were taken away in handcuffs for interrogation, but none spent any time behind bars. Yet, they had accumulated through criminal behavior tens, even hundreds, of millions of dollars. They caused bankruptcies that drove some redundant employees to suicide, ruined hundreds of thousands of lives, and cost taxpayers hundreds of billions of dollars. Meanwhile, for minor crimes such as shoplifting, tens of thousands of ordinary US citizens languish in overcrowded jails.

Between Bush and his predecessor, Bill Clinton, the politics of double standards has carried on regardless: prison for the poor and golden retirements for rich friends. In January 2001, President Clinton, three days before leaving the

White House, amnestied Mark Rich. This US, Belgian, and Spanish citizen, a multibillionaire through speculating on raw materials, had been wanted by US authorities for seventeen years for a host of crimes. These included providing strategic goods to regimes under international embargo (South Africa during apartheid and North Korea), tax evasion, racketeering, etc. (Ziegler 2002, 98). It must be said that Clinton, mixed up with the law himself, had received a fine gift from Mark Rich's ex-wife. Hoping to obtain the presidential pardon for her ex-husband, she had just paid $450,000 into Clinton's presidential library fund.

In September 2002, Congress passed a law called the Sarbanes-Oxley Act, with the aim of preventing further behavior such as that revealed by the affairs of Enron, WorldCom, etc. The law provides for tougher sentences for different financial crimes. Penalties for obstructing justice and destroying vital evidence, of which the firm Arthur Andersen was found guilty in the Enron affair, were doubled to a maximum of twenty years in prison. Concerted operations with the intent to deceive shareholders are henceforth considered criminal offenses liable to ten years' incarceration. CEOs now have to certify and sign off on their company's accounts. A false declaration is punishable by twenty years' imprisonment. Banks and brokerage firms are forbidden from penalizing analysts who produce unfavorable opinions on client companies. Directors are no longer entitled to privileged loans from their companies. On this last point, Bush could have been sued for the privileges he enjoyed when he was a director of Harken, if such legislation had existed at the time.

In the end, CEOs and capitalist companies alike got off lightly with regard to the law. The fines that companies were (or will be) condemned to pay can be deducted from taxable income. If this weren't enough, in 2002 Bush passed a law by which dividends distributed among shareholders are now also deductible. Just a little booster to get the motor started again, with the usual suspects in the driver's seat.

Watchdogs in the dog house

The crisis has directly hit the main institutions whose job it is to put the economic house in order. In November 2002, Harvey Pitt, president of the SEC, resigned. Robert Herdman, chief accountant of the SEC also resigned. A few days later, he was followed by William Webster, newly appointed president of the Public Company Accounting Oversight Board, founded in summer 2002 to oversee the cleanup. Webster, former director of the CIA and the FBI, threw in the towel after the council's first meeting! He fell foul of unfortunate revelations: he headed the audit committee of the company US Technologies, accused in court of accountancy malpractice (*Le Monde*, November

14, 2002). Furthermore, the special anticorruption financial squad created by the Bush administration came in for violent criticism. Its head, Larry Thompson, a deputy attorney general in the Justice Department, had been a director of Providian Financial, a company involved in fraud charges. Under his watch, Providian Financial, specialized in credit cards, was forced to pay the treasury $400 million to escape prosecution for fraud.

Another gem of information: The head of the antitrust division of the Justice Department, Charles James, resigned in October 2002 to join the oil group ChevronTexaco as vice president and legal adviser. He had been appointed in June 2001 by George W. Bush and was the architect of the out-of-court settlement between the Justice Department and Microsoft. Needless to say, the settlement was highly favorable to Bill Gates's company.

US pension problems

While the bosses got off lightly, thanks to the good graces of the executive and legislative authorities, things were less rosy for workers. Company profits were on the rise again in 2002, according to the World Bank *Global Development Finance* report of April 2003. On the other hand, workers' pensions are under threat. The "pay as you go" system of pensions is rare in the United States, and those who are entitled to it draw only a small income amounting to about 40 percent of their salary. Under Ronald Reagan's administration, the system of pensions by capitalization, already widespread, was strongly encouraged within the framework of what were known as "401(k) plans" (enacted in 1982). As long as the stock markets were rising, even euphoric, this system seemed highly attractive to some, as a large proportion of workers' savings was invested in the form of shares.

Then, what was bound to happen happened: forty million workers with a 401(k) plan pension scheme found themselves in trouble, as they had neither guarantee nor security. Their savings, which totaled about $1.5 trillion, were put on a forced slimming diet to the tune of $175 billion a year following a series of auditing scandals, bankruptcies, and a creeping stock market crash. Workers with 401(k) plans from Enron, Global Crossing, and WorldCom lost practically everything. In recent years, many companies have invested their employees' savings in their own shares, barely consulting the workers. In 2001, Procter & Gamble's 401(k) plan involved the investment of 94.7 percent of savings in the company; Coca Cola, 81.5 percent; General Electric, 77.4 percent; Texas Instruments, 75.7 percent; McDonalds, 74.3 percent; and Enron (as was), 62 percent.

Forty-four million private-sector workers form the other major category of workers whose pension depends on the system by capitalization. They are part of a pension scheme known as "defined benefit," which predates the "defined contribution" 401(k) plans. A large number of workers in the automobile, air transport, metallurgy, petroleum, pharmacy, and telecommunications sectors depend on this system, which guarantees a fixed monthly income paid by the employer. In theory, and unlike the 401(k) plans, these pensions do not depend on the ups and downs of the stock market.

The trouble is that the companies responsible for financing these funds have not done so to a sufficient degree. The situation is made more serious as company revenues fall and a large proportion of the pension funds come from profits made on capital placed on the stock exchange by the companies. According to studies published in 2002, twenty-six large companies should see their financial situation deteriorate when they refloat their pension funds (Ford should see a loss of an estimated $6.5 billion), and some would be forced into insolvency.

This problem does not only concern US companies. For example, researchers from Morgan Stanley have estimated that the ratio of debt to capital for the Swiss-Swedish multinational ABB would go from 202 percent to 374 percent if due pension outlay was included and considered on the same level as other debts. "This is a ticking time bomb. It is not a question as to whether it will explode, but when it will," declared Michael Hirsch, a vice president of the Lynnvest Group, in the October 1, 2002, *Financial Times*. In its March 12, 2003, issue, the *Financial Times*, which reports regularly on the catastrophic situation of private pension funds, announced a shortfall of $300 billion in the treasuries of US companies for honoring their pension commitments. In one year, the shortfall had doubled. The same source claims that in Great Britain, the shortfall totaled $136 billion for the country's one hundred main companies. Meanwhile, the European Commission has managed to get the European Parliament to allow private pension funds to operate in the EU.

The largest pension funds in the United States are those of the civil service. The biggest of these is CalPERS (California Public Employees' Retirement System), which, in 2002, had assets of $150 billion spread over 1,800 companies. Total assets for all of the different civil service pension funds came to more than $1.5 trillion. CalPERS lost $585 million in the bankruptcy of WorldCom alone. Enron's failure resulted in a loss of $300 million for the third-largest pension fund.

The bosses are less concerned about their pensions; clearly, they do not share the same worries. Take the case of the former CEO of General Electric, as reported by economist Paul Krugman:

> The messy divorce proceedings of Jack Welch, the legendary former CEO of General Electric, have had one unintended benefit: they have given us a peek at the perks of the corporate elite, which are normally hidden from public view. For it turns out that when Welch retired, he was granted for life the use of a Manhattan

apartment (including food, wine and laundry), access to corporate jets and a variety of other in-kind benefits, worth at least $2 million a year. The perks were revealing: they illustrated the extent to which corporate leaders now expect to be treated like *ancien regime* royalty. In monetary terms, however, the perks must have meant little to Welch. In 2000, his last full year running GE, Welch was paid $123 million, mainly in stock and stock options. (*New York Times* magazine, October 20, 2002)

Salaries: An adjustment variable

During periods of economic slowdown, when companies face falling profits and exacerbated competition, bosses like to cut costs, first to salaries and number of staff. The workforce is the main adjustment variable to ensure improvement or stabilization of the company's results. Shareholders do not want to suffer from economic uncertainty. They want workers to bear the burden of risk.

Astronomical pay and golden handshakes for corrupt bosses

Since the Reagan and Thatcher years, the gap between workers' pay and that of CEOs (who are capitalists, although they are paid a salary) has widened dramatically. According to *BusinessWeek*, in 1980, the average CEO earned forty-two times more than a blue-collar worker; in 1990, the average CEO earned 85 times more, and 531 times more in 2000.[7]

The AFL-CIO compared the incomes of three CEOs to the fortunes of their company's share prices on the stock exchange from 1996–2000. Whereas the share prices of the companies they were managing fell sharply (despite a period of strong growth in general), their incomes were nothing short of amazing (see table 5.2).

TABLE 5.2. CEO INCOME COMPARED TO COMPANY STOCK PRICES

Company	Director	Period	Cumulated revenue (in dollars)	Share prices (%) compared to S&P 500
Bank of America	Hugh McColl	1996–2000	95.6 million	-34
Sprint	William Esrey	1996–2000	218.4 million	-34
Conseco	Stephen Hilbert	1995–1999	146.2 million	-50

Source: AFL-CIO, www.aflcio.org/paywatch/ceopay.htm

Figure 5.1 presents the overall evolution of CEO pay, of profits, and of stock market capitalization. The figure reveals what a farce corporate governance turns out to be. The evolution of CEO salaries should follow that of their company's results; however, what can be seen is quite the reverse.

A similar state of affairs exists beyond the borders of the United States. In 2001, while Vivendi Universal was sliding into the red, Jean-Marie Messier's salary increased by 19 percent (a 66 percent rise after tax). Unbeknownst to shareholders, Messier sold more than 300,000 shares at the end of December 2001; yet, in May 2002, he claimed he was still buying them. In Switzerland, Mario Corti, top director of Swissair, received 8.3 million euros to turn the failing airline company around—a few months later, it went bankrupt.

CEO pay is comprised of a salary, stock options (which, in 1999–2000, represented twice the salary on average), and bonuses. Add to that a golden retirement pension, one or several residences, an unlimited expense account, one or more cars, a chauffeur—sometimes even an airplane. To a CEO's pay should be added the revenue earned from their capital. And don't forget gifts from client companies (for example, packages of free shares).

Stock options were all the rage in the 1990s, and until 2001. They netted colossal sums of money for several thousand CEOs. In 2000, Jeffrey Skilling, former Enron CEO, pocketed $62.5 million thanks to stock options. In December 2002, the *Wall Street Journal* drew up a list of the five bosses who benefited most from stock options between 1998 and 2002 in the United States. The results, which follow, do not include other forms of remuneration. Lawrence J. Ellison, Oracle CEO, received $706 million; Michael D. Eisner, Walt Disney CEO, $570 million; Michael S. Dell, Dell Computer CEO, $233 million; Sanford I. Weill, Citigroup CEO, $220 million; and Thomas M. Siebel, Siebel Systems CEO, $174 million. Obviously, if there are winners, there must be losers. These are on the side of the public treasury and modest taxpayers. Indeed, the way stock options were accounted by companies beat the US Treasury out of $56.4 billion in 2000.

What crowns it all are the fabulous severance packages for bosses who led their companies to bankruptcy. Percy Barnevik, CEO of ABB, received $88 million as a severance package in 2002. It is worth noting that this is the same Percy Barnevik who provided an infamous definition of globalization:

> I would define globalization as the freedom for my group to invest wherever it likes, for as long as it likes, to produce whatever it likes, buying and selling wherever it likes, and having to bear the fewest possible constraints as regards labor laws and social conventions.

Barnevik, omnipresent at every Davos Forum, created the Global Compact in 2000 with UN secretary-general Koffi Anan. This informal agreement, drawn up between the UN and the planet's main multinational corporations (MNCs), is officially designed to promote a "code of good conduct" for MNCs in the Third World. In fact, it ensures extra money for the UN from the private

FIGURE 5.1

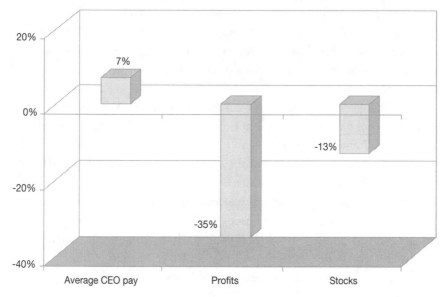

CEO pay rises while profits and share values fall

Source: New York Times (see also AFL-CIO Executive Paywatch, available online at www.aflcio.org/corporateamerica/paywatch)

sector in exchange for increased respectability for the donor MNCs. Thus, the idea of a UN sponsored by MNCs is one of Barnevik's finds. Until 2002, the CEO of ABB could do no wrong, as far as the pro-globalization press was concerned. The *Financial Times* wrote, with a spot of irony, "The only reason Mr. Barnevik does not walk on the water between Denmark and Sweden is that he doesn't have the time" (quoted in Ziegler 2002, 115).

Even CEOs who are not given generous severance packages are not hard up. Dennis Kozlowski, former Tyco CEO, did very well indeed. According to legal authorities, he had pinched $170 million from his company's till, as well as pocketing $430 million reaped from the fraudulent sale of company shares. His ex-wife magnanimously paid bail of $10 million in September 2002. He had not been in jail for long. In June 2002, he had organized a party in Sardinia at the expense of his company, for the tidy sum of a million dollars (*Financial Times*, September 20, 2002). Fancy that!

Need Enron and Co. concern the rest of the world?

Twenty years of deregulation and market liberalization on a planetary scale have eliminated all of the safety barriers that might have prevented the cascade effect of crises of the Enron type. The capitalist companies of the Triad and emerging markets have evolved, with some variations, along the same lines as those in the United States. The planet's private banking and financial institutions (as well as insurance companies) are in a bad way, adopting ever-riskier practices. The big industrial groups have all undergone a high degree of financialization and they, too, are vulnerable. The succession of scandals shows just how vacuous are the declarations of US leaders and their admirers around the world.

A mechanism equivalent to several time bombs is under way on the scale of all the economies on the planet. To name just a few of those bombs: overindebtedness of companies and households, derivatives (which, in the words of the billionaire Warren Buffet, are "financial weapons of mass destruction"), the bubble of property speculation (most explosive in the United States and the UK), the crisis of insurance companies, and the crisis of pension funds. It is time to defuse these bombs and to think of another way of doing things, in the US and elsewhere. Of course, it is not enough to defuse the bombs and dream of another possible world. We have to grapple with the roots of the problems by redistributing wealth based on social justice.

---

1   At the end of the 1980s, Japan and Germany were seen as the models to imitate. A few years later, Japan sank into a deep crisis and still had not reemerged in 2003. Germany, although in a better situation than Japan, has still not completed the reunification process begun in 1991. Between 1993 and mid-1997, South Korea, Thailand, and Malaysia were held up as models, until they were later hit by the crisis. In short, models come and go like fashions—they may be all the rage, but do not usually last long.

2   An indication of the extent of the fiasco: Paul O'Neill was forced to resign by G.W. Bush in December 2002 and replaced by John Snow.

3   Phil Gramm was put forward as a possible replacement for treasury secretary Paul O'Neill (*Financial Times*, December 9, 2002).

4   The organization Public Citizen called for Phil and Wendy Gramm to be summoned to appear in the Enron trial (see Public Citizen 2001).

5   The firm Williams Co., based in Oklahoma with operations in California, was prosecuted for closing down one of its California electricity plants, thus enabling it to demand a price twelve times higher for electricity from its other power station located nearby! (Public Citizen 2001)

6   A Stage 3 alert is declared when operational reserves of electricity fall below 1.5 percent. This forces the authorities to carry out massive electricity cuts to increase the "reserves."

7   See the Executive Paywatch section of the AFL-CIO web site at www.aflcio.org.

6

Globalization and the Growing Debt Burden

Global indebtedness has rocketed over the last decades. Between 1970 and 2002, the external debt of the developing countries (DC) was multiplied by thirty-five, while the public debt of the United States and other industrialized countries was multiplied by ten. In 2003, total debt worldwide (about $60 trillion) represented almost twice the gross global product and ten times the annual global volume of commercial exports. In a way, neoliberal globalization has taken place in an ocean of debt.

The total debt of a country is divided into internal debt, contracted with a creditor within the country, for example, a local bank, and external debt, contracted with an external creditor. The external debt of the DC is divided into external public debt and external private debt. The first is contracted by the government—state, local organizations, and other public bodies—or by private organizations for which the state guarantees the debt. The external public debt is also known as sovereign debt. External private debt is contracted by private bodies—for example, the local branch of a multinational of the North implanted in a DC—and is not guaranteed by the state.

External public debt can be broken down into three parts, according to the type of creditor. In the multilateral part, the creditor is a multilateral institution such as the IMF or the World Bank. In bilateral part, the creditor is another state. In the private part, the creditor is a private institution such as a bank or the money comes from the money markets.

According to data from the World Bank in 2003, the external debt of the DC (Third World and former Soviet Bloc) came to about $2.4 trillion at the end of 2002.

In figure 6.2, the distribution is represented from the creditors' point of view. Figure 6.3 illustrates the debtors' point of view.

Between 1980, the start of the crisis, and 2002, the external debt of the DC was multiplied by four (from $600 billion, to $2.4 trillion).

If we compare the external DC debt to total world debt, we see that the

FIGURE 6.1. BREAKDOWN OF THE TOTAL DEBT OF A COUNTRY

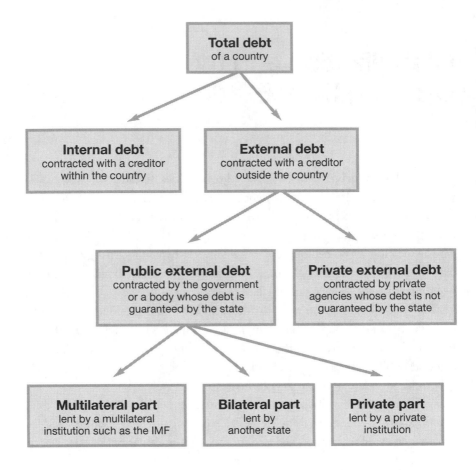

former is only a marginal amount of global indebtedness. In 2002, the proportion represented by the total external public DC debt with regard to total global public and private debt (about $60 trillion) was less than 3 percent. Even if we add public and private external DC debt ($2.4 trillion), it still only comes to 5 percent of total global debt.

The external debt of the United States (285 million inhabitants) represented, in 2002, about $3.4 trillion, i.e., more than twice the total external public debt of the Third World and former Soviet Bloc added together (about $1.6 trillion). Total public and private debt in the United States represents about $30 trillion (public debt, about $7.4 trillion; household debt, about $8.2 trillion; debt of private companies, about $14.4 trillion), that is, more than ten times the total external debt (private and public combined) of the DC.

The internal debt of the most industrialized countries is much greater than

The World Bank cooks the books

The figure given by the World Bank for 2002 was $2.384 trillion. A year earlier, the figure given was $2.442 trillion. This apparent reduction is likely to lead readers to mistaken conclusions. In fact, the external DC debt increased by $50 billion between 2001 and 2002. Intrigued by the inconsistency of these figures, for which we could find no explanation, we asked the relevant authorities of the World Bank in Washington why this sudden change in the data on the debt. They replied that South Korea had received some good news: it no longer counted as a DC, as its annual per capita income had crossed the threshold of $9,265! Consequently, its debt (about $110 billion) was no longer included in the total. Now that is radical.

This leads us to make the following comments. The criterion of per capita income to determine whether a country is a DC is arguable. Paradoxically, when the per capita income of South Korea was less than $9,265, the general situation, from 1990 to 1997, justified a change of category because its economic capacity and its ability to conduct independent policies were far greater than today. The crisis that struck in 1997–98 enabled the multinationals of the Triad to buy up Korean businesses at low prices. The agreement signed between South Korea and the IMF in 1998 meant that the latter could dictate policies that were in line with the Triad's interests, reducing Seoul's freedom of decision. Additionally, living conditions in Korea have worsened since 1998. In the end, there is room for reasonable doubt as to the World Bank's motives in the affair. Slyly deducting South Korea's debt from the total amount of DC debt allows the World Bank to produce a "reassuring" picture.

This is by no means the first such trick. In 1999, the World Bank withdrew Nigeria from the category of heavily indebted poor countries (HIPC, see glossary), composed of forty-one nations at the time, and replaced it with Malawi. Without changing the overall number of HIPC, they were able to reduce the figure of debt stock for the HIPC, since Malawi's debt was $3 billion while Nigeria's was nearer to $30 billion. At the time, journalists announced that the debt of poor countries had been reduced as part of the debt reduction decided by the G7 in 1996 in Lyon, which was not what had happened at all. We denounced this story in *Le Monde Diplomatique* (September 1999).

Furthermore, the calculation of the debt for certain countries that do

Continued, next page ▶

FIGURE 6.2. EXTERNAL DEBT OF THE DC AT THE END OF 2002
FROM CREDITORS' POINT OF VIEW

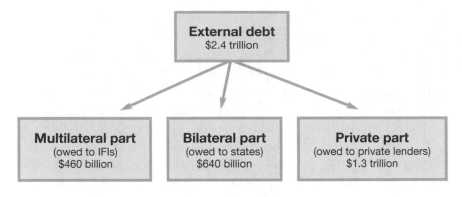

▶*Continued from previous page*

not follow the World Bank's statistics system is most mysterious. This is
the case for Iraq, Libya, or even more surprisingly, Saudi Arabia, which
is a permanent administrator of the World Bank. According to the Center for Strategic and International Studies (CSIS) in 2003, the external
debt of Iraq should come to $127 billion, not including the colossal sum
of $199 billion in compensation claimed by Kuwait and Saudi Arabia
after the first Gulf War of 1991. That places Iraq among the most heavily indebted developing countries!

How much of this debt is the World Bank now taking into account?
It is impossible to find out; however, a small calculation will prove revealing. Concerning the Middle East and North Africa, the declared
debt is $200 billion. Adding available data for the countries in the region
gives $141 billion. Consequently, the World Bank estimates at $59 billion the total debt of Libya, Iraq, and Saudi Arabia. Either the amount is
correct and the information provided by the CSIS is wrong, or the
World Bank has grossly underestimated Iraq's debt in its 2003 report,
which promises surprises in the 2004 edition.

Above all, it shows that the figures concerning the exact amount of
DC debt are subject to evaluations that can vary considerably, according
to the message that the World Bank or other bodies want to get across.
In the rest of this book, we shall normally refer to figures provided by
the World Bank in order to use the same data as are generally used by
the press or in negotiations between creditors and borrowers. However,
the reader is warned that the data is arguable and contested.

FIGURE 6.3. EXTERNAL DEBT OF THE DC AT THE END OF 2002
FROM DEBTORS' POINT OF VIEW

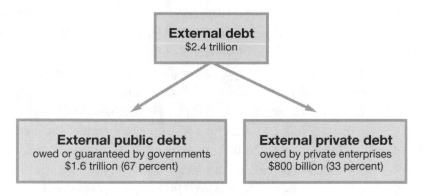

their external debt. In 2002, the public debt of the United States alone (about
$7.4 trillion) represented more than four and a half times the total external
public debt of the DC. Japan's (about $7.2 trillion) also represented more than
four and a half times that sum. One might also compare Japan's public debt to
the external public debt of all the DC of Asia and the Pacific. The public debt
of the twelve member states of the EU that form the euro zone came to about
$5 trillion in 2002, that is, more than three times the total external public debt
of the DC (see figure 6.4).

FIGURE 6.4. DEBT OF TRIAD COUNTRIES VS. DEBT OF DC REGIONS

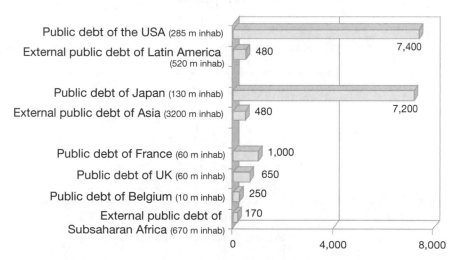

Calculated by Damien Millet and Eric Toussaint on the basis of World Bank GDF 2003, Federal Reserve, and BIS

The phenomenon of globalization described thus far and the debt problem are inextricably linked. The process of globalization began in earnest in 1982 with the eruption of the Third World debt crisis (see chapter 8), following on the about-face in US Federal Reserve policy under Paul Volker in October 1979. The two developments were tightly intertwined. Debt crisis management after 1982 was very much part of neoliberal globalization; it was an integral part of the realignment in the relationship of forces between countries of the North and South. The countries of the South entered a phase of heightened dependence.

Debt securitization (see glossary) is another key element of the link between the way in which the Third World debt crisis has unfolded and other globalization-related phenomena. This securitization concerns a significant part of OECD country public debt, along with both the external and internal debt of Third World countries—at least for those still not excluded from international financial markets. Securitization is a key feature of globalization.

What is securitization?

The term "securitization" is used to describe the new privileged position occupied by security issues in market activity. Security issues are traditional international bonds issued by a foreign borrower on the financial markets and in

FIGURE 6.5. SOURCES OF GOVERNMENT-GUARANTEED LONG-TERM LOANS

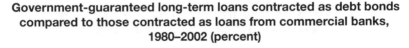

Government-guaranteed long-term loans contracted as debt bonds compared to those contracted as loans from commercial banks, 1980–2002 (percent)

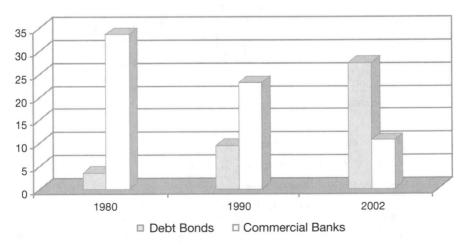

Debt Bonds   Commercial Banks

Calculated by Damien Millet and Eric Toussaint on the basis of World Bank GDF 2003

the currency of a given lender country. They may also be euro bonds denominated in a currency other than the market for which they are issued, or they may be international stocks. In addition, former bank debt has been converted into tradable securities, thus freeing banks from their responsibilities to developing countries in the wake of the debt crisis.

Sharing out risk is the main feature of this securitization trend—in numerical terms, above all, since the risk of loan default is not borne solely by a small number of multinational banks closely linked to one another; in qualitative terms, too, since each element of risk linked to a given issue can itself be the object of another financial instrument that can also be traded on the markets. Negotiable futures contracts exist, for example, to hedge against currency and interest rate fluctuation. There are also options, which are negotiable on the market. The list of such products continues (Adda 2001).

The progress of securitization has been impressive. Between 1980 and 2002, the volume of securities increased tenfold from about $3.1 trillion, to more than $30 trillion (see figure 6.5). The big financial players invest a growing share of their holdings in the government bonds of the major industrialized countries and of those Third World countries that have achieved a certain level of industrial development. These Third World countries, in fact, have the highest external debt in absolute terms; however, the total of international se-

FIGURE 6.6. DEBT BONDS VERSUS CREDITS TO COMMERCIAL BANKS

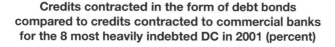

**Credits contracted in the form of debt bonds
compared to credits contracted to commercial banks
for the 8 most heavily indebted DC in 2001 (percent)**

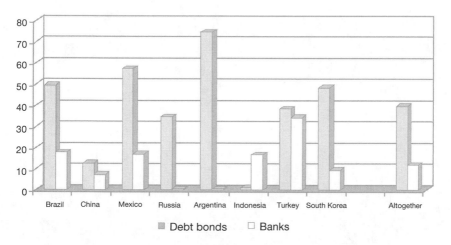

Calculated by Damien Millet and Eric Toussaint on the basis of World Bank GDF 2003

curities issued by governments and private companies in the periphery is only a small part of the global total of securities issued—less than 10 percent. This percentage was halved between 1997 and 1999, from 10 percent to about 4 percent (UNCTAD 2000b, 48).

A growing number of Third World countries issue debt paper—in the main financial markets of the highly industrialized countries, in their own domestic securities exchanges, and even through private and public banks present on their soil. Most of these issues involve debt instruments that have the advantage of extreme liquidity; the purchaser can off-load them at a moment's notice to a host of players on the secondary markets.

Designed to reduce and spread the risk for the creditor, the development of securitization makes the international system vulnerable. When a crisis erupts, a large part of holders will try to sell off their securities, which will lead to a speculative wave that is difficult to contain. All security holders suddenly try to unload them and can do so only at a very low price. The phenomenon is even clearer if we consider the eight DC whose external debt exceeds $100 billion. For these eight countries taken as a whole, the part of government-guaranteed long-term loans contracted as debt bonds is about 40 percent, as against about 12 percent to commercial banks.

7

Retrospective on the debt crisis

Public debt, international credit, and the origins of industrial capitalism, fifteenth–nineteenth centuries

In the footsteps of Adam Smith and David Ricardo, Karl Marx spent considerable time studying the creation of an international credit system and the role of public debt in capitalist accumulation on a world level. In the first volume of *Capital*, he devotes several pages of spirited analysis to the subject. In chapter 31 (Marx 1976 [Penguin edition]), he particularly focuses on colonial expropriation, public debt, and the international credit system as the sources of primitive accumulation that made industrial capital prosper the world over.

On the role of colonial expropriation, it is worth quoting *Capital*. Thankfully, Marx's analysis breaks with the presentation in the *Communist Manifesto* of capitalism as a civilizing force in the periphery:

> The discovery of gold and silver in America, the extirpation, enslavement and entombment in mines of the indigenous population of that continent, the beginnings of the conquest and plunder of India, and the conversion of Africa into a preserve for the commercial hunting of blackskins, are all things which characterize the dawn of the era of capitalist production. (Marx 1976, 915)

In the same chapter, Marx makes a dialectical link between the oppressed in the center and those in the colonies: "In fact the veiled slavery of the wage-laborers in Europe needed the unqualified slavery of the New World as its pedestal." He concludes, "[C]apital comes dripping from head to toe, from every pore, with blood and dirt" (Marx 1976, 925, 926).

According to Marx, "The different methods of primitive accumulation of the capitalist era can be assigned in particular to Spain, Portugal, Holland, France and England, in more or less chronological order. These different moments are systematically combined together at the end of the seventeenth century in England; the combination embraces the colonies, the national debt, the modern tax system, and the system of protection" (Marx 1976, 915).

He devotes several pages to colonial pillage and then examines the question of international credit:

> The system of public credit, i.e. of national debts, the origins of which are to be found in Genoa and Venice as early as the Middle Ages, took possession of Europe as a whole during the period of manufacture.... The national debt, i.e. the alienation [*Veräusserung* = alienation by sale] of the state—whether that state is despotic, constitutional or republican—marked the capitalist era with its stamp....
>
> The public debt becomes one of the most powerful levers of primitive accumulation....
>
> Along with the national debt there arose an international credit system, which often conceals one of the sources of primitive accumulation in this or that people.... A great deal of capital, which appears today in the United States without any birth-certificate, was yesterday, in England, the capitalized blood of children. (Marx 1976, 919–20)

Twentieth-century Marxist scholars have expanded on this question of global primitive accumulation (Amin 1993; Gunder Frank 1971; Mandel 1968a, 1968b). Ernest Mandel's article "L'accumulation primitive et l'industrialisation du tiers monde" ("Primitive accumulation and the industrialization of the Third World") provides a particularly interesting summary. Based on calculations by other researchers, he estimates that between 1500 and 1750, some one billion English pounds (gold sovereigns) were transferred from the colonies to Western Europe. This is more than the total value of capital invested by 1800 in all European industrial companies (Mandel 1968, 150–51).

Debt crises in the nineteenth and early twentieth centuries

Semi-periphery and financial dependence

The policies of the main capitalist powers in the late nineteenth and early twentieth centuries used foreign debt as a weapon of domination toward subordinate powers that could have themselves become central capitalist powers. The Russian Empire, the Ottoman Empire, and China took in foreign investment to deepen capitalist development. They took on heavy debts in the form of government bonds issued in the financial markets of the main industrial powers. In the cases of the Ottoman Empire and China, difficulties meeting debt payments progressively led them to be placed under foreign tutelage. European officials set up and oversaw special debt repayment accounts in these countries. They had virtual control over government revenues, which they ensured went toward fulfilling international debt obligations. This loss of financial sovereignty led the Ottoman Empire and China to negotiate their debt away against port, railway, and trade concessions. Russia, facing the same fate, chose another path after the 1917 revolution: it repudiated all debts taken on by the czarist dictatorship (Adda 2001, table 1, 57–58).

Unlike China, the Ottoman Empire, and Russia, Japan did not take on foreign debt. As such, it is the only example of successful capitalist development in the late nineteenth century by a country from the "semi-periphery." Japan experienced genuine autonomous capitalist development in the wake of a bourgeois revolution in 1868 that prevented Western finance from taking hold on its soil, among other things, while eliminating obstacles to the circulation of domestic capital. By the late nineteenth century, Japan had emerged from its autarchy of yore to become a rapidly expanding imperialist power.

Latin American external debt crises in the nineteenth and twentieth centuries

Since gaining independence in the 1820s, the countries of Latin America have gone through four debt crises (Vilas 1993). The first crisis took place during the 1820s, while the different countries were attaining independence. The second took place in the 1870s. During this crisis, Venezuela refused to meet its payments and entered into direct conflict with US, German, British, and French imperialism. In 1902, these countries sent a multilateral naval force to blockade the port of Caracas, and this gunboat diplomacy forced Venezuela to resume debt payments. These debts were not paid off until 1943. This chapter will provide an analysis of the third Latin American debt crisis, which took place in the 1930s. The fourth crisis, which began in the 1980s and was still raging at the time of writing, will be discussed in a later chapter.

A link exists between the outbreak and deepening of these four crises, on the one hand, and the long waves of capitalism, on the other. The long waves of capitalist development since the early nineteenth century have been analyzed by a number of authors, including Ernest Mandel, who made a major contribution, especially with respect to the role of political factors in the development and conclusion of long waves (Mandel 1971, 1978). Much work remains in this line of study. The link seems very strong between:

- the first modern crisis of commodity overproduction (1826), which opened the door to a long wave of slow growth (1826–47), and the first Latin American debt crisis, which began in the 1820s;

- the long depression of the industrialized economies from 1873 to 1893, and the Latin American debt crisis in the 1870s;

- the worldwide depression in the 1930s, and the Latin American debt crisis, which this time, however, opened the way for higher levels of growth than in the crisis-ridden economies of the center (one key reason for this growth was the decision by fourteen Latin American countries to suspend debt payments);

- the long wave of slow growth beginning in 1973–74, and the current Latin American (and Third World) debt crisis.

Why these crises erupt, and when, is intimately linked to the rhythms of the global economy, mainly the economies of the highly industrialized countries. Each debt crisis was preceded by a period when the economies of the industrialized countries of the center overheated and part of the excess capital was recycled into the economies of the periphery. During the preliminary phases, immediately preceding each crisis, debt increases sharply, corresponding to the end of a long cycle of expansion in the industrialized countries. A recession or a financial crash that hits one or more of the main industrialized economies usually triggers the crisis. The first crisis, in 1826, was caused by the London Stock Exchange crash of December 1825. The second crisis erupted in 1873, following stock exchange crashes in Vienna, then New York. The third, in 1931, was part of the fallout after the 1929 Wall Street crash. The fourth crisis, in 1982, resulted from the combined effects of the second global recession (1980–82) after the Second World War and the rise in interest rates decided by the US Federal Reserve in 1979. Each of these four crises lasted from fifteen to thirty years and affected the independent states of Latin America and the Caribbean, almost without exception.

During these crises, suspensions of payment were frequent. Between 1826 and 1850, during the first crisis, almost all countries suspended payment. In 1876, eleven Latin American countries were in cessation of payment. In the 1930s, eleven countries of that continent declared a moratorium. Between 1982 and 2002, Mexico, Bolivia, Peru, Ecuador, Brazil, Argentina, and Cuba suspended repayment at one time or another for a period of several months. Suspension of payment allows debtor countries to prepare the necessary conditions to resume payments in the future, after renegotiating terms with their creditors.

The debt crisis in Latin America and the Caribbean in the first half of the 20th century

Mexico 1914–42, or How a firm attitude can pay off for an indebted country

In 1914, during the revolution led by Emiliano Zapata and Pancho Villa, Mexico—the major indebted country of the continent with regard to its neighbor in the North—completely suspended external debt repayment. Between 1914 and 1942, Mexico only repaid symbolic amounts while playing for time. Long negotiations between Mexico and a consortium of creditors, conducted by the director of the US bank JPMorgan, were held between 1922 and 1942…twenty years! Meanwhile, in 1938, Mexico, under president

Lázaro Cárdenas, had nationalized the petroleum industry, previously owned by North American companies, without compensation. This measure, all to the advantage of the Mexican population, triggered the protests of the creditor. In the long run, Mexico's tenacity paid off: in 1942 the creditors wrote off more than 90 percent of the value of their loans and accepted small indemnities for the companies they had lost.[1]

The Latin American debt crisis in the 1930s

The debt crisis that erupted in 1931 was preceded by a period during which the United States significantly reinforced its economic and financial presence, particularly in Central America, the Caribbean, and several Andean countries. Until then, European financiers had been preponderant in these areas. Since 1898, the United States had exercised de facto protectorates in Cuba and Puerto Rico. It now intervened militarily in Panama, San Domingo, Haiti, and Nicaragua. Furthermore, in the 1920s, North American governments administered customs and, in some cases, internal revenue services of seven countries: Haiti, Peru, San Domingo, Nicaragua, Bolivia, Ecuador, and Honduras. For Latin American governments, the 1920s were a decade of new loans that were regularly repaid.

In 1930, before a US congressional commission, a certain Mr. Dennis, employed by the finance company Seligman Brothers of New York, gave an enlightening account of the financial flows between Europe, Latin America, and the United States:

> It so happened, after the war, that England and France, and the creditor countries of Europe had to pay for a heavy surplus of imports from America. Where were they to get the necessary dollars? They got them very largely from South America and other fields in which they had invested capital. They drew their income from investments in Latin America in dollars to pay the United States for an excess of imports from this country and also on war-debt payments.... We loaned the money to Latin America and thus Europeans acquired dollars to pay us.... It was a triangular movement. (US Congress, Sale of Foreign Bonds, 1606–1607, quoted in Marichal 1989, 189)

In 1931, crisis struck, after a decade in which substantial foreign loans had been made to Latin America, primarily from the United States. In fact, following the First World War, the United States had replaced Britain as the biggest exporter of capital to Latin America. Britain held a significant portion of Brazilian and Argentinean debt, but the United States dominated the rest of the continent. Due to its payment of reparations after the First World War, Germany was a diminished financial power. Yet, along with Britain, it had been Latin America's main creditor until the early twentieth century.

At the time, securities and bonds issued on the financial markets of the main capitalist powers made up Latin American debt. This is similar to the situation in the 1990s, but unlike that of the 1970s and 1980s, in which debt largely took the form of bank loans (see chapter 8). A number of factors explain the increased supply of loans from Europe and the United States after the First World War. Latin America's ruling classes inspired enormous confidence, guided as they were by a positivist philosophy of progress. There were great hopes in the development of the continent: huge tracts of land had been devoted to export-oriented production, especially of foodstuffs; massive infrastructure was developed, including ports, railways, and electricity; and finally, progress in intercontinental transport afforded greater integration into world markets. In the 1920s, investment boomed in the three biggest economies of the continent—Brazil, Argentina, and Mexico—financed by debt paper issued on the US and European markets. These countries accumulated huge debts; however, all concerned—lenders, borrowers, financial market operators—were convinced that exports would increase indefinitely, providing solid growth and regular debt service payments. The same reasoning held sway in the 1970s (see chapters 8 and 10).

In 1914, half of industrial exports from the imperialist center went to countries that primarily produced and exported foodstuffs and raw materials. A fundamental change has taken place from as far back as the 1970s: imperialist countries largely export to one another. In 1914, half of the periphery's exports went to only four countries of the center: Britain, Germany, France, and Belgium. If Italy, Japan, the United States, and Austria-Hungary are included, 70 percent of the periphery's exports at the time are accounted for.

In 1928, investment flows slowed down considerably due to the saturation of financial markets by Latin American securities. Soon after the 1929 stock market crash, such paper was no longer issued. With the financial tap tightly closed, Latin American countries were unable to meet their debt obligations.

External debt payments suspended by fourteen Latin American governments

On January 1, 1931, the Bolivian government announced that it would stop its debt payments. A number of other countries followed suit (Marichal 1989; Vilas 1993; Ugarteche 1997, 117). By 1932, twelve countries had partially or fully suspended debt payments; by 1935, fourteen had done so. The decision to suspend payment was made primarily because the price of exported products fell (Fishlow 1985) and investment from imperialist countries dried up.

There is a striking contrast with the situation fifty years later. One-third of all Latin American countries unilaterally suspended debt payments in the 1930s. In general terms, this decision proved correct. Most of the countries that ended debt payments experienced renewed economic growth in the

1930s, despite the halt in foreign lending. Following the Second World War, the multilateral world trading system recovered; yet, private capital markets did not reopen to Latin American borrower countries. Alternative channels were put in place at Bretton Woods in 1944. Multilateral government loans replaced financial markets. Not until the 1960s did private banks in the center begin lending directly to Latin America.

For a while, then, Latin American countries kept the international financial system at arm's length. Even those countries that had never stopped debt payments recognized the unlikelihood that global financial flows could work in their favor. Financial disarray in the United States itself heightened such feelings. Furthermore, the war between the main imperialist powers (1940–45) meant that the main lenders, Britain and the United States, could not muster the additional strength to recover their unpaid Latin American debts by force.

Although a few countries that repudiated their debts could have met their payments, they determined that the domestic social cost would have been too high. Because they suspended payments, the countries concerned could use these considerable financial resources to pursue a policy of economic expansion. If they had continued to service their debts, they most certainly would not have been able to implement exchange controls and protectionist policies against a variety of products from the North. These latter measures led to real development, thanks to a process of "industrialization through import substitution" (see glossary). Countries produced domestically many of the items previously imported from the North.

Had they not suspended foreign debt payments, these countries would not have been able to undertake the wide-ranging public works programs that would play an important role in the economic recovery of the region. Interestingly, a variety of dissimilar political regimes pursued this line of action. As Carlos Vilas has noted, however, such converging policies were not part of some preconceived plan. Only later, especially with the creation of CEPAL (Comisión Económica para América Latina [Latin American Economic Commission]), did industrialization through import substitution become part of a common strategic vision, replacing the approach of export-driven industrialization (Vilas 1993, 11).

Debt repudiation and economic recovery

The following question must now be asked: How closely is economic recovery linked to debt repudiation? A study by David Felix (1987) compares the evolution between 1929 and 1939 of five countries that totally repudiated their debts (Brazil, Colombia, Chile, Mexico, and Peru), with that of Argentina, which only repudiated a part of its debts. The study shows better economic results for the five countries than for Argentina.

Whether total or partial, repudiation led to a recovery of production in the countries concerned. Between 1929 and 1939, GNP in Brazil, Colombia, and Mexico rose more quickly than in the United States, France, and Canada. After 1932, industrial growth in Mexico, Colombia, and Chile was stronger than in Argentina. After the Second World War, the countries that had suspended external debt payment entered into negotiations with the imperialist countries and obtained substantial debt reductions along with payment facilities.

Argentina's approach, however, was not rewarded by the imperialist countries. Argentina's main economic partner in the North was Britain, which had obtained credit from Argentina to pay for products Britain needed for the war effort (Vilas 1993, 11). Yet, after the Second World War, with help from the United States, Britain pursued a policy that only knocked off a marginal portion of Argentina's debt. (For a detailed description of this episode, see Olmos 1995, 42–45.)

How US and European creditors took debt repudiation

The United States adopted an attitude of tolerance toward the fourteen Latin American countries that unilaterally suspended debt payments. Note that, from 1934 on, several European governments also stopped repaying the debts they had contracted with the United States during the First World War.

The crisis that began in 1929 was so far-reaching that it gradually strangled the public treasuries of Europe. It started with Germany. Through the Treaty of Versailles, the victors had imposed draconian conditions on that country, including huge reparation payments. Germany, squeezed by the effects of the 1929 crisis, asked to renegotiate its debt. An international conference met in Lausanne in 1932 (this was when the Bank for International Settlements was established) and decided to drastically reduce the amount Germany owed its European creditors. The amount due was reduced from $31 billion to $1 billion. This decision was an effort to avoid multiple bankruptcies of German (or Austrian) banks whose shock waves would endanger the entire financial system of the other industrialized countries.

The economic situation did not improve, and the European countries that had won the First World War were also in difficulty. They suspended payments to the United States, though that country had been their ally. The war debt owed to the United States came to $10 billion. Tensions grew between the European and North American allies until, on June 4, 1934, Great Britain, followed closely by France, Belgium, and Italy, announced suspension of all future repayments to the United States.

The Latin American governments that had suspended their repayments to both North American and European creditors as of 1931 had not expected the Europeans to suspend repayments to the United States. The internal divisions among the creditor states of the North from 1932 made things easier for them.

A clear contrast exists between the debt crisis of the 1930s and that of the 1980s in the way they were handled. In the 1980s, the United States decided to pull out all stops to prevent a repetition of the 1930s. Backed by the other G7 countries, the Reagan administration went on the offensive with a number of initiatives in the wake of the 1982 Mexican crisis. The Baker and Brady Plans were instituted in close succession (see box above). US policy makers

The Brady Plan

The Brady Plan, named for Nicholas Brady, US treasury secretary in the 1980s, led to a number of bilateral agreements between US authorities and Latin American governments on debt rescheduling and reduction. The privatization of state-owned firms was one of the central components of the Brady method. The method won over the IMF and World Bank, which have since applied it the world over. Indebted countries repay debts by selling off entire sections of their industrial apparatus, communications firms (telecommunications, airlines, ports, and so on), and banking system.

Apparently never lacking chutzpah, Brady threw in a further twist in the case of Mexican debt: Mexican authorities were forced to buy US treasury bonds as a guarantee for new loans from private banks in the North and from the IMF and World Bank. In other words, among other methods for financing its gargantuan debt, Mexico is obliged to loan the United States money through the purchase of US treasury bonds. In return, Mexico is authorized to borrow on international markets to finance debt repayment! Through it all, Mexico's debt rose from $95 billion in 1982, to nearly $130 billion in 1994.

Meanwhile, members of the Mexican ruling elite did not fail to cash in on the myriad of financial transactions and privatization sell-offs. Indeed, by 1996, twenty-four Mexican families had joined the ranks of the world's one hundred wealthiest families, breaking all records of speed— and greed. These twenty-four families own the means of production responsible for creating 14 percent of Mexico's GDP. At the same time, some 35 million Mexicans live on less than one dollar per day. No retirement to a dream home on the Cayman Islands for them!

had concluded that the American attitude in the 1930s had paved the way for too much autonomous economic development in a number of countries in their traditional sphere of influence. This time, the United States rejected cancellation and dealt with debtor countries on a case-by-case basis.

The governments of the indebted countries failed to form a united front, despite appeals made by the Cuban government in 1985. By adopting attitudes of disciplined subordination (as did, for example, Mexico and Argentina) or ineffectual resistance (Brazil and Peru), they helped to strengthen US leadership and were responsible for a massive transfer of wealth from the South of the continent to the North. They creamed off a not inconsiderable share for themselves on the way.

---

1   For a detailed analysis, see Carlos Marichal, *A century of debt crises in Latin America: From independence to the Great Depression, 1820–1930*, Princeton University Press: 1989; and, by the same author, "La deuda externa: El manejo coactivo en la política financiera mexicana, 1885–1995," *Revista Ciclos en la Historia, la Economía y la Sociedad* 9:17 (1999): 29–46.

8

The Third World debt crisis of the 1980s and 1990s

The debt surge of the 1960s and 1970s

Between 1961 and 1968, the total external debt of the Third World more than doubled, from $21.5 billion to about $47.5 billion. Between 1968 and 1980, the Third World's total external debt was multiplied by twelve in as many years—from $47.5 billion to more than $560 billion.[1] Yet, neither the media nor the international financial institutions talked about the Third World debt crisis before August 1982—when the Mexican government announced that it could no longer meet its regular external debt payments. This created serious problems for the international financial system, especially for the North's private banks. The crisis, however, had much earlier origins.

The birth of the Eurodollar market and the origins of the debt crisis

In the 1960s, a growing number of banks operating outside the United States, especially in Europe, began to accept deposits and provide loans in dollars. This helped to absorb and recycle the huge quantity of dollars circulating around the world as an instrument for international payments (Adda 2001, vol. 1, 94ff.; Chesnais 1996, 14; de Brunhoff 1996, 47; Norel and Saint-Alary 1992, 41ff.). Eurodollars were dollars held on account by banks with operations centered outside the United States. This newcomer to the financial markets signaled the beginning of the deregulation of capital flows, since the banks in question were not subject to the control of any state body—neither the US Federal Reserve nor Western European governments. They were also outside the ambit of interstate bodies, with the IMF opting for noninterference. In so doing, the IMF failed to respect its own statutes; article VI explicitly calls for controls on capital flows.

Handling costs for Eurodollar-denominated financial products were lower than those for other currencies, since "Eurobanks" were not obliged to set up mandatory reserves. Therefore, they could offer high returns to depositors and competitive rates to borrowers, while posting high profits—all at a risk, however.

Early signs that the long wave of rapid growth was winding down included high levels of bank liquidity. The banks received increasing amounts of capital, since the drop in profit levels meant fewer and fewer attractive investments in production. At the beginning of the 1970s, a major upswing in Eurodollar loans occurred. They jumped 212 percent between 1970 and 1971, 58 percent between 1971 and 1972, and 207 percent between 1972 and 1973.

Increase in World Bank loans

During the first twenty-two years of its existence, the World Bank provided loan financing for only 708 projects, to the tune of $10.7 billion. From 1968 on, however, loan totals skyrocketed. Between 1968 and 1973, the World Bank loaned $13.4 billion for 760 projects (George and Sabelli 1994; McNamara 1973).

Recycled petrodollars

Many analysts and opinion makers in the North have incorrectly blamed the surge in Third World debt on the 1973 increase in the price of oil, decided by the OPEC cartel of oil-producing countries from the South. As we have just shown, however, debt had increased much earlier.

Two factors linked to the oil shock did accelerate indebtedness. First, the governments of the South transferred most of the revenues obtained by oil-producing countries into the North's financial system, which further heightened the excess liquidity of the North's banks. As a result, these banks sought to loan money to the South even more aggressively than in the late 1960s and early 1970s. Second, non–oil-producing countries of the South were hit by the increase in their oil bills, creating a deficit in their trade balances. To finance this deficit, they were forced to borrow in the North's financial markets.

It is one thing to identify these two factors, but quite another to blame OPEC countries. Blaming OPEC countries for the Third World debt crisis lets decision makers in the North off the hook. It also opens the way to blame OPEC for the 1974–75 world economic crisis. At the time, Ernest Mandel warned against such an explanation for the crisis. (See, in particular, Mandel 1975, 1982; see also Norel and Saint-Alary 1992.) Regulationist economist Michel Aglietta has provided a similar explanation (Aglietta, Brender, and Coudert 1990).

The responsibility of the North's bankers

The banks in the North pursued increasingly audacious (and risky) loan policies, especially with respect to Third World countries (both their governments and private companies). Policy makers in Third World countries soon grew accustomed to a situation in which banks "offered" them loans at low rates (3–8 percent until 1978, Norel and Saint-Alary 1992). Factoring in inflation, interest rates were almost nil, and even negative at times, making borrowing an attractive proposition. Any number of the South's leading government officials and enterprise heads from the time can be found to testify that representatives from the North's banks descended upon them to offer loans, tripping over one another to offer the most attractive terms. By the time the crisis hit in 1982, more than five hundred banks had made loans to Mexico, and more than eight hundred to Brazil.

Easy money and the world economic crisis

When the global recession hit in 1974–75, the North's governments implemented the kind of pump-priming measures that were very common at the time, with the aim of boosting production through an increase in demand. The policy of easy credit for the Third World was continued in this overall framework. In addition, several countries in Central Europe and the Balkans (Yugoslavia, Poland, Hungary, Romania, and others) were granted big loans.

Now, it was the turn of the North's governments to offer attractive loans, especially in the form of export credits for the South. The loans were provided to Third World countries on condition that the countries make purchases from the industries of the creditor countries—of industrial goods and other products, including military hardware disguised in one way or another. Such bilateral loans (from governments of the North to those of the Third World) aim to boost Third World demand for products from the North. Because of this policy, between 1976 and 1980, the South's total debt grew at an annual rate of 20 percent.

What were the loans for?

The World Bank and the governments and banks of the North provided loans, above all, for large infrastructure projects—energy megaprojects, for example. They also provided loans to finance the balance of payments deficit of countries of the South. Export credits were provided to back the North's exporting industries.

All of these loans obeyed the same overall logic: strengthen the link between the countries of the periphery and the world market, and further steer these countries toward export-oriented production. In the South, this meant abandoning local food crops and industrial undertakings aimed at meeting the needs of the domestic market. It also meant abandoning projects aimed at exporting high value-added products that could compete with those manufactured in the North.

The loans sought to induce each country of the South to specialize in the production of a few export products. The least advanced Third World countries were the most vulnerable; they specialized the most, thereby further heightening their dependence. This was also the case for more developed countries such as Algeria, which had been in the midst of a genuine industrial takeoff but was driven to concentrate in large measure on oil and gas extraction.

By steering the countries of the South to focus on the export of raw materials and basic manufactured goods, the North put them in competition with one another. This could only lead to a short-term drop in the price of the exports. The only possible consequence was a drop in export earnings and, above all, deterioration in the terms of trade (see chapter 9).

Corrupters and the corrupted

It is difficult to determine how large a share of these loans went toward the personal enrichment of people holding public posts in the South. Norel and Saint-Alary (1992, 40) ask, "How many bankers so much as batted an eyelid when they saw that loans destined for Mexican or Filipino state firms were actually deposited directly into the Boston and Geneva accounts of highly placed government officials?"

By the time Filipino dictator Ferdinand Marcos was toppled after twenty years in power, he had accumulated a personal fortune of some $10 billion. Post-Marcos governments and the Filipino people inherited an external debt of about $30 billion.

The Mobutu dictatorship of Zaire is another textbook case. In 1960, Mobutu earned the salary of an army corporal. Thirty years later, his personal fortune totaled some $8 billion (estimates vary, since banks from South Africa and the North have refused to reveal the extent of Mobutu's holdings). When Mobutu was toppled in May 1997, the external debts of the new Congolese government and the Congolese people totaled nearly $13 billion.

Later, we examine Argentine debt under the 1976–82 dictatorship. Clearly there was systematic complicity between the banks of the North, the IMF, US officials, and the Argentine dictatorship to steep the country in debts while enriching Argentine officials and the North's financial institutions.

Examples of such practices abound. They are part of the "system" and are now considered normal and legal. A considerable share of money loaned by the North (almost 80 percent, according to Vilas [1993] and other writers) never reached the target countries—let alone the people of these countries.

In 2002, the total amount deposited by developing countries in Northern banks came to twice the amount lent to the DC by those same banks (see chapter 9, table 9.8). Without a doubt, a significant share of this money comes from the funds loaned to developing countries and subsequently embezzled by government officials and businesspeople.[2]

One also has to take into account the loan money used for projects aimed at increasing the prestige of dictatorial and nondictatorial regimes. In the Ivory Coast, for example, Félix Houphouët-Boigny built a replica of Saint Peter's Basilica in the village where he was born. Mobutu had the Gbadolite palace built. These examples are just the tip of the iceberg.

Finally, account should be taken of the environmental and human damage caused by the building of energy megaprojects and communications infrastructure. Most of the spending on these projects went toward importing equipment from the North and paying the salaries of experts from the North. Very little money actually made it to the South. To top it off, many of these projects were never completed or operate way under capacity, since they were not drawn up in accordance with the real needs of the countries in question.

Corruption also made headway within private business, where individuals from both the North and the South filled their pockets. A revealing example is that of Elf Aquitaine in Congo-Brazzaville. Former Congolese president Pascal Lissouba opened a can of worms when he lodged a complaint against the Elf group for involvement in a coup d'état—their way of "punishing" Lissouba for considering the sale of a series of oil wells to an American oil company. Lissouba's complaint reads: "It would not be difficult to find the account-book proof of Elf's financial support to the coup d'état. This is because the preparation and execution of such a large-scale operation cost, directly or indirectly, somewhere between 100 and 200 million dollars." He denounces the financial circuits (from which he himself benefited) that went through the Paris-based FIBA bank, the Luxembourg-based SIBA, and the Belgian bank Belgolaise (*Le Monde*, November 27, 1997). This scandal ties in with the revelations concerning payoffs made by Elf into the Swiss bank accounts of some forty highly placed French officials. The list of officials includes a former minister of a right-wing government, a close associate of the right-wing former minister of the interior Charles Pasqua, and a friend of former president François Mitterrand (*Le Monde*, December 1, 1997).

In the world of corruption, it takes two to tango. Belgium (along with

Luxembourg) and France rank first and second in the list of corrupting nations compiled by Johann Lambsdorff, professor of economics at Göttingen University, for Transparency International. A whole host of laws in the North explicitly allow companies to account for commissions paid overseas and deduct them from their taxable profits (*Le Soir*, August 30–31, 1997). Furthermore, a portion of the aid "granted" by France to countries in its orbit returns directly into government coffers.

The October 1979 U-turn

The Latin American debt crisis in the 1980s was brought about by the huge increase in interest rates, a result of Federal Reserve Chairman Paul Volcker's tight money policy in the United States.

—Joseph Stiglitz, *Globalization and Its Discontents*

In the 1970s, global inflation reached levels intolerable from the standpoint of the capitalist system (Adda 2001, 99ff.; de Brunhoff 1996, 49). Real interest rates on loans, accounting for inflation, were negative, which was damaging to creditors.

A radical U-turn was made in October 1979, under the guidance of US Federal Reserve head Paul Volcker and British prime minister Margaret Thatcher. Volker and Thatcher represented, respectively, the biggest financial power and the country with the biggest international currency market. Interest rates were sharply increased. The primary objective of the "second October revolution," as some commentators called it, was to stamp out inflation in the United States. The result was an increase in interest rates on short-term loans to unprecedented levels.

This policy was promoted worldwide from 1980 onward by the Reagan administration and Thatcher government. Neoliberal policies were progressively imposed the world over, leading to a fundamental overhaul in the way national economies were financed internally and externally. This change in financial policy had a major impact on the most vulnerable countries (in the form of the Third World debt crisis), and on employment, salaries, social spending, and the public debt in the developed capitalist countries.

Financial suffocation of the Third World

Effects of the increase in interest rates

For Third World countries, this new policy meant a tripling of payments on the same levels of debt, because the interest rates they paid followed the upward march of the prime and LIBOR rates (see glossary). Loans contracted during the 1970s contained a clause whereby interest rates would be pegged to

The Inga Dam in Congo-Zaire

Long on the project books when Congo-Zaire was a Belgian colony, the Inga hydroelectric complex got under way in 1965, after General Mobutu took power, and remained under the wing of the president's office throughout. By late 1971, the project needed new financing to reach completion. The first phase of Inga cost $163.35 million, 125 percent more than initial estimates. By the end of 1980, the Inga central station was using only half its capacity; almost none of the industrial projects destined to be powered by the new complex had materialized.

Still, at that time, a group of industrialists set about building Inga II, which was intended to provide three times as much power as Inga I. Its initial estimated cost was $360 million; it ended up costing $460 million. Inga II was financed by bank and commercial loans. The bank Société Générale de Belgique provided the biggest loans—some $167 million—at interest rates between 6 percent and 8 percent. Problems with silting up significantly increased Inga II's operating costs. Furthermore, the industrial development that would have justified the second complex never came about (Galand and Lefèvre 1996, 30).

Inga did indeed generate electricity—transmitted through a network of thousands of kilometers of power lines linking up strategic industrial centers. The worst thing about this classic "white elephant" tale is that Inga was neither designed nor used to provide even a spark of electricity to power village water pumps, to light local health clinics, or to improve in any way the lot of the hundreds of thousands of people living under the web of high-voltage power lines.

A study carried out at the request of the Belgian minister for cooperation and development makes the origin of such risky ventures quite clear:

> In the context of crisis in Western countries, excess liquidity in the international monetary system—combined with the near-total absence of controls over financial markets—bankers redirected their financial surplus into the Third World. As such, they became specialists in the transformation and recycling of savings from the Third World into loans to the Third World. The resulting debt was highly concentrated in a small number of countries, and owed to a small number of largely American lender banks.
>
> Big American banks had already begun to loan to Third World countries in the late 1960s. But the flood of petrodollars onto international capital markets led to lending of epidemic proportions, with door-to-door "money salesmen" crisscrossing the Third World in the hunt for borrowers. (Simons 1981)

changes in these rates.

This evolution of interest rates can be seen clearly in table 8.1. In table 8.1 and figure 8.1, the real interest rate was calculated by subtracting the rate of US inflation from the nominal interest rate. For our purposes, the prime rate provides a good estimation of the rates practiced on international financial markets. Like the London LIBOR rate, it is used as a reference for setting the rates on loans to the Third World.

TABLE 8.1. NOMINAL INTEREST RATES,
REAL INTEREST RATES, AND INFLATION (PERCENT)

Year	Prime Rate (%) Nominal	Real	US Inflation (%)
1970	7.9	2.0	5.9
1971	5.7	1.4	4.3
1972	5.2	1.9	3.3
1973	8.0	1.8	6.2
1974	10.8	-0.2	11.0
1975	7.9	-1.3	9.2
1976	6.8	1.1	5.7
1977	6.8	0.3	6.5
1978	9.1	1.4	7.7
1979	12.7	1.4	11.3
1980	15.3	1.8	13.5
1981	18.9	8.6	10.3
1982	14.9	8.7	6.7
1983	10.8	7.6	3.2
1984	12.0	7.7	4.3
1985	9.9	6.4	3.5
1986	8.3	6.4	1.9
1987	8.2	4.5	3.7
1988	9.3	5.2	4.1
1989	10.9	6.1	4.8
1990	10.0	4.6	5.4
1991	8.5	4.3	4.2
1992	6.3	3.3	3.0
1993	6.0	3.0	3.0
1994	7.7	5.1	2.6

Source: CEPAL in Ugarteche 1997, 230.

The figures illustrate how low interest rates were in the 1970s (in both nominal and real terms). In 1974–75, real interest rates were negative. The upward trend began in 1979–80, with a rise in nominal rates. Inflation began to drop in 1981, leading to a strong surge in real interest rates that ultimately financially asphyxiated the debtor countries of the South.

Real interest rates were higher throughout the 1980s and 1990s than they were in the 1970s. This means that new loans granted in the 1980s and 1990s to finance servicing of 1970s debts usually had higher real interest rates than those of the loans they were meant to service.

Even more damning is the study made by Sebastian Edwards, World Bank economist and head of the bank's Latin American economics division until 1996. Far from contradicting the preceding estimate, it magnifies it. Edwards calculates the real interest rates used for Latin American loans by subtracting the inflation rate for Latin American exports from the nominal LIBOR rate. This is an astute calculation, since Latin America services its debts with its export earnings. Edwards writes, "[I]n the case of Latin America, the real interest rate went from an average of -3.4 percent [a negative rate favorable to

FIGURE 8.1. EVOLUTION OF PRIME RATE (NORTH AMERICAN INTEREST RATE) BETWEEN 1970 AND 1981 (PERCENT)

Source: Graph prepared by Damien Millet (data from table 8.1).

debtors] between 1970 and 1980 to +19.9 percent in 1981, +27.5 percent in 1982 and +17.4 percent in 1983" (Edwards, 1997).

Trade deficits for the countries of the South

In 1980–81, the first generalized recession since the one in 1974–75 caused export markets to contract (Mandel 1982, 214ff.). Coupled with the sharp fall in the price of raw materials from August 1982 on, this financially throttled the countries of the Third World. These countries were hit by a drop in export earnings and an increase in interest payments, which in turn created a trade deficit that had to be financed with new loans. At the same time, credit sources were drying up, as banks became aware of the risks that they had taken. The earnings of oil-producing countries plummeted; petrodollars were no longer available for recycling into loans.

The spectacular increase in the US budget deficit under Reagan was financed by masses of capital that flooded into the United States and away from Third World countries. The United States overtook Third World countries as

FIGURE 8.2. PRICES FOR SOME GROUPS OF PRODUCTS
IN 1990 DOLLARS (BASE VALUE 100 IN 1990)

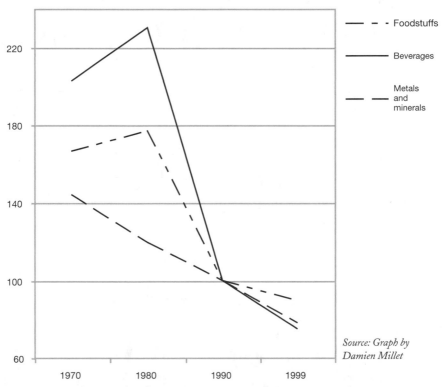

Source: Graph by Damien Millet

the main borrower on global financial markets, while West Germany and Japan overtook OPEC as the world's main moneylenders.

Not surprisingly, the decision by banks to stop abruptly all loans to Third World countries led to the suspension of debt-service payments that these banks feared. In August 1982, Mexican officials announced that they could no longer meet their international financial obligations. Other Third World governments the world over would soon follow.

The Third World debt crisis posed a serious problem to the governments of rich countries. Barely emerging from several years of crisis, they had another thorn in their sides. Banks had lent so much money to the Third World that the debt crisis threatened to plunge them into another crisis. For example, in 1982, loans to Brazil, Argentina, Venezuela, and Chile represented 141 percent of Morgan Guaranty Bank's own capital; Chase Manhattan, 154 percent; Bank of America, 158 percent; Chemical Bank, 170 percent; Citibank, 175 percent; and Manufacturers Hanover, 263 percent.

The situation was soon contained, however, when the IMF and the World Bank jointly stepped in as the main Third World debt-collection agency. Within the Paris Club, which works closely with the IMF and the World Bank, the North's creditor countries set about renegotiating their bilateral loans with debtor countries. The London Club oversaw the withdrawal of private banks from the Third World debt market and guaranteed that the interests of these banks would be fully looked after.

Almost all of the countries of the South agreed to debt-repayment plans that actually increased the amounts to be paid over the medium and long term.

---

1 The different international bodies (the World Bank, the IMF, the OECD, the UN Secretariat) regularly publish reports on debt, but their figures often differ significantly. These differences stem from (1) different methods of adding up incomplete available figures, (2) differences in the nature of debt taken into consideration, and (3) different sample countries. For example, in 1983, the OECD estimated that total Third World debt was $552 billion in 1982, while the World Bank calculated it at $596 billion. Subsequently, the OECD changed its method of calculation to include short-term debt. Consequently, its figure for 1982 jumped to $820 billion in its subsequent report. The OECD change further boosted the 1982 Third World debt figure in its 1990 report to $854 billion. For each year in the 1980s, there is a difference of at least $100 billion between IMF and OECD figures! (See Norel and Saint-Alary 1992, 19ff.)

2 Another share, undoubtedly the largest, comes directly from the exploitation of waged workers and small local producers by the local capitalist class, who then sends the money to the North for safekeeping.

9
Transfers from periphery to center, from labor to capital

n the countries of the North, the public is told that the North is trying to help the South. However, at the G7 Summit in Naples in July 1994, even former French president François Mitterrand saw fit to declare: "Despite the considerable amounts spent on bilateral and multilateral aid, the flow of capital from Africa towards the highly industrialized countries is greater than that which flows towards the developing countries." In fact, there is a massive transfer of the social surplus created by salaried workers and small producers in the South toward the ruling classes of industrialized and Third World countries.

This chapter begins with a general overview of the different forms of transfer from the South to the North. This includes transfers from salaried workers and small producers in the South toward the capitalists in the North and the South, as well as the loss of potential income in hard currency suffered by the South due to the protectionist policies of the North. Finally, the chapter will address money sent to the developing countries by migrants, and certain aspects of official development aid.

The transfer of wealth

Debt repayment

In 1980, according to the World Bank, the total external debt of the developing countries came to about $580 billion. At the end of 2002, it came to about $2.4 trillion, a fourfold increase. Table 9.1 breaks it down by region.

The proportional increase per region during this period is impressive, as shown in figure 9.1.

TABLE 9.1. EXTERNAL DEBT OF DC BY REGION (IN BILLIONS OF DOLLARS)

	1980	**2002**
Southeast Asia and the Pacific	64.6	509.5
South Asia	37.8	166.8
Middle East and North Africa	102.5	317.3
Sub-Saharan Africa	60.8	204.4
Latin America and the Caribbean	257.4	789.4
Former Soviet Bloc	56.5	396.8

Source: Calculated by Damien Millet and the author, based on World Bank 2003a.

FIGURE 9.1. FACTOR OF DEBT INCREASE BY REGION FROM 1980 TO 2002

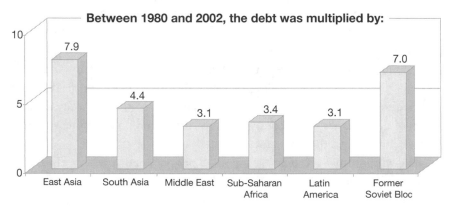

Source: Calculated by Damien Millet and the author, based on World Bank 2003a.

Between 1980 and 2002, the developing countries repaid their creditors a little more than $4.6 trillion.[1] Thus, countries in the periphery have repaid eight times the amount they owed, only to find themselves four times more indebted. The proportional increase between the debt owed in 1980 and repayments since that date is telling (see figure 9.2).

Between 1980 and 2002, the populations of periphery countries have sent the equivalent of fifty Marshall Plans to creditors in the North (with the capitalists and the governments of the periphery skimming off their commissions on the way).

How can repayments be higher than the amount due in 1980? This is the transfer mechanism set up by the bankers of the North, with the help of the Paris Club and the IMF/World Bank duo. In general, the interest rates applied to the repayment of capital borrowed by countries of the periphery are so high that the borrowers must systematically increase their indebtedness in order to meet the repayments. They contract new debts to pay off the old.

How can this situation continue without leading to refusal to pay on the part of the leaders of the South? Here, a new logic comes into play. The ruling classes of the periphery, whose interests are served by most of the governments of the South and the former Eastern Bloc, take advantage of the external indebtedness of their own countries. They export toward the banks of the center a large portion of the capital they have accumulated in the periphery through various means, including embezzlement of international loans; exploitation of salaried workers and small producers; theft of public property, as occurred on a large scale in the former Soviet Union; aid received from the governments of the periphery; oil or other revenues paid by transnational companies, which exploit the country's resources; and criminal activities (trafficking in drugs, arms, and human beings, etc.). The aim of the scheme is to place the capital somewhere safe and confer upon it, in some cases, a legal status that it did not have to begin with. This export of capital contributes to the accumulation of capital in the center of the system and strengthens it.

Subsequently, part of this exported capital is lent to the states and businesses of the periphery. The ruling classes of the developing countries are thus the creditors of part of their country's external debt. In their capacity as capitalists of the periphery, they borrow from the banks and on the money markets of the center capital that they placed there.[2]

The wheel turns. The elite classes of the periphery borrow from the center at higher interest rates than those paid by the residents of the center, but lower rates than those imposed in their own country by the central bank as a result of agreements with the IMF and the World Bank. To cap it all, they then lend the money borrowed from the center at exceedingly high interest rates to their own governments (as well as to small businesses and the middle

FIGURE 9.2. DEBT SERVICE BETWEEN 1980 AND 2002
MEANT THAT THE DEBT OF 1980 WAS REPAID SEVERAL TIMES OVER

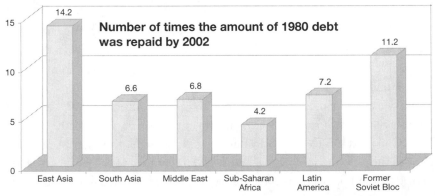

Source: Calculated by Damien Millet and the author, based on World Bank 2003b.

The Marshall Plan (1948–51)

Initially known as the European Recovery Program, the Marshall Plan, brainchild of the Democratic Truman administration, later became known by the name of then secretary of state George Marshall (formerly chief of staff, 1939–45), who was charged with its implementation. The Marshall Plan was meant to help with European reconstruction after the devastation of the Second World War. Between April 1948 and December 1951, the United States granted aid, in the form of loans and grants worth $12.5 billion, to sixteen European countries.

In 2003 dollars, the Marshall Plan would come to $90 billion. Considering the total amount of repayments made by the developing countries in 2002 alone ($343 billion), they paid their creditors in the highly industrialized countries the equivalent of nearly four Marshall Plans in a single year. In the same vein, since 1980, the peoples of the periphery have sent $4.6 trillion (more than fifty Marshall Plans) to their creditors in the center.   *Source: World Bank 2003a.*

class) in the periphery.

The capitalists of the periphery accumulate capital by exploiting the salary earners and small producers of their region, and squandering the country's natural resources. Then, they export part of this capital to the banks of the center. Then, they borrow the capital and they import it into their country and lend it to their compatriots at high rates, greatly increasing the internal debt. Furthermore, they buy external debt bonds on the New York or London money markets, where most of the debt bonds issued by entities of the periphery are traded. Thus, they make up part of the club of creditors for the public and private external debt of the periphery.

A simple example will serve to illustrate this. Capitalists of the periphery (A) deposit with (lend) B, a bank of the North, $200 million at an interest rate of 4 percent. After a year, they pocket $8 million in interest. They borrow $100 million from this same B at 9 percent interest. They pay $9 million, transferring $1 million to the profit of B. These same capitalists lend the $100 million to C (a government in the South, salary earners, small or medium-sized businesses) at 15 percent interest. When they receive $15 million at the end of the year, they use $9 million to repay B and pocket $6 million. Conclusion: B (banks/capitalists of the North) makes more profit than A (capitalists of the South) who makes more profit than C (a government in the South,

FIGURE 9.3. DIRECTION OF FINANCIAL FLOWS
INVOLVING FINANCIAL ACTORS OF NORTH AND SOUTH

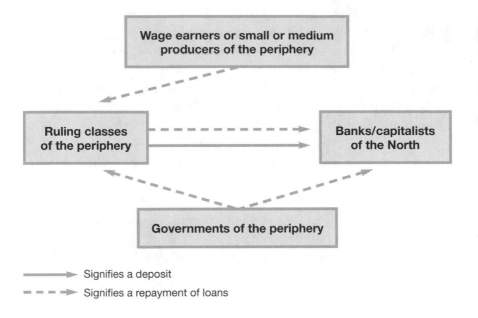

salary earners, small or medium-sized businesses). (See figure 9.3.)

That is why the ruling classes of the periphery and the governments that serve their interests do not demand the cancellation or fundamental renegotiation of the external and internal debts of their countries.

In economics classes in the so-called developing countries and in the documents of the World Bank and the IMF, they have the cheek to claim that local savings are insufficient, obliging the country to have recourse to external indebtedness to compensate for this lack. The real need is for measures to prevent capital escaping and to redistribute wealth in such a way as to enable people to build up local savings that could be used for socially just and ecologically sustainable development.

Debt servicing far outstrips net ODA

Since 1997, debt servicing (private and public) paid by the periphery (Third World and former Eastern Bloc) drains $300 billion to $400 billion, of which $200 billion to $250 billion is repayment of capital toward private banks, other institutional investors, the IMF, the World Bank, or the industrialized states. Repayments made by governments of the developing countries have oscillated between $180 billion and $200 billion a year since 1997. The total share of official development assistance (ODA; see end of chapter for a more detailed analysis) that actually reaches the developing countries is less than $40 billion. For 2002, the debt servicing paid by the developing countries came to $343 billion, whereas net ODA was approximately $37 billion. The imbalance is obvious: in 2002, the countries of the periphery repaid almost nine times what they received in ODA!

While the ODA has stagnated in absolute terms (in real terms, it has dropped sharply), debt service paid by the developing countries has increased considerably (see figure 9.4).

If the sum of the loans granted in 2002 to the countries of the periphery is subtracted from the sum of repayments they made in the same year, the result is an impressive $95 billion in favor of the lenders (World Bank 2003a). The transfer is distinctly from the periphery to the center, and not the reverse.

A key period: 1998–2002

Now let us examine the period that followed the Southeast Asian crisis. Between 1998 and 2002, the total of negative net transfers from the developing countries toward their creditors came to $560 billion.[3] In short, between 1998 and 2002, the developing countries sent the net equivalent of more than six Marshall Plans to their creditors. This is a huge net transfer of wealth that is kept systematically under wraps.

In April 2003, it seemed as though a corner of the veil might be lifted. In its 2003 *Global Development Finance* report, the World Bank declared, "[D]eveloping countries overall have become net capital *exporters* to the developed world, running a modest current-account surplus in most years since 1998" (italics in the original). In other words, the indebted countries finance their creditors. The World Bank made this admission with great discretion, for the existence of negative net transfers is in total contradiction with the objec-

Net transfers on debt

By definition, net transfers on debt are the difference for a developing country, or group of developing countries, between new loans received and the debt service paid (total repayments of capital and interest over the period concerned). When everything is taken into account concerning the debt, net transfers since 1998 for all of the developing countries taken as a whole are negative. The debt leads to a bleeding of capital out of the periphery—capital desperately needed at home for human development.

FIGURE 9.4. EVOLUTION OF DC DEBT SERVICE

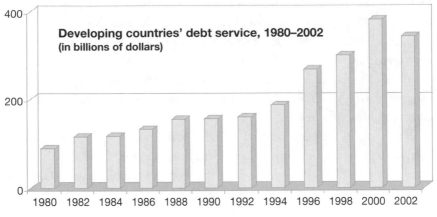

Source: *World Bank 2003b.*

tives in whose name multiple sacrifices are imposed upon the populations of developing countries.

It is nothing short of scandalous that no large daily newspaper of a lender country, and no television channel, has given the space deserved by such avowed failure. This vital information was provided only to an infinitesimally small segment of world opinion, via a few media in a few developing countries. This conspiracy of silence must be denounced. It conceals the existence of a methodical pumping of much of the wealth produced by the populations of the developing countries via instruments that should be considered authentic weapons of mass destruction.

Debt repayment sucks up part of the social surplus produced by the workers of the South (whether salary earners, small individual or family producers, or workers in the informal sector) and directs this flow of wealth toward the holders of capital in the North, with the ruling classes of the South taking their commission. Thus, the latter grow rich, while the national economies they head stagnate or regress and the populations of the South grow poorer.

So far, we have considered private and public debtors in calculating net transfers on debt. We can refine the analysis by calculating the difference between what governments have borrowed and what they have repaid. Indeed, with a view to finding a way for the cancellation of the external public debt of the developing countries, it would be worthwhile to see what governments would save by ending the repayment of the public debt. We have to account for the fact that they would likely receive no further loans. Official wisdom has it that governments of the developing countries would lose significant sources of funding if they stopped repaying the debt. What follows shows that the reverse is true:

▶ **Amount lent** to governments of developing countries by all types of lenders between 1998 and 2002: $705 billion.

▶ **Amount repaid** by governments of developing countries to all types of lenders between 1998 and 2002: $922 billion.

▶ **Difference:** $217 billion.

Governments of developing countries repaid $217 billion more than they received in the form of new loans over the same period. Imagine that instead of repaying $922 billion, they had stopped the payments in order to prioritize the satisfaction of their citizens' basic social needs. Imagine that, by way of reprisal, the creditors had turned off all of the loan taps. What would have happened? Governments of the developing countries would have saved $217 billion that they could have used to implement socially just, ecologically sustainable policies.

Let us take this argument further. If the creditors, not content with turning off the taps, had persuaded the governments of the North and the NGOs to end official development assistance, what then? Would the governments of developing countries still have come out as winners, or would they lose? Despite the cessation of ODA, they would still have been winners, as between 1998 and 2002, the "donations" part of ODA only came to $150 billion[4] (World Bank 2003a, 201). In short, $217 billion less $150 billion still leaves savings of $67 billion in favor of the governments of developing countries.

An analysis by continent is useful, as it shows how the $217 billion breaks

FIGURE 9.5. PROJECTED SAVINGS BY REGION IF DEBT REPAYMENTS HAD CEASED 1998–2002 (BILLIONS OF DOLLARS)

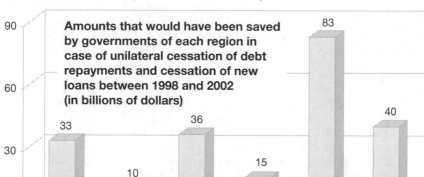

Source: Calculated by Damien Millet and the author, based on World Bank 2003a

down and clarifies what colossal sums might have been saved in the case of unilateral cessation of repayment.

Difference in interest rates between North and South

In the 1980s, the bankers of the North made the indebted countries of the South pay risk premiums. They tacked these premiums on to new loans granted to countries of the South to ensure that they paid their debt service. Moreover, loans contracted in the 1970s were at variable interest rates indexed on the fluctuations of the LIBOR (London's finance market) or the prime rate (New York's

An important comparison: Repayment of the public debt in the North

Although not the focus of this section, it seems appropriate to mention here the parallel between repayment of the Third World external public debt and repayment of the public debt in the highly industrialized countries. The latter constitutes a mechanism for pumping off part of the earnings of workers and their families to the profit of the institutional holders of public debt paper (banks, pension funds, insurance companies, mutual funds, etc.), owned and controlled by the capitalists.

This pumping works through the state's use of an increasing share of tax revenue (mainly levied on wages and salaries and by indirect taxation such as VAT and other taxes that predominantly hit low- and middle-income households) to repay the public debt. François Chesnais elaborates on the same idea:

> Part of the growth in the financial sphere is due to the following chain of events. First, the flow of wealth begins as salaries and wages, or farmers' and small-business earnings. Then it is siphoned off by the state via taxation. Finally, it is transferred to the financial sphere as repayment of the interest or the principal of the public debt. (Chesnais 1996, 15)

> Public debt bond markets set up by the main countries benefiting from financial globalization and imposed on the other countries (usually without much difficulty) are, in the words of the IMF itself, the "cornerstone" of financial globalization. Put simply, it is the most solid mechanism for transferring the wealth of certain classes and social strata in certain countries to others, a pure product of financial liberalization. Attacking the foundations of financial power means dismantling these mechanisms and, consequently, canceling the public debt, not only in the poorest countries, but also in any country where the vital social forces refuse to allow their government to continue to impose austerity budgets on citizens in the name of servicing the public debt. (Chesnais 1998)

finance market). According to the UNDP, this created major differences between rates in the North in the 1980s and those applied to loans in the South:

> During the 1980s, while interest rates were 4 percent in the highly industrialized countries, the effective interest rate paid by developing countries was 17 percent. On total debt worth more than $1 trillion, this meant a special interest premium of $120 billion annually. This merely aggravated a situation in which net transfers to pay the debt totaled $50 billion in 1989. (UNDP 1992, 74)

The 1997–98 Southeast Asian crisis sparked a sharp increase in the risk premiums the countries of the region had to pay in order to borrow the money needed to pay off short-term debt. In June 1997, Thailand was paying 7 percent to its lenders; by December 1997, it was paying 11 percent. By late 1997, Brazil and Russia, two countries at opposite ends of the planet, had to double the yield on their debt issues in order to remain attractive to foreign investors. At the high point of the crisis (August 1998), Russia had to pay a risk premium of 45 percent (UNCTAD 2000b, 46).

In 2000–01, countries such as Argentina, Brazil, Turkey, and Nigeria had to promise to pay interest ranging from 9 percentage points (Brazil in April 2001) to 21 percentage points (Nigeria in April 2001) above that paid by the highly industrialized countries for loans. In the financial section of the Spanish daily *El Mundo* (April 25, 2001), it was claimed:

> Calm has been restored to the debt market: the difference of interest between Argentine debt bonds and those of the US Treasury—which indicates the risk that investors take in this Latin-American country—has fallen to 13 percent, from the historic peak of 18 percent reached on Monday 23 April 2001.

In September 2002, in the home stretch of an electoral campaign, Brazil underwent a destabilization offensive: a massive capital exodus, an attack on the national currency. The spread, or interest rate differential, reached 24.5 percent. It was a sort of risk premium for those who do not inspire confidence in potential lenders.

Three American agencies, Moody's, Standard and Poor's, and Fitch Ratings specialize in "country risk" ratings. They have significant influence on risk premium levels. On December 22, 1997, Moody's decided to downgrade South Korea by several notches in its country risk tables. Until that date, South Korea had been given the same ranking as reliable highly industrialized countries. Overnight, it became a high-risk country on a par with the Philippines. Ever since, South Korean debt paper has had the same risk rating as junk bonds.

We are seeing a repeat of the 1982 crisis at the start of the new millennium. Third World countries must henceforth pay higher interest rates for their loans than the North pays. The phenomenon has been exacerbated by the "flight to security." Consequently, since the end of 1997, institutional investors have preferred debt issues from the most industrialized states to those from the economies of the periphery. This growing demand has sparked a generalized fall in the rates offered by the Triad (i.e., what they pay to those who lend them money). The US Federal Reserve's attempts, from the end of 2000, to relaunch the American economy by reducing its leading rates on more than ten occasions has intensified the downward tendency of interest rates in the center. The European Central Bank also reduced its leading rates in June 2003. In Japan, the central bank maintained interest rates at zero. The effect of this was a generalized fall in the interest rates paid by the states of the North for the new loans they issued.

Thus, the gap has widened still further between the interest rates paid by the periphery and those found in the center. Capital flight from the periphery to the center enabled the latter's state treasuries to make savings while the treasuries of the developing countries were forced once again to cough up more money.

Deterioration in the terms of trade

The world market is characterized by the fact that the majority of countries in the South have continued to export raw materials and low value-added manufactured goods. Conversely, these countries import high value-added industrial goods and technology. They are also net importers of farm products destined to feed the population and livestock—livestock largely exported to the North.

The "terms of exchange" of basic commodities have deteriorated over the long term. That is, the prices of products exported by the countries of the periphery have fallen compared to the prices of manufactured goods, services, and patents imported from the highly industrialized countries. According to the UN Secretariat, the ratio of prices (in terms of trade) between a basket of goods exported by the South and one it imports from the North went from an index of 100 in 1980, to 48 in 1992. Therefore, if 100 units from the South could be traded against 100 units from the North in 1980, by 1992 the same 100 units from the South could obtain only 48 units from the North. In other words, a country in the South must export twice as much to obtain in exchange the same quantity of goods from the industrialized world.

OPEC member countries have seen their terms of trade plummet even further. In 1992, the real price of crude oil was one-third of the price in 1981. In the four years from 1986 to 1989, the fall in the terms of trade meant $55.9 billion in lost earnings for sub-Saharan Africa. Ninety percent of exports from half the countries of Africa are made up of raw materials.

Fifteen countries belong to the category of severely indebted medium income country (SIMIC): Argentina, Bolivia, Brazil, Chile, Colombia, Ivory Coast, Ecuador, Mexico, Morocco, Nigeria, Peru, the Philippines, Uruguay, Venezuela and Yugoslavia. Between 1981 and 1989, the deterioration in the terms of trade cost them $247.3 billion.

Table 9.2 illustrates the decline in prices between 1980 and 2000. Alfred Maizels, a specialist on terms of trade, put these changes into perspective in the following declaration, presented at UNCTAD X in Bangkok in February 2000:

> A major change occurred, however, after 1980, when the dominant feature of the commodity markets was a drastic general fall in real commodity prices which have remained at depressed levels ever since. By the end of the 1980s, the commodity price recession was more severe, and considerably more prolonged, than that of the Great Depression of the 1930s. From 1990 to 1997, there was no significant trend, upwards or downwards, in the commodity terms of trade, but there was a further sharp deterioration during the following two years as a result of the Asian financial crisis and the consequent depreciation of the currencies of the major Asian economies.

TABLE 9.2. PRICES OF CERTAIN BASIC PRODUCTS BETWEEN, 1980–2001

Product	Unit	1980	1990	2001
Cafe (Robusta)	cents/kg	411.70	118.20	63.30
Cocoa	cents/kg	330.50	126.70	111.40
Groundnut oil	dollars/ton	1090.10	963.70	709.20
Palm oil	dollars/ton	740.90	289.90	297.80
Soya	dollars/ton	376.00	246.80	204.20
Rice (Thai)	dollars/ton	521.40	270.90	180.20
Sugar	cents/kg	80.17	27.67	19.90
Cotton	cents/kg	261.70	181.90	110.30
Copper	dollars/ton	2770.00	2661.00	1645.00
Lead	cents/kg	115.00	81.10	49.60

Source: Table by Damien Millet, based on World Bank 2002.

According to the IMF, the prices of basic products (not including oil) fell by 30 percent between 1996 and 2000 (IMF 2000b, 11). UNCTAD makes the same diagnosis (UNCTAD 2000b, 34).

In addition to this downward tendency and market sensitivity to marginal fluctuations, highly industrialized countries have aggravated the problem by manufacturing substitutes: synthetic fibers, artificial sweeteners, and so on. The most recent substitute, and not a minor one at that, would allow countries of the North to label as "chocolate" a product that has virtually no cocoa in it. The European Commission has authorized European chocolate makers to substitute fat for cocoa butter (which is produced in the South), up to 5 percent of the product's net weight. The commission realizes that this would trigger a fall in cocoa exports to the EU, leading to an inexorable fall in the price of cocoa on the world market and severe poverty for the South's cocoa farmers. However, the European lobby is very powerful. This is a clear example of EU protectionism against the South.

Even when they export manufactured goods, countries of the South generally lose out in trade with the North. Between 1980 and 1990, the price of the South's manufactured exports increased in nominal terms by 12 percent. During the same time, the price of the G7's manufactured exports rose 35 percent (UNDP 1992). In real terms, the South's manufactured exports dropped in price, while the North's rose.

The deterioration of the terms of trade is a sign of the unequal character of global trade. The most highly industrialized countries have an advantageous position in their trading relations with the South. A study of France's foreign trade, *Le Commerce extérieur de la France*, published by the French statistical institute INSEE (1997), provides confirmation of this state of affairs. France's trade with countries of the North is balanced, but it recorded a surplus in 1996—40 percent thanks to its trade with Africa; 25 percent, with the Middle East; and 15 percent, with Eastern Europe. Yet, 80 percent of France's trade is carried out with other highly industrialized countries. In other words, the remaining 20 percent of the country's foreign trade—with the Third World and Eastern Europe—generated France's trade surplus.

The policies adopted by the ruling classes of the countries of the center in the Thatcher-Reagan era of the early 1980s, the deterioration of terms of trade, the debt crisis, and the structural adjustment policies imposed by the Bretton Woods institutions are inextricably linked. In the following passage, Maizels (2000) shows how the deterioration in terms of trade, far from being a fluke of fate, is the result of a series of policies decided upon in the highly industrialized countries:

> The immediate cause of the fall in commodity prices in the early 1980s was the imposition of restrictive monetary policies in the main industrial countries in order to reduce inflationary pressures. This resulted in a marked slowdown in their economic growth rates, and in a sharp contraction of the growth in demand for raw materials. Since then, their growth rates have remained low by postwar standards, which is one reason why commodity prices have failed to show any substantial recovery.
>
> The other main reason for the failure of commodity prices to recover is that the volume of commodity exports from developing countries rose rapidly, by over 40 percent, from 1980 to 1990. With prices depressed, it would seem perverse for supply to expand at all, but a new factor came into play. A foreign exchange squeeze—largely a result of the earlier collapse in world commodity prices—together with the high interest charges on foreign debt and the virtual cessation of new commercial loans until the early 1990s, put pressure on commodity exporting countries to

expand exports. At the same time, loans from the IMF were usually accompanied by strict conditionality, including currency devaluation aimed at promoting exports.

Commodity prices in real terms have now been at historically depressed levels for two decades. One result has been that commodity-exporting countries have suffered large terms-of trade losses over this period. The rate of loss has risen sharply, from about $5 billion a year for the period 1981–1985 to almost $55 billion a year for the period 1989–1991. Total terms-of trade loss from 1980 to 1992 was about $350 billion, with a considerably greater cumulative loss since then. This terms-of-trade loss was a major factor in the rise of their foreign debt as these commodity-exporters strove to maintain a minimum of essential imports. Moreover, the burden of the commodity price recession has fallen disproportionately on sub-Saharan Africa, the poorest developing region, and the least able to make the necessary structural adjustments.

World trade controlled by the North's MNCs

The MNCs of the highly industrialized countries control global transport, trade, and the distribution of goods and services. These companies take in a large share of the earnings obtained through the sale of commodities, since Third World countries must pay astronomical amounts for the transport, insurance, packaging, and marketing of the products they export and import. The shipping companies of the highly industrialized countries belong to well-organized cartels and charge high fees for transport services. These companies control 85 percent of the world's merchant fleet. The air freight industry is even more dominated by the MNCs of the highly industrialized countries.

Several studies have shown that Third World countries receive on average only 10 percent to 15 percent of the retail sale price of their products in the North. Let us take two typical examples. In the price of a Nike sports shoe, less than 2 percent on average serves to pay the labor costs (usually in an Asian country), while 4.5 percent goes toward advertising and almost 40 percent to the retailer, usually in the North. Moreover, according to Fair Trade labeling association Max Havelaar, for a packet of 250 grams of Arabica coffee sold for between 1.8 euros and 3 euros in traditional trade circuits, the share that goes to the small producer is less than 0.15 euro, i.e., between 5 percent and 8.5 percent.

Profit repatriation by MNCs operating in Third World countries

Between 1998 and 2002, net repatriation of MNC profits totaled $334 billion (World Bank 2003a). While the net inflow of foreign direct investment (FDI) to the developing countries began to drop in 1999, the total amount of profits repatriated increased. A share of the total value that appears in the data of imperialist countries as domestically produced profit is, in fact, surplus created in the Third World.

Since MNCs do a lot of internal undercharging and overcharging, it is difficult to determine the exact value of profit repatriation. Some MNCs (those in a monopoly or oligopoly situation) handle everything from the extraction of raw materials to their sale to the manufacturing and distribution sector. For them, it does not matter if profits appear on the books of the extraction subsidiary, of the transport division, or of the refinery. However, numerous creative accounting techniques exist to shift a company's profits to one of its production and marketing locations, depending on a variety of factors. Corporate tax rates are one such factor, as is the need to repatriate profits to company headquarters in the North. The same MNC might switch from one technique to the next, at a particular time or place, depending on which one best corresponds to its interests.

One technique is for the headquarters of an MNC to sell goods and services to one of its Third World subsidiaries at prices above world market levels. Augustin Papic has calculated, for example, that pharmaceutical MNCs make internal sales to their Latin American subsidiaries at prices between 33 percent and 314 percent above world market levels. In Colombia, subsidiaries of multinational pharmaceutical companies import products from headquarters at prices 155 percent higher than usual export levels. Other examples include 40 percent price increases in the rubber industry, 26 percent in the chemicals industry, and between 258 percent and 1,100 percent in the electronics industry.

In the other direction, subsidiary exports to company headquarters are tremendously underpriced. A study revealed that 75 percent of MNC subsidiaries in Mexico, Brazil, and Argentina underpriced their exports by about 50 percent in comparison to local companies (Mandel 1975b).

Over the last twenty years, the development of industrial free-trade zones in a number of Third World countries, including China, and the former Eastern Bloc has made it much easier for MNCs to repatriate their profits.

Privatization of state-owned companies in the South

Governments of the South and the former Soviet Bloc have sold off and continue to sell off their state-owned companies, a great number of which are bought up by public or private MNCs of the Triad. In view of the underestimation of the true value of the companies privatized, this is undoubtedly another form of transfer of the wealth and strategic levers of the periphery to the center. Some public companies have been sold into foreign ownership for a song, only to be dismantled soon afterward.

The sale of the Argentine national airline company, Aerolineas Argentinas, to the Spanish company Iberia is a case in point. The infrastructure, air routes, and aircraft belonging to the Argentine company were acquired by Iberia for far less than their value. Then, Iberia took over the air routes and subcontracted the aircraft at a high price (*Financial Times*, June 13, 2001). Whereas the Argentine government had taken on the airline company's debts and sold Aerolineas unencumbered, Iberia saddled Aerolineas with the loans contracted to buy it (*Clarin*, June 21, 2000)! Finally, by 2001, Aerolineas Argentinas was on the verge of bankruptcy, with debts totaling $900 million. It owned only two of the twenty-nine aircraft it held at the time of privatization in 1990.

According to the World Bank, all of the privatization sell-offs in the periphery between 1990 and 1999 earned a little more than $315 billion for the governments in question. How much of that money went to cover the debts of the privatized companies (as in the case of Aerolineas Argentinas)? The World Bank does not say. What was the true value of the companies that passed from the public into the private domain? Exactly what portion passed into the hands of foreign firms? The World Bank is not telling. What is certain is that the MNCs of the center have progressively become the main owners of the privatized companies of the periphery. In 1999, the MNCs of the center made 76 percent of acquisitions (World Bank 2001, 189).

In numerous areas, the MNCs of the center have taken control of strategic economic sectors. In 2000, Spanish banks controlled 40 percent of the assets of the Latin American banking system, as against 10 percent in the mid-nineties (BIS 2001a, 52). Concerning privatization, between 1990 and 1999, telecommunications was the sector most affected ($76 billion), followed by the electricity production sector ($53 billion), oil and gas ($45 billion), banks ($34 billion), the iron and steel industry ($9.6 billion), mines ($9 billion), and the chemical industry ($6 billion). Latin America leads in privatization programs ($177 billion): "The region has already conceded a large part of its infrastructure and financial establishments to private sector management" (World Bank 2001, 186). It is followed by Central and Eastern Europe ($61 billion), East Asia and the Pacific ($44 billion), South Asia ($11 billion), and North and sub-Saharan Africa ($8 billion each).

The crises that hit periphery countries are opportunities for the Triad's MNCs to buy up businesses for a song. After the East Asian crisis of 1997–98, Korean companies were sold for 6 percent of their pre-crisis value. According to the French language magazine *Jeune Afrique L'intelligent* of March 9, 2003, commenting on the African Development Bank and OECD report, *Economic Perspectives in Africa*, "2,700 public companies have been sold off, and of 53 African countries, only nine have not privatized.... [However], the privatizations have only netted $8 billion to date, i.e., barely 1.5 percent of the African GDP." *Le Monde* (April 1, 2003), commenting on the same report, writes, "Employment seems to have been the greatest victim of private-sector transfers.... A World Bank study of 54 privatized companies in Benin, Burkina Faso, Ghana, Togo, and Zambia shows an average 15 percent fall in employment." Altogether since 1985, when the wave of privatizations started, several trillion dollars in assets of companies in the periphery have been transferred into the hands of Triad companies for a few hundred billion dollars. The only way for the populations of the periphery to reverse this vast pillage would be to oblige their governments to resort to expropriation without compensation. This would restore lost national treasures to their rightful owners.

Patents, royalties, and intellectual property rights

Another net transfer of resources from the South to the North stems from the payments the South must make to acquire or use technologies from the North, part of what Mandel (1978) refers to as "technological rent." MNCs benefit, thanks to the technological advantage they have acquired.

MNCs are often engaged in intense research and development and product-development battles with one another (in the computer industry, for example). While there are both winners and losers in the North, the countries of the South usually lose. They cannot hold their own against the research and development muscle of the MNCs and governments of the North (more than 95 percent of research and development is carried out in OECD countries). The latest set of GATT agreements (which laid the basis for the World Trade Organization) further worsened the situation—on the question of intellectual property rights, for example.

Intellectual property rights: The view from the South

Most Third World countries see genetic resources as part of their collective heritage. For millennia, small farmers have selected seeds to work the land in perfect harmony with their needs, while respecting nature. They have never claimed these seeds and the resulting produce as their intellectual property.

Intellectual property rights: The view from the North

Biochemical and agribusiness MNCs—Monsanto, Aventis, Novartis, and Cargill, to name the biggest ones—scour the planet to "discover" seed varieties and claim all patent rights. In this way, they stake their control over the patiently developed genetic heritage of humankind. A revealing case is that of "basmati" rice. This ancient variety of high-quality rice from North India and Pakistan has become a reference after centuries of constant labor by Indian and Pakistani peasants. Yet, in 1997, the US company Rice Tec, which belongs to the prince of Liechtenstein, patented the seed and lineage of basmati rice. After a costly legal battle engaged by India, the US Office of Patents validated the patents on three specific sorts of rice derived from traditional basmati. Thus, the Texan company has officially become the owner, in contempt of the peoples of the South whose generations of expertise produced it.

The United States and other developed capitalist countries have harnessed the Third World's biological diversity to make millions of dollars in profits, without returning a single dollar to the original "owners" of the seeds—the countries or local communities in question. For example, a variety of wild tomato was taken out of Peru in 1962. It made $8 million per year for American canning companies due to its higher concentration in soluble solids. None of the profits were shared with Peru, the origin of the genetic material.

According to Vandana Shiva (1994), between 1976 and 1980, wild varieties taken from the South brought in $340 million annually for the American agricultural sector. Since the beginning of the 1970s, agrochemical companies have taken over more than four hundred seed companies, mainly through tougher legislation in defense of intellectual property rights.

MNCs work for homogeneity and uniformity through genetic engineering, with the specific aim of dominating the markets. It is easier for a laboratory-induced variety of rice to be traded on stock markets than for the innumerable strains of rice that correspond to local conditions and tastes the world over. This is especially true when the laboratory-induced variety becomes private property, thanks to intellectual property rights. It can then be the object of a production monopoly, as can all of its subsequent generations. Indeed, a farmer who buys wheat seeds cannot use the seeds from the harvest to replant for the following season.

Furthermore, the monopoly extends to an entire range of related products. It is no coincidence, for example, that the only herbicide tolerated by the variety in question is produced by the same MNC. The thirst for captive markets is so great that sterile seeds are created in order to oblige farmers to purchase a new batch each year—since batches lose their genetic characteristics with each harvest. Thus, the circuit is complete: small farmers are no longer producers and owners, but rather buyers and consumers. They become slaves of patents and the MNCs that hold them.

Property rights are said to improve products and preserve biodiversity. In fact, biotechnologies are used to harness properties that have already been attained by nature—primarily to create uniformity through the selective breeding of high-yield varieties. Such uniformity is disastrous for crops. Plants become clones; all share the same weaknesses. In 1970–71, a rust infestation destroyed 15 percent of US corn crops, whose genetic uniformity made them vulnerable.

Similar devastation has occurred with "green revolution" varieties of rice in Asia.

High-yield varieties are also of dubious merit. International programs for eucalyptus plantations, for example, were clearly designed to back the pulp and paper industry's need for rapid growth. Eucalyptus yields almost nothing in biomass, needed to feed animal life. Furthermore, in the eyes of a forestry expert, naturally diverse tropical forests could even be described as "unproductive." Industry is not interested in diversity, it only cares about the yield in profitable natural resources.

MNC laboratories always defend technological changes in biodiversity by saying that they improve and increase economic value. The laboratory creation of seed varieties is seen as "production," in keeping with the logic of assembly-line production. The reproduction of the required raw material by nature and the Third World's farmers and forest dwellers is seen as "conservation." The only value registered is that created through work carried out in the laboratory. Centuries of innovation are totally devalued in order to grant monopolistic control over life forms solely to those using new technologies for genetic modification. Bio-uniformity (as opposed to biodiversity) is the unavoidable outcome of such an approach in a context where domination and profit hold sway.

Intellectual property rights and the TRIPS agreement

The Trade-Related Aspects of Intellectual Property Rights (TRIPS) agreement (see glossary) became effective in 1995 within the framework of the World Trade Organization (WTO). It is one of the mainstays of the Uruguay Round of negotiations, but also one of the most controversial. Drawn up by twelve US transnational companies, it was forced through by North American, Japanese, and European governments despite the opposition of the South. Its aim is to reinforce protection of patented products and techniques in order to prevent other companies in the world from copying them (mainly in the least developed countries). While reinforcing intellectual property rights, the TRIPS agreement also introduces the notion of an enforceable global norm associating intellectual property rights with trade. Thus, intellectual property rights become obligatory, but without ensuring the parallel defense of the interests and health of society, and the rights of indigenous peoples.

TRIPS mainly benefits the highly industrialized countries, with their technological advances, and so perpetuates unequal development. Payment for intellectual property rights makes the transfer of technology more expensive and leaves the developing countries further marginalized. The highly industrialized countries hold 97 percent of patents, and the MNCs hold 90 percent of all technology and invention patents. So far, nothing indicates that the system of patents has stimulated research and development activities in poor countries or has been to their advantage, or that it ever will. For example, in the pharmaceutical sector before the TRIPS agreement, countries such as China, Egypt, and India patented procedures, but not the final products. This approach encouraged local companies to work on developing generic medicines, analogous to but much cheaper than the original brands. The result is that in Pakistan, where patents exist, medicines cost up to thirteen times more than they do in India, where patents do not exist.

Now, under the TRIPS agreement, a medicine may not be produced or purchased abroad without the authorization of the patent owner (i.e., the payment of royalties), who enjoys this right for twenty years. It is true that some clauses allow for exceptions. In the case of a health emergency or unfair competition (exorbitant prices or refusal to sell on the part of the inventor), governments have the right to resort to contractual licenses or parallel imports. In practice, this right does not seem to be much used. On the other hand, the WTO has put such strong economic pressure on India that it has had to renounce price control and production of generic medicines (ATTAC 2001c).

The United States under George W. Bush is among the most savage defenders of the interests of the pharmaceutical laboratories. Yet, when the United States is the one with a health crisis, things are quite different. In October 2001, a brief outbreak of anthrax in the United States led the government to oblige the transnational company Bayer to halve the price of Cipro, the antibiotic used to treat the disease, on pain of lifting the drug's patent and authorizing generic production. The South, of course, does not have the means to impose such measures, however salutary they would be for the poorest populations. As proof of this injustice, in December 2002, the same US government blocked the modest compromise agreed to at Doha in November 2001 concerning the right to countries of the South to produce certain medicines in generic form to fight certain illnesses (particularly AIDS, tuberculosis, and malaria).

TRIPS also raises questions of compatibility with human rights legislation and environmental agreements. The Universal Declaration of Human Rights; the International Pact on Economic, Social and Cultural Rights; and the International Pact on Civil and Political Rights recognize the right to share in scientific progress. Furthermore, the Convention on Biological Diversity requires states to protect the rights of indigenous populations in the use of biological resources and systems of knowledge. It also states that the benefits of the commercial use of biological resources and the knowledge of local communities shall be shared out fairly. (UNDP 2000a, 84). Already in 1999, the Global Human Development Report recommended that the "implacable advance of intellectual property rights must therefore be called into question and stopped" and that the "principle of caution must override profit" (UNDP

1999, 73, 75). This recommendation has so far been ignored.

Applications for patents have increased considerably over the last twenty years. They mainly stem from a few highly industrialized countries that, strange to say, had vague rules on the matter when they set up their national industries. They changed their tune once they began to export technology.

As for the quest for knowledge, patents obstruct research likely to make new discoveries that would profit everyone. The "piling up" of patents chops up and fences off research areas. Ideas no longer circulate freely among different groups of researchers. On the other hand, the profit linked to the commercialization of patented products is prioritized and protected.

When new research programs are decided upon, money speaks louder than the needs of millions of people. New technology is designed for those who have the money to access it; therefore, research targets high-income markets. According to ATTAC (2001c):

> The profitability compass of finance...shows which diseases are worth treating and which, on the contrary, would be a waste of the pharmaceutical companies' time. Thus, out of the 1,223 new molecules marketed between 1975 and 1997, only 13 were specifically aimed at tropical diseases and of those, five result from veterinary research.... More worrying still, when medicines exist but only target poor countries, the profitability compass leads to stopping their manufacture. For example, for sleeping sickness, which kills 150,000 people a year, there is a drug developed in 1985 by the US firm, Merell Dow. When they bought up the firm, Marion Roussel inherited the molecule but stopped making the drug. Similarly, a drug to treat bacterial meningitis, particularly common in the South, has existed for several years. But there again, Marion Roussel decided to stop making it, as it is not profitable enough.

Environmental debt versus financial debt

Pillage of genetic material, excessive exploitation of natural resources, and colossal attacks against the environment have had disastrous effects on the countries of the periphery. To get the hard currency needed to repay debts, which the rich countries and the international financial institutions insist must be given top priority, the governments of the indebted countries have been obliged to sell off their natural resources to the highest bidder, at the same time seriously overexploiting them, with no consideration of medium- and long-term consequences.

In many cases, the centers of economic and political power in the North did not have to coerce the governments of the South, for the latter themselves organized environmentally destructive economic activities in exchange for a percentage of the revenues they generated. (The governments in power in Congo-Brazzaville, Liberia, Sierra Leone, and Angola spring to mind.) The periphery's capitalists have often taken part in the dilapidation of natural wealth and the destruction of the environment to make maximum profit. This has led to accelerated desertification. The future of large areas of primary forests is uncertain (especially in Amazonia, Central Africa, and Southeast Asia). Soil erosion destroys the livelihoods of whole populations in these heavily rural areas. Much light has been shed on the environmental ravages of oil extraction, for example, and of the mining industry (such as mercury pollution after treating gold in the mines). Worse still, certain countries of the periphery have agreed to become the dustbins for certain highly industrialized countries, allowing disposal of highly dangerous and polluting industrial waste on their land, often without the slightest precaution.

The capitalist system and its corollary, the debt, have led the periphery countries into an impasse, threatening the ecological balance of the world itself. In such conditions, it is legitimate to introduce the notion of environmental debt, owed by the governments of the highly industrialized countries, transnational firms, governments of the periphery, and local capitalists to the populations of the periphery. Indeed, this environmental debt is real, since such environmental degradation thrusts the people of the periphery each day deeper into hardship.

Capital transfer from the periphery to the center

The IMF estimated that, in 1988 alone, in the thirteen most heavily indebted countries, capital flight represented about $180 billion. Later, in the 1990s, complete liberalization of capital movement resulted in a huge displacement of capital from the periphery toward the highly industrialized countries. The World Bank, in its 2001 *Global Development Finance*, observes, "Although the rise in capital inflows to developing countries in the first half of the 1990s received most of the attention, *capital outflows also increased*. And at least a part of the decade's increase in capital inflows may reflect transactions tied to capital outflows, perhaps to avoid taxes" [emphasis added].

Rubens Ricupero, secretary-general of UNCTAD, in the Overview to UNCTAD's 1998 *Trade and Development Report*, made a clearer observation:

> Opening up the capital account is not likely to bring back flight capital, which on some estimates accounts for 70 percent of non-land private wealth in [sub-Saharan Africa]. Much of the flight capital appears to have originated from the illicit diversion of public funds rather than to have been constituted by business incomes seeking economic stability or high yields abroad.

In a remarkable study entitled "Is Africa a Net Creditor?" James K. Boyce and Léonce Ndikumana draw the conclusion that between 1970 and 1996, the equivalent of $285 billion was placed abroad by the ruling elite of Africa. The authors deduce that once the external debt of the twenty-five countries of the study (representing 92 percent of the sub-Saharan population, 91 percent of the debt, and 93 percent of GDP—not including South Africa) was subtracted, the countries concerned were creditors of the rest of the world for a sum of about $106 billion. They reckon that in 1996, the capital placed abroad by the capitalists of Nigeria represented four times the country's external debt. In the case of Rwanda, in 1996, capital placed abroad represented triple the total external debt. For the Democratic Republic of the Congo and Sierra Leone, capital placed abroad represented twice the country's external debt. For Angola, Cameroon, Ivory Coast, and Zambia, it was a little less than double. The two authors, as well as several others, note a marked correlation between international loans and capital flight. They cite the work of N. Hermes and R. Lensink, who studied capital flight for six African countries from 1976–89 and claim that for every dollar borrowed by the governments (or with their backing), 75 cents to 90 cents was reexported through capital flight. Other authors make similar observations for Latin America, Asia, and the former Soviet Bloc.

In 2000 alone, fresh deposits by capitalists of the periphery in banks of the center came to $145 billion (BIS 2001a, 125). Holders of capital in the South have shifted a large part of their assets onto the North's financial markets, into numbered bank accounts in offshore locations, and into real estate in the North. If the external debt stock owed by developing countries to banks of the center is compared to the assets that rich citizens of those countries hold in the same banks, the result gives a completely different picture than that commonly imagined.

Figure 9.6 gives a clear indication of the colossal size of the assets that the rich of the developing countries hold in the countries of the Triad. The figure for deposits by residents of the developing countries in banks of the Triad comes from quarterly statistics of the Bank for International Settlements. These deposits are classed as debts of the same banks owed to the developing countries.

The amounts shown in figure 9.6 only concern cash deposits, which are in fact only a part of total assets. The money deposited comes partly from the normal business activities of companies of the developing countries (mainly trade) and is partly money embezzled by the corrupt elite. Even assuming that only 25 percent of the deposited money is illicitly or criminally obtained, acquired at the expense of poor citizens and the nation as a whole, that amounts to $350 billion, which, if returned to its rightful owners, could finance human development in the developing countries.

To make it more difficult to accumulate ill-gotten gains, democracy and citizens' control of public spending are required, with a complete arsenal of legal and judicial measures (including lifting bankers' secrecy and establishing a wealth register) and capital movement controls. Public trustees should be re-

FIGURE 9.6. DC DEPOSITS IN—AND DEBTS TO—BANKS IN RICH COUNTRIES

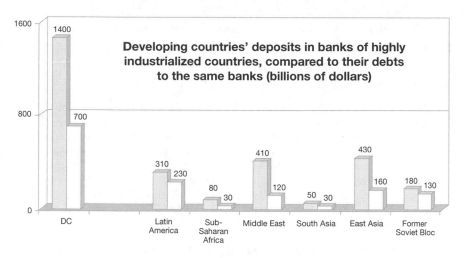

Source: Calculated by Damien Millet and the author, based on BIS 2003.

quired to produce an annual statement of their wealth. The decision to borrow should be subjected to parliamentary debate. An independent organization should conduct a yearly audit on the state of the debt. Creditors should answer the following questions: Who contracted the loans? What were the terms of the contract? Who received the borrowed money? How? Into which account? Who, in the indebted country, holds money in deposit in the creditor banks?

From the late 1990s to the early 2000s, some positive initiatives of this kind have been taken as a result of international campaigns and the tenacity and courage of certain magistrates. More than $600 million placed in Swiss banks by Ferdinand Marcos (Philippine dictator from 1972–86) was frozen (only a fraction of the Marcos hoard), then returned to the Philippine authorities (*Financial Times*, July 16, 2003).[5] Other, if smaller, amounts have also been returned by Swiss banks to countries of the periphery. For example, in 2002, $67 million stolen by Peru's former president Alberto Fujimori and his soul mate Vladimiro Montesinos, head of the secret services, were returned to Peru.

Other big files under "negotiation" include money in Switzerland, Great Britain, Luxembourg, and Liechtenstein of the late General Sani Abacha, dictator of Nigeria from 1993 to 1998. More than $4 billion are at stake. A look at the case illustrates the extent to which the big international banks and the legal and political authorities of the North have connived to deny the people of Nigeria their due.

A *Financial Times* survey carried out in 2000 revealed that at least fifteen banks based in London were giving full cooperation at the time to Abacha's circle in laundering the money he had embezzled (*Financial Times*, September 29, 2002). *Le Monde* claimed in its account of a report by the Financial Services Authority (FSA), an official British body that monitors the banking sector, that two major French banks, BNP-Paribas and the Crédit Agricole Indosuez, actively collaborated with the dictator Abacha. According to *Le Monde* (October 6, 2001):

> Between February 1997 and January 1998, $36 million are believed to have transited through the former Paribas bank in ten payments made into a Swiss account. Apparently these were bribes paid to the former leader's circle by French businessmen of the BTP group (a construction and public works firm). The former Banque nationale de Paris is also believed to have transferred $7 million from London to the Geneva account of a phony import-export company set up by the dignitaries of the military regime. Lastly, the Crédit Agricole Indosuez is thought to have served as the go-between in the payment of $92 million linked to falsified Nigerian debt paper.

According to the *Financial Times*, the FSA's confidential report accused twenty-three London banks of helping Abacha during his dictatorship to stash away $1.3 billion in stolen funds. In Switzerland, in October 1999, at the demand of the new Nigerian government, the attorney general of Geneva blocked 130 bank accounts, containing $645 million, related to the circle of the late dictator. In September 2000, the Swiss public bank–monitoring commission censured fourteen banks, including Credit Suisse, for their past dealings with Abacha. In 2001, the British banking authorities finally ordered the sequestration of Abacha's accounts in nineteen London-based banks (including Barclays Bank, Citibank, Deutsche Bank, and Merrill Lynch). Too late— only $30 million remained in these accounts. The case of the funds embezzled by Abacha is far from settled.

The examples mentioned above show that it is possible to fight for the recovery of ill-gotten gains. However, without active parliamentary and citizens' control of such procedures, there can be no guarantee that the returned money will be used directly to the advantage of the populations who need it.

The "brain drain" from South to North

Although the North has gradually closed its borders to the South's citizens, some countries in the North—especially the United States—have made exceptions to allow for a brain drain from the South (and East). Recipients of publicly funded training and professional experiences in their home countries, citizens from the periphery are welcomed in the North. In some cases, the number of people involved is staggering. In 1987 alone, Sudan, for example, lost 17 percent of its doctors and dentists, 20 percent of its university teaching staff, 30 percent of its engineers, and 45 percent of its land surveyors to the

North (UNDP 1992). A large number of scientists from the former Eastern Bloc have gone to the United States since the beginning of the 1990s.

In 2000–01, the transfer of qualified staff from countries of the periphery to the countries of the center increased. Computer analysts, on the one hand, and medical staff (doctors, nurses, etc.) on the other, are especially sought after. Moreover, a study cited by the World Bank in its 2003 *Global Development Finance* report estimates that more than a third of people with higher education diplomas in Africa, Central America, and the Caribbean have emigrated to the United States or other OECD countries.

Losses sustained by the South due to protectionism

Protectionism in the North against products from the South

The capitalist governments of the North impose restrictions on the flow of goods through tariff (duty) and nontariff (quotas and regulations on standards and quality) barriers. According to UNCTAD, this represents an annual loss of several hundred billion dollars (UNCTAD 1999; Horman 2001, 27; UNDP 2000a, 51). The average rate of effective protection of the markets of the highly industrialized countries, according to a study by UNCTAD, is twice as high regarding developing countries as it is for other industrialized countries.

As for farm products, the European Union (through the Common Agricultural Policy), the United States, and Japan subsidize agricultural production, making farm-product imports from the South less attractive. The EU and United States have become net exporters of farm products to the rest of the world. Their subsidies (more than $360 billion in 2002) to the agricultural sector (largely to agribusiness) make their products more affordable in the South's markets than some locally produced items (Kroll 2001, 10).

The solution is not to open all borders and lower customs tariffs. The suggestions put forward by the international movement Via Campesina (1998; see also Berthelot 2000, 2001; Bové and Dufour 2000; and Via Campesina 2002) should inspire alternative proposals to the free-trade creed of the WTO and the highly industrialized countries (see chapter 18).

Limits on the right of the South's citizens to look for work in the North

We have already seen how the governments of the North skim off the cream of the "brains" from the South and the East. At the same time, they strictly limit the right of people from the South to sell their labor in the North. The 1992 edition of the UNDP's *Global Human Development Report* clearly challenges restrictions on the freedom of movement of people from the

South to the North put in place by the governments of the industrialized capitalist countries.

One of the major sources of lost revenue for the Third World is restriction of the labor force. According to a conservative estimate from the UNDP, the cumulative loss of hard-currency remittances for countries of the South, due to the suspension of legal immigration in the 1980s, is in the range of $250 billion (UNDP 1992).

Showing equal caution, the UNDP 1992 report calls for the abrogation of restrictive measures taken by governments of the North to limit the free movement of people from the South to the North. Were these measures lifted, the UNDP estimates that every year, two percent of the Third World workforce would decide to emigrate. If these workers earned the minimum wage, in line with the poverty threshold in industrialized countries (about $5,000 per year), their annual income would total some $220 billion. They would send between $40 billion and $50 billion to their countries of origin; the UNDP calculates that after five years, such remittances could total at least $200 billion per year (UNDP 1992, 63–64). If this recommendation by the UNDP had been implemented from 1992, the extra funds sent would have represented more than $2 trillion for the period 1992–2002. The UNDP rightly points out that the effects of these losses are cumulative, given that the cost of opportunities denied in the present increases with time.

Stagnating ODA versus the amount sent home by migrants

In 2002, despite the draconian obstacles to people's freedom of movement and settlement, migrants sent $80 billion to their home countries in the periphery, while net official development assistance to these countries was $36.7 billion.[6] Even considering total ODA, which came to $57 billion in 2002 according to the OECD Development Assistance Committee, it remains clear that migrants were more generous than the governments of the highly industrialized countries. The total amount sent to the developing countries by migrants is so great that it has given rise to numerous studies in recent years and attracted the attention of private bankers, governments, and institutions such as the World Bank. Profit beckons yet again, as we are about to see.

The worsening of the international economic situation and the deterioration of living conditions in the developing countries have prompted increased solidarity on behalf of the migrants established in the "rich" countries. Though their own situation has suffered as a result of the economic depression affecting the Triad countries, migrants have increased the amounts they send to their families. Whereas, the total amount sent remained fairly stable from

1997–2000, there was a marked increase of 20 percent over the two-year period 2001–02 (see figure 9.7). Over the same period, ODA did not increase,
investment flows dried up, and bank and public bilateral flows became negative from the end of the 1990s. Over a longer period, from 1990–2002, ODA
actually *stagnated* (in fact, in real terms, it fell more than 30 percent), while migrants' remittances increased by 160 percent.

Entire regions of developing countries receive more through donations on
the part of migrants living in rich countries than they do through bilateral
ODA donations. World Bank and IMF data show that, in 2002, South Asia
received four times more from migrants than through bilateral ODA (see figure 9.8). That ratio is four times more for North Africa and the Middle East,
five for East Asia and the Pacific, and eight for Latin America and the
Caribbean (World Bank 2003a, 201–06).[7]

Another calculation that illustrates the harsh truth is a comparison of the
declared budget cost of the donation part of ODA to the real cost. In 2002,
the treasuries of the Triad states received twice as much money in the form of
repayment as they paid out in the form of loans. In 2002, they lent $18.8 bil-
lion to the developing countries, while the latter repaid $36.9 billion on previ-
ous loans. Therefore, the treasuries of the Triad states made a surplus of $18.1
billion. The same year, the same treasuries paid out $32.9 billion in the form
of donations to the developing countries.[8] They were thus able to finance
more than half their donations using the above-mentioned surplus, making
the net cost of the donation part of ODA $14.8 billion.[9]

Migrants' remittances are a source of juicy profits for banks. It is estimated
that in order to send $72 billion to the developing countries in 2001, migrants

FIGURE 9.7. AMOUNTS SENT HOME BY MIGRANTS

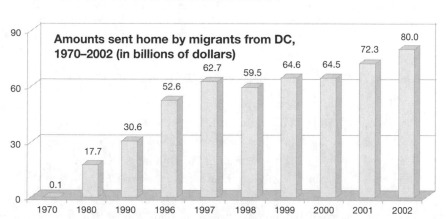

Source: World Bank 2003a.

FIGURE 9.8. AMOUNTS SENT BY MIGRANTS COMPARED TO BILATERAL ODA

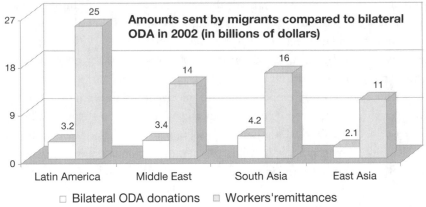

Source: World Bank, GDF 2003a

had to pay the banks the heavy tribute of $12 billion. Banks keep between 7 percent and 18 percent of the amount sent by migrants—and these are the same banks who scream bloody murder at the proposal of a Tobin-style tax of 0.1 percent on foreign currency transactions.

US banks make huge profits on *remesas*, the remittances sent home by Latin American immigrants. In 2001, $28.4 billion were sent to the developing countries from the United States. Nearly a third of this went to Mexico, procuring about $1.5 billion for US banks. The authors of the 2003 *Global Development Finance* report observe a cause and effect relationship between Citigroup, the biggest bank in the United States (and the world), taking over the Mexican bank Banamex in 2001, and the size of the profits made on Mexican immigrants' remittances.

> The large and fast-growing business opportunities associated with workers' remittances have attracted at least two major FDI deals in Mexico recently. Valued at

Migrants send more money than governments

The United States devoted $11.4 billion to ODA (concessional loans plus donations), whereas the migrants living there sent $28.4 billion to the developing countries. Every year, Belgium and Switzerland each give a little under $1 billion in ODA, including $0.9 billion each in 2001. In the same year, the migrants living on their territory sent $16.2 billion to the developing countries ($8.1 billion from Belgium and the same amount from Switzerland)—nine times more (World Bank 2003a, 160, 199).

$12.5 billion, the Citigroup-Banamex deal in 2001 is the single biggest investment south of the border for any US company.... In December 2002, Bank of America paid Santander $1.6 billion for part of Serfin. (World Bank 2003a, 161)

Hard currency coming into the developing countries from migrants' remittances serves as a basis for other deals. In August 2001, the Bank of Brazil issued a loan of $300 million based on the future remittances of Brazilian migrants living in Japan. Bolstered by the certainty of receiving a specified sum from migrants, the developing countries have regularly issued international loans in the form of bonds. Suhas Ketkar and Dilip Ratha (2001), World Bank specialists in securitization, claim that this is the case not only for Brazil, mentioned above, but also for El Salvador, Mexico, Panama, and Turkey. They encourage other developing countries to follow suit, reckoning that it is the only way for some sub-Saharan and South Asian countries to get access to the finance markets.

Hard currency inflow from migrants has reached such proportions that the World Bank is proposing that its consultants be brought in to better manage the flow. Watch your wallets!

Another important consideration is that the migrants' remittances procure the governments of the developing countries large amounts of tax. Since the families receiving the migrants' money mainly spend it on consumer goods, it also contributes to increasing tax revenue. One study concluded that, in Mexico, the equivalent of 15 percent of migrants' remittances finds its way into the state coffers in the form of value added tax (VAT).

Comparing the behavior of migrant workers to that of the capitalists of the periphery, one can only conclude that while the former send considerable amounts back to their country of origin by way of solidarity, the latter are busy doing everything in their power to send their accumulated capital the other way.

The real beneficiaries of ODA

The share of ODA that remains in developing countries is very small. Almost all the money provided quickly returns to rich countries in exchange for products purchased from them.

—*Robert McNamara, president of the World Bank, September 30, 1968*

Official development assistance is made up of the grants and soft loans (at favorable rates) provided by the public bodies of the OECD grouped together within the Development Assistance Committee (DAC). It is sufficient that a loan be made at below-market rates for it to be seen as assistance, even if every cent is paid back by the borrower country.

The DAC designates the countries to receive assistance; not all developing

countries are included. DAC members have now created a second list of beneficiaries, including most of Central and Eastern Europe; countries such as Israel; colonies such as New Caledonia, French Polynesia, the Dutch Antilles,
and the Virgin Islands (GB). They receive what is known as official aid
(OA).[10] This aid is made conditional upon the reduction of the public deficit,
privatization, environmental good conduct, policies aimed at the poorest sectors of the population, and democratization, among other things. All such
conditions are laid down by the main governments of the North, and the
World Bank and IMF. Recent additions to the rhetoric are the notions of
good governance and the fight against poverty.

The member states of the DAC provide this aid entirely through two
channels. The first is directly administered by the states in the DAC and
counts as their bilateral aid. The second is managed by the multilateral institutions. Bilateral aid represents about two-thirds of ODA, and multilateral aid
the rest. As far as multilateral aid is concerned, the international financial institutions (the World Bank, the IMF, and regional development banks) take
the biggest share (about 45 percent), followed by the European Development
Fund (about 30 percent) and the various specialist institutions of the UN,
which represent only about 25 percent.

A small portion of bilateral aid is allocated to NGOs of the DAC member
states, which are responsible for getting it to the developing countries. According to the World Bank, the donations that the NGOs make to the populations of ODA beneficiary countries totaled a little more than $7 billion in
2001 (part of this amount comes from member states of the DAC via the public subsidies that the NGOs receive; the rest is collected directly by NGOs
from the public and/or private foundations).

ODA dropped by more than 30 percent in real terms between 1992 and
2000, even though the heads of state of the North who were present at the
1992 Rio Summit promised to increase annual ODA by $125 billion, tripling
its volume.

By our calculations, ODA provided by industrialized countries and multilateral institutions to the developing countries as a whole came to $36.7 billion
in 2002. This amount is much smaller than the total of migrants' remittances
(see figure 9.9). Moreover, only when we put on the other side of the scales
capital outflow due to net transfers on debt ($95 billion in 2002), repatriation
of profits by multinationals ($66 billion in 2002), and *capital flight* (about $150
billion in 2002) can we begin to weigh the net transfer of capital from the developing countries to the center. The net contribution of ODA represents
about a tenth of capital outflow for that year. That does not include the

straightforward pillage of certain natural resources, the effects of the brain drain, losses due to unfair trading, etc.

ODA equals "tied aid"

ODA is usually "tied aid," which means that funds given or loaned will be used to buy products or services from the donor country. Multilateral ODA is not exempt from the same criticism, as the most influential countries in the international financial institutions systematically seek to promote export firms based in their own countries. In a press release dated April 13, 2000, Larry Summers, then US secretary of state, revealed that US firms in 1998 had received orders worth $4.8 billion within the framework of loans and investments made by the World Bank and the IMF. On the other side of the Atlantic, a report read at the French National Assembly, December 13, 2000, by the World Bank and the IMF included the following passage:

> Global results in terms of return rates or market shares profiting French firms are good, but conceal significant geographical and sectorial disparities.... France is affected by specific factors reflecting the commercial presence of French firms: a high concentration in Africa which contributes largely to global results (45 percent of Bank payments to Africa go to French companies).

ODA thus appears as aid from the industrialized countries to their export firms.

Bilateral ODA can also be used to compensate exporters from the "donor" country. To promote exports from their country's firms, the governments of the North have set up export credit agencies (public or private, but acting on behalf of the state) that guarantee payment to the exporters from the center in case of default on the part of the importers of the periphery.[11] A considerable part of the developing countries' external debt consists of debts covered by ex-

FIGURE 9.9. FINANCIAL TRANSFERS BETWEEN NORTH AND SOUTH

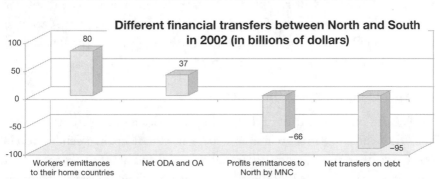

Source: Graph drawn by Damien Millet and the author, based on the World Bank 2003a.

FIGURE 9.10. NET TRANSFERS ON BILATERAL ODA/OA, 1996–2002

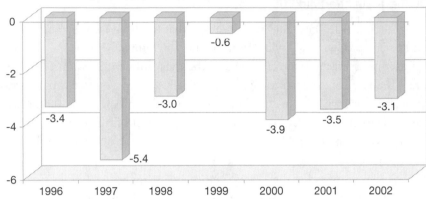

Net transfers on bilateral ODA/OA
(–22.9 billion dollars between 1996 and 2002)

Source: Graph by Damien Millet and the author, based on World Bank 2003a.

port credit agencies. According to the Export Credit Agencies (ECA) Watch campaign, in 1998, the outstanding debt guaranteed by export credit agencies represented 24 percent of the developing countries' long-term debt and 56 percent of credit held by official bodies (states, multilateral agencies, etc.), i.e., about $460 billion.[12]

Governments of DAC member countries regularly make use of overseas development money by transferring it to export credit agencies that compensate export firms. They justify this transfer on the pretext that it reduces the external debt for certain countries. They charge the cost of transferring monies from one account to another within the same country of the center to ODA. In fact, it is a transfer from a public fund (the state budget in this case) to a private account (the export company) via an export credit agency. This type of operation is used in debt-reduction initiatives. The Belgian government, for example, registers the cost of compensating the Belgian export guarantee agency as an ODA expense, and then the agency compensates the Belgian exporters who have not been paid by indebted countries.

ODA as a source of indebtedness

The external public debt of developing countries resulting from multilateral ODA came to $144.4 billion in 2002. The external public debt of developing countries resulting directly from bilateral ODA and OA (concessional loans) then came to $243.7 billion. A crucial fact is that every year between 1996 and 2002, the developing countries repaid more as bilateral ODA/OA loans than they received from DAC member countries! The World Bank's 2003 *Global Development Finance* report gives a total negative net transfer of $22.9 billion in seven years (see figure 9.10).[13] This figure lifts the veil hiding one of the facets of aid: via ODA/OA loans, the donor countries make money on the backs of the countries they are supposed to be helping.

ODA hides behind humanitarian rhetoric

Since the early 1970s, member countries of the OECD and the DAC pledged 0.7 percent of their GDP to ODA. To inflate their statistics, the governments of the North count everything they can as ODA: technical aid, debt reduction (see above), the cost of student grants allocated to residents of developing countries who come to study in the center, the maintenance costs of political asylum seekers. Some governments, such as the that of the United States, even add the cost of the so-called war on terror (combating international terrorism). This includes, for example, the expenses incurred by reinforcing the security of their staff in Pakistan after September 11, 2001. Several governments include (or propose to in the future) the cost of their participation in peacekeeping operations. By doing this, they count the military spending involved in sending troops as ODA! On paper, this looks like a reduction in military spending in favor of an increase in the overseas development budget. (This was clearly the intention of the Spanish government under José María Aznar.) In 2002, the Aznar government also proposed to include in ODA the losses in tax revenue incurred by the possibility for donors, individual or institutional, to deduct the donations they make to NGOs from their taxable income.

More than thirty years after the pledge was made, it is far from fulfilled (see figure 9.11). To try to deal with this evident failure, the UN organized an In-

FIGURE 9.11. ODA FOR SOME DAC COUNTRIES IN 2002

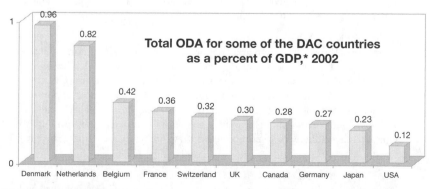

Total ODA for some of the DAC countries
as a percent of GDP,* 2002

	0.96	0.82	0.42	0.36	0.32	0.30	0.28	0.27	0.23	0.12
	Denmark	Netherlands	Belgium	France	Switzerland	UK	Canada	Germany	Japan	USA

*ODA for total DAC in 2002
was 0.23 percent of GDP.

Source: World Bank, Global Development Finance 2003

ternational Conference on Financing for Development in Monterrey, Mexico, in March 2002, where ODA was much discussed. The conference concluded that "a significant increase in ODA is needed," but the idea of doubling ODA (to about $100 billion), which was proposed by the UN secretary-general and the World Bank, was not retained. Yet, it must be doubled, if only to fulfill the modest Millennium Development Goals (one of which is to halve the percentage of people living in extreme poverty by 2015). The United States categorically refused any commitment even to reach the existing target of 0.7 percent of GDP. Instead, it chose to put the emphasis on private investments, which everyone knows are avid for profit and deaf to social needs. In short, the Monterrey Consensus, which emerged from this gathering, does nothing to question the sinister Washington Consensus of the 1980s and 1990s.

ODA in line with the major political strategies of the center

In his book *Give and take: What's the matter with foreign aid?*, David Sogge (2002, 41–42) provides an outline of the different motives behind the provision of ODA by governments of the center. This is how he lays them out:

STRATEGIC SOCIO-POLITICAL MOTIVES
Short term: Abroad, to reward and keep a client "on side" politically during negotiations, wars or other crises; to defuse public protest and insurrection; to provide a base for intelligence-gathering; to influence decision-making in international fora. [Author's note: See how the United States and others "buy" votes to support their policies at the UN Security Council, WTO, etc.] At home, to reward or retain loyalty of ethnic/political constituencies, to be seen to be "doing something" during a crisis.
Longer-term: Abroad, to gain regular access to and loyalty of leadership at the receiving end; to win or deepen acceptance of a doctrine or model of development; to reinforce a country's place in a larger economic, political and military system; to stabilize economic or demographic trends in a country or region in order to stem unwanted effects such as terrorism and migration; in international institutions, to set and steer economic and political agendas. At home, to consolidate political support of voter and contributor constituencies, particularly the private sector, but also those with ethnic ties to aid recipients.

MERCANTILE MOTIVES
Short-term: Abroad, to seize market opportunities. At home, to promote interests of a sector of business and related employment; to improve the lender/donor's balance of payments; to assure the solvency of creditor banks, public or private.
Longer-term: Abroad, to win, expand, protect trade and investment opportunities, including strategic access to raw materials and cheap labor; to shape and stabilize North-South economic roles and hierarchies; in international institutions, to win and stabilize adherence to economic rules. At home, to consolidate and protect economic sectors.

HUMANITARIAN AND ETHICAL MOTIVES
Short-term: To show concern and compassion for victims of war, upheaval and natural catastrophes.

Longer-term: Abroad, to demonstrate concern about poverty, human rights abuse including the human rights of women; to compensate for damages. At home, to show solidarity with a particular country or group, to claim the moral high ground.

The more a country in the South spends on arms, the more ODA it receives

One of the most striking examples of "tied" bilateral aid is that of the arms trade. The more arms a Third World country buys, the more aid it receives from industrialized countries. Industrialized countries have an iron grip on most of the global arms trade. The United States dominated the market with 50 percent of arms exports in the period 1995–99, distantly followed by the Russian Federation, with 13 percent; France, 10 percent; and Great Britain, 6.5 percent (Serfati 2001, 165). These economic giants all have public-sector companies or MNCs in the arms trade constantly on the lookout to conquer new markets. While companies in other sectors are being privatized one after the other, the arms industry is quite happy to remain under state control. Private arms manufacturers also derive tremendous advantages from the military and economic power of their respective states, which help them to find customers for their killing machines.

US weapons manufacturers are highly concentrated. Seven rule the market: Lockheed Martin, Boeing, Raytheon, General Dynamics, Northrop Grumman, TRW, and United Technologies. Lockheed Martin, world leader in arms production, enjoyed $855 million of public aid from the US government to absorb Martin Marietta, another North American arms manufacturer. (That is almost equivalent to the entire debt of Chad, a country with seven million inhabitants.)

Claude Serfati (2001, 165) writes the following:

It has to be said that ties between leaders of industrial groups and US political decision makers are all the closer since the former generously finance the latter.

During the 1996 presidential campaign, records were broken, with $13.9 million donated by arms manufacturing groups, $9.1 million to the Republicans and $4.8 million to the Democrats.

Serfati (2001, 84) also notes that "today the top five groups get 40 percent of the $60 billion in annual orders from the Defense Department and about a third of the $38 billion set aside for military research and development."

Developing countries account for about 15 percent of global arms purchases. While in no way justifying such spending, this figure is important to keep in mind, given the share of the world's population (85 percent) that lives in developing countries. Contrary to what many in the North often hear and think, Third World countries are not the world's main spenders on arms. In

2001, military spending in the United States (with less than 5 percent of the world's population) accounted for 36 percent of global military spending. The G7 countries accounted for 63 percent; the Russian Federation and China, 3 percent each (Serfati 2001, 86; *Upstream Journal* May/June 2001, 9; for the years 1985 and 1996, see Achcar 1999, 18–20). It is significant that "countries that devote major spending to the military (more than four percent of GNP) receive about twice as much ODA per capita as those whose arms spending is less (between two and four percent of GNP)" (UNDP 1992, 46).

In its 1994 *Global Human Development* report, the UNDP returns to this subject:

> Assistance more frequently goes to strategic allies than to poor countries.... Until 1986, donor countries provided on average five times more in bilateral aid to countries with high arms spending than to those whose arms spending was low.
>
> In 1992, [high arms spenders] were still receiving two-and-a-half times more aid per capita than [low arms spenders].

Israel, for example, an American strategic ally in the Middle East, receives $176.00 in US aid for each poor person, while Bangladesh only receives $1.70.

The authors of the 1994 UNDP report draw attention to the double standards of the industrialized countries' governments:

> Some donors argue that discrimination against countries with high military spending would violate their national sovereignty. This is a surprising argument given that donors are not so reluctant to violate national sovereignty in a large number of other government policy fields.

Examples given include demands made on aid recipients to eliminate food subsidies, to devalue their currencies, or to privatize state-owned companies. The report continues:

> This contrast was particularly in evidence during the period of structural adjustment in the 1980s. Many donors watched in silence as dramatic cuts were made in social spending, while military spending continued to climb. In sub-Saharan Africa, military spending went from 0.7 percent to 3.0 percent of GNP between 1960 and 1990. Thus, some developing countries preferred to balance their budgets by compromising human lives rather than by reducing their military spending.

In the early 2000s, governments of the North and their arms industries made the countries of the periphery increase their arms orders. At the same time, arms spending in the highly industrialized countries, after a fall between 1986 and 1997,[14] began to climb again significantly. In the United States, the Clinton administration started the upward trend sharply. His successor, Bush Junior, intensified the increase, particularly by investing in antimissile defense (National Missile Defense [NMD] and Theater Missile Defense [TMD]), a central instrument of North American military strategy.

In 2003, the US defense budget alone represented about twice the amount of the entire external debt of sub-Saharan Africa (which came to about $205 billion in 2002, for a population of more than 600 million). The arms manufacturers of the North press their governments to win new contracts in the East. According to Serfati (2001, 130):

A fine mixture of military and industrial interests is revealed by the fact that the US Committee to Expand NATO is presided by none other than the vice president of Lockheed Martin (which received $18.5 billion worth of orders from the Pentagon in 1999). Now one of the conditions placed on NATO admission for those countries is that they increase their military spending in order to modernize equipment, leftover from the time of the Warsaw Pact and considered obsolete, and especially to make them compatible with NATO armaments. In other words, that they acquire US equipment.

Serfati mentions that Poland, the Czech Republic, and Hungary bought a hundred F-16 aircraft (produced by Lockheed Martin).

The American offensive has become virulent: the Pentagon has bought up Mig-29 and Sukhoi 27, 30, and 37 craft from the former so-called socialist camp and replaced them with US weaponry. The US military-industrial complex is launching a new generation of weapons, they are therefore trying to clear out the arms stocks of the preceding generation (F-16s, for example). Countries will be getting arms that, from a technological point of view, will be obsolete within a few years, though they will have hardly begun to pay for them. Also, the new generation of arms will give the United States a strategic advantage in case of conflict, as it will completely dominate the arms technology of the others. It will provide its clients with spare parts and technical assistance for the outmoded equipment, while progressively arming itself with weapons of the new generation.

In the Third World, US manufacturers have also scored points off their competitors in the North. The United States accounted for 48.9 percent of arms sales to the Third World in 1991, 56.8 percent in 1992, and almost 75 percent in 1993. Between 1996 and 1998, the pages of the American and Latin American press were filled with a heated debate on the arms trade. In 1977, in the heyday of Latin American dictatorships, President Jimmy Carter had decreed an embargo on arm sales to Latin America. This legislation has been called into question by the North American war industry, which wants to profit from a Latin American market also coveted by European arms industries. In South America, the political and geostrategic offensive of the United States takes the form of Plan Colombia, whose regional implications are enormous. (Colombia, Venezuela, Brazil, Ecuador, and Peru are all directly concerned.) The United States wants to lend or give money to the Colombian government to purchase more American military hardware on the pretext of combating drug production and trafficking.

The United States is also busy elsewhere in the Third World. Of course, it has a strong presence in the Mediterranean region, especially in Turkey, and in the Middle East. Israel is the country that proportionately receives the most US ODA, a large portion of which is spent on arms. Saudi Arabia is one of the American military sector's main customers. Asia is also at the center of US attention (particularly Southeast Asia). If there were any need to demonstrate the extent of US military presence abroad, it would suffice to say that the United States has more than a hundred foreign military bases and, in recent years, it has multiplied its military interventions (Afghanistan in 2001; Iraq in 2003).

The invasion of Iraq in March 2003 was in total violation of the UN Charter, transforming the country into a de facto US protectorate. The cost of occupation is between $3 billion and $4 billion a month. What the US government presented in 2003 as a rescue operation for the Iraqi people is in fact expanding US oil companies, its military-industrial complex, and construction companies such as Bechtel. The Bush administration intends to saddle Iraq with the cost of the destruction and the reconstruction of the country and to take repayments out of Iraqi oil revenue for the near future.

As for the Western European military industry, in the period 1980–90, a wave of mergers gave rise to two big European groups in the defense and aeronautics sector: BAE Systems of Great Britain and the European Aeronautic Defence and Space Company (EADS, composed of Aerospatiale Matra of France, Dasa of Germany, Finmeccanica of Italy, and CASA of Spain). These two companies plus the French firm Thompson-CSF and their seven North American counterparts mentioned above form the ten principal "military" companies of the planet.

The former European colonial powers all include a military section in their external cooperation policies, especially in Africa. France and Great Britain are the most active in this field. Indeed, France maintains a formidable military presence in Africa (see the work of François-Xavier Verschave). The decision to create a "rapid reaction force," made at the Nice summit by the EU heads of state in December 2000, will undoubtedly lead to significant increases in military spending for the member countries. It is also likely to become an important dimension of the EU's external cooperation with the countries of the periphery.

---

1   When South Korea is included, this amount increases to $4.9 trillion.

2   That is, in a manner of speaking. The banks of the center lend capital, part of which comes from deposits made by the capitalists of the periphery. In some cases, the depositors and the borrowers

are the same capitalists who, to make the accumulated capital secure, prefer to use separate bank accounts.

3   Five hundred sixty billion dollars represents the difference between loans received between 1998 and 2002, and the amounts repaid during the same period. If we only consider repayments between 1998 and 2002, we get the pharaonic sum of $1.9 trillion! (During this period, South Korea was classified as a developing country; therefore, we have incorporated it in the figures given.)

4   We shall see later that what ODA actually contributes is far less than the amounts officially announced.

5   The procedure was long—seventeen years—and complex. The *Financial Times* claims that the amount returned to Philippine authorities came to $658 million; whereas, the wealth accumulated by Marcos is estimated to be $5 billion–$10 billion. The procedure was complex because the Swiss Supreme Court demanded that a Philippine court should pronounce judgement on the sum transferred by Switzerland to a Philippine bank account. Close associates of the late Marcos tried to get their hands on the money. In July 2003, the Philippine Supreme Court finally decided, by a 12–0 vote with one abstention, that the money in question had been acquired illicitly by Marcos and should therefore be made available to the Philippine authorities.

6   This figure includes about $32.9 billion in donations and $3.8 billion of net transfers on the concessional debt, as calculated by the author based on World Bank 2003a. (Net transfers on the concessional debt are positive thanks to loans granted by the International Development Association, a member of the World Bank.) These figures for ODA hardly reflect the reality of financial transfers, as they grossly overestimate the exact amount of aid. Indeed, if the amounts registered as ODA concern a planeload of food and medicines, only the food and medicine actually go to the country. The pilot's salary, the cost of chartering the airplane, the cost of buying the food from an agribusiness multinational and the medicines from a big pharmaceutical laboratory remain in the North. So it is important to remember that the sums given do not actually arrive in the DC as such, unlike the money sent by migrants to their families back home (even allowing for intermediaries taking a cut on the way).

7   For sub-Saharan Africa, reliable figures are available for too few countries to enable a meaningful calculation of the ratio of migrants' remittances to ODA.

8   Debt reductions are counted as part of these donations, with not a penny leaving the country that grants the reduction to the developing country.

9   How does this relate to the GDP of the Triad countries? The Triad's total GDP comes to about $27 trillion; therefore, $14.8 billion represents about 0.06 percent. It should be recalled that the rich countries promised to commit 0.7 percent of their GDP to ODA. Migrants are generally estimated to send between 10 percent and 20 percent of their income to their families back home. The generosity of the meek contrasts with the avarice and greed of the powerful.

10 This list includes the following: Belarus, Bulgaria, Czech Republic, Estonia, Hungary, Latvia, Lithuania, Poland, Romania, Russia, Slovakia, Ukraine, the Dutch Antilles, Aruba, the Bahamas, Bermuda, Brunei, the Caymans, South Korea, Cyprus, the United Arab Emirates, the Falklands, Gibraltar, Hong Kong, Israel, Kuwait, Libya, Macao, Malta, New Caledonia, French Polynesia, Qatar, Singapore, Taiwan, and the Virgin Islands (GB).

11 In the United States, the analogous body is Ex-Im Bank; in Germany, it is Hermès; in Britain, ECGD; in France, COFACE (which was privatized in 1994); in Belgium, Ducroire.

12 See www.eca-watch.org.

13 See the summary table on the debt entitled "All Developing Countries," in World Bank 2003a, vol. 2.

14 Between 1986 and 1994, arms spending fell 21 percent in the United States against a reduction of 69 percent for the former Warsaw Pact countries and China.

10

The World Bank and the IMF: Sixty years is enough!

Bretton Woods: Birth of the IMF and World Bank

On the evening of June 30, 1944, two special trains left Washington and Atlantic City. Both were bursting with hundreds of gentlemen (there were very few women) in fashionable suits and ties. Their conversations were in so many languages that local reporters referred to the trains as "the Tower of Babel on wheels." Their destination was Bretton Woods, in the picturesque hills of New Hampshire. They were on their way to the UN Monetary and Financial Conference.

This meeting of forty-four countries had been organized by US president Franklin D. Roosevelt. The goal was to lay down the rules for a new postwar international economic order. The inaugural session of the conference was held in the grand ballroom of the Hotel Washington, with ample room for the hundreds of delegates.

Henry Morgenthau, US treasury secretary and conference chair, read a welcome message from Roosevelt. Morgenthau's opening speech set the tone for the gathering and reflected the guiding spirit behind it. He called for the "creation of a dynamic world economy in which the peoples of every nation will be able to realize their potential in peace and enjoy, increasingly, fruits of material progress on an earth infinitely blessed with natural riches." He stressed the "elementary economic axiom that prosperity has no fixed limits. It is not a finite substance to be diminished by division." Morgenthau concluded: "The opportunity before us has been bought with blood. Let us meet it with faith in one another, with faith in our common future, which these men fought to make free." The seven hundred delegates rose as the orchestra played the "Star-Spangled Banner."

This consensual address obscured the heated debates that had been raging for months between the heads of the British (above all J.M. Keynes) and American (Morgenthau and Harry White[1]) delegations. The United States wanted to ensure definitively their supremacy in the world over the British. The debate between the Americans and the British had begun before American entry into the Second World War. Winston Churchill had told Roosevelt, "I believe you want to abolish the British Empire.... Everything you say is confirmation of this fact. Yet we know that you are our only hope. And you know we know it. Without America, the British Empire will perish" (in George and Sabelli 1994, 31). The United States fulfilled its objectives, and the positions put forward by J.M. Keynes, while officially praised, were actually marginalized by Morgenthau.

The first weeks of the gathering were almost exclusively taken up by the drafting of IMF statutes, which had been the subject of debate for some months. The main objective of the United States was to set up a system to guarantee postwar financial stability. It wanted competitive devaluation, trade restrictions, import quotas, and all other measures inhibiting trade to end. It wanted free trade without discrimination against US products, a demand that had to be met since the United States was the only Northern country at the time to have a surplus of basic foodstuffs. The United States also sought a favorable climate for its investment in foreign countries and free access to other countries' raw materials, which it had been denied by European colonial empires.

The International Bank for Reconstruction and Development (IBRD), or the World Bank, as it is known, was the first institution of its kind. Its basic structure, as spelled out in the articles of its charter, has remained unchanged. The main goals of the bank were to "assist in the reconstruction and development of territories of members by facilitating the investment of capital for productive purposes" and to "to promote the long-range balanced growth of international trade...by encouraging international investment" (IBRD Articles of Agreement, Article I).

How the IMF and World Bank are run

According to the statutes, the highest governing body in the World Bank (and in the IMF) is the board of governors, where a governor represents each country.[2] The governors of the World Bank and IMF are usually ministers of finance or central bank presidents. In theory, the governors choose the World Bank president; in practice, however, the president has always been a US citizen and is chosen by the US government, usually by the treasury secretary. The head of the IMF is typically European. The managing director of the IMF is assisted by a first deputy managing director, traditionally from the United States, designated by the US Treasury. Annual meetings between the World Bank and the IMF are an occasion for all of the governors of the two

FIGURE 10.1. VOTING RIGHTS OF IBRD ADMINISTRATORS, 2003*

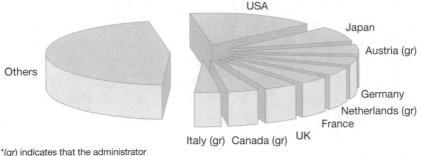

*(gr) indicates that the administrator
presides over a group of countries

Source: World Bank.

institutions to gather in one place.

On a day-to-day basis, most of the governors' powers are delegated to the board of executive directors. In the beginning, the World Bank had twelve executive directors who represented the forty-four founding member countries.

The World Bank's charter stipulates that each of its five biggest shareholders nominate its own executive director,[3] while each of the remaining directors is elected by and represents a number of countries. The World Bank has continually acquired new members (in 2003, it had 184 member countries), and consequently, it now has 24 executive directors.[4] The weight of each director's vote is essentially proportional to the share of funds provided to the World Bank by the country or countries they represent (see table 10.1).

TABLE 10.1. DISTRIBUTION OF VOTING RIGHTS
BETWEEN WORLD BANK ADMINISTRATORS IN 2003

Country	Percent	Group presided by	Percent	Group presided by	Percent
United States	16.41	Austria	4.80	Thailand	2.54
Japan	7.87	Netherlands	4.47	Kuwait	2.72
Germany	4.49	Venezuela	4.50	Switzerland	2.97
France	4.31	Italy	3.51	Brazil	3.60
UK	4.31	Canada	3.85	India	3.40
Saudi Arabia	2.79	Denmark	3.34	Pakistan	3.35
China	2.79	Australia	3.45	Argentina	2.32
Russia	2.79	Uganda	3.41	Guinea-Bissau	2.00

Source: World Bank [Somalia did not take part in the vote in 2002].

The US vote accounted for 36 percent of the total when the World Bank was founded; it has now been reduced by stages to 16.41 percent. In 2003, the richest industrialized countries controlled more than 50 percent of all votes (see figure 10.1), while forty-five African countries together controlled only 5.41 percent and two executive directors of twenty-four.

Executive directors live in Washington DC, meet often (at least once per week), and must approve each loan and the World Bank's main policies. Day-to-day decisions require a simple majority on the executive board, but any change to the constitutive charter requires the approval of at least three-fifths of members and 85 percent of total vote shares. This means that the United States, with 16.41 percent of votes, has veto power on all changes to the statutes and distribution of voting rights—indeed on any reform of the Bretton Woods institutions.[5]

The World Bank's beginnings: Foiled by the Marshall Plan

Keynes wanted the "reconstruction" component of the World Bank to make it an institution that loaned capital to countries "devastated by the war, to help them rebuild their ruined economies and replace lost or destroyed means of production." Consequently, the World Bank was expected to start by focusing on European reconstruction, with a priority to back private investment. Direct lending was expected to be a secondary activity at best.

Under US pressure, however, the World Bank did not really participate in European postwar reconstruction. The Marshall Plan, set up by the United States alone, occupied this function. The World Bank made only four loans, totaling $497 million, for reconstruction, while the Marshall Plan pumped in $12.5 billion.

As an institution for reconstruction, the World Bank was a failure. A war-destroyed Europe did not need interest-bearing loans for specific projects that took a long time to prepare. Rather, it needed quickly available grants and low- or zero-interest loans in order to strengthen its balance-of-payments position and purchase the basic goods it urgently needed.

The World Bank and development

The ultimate objective of the World Bank, as laid down in its statutes, was also to assist in the development "of the productive resources of members, thereby assisting in raising productivity, the standard of living and conditions of labor in their territories" (IBRD Articles of Agreement, Article I).

In the decades after this failure in the phase of "reconstruction," the World Bank focused on the second component of its name: "development." However, since it has always been firmly under the control of the main capitalist powers, its conception of development has never been concerned with efforts aimed at emancipating the peoples of the Third World while ensuring egalitarian social development.

To finance development, the World Bank loans money to governments. The form of these loans has changed over time, but one crucial factor has not changed: the World Bank has never allowed anyone to get away with not paying their debts.

Politics and geopolitics

After 1955, the spirit of the Bandung Conference was alive in many areas of the planet. The conference took place after the French defeat in Vietnam (1954) and came just before Nasser's nationalization of the Suez Canal. After that came the Cuban (1959) and Algerian (1954–62) revolutions and a new phase in the Vietnamese liberation struggle. In more and more areas of the Third World,[6] import substitution policies were put in place and internal markets were developed. Consequently, dependence on the most industrialized capitalist countries decreased. A wave of bourgeois nationalist governments (Nasser in Egypt, Nehru in India, Perón in Argentina, Goulart in Brazil, Sukarno in Indonesia, Nkrumah in Ghana, among others) implemented populist programs, while new revolutionary governments (Cuba, China) pursued an even more radical course.

World Bank projects had a strongly political content: to prevent the development of anti-imperialist movements by applying the lessons learned in South Korea and Taiwan. At the time, however, the World Bank had a relatively small amount of funds at its disposal. Its financial power was given a boost only later, under Robert McNamara (World Bank president, 1968–81).

The World Bank and the Green Revolution

The World Bank's approach to development is heavily productivist. The official aim of the Green Revolution of the 1960s was to increase agricultural production in the countries of the South in order to meet the food needs of local populations. National governments and institutions of the international community—the Ford Foundation played an active role here—established centers in the Philippines (for Asia) and Mexico (for Latin America) with the mission of seeking out and selecting high-yield varieties of grain. These varieties were expected to fulfill the food requirements of the inhabitants of these countries, based on the argument that traditional varieties were not able to meet rising demand due to population growth.

However, the Green Revolution had disastrous effects on the environment and has actually increased the dependence of the countries involved on agribusiness MNCs. The construction of huge dams and power stations and gigantic roads (e.g., the Trans-Amazon Highway) went ahead without any consideration of environmental impact. Exportable cash crops were given priority to the detriment of food crops.

This "revolution" was not brought about by the people of the countries in question; it was imposed on them. In India, the 1965 drought provided the ideal pretext. Growth curves on Indian agricultural production show that there had been uninterrupted growth—until 1965, which indicates a small drop caused by the drought. India requested limited food aid from the United States, which seized the opportunity to impose a series of ecologically unsustainable techniques. Indeed, from the beginning of the 1960s on, capitalists had been promoting chemical-intensive export-oriented agriculture. The World Bank claimed that it saved India from famine, which is patently untrue. Although India was not exporting its farm products, its subsistence crops were enough to meet the country's needs. It is worth recalling that the Great Bengal Famine of 1943 (which left two million to three million people dead) was not caused by a lack of food, but by an increase in the price of foodstuffs caused by inflation—itself caused by the war effort and speculation on food stocks.

Vandana Shiva has clearly condemned the Green Revolution as the project

The UNDP praises the Green Revolution

In spite of these arguments, backed by demonstrations of hundreds of thousands of peasants and small farmers, the 1997 *Global Human Development* report contains deplorable praise for the "progress" brought about by the Green Revolution: "The first Green Revolution has helped millions of small farmers and urban consumers get out of poverty, thanks to technological breakthroughs in wheat, corn and rice farming in high-potential agricultural areas."

Yet, only three years before, the 1994 UNDP report had explained the 1943 famine in the following way: "Nature is doubtless responsible for local food shortages, but it is human beings that turn these shortages into large-scale famines. Hunger is not due to an absence of food, but to a lack of means for acquiring this food."

Now the UNDP is calling for a second Green Revolution—this time to benefit poor farmers in the poorest areas! This very argument was used by the World Bank to promote the first Green Revolution.

that upset the fragile balance that India had achieved over centuries. She rejects the claim that traditional structures were and remain unable to fulfill the country's food requirements. She has put forward well-supported arguments to the effect that the real problem in the countries of the Third World is the distribution of land and wealth.

In fact, the Green Revolution was the tool chosen by the agribusiness MNCs as a profitable response to these problems, using science and technology—and, above all, without making any changes to the organization of agrarian society. (In other words, no land reform.) Shiva has noted that as the Green Revolution has grown in strength, traditional community structures have become dependent on technology that they neither created nor control. This so-called revolution has been a major boon to multinational corporations.

The agribusiness industries of the North have imposed various seed varieties on countries such as India. These varieties did produce favorable short-term results; however, over time, they have been disastrous in a number of ways. First, they require ever-greater purchases of chemical fertilizers, pesticides, herbicides, and so forth, since these imposed varieties of rice are genetically programmed to degenerate after a generation. Second, when the costs are calculated, the performance of these varieties is no better than those obtained through traditional selection and improvement techniques. Dependence, on the other hand, has grown enormously—on machinery and fertilizers, all provided by the industries of the North.

Finally, the Green Revolution has produced a number of other harmful effects. It was carried out to the detriment of communal lands (forests, grazing lands). It has led to a severe impoverishment of biodiversity, an increase in plant diseases (traditional varieties were more resistant), and soil exhaustion (intensive crops have removed certain vital microelements). It requires much greater irrigation than traditional crops (in regions where drought is a real risk), and the massive use of inputs has made huge tracts of land saline. Consequently, the ecological balance has been irremediably destroyed through the intensification of these monocultures. Before the Green Revolution, the Ford Foundation had concluded that land in Punjab was under-utilized. In fact, peasants and small farmers had been using the land in a balanced way in order to avoid soil exhaustion. Only after the disaster of the Green Revolution did the Ford Foundation and the World Bank discover the virtues of organic fertilizers—rather late in the day.

In a number of works, Shiva has decried the violence of the Green Revolution. She places this entire episode within a historical perspective that reveals it as part of the plunder and exploitation of the peasantry for the benefit of the trade and industry of the countries of the center. In the eighteenth century, Indian agriculture was thriving. Until 1750, those who worked the land kept seven hundred of every thousand units produced. Of the remainder, only 50 left the village, while 250 remained for the upkeep of the community. By the nineteenth century, after fifty years of British colonization, this pattern of distribution had been overturned. For every 1,000 units of production, peasants handed over 600, of which 590 went to the central authority, Britain. In spite of this tax grab on peasant production and outside control of any surplus production, the peasantry at the time could still keep 40 percent of the harvest in order to ensure the following year's production. Compared to the Green Revolution, this actually appears rather generous.

The real objective of the Green Revolution was to limit the spread of the Chinese Revolution. The Green Revolution burdened the peasantry with debt, making them dependent. To produce one thousand units, peasants and small farmers are obliged to take on debts equivalent in value to three thousand units. They have to borrow to buy seeds (every year), fertilizers, pesticides, herbicides, tractors (which often must be abandoned due to the lack of spare parts), and so on. They rarely produce enough to pay back their loans. After two growing seasons, they sell their land to the banks and big landowners, and move on to swell the ranks of the urban slums.

Priority given to cash crops, livestock, and forestry

Throughout its existence, the World Bank has contributed powerfully to intensifying agricultural production for exportation. Food crops have been replaced partly by rubber in Thailand and Malaysia, cotton in West Africa, soy beans in the South of Brazil, groundnuts in Senegal, cocoa in Ivory Coast, etc. Countries with a tradition of self-sufficiency in cereals and vegetables have gradually become net importers of those products, leading to loss of food security and food sovereignty. The deliberate wish of the United States to end the food security of the developing countries was crudely expressed by John Block, then US agriculture secretary, in 1986 at the Uruguay Round: "[The] idea that developing countries should feed themselves is an anachronism from a bygone era. They could better ensure their food security by relying on US agricultural products, which are available, in most cases at much lower cost" (cited in Bello 2002, 53).

The intensification of export-oriented activities went hand in hand with the dispossession of small landowners (at the same time increasing the number of landless peasants and the rural exodus to towns) and the development of large export-agriculture companies (plantations). In some countries, projects supported by the World Bank have meant the colonization of forested areas to develop export agriculture. This has affected several Amazonian states in

Brazil, Thailand, Malaysia, and Indonesia. The consequences are deforestation; displacement of population; destruction of the ecological balance; reduced biodiversity; and degradation of living conditions of the populations sustained by the forest, especially indigenous peoples. The World Bank has also systemati-

The Chad-Cameroon pipeline

The Chad-Cameroon pipeline is emblematic. The project directly serves the interests of the multinational petroleum corporations and the United States. Work began in 2000 and was completed by the end of 2003. The consortium, supported and partly financed by the World Bank, is led by ExxonMobil (United States) and includes ChevronTexaco (United States) and Petronas (Malaysia). The idea is to transport crude oil by pipeline over 1,000 km from Chad to the Atlantic Ocean via Cameroon. On the Cameroon coast, the crude oil is to be loaded onto tankers and transported to the refineries.

The project is part of the new US strategy to diversify its petroleum supply zones, in particular by strengthening the relative importance of certain African countries such as Nigeria, Angola, Equatorial Guinea, and Chad. This is just one of innumerable projects for the extraction of raw materials with no local processing. The project will generate a tiny number of permanent jobs (a few hundred) in the two countries concerned, although the initial investment was $3.5 billion. All of the equipment and the entire specialized workforce are foreign. In Cameroon, the pipeline crosses or passes near fragile forests where dozens of Pygmy communities live. The populations affected are given little compensation (see *Los Angeles Times*, June 17, 2003).

The project has received the enthusiastic support of the Chad and Cameroon governments, as the contract stipulates that, over a period of thirty years, Chad (where the oilfields are) will get $2.5 billion, and Cameroon $500 million. The World Bank and the US government are engaged in an active propaganda campaign vaunting the supposed benefits of the project, while the Chad and Cameroon authorities do the same at home.

The international press is doing its bit, too. An article that appeared on the front page of the *Wall Street Journal*, June 26, 2003, illustrates the present neocolonial period:

> In a different desert, the dust of another nation-building project rises. Massive trucks and drilling rigs deployed by an Exxon Mobil-led consortium

cally supported forest-exploitation projects for export. This is the case for Brazil, Congo, Ivory Coast, and Indonesia, often involving real pillage of forest resources, which adds to the negative effects already mentioned.

Another project cherished by the World Bank is the development of stock-

rumble through the sand and bush of Kome, Chad, rushing to complete one of the largest private-sector investments—$3.5 billion—in Sub-Saharan Africa.

The WSJ takes us back to the days of Livingstone and Stanley:

The crude is set to flow 663 miles through a pipeline that slithers under hippo-filled rivers, parched savannas, tropical rain forests and the hunting grounds of the Bakola pygmies, before emptying into storage tanks anchored in the Atlantic surf off the coast of Cameroon....

Next, comes the neocolonial humanitarian touch:

For the first time, a nation has agreed to surrender part of its sovereignty over how to spend the money earned by unlocking its oil wealth. Proceeds from Chad's sale of oil from the first three fields—expected to exceed $100 million a year, nearly doubling the nation's fiscal revenue—will travel a financial pipeline designed by the World Bank and other outsiders and monitored by a Chadian committee that includes Muslim and Christian religious figures and other community leaders. Their job is to ensure the money is spent on development projects such as schools, clinics and rural roads, and isn't siphoned into secret overseas bank accounts....

Then, there is the strategic dimension: "If it succeeds, the project... could offer the world a blueprint for how multinational companies, aid groups and governments can join hands to beneficially exploit the mineral wealth of Iraq and other countries."

US interests are not forgotten: "For the U.S., the Chad project represents an important new oil source beyond the Middle East, and, through Exxon, another American foothold in Africa."

Finally, the bit about fighting poverty: "The project could also open a vital new front in the battle against the poverty that can breed the anger on which terrorists prey."

What the *Wall Street Journal* does not mention is that the World Bank had to suspend remittances temporarily in 2000. It seems the dictator of Chad, Idriss Deby, had used the first few millions of dollars to buy arms to back up his regime. In 2003, Idriss Deby discharged the president of the steering committee responsible for ensuring that the funds were put to good use.

breeding on large farms, which also involves deforestation. In general, the World Bank does not consider the social and environmental impact of projects it supports. (For a systematic analysis of these projects, see Rich 1994.)

The frenzy of energy megaprojects

The list of big dams and power stations that have enjoyed the World Bank's support is impressive. The cost of these big construction projects constitutes a far from negligible share of the external public debt of many indebted countries. As for the damage caused to the environment and the populations, the list of negative effects is long and growing. On the global scale, several tens of millions of people have been forcibly displaced, often with little or no compensation. Since the end of the 1980s, certain projects have had to be abandoned—or, at least the World Bank has had to withdraw its support. The dams on the Narmada River in India are one example. In some cases, the World Bank was forced to back off by the actions of certain people who made it aware of the scale of the damage caused and of the population's ability to organize protests, as well as the solidarity of citizens' movements in the highly industrialized countries. Yet, the World Bank still has not given up on its grand infrastructure projects.

Blind faith in the productivist model

The World Bank (and the IMF) have always sworn by economic growth. Growth is the sine qua non condition of development; development is synonymous with growth. In 1987, Barber Conable declared, "A basic truth is that development cannot be stopped, only directed" (cited in Rich 1994, 199). At the controls in the World Bank and the IMF, there seem to be only two indicator lights: one for the growth rate (measured by the rate of growth of the GDP), and one for the rate of debt repayment.[7] The resources of the planet seem infinite and the environment seems capable of bearing all of the outrageous industrial procedures used in productivist models.

World Bank theorists uphold that all of the environmental problems will find a solution thanks to technical progress. They maintain that the Cassandras who claim that some resources (such as fossil fuels) exist in limited quantities will be contradicted by the facts. Oil and gas stocks are colossal, they insist; we have only yet discovered a small part. Recently, in 2003, Anne Krueger, first deputy managing director of the IMF (formerly chief economist of the World Bank in the 1980s), was turning out this kind of rubbish (see chapter 18). On June 18, 2003, at the Seventh St. Petersburg International Economic Forum, Krueger explained that petroleum reserves are greater today

Growth can lead to poverty

"The very concept of growth, as it has been defined, theorized, and formalized over the last thirty years, reveals how radically inadequate it is to serve as the basis of a political economy, either to use with the developing countries or for them to put into practice. The phenomena it uses and isolates in its theoretical constructions are themselves inappropriate for defining a strategy that the rich countries might use, even less the poor countries.

"*Why* growth? Growth *to what end*? Under what *conditions* is growth beneficial? Growth *for whom*? For certain members of the international community, or for *all*? How can any pertinent answer be found if we are dealing with aggregates supposed by theoretical construction to be homogeneous?

"Not only do these questions underlie the developing countries' demands, but clearly they are unavoidable for anyone who is concerned that models should be operational and politics concrete.

"Into the world of *objects* or *things*, these unusual approaches introduce the *human being*, the *individual*, the *actor*, not simply the producer or the consumer, slave of the market and subject to the general system of prices, but individuals and their groups, able to change their environment by deliberate, organized actions. Today, everyone knows that growth can lead to poverty if, for example, it means the destruction or deterioration of natural resources. Everyone knows that growth does not take into account possible deterioration or destruction by humankind, since it ignores everything that might be included in the metaphor 'human depreciation'....

"Before development can seriously be considered, the risks that growth without development entails have to be clearly understood. These are manifest when the economic activity of a developing country turns on the setting up of foreign firms or big construction projects, with no fallout for the rest of society."

*Excerpted from François Perroux, Pour une philosophie du nouveau developpement
(For a philosophy of new development). Paris: Aubier, 1981.*

than they were in 1950, and that no irreparable damage has been caused to the global environment. She claims that we will discover more petroleum reserves as time goes by and, after a normal phase of environmental deterioration, the situation will improve according to objective economic laws. She even goes so far as to claim that once growth reaches the critical threshold point of $5,000 per capita GDP, people begin to spend what is necessary to reduce pollution.

The World Bank and the IMF add that the reduction of poverty can be attained only through growth (and free trade, as we shall see further on). Those who criticize this blindness about growth are accused of not caring about the poor: surely, you are not suggesting that they should be deprived of growth! The emptiness of productivist ideology has been particularly well demonstrated by François Perroux (see box).

The power to intervene in national economies

Although the World Bank had only limited means at its disposal in the period preceding McNamara's stewardship, it was able to set up a network of influence that would be of great service later on. It set about creating demand for its services in the Third World. The influence the World Bank enjoys today derives in large part from the patronage networks it established in countries that later became its customers and, of course, its debtors. The World Bank pursued a policy of active influence peddling in order to build up its network of debtors.

From the 1950s on, one of the main objectives of the World Bank was to "build up institutions." This usually involved the creation of autonomous agencies within governments, agencies that became long-term borrowers from the World Bank.[8] Such agencies were intentionally founded in such a way as to be relatively independent financially from their governments and free from the control of local political institutions. They became natural relays for the World Bank, to which they owed their existence.

The creation of these patronage networks was a cornerstone of World Bank strategy to become involved in the economic policies of Third World countries. Obeying no rules but their own (often drawn up in keeping with World Bank recommendations), staffed by big-name local technocrats who shared World Bank aims, championed and admired by the World Bank, these agencies served to create a stable and reliable source for what the Bank needed most: "viable" loan proposals. They also provided a parallel power base through which the World Bank was able to transform national economies— even entire societies—without bothering with the "cumbersome" process of democratic control and debate.

In 1956, the World Bank founded the Economic Development Institute, with generous financial support from the Rockefeller and Ford Foundations. The institute gave six-month training courses to official delegates of member countries. According to Rich (1994, 76), "Between 1956 and 1971, more than 1,300 official delegates had passed through the institute; some of them had become Prime Minister or Minister of Planning or Finance."

The implications of such a policy are most worrying. The International Legal Center (ILC) in New York carried out a study of World Bank involvement in Colombia between 1949 and 1972. The ILC report concludes that the World Bank's autonomous agencies had a profound impact on political structure and social development throughout the region. They weakened "the system of political parties and the respective roles of the legislature and judiciary" (Rich 1994).

By the 1960s, the World Bank had set up its own new mechanisms for continual intervention in the internal affairs of borrower countries. It, however, emphatically denies that such interventions are political in nature. On the contrary, it insists that World Bank policies in no way impinge on power structures, and that political and economic matters occupy two discrete spheres.

World Bank support for dictatorships

Article IV section 10 of the World Bank statutes stipulates:

The Bank and its officers shall not interfere in the political affairs of any member; nor shall they be influenced in their decisions by the political character of the member or members concerned. Only economic considerations shall be relevant to their decisions, and these considerations shall be weighed impartially in order to achieve the purposes stated in Article I.

The obligation to disregard political and noneconomic factors in World Bank operations—a key element of the institution's charter—has been systematically violated since the World Bank first came into existence. It refused to lend any money to France in the aftermath of the Second World War as long as communists sat in the government of national unity. The day after the communists left the government, loans were granted. Yet, in 1947, it lent $195 million to the Netherlands, despite the fact that the Dutch government was engaged in a military offensive against the Indonesian nationalists. The Dutch had launched their attack two weeks before the World Bank approved the loan. Over the next two years, the number of Dutch occupation troops rose to 145,000. Even after the UN decreed a cease-fire in 1948, the Dutch army went ahead with several airborne and land attacks. Voices were raised at the UN, criticizing the World Bank's loan to the Netherlands.

When responding to charges that it plays political favorites, the World Bank has pointed to articles from its charter that prohibit interference in the political affairs of member states. In fact, these parts of its charter have often been little more than a smoke screen for World Bank support of dictatorial regimes. Indeed, article IV did not prevent the World Bank from refusing loans to Brazil and Chile when their governments were not to its liking. At the beginning of the 1960s, the World Bank denied credit to the democratically elected Goulart government in Brazil. After the 1964 military coup (which set up a military dictatorship that lasted for twenty years), however, loan totals from the World Bank went from zero to an annual average of $73 million for the remainder of the 1960s, and to just under $500 million per year in the mid-1970s. Under the democratically elected government of Salvador Allende (1970–73), Chile did not receive loans from the World Bank. After the 1973 military coup, under the Pinochet regime, the country suddenly became creditworthy.

In the late 1960s and during the 1970s, under the presidency of Robert McNamara, the World Bank gained notoriety for backing antidemocratic regimes that tortured and murdered their own citizens. In 1965, for example, the World Bank openly defied a resolution from the General Assembly of the United Nations calling on all UN-affiliated agencies (including the World Bank) to suspend financial assistance to the South African apartheid regime. However, the World Bank argued that its article IV legally obliged it to ignore UN resolutions. Even a personal plea from UN secretary-general U Thant to George Woods, then World Bank president, was of no use. The World Bank also ignored the UN resolution of that period to refuse financial support to Portuguese dictator Salazar for exercising colonial domination over Angola, Mozambique, Guinea-Bissau and Cape Verde, and East Timor. McNamara (1973, 23) insisted that the World Bank provide credit to the brutal Indonesian dictatorship established in the wake of the 1965 massacre of more than 500,000 communists. Following his departure, the World Bank pursued the same policy, in line with US foreign policy.

Another UN institution, the UNDP (1994, 81), has a thing or two to say about US and World Bank support for dictators:

> In fact, aid provided by the USA in the 1980s is inversely proportional to respect for human rights. Nor have multilateral donors [the World Bank and the IMF] seemed to be overly concerned with such considerations [democracy]. Indeed, they seem to prefer authoritarian regimes, they argue without batting an eyelid that such regimes promote political stability and are better able to manage the economy. When Bangladesh and the Philippines ended martial law, their respective share in overall World Bank loans fell.

World Bank power surges during McNamara stewardship

In 1968, McNamara said, "The only limitation on the activities of the World Bank would be the ability of member-countries to use our assistance in an efficient way and to pay back our loans according to the terms and conditions that we determine." In 1969, he said, "The International Bank for Reconstruction and Development is a body that makes investments whose objective is development, it is neither a philanthropic institution nor a social welfare agency" (McNamara 1973, 21, 155).

The World Bank's activities grew in number in the 1960s and particularly in the 1970s. From 1968 to 1981, under McNamara (US secretary of defense during the Vietnam War), the World Bank was engaged in a lending frenzy. He made it clear that the career prospects of loan officers were linked directly to the number of projects in their portfolios.

The bigger the project, the greater the likelihood of receiving World Bank financing (George and Sabelli 1994; Rich 1994). This quantitative approach, and the pressures applied on World Bank associates to draw up and promote expensive projects to borrower countries, led these countries to take on excessive debt.

During the first twenty years of its existence, the World Bank (IBRD and IDA) only loaned out $10.7 billion. During McNamara's first five years as president, the World Bank backed projects worth $13.4 billion (George and Sabelli 1994, 52; McNamara 1973, 22–26, 144, 150–60). He had an almost fanatical belief in quantitative methods and administrative models seen as universally valid and capable of solving a whole range of problems. At the beginning of the 1960s, he said: "Running any department of an organization is exactly the same, whether one is dealing with the Ford Motor Company, the Catholic Church, or the Ministry of Defense.... At a certain stage, all problems are the same." In 1967, he said, "Management is the way social, economic, and political change—indeed, change of all kinds—is spread throughout society."

McNamara saw himself as a "development planner." In his eyes, the World Bank was playing a "vanguard" role in development assistance by planning it from start to finish (McNamara 1973, 31, 34). The planning mechanism was central to his approach: the World Bank should lay down effective methods for "family planning and for the public administration responsible for population control" (p. 33); the Green Revolution begun in the mid-1960s should be better planned across the board (p. 78ff.); planning for major public works would provide work for the unemployed and build up infrastructure (p. 42).

McNamara also got the World Bank to draw up plans for massive five-year loans to borrower countries. These plans were detailed in the country program papers, which set objectives and priorities for all World Bank lending to a given country, based on the work of "economic missions in the countries" and the reports they produced. These economic reports and the overall country files joined the ranks of the most confidential documents of the World Bank, just a step below its internal memoranda. In some cases, even government ministers of the country concerned could not examine these major plans. In the poorest and smallest countries, such secrecy was seen as proof that their economic fate had been taken over by international trustees.

McNamara's point of view greatly amplified tendencies that already existed in the World Bank. These tendencies bolstered its institutional power, while further neglecting the complex and distinct social realities of countries lumped together in the "developing countries" category. Easily quantifiable objectives were defined to measure progress. Complex social realities were reduced to so many sets of target figures and group totals. Everything came to be seen in terms of profitable undertakings, gradual increases in production and productivity, the evolution of earnings, and so on.

It was not difficult to foresee the results of such an approach, applied everywhere in an identical fashion. At best, it would be ineffective; at worst, it was so inappropriate from a social and environmental angle as to condemn many projects to failure.

Development and the security of the "free world"

It was also under McNamara's stewardship that the World Bank began to build up its "new style" portfolio of projects aimed at combating poverty. The main objective was rural development and agriculture—a sector whose share of World Bank loans rose from 18.5 percent in 1968, to 31 percent ($3.8 billion) in 1981.

The World Bank joined the struggle against the spread of communism in the Third World. It set up projects aimed at alleviating poverty in both the cities and the countryside. These included housing improvements, and the installation of water pumps and power lines. For the first time, health and education projects also accounted for a significant share of the World Bank's portfolio.

It was as part of his crusade against communism that McNamara opted to tackle the scourge of absolute poverty. Never before had the World Bank seen its work for development as part of a program to alleviate poverty. However, McNamara was convinced that if steps were not taken against growing inequality in the distribution of wealth in developing countries (see his description in McNamara 1973, 128), from time to time popular uprisings would threaten capitalist countries in the center.

McNamara's time at the helm of the World Bank coincided with the spread of struggles for liberation and revolution: the Portuguese Revolution of 1974, freeing Africa's last colonies; final defeat for American troops in Vietnam in 1975; and the Nicaraguan Revolution of 1979. There were also major social and political crises, even in the capitalist heartland: the Black civil rights movement and the anti–Vietnam War movement in the United States in the late 1960s and early 1970s, and the 1968 student movements in France, Germany, and Mexico. There were also massive workers' strikes in France (May 1968), Italy (1969–70), and the so-called socialist countries (the Prague Spring of 1968). McNamara was an old hand at such things, having ordered mass napalm bombings of Vietnam. These liberation movements threw a wrench into the works of World Bank "development" plans. As a result, it pumped in increased credit to strengthen the Third World's economic ties to the world market and its political ties to the capitalist world. These new loans were part of a strategy aimed at "containment" of the spread of the broad movement for emancipation.

In 1968, while still secretary of defense, McNamara declared: "Ernesto Che Guevara's death in Bolivia in the fall of 1967 delivered a severe blow to the hopes of the Castroite revolutionaries. But this is not a sufficient response to the problem" (McNamara 1968, 29). In 1972, he made a clear speech in this regard at the meeting of World Bank governors:

> Too little, too late, is history's most fitting epitaph for regimes that have fallen in the face of the cries of the landless, unemployed, marginalized, and oppressed, pushed to despair. As such, there must be policies designed specifically to reduce the poverty of the poorest 40 percent of the population in developing countries. This is not just the principled thing to do, it is also the prudent thing to do. Social justice is not only a moral obligation, it is also a political imperative. (McNamara 1973, 139–40)

Thereafter, McNamara called for agrarian reform to provide land to poor farmers and limit the land holdings of big landowners. He proposed that the credit systems of developing countries be reformed to give small farmers access to loans. He backed public works projects aimed at improving the lot of the poorest sectors. In short, McNamara wanted the multilateral public institution he headed to pursue a growth strategy requiring that the World Bank itself be given greater funds and power. He was scarcely interested in the governments of the South playing a role in redistributing wealth. Rather, he wanted the World Bank to compensate for the ingratitude of the North toward the South, as well as for the weakness of the South's governments.

McNamara's above-mentioned proposals were not implemented anywhere by the World Bank. Furthermore, McNamara's development plan never considered the potential of increased trade between the countries of the South. He never acknowledged the need to build up regional blocs in the South— blocs that could create complementarities favoring a cumulative process of regional growth that would reduce the South's dependence on the North. The only relationship worthy of his attention was between the countries of the South and those of the North—in which those from the South always come off worse, since the developed countries set the rules of international trade.

It is nonetheless noteworthy that McNamara's declarations and proposals stood in sharp contrast to the aggressive neoliberal turn taken in the 1980s. In his own way, McNamara belonged to the old school. This does not change the fact that he played an important role in laying the groundwork for the neoliberal offensive. The waning gap between his words and his deeds was eliminated by the neoliberals, who jettisoned all talk of planning, state control, and development.

Note that Joseph Stiglitz, in *Globalization and Its Discontents* (2002, 13), takes the part of McNamara and the team he gradually assembles:

> The most dramatic change in these institutions occurred in the 1980s, the era when Ronald Reagan and Margaret Thatcher preached free market ideology in the United States and the United Kingdom. The IMF and the World Bank became the new missionary institutions, through which these ideas were pushed on the reluctant poor countries that often badly needed their loans and grants. The ministries of finance in poor countries were willing to become converts, if necessary, to obtain the funds, though the vast majority of government officials, and, more to the point, people in these countries often remained skeptical. In the early 1980s, a purge occurred inside the World Bank, in its research department, which guided the Bank's thinking and direction. Hollis Chenery, one of America's most distinguished development economists, a professor at Harvard who had made fundamental contributions to research in the economics of development and other areas as well, had been Robert McNamara's confidant and adviser. McNamara had been appointed president of the World Bank in 1968. Touched by the poverty that he saw throughout the Third World, McNamara had redirected the Bank's effort at its elimination, and Chenery assembled a first-class group of economists from around the world to work with him. But with the changing of the guard came a new president in 1981, William Clausen, and a new chief economist, Ann Krueger, an international trade specialist, best known for her work on "rent seeking"—how special interests use tariffs and other protectionist measures to increase their incomes at the expense of others. While Chenery and his team had focused on how markets failed in developing countries and what governments could do to improve markets and reduce poverty, Krueger saw government as the problem. Free markets were the solution to the problems of developing countries. In the new ideological fervor, many of the first-rate economists that Chenery had assembled left.

Reading Stiglitz's opinion here, one cannot but wonder if his positive assessment of McNamara's role at the head of the World Bank is not inversely proportionate to his rejection of the policies applied by his successors during the time when Reagan and Bush Senior were in power. One can share his negative opinion of the latter, but without losing sight of the fact that McNamara's policies prepared the terrain. The virtues that Stiglitz attributes to McNamara are not proven; on the other hand, McNamara's active participation in drawing up and implementing nefarious policies has been demonstrated by a variety of authors whose conclusions we share. McNamara and other high officials in the World Bank and IMF should be called to account for their acts before a court of justice.

1   In 1942, Harry White had drawn up proposals for a new financial and monetary international architecture, at the request of the US Treasury (see Aglietta and Moatti 2000, 10–24).

2   All that follows is also valid for the IMF. When the IMF functions differently from the World Bank, it will be mentioned explicitly in the text.

3   In 2003, the five biggest shareholders were the United States, Japan, Germany, Great Britain, and France.

4   In addition to the directors directly designated by the five countries mentioned above, China, Russia, and Saudi Arabia each have the right to designate an executive director. Therefore, of the twenty-four executive directors, eight are individual representatives of a country and sixteen are designated by groups of countries.

5   The number of votes required for a decisive majority has been modified three times since 1945, as the number and importance of new members has changed, in order to maintain the veto power of the United States. When the World Bank was founded, the required majority was 65 percent of votes, and the United States had 36 percent. When the US quota was reduced to just over 20 percent, the required majority was raised to 80 percent. Since 1989, when the US quota fell below 20 percent, the required majority was increased to 85 percent.

6   The expression "Third World" is thought to have been coined by French demographer Alfred Sauvy, in an article that appeared in *L'Observateur*, August 14, 1952: "We often talk of the two worlds [capitalist and socialist], of the possibility of war between them, of their co-existence, etc., forgetting that there is a third one, much bigger, and chronologically, the first. I mean what the United Nations refers to as the under-developed countries.... The under-developed countries, the Third World, have entered a new phase.... For at last, this Third World, ignored, exploited and despised as was the Third Estate, also wants to be something."

7   In March 2000, at the University of Prague, I faced Matt Carlson, vice president of the World Bank, responsible for relations with civil society, in a public debate. He told me that I needn't worry about the situation in Mozambique, as that country had registered an exceptional rate of growth for its GDP. On several occasions, I have seen how far representatives of the World Bank and IMF cling to this approach, though it is now widely recognized that economic growth coexists with a deterioration or stagnation of living conditions for the majority of the population.

8   Bruce Rich (1994, 13, 41) gives examples of agencies founded through the World Bank: in Thailand, the Industrial Finance Corporation of Thailand (IFCT), the Board of Investment (BOI) of Thailand, the National Economic and Social Development Board (NESDB), and the Electricity Generating Authority of Thailand (EGAT); for India, the National Thermal Power Corporation (NTPC) and Northern Coal Limited (NCL).

11

The debt crisis and World Bank legitimacy

As far back as the beginning of the 1970s, Robert McNamara identified increasing Third World indebtedness as a problem. He wrote in 1973:

> By the end of 1972, the debt totaled $75 billion and annual servicing was more than $7 billion. Debt servicing rose by 18 percent in 1970 and by 20 percent in 1971. The average rate of increase of the debt since the 1960s has been almost twice as high as the rate of increase in the export revenues that these countries must use to service the debt. This situation cannot continue indefinitely.

Between 1968 and 1981, the sums loaned annually by the World Bank increased constantly, from $2.7 billion in 1968 (the year McNamara became World Bank president), to $8.7 billion in 1978, to $12 billion in 1981, on the eve of the crisis (Bello 2000, 39). The World Bank actively contributed, by its policies, to creating the conditions that led to the debt crisis. For example, it encouraged further indebtedness on the pretext of increasing exports. Now the increase in the volume of debt and in debt service was certainly a cause of the crisis, as indebted countries repay their external debt with hard currency earned through exportation. Indeed, the continued increase in the volume of exports combined with little or no increase in demand from the industrialized countries could only result in falling prices of products exported from the periphery. It was bound to generate an unsustainable situation. The fall in prices of exports and the ensuing loss of income led to repayment difficulties. Add to this the factor that was to set it all off: the sudden increase in interest rates imposed by the US Federal Reserve from the end of 1979 (there are close ties between the World Bank, the Federal Reserve, and the US government). Crisis was inevitable.

Does this mean that there has been a plot deliberately hatched by the World Bank? The answer has to be modulated. Although no such plot has yet been uncovered, it is clear that the World Bank and the powers that oversee it—with the US government in the forefront—carry the major part of the responsibility, as much in the succession of events leading up to the crisis as in the use of the crisis to further subordinate periphery countries to the highly industrialized capitalist countries.

The rise in interest rates caused the crisis to break out in 1982, with the combination of a huge increase in the amounts the debtors had to repay and a dramatic fall in their income. Who made the decision to raise interest rates so steeply at the end of 1979? The US Federal Reserve along with the treasury department. Why were the periphery countries hit by a fall in export revenues? It was the direct result of the "all export" policies recommended by the World Bank, and of US tactics against the cartel of petroleum-producing countries, aimed at dividing OPEC and lowering the price of oil. It is common knowledge that the US treasury department mainly determines the directives applied by the World Bank. The shady dealing of certain states of the South, the embezzlement of funds by the ruling classes of the periphery countries—all of that existed (and still does), and the guilty parties must be brought to justice. However, let it not be forgotten that the World Bank, the IMF, and the authorities of the industrialized countries turned a blind eye, when they did not actively support the regimes concerned. The true causes of the crisis are unmistakable. The crisis was mainly the result of decisions made in the creditor countries.

Where was the World Bank when crisis struck? It proved incapable of assessing its amplitude or proposing policies to protect the interests of debtors faced with the fait accompli of increased interest rates. Yet, far from seeing its power diminish, the World Bank grew in stature. Clearly, the US government and colleagues from the other major capitalist powers were not dissatisfied with the World Bank's work. If they had been, they would have limited its role. On the contrary, they gave the World Bank and the IMF their full backing during and after the crisis. Furthermore, the World Bank and IMF raked in considerable profits, in the form of "reserves," on the backs of the indebted countries.

Since the debt crisis, the World Bank and IMF have served as instruments to increase the subordination of the periphery countries to the countries of the center. This has been done by systematically implementing policies that open and deregulate the economies of the periphery (structural adjustment), with the connivance of the ruling classes of those countries. The sum of these policies has taken a human toll of dramatic proportions.

All of that is part of the debt owed by the World Bank, the IMF, the governments behind their policies, and those of the periphery that serve as their accomplices to the citizens of this planet and, above all, to those citizens who suffer daily because of the debt crisis.

World Bank justification for increased indebtedness

Until 1973, McNamara argued that the growth-oriented programs of developing countries had to be backed. Government assistance from the developed countries was insufficient, he said, and these same developed countries were not dismantling discriminatory measures against imports from developing countries in spite of promises to do so. McNamara even publicly criticized the protectionism of the North and the low level of official development assistance (ODA) on numerous occasions (see McNamara 1973, 127). The World Bank, he argued, should therefore loan increasing sums to developing countries to help them achieve consistent growth rates, despite all the obstacles, and earn sufficient revenues to pay back their debts. Consequently, the World Bank set itself the mission of providing as much credit as possible to developing countries, as a way to make up for inadequate levels of ODA. This approach was clearly at odds with McNamara's warnings concerning debt levels that outstrip the rate of growth of export earnings (see above).

From 1973 on, following the rise in the price of oil and other raw materials, McNamara argued that developing countries could use borrowed funds to develop their communications infrastructure, increase electricity production, and boost export-oriented activities. His underlying assumption was that prices of the exported goods of these countries would continue to increase on the world market, or remain stable at the least. As a result, he forecast that

FIGURE 11.1. DEVELOPMENT AS ENVISAGED BY THE WORLD BANK VS. REALITY, 1968–80

their export earnings would continue to rise thanks to increases in export volumes. These increased earnings, he said, would enable developing countries to service their debts (interest and principal), while reinvesting a portion in the improvement of export-oriented industries. This was expected to have a cumulative effect, leading to or accelerating development while anchoring these countries firmly in the camp of the Western countries.

McNamara argued that debt obligations were a powerful material incentive for developing countries to modernize their export-oriented agricultural and industrial sectors. This line of reasoning was repeated in a number of his talks and writings. The virtuous circle of "debt/increased exports/debt servicing" would develop the South and boost world economic growth. The actual course of events has given the lie to this approach: as we have seen, the prices of exported goods plummeted in the 1980s, while interest rates rose sharply at the same time. This led to the financial asphyxiation of indebted countries (see figure 11.1).

World Bank tunnel vision

Although the debt crisis only burst into the open in August 1982, there had been no shortage of ominous signs. Warnings had been given, but the World Bank obviously underestimated the dangers of the situation. One need only look at its 1981 annual report on global development: "These trends suggest it will be more difficult for developing countries to manage their debt, *but they do not presage any generalized problem*. This analysis is confirmed in projections for the balance of payments in the 1980s, based on various probable scenarios" [emphasis added].

The 1982 report was released a few weeks before the explosion of the Mexican crisis. It provided an even more blinkered and optimistic analysis of the situation (Edwards 1997, 31). In its 1983 report, the World Bank said that liquidity problems had affected only specific countries, not entire regions or groups of countries. Yet, about thirty countries followed closely in Mexico's footsteps. The 1984 report provided optimistic projections through 1990 concerning the relationship between Latin American export earnings and debt-service payments. In fact, the exact opposite occurred (Edwards 1997, 96).

For a number of years, the World Bank continued to promote the illusion that the debt crisis was above all a liquidity crisis, instead of recognizing that the debtor countries were insolvent. These debtor countries were not simply experiencing liquidity problems, they were in the midst of a full-fledged crisis of a long-term structural nature. The only way out without calling the system into question was to continue borrowing, to get enough money to keep up the debt repayments, and to spend an ever-greater proportion of tax revenues on debt repayment. Once the crisis started, only Ceausescu in Romania opted for repaying without recourse to further loans. To honor his debts, Ceausescu levied taxes on an unprecedented scale on the wealth produced by the Romanian people, with catastrophic results for society.

In 1986, with the debt of developing countries greatly exceeding $1 trillion, the World Bank claimed that by the mid-1990s, this debt total would be, at worst, about $864 billion. By 1995, however, total Third World debt was $1.94 trillion—twice the forecast amount.

The IMF made the same errors. In its quarterly *World Economic Outlook* of April 1982, the IMF argued that in spite of a number of payment problems, Latin America would obtain major loans from the international financial community. In its October 1982 report, the IMF predicted that recession would be avoided. In its 1984 reports, the IMF seconded the World Bank in calculating that the ratio between debt servicing and export earnings would improve for Latin America. The opposite, in fact, occurred.

Wrong forecasts on world market prices

The World Bank was equally arbitrary and wrong in its forecasts of the export revenues meant to rescue developing countries from debt. Its 1981 predictions for the price of African raw materials were off by 62 percent for minerals and metals; 156 percent for oil; 180 percent for fats and food oils; 103 percent for beverages; 60 percent for lumber; and 97 percent for nonfood agricultural products (George and Sabelli 1994, 100–01). The World Bank could have easily foreseen—with all countries of the South seeking to maximize exports in order to meet debt obligations—a drop in the prices of exported products.

The IMF did no better than the World Bank. UNCTAD's *Least Developed Countries Report* (2000d, 70) mentions an internal IMF study reporting that the latter had, in 1983, negotiated an agreement with Zambia based on pure fantasy. According to the agreement proposed by the IMF, the price of copper exported by Zambia was to rise by 45 percent over four years. This would enable the country to repay its creditors. In fact, the price of copper dropped by about 12 percent, leaving the African country with a debt burden even heavier than before the agreement (Brooks 1998).

In 1991, the World Bank repeated the same mistake. Its international economy division continued to put out optimistic forecasts that were also revealed, within two years, to be thoroughly groundless. Real market prices were significantly lower than predicted: 47 percent lower for coffee, 56 percent for cocoa, 74 percent for sugar, 35 percent for rubber, and 52 percent for lead, to name but a few. The World Bank's 1991 report persists in forecasting a continued increase in raw material prices during the 1990s, claiming that the GNP of developing countries would rise by 5 percent annually between 1992 and 2002. In fact, the reverse happened as far as raw materials were concerned, since they fell by 30 percent between 1996 and 1999. As for the growth rate of the GNP in developing countries, it was 3.2 percent in 1998, and 3.8 percent in 1999 (IMF 2000b, 11–12).

The World Bank siphons off the resources of the South

World Bank leaders have calculated the return on funds deposited by industrialized countries in the World Bank as their participation in its capital. The official publications of the World Bank say nothing about this, but specialized publications aimed at the business community provided an idea of its profits. The following is an excerpt from a speech given to an audience of Belgian employers in 1986, which was published in the bulletin of the Belgian employers' federation, by Jacques de Groote, formerly Belgium's executive director at the IMF and also at the World Bank:

> The advantages that Belgium, like all World Bank member countries, acquires through its participation in the group's institutions can be measured by looking at the flow-back. The flow-back is the relationship between, on the one hand, total spending by the International Development Association (IDA) and the World Bank on a country's companies based on contracts secured by these companies and, on the other hand, this country's contribution to the World Bank and IDA. As a result, the flow-back is the relationship between what companies obtain through the sale of equipment and consulting services, and what Belgium contributes to the World Bank and IDA. The flow-back from the World Bank to the industrialized countries is significant and continues to rise; from late 1980 to late 1984, it has risen from seven to ten for all industrialized countries taken together. Which means that for every dollar put into the system, industrialized countries got back seven in 1980 and 10.5 now. (FEB, 1986, 496–97)

Chris Adams (2000, 27), a research associate with Focus on the Global South (Bangkok), has analyzed the lending policy of the Asian Development Bank (ADB), which, like the African and Inter-American Development Banks, is connected to the World Bank. Among the main shareholders (so-called donors) of the ADB are Japan, the United States, Germany, Canada, Australia, the UK, Italy, and France. According to Adams, "[M]ost of the donor countries get more money from the ADB in the form of contracts obtained by their companies than they provide as their total contribution to the bank."

US preeminence over the World Bank
and multilateral regional banks

Henry Kissinger (head of the National Security Council, 1969–75, and secretary of state, 1973–77), speaking in Berne, Switzerland, in 1985, on the external debt, said:

> There is no painless solution for the indebted countries to find a way out of their critical situation, but we must propose certain amendments to the IMF's adjustment program. The solution will mean a sacrifice; I prefer the indebted nations to fulfil their external obligations to creditors by using real assets, through the transfer of property belonging to public companies. (Cited in Olmos 1990, 51)

A 1982 US Treasury report expresses satisfaction at the preeminence of the United States within the multilateral financial institutions:

> The United States was instrumental in shaping the structure and mission of the World Bank along Western, market-oriented lines.... We were also responsible...for the emergence of a corporate entity with a weighted voting run by a board of directors, headed by a high-caliber American-dominated management, and well-qualified professional staff. As a charter member and major shareholder in the World Bank, the United States secured the sole right to a permanent seat on the Bank's Board of Directors.... Other significant actors—management, major donors, and major recipients—have recognized the United States as a major voice in the (multilateral development) banks. They know from past experience that we are capable and willing to pursue important policy objectives in the banks by exercising the financial and political leverage at our disposal. (Cited in Bello 2002, 59–60).

Walden Bello calls attention to another passage from this treasury document:

> In a study of fourteen of "the most significant issues" that sparked debate at the Bank—ranging from blocking observer status for the Palestine Liberation Organization (PLO) to halting Bank aid to Vietnam and Afghanistan—the United States was able to impose its views as Bank policy in twelve cases. (Bello 2002, 60)

US government domination over the World Bank has also meant that the president of the World Bank has always been a US citizen, designated by the administration. The class origins of and offices held (before and after) by the various US citizens chosen to preside at the World Bank are revealing. The first president, Eugene Meyer, who only lasted eight months, was editor of the *Washington Post* and formerly with Lazard Freres. The second, John J. McCloy, was a major Wall Street lawyer and was later designated US high commissioner for Germany, then director of Chase Manhattan Bank. The third, Eugene R. Black, became a special adviser to President Lyndon B. Johnson. The fourth, George D. Woods, had been a director of an investment bank. Robert S. McNamara had been CEO of the Ford Motor Company then secretary of defense under Kennedy and Johnson. His successor as World Bank president, Alden W. Clausen, had been president of Bank of America (one of the main US banks, highly implicated in the Third World debt crisis), where he returned after his World Bank term. In 1986, Barber Conable succeeded him, a former Republican member of Congress. Then Lewis T. Preston took office in 1991, a former chair of the executive committee of JPMorgan bank. James D. Wolfensohn, a Wall Street banker with Salomon Brothers, has been president since 1996. In short, as a general rule, there are close ties between US political power, big business (the hard core of the US capitalist class), and the presidency of the World Bank.

The Wapenhans Report (1992) and the Meltzer Commission (2000) on World Bank failures

In February 1992, the vice president of the World Bank, Willi Wapenhans, carried out a confidential study evaluating projects financed by the World Bank—some 1,300 projects in 113 countries. The conclusions of the study are shocking: 37.5 percent of projects are evaluated as unsatisfactory upon conclusion (up from 15 percent in 1981), with only 22 percent of financial commitments seen to be in line with World Bank directives. Then, in February 2000, a US congressional commission led by Alan Meltzer presented a report on the World Bank and IMF. It found that 65 percent to 70 percent of World Bank projects in the poorest countries failed (55 percent to 60 percent failed in the developing countries taken as a whole).

Yet, the profits keep rolling in

As McNamara remarked, the World Bank does not operate in a spirit of philanthropy. Although it is coy about drawing attention to the fact, year in, year out, it has a surplus of more than $1.5 billion that are added to its reserves. Where does this surplus come from, if not from the transfers made by the peoples of the periphery in the form of debt repayments?

A succession of financial crises: 1994–2001

In 1994, the second Mexican crisis unfolded (the first had been in 1982); in 1997, the East and Southeast Asian crisis; in 1998, the Russian crisis; late 1998–early 1999, the Brazilian crisis; late 2000–early 2001, crises in Argentina and Turkey; end of 2001, another crisis in Argentina. In each case, the World Bank failed to predict the imminent crisis. When Thailand and the three other Asian "dragons" (Indonesia, Malaysia, and the Philippines) began to wobble, the World Bank made the following declaration in its 1997 report on global indebtedness:

> The debt situation remains healthy. Although growth of overall debt has surpassed export growth, the ratio between total debt and export earnings has been maintained at moderate levels. Total debt was worth 99 percent of annual export earnings in 1996, much lower than the 146 percent average in middle- and low-income countries. (World Bank 1997b, 160)

However, serious examination of the figures provided by the World Bank in that same document should have led to a very different conclusion. It was apparent that private-sector debt had rocketed in 1996, despite the fact that it was backed by no guarantee. Short-term debt (at a high interest rate) had also shot up. There was also an increased flow of particularly volatile portfolio investments.

In fact, the policies recommended by the World Bank (and the IMF) were directly responsible for the repeated crises. Worse, when these crises did break out, the World Bank (and the IMF) dictated remedies that aggravated the situation. These institutions heightened human suffering and had the governments of the periphery gradually abandon the main instruments of national sovereignty (exchange control, control of capital movement, production and credit in the public sector, control of the central bank, etc.).

1996 launch of debt-reduction initiative for the HIPC

In 1996, the World Bank and IMF launched a debt-reduction program for the heavily indebted poor countries (HIPC). This concerned 42 countries of more than 180 periphery countries. The sum total of their debts represents about a tenth of the DC debts. Media gave the program a lot of coverage. The idea was to make the payment of debt service "sustainable" for those of the forty-two countries that would finally benefit. There was no generosity in this decision of the creditors—merely a cold calculation as to how to keep the payments flowing in.

Within this framework, the G7, the IMF, and the World Bank promised to cancel 80 percent of the HIPC debt at the G7 Summit in Lyon, France, in June 1996. Three years later, at another G7 Summit, in Cologne, Germany, they announced an even greater reduction of 90 percent of the debt. This figure was put forward after pressure from the worldwide campaign for the abolition of the debt of the poor countries, known as the Jubilee 2000 campaign.

At the time, the UNDP reported that the sum the World Bank and the IMF planned to raise was less than the cost of a single US stealth bomber. As another basis for comparison, it was equivalent to the construction costs of the Euro Disney adventure park in the Paris area (UNDP 1997, 103). In five years (1996–2000), the amount that the IMF actually deposited in the trust fund serving to finance debt reduction was less than the amount required to pay their 2,300 civil servants for the year 2000. Yet another comparison: the amount spent by the IMF over five years to finance HIPC debt reduction was less than 2 percent of the sum committed to rescuing the creditors of Southeast Asia, Brazil, Russia, and Argentina over the same period. As for the World Bank, the amount it contributed was less than its annual profits of about $1.5 billion. In any case, what the World Bank and IMF pay out comes back to their coffers in the form of repayments, as neither of the two institutions ever gives up on a debt.

UNCTAD points out that none of the various debt-reduction measures has provided an acceptable solution to the problems of indebtedness and drastic austerity that dog the social budgets of the indebted countries.

> Current expectations regarding the implementation of the enhanced HIPC Initiative are unrealistic. The scale of debt relief will prove insufficient to ensure debt sustainability in the medium term...; moreover, the magnitude of debt relief, and its manner of delivery, will not have major direct effects on poverty reduction. (UNCTAD 2000d)

The OECD, which usually adopts the same position as the World Bank and the IMF, nevertheless warned against an optimistic interpretation of the results of the HIPC initiative in the short and the middle term in its *External Debt Statistics*, 1998–99: "The complete implementation of the initiative will not result in a reduction in value...of the debt, as the reductions will mainly take the form of remissions of interest payments and donations destined to finance debt servicing, and not direct reductions of the debt stock."

Aside from the extremely limited nature of the effort made by the creditors, there are two fundamental criticisms of the initiative. First, it forces the beneficiaries to renounce all sovereignty in matters of economic and social policy. The HIPC initiative means applying extra doses of neoliberal policies (see below). Second, the HIPC initiative increases the power of the World Bank and the IMF over the countries concerned.[1]

An unprecedented legitimacy crisis

Since 1997–98, the World Bank and the IMF have been suffering the worst legitimacy crisis of their history. Countless demonstrations of opposition have been held, both in countries subjected to their policies and in the highly industrialized countries. Since 1999, every one of their twice-yearly meetings (one in April, the other in September) has seen massive, radical counter-demonstrations. Both institutions are also undergoing an internal crisis. In 1999–2000, Joseph Stiglitz, chief economist and senior vice president of the World Bank, resigned, as did Ravi Kanbur, the director of the annual *World Development Report*. Both had been reformist elements within the World Bank. Finally, in the United States, the two institutions have been severely criticized by the majority of Republicans in Congress, as well as many Democrats. In 2000, the US congressional commission led by Republican Allan Meltzer, in which Jeffrey Sachs represented the Democrats, published its findings. It was revealed that, far from giving priority to the poorest countries, the international financial institutions devoted 80 percent of their operations to periphery countries that already have access to the money markets.

Back into the field with the Poverty Reduction Strategy

In an attempt to head off the legitimacy crisis, while at the same time keeping their neoliberal objectives firmly in view, in September 1999, the Bretton Woods institutions launched a new initiative: the Poverty Reduction Strategy. They ask the governments of the HIPC that wish to reduce their debts to draw up a Poverty Reduction Strategy Paper (PRSP; see glossary), to be handed over to (part of) civil society in their country. Officially, the idea is to give structural adjustment a human face by increasing health and education expenditure for ordinary people and special programs targeting the very poor. However, the PRSP must not in any way deviate from structural adjustment. This means fast-lane privatization of services (water, electricity, telecommunications, public transport); privatization or closure of public industrial companies, where such exist; increased taxation of the poor through generalized VAT (at a single rate of 18 percent, as is already the case in the West African Economic and Monetary Union); an end to tariff barriers (thus placing local producers in competition with the multinationals); liberalization of capital inflow and outflow (which generally results in a massive exit of capital); privatization of land; and cost-recovery policies in health and education.

That the HIPC accept these policies is the absolute condition laid down by the IMF, the World Bank, and the Paris Club in exchange for future reductions of payments and fresh adjustment loans. Moreover, since 1999, the IMF has proposed structural adjustment loans—relabeled Poverty Reduction and Growth Facility (PRGF)—to about ninety countries. These policies (PRSP and PRGF) will do no more than their predecessors in reducing real poverty. The Bretton Woods institutions behave like vandals, creating social mayhem, doing untold damage, then leaving the NGOs and local communities to pick up the pieces.

The World Bank is particularly concerned by NGOs and certain local authorities. Its strategy has been to win them over with "soft loans," destined to encourage microcredit (particularly for women's NGOs), to support health or education projects at a local level, or to better manage the remittances sent by migrant workers. The World Bank has created an agency for loans and donations to support NGOs and targets local authorities with loans for projects such as improved sanitation. Good governance has become one of its pet themes, to the extent of citing Porto Alegre, Brazil, in 2001 as an example of good town governance, thanks to its participatory budget system.

The results of this offensive World Bank strategy to win over civil society and gain legitimacy are not negligible. A number of NGOs and local authorities are collaborating with the World Bank.

The US administration discusses the World Bank's future

So many crises have erupted since 1994–95, and the competence of the IMF and the World Bank to deal with them has been so often called into question, that a heated debate has begun to unfold around the future role of the Bretton Woods institutions. Various high-level commissions have worked on the subject. In 1994, the Bretton Woods commission presided over by Paul Volcker (former president of the Federal Reserve) envisaged the possible merger of the IMF and the World Bank, but finally concluded that it was not advisable. As mentioned earlier, in 1999–2000, the Meltzer Commission, in which the Democrats took part, produced a consensual report pleading for the redefinition of the role of each of the international financial institutions. It was suggested that the World Bank should limit its activities to the poorest countries that do not have access to the financial markets and the IMF should center its activities on the other countries of the periphery. The World Bank would only provide aid via donations and would cease to make loans which, the commission found, only led to worse indebtedness. The HIPC debt should be canceled definitively. The conclusions of the Meltzer Commission were not heeded by the government, and the debate is far from over.

Anne Krueger (1998), appointed to the number two position in the IMF in 2001 by the Bush administration, calls attention to the differences between the 1970s and the late 1990s. She helps to clarify certain terms of the issue. In the early 1970s, the United States decided to raise the profile of the World Bank and IMF by reducing bilateral aid and increasing multilateral aid. Krueger goes on to say that, since then, global-scale liberalization has considerably reduced the scope for maneuver of the institutions, as private capital flows have taken over and the Cold War ended. She notes:

> Until the end of the Cold War, political support for development assistance through the IFIs and bilateral agencies originated from two groups: those on the right concerned with security, and those on the left supporting development objectives on humanitarian grounds. With the end of the Cold War, support from the right eroded and the Bank's effort to spread itself into new issues may reflect a search for a broader political support base.

She describes changes in the World Bank:

> Many of the accusations about the Bank's organizational ineffectiveness may originate from its efforts to extend into all directions in all countries. A strong case can be made that, in getting as involved as it has with environmental matters, coopera-

tion with NGOs, combating corruption, and embracing other "new issues," the Bank has moved far beyond its essential competence in addressing many of these issues, and in so doing, has over-stretched the capacity of its staff.

The World Bank, she explains, wants to keep a finger in all the pies; whereas, in fact, it should choose between three options:

(1) continue to be a development institution, focusing only on those countries that are truly poor and gradually phasing out activities in the middle-income countries; (2) continue to operate in all client countries, focusing on the "soft issues" of development such as women's rights, preservation of the environment, labor standards, and encouragement of non-governmental organizations (NGOs); or (3) to close down.

Krueger does not favor the third option and leaves the remaining two open for discussion. She does say, however, that eventually the decision will have to be made. Clearly, development is not the fundamental issue in her eyes. As for the way the two institutions are run, she insists that there is no question of modifying their constitutions by instigating "one-country one-vote." A merger between the World Bank and the IMF is not excluded, but would open a can of worms, as a new constitution would have to be debated, with the risk of one-country one-vote rearing its ugly head (Krueger 1998, 2015). Her view is that things should remain in the hands of the major powers.

In 2001, the year she became first deputy managing director of the IMF, Krueger was faced with the Argentine crisis. The popular uprising of December 19, 2001, brought down Argentine president Fernando de la Rúa and his minister of economy, Domingo Cavallo, both excellent pupils of the IMF. The ensuing suspension of repayments activated the internal IMF debate at the management level over a proposal Krueger made in November 2001. She suggested instigating a sovereign debt restructuring mechanism. In the spirit of the Bankruptcy Code in force in the United States at the time, especially its chapter 11, the indebted country faced with insolvency would be granted a period of respite. This would allow the bankrupt country, under the auspices of the IMF, to negotiate an agreement with its creditors (including the IMF). To implement Krueger's proposal, the IMF's statutes would have to change, requiring a majority vote of 85 percent.

In April 2003, at a meeting of the board of governors of the IMF in Washington DC, the Krueger proposal was officially dropped. The top management of the IMF was completely isolated. The Bush administration had expressed its opposition to the proposal, thus disavowing the woman who was supposed to enjoy Washington's full support. In fact, major US (and foreign) banks had made clear their opposition to the proposal. They did not approve the idea of strengthening a public multilateral body, not even the IMF, generally favorable to the interests of the large private financial organizations. Some indebted countries of the periphery also showed reticence at the idea of an even more powerful IMF.

This U-turn on the part of the Bush administration, which had originally given its support to Krueger's proposal, was undoubtedly motivated in part by tensions surrounding the war against Iraq, which began March 2003. Had the administration wanted to pass the Krueger proposal, they would have had to enter into negotiations with a large number of interlocutors within the IMF to obtain 85 percent of the votes. During these exchanges, governments of the periphery might have made certain embarrassing demands, for example, the guarantee that the voting quota of such and such country would be increased. Nevertheless, the isolation of the top management of the IMF certainly contributed to the enduring crisis of legitimacy of the Bretton Woods institutions.

Something else occurred to entrench this situation. In June 2003, the management of both the World Bank and the IMF had to state their position concerning a proposal made by a number of African governments, backed by several others. The proposal called for one or two extra seats for Africa on the respective executive boards of the two institutions. The IMF and the World Bank did not publicize the heated internal arguments caused by the proposal. Sub-Saharan Africa, with only two representatives for more than forty member states, failed in its bid. The crisis that the Bretton Woods institutions are going through is far from resolved, and the chances of democratic self-reform are remote.

The future of the World Bank and the IMF is a major issue for the social movements, as is the future of other big international institutions (the WTO, UNCTAD, the United Nations). The stakes are astronomical. Opinions are divided both among those in power and within the movements seeking alternatives. As for the latter, their decisions should hinge on which international institutions are able to promote the satisfaction of basic human rights, peaceful relations between peoples, social justice throughout the world, and protection of the environment.

---

1   For a detailed analysis of the HIPC initiative, see Damien Millet and Eric Toussaint, *Who Owes Who? 50 Questions about World Debt* (Zed Books 2004), also published as *The Debt Scam* (VAK Publications, 2003), especially questions 25–27.

12

World Bank and IMF structural adjustment programs

t is noteworthy that the same word appears indiscriminately in economic policy recommendations—whether made to the highly industrialized countries, the Third World, or countries of the former "socialist" camp. The neoliberal tendency has given rise to a near-monolithic slate of recipes for all of the countries of the world, whether in the North or South. The watchword is "flexibility." In the North, this has meant dismantling a number of important institutional safeguards and gutting the social gains that had initially gone hand in hand with the successes of postwar growth but progressively became a hindrance to capitalist profitability and accumulation. In the South, state intervention as such has become the target of the "letters of intention" that debtor countries negotiate with the IMF, which demand policies of social austerity.

While the IMF has had ties with the countries of the periphery for a long time, it has focused much more attention on them, and seen its power there grow, since the outbreak of the debt crisis in the 1980s. As for the World Bank, we have seen how it has played an ever more important role in the periphery since the end of the 1960s.

From the beginning of the 1980s on, the World Bank and IMF have teamed up to manage the debt crisis and implement adjustment policies. They have become, at the same stroke, large-scale debt collectors. One major paradox is that the IMF and World Bank have continued to tighten their hold over the countries of the periphery despite failure to meet their stated objective of restoring long-term growth, and though their policies have actually heightened financial instability. This has a boomerang effect: even as they tighten their grip on the indebted countries, the resulting crisis is undermining the two institutions, with an internal crisis and an external crisis of legitimacy.

However, since the 1994 Mexican crisis, the IMF has had the upper hand over the World Bank when it comes to defining government policies. It has come out even further on top in the wake of the 1997–98 Asian crisis. The

World Bank remains in charge when it comes to dealing with the poorest countries and with NGOs (in order to "co-opt" them), and setting up programs for the poorest sectors of the population in periphery countries.

As for the other omnipresent word, "adjustment," to what exactly are countries of the South expected to "adjust"? The world economy is not a united whole; it has a hierarchy. Developing countries cannot merely imitate policies pursued in industrialized countries at some point in the past. Therefore, the structural adjustment of these countries cannot offer any real prospects for development. Quite the opposite is true.

The stated objectives of adjustment loans

The defining essence of adjustment loan objectives can be found in Article I of the IMF Articles of Agreement: priority must be given to "balanced growth of international trade." As such, countries that always import more than they export need financial support so they are not excluded from international commerce. Without loans, they cannot buy. The IMF explains that such interventions not only enable these countries to continue to participate in international trade, but also, as a result of structural adjustment programs, lead them to increase such participation (Lenain 1993; Christin 1995; Norel and Saint-Alary 1992).

A fundamental passage in the second paragraph of Article I is systematically ignored: "*to contribute thereby to the promotion and maintenance of high levels of employment and real income.*"[1] Later we will see that the policies recommended and imposed by the IMF (and the World Bank) pull in exactly the opposite direction.

The IMF Articles of Agreement also stipulate:

"*The Fund shall adopt policies on the use of its general resources, including policies on stand-by or similar arrangements, and may adopt special policies for special balance of payments problems, that will assist members to solve their balance of payments problems in a manner consistent with the provisions of this Agreement and that will establish adequate safeguards for the temporary use of the general resources of the Fund.*"[2]

It is on this basis that the IMF intervenes directly in borrower countries to set their economic policies.

Adjustment programs are the best possible guarantee that a country will continue to service its debts. Indeed, the central priority of these programs is export revenue. A high percentage of these export earnings soon find their way back into IMF and World Bank coffers—since they have priority over other lenders—then into coffers of the private banks (in the London Club) and those of the Paris Club member states. Members of the London and Paris Clubs clearly have a stake in working with the IMF and World Bank.

Since the WTO was established in 1995, the G7 has instigated the holy trinity of neoliberal world order. The three institutions join forces to push forward the neoliberal agenda, which consists of subjecting every area of human activity and every type of natural resource to commercial trading. So-called adjustment programs contain a large section of structural reforms aimed at fulfilling certain objectives: to ensure regular debt payments, open up all of a country's areas of activity to trade and foreign capital, protect MNCs against nationalization measures or any specific constraints imposed by a given country, etc.

Debt and structural adjustment

Once countries are in debt, the IMF and the World Bank can force them (through a kind of economic blackmail) to reorient their macroeconomic policies in the way most in step with the interests of international creditors. The objective is to impose a relationship in which debt servicing becomes a matter of course, while debtor nations are kept in a straitjacket that prevents them from embarking on an independent national economic policy (Chossudovsky 1994).

Structural adjustment policies have been implemented on a grand scale. Although conditions vary greatly from one "adjusting" country to the next, the same economic remedies are applied the world over. Acceptance of IMF prescriptions—spelled out in economic stability pacts—is not only a precondition for obtaining loans from multilateral institutions, but also a green light for the London and Paris Clubs, foreign investors, commercial banking institutions, and bilateral lending agencies (Lenain 1993).

Not surprisingly, countries that do not accept the IMF's corrective measures encounter tremendous difficulties in restructuring their debts and obtaining new development financing and international aid. The IMF can also seriously undermine a country's economy by blocking access to the short-term credit needed for financing ongoing trade in basic goods. This is what happened in Argentina in December 2001, with terrible consequences (see chapter 16).

The IMF and World Bank have increasingly been called upon by holders of capital in the North to collect "bad loans" owed to commercial banks. Fresh funds in the form of short-term loans were aimed to force developing countries to pay their debts to commercial banks and foreign governments. New funds were provided to pay off old debts. The international financial institutions refinanced old debts, which became a method for forcing Third World countries to pay their debts as well as overdue payments on these debts. For example, after the brutal repression of the riots of 1989, the Venezuelan government had its "bad debts" turned into shares guaranteed by the international financial institutions. Not a penny from this IMF and World Bank rescue package actually remained in the country.

More recently, loans have been made to Korea, Thailand, Indonesia, the Philippines, Brazil (1999 and 2002–03), and to Argentina and Turkey (2000) by the IMF, World Bank, and other moneylenders. They are to be used to repay the short-term debt owed by these countries (above all their private companies) to the big speculators and institutional investors from the North and from within the region. The case of the Democratic Republic of the Congo (DRC) deserves special mention. Between 1993 and 2002, under three successive presidents (end of Mobutu's dictatorship, Laurent Désiré Kabila's presidency from 1997–2001, then the beginning of his son Joseph Kabila's), Zaire, soon to become the DRC, suspended its payments. In 2002, the World Bank and IMF turned on the credit taps to get the transfer of wealth from the Congo to its creditors flowing once more. New loans were granted on condition that the DRC resume payments and apply structural adjustment under its new name, the Poverty Reduction Strategy.

Macroeconomic reform and the structural adjustment program

Loans from international financial institutions (including the regional development banks linked to the World Bank) are provided as support for balance of payments—that is, short-term loans to finance imports and debt servicing. These loans are usually provided on condition that a certain set of policies will be implemented. In other words, these are political loans provided by the international institutions on condition that the government in question adopts a program of economic stabilization and structural economic reforms in line with their demands. Agreements for such political loans explicitly call for a scaling down of internal undertakings. Unlike conventional loans, these loans are never linked to investment projects.

Invariably, governments must prove to the IMF that they are "genuinely engaged in implementing economic reform" before loan negotiations can really begin. This process often unfolds in a framework known as the "IMF's secret program." The IMF lays down a series of policy guidelines and gives technical advice to a government—without the slightest backing in the form of a loan. The Indonesian government, for example, had to close a number of large banks in November 1997, before it could receive the funds promised by the IMF. The forced bankruptcy of these banks provoked panic within the population. The IMF had to recognize this tactical error at the beginning of January 1998 (*New York Times*, January 14, 1998). It then got the Indonesian dictator to sign an agreement of submission to the IMF under the imperious gaze of Michel

Camdessus, broadcast live on national and international television.

Once the loan is disbursed, the policy conditions are closely monitored on a quarterly basis by the Washington-based institutions. Loan payments are made in several installments and can be suspended if the required reforms no longer appear to be on track.

The division of labor between the IMF and World Bank

The IMF and the World Bank stand shoulder to shoulder when it comes to implementing structural adjustment programs. In a number of debtor countries, the government sets out its priorities in what is known as a letter of intent. Officially, the letter is drawn up by the debtor country; in reality this takes place under the supervision of the Bretton Woods institutions (Aglietta and Moatti 2000, 78).

There is a clear division of labor between the two Bretton Woods sister institutions. On the one hand, the IMF takes care of key negotiations over structural matters, keeping in mind the exchange rate and the budget deficit. On the other hand, the World Bank directly involves itself in structural reform through its local representatives and various technical missions. Moreover, the World Bank also has people working in the government ministries that are responsible for laying down the specific framework of the structural adjustment. Reforms to health care, education, industry, agriculture, transport, and the environment are all drawn up under the watchful eye of the World Bank.

The Bretton Woods institutions have a variety of lending mechanisms at their disposal and are quite prepared to use them, on condition that the country in question follows their policy recommendations.[3]

---

1   IMF, Articles of Agreement, Article I – Purposes, second paragraph http://www.imf.org/external/pubs/ft/aa/aa01.htm.

2   IMF, Articles of Agreement, Section 3. *Conditions governing use of the Fund's general resources. http://www.imf.org/external/pubs/ft/aa/aa05.htm#3.*

3   I have based this section, and the description in chapter 13 of the two phases of adjustment, on the work of Michel Chossudovsky in *La pauvreté des nations* (1994) and *The Globalization of Poverty* (1997). I have supplemented his analysis with my own, additions for which I am solely responsible.

13

The two phases
of structural adjustment

> *[S]taff members pore over numbers in the finance ministries and central banks and make themselves comfortable in five-star hotels in the capitals.... One should not see unemployment as just a statistic, an economic "body count," the unintended casualties in the fight against inflation or to ensure that Western banks get repaid. The unemployed are people, with families, whose lives are affected—sometimes devastated—by the economic policies that outsiders recommend, and, in the case of the IMF, effectively impose. Modern high-tech warfare is designed to remove physical contact: dropping bombs from 50,000 feet ensures that one does not "feel" what one does. Modern economic management is similar: from one's luxury hotel, one can callously impose policies about which one would think twice if one knew the people whose lives one was destroying.*
>
> —*Joseph Stiglitz*, Globalization and its Discontents[1]

An argument can be made that structural adjustment is divided into two distinct phases: "short-term" macroeconomic stabilization—involving currency devaluation, price liberalization, and budget austerity—followed by the implementation of a number of more fundamental structural reforms. Often, however, these structural reforms and the "economic stabilization" are implemented at the same time.

Phase I: Short-term economic stabilization in five steps

1. Devaluation and raised interest rates

Devaluation and the creation of a uniform exchange rate (eliminating exchange controls and multiple exchange rates) are vital tools in government policy. The Bretton Woods institutions explicitly carry out devaluation; the

IMF plays a central role in the decision to devalue. The exchange rate determines both the real prices paid to direct producers and the real value of their earnings. Price increases and the IMF-dictated de-indexing of salaries reduce these real earnings.

In some cases, devaluation provides a basis for the short-term reactivation of the entire export-oriented commercial agriculture sector. More often, however, profits only go to the big commercial operations and agricultural and industrial exporters. In French-speaking Africa, such devaluation is often called "tam-tam" devaluation. The wealthy classes receive enough advance warning to convert their local currency into hard currencies before the local currency is devalued. When the CFA franc (the currency used in thirteen of France's former West African colonies) was devalued by 50 percent in January 1994, those holders of capital who had changed their money into hard currency in time saw the value of their capital double.

Such devaluation usually encourages speculation against the national currency. The wealthy who sell national currency to buy hard currency and/or to invest their capital on the financial markets of the North make juicy profits immediately following devaluation by repatriating some or all of the money they had tucked away in a safe haven. The rich get richer, the poor poorer. A country's short-term gains after devaluation are inevitably erased once other competing Third World countries are forced to devalue. The Bretton Woods institutions often demand currency devaluation as a condition for entering into negotiations on structural adjustment loans.

The IMF also imposes significant increases in interest rates, both real and nominal, which affect domestic prices. This policy results in a collapse of credit for the country's agriculture and industry. Local businesspeople are put off by high interest rates and the lower classes, and even the middle classes, see a sharp fall in their access to credit, with a negative effect on consumption. Short-term credit remains available for external trade, but the national banking sector tends to cut itself off from the real economy. A policy of high interest rates adopted in countries such as Brazil and Mexico mobilize capital in the form of small investments. Indebted companies faced with rocketing credit repayments are often driven to bankruptcy. Part of the money owed to local banks becomes irrecoverable, which may also lead to bankruptcy. Higher interest rates also affect public authorities with debts on the local market (internal public debt): interest charges steeply increase. According to Stiglitz (2002, 17), "[T]he IMF's insistence on developing countries maintaining tight monetary policies has led to interest rates that would make job creation impossible even in the best of circumstances."

2. Budget austerity

The IMF imposes precise guidelines, taking stock of the budget deficit and the breakdown of government spending. These guidelines affect both operational spending and development spending. The Bretton Woods institutions dictate the dismissal of public-sector employees and drastic cuts in spending on social programs. These austerity measures affect all categories of public spending.

When the debt crisis began, the international financial institutions (IFIs) restricted their intervention to setting budget-deficit objectives that would enable the country in question to meet its debt-servicing obligations. Since the end of the 1980s, the World Bank has tightly controlled the very structure of public spending through what are known as public expenditure reviews. In this way, the breakdown of each ministry's spending is supervised by the Bretton Woods institutions. The World Bank recommends an "effective transfer of costs" from regular areas of spending to those "with a specific objective." According to the World Bank, the goal of "public-spending supervision" is to "promote poverty reduction through effective and efficient spending."

In addition, the structure of investment spending is forced to target a "specific objective." The public investment program, also under the supervision of the World Bank, demands that governments severely reduce the number of investment projects. The concept of "investment to meet an imposed objective" is used to reduce spending on basic economic and social infrastructure to the bare minimum.

As for spending on social programs, the IFIs have made a principle of recovering operating costs from users (patients in health care and the parents of children in education) and gradually withdrawing the state from basic health-care and education services. In the area of social spending, the concept of "loans granted to meet an imposed objective" is applied to what are known as "vulnerable groups." Austerity measures in the social sectors mean a shift from regular programs to specific-objective programs, which is largely responsible for the deterioration of user services such as schools, clinics, and hospitals. At the same time, austerity measures appear to legitimate the Washington-based institutions.

The budget deficit as a moving target

The IMF sees the budget deficit as a moving target. First, it fixes a budget-deficit target of 5 percent of GNP. The government meets this objective. In subsequent negotiations—or within the same loan agreement—the IMF reduces the target to 3.5 percent of GNP, arguing that the government's spending plans are inflationary. Once the government reaches the 3.5 percent goal, the IMF wants the deficit reduced to 1.5 percent of GNP, and so on. The rationale behind this whole exercise is obvious: ensuring that state revenues go toward servicing the foreign debt (Chossudovksy 1997).

Stiglitz (2002, 12) writes:

> Over the years since its inception, the IMF has changed markedly. Founded on the belief that markets often worked badly, it now champions market supremacy with ideological fervor. Founded on the belief that there is a need for international pressure on countries to have more expansionary economic policies—such as increasing expenditures, reducing taxes, or lowering interest rates to stimulate the economy—today the IMF typically provides funds only if countries engage in policies like cutting deficits, raising taxes, or raising interest rates that lead to a contraction of the economy. Keynes would be rolling over in his grave were he to see what has happened to his child.

3. Price liberalization

This measure aims to eliminate subsidies and/or price controls. It has an immediate impact on real earnings, whether in the formal or informal sector. The deregulation of prices on grains for household use and import liberalization on food reserves from the North are key components of this process. Subsidized European and North American agricultural products (Common Agricultural Policy subsidies in the case of the European Union) invade local markets. This reduces the earnings of local farmers and drives many of them to bankruptcy. In fact, it is not rare for the North's agricultural surpluses to be sold to the South at cut-rate prices.

Liberalization programs also have an effect on the prices of imported goods and raw materials. When combined with currency devaluation, liberalization measures boost the local price of imported inputs (fertilizers, herbicides, seeds, equipment, and so forth) and have an immediate impact on the price structure in most areas of economic activity. Stiglitz (2002, 77) evokes case of Indonesia, where "the IMF insisted on abolishing subsidies for food and kerosene (the fuel used for cooking by the poor) just as IMF policies had exacerbated the country's recession, with incomes and wages falling and unemployment soaring."

4. Setting the price of gas and public services

The state, under the supervision of the World Bank, sets the price of gas. Increases in the prices of gas and public services (often by several hundred percent) destabilize local producers. High domestic prices for gas—often pushed higher than the world market price—are felt throughout the cost structure of domestic industry and agriculture. Consequently, production costs are inflated well above prevailing local prices for goods, driving many companies to bankruptcy.

Periodic jumps imposed by the World Bank in the prices of gas and oil products (implemented alongside import liberalization for basic goods) create an "internal transit tax," intended to isolate local producers from their own internal market. In many developing countries, the high cost of gas paralyzes the transport of goods within the country. The high cost of transport—imposed by the IFIs—is a key factor preventing small local producers from selling their products in city markets, where they compete directly with agricultural products imported from Europe and North America.

As mentioned in step 2, the World Bank (and the IMF) has been pushing for all government services to be offered at cost or transferred to the private sector. This not only includes health care and education, but also communications, roads, electricity, and water. "The fact that *even the poor are entirely prepared to pay for most infrastructural services* makes it all the more possible to charge fees. Private-sector participation in management, financing and ownership will, in most cases, be necessary to give a commercial edge to infrastructure use" (World Bank 1994, 3) [emphasis mine].

5. De-indexation of salaries

The IMF imposes a reduction in real wages by de-indexing salaries and liberalizing the labor market. This means removing cost-of-living adjustment clauses from collective agreements and eliminating minimum-wage laws. Let us not forget that while real wages are one-fifth (in South Korea or the Czech Republic, for example), or even one-twentieth (in Mali or Haiti), of what is paid in the advanced capitalist countries, structural adjustment programs (SAPs) boost the price of basic household goods to levels seen in the developed capitalist world. In some cases, the prices are even higher.

Phase II: Structural adjustment proper in ten additional steps

Implementing "macroeconomic stabilization" is the condition for receiving IMF funds and renegotiation of the external debt with the Paris and London Clubs. Implementation of "necessary" structural reforms always follows. A division of labor exists between the IMF and the World Bank. The "necessary" economic reforms are "encouraged" with structural adjustment loans from the World Bank, through sectoral adjustment loans and Poverty Reduction and Growth Facility (PRGF) loans. The structural reform package has the following main components:

1. Trade liberalization

Stiglitz (2002, 16–17) writes:

Most of the advanced industrial countries—including the United States and Japan—had built up their economies by wisely and selectively protecting some of

> their industries until they were strong enough to compete with foreign compa-
> nies.... Forcing a developing country to open itself up to imported products that
> would compete with those produced by certain of its industries, industries that
> were dangerously vulnerable to competition from much stronger counterpart in-
> dustries in other countries, can have disastrous consequences—socially and eco-
> nomically. Jobs have systematically been destroyed—poor farmers in developing
> countries simply couldn't compete with the highly subsidized goods from Europe
> and America—before the countries' industrial and agricultural sectors were able to
> grow strong and create new jobs.... And because trade liberalization occurred be-
> fore safety nets were put into place, those who lost their jobs were forced into
> poverty. Liberalization has thus, too often, not been followed by the promised
> growth, but by increased misery.

Protectionist tariff barriers are eliminated in order to make the domestic economy more "competitive." In reality, trade liberalization destroys industrial production for the domestic market and "liberates" domestic capital from
genuinely productive activities.

2. Liberalization of the banking system, independence of the central bank, end of control of capital movement and exchange

This means privatizing state-owned banks and deregulating the commercial banking sector. The central bank loses control of monetary policy; interest
rates are set on the free market by commercial banks. It is worth recalling that
international agreements have opened domestic banking to foreign commercial banks. The tendency is toward a weakening of domestic banking institutions, whether state-owned or private.

The central bank is made independent of the executive and legislative authorities, which usually implies a change of constitution (as in Brazil, 2003).
Consequently, the government loses control of monetary policy and interest
rates. Central bank management is, in fact, directly accountable for its policies
to the major private banks—national and, above all, transnational—and to the
IMF.

> In some cases the agreements stipulated what the laws the country's Parliament
> would have to pass to meet IMF requirements or "targets"—and by when....
> .... In the case of Korea, for instance, the loans included a change in the charter
> of the Central Bank, to make it more independent of the political process....
> When, in Seoul, I asked the IMF team why they were doing this, I found the an-
> swer shocking (though by then it should not have come as a surprise): We always
> insist that countries have an independent central bank focusing on inflation."
> (Stiglitz 2002, 43–45)

The IMF and the World Bank also condition adjustment loans on ending
the control of capital movements and exchange control. According to the Bretton Woods institutions, this is to create a climate of confidence with regard to

potential investors. In reality, these two measures make the countries that adopt them easy prey for speculative attacks. Furthermore, they facilitate tax evasion and capital flight. Last, they encourage the transfer of funds linked to illegal trade and lead to an influx of dirty money. Laundering is made easy too, thanks to these reforms (deregulation of the banking sector, no more controls, etc.).

Another measure in the same vein is the encouragement, in exchange for impunity, of the "repatriation" to the South of capital deposited in secret accounts, including huge quantities of dirty money. Once it has been through the interbank market, the money is converted into local currency and used to buy the state assets and public land that the Bretton Woods institutions have decided must be sold as part of their policy of privatization.

> [T]he influx of hot money into and out of the country that so frequently follows after capital market liberalization leaves havoc in its wake. Small developing countries are like small boats. Rapid capital market liberalization, in the manner pushed by the IMF, amounted to setting them off on a voyage on a rough sea, before the holes in their hulls have been repaired, before the captain has received training, before life vests have been put on board. Even in the best circumstances, there was a high likelihood that they would be overturned when they were hit broadside by a big wave. (Stiglitz 2002, 17)

3. Privatization of state-owned firms

The privatization of state-owned companies and the renegotiation of a country's foreign debt are always linked. The most profitable of these companies are snapped up by foreign capital or consortiums (involving foreign and domestic capital). The proceeds from these sales go toward the Paris and London Clubs. In this way, international creditors and MNCs come to control state-owned concerns with practically no real investment (see the Argentine case in Chapter 16).

In the countries of the former Soviet Bloc, privatizations linked to measures such as those mentioned above led to massive buying up of public property by the new national capitalists (some of whom were members of the *nomenklatura* in power under the old bureaucratic regime). Criminal methods of accumulation of capital were systematically employed. The judicial affairs surrounding such Russian firms as Yukos, Sibneft, Menatep, and the oligarchic capitalists Khodorski, Abramovich, etc., are emblematic of the process encouraged by IMF and World Bank policies.

4. Tax reform

Reforms aim to undermine domestic production, on both the demand and supply sides. The introduction of value-added taxes (VAT) and sales taxes, alongside changes in the structure of direct taxation, means a greater tax burden for middle-income groups. Registering small producers, as well as workers and vendors in the informal sector, is part of World Bank policy aimed at increasing taxes.

One author who supports IMF fiscal policies presents them in the following way:

> The IMF encourages developing countries to undertake tax reforms in order to improve the allocation of economic resources. It therefore calls for the elimination of highly progressive income-tax schedules, since they create costly distortions in the way resources are allocated, open the door to tax fraud, and boost administrative spending on debt collection. IMF-recommended tax reforms also include an overhaul of taxes on foreign trade. (Lenain 1993, 55)

The author, Patrick Lenain, was at one point an IMF official. His remarks need no comment.

5. Land privatization

This policy involves issuing land titles while raising the ceiling below which access to property is denied. Such measures concentrate land in the hands of the wealthy few, while small farmers give up their land or mortgage it—only to become tenant farmers (sharecroppers) and seasonal agricultural laborers, or to join the ranks of the urban poor. The policy violates traditional land rights (in Africa and India, for example) and undermines the gains of authentic revolutionary transformations. In Mexico, for example, article 27 of the constitution, which enshrined the rights of indigenous peoples and poor farmers over collective lands known as *ejidos* (see chapter 15), was reformed in the early 1990s. This kind of land counterreform has been the object of huge mobilizations of poor farmers in Egypt since 1997.

Land privatization is also a way to repay the debt. The public-land sell-off generates state revenues, which are channeled to international creditors. Additional dirty money is also repatriated and laundered in the process, no questions asked.

6. Labor market reforms

The IMF and the World Bank recommend a loosening of labor-market regulations (usually hard-won through workers' struggles), arguing that institutional rigidities limit labor mobility and therefore cause unemployment (Lenain 1993; Decornoy 1995; Valier 1996). In 1995, the World Bank devoted its entire *World Development Report* to the question of work, under the title *Workers in an Integrating World*. The report does not beat around the bush—far from it: "The quest for greater worker mobility will often mean implementing measures that allow the process of job destruction—which will include dismissals in the public sector—to follow its course (*sic*) (World Bank 1995a, 8). The World Bank is fiercely opposed to establishing or maintaining benefits for the long-term unemployed. Such benefits, goes the argument, are themselves a cause of unemployment.

The World Bank defines a "voluntarist" labor market policy as a policy that

> seeks to help the unemployed find work and to improve the future prospects of those already working. This involves job-search assistance, training and job-creation initiatives. [On the other hand], a passive policy seeks to support the standard of living of those not working through monetary and other forms of assistance. (World Bank 1995a, VIII)

On the subject of wages, the World Bank comes out clearly against minimum-wage legislation in Third World countries. It argues that in places where a minimum wage exists, it is "too high in relation to the country's earnings and to other wages; even a small increase would reduce employment." The conclusion is unbending: "The establishment of a minimum wage may be of some use in industrialized countries, but it is difficult to justify in low- and middle-income countries" (World Bank 1995a, 88, 93).

7. Trade unions

According to the World Bank, trade unions heighten the "privileges" of workers in the formal sector and, as a result, "skew revenue distribution" to the detriment of that "mass of workers who make up the active population in the informal and rural sectors." It also finds that "trades unions have on occasion used their political power to oppose structural adjustment." Nevertheless, the World Bank is generous enough to tolerate the existence of unions: "It is not necessary to refuse to recognize the rights of workers for revenue growth to occur" (World Bank 1995a, 95, 96, 101).

8. Pension systems

In recent years, the World Bank has turned its attention to pension reform. It actively promotes capitalization-style (funded) pension systems based on the development of private pension funds and the reduction of pension costs for the state. In the countries where distributional pension schemes exist and are the financial mainstay of the pension system—i.e., the highly industrialized countries (especially Western Europe), the former Soviet Bloc, and some Third World countries (including China)—the World Bank actively encourages a counterreform to push back retirement age, reduce payouts, and create a private complementary scheme. Robert Holzmann (1999) explains, "As is well known, the staff study [of 1994] recommended a multi-pillar pension system—optimally consisting of a mandatory, publicly-managed, unfunded and a mandatory, but privately-managed funded pillar, as well as supplemental voluntary private funded schemes."

The World Bank has saluted the neoliberal reforms launched in France, Austria, the Czech Republic, and Brazil in 2002–03. Private pension funds, encouraged by the World Bank and big capitalist institutions, have been on the rise over the last two decades, for instance in Brazil, Chile, Argentina, Mexico, and also in South Africa, Eastern Europe, and some Asian countries. Holzmann (1999) admits "[M]any schemes that have been funded to some degree have been depleted of accumulated assets through outright diversion or a low rate of return, making the originally-promised benefits impossible." This has not led the World Bank to review its position, all the more since "repeated increases in the level of generosity can only reduce capital formation and, hence, the output level for current and future generations" (Holzmann 1999). Once again, the World Bank prioritizes the accumulation of capital with minimal recourse to solidarity mechanisms.

The pension reform carried out in Argentina in the 1990s, under the auspices of the IMF, ended in disaster. The private pension fund, known as AFJP, that was managing the capitalization-based pension scheme invested a considerable part of the contributions in Argentine public-debt bonds. Devaluation in early 2002, combined with the suspension of debt payments, reduced Argentine workers' savings to next to nothing. The development of AFJPs has also considerably reduced the state's tax revenues.

In Nicaragua, a similar reform was applied in the early 2000s. Workers under age forty-three pay into an obligatory private pension scheme. The private pension fund invested workers' savings in internal public-debt bonds; this debt will soon become unpayable, swelling beyond belief under World Bank and IMF policies. As for the public pension fund, it is now only supplied by the contributions of workers over forty-three years of age. The decision to do away with the contributions of workers under forty-three is bound to drive the public retirement fund to the wall, as it will have increasing numbers of retirees to pay out of an ever-diminishing kitty.

9. Poverty and the social safety net

The Bretton Woods institutions have abandoned the goal of poverty eradication, or even of generalized poverty reduction. Now, the goal is "managing poverty" to make it "bearable." At the same time that cuts are made in social spending, programs aimed at the poorest sectors are put together. This is meant to be a more effective system; yet, these targeted programs are combined with "cost recovery" and the "privatization" of health care and education (so people must now pay for medicine, medical visits, and school tuition).

The state has withdrawn from a number of sectors. Civilian organizations and NGOs now manage several programs previously run by government ministries, taking on the functions of local government. With funding frozen by SAPs, small-scale production and handicrafts, sub-contracting for export houses, training in local community groups, local employment schemes, and other such activities have been incorporated into the "social safety net." In this way, the fragile conditions for survival of the local populations are maintained, while the danger of social upheaval is contained.

10. Good governance

Although the World Bank denies it, since the beginning of the 1990s, the granting of loans has been linked explicitly to a series of political conditions. Good governance is one such condition. Although the implementation of SAPs absolutely requires a toughening of state authoritarianism, a facade of "democratization" is demanded as an adjunct to the "free" market. After SAP implementation caused popular revolts in a number of countries, the World Bank has made good governance a priority. No surprise here: governments that implement SAPs lose legitimacy in the eyes of the people, in as much as they appear to lose all autonomy in their relations with the IFIs. The World Bank's response is to wash its hands of the entire matter, holding the defects of the governments concerned responsible for popular disturbances. Good governance has become another way to keep debtor countries in line.

In 1990, Barber Conable, World Bank president from 1986–91, made the following declaration to a number of the World Bank's African governors:

> Let me be frank: political uncertainty and arbitrary rule in so many sub-Saharan African countries are major obstacles to their development.... In saying this, I'm not talking politics. Rather, I'm speaking as a defender of increased openness and responsibility, of respect for human rights and the rule of law. Governability is linked to economic development. Donor countries are increasingly indicating that they will cease to back inefficient systems which do not meet the population's basic needs. (Quoted in Lancaster 1993, 10)

For the World Bank, good governance is advantageous in two other ways: first, as a way to respond to ever more virulent international criticism (it reassures critics that funds provided to governments are managed so that the "aid" reaches the target groups, whether they are the poor or industrialists); second, as a strategy to establish a local network of nongovernmental bases of support to meet its objectives (local and foreign NGOs, the media, religious institutions, chambers of commerce, and employers' organizations). Good governance has become such a priority for the World Bank that it published a special report in 1992, *Governance and development.*

In 1985, Jean Leca provided the following definition of "good governance":

> The conformity of the governed results from a process complementary to that of
> the instrumental exchange of resources: the establishment of a reservoir of loyalty
> [within a framework of submission—*Toussaint*] that allows for the temporary ac-
> ceptance of an unfavorable exchange…. The legitimation of power can be defined
> as a process through which those that govern produce (or use) one (or more) sys-
> tem(s) of justification that enable them to appeal, should the need arise, to other
> centers of social power—to obtain effective obedience. (Leca and Papeni 1985, 19)

In fact, the development of good governance has nothing to do with democracy. Rather, it is a set of policies aimed to obtain consent from the oppressed. In many cases, talk of good governance is a flimsy cover for bolstering
executive power and undermining social movements.

The feasibility of austerity policies

The OECD's manual for governments

In a report intended for government eyes, Christian Morrisson (1996), an
official in the Organization for Economic Cooperation and Development
(OECD), provides a number of recommendations. The document makes one's
blood boil and requires little comment. Following are some extracts (the sub-
heads are mine).

First, on the objective of the report, called "The political feasibility of adjustment":

> The Development Center strives to identify and analyze the problems that will
> arise in the medium term, both for OECD member-countries and nonmember
> countries, and to determine trends in order to facilitate the development of appro-
> priate policies. This series of Economic Policy Notebooks provides the results of
> the Center's research work and is primarily meant for political leaders and deci-
> sion-makers concerned by its recommendations.
>
> Economic stabilization and adjustment policies may cause social disturbances;
> they may even endanger a country's stability. In this Economic Policy Notebook,
> the political consequences of such programs are analyzed. From five in-depth
> studies and two key country samples in Latin America and Africa, it can be ob-
> served that the political costs in terms of strikes, demonstrations, and riots are very
> different from one stabilization measure to the next. Our research has allowed us
> to define what a politically effective stabilization program should look like. It is
> possible to obtain the desired results while minimizing political risks. (3)

> [The] distinction between stabilization and structural adjustment is important
> from the political standpoint. In fact, a stabilization program is a kind of emer-
> gency treatment and necessarily includes many unpopular measures: household in-
> comes and consumption are sharply reduced through reductions in public-sector
> wages, subsidies and employment in the building industry. Structural adjustment
> measures, in contrast, can be spread over many years, and each measure creates at

the same time both winners and losers, so that the government can easily rely on a coalition of beneficiaries to defend its policy. (3)

In the case of adjustment..., [t]he government can compensate for [a] fall in popularity by repression in the case of unrest, but this entails numerous costs (increased dependence on the military, negative reactions abroad). (6)

Timing

We see a close link, with a delay of three to six months, between the announcement of stabilization measures and unrest, strikes or demonstrations. This delay is interesting, since it proves that, contrary to the theory of rational expectations, political reactions appear at the time when measures are actually applied, rather than when they are announced. (8)

A worthy role model

There are examples of success, however, where a government manages to avoid this risk, as in Morocco in 1983–85....
    .... This political success is explained by two factors: prudence and a good communication strategy.
    First, the price increases were planned with care....
    Second, the government was able to influence public opinion at the right times.... [I]n December, the king proclaimed that the poor should be protected against the adverse effects of adjustment.... In autumn 1985, when the prices of basic products were increased, the king made a speech on the theme "Yes to austerity, no to pauperization." (13)

The easiest to impose

[A] restrictive monetary policy, sharp cuts in public investment or a reduction in operating expenditures entail no risk for a government. This does not mean that these measures have no negative economic or social consequences.... Here, however, we are arguing in terms of only one criterion: minimizing the risk of unrest....
    Cuts in investment budgets rarely trigger any reaction, even when they are very severe: -40 percent in Morocco in three years, -40 percent in [Ivory Coast] in two years, -66 percent in Venezuela between 1982 and 1985, and -60 percent in the Philippines in two years. (14)

Errors to avoid

In this sense, a program which affected all groups equally (i.e. one which would be neutral from the social standpoint) would be more difficult to apply than a discriminatory program, which makes certain groups carry the cost of adjustment while others are spared so that they will support the government. (15)

Total control is best

In the case of real confrontation, the exceptional political weight of a head of state can be a decisive factor for the success of the adjustment. Governments always have a real capacity for resistance, of course, thanks to the police and the military. In several cases, including that of Ecuador, they did not yield when faced with riots. When unrest is such as to threaten the regime, however, the authority of the head of state is a very important factor. This was the case in Morocco, Côte d'Ivoire and Venezuela, where the President had this authority in 1990 because the same party controlled the presidency, the parliament and the biggest union. (15)

Massive privatization and dismissal: A realistic agenda

The problem of the reform of public enterprises, through restructuring or privatization, arises in many countries and always gives rise to strong opposition because it runs counter to a number of vested interests....

.... In certain cases, however, governments have managed to implement restructuring plans which would be rejected in developed countries. In Bolivia, for example, President Paz introduced extremely harsh measures in 1987: two-thirds of the workforce of the state tin-mining company were dismissed because this enterprise was responsible for one-third of the total fiscal deficit. This decision triggered a series of strikes and demonstrations, but the government held firm against the miners and remained in power for another three years. (18–19)

Use the IMF threat

[A]ny adjustment is a risky operation in political terms.... On the one hand, the opposition will impute all the costs of adjustment to the government, even if exogenous factors are partly responsible for the macroeconomic imbalances; while on the other, if the government waits for a financial crisis before adjusting, through fear of the opposition, it will have much less room for maneuver in a political crisis. At the extreme, it can in principle make no more concessions once it has made commitments to the IMF in order to obtain its help. In fact, such a decision may actually help a government, since it can then say to its critics that the agreement reached with the IMF was imposed on it, like it or not. (20)

The government nevertheless has ways of appealing to the pragmatism of civil servants. It can, for example, explain that since the IMF has imposed a cut of 20 per cent in the public-sector payroll, the only options open are either redundancies or pay cuts, and it prefers the second solution in the interest of all. (27)

North and South: How to undermine trade unionism

[I]f the workers in these [public-sector] enterprises are well organized, they can provide effective opposition to the government decision [to dismiss thousands of workers or to privatize]....

Any policy which weakens this type of corporatism[2] is desirable: from the economic standpoint, this would eliminate obstacles to growth, while from the political standpoint, the government would gain a certain freedom of action which could be important to it in a period of adjustment. It can be objected that this policy will arouse opposition, but it is better for the government to fight this battle when the economic situation is satisfactory than in a time of crisis, when it is weakened. Such a policy can take diverse forms: guarantee of minimum service, training of additional skilled workers, privatization or splitting into several competing enterprises, where this is possible. (21)

Measures to avoid

Many of [the inhabitants of the shantytowns or the poor districts] feel frustrated and excluded in comparison with the rest of the urban population. Vandalizing and looting shops in the more prosperous districts thus enables them to vent their feelings. If a stabilization measure—a cut in subsidies, for example—causes a sharp increase in the prices of basic foodstuffs, these populations will react violently in their despair. Such a measure suddenly reduces their already extremely low standard of living, and once they have arrived at this point, the poor have nothing more to lose. (24)

[T]he first precaution to take is to avoid laxist policies in periods of prosperity, because such policies create "acquired rights" which are difficult to call into question later on. (26)

If it is impossible to avoid a price increase, a number of precautions must be taken. It is necessary, as in Morocco in 1983–84, to increase the prices of intermediates first, not those of basic products consumed by poor households. If the prices of the latter are to be increased, it is necessary to proceed by imposing moderate increases (less than 20 percent) over a period of time. (25)

Teachers' strikes: Innocuous were it not for the kids

A teachers' strike does not in itself cause much trouble for the government, but it is indirectly dangerous, as we have seen, since it frees young people to demonstrate. (27)

A winning strategy for cutting salaries: Divide and rule

[B]onuses can be eliminated in certain departments, using a discriminatory policy so that all civil servants will not join together in a common front. It is obviously inadvisable to eliminate the bonuses paid to security forces in difficult political circumstances when the government may have need of them. (27)

Nothing is politically more dangerous than taking economy-wide measures to solve a macroeconomic problem. For example, if civil service wages are to be reduced, the government should cut them in one sector, freeze them in nominal terms in another and even increase them in a politically sensitive sector. (28–29)

Easy measures to apply

[W]e can now recommend many measures which cause no political difficulty. To reduce the fiscal deficit, very substantial cuts in public investment or the trimming of operating expenditure involve no political risk. If operating expenditure is trimmed, the quantity of service should not be reduced, even if the quality has to suffer. For example, operating credits for schools or universities may be reduced, but it would be dangerous to restrict the number of students. Families will react violently if children are refused admission, but not to a gradual reduction in the quality of the education given, and the school can progressively and for particular purposes obtain a contribution from the families, or eliminate a given activity. This should be done case by case, in one school but not in the neighboring establishment, so that any general discontent of the population is avoided. (28)

How to ensure a strong government

If a government is to have sufficient room for maneuver to adjust, it must be supported by one or two big parties in the parliamentary majority, not by a coalition of small parties, which means that a straight majority system for parliamentary elections is to be preferred to proportional representation (or at least it is advisable to have a combination of the two). There are other methods of reinforcing the executive, such as the possibility of temporary special powers or *ex post* control by the judicial power, to prevent the *ex ante* blocking of the program by the judiciary. A referendum may be an effective weapon for a government provided that only the government can initiate it. (32)

Overall effects of IMF and World Bank policies

Social consequences of structural adjustment programs

1. Education

Educational institutions have deteriorated; some have closed, and teachers have either been dismissed for lack of funds or gone months without pay. The shortage of funds has been compensated for through tuition fees and special charges collected through parent associations and local communities. This has meant the partial privatization of essential social services and the de facto exclusion of broad sectors of the population, especially in rural areas.

Two explicit conditions for adjustment loans are a freeze in the number of diplomas awarded in teaching colleges and an increase in the number of students per teacher. Education budgets are being slashed, and children spend only a half-day at school. "Two-way flow classes" are created as a result, with each teacher taking separate morning and afternoon classes (Ndiaye 1994). Each teacher now does the work of two, and the money saved goes toward repaying government debt. These measures—carried out in the name of "cost efficiency"—are still seen as falling short of the mark. In sub-Saharan Africa, some lenders have proposed a system whereby teachers would lose their salaries in exchange for small loans to set up their own "private schools." In this system, however, the ministry of education would still be responsible for maintaining the "quality" of teaching.

In Africa, primary school enrolment had risen from 41 percent of eligible children in 1965, to 79 percent in 1980. By 1988, however, it had fallen back to 67 percent (UNDP 1992). In Zambia, between 1990 and 1993, the government spent $37 million on primary education and $1.3 billion on debt servicing. In other words, for every dollar invested in primary education, $35 left the country to repay the debt. By 1995, the government was spending six times less on primary education than it had ten years earlier. In fact, 80 percent of primary-school expenses were borne by the children's families.

Stiglitz (2002, 51–52) recalls:

> In 2001, Congress passed and the president signed a law requiring the United States to oppose proposals for the international financial institutions to charge fees for elementary school (a practice that goes under the seeming innocuous name of "cost recovery"). Yet the US executive director simply ignored the law, and the se-

crecy of the institutions made it difficult for Congress—or anyone else—to see what was going on. Only because of a leak was the matter discovered, generating outrage among congressmen and women accustomed to bureaucratic maneuvering.

2. Health care

The international institutions claim that state subsidies to health care create undesirable "market distortions," which "benefit the rich." Moreover, in the name of "greater equity" and "efficiency," they argue that users of primary health-care services should pay fees, even if they are from impoverished rural communities.

The World Bank also calculates that total annual spending of eight dollars per person is more than enough to provide acceptable standards of clinical care. This has meant an across-the-board collapse of preventive and curative medicine: medical supplies are lacking, working conditions are horrendous, and staff are poorly paid—if they are paid at all. Public health facilities in sub-Saharan Africa, and some countries of Latin America and Asia, have actually become breeding grounds for sickness and infection. Indeed, lack of funding for medical supplies (including syringes and bandages) and equipment, and price increases (recommended by the World Bank) for electricity, water, and fuel (necessary for sterilizing instruments, for example) have increased the likelihood of infection (including HIV).

Thanks to these draconian austerity measures, tremendous social inequality now exists in access to health-care services. The state has significantly withdrawn itself from health matters, the already high percentage of people lacking health care has grown even higher, and once-eradicated infectious diseases are on the rise. The rise in infectious disease is also linked to drops in public spending on preventive measures—such as improved sewers and access to drinking water.

The infant mortality rate (IMR) is a reliable indicator of a country's well-being. The implementation of SAPs in African countries has eliminated entirely the advances made with great difficulty during the previous fifteen years. The most striking example is in Mali, where the IMR had dropped by 23 percent between 1960 and 1980, but increased by 26.5 percent between 1980 and 1985. Nutrition and food security are two key factors in health. A UNICEF study in ten countries on the effects of adjustment on health concluded that children's nutrition had declined in eight of the ten countries. In Zambia, between 1980 and 1984—the period when SAPs were being implemented—death from malnutrition rose from 2 percent to 6 percent for children ages 0–11 months, and from 38 percent to 62 percent for children ages 1–14 years. By 1995, the Zambian government was spending 30 percent less on health care than ten years earlier. One consequence: infant mortality rose by 20 percent in ten years.

The IMF and the World Bank argue that users should pay for health-care services. Consequently, in Mozambique, the number of consultations at the Maputo Central Hospital dropped by 24 percent between 1986 and 1987. In Malaysia, even before the crisis that broke in 1997–98, 40 percent of the population could not afford private health-care services (Balasubramaniam 1996). As for maternal health, the number of women in Nigeria using the capital city's main maternity ward for childbirth dropped from 6,535 in 1983 (beginning of SAP), to 4,377 in 1985, and 2,991 in 1988 (Bruno Dujardin, Antwerp Institute of Tropical Medicine).

There is a direct link between the spread of AIDS, malaria, and tuberculosis and structural adjustment programs. As a crowning irony, the World Bank has been entrusted with running the Global Fund, founded by the UN in June 2001, and highly promoted at the G7 summit in Genoa, Italy, that July. The purpose of the Global Fund is to take the lead in fighting AIDS, malaria, and tuberculosis.

Social costs described as "side effects"

In macroeconomic terms, these health and education measures lead to the disintegration of a debtor country's human resources. According to the UNDP 1992 report: "As a result of the economic crisis of the 1980s and the SAPs adopted in response, social spending has been sharply reduced in a large number of heavily indebted countries. This has had a direct effect on the population's standard of living, infant mortality, school enrollment and nutrition."

Through the prism of IMF and World Bank ideology, however, the "social costs" of SAPs are a "separate" matter. "Undesirable side effects" cannot be blamed on the economic model. They belong to a "separate sector": the social sector. According to the IMF and World Bank, the social costs are compensated for by the "economic benefits" of macroeconomic stabilization. Social costs are "short-term" while "economic benefits" are long-term.

Economic consequences of adjustment policies

Production for the domestic market is severely depressed as a result of reductions in real salaries, import liberalization, and tax and price reform. IMF measures are theoretically designed to help countries restructure their economies in order to create a surplus in their trade balance—thereby enabling them to repay their debts and embark upon a process of economic reconstruction. In fact, the exact opposite occurs. Austerity undermines a country's capacity for recovery and prevents it from reducing its debt burden. The only thing austerity more or less ensures is that interest payments on debt will be met.

IMF measures actually increase a country's debt burden:

- loans granted on the basis of adjustment policies, in order to repay old debts, increase both total debt and debt servicing;

- in a context of trade liberalization and the destruction of domestic production, short-term loans are granted to enable the country to continue importing goods from the world market;

- total import costs increase following currency devaluation;

- there is little or no capital accumulation in sectors not tied directly to the export sector.

Macroeconomic stabilization and SAPs are powerful tools in the service of an economic restructuring that adversely affects the living standards of millions of people. SAPs are directly responsible for the process of mass impoverishment described thus far. The implementation of the "economic remedies" of the IMF and World Bank has led to the slashing of real wages and the strengthening of an export economy that feeds off a low-wage workforce. The same "recipe" of budget austerity, trade liberalization, and privatization has been implemented simultaneously in more than one hundred debtor countries in the Third World and the former Soviet Bloc.

Political consequences

Most debtor countries lose part or all of their economic sovereignty, along with control over economic and monetary policy. The central bank and ministry of finance are reorganized; some state institutions fall apart, paving the way for outside "economic supervision." The local teams and missions of the IMF and World Bank come to form a "parallel government," which overrides local organizations and the national parliament. Countries not respecting the IMF's "performance goals" are blacklisted. Sudan is on such a list today, as was Nicaragua between 1979 and 1990.

The IMF demands that the internal security apparatus be strengthened (c.f. the case of Algeria). Political repression—with the collaboration of the ruling classes of the Third World—supports the parallel process of economic repression. The tremendous despair of a population pauperized by the market economy is a source of riots against SAPs and brutally repressed uprisings.

Structural adjustment is one of the main techniques for economic constraint used by states in the center against the periphery. Structural adjustment—implemented in more than one hundred countries simultaneously—has a devastating social impact, negatively affecting the living and working conditions of some four billion individuals (Chossudovsky 1994, 1997).

The implementation of SAPs in many debtor countries leads to the "internationalization" of their macroeconomic policy, under the direct control of the IMF and the World Bank—which represent powerful financial and political interests (the Paris and London Clubs, the G7, and the closed circle of the main MNCs). This new form of political and economic domination—a kind of market colonialism—oppresses peoples and governments through the impersonal interaction (and deliberate manipulation) of market forces. The Washington-based bureaucracy is given the task of carrying out an overall economic enterprise affecting the living and working conditions of more than 80 percent of the world's population.

At no point in history has the "free" market—given global reach through macroeconomic processes—played such a huge role in the destinies of "sovereign" nations. The restructuring of the global economy under the watchful eye of the Washington-based financial institutions has increasingly denied the countries of the Third World the possibility of building a national economy. The internationalization of economic policy has turned these countries into economic open territory and their national economies into reservoirs of cheap labor and raw materials.

Price unification and compartmentalization of the labor market

While the standard of living between countries of the North and those of the South differ significantly, the devaluation of national currencies (see above) and the deregulation of internal markets (through SAPs) lead to the dollarization of domestic prices. Domestic prices for food are increasingly aligned with world-market prices.

This new global economic order—based on the internationalization of commodity prices and a fully integrated world market—operates with two distinct "labor markets," increasingly cut off from one another. In other words, this global market system is characterized by a dual structure for wages and labor costs, separating countries of the periphery and those of the center. While prices are unified and aligned with those of the world market, wages (and the cost of labor) in the Third World and Eastern Europe are, on average, ten to twenty times lower than those in OECD countries. Furthermore, with the shutting of US and Western European borders, the South's workforce can no longer circulate freely and sell its labor in the countries of the North. This fortifies the barriers separating labor markets on a global scale.

Reducing the role of the state
and eliminating autonomous national projects

The World Bank (1995) stresses the sheer scale for humankind of reducing the role of the state: "Of the world's 2.5 billion workers, 1.4 billion live in countries facing the difficult task of definitively emerging from a system of state intervention, excessive protectionism and centralized planning." (7)

> In sub-Saharan Africa, Latin America and South Asia, most countries have pursued differing degrees of autonomous development that protected certain industries and discriminated against agriculture. These strategies benefited a limited number of privileged people (holders of capital and workers employed in the protected sector). Privileges were often defended with intervention of an institutional sort (bans on dismissal in Latin America, excessive public-sector hiring in sub-Saharan Africa and South Asia) instead of being based on an increase in demand for labor or improvements in productivity. (16)

> Nothing is better for growth and improvements in the standard of living of workers than developments of the market that encourage companies and workers to invest in physical capital, new techniques and training. Some countries attempted to help workers with investment policies benefiting industry to the detriment of agriculture—through protecting from international competition the jobs of a small number of favored workers in the industrial sector, decreeing salary rises and creating excess jobs in the public sector. These attempts have ended in failure, whether in Latin America, the former Soviet Union or elsewhere. (3)

A number of observations can be made about these statements from the World Bank. First, there is systematic wangling to present workers in the formal sector as privileged to the same degree as holders of capital. In the world according to the World Bank, there is no class antagonism between capitalists, on the one hand, and workers (whether small farmers, factory workers, education and health-care workers, or unemployed), on the other. According to the World Bank, the real antagonism is between those with "privileges" (workers in the protected sector, state-sector employers, and private employers protected by the state), on the one hand, and the poor (the unemployed, informal-sector workers), on the other. Second, the state played a negative role in most of the economies of the South and East; its role must therefore be cut back. Third, attempts at autonomous development all ended in failure. Fourth, one can sense the glee of the report's authors over the enormous opportunities opened up for neoliberal policies in regions as different as Latin America, Africa, South Asia, and the former Soviet Union. This jubilation even takes on a ruthlessly vengeful tone in the following passage on the countries of the former Soviet bloc: "Considering themselves to be the champions of labor, they guaranteed their workers periodic wage increases and cradle-to-grave social protection—and therefore saw no need for free and independent trade unions" (World Bank 1995, 16).

Need we point out that it is sheer demagogy for the World Bank to mention the absence of free trades unions, given that it has supported (and continues to support) any number of dictatorships, for instance, Chile under Pinochet or Romania under Ceausescu, to name only two examples? Clearly, the World Bank's main priority is eliminating state interventionism and attempts at autonomous development and planning.

Yet, as a rule, countries in the periphery that have scored successes have done so largely by relying on the active role of the state. This is particularly true of countries not long ago seen as models of success: South Korea, Taiwan, Malaysia, Thailand, Brazil, and Mexico. Whether run by the national bourgeoisie, sections of the petty bourgeoisie, or a dictatorial bureaucracy in the countries of the so-called socialist bloc, the state played a central role in spurring real, if deformed, development. The "overdevelopment" of the state in the countries of the periphery (leaving aside the socialist bloc) is a function of the weakness of the local capitalist class. The state was a crutch for a local bourgeoisie handicapped by long years of colonial exploitation. By shrinking the role of the state in the periphery, the World Bank seeks to heighten the dependence of these countries on big capital at the center.

For those seeking a progressive answer to this challenge, a number of pitfalls must be avoided. It is wrong, for example, to defend the state per se, as if its social content were neutral and its role globally positive. In the capitalist countries of the South, the state is a force for domination in the hands of the local exploiting classes. This state organizes the repression of people's movements and enables the capitalist class to amass profits in peace. The neoliberals should not have a monopoly on criticism of the state.

Indeed, Karl Marx was not the only one to decry the exploitative character of the capitalist state. The classical economist Adam Smith wrote, "Civil government, so for it is instituted for the security of property, is in reality instituted for the defense of the rich against the poor, or of those who have some property against those who have none at all" (Smith 1983). The World Bank and the neoliberals might be able to claim this passage as their own, on condition that the last part is removed. In their demagogic worldview, "the rich" are state-sector workers; these workers use the state to exploit the poor. However, it is pure communist heresy to say that the state was set up to defend the private property of the rich against those who have none.

There is good reason to fight the state, and replace it. The overthrow of the capitalist state comes as part of an authentic emancipating revolution. This revolution must also end with the withering away of the new state structures, which are established for a transitional period. The objective is indeed the elimination of the state—not to give free reign to market forces, but rather to replace class dictatorship with a free association of working people.

This brings us to the following question: what do the World Bank and the neoliberals have in mind when they vituperate against the state? Is it not the system of social security partially financed from state funds? Of overly accessible public education and health-care programs? And of labor laws that more or less

The causes of underdevelopment
and the strategic significance of neoliberalism

A hierarchical world economy was progressively established between the sixteenth century and the beginning of the twentieth century. The violence that accompanied Western European expansion connected the different regions of the planet. At the beginning of the twentieth century, three centers of power emerged as the world's dominant powers: the Euro-

Continued, next page ▶

protect workers against unjust dismissal? The main targets for neoliberal ire are the fragments of democracy and collective solidarity that exist within the state, and whose existence the state guarantees. These fragments of democracy and collective solidarity stem from a mix of social gains secured through tremendous struggle by the oppressed and concessions made by the rulers to maintain social peace. We must protect these fragments of democracy and solidarity.

The World Bank seeks to dismantle other areas of state authority. It insists on the elimination of remaining legislation protecting domestic markets in the countries of the South. It seeks to eliminate the control that some states in the South still have over strategic industries and natural resources. For the World Bank, these things must be eliminated to allow for the totally free circulation of capital—which can only bolster the supremacy of MNCs and the economies of the North.

In this respect, we must learn to handle certain lines of argument with caution, lest we give credence to World Bank demagogy. The World Bank argues, for example, that the privatization of state-run enterprises reduces corruption, increases company efficiency, and curtails corrupt state bureaucracy. Let us not jump from the frying pan into the fire: there is surely no need, on the eve of the third millennium, to demonstrate that private capitalist management is inefficient and corrupt. Rather, there is a need for strict control of public administration. This means building active social movements and carrying out thoroughgoing political and legal reforms.

---

1   This chapter is rich in quotations from *Globalization and Its Discontents* (Stiglitz 2002). This is justified by the fact that he was both an actor and a privileged witness of the World Bank/IMF policies analyzed in this chapter. However, the solutions suggested by Stiglitz tend to let the World Bank off the hook in several areas, as his criticism is directed mainly at the IMF; and the solutions he proposes are not equal to the challenges he identifies so well. Nevertheless, Stiglitz's book is a precious tool and recommended reading.

2   Morrisson uses the term "corporatism" in reference to the trade union movement.

▶ *Continued from previous page*

pean continent, led by Great Britain; the United States (British colonies until the end of the eighteenth century); and Japan. Together they constitute the "center," in contradistinction to the "periphery" they dominate.

This process involved the pillage of entire peoples by Europe's colonial powers; it also destroyed advanced civilizations that could otherwise have evolved in a pluralistic framework in a potentially noncapitalist direction. The Inca, Aztec (Galeano 1970), Indian (South Asian), and African civilizations were partially or totally destroyed. It was not, however, for lack of resistance. Karl Marx described Indian and Chinese resistance in the following terms:

> The obstacles that the internal solidity and articulation of pre-capitalist national modes of production oppose to the solvent effect of trade are strikingly apparent in the English commerce with India and China. There the broad basis of the mode of production is formed by the union between small-scale agriculture and domestic industry, on top of which we have in the Indian case the form of village communities based on common property in the soil, which was also the original form in China. In India, moreover, the English applied their direct political and economic power, as masters and landlords, to destroying these small economic communities. In so far as English trade has had a revolutionary effect on the mode of production in India, this is simply to the extent that the low price of English commodities has destroyed spinning and weaving, which form an age-old and integral part of this unity of industrial and agricultural production. In this way it has torn the community to pieces. Even here, their work of dissolution is succeeding only very gradually. These effects are felt still less in China, where no assistance is provided by direct political force." (Marx, *Capital*, vol. 3, 451–52).

The accumulation of capital also took place within the countries of Europe. The bourgeoisie enriched itself through the impoverishment of other social classes (including the nobility). It expelled a section of the peasantry from the lands peasants worked to make them work in factories.

Nor did this process occur without resistance in Europe. There were peasant revolts, and the bourgeoisie had to oblige a sizeable number of proletarians to work in the factories (thus the laws against begging, punishable by forced labor).

Back to the international arena, the worldwide primitive accumulation of capital occurred not only through outright pillage, but also through unequal exchange. Marx describes this process in *Capital*, vol. 3, in the section on foreign trade.

> Capital invested in foreign trade can yield a higher rate of profit, firstly, because it competes with commodities produced by other countries with less

developed production facilities, so that the more advanced country sells its goods above their value, even though still more cheaply than its competitors. In so far as the labor of the more advanced country is valorized here as labor of a higher specific weight, the profit rate rises, since labor that is not paid as qualitatively higher is nevertheless sold as such. The same relationship may hold towards the country to which goods are exported and from which goods are imported: i.e. such a country gives more objectified labor in kind than it receives, even though it still receives the goods in question more cheaply than it could produce them itself. (Marx, *Capital*, vol. 3, 344–45)

Marx is talking about the advantages that capitalists secure from foreign trade, not only as a result of unequal trade, but also as a way to reduce production costs—enabling the capitalist system to counterbalance the tendency of profit rates to fall.

Marx's analysis of the nineteenth century remains valid today for understanding unequal exchange between countries with different levels of productivity—in particular, between industrialized capitalist countries and the countries of the periphery. Indeed, the most industrialized countries export to less industrialized countries goods that can be sold at a lower price than what it would cost the countries of the South to produce them. For example, when capitalists in the most industrialized countries sell industrial goods to the countries of the South, they can make surplus profit while remaining competitive. For a country of the South to begin to produce industrial goods without confronting competition from the North, it would need to subsidize domestic industry and erect protectionist barriers—in the way that the United States did when it broke from the British Crown in the late eighteenth century. Such an approach gives less industrialized countries time to reach a stage in the cumulative process of industrialization where they can produce goods at comparable levels of productivity to their competitors in the North. This is what South Korea managed to accomplish for certain types of goods.

Countries of the periphery have faced a twin difficulty: in the first place, they were pillaged; second, the only path left open to them was that of entering the world market under the wing of the center's main powers. Countries electing to industrialize have had to do so within the framework of a world market flooded with Western industrial goods. Ernest Mandel (1968a, 153–54) explains:

In other words, while the world market and global economy powerfully stimulated the industrialization of the West from the sixteenth century to

Continued, next page ▶

▶*Continued from previous page*

the nineteenth century..., since the end of the nineteenth century the world market and global economy have been among the biggest obstacles to the industrialization of the Third World, precisely in so far as they act as a brake on the accumulation of industrial capital.

To understand this brake on development, one must consider the social structure of societies in the periphery—clearly analyzing this structure with the precise features of each country and bloc of countries in mind. For example, a world of difference exists between two large components of the periphery: Latin America and Africa. Latin America has had formal independence since the nineteenth century, the point at which the colonization of Africa began in earnest. Latin America saw the beginnings of industrialization in line with the first phase of the industrial revolution in Europe. Whatever industrialization exists in Africa—and in some countries of sub-Saharan Africa there is none—goes back no further than the first half of the twentieth century. Latin America's bourgeoisie has a long history behind them; those of Africa are still in the process of formation in a number of countries. Indeed, they often trace their roots back no further than the new state machinery that emerged in the wake of their countries' national independence in the 1950s and 1960s. Between these two continents, the differences are striking. Yet, they have enough in common (along with most of Asia) to belong to the periphery.

The brake on development does not only stem from the periphery's subordinate relationship to the center; it also results from the class structure of the countries of the periphery and the inability of the local bourgeoisie to unleash a cumulative process of growth involving the development of the domestic market.

With this in mind, one can understand the strategic significance of the neoliberal onslaught of the last twenty years of the twentieth century. For the overwhelming majority of countries in the South and from the former socialist bloc, the possibilities for autonomous development are smaller than during the previous historical period. The economies of these countries are more than ever before faced with competition from the goods and capital of the countries of the center.

The drastic slimming treatment—and even plain and simple dismantling—imposed on the states of the periphery aims to eliminate obstacles to the expansion and two-way flows of capital controlled by the countries of the center. The objective of the dominant classes in the North—with the complicity of the rulers of the South and the East—is clear. This does not mean that some governments in the periphery will not try to maneuver their way to retain control over some strategic sectors of "their" economies. More importantly, nor does it mean that the oppressed will not show a tremendous capacity for resistance—which could take matters in a different direction: toward a socially just form of development.

14
Neoliberal ideology and politics: Historical perspectives

Since the 1970s, neoliberal ideology has progressively come to dominate economic and political thinking. It is promoted by universities, the main economic journals, and the media. Both right-wing and left-wing governments—with perhaps a few exceptions—have adopted it. Neoliberal ideology appears to be all-conquering not only in the industrialized countries of the North, but also in Eastern Europe (including the Russian Federation) and the countries of the Third World. Numerous Third World regimes that previously promoted socialist-type (or even "Marxist-Leninist") ideas of the pro-Moscow or pro-Beijing variety have now jumped onto the neoliberal bandwagon.

Purveyors of the current neoliberal fashion identify with an incoherent and eclectic set of economic and political ideas originating with David Hume (1711–76), Adam Smith (1723–90), Jean-Baptiste Say (1767–1832), David Ricardo (1772–1823), and even Immanuel Kant (1724–1804). However, before analyzing the new neoliberal fashion, it is useful to examine what immediately preceded it.

1930s–1970s: Liberalism eclipsed

After occupying the center stage in the nineteenth century and the first third of the twentieth century, liberal thought was eclipsed for the long period that lasted from the middle of the 1930s to the end of the 1970s.

During this time—from the 1930s in North and South America; after the Second World War in Europe—policies involving strong government intervention in the economy came to hold sway. This was true of the United States under Franklin Roosevelt's New Deal in the 1930s (see glossary) and thirty years later under the Kennedy administration. It was true of Britain under Beveridge (advised by J.M. Keynes) during the Second World War and under subsequent Labour governments. After the Second World War, it was true of France, Germany, Holland, Belgium, and the Scandinavian countries. Keynesianism, whether of the social-democratic, "socialist," or social-Christian variety, dominated economic thinking.

In the countries of Eastern Europe, a dogmatic and authoritarian version of Marxism backed by bureaucratic regimes came to dominate. Large-scale nationalizations of private companies followed the establishment of "people's democracies" after the Second World War.

In a certain number of key Third World countries, developmentalist, nationalist, and even socialist policies came to the fore, as in China after the 1949 revolution. Anticommunist regimes in the Third World, such as those in South Korea and Taiwan, carried out radical agrarian reforms and built a strong industrial sector under the wing of the state. This is the central (and well-hidden) reason for the economic "miracle" that took place in these two "tiger" economies. The policies that created the past successes of South Korea and Taiwan stand in stark contrast to neoliberal prescriptions—a point that cannot be overemphasized.

The eclipse of liberalism came about as a result of the prolonged economic crisis that began with the Wall Street crash in 1929, and of the victory of fascism and Nazism and their defeat at the hands of the masses and Allied forces (United States, USSR, Britain, France). The war and the defeat of fascism opened the way to significant political and social changes in the world. These began with concessions to the working class, the crisis of the colonial empires, and the liberation struggles of dominated Third World peoples. To this add the relative success of import substitution industrialization in Latin America, the economic dynamism of India after it won independence from Britain in 1947, Algeria after it won independence from France in 1962, and Egypt under Nasser in the 1950s and 1960s, until the 1970s. There was also economic progress in the so-called socialist countries (Eastern Europe after the war; the USSR from the 1930s on).

This period shows a number of striking features. First, a large number of private companies came under public control ("nationalizations"), beginning in Western Europe in the wake of the victory over the Nazis and extending into the Third World until the mid-1970s. Second, social-welfare systems were set up and expanded as part of what became known as the "welfare state" (see glossary). Such reforms were also carried out in a number of Third World countries, such as Mexico in the 1930s under Lázaro Cárdenas. Third, the economic model in place was "Fordist," in that it involved the development of mass consumption of durable goods in the industrialized countries. Fourth, a social compromise was reached in these countries between the leadership of the labor movement (parties and trade unions) and "their" capitalist classes. This compromise took the form of agreements contributing to social harmony. These features arose and prospered within a framework of sustained growth—in the developed capitalist countries, the Third World, and the so-called socialist countries.

These wide-ranging political and economic developments also included a worldwide renewal of nondogmatic Marxism. In the developed capitalist countries, the works of Ernest Mandel, Paul Sweezy, Paul Baran, Andre Gunder Frank, to name but a few, were published. In Cuba, after the revolutionary victory, came the works of Ernesto Che Guevara in the 1960s. In Eastern Europe, Jacek Kuron and Karol Modzelewski in 1960s Poland, Karel Kosik, Rudolf Bahro, and others gave the foundation to a nondogmatic Marxism that emerged in opposition to the fossilized Stalinist system. It is also worth noting the emergence of the Marxist-influenced dependency school of thought in Latin America (Theotonio Dos Santos, Ruy Mauro Marini, Fernando Henrique Cardoso). Finally, there is the work of Samir Amin on delinking.

Liberal ideology returns with a vengeance

Liberal ideology returned with a vengeance in the 1970s, in response to the economic crisis in the main industrialized capitalist countries. The crisis marked the beginning of a long wave of slow growth, or rather a long downturn. The liberal counteroffensive picked up steam with the Third World debt crisis in the early 1980s and the implosion of the bureaucratic regimes of Eastern Europe at the end of the 1980s.

This liberal (or neoliberal) resurgence has underlain and justified the massive worldwide offensive waged by capital against labor. This offensive began in the second half of the 1970s in the industrialized capitalist countries and continued with the progressive restoration of capitalism resulting from the collapse of the bureaucratic regimes of the East at the end of the 1980s. It included the crisis of the "developmentalist" models in the countries of the South, aggravated by the foreign-debt crisis—leading to a new cycle of heightened dependence for countries that had experienced partially autonomous industrialization (such as Mexico, Argentina, Brazil, India, and Algeria). South Korea may soon join the ranks of these latter countries.

As for the most dependent and least industrialized countries (Central America; the Caribbean, except Cuba; sub-Saharan Africa; and South Asia, except India), they never really escaped dependence on the North's capitalist powers. They are now fully under the thumb of the international financial institutions (including Nicaragua and Vietnam, which had indeed experienced authentic revolutions). Institutions such as the Economic Commission for Latin America (CEPAL) and the United Nations Conference on Trade and Development (UNCTAD) have slowly joined the neoliberal chorus—though this process has not always been smooth (witness, for example, the 1995

UNCTAD report cited elsewhere in this book). As for the Nonaligned Movement (NAM), it has not survived the Yugoslav crisis, the Third World debt crisis, and the overall neoliberal offensive.

Neoliberal ideology is not a product of the crisis

Liberal (or neoliberal) ideology is not a product of the crisis. It existed long before the crisis broke. Various economists and political leaders continued to identify with liberal ideas in spite of the preeminence of Keynesian and proto-socialist policies. A number of them had long been sharpening their theoretical wits, engaged in a wide-reaching ideological battle with the Keynesian ideas favored in the North, the "developmentalist" ideas in the South (personified by such people as CEPAL head Raúl Prebisch), and socialist and Marxist ideas in general in various parts of the world.

The theoretical foundation of the different neoliberal currents

Methodologically speaking, the main tenets of neoliberal thought are not easily defined. The same goes for Keynesian and Marxist thought. Each of these schools of thought has many different currents. Profound differences exist between the different currents of liberalism, and the same can be said for Keynesianism and Marxism. There have also been attempts to synthesize liberal and post-Keynesian ideas, on the one hand, and liberal and post-Marxist ideas, on the other.

In general, the liberal (and neoliberal) school of thought is grounded in a vast and eclectic body of works—including neoclassical notions such as the quantitative theory of money, Say's law, the theory of prices based on the interaction of supply and demand, and the theory of comparative advantages.

Friedrich von Hayek (1899–1992) and Paul Samuelson are good examples of why it is so difficult to define clearly the parameters of neoliberalism. Hayek currently enjoys enormous popularity as an ultraliberal, yet he rejects many key hypotheses of neoclassical thought. Samuelson does not belong to the liberal school, yet in the 1950s he pushed for a synthesis of neoclassical thought.

Forerunners of the neoliberals

Adam Smith

Adam Smith (*An Inquiry into the Nature and the Causes of the Wealth of Nations*, 1776) carried out a synthesis of the contributions of a number of schools of economic thought, including that of the French physiocrats. He opposed mercantilism, which had been responsible for two centuries of protectionism and state intervention. The main expressions of mercantilism were Colbertism in France, bullionism in Spain, and the policies of Oliver Cromwell and William Pettyin England. Smith is best remembered for his allegory of the "invisible hand." According to Smith, each individual fulfills "an objective that is entirely independent from his intentions.... While seeking only his personal gain, he often works in a much more efficient way in society's interests than had society's interest been his real motivation" (Smith 1776, 256).

For Smith, public spending should be limited to defense, justice, and public works, when private entrepreneurs are not willing to take charge themselves, "given that, in these matters, profit would never be enough to return monies spent" (Smith 1776, 370). Smith's ideas correspond to the strong development of English capitalism in the eighteenth century and laid part of the foundation for "economic liberalism."

We should recall that Smith has been a source of inspiration not only for liberals (and neoliberals); some parts of his analysis (and that of the mercantilists he fought) were taken on by Karl Marx in his critique of political economy. Indeed, for Smith, "Labor is the true measure of value" (Smith 1979, 31). David Ricardo expanded on this notion, and Marx further developed it while acknowledging his debt to Smith and Ricardo. Unlike Smith, Marx also used a number of contributions from the mercantilists (see Labica and Bensussan 1985, 740).

Smith also makes a number of statements that today's neoliberals would find extremely irritating:

> English businessmen frequently complain about the high level of wages in their country. They say that this high level is the reason why they cannot sell their goods at prices that are as competitive as in other countries. But they remain quite silent about their high profits. They complain about the high profits of others but are very quiet about their own. In many cases, the high profits made by capital are much more to blame for price rises than are exorbitant wages. (Smith 1979, 534)

This statement is truly blasphemous for today's neoliberals, for whom wages are always far too high and the cause of inflation and poor competitiveness.

Jean-Baptiste Say

In 1803, Jean-Baptiste Say described a law whereby the role of money is neutral in the economy and "supply creates its own demand." Therefore, no crisis of overproduction is possible in a free market economy. Say's law is a key reference for liberal (and neoliberal) economists. Yet it was proved wrong by events in Say's time, a point that has been raised by a wide range of economists from Malthus (*Principles of Political Economy Considered with a View to Their*

Practical Application, 1820), to Sismondi (*Nouveaux principes d'économie politique, ou, De la richesse dans ses rapports avec la population*, 1819), and Marx.

David Ricardo

In David Ricardo's theory of competitive advantages (Ricardo 1977[1817], chapter 7), he critically enhances Smith's stance in favor of free trade and an international division of labor. For Ricardo, a country does well to specialize in areas of production whose relative costs are lowest—in other words, in areas where it has the greatest comparative advantage. Unlike Smith, he argues that countries with competitive advantages in all areas of production should nonetheless specialize:

> In a well-known example, Ricardo shows that if Portugal is more efficient than England in the production of both wine and fabric, it should still abandon the latter if its price advantage in wine production is greater. Inversely, England should specialize in the production of fabric, where its handicap is the least great.

Other influences on neoliberalism

Today's neoliberals draw inspiration not only from Smith, Say, and Ricardo, but also other economists such as William Stanley Jevons (*The Theory of political Economy*, 1871), Carl Menger (*Grundsätze der volkswirthschaftslehre*, 1871), and Léon Walras (*Éléments d'économie politique pure; ou, Théorie de la richesse sociale*, 1874). These economists criticize both Ricardo's (and Marx's) analysis of value and his analysis of distribution. They developed a theory of prices based on the principle of decreasing marginal utility. Dominant economic thought refers to this theory as signaling the "marginalist revolution." Within this framework, Walras also postulated a system of general equilibrium, which is in vogue among today's neoliberals. In such a system, society is defined as a natural mechanism (akin to a biological organism and the solar system) within which individuals freely ensure the most effective allocation of resources, thereby guaranteeing optimum economic performance.

To complete the list of references for today's neoliberals, we must add the quantitative theory of money. This theory, around since at least the sixteenth century, can be found in the works of Smith and Ricardo. It explains price movements as a result of the quantity of money in circulation.

Some economics describe all of these references taken together as a "neoclassical" synthesis. As Michel Beaud and Gilles Dostaler (1995) have pointed out, "Through it all, real life has persistently contradicted the analysis of many classical and neoclassical economists whereby the free functioning of the markets is enough to guarantee the full use of resources and their optimum allocation."

Marxist scholars, beginning with Marx and Engels themselves, refuted the different component parts of this rather eclectic body of theoretical work—at a time when Marxism influenced a large part of the international working-class movement.

By his own admission, Keynes had originally championed the liberal cause. Yet seventy-five years after Marx and Engels, he developed a radical critique of several of the central tenets of the classical (liberal) economic creed. In response to Smith and Say, for example (and like Marx), Keynes (1945 [1936]) highlights the important contributions of the mercantilists. However, he stood by the liberal creed on a number of other matters—on such key questions, for example, as the definition of real salaries as equal to the marginal productivity of labor (see Beaud and Dostaler 1995, 54).

More on the eclipse of liberalism

As a result of the depression of the 1920s and 1930s, a new wave of critics tackled the neoclassical creed on a largely pragmatic basis. This new wave was international and involved political leaders and economists who belonged to various currents: enlightened bourgeois thinkers, socialists, and Marxists. In a context of mass unemployment and depression, proposals came forward for major public works, anticyclical injections of public money, and even bank expropriations. Such proposals came from a wide variety of sources: Germany's Dr. Hjalmar Schacht; the Belgian socialist Henri De Man; the founders of the Stockholm School, backed by the Swedish social democrats; Fabian socialists and J.M. Keynes in Britain; Jan Tinbergen in the Netherlands; Ragnar Frisch in Norway; the groupe X-Crise in France; Lázaro Cárdenas, Mexican president (1935–40); adepts of Perónism in the Argentina of the 1930s; Franklin D. Roosevelt, US president (elected in November 1932), and his New Deal.

The entire range of proposals and pragmatic policies was partially summed up in Keynes's 1936 work, *General Theory of Employment, Interest and Money*.

The Keynesian revolution

The preparatory work carried out by Keynes (1883–1946) in laying the groundwork for his *General Theory* was fueled by the need to find a solution to the spreading crisis of the capitalist system. Moreover, this solution had to be compatible with the continued survival of the system. The work was partially the result of a wide-ranging collective process wherein groups and individuals ended up in different Keynesian currents, often very much at odds with one another. Some leaned more towards Marxist positions, such as Joan Robinson of England and Michal Kalecki of Poland, who had actually formulated the key components of the *General Theory* before Keynes. Others grew progressively closer to the tenets of liberalism and neoclassical economics that Keynes decried.

In one of his works, Keynes pays homage to the English philosopher George Edward Moore, whom he credits with freeing him from the prevailing morality of the day, and having "protected us all from that final *reductio ad absurdum* of Benthamism known as Marxism" (quoted in Beaud and Dostaler 1995).

Keynes had been politically active since the First World War. As an employee of the British Exchequer, he actively participated in negotiations on the Treaty of Versailles, which marked the end of the war in 1918. He resigned from the British delegation in protest against the scale of reparations imposed on Germany. Soon after, he wrote *The Economic Consequences of the Peace* (1919). In the 1926 pamphlet *The End of Laissez-faire* he writes: "It is in no way accurate to deduce from the principles of political economy that enlightened personal interest always works in favor of the general interest" (quoted in Beaud and Dostaler 1995).

In the 1920s, Keynes condemned the policies of Winston Churchill's Tory government. He opposed the liberal (neoclassical) policies that provoked the miners' strike, followed by the 1926 general strike. Thereafter, he called for a policy of major public investment. He supported the Liberal Party while maintaining friendly ties with the Labour Party. In 1929, in the wake of Tory defeat, the new Labour government appointed him to the MacMillan Commission on the economic situation. In 1930, he became an adviser to the same government.

The economic crisis deepened following the 1929 Wall Street crash, leading Keynes to produce an analysis of employment, interest, and money, which strengthened his conviction that state intervention should increase. The state should increase spending to compensate for the shortfall in demand and boost the economy and employment. Thereafter he became involved in a major polemic with Friedrich von Hayek. Although, like Keynes, Hayek had come to reject a number of the ideas of Smith, Ricardo, Walras, and Jevons, he fashioned, with Ludwig von Mises (1881–1973), a set of ultraliberal ideas that stood in fierce opposition to the main tenets of the Keynesian revolution.

Whereas Keynes and his fellow economists were convinced that the collapse in investment had caused the Great Depression, Hayek and his supporters saw overinvestment rooted in slack monetary policies as the cause. For Keynes, consumption and investment had to be sparked by strong state intervention. For Hayek, state intervention reduced the funds available for private investment. For Keynes, wages had to be increased to stimulate consumption. For Hayek, they had to be lowered to ensure renewed full employment. The polemic hit the pages of the British press in 1932 (*Times*, October 17 and 19).

Keynes believed that economic policy should be geared toward reducing the high unemployment rate and distributing revenues in a more egalitarian manner. If the government did not pursue the objectives of full employment and greater equality, he argued, there was a serious danger that either fascism or Bolshevik communism would win the day. Government policy had to be aimed at reducing high interest rates, which channeled vital resources into the financial sector. By lowering interest rates, the aim was to favor the destruction of the rentier class, the scourge of the capitalist system. At the same time, however, Keynes states quite clearly that the consequences of his theory are:

> moderately conservative in its implications. For whilst it indicates the vital importance of establishing certain central controls in matters which are now left in the main to individual initiative, there are wide fields of activity which are unaffected. (…) I conceive therefore, that a somewhat comprehensive socialisation of investment will prove the only means of securing an approximation to full employment (…). But beyond this no obvious case is made out for a system of State Socialism which would embrace most of the economic life of the community. (Keynes, 1936, p. 377-378)

Keynes's prescriptions were put into practice in many regions of the world until the 1970s. They also strongly influenced a number of economists, such as Paul Samuelson, John Kenneth Galbraith, James Tobin, and Raùl Prebisch.

Preparing the neoliberal counterrevolution

There was a swift reaction to the policies of state intervention aimed at boosting demand and moving toward full employment. From the beginning of the 1930s, Hayek and von Mises set out to demolish Keynes's proposals.

> Since 1945, in various academic and business circles, different projects have emerged simultaneously to bring together the qualified defenders of liberalism (neoclassical economics) with the aim of organizing a joint response to the advocates of state intervention and socialism. Three centers where this postwar resistance was organized were the Institut universitaire de hautes études internationales (IUHEI) in Geneva, the London School of Economics (LSE), and the University of Chicago. (Udry 1997)

At the end of the Second World War, Hayek was teaching at the LSE. In 1947, he and von Mises founded the Société du Mont-Pèlerin (Mont Pelerin Society). The first meeting was held in April 1947, bringing together thirty-six liberal luminaries at the Hôtel du Parc at Mont-Pèlerin near Vevey in Switzerland. The gathering was financed by Swiss bankers and industrialists. Three major US publications (*Fortune*, *Newsweek*, and *Reader's Digest*) sent delegates. In fact, *Reader's Digest* had just run an abridged version of one of Hayek's main works, *The Road to Serfdom* (1944). Among other things, the book argues:

> In the past, man's submission to the impersonal forces of the market made possible the development of a civilization which otherwise would not have emerged. It is

through submission that we participate everyday in the building of something much bigger than what we can all fully understand.

Right-wing economists and philosophers from different "schools of thought" participated in the gathering. "At the end of the meeting, the Société du Mont-Pèlerin was founded—a kind of neoliberal Freemasonry, very well organized and devoted to the dissemination of the neoliberal creed, with regular international gatherings" (Anderson 1996). Among the organization's most active members were Hayek, von Mises, Maurice Allais, Karl Popper, and Milton Friedman. It became a think tank for the neoliberal counteroffensive. Many of its members went on to win the Nobel Prize in economics (Hayek in 1974, Friedman in 1976, and Allais in 1988).

The neoliberal resurgence

The neoliberal current made the University of Chicago one of its bastions. Friedman spent his entire academic career there, while Hayek taught there between 1950 and 1961. Later, people began to refer to the neoliberals as the Chicago School and spoke of Friedman's "Chicago Boys." In 1970, Friedman declared that he had seen through the victory of the "counter-revolution in monetary theory," defined by him as the "renewed accent placed on the role of the quantity of money" (Friedman 1970). In *The Counter-revolution in Monetary Theory*, Friedman argues that all variations in the money supply are followed by corresponding changes in prices, production, and revenues. He argues that this law has been observed for centuries and can be compared to the laws of natural science. He concludes that the state cannot boost demand through the creation of money, lest unemployment rise in the same proportions. He proposes a constitutional amendment whereby the money supply should change at a constant rate, equal to the long-term rate of growth of national production (Beaud and Dostaler 1995).

Following in the footsteps of Say, Friedman argues that the free functioning of the market is enough to ensure the optimum allocation of resources and the full use of production capacity. This view has been refuted by real life, but this has not stopped it from gaining wide currency as a matter of "common sense."

Friedman did not remain aloof from politics; he put himself squarely in the reactionary camp. In 1964, he was economic adviser to Republican presidential candidate Barry Goldwater. He held the same post alongside Richard Nixon in 1968, and Ronald Reagan in 1980. After the government of Salvador Allende was overthrown by a military coup in Chile in 1973, he was adviser to General Pinochet. He supported the repression that was carried out and called for measures of extreme austerity. Hayek also expressed support for the general's dictatorial and bloodthirsty methods. In response to a Chilean journalist's questions in 1981, he said: "A dictator may rule in a liberal way, just as it is possible for a democracy to rule without the slightest liberalism. My personal preference is for a liberal dictatorship rather than a democratic government thoroughly lacking in liberalism" (quoted in Salama and Valier 1994). After ten years of application of his economic prescriptions, Chile entered a recession that saw its GDP plummet by 15 percent in 1982–83, and unemployment of 30 percent (Ominami 1996). Indeed, Chile was only able to become something of an economic success story in the 1990s by breaking cleanly with the approach of the Chicago Boys.

While Ronald Reagan was inspired by Friedman, Margaret Thatcher was a disciple of Hayek:

> It was only in the middle of the 1970s, when Hayek's works figured prominently in the readings that Keith Joseph [Thatcher's economic adviser and participant at Mont-Pèlerin meetings] gave me that I really grasped his ideas. It was only at that point that I considered his arguments from the point of view of the type of state dear to Conservatives (a limited government based on the rule of law), as opposed to the point of view of the type of state to be avoided (a socialist state where bureaucrats ruled unchecked). (From *The Path to Power* [1995]; quoted in Udry 1997)

Robert Lucas and the denial of involuntary unemployment

The neoliberal counterrevolution has added a new dimension to reactionary ideas. According to Robert Lucas, who describes himself as a partisan of "new classical macroeconomics," involuntary unemployment does not exist. For Keynes, the existence of involuntary unemployment was a given. However, according to Lucas, unemployment is caused by the choices a worker makes between work and leisure. Lucas argues that any economist seeking to understand changes in the labor market must postulate that workers make rational choices about amounts of work time versus leisure time. In other words, an unemployed worker is a person who has chosen to increase leisure time, even if this means their income falls or disappears.

In line with the classical orthodoxy targeted by both Marx and Keynes, Lucas argues that there is a natural rate of unemployment, and that it is counterproductive for governments to seek to influence this rate with pump-priming, job-creation measures.

In 1995, Lucas, a professor at the University of Chicago, was rewarded with the Nobel Prize for economics for his contribution to the neoliberal offensive. He and his colleagues made a radical critique of Reagan's policies, rightly arguing that they had strayed from monetarist orthodoxy. They approved Reagan's monetarist plans to reduce the money supply but said that tax cuts and high military spending—which could only widen the public deficit—

were incompatible with this objective. They backed cuts in social spending and opposed the increase in military spending.

There was nothing ethical about their opposition to military spending, yet it revealed the striking incoherence between Reagan's monetarist convictions and his actual policies involving an increase in the public deficit. He partially applied Keynesian methods to get the United States out of recession with an increase in public spending. He did so in a reactionary manner, channeling the increased public funds into arms spending (and space research for the Strategic Defense Initiative [Star Wars] project). As far as the interests of US imperialism were concerned, Reagan's approach—much criticized by the neoliberal keepers of the faith—ended up serving them quite well. The social costs, however, have been enormous.

A key postulate of neoconservatism: Free markets ensure optimum resource allocation

> *For the hand to remain invisible,*
> *the eye must be blind.*
>
> —*Daniel Bensaïd, 1995*

Of course, it is easy to argue that there is no example of a fully free-functioning market. This is obviously true in those countries where the authorities and organized workers refuse neoliberal dogmas and have managed to defend their social welfare system and retain reasonably stable employment and intact public services. Yet, it is also true in the countries where neoliberal policies have been implemented most aggressively.

The neoliberals in power in the United States since 1980 have indeed cut back on what they see as obstacles to the free functioning of the market—for example, by diminishing the strength of the trade-union movement and rolling back social welfare. However, they have strengthened other such "obstacles": through the greater concentration of companies, creating oligopolies in certain sectors; the privatization of state-owned companies, eliminating any form of democratic control; the maintenance of protectionism against foreign competitors (tariff barriers and other constraints on the free market); the strengthening of the power of financial players, leading toward a "tyranny of the markets"; the restriction of the free circulation of labor; and through a multiplicity of acts of financial delinquency that obstruct the working of the free market (insider trading; see Enron, Global Crossing, and other affairs).

Meanwhile, in the case of the United States, inequalities have increased and poverty affects a larger portion of the population. A significant share of new jobs is poorly paid and short-term. The prison population rose from

250,000 in 1975, to 744,000 in 1985, to 1.6 million in 1996; according to prison authorities, "a black man is seven times more likely than a white man to go to prison" (*Le Monde*, August 13, 1997). Never before have their been so many economic activities of a criminal character by company heads and public officials—encouraged by the deregulation of capital flows.

In defense of their record, neoliberals always retort that resources are not optimally allocated since the market does not function anywhere unfettered. The task, therefore, is to struggle against obstacles to the market in view of achieving universal prosperity at some point in the distant future. In fact, in the name of the quest for a free market (the neoliberal promised land), the objective is to destroy the gains of workers and the oppressed generally—gains that are described as so many reactionary "rigidities."

Neoliberal sleight of hand: Portraying the oppressed as oppressors

There is nothing new about this line of argument. The idea is to single out as oppressive mechanisms the trade-union movement and legislation that defends workers. These mechanisms, the argument goes, were established by the

The IMF and the nonexistence of involuntary unemployment

According to Joseph Stiglitz (2002), winner of the 2001 Nobel Prize for Economics, the doctrine of the nonexistence of involuntary unemployment is still deeply ingrained within the IMF:

In some of the universities from which the IMF hires regularly, the core curricula involve models in which there is never any unemployment. After all, in the standard competitive model—the model that underlies the IMF's market fundamentalism—demand always equals supply. If the demand for labor equals supply, there is never any *involuntary* unemployment. Someone who is not working has evidently chosen not to work.... While these models might provide some amusement within academia, they seem particularly ill suited to understanding the problems of a country like South Africa, which has been plagued with unemployment rates in excess of 25 percent since apartheid was dismantled.

The IMF economists could not, of course, ignore the existence of unemployment. Because under market fundamentalism...there cannot be unemployment, the problem cannot lie with markets. It must lie elsewhere—with greedy unions and politicians interfering with the workings of free markets, by demanding—and getting—excessively high wages. There is an obvious policy implication—if there is unemployment, wages should be reduced.

The absurdities of neoliberal and neoclassical thought

The imperialism of neoclassical economics (excerpts from Beaud and Dostaler 1995, 183–85):

Neoclassical theory has long been criticized for its reductionism, which makes it unable to take into account the complexities of the world in which we live. Paradoxically, some neoclassical theorists linked to the Chicago School have reacted to this critique by pushing their reductionism to the extreme—making their theory the key to all knowledge of all social phenomena. The other social sciences—such as sociology, political science, history, and psychology—are seen as superfluous.

According to this view of things, society is a collection of independent agents (individuals, households, and companies). Each agent has free will; it is the interaction of the different individual decisions that determines the course of economic, social and political life. Each agent is subjected to a series of constraints, both cognitive and material in nature. The resources available to each agent (goods and services, productive resources, information) are limited. Behavior can be foreseen based on the hypothesis that each agent will act rationally. This hypothesis, in fact, is the core of neoclassical analysis....

.... The big step was taken by Becker (who won the Nobel Prize for economics in 1992) and Mincer, both from the Chicago School. They have applied this approach, based on the rational behavior of each independent agent, to all human activities. This enables them to explain all human behavior, including criminal activities. Such activities, like all others, are seen to be the result of a rational calculation, wherein profits (high and short-term) are compared to costs (the danger of being apprehended and punished). Becker and his colleagues have generalized this analysis to include marriage, childbearing and rearing, divorce, and the division of household chores. In each case, it is a matter of making a rational cost-benefit analysis. The emergence of such specialities as the "new economy of the family" (Becker 1968; Becker and Landes 1974) shows how wide the net of *homo economicus* and rational choices has been cast....

.... In addition to being called "revolutionary," these changes have also been labeled "imperialist" (Stigler 1984). The further afield Becker and his colleagues travel, the less room there is for genuine research in anthropology, psychology, political science, sociology and all the social sciences and humanities—for this approach to economics sees itself as a general theory for all human behavior:

> There is only one social science. What gives the economic sciences their capacity for imperialist expansion is the fact that our analytical categories—scarcity, cost, preference, opportunity—are truly universally applicable. [...] In this way, the economic sciences are the universal grammar of social science' (J. Hirschleifer, "The Expanding Domain of Economics," *American Economic Review*, vol. 75, no. 6, 1985, 53).

privileged sectors of the population with well-paid jobs against those who merely want to accept the jobs they are offered. In 1944, Hayek wrote in *The Road to Serfdom*:

> Never has a class been so cruelly exploited as are the weakest sectors of the working class by their privileged brothers—a form of exploitation made possible by the "regulation" of competition. Few slogans have done as much damage as the "stabilization" of prices and wages. By ensuring the wages of the few, the situation of the many is made increasingly precarious. (Hayek 1944)

The World Bank in essence said the same thing fifty years later, in its 1995 *World Development Report*, "Workers in an Integrating World:

> Through the obstacles it places to job creation, overly restrictive job-security regulations threaten to protect those in salaried positions *at the expense of excluded sectors, the unemployed and workers in the informal and rural sectors*. (104) [emphasis added]

Down with job security! It thrives at the expense of the oppressed!

> There is good reason to fear that those who most benefit from social security—usually well-off workers—do so *at the expense of other workers*. (104) [emphasis added]

Down with social security!

> There can be no doubt that trade unions often behave like monopolies to secure improvements in wages and working conditions for their members *at the expense* of holders of capital, consumers *and the non-unionized work force*. (95) [emphasis added]

Down with the trade unions!

Hayek and Friedman now have imitators in the East. Former Czech prime minister Vaclav Klaus, who became president in 2003, told the British weekly *The Economist*:

> The Western European social system is too much a prisoner of rules and excessive controls. The Welfare State, with all its generous transfer payments unconditioned by criteria relating to the efforts and merits of the people concerned, destroys the work ethic and feelings of individual responsibility. Public-sector workers are too protected. The Thatcher revolution—that is, the liberal, anti-Keynesian revolution—is in midstream in Western Europe. It has to be taken to the other shore. (Quoted in Anderson 1996)

In another document drawn up by the World Bank for the Global Summit on Social Development, organized by the UN, in Copenhagen in March 1995, the World Bank argues that for Third World countries: "Minimum wages, unemployment insurance, redundancy payments and job-security legislation are of no use to rural and informal workers, who account for the majority of the poor in developing countries" (World Bank 1995b).

This type of statement is in perfect harmony with those made by another champion of neoconservatism, George Gilder (1981, 127), for whom "[s]ocial security now erodes both work and the family, keeping the poor in poverty." It is worth pointing out that Gilder favors such an approach for the entire planet, including the industrialized countries! Such declarations are reminiscent of something Thomas Robert Malthus, in his *Principles of Political Economy* (1820) wrote: "To be sure, the Poor Laws can be seen as weakening the willingness and ability of the common people for uplift. In this way, they weaken one of the most powerful motives for work."

15

The debt crisis at the start of the new century: Latin America and sub-Saharan Africa

The fourth Latin American debt crisis

In contrast to what occurred during the crisis of the 1930s, after the 1982 Mexican crisis, Latin America's leaders resigned themselves to negotiating separately with their private foreign creditors (who held most of the region's external debt). The United States was heavily involved in this process. Latin American leaders justified this approach by arguing that they had to prevent external lines of credit from being cut off one after the other. In fact, Latin America has seen the worst of both worlds: there has been a huge drain of wealth into the coffers of private creditors, but this has not prevented foreign banks from cutting off their lines of credit. The Economic Commission for Latin America and the Caribbean (ECLAC) estimates the net transfer of capital (see glossary) from Latin America to the North between 1983 and 1991 to be more than $200 billion.[1] A colossal transfer of wealth from the countries of Latin America to the North's financial institutions has occurred. Between 1982 and 2000, Latin America made $1.45 trillion in debt servicing payments—about four times its total debt stock, which came to $333.2 billion in 1982. Latin American debt has continued to grow (see table 15.1).

Latin American government policy in the 1990s

According to the UNDP *Global Human Development Report 1997*, "The rate of poverty dropped in the 1950s and even more quickly in the 1960s and 1970s. The 1980s were disastrous. In the 1990s, only a few countries have registered a fall in poverty (Chile, Colombia)." In 1993–94, almost every financial commentator, along with many reputable economists, backed the self-satisfied claims of the World Bank and IMF that Latin America was in the midst of a

TABLE 15.1. PROGRESSION OF THE EXTERNAL DEBT
OF LATIN AMERICA AND THE CARIBBEAN (BILLIONS OF DOLLARS)

Total Latin America + Caribbean

1970	1980	1990	1996	1999	2001	2002
32.56	257.37	475.37	670.87	794.84	764.88	789.40

Main indebted countries

	1970	1980	1990	1996	1999	2001
Brazil	5.73	71.53	119.96	181.32	243.71	226.36
Mexico	6.97	57.38	104.44	157.50	167.25	158.29
Argentina	5.81	27.16	62.23	111.38	145.29	136.71
Venezuela	1.42	29.36	33.17	34.49	37.26	34.66
Peru	3.21	9.39	20.06	28.98	29.21	27.51
Colombia	2.24	6.94	17.22	28.90	34.42	36.70
Chile	2.98	12.08	19.23	23.05	34.27	38.36
Subtotal	28.36	213.84	376.31	565.6	691.41	658.59
Subtotal as percent	87	83	79	84	87	86

Medium-sized countries

	1970	1980	1990	1996	1999	2001
Ecuador	0.36	6.00	12.11	14.50	15.31	13.91

Small countries

	1970	1980	1990	1996	1999	2001
Bolivia	0.59	2.70	4.28	5.20	5.55	4.68
Haiti	0.04	0.35	0.91	0.90	1.18	1.25
El Salvador	0.18	0.91	2.15	2.91	3.80	4.68
Guatemala	0.16	1.18	3.08	3.77	4.21	4.53
Nicaragua	0.20	2.19	10.75	5.96	6.91	6.39
Paraguay	0.11	0.96	2.11	2.57	3.39	2.82
Uruguay	0.36	1.66	4.42	5.90	7.50	9.71

Source: Table drawn up by Damien Millet, based on World Bank 2003a.

full-fledged economic recovery. (They were similarly complacent with respect to the Southeast Asian "dragons" until June 1997, though the crisis there had already begun in April of that year.) They pointed out that significant funds were making their way back into Latin America—which, they argued, signified the end of the lost decade of the 1980s.

After leaving his job as an IMF administrator, and only a few months before the Mexican crisis of December 1994, Jacques de Groote told the Belgian daily *Le Soir* (March 28, 1994):

> There are countless success stories. The best example is Mexico. In October 1982, this country was hit by a major debt crisis. The joint action of the IMF and World Bank quickly got the country on its feet again, got its balance of payments back in shape in exchange for a limited and short-term drop in the population's wages. Today, investment has returned to Mexico and the World Bank is running a program that aims to diversify production.... In fact, all the countries of Latin America...are doing very well economically.

In fact, however, these investment flows were (and are) volatile. They were attracted primarily to these countries for two reasons: a policy of high interest rates pursued by the IMF's best pupils (Brazil, Mexico, and Argentina, to name a few), and an unprecedented wave of privatization (large state-owned companies sold for a song). In order to sweeten the pot, the government declared a fiscal amnesty for all nationals who returned capital that had been invested abroad.

All along, the Mexican trade deficit was worsening, which ultimately shook private investor confidence and led them progressively to withdraw their money throughout 1994. Stock market shares were sold off, and Mexico plunged into crisis again. To avoid a similar fate, the governments of Brazil and Argentina pursued an aggressive policy of high interest rates in an attempt to keep investment from going elsewhere. It was not enough. Brazil was sucked down in late 1998 to early 1999, when massive capital flight from the country occurred. Argentina, already shaken by the "Tequila effect" of the 1995 Mexican crisis, plunged again in 1999. In 2002, the effects spread to Brazil and Uruguay.

Debt nationalization, company privatization, domestic-market doldrums, and increased dependence on foreign capital

Local capitalists reaped enormous benefits when their governments nationalized private debt. In Argentina, this operation took place between 1980 and 1982, and cost the equivalent of 25 percent of GDP; in Mexico, rescuing the banks in the last half of the 1990s cost 15 percent of GDP. In this way, local capitalists not only earned huge savings, but were also able to export much of their capital to the North's financial markets. In addition, since the state took over company debts, companies were able to use their new margin for maneuver to buy up state-owned enterprises that were privatized from the mid-1980s on. Some countries, such as Mexico and Argentina, privatized faster than others. Brazil and Venezuela only began large-scale privatization in 1996–97.

As has already been pointed out, since the beginning of the 1990s, most Latin American governments have pursued a policy of high interest rates. The objective is to attract foreign investment and to persuade local capitalists to repatriate a part of the funds they have invested in the North. The social costs of such a policy are high. Small and medium-sized producers, let alone households, cannot borrow, which has led to a downturn in production for the domestic market.

Growth is pulled along by exports, on the one hand, and by imports aimed at satisfying the needs of the capitalists and the upper middle classes, on the other. Due to the high domestic interest rates in effect in most Latin American countries, the government and local state bodies pay a high price for money borrowed from local capitalists. These borrowed funds are used to service both foreign and domestic debt owed to these same capitalists and capitalists from the North.

Since state bodies have to pay so much for money borrowed on domestic financial markets, and since this money is not enough to pay off previous debts, governments and private companies issue debt paper on international markets. This is actually less costly, since interest rates in the North are not currently lower than in countries such as Brazil, Mexico, and Argentina. The problem, of course, is that these countries become even more dependent on external markets and trends. Several times per year, the big Latin American countries issue debt paper on international markets. The money collected through such issues goes mostly toward paying off holders of previous debt issues. In a striking example of dependence on the United States, some Latin American countries—especially Mexico—have to purchase US treasury bonds to guarantee their own borrowing on international markets.

The fundamental problem is that such policies do not lead to a process of cumulative development, through which these countries could catch up with the industrialized powers of the North. Trade imbalances have actually grown, despite the optimistic pronouncements of Latin American leaders. This is due to the structure of Latin American exports to the world market. Whatever the level of industrialization, these countries remain far behind the North—and the gap is widening. According to Peruvian economist Oscar Ugarteche (1997), there has been a "reprimarization" of Latin American exports in recent years, which means that, proportionally, Latin America exports more low value-added ("primary") products than before.

Note that John Saxe-Fernández and Omar Núñez Rodríguez advance a different opinion from Ugarteche's: "We should point out that this policy of disindustrialization does not entail a return to a primary exporter model for

TABLE 15.2. NEGATIVE NET TRANSFER ON DEBT IN LATIN AMERICA AND THE CARIBBEAN, 1996–2002 (BILLIONS OF DOLLARS)

	1996	1997	1998	1999	2000	2001	2002	Total (1996–2002)
Latin America + Caribbean	-3.21	-17.23	-9.08	-40.00	-55.87	-42.32	-38.29	-206.00

	1996	1997	1998	1999	2000	2001	Total (1996–2001)
Argentina	7.87	9.81	2.77	-3.90	-7.32	-15.96	-6.73
Bolivia	0.15	0.27	0.04	0.02	0.13	0.00*	0.61
Brazil	8.79	-13.44	-8.72	-23.63	-21.29	-11.84	-70.13
Chile	-0.12	0.88	3.35	0.51	0.17	-0.58	4.21
Colombia	2.36	1.61	-1.13	-1.41	-2.40	0.59	-0.38
Costa Rica	-0.25	-0.13	0.20	0.06	0.03	-0.10	-0.19
Ecuador	-0.02	0.41	-0.85	-1.69	-0.28	-0.05	-2.48
Haiti	0.09	0.15	-0.02	0.10	0.00†	0.08	0.40
Honduras	-0.12	0.17	-0.02	0.25	0.17	0.05	0.50
Jamaica	-0.37	-0.12	-0.19	-0.34	0.18	0.49	-0.35
Mexico	-16.54	-16.22	-2.34	-5.32	-21.88	-11.21	-73.51
Nicaragua	0.00	0.25	-0.19	0.39	0.24	-0.01	0.68
Paraguay	-0.05	-0.11	0.18	0.45	-0.33	-0.36	-0.22
Peru	-1.25	0.12	-0.77	-2.76	-1.13	-1.42	-7.21
Uruguay	0.32	0.50	0.34	-0.61	-0.10	0.97	1.42
Venezuela RB	-2.30	-0.06	-0.73	-2.29	-1.75	-4.82	-11.95

* $3 million.
† $4 million.

Source: World Bank 2003a.
Table by Damien Millet.

the continent's economies." However, in their valuable study, the authors observe that the dominant policy

> diverts public investment to debt servicing and other non productive expenses, drawing in its wake a complete process of denationalization through privatizations, which are nothing less than the stages whereby industry, agriculture, mining activities and the infrastructure fall into the hands of foreign capital. (Saxe-Fernández and Núñez Rodríguez 2001)

At the same time, industries targeting the domestic market have stagnated or declined, whether they remain in domestic hands or were sold off to foreign interests. Foreign investors are rarely interested in boosting both employment and production. There are exceptions—the automobile sector in Argentina, Brazil, and Venezuela, and some investments in the oil sector—but these are marginal. Multinationals, with American MNCs in the lead, seek to bolster their control over local economies, not to develop them.

Claudio Katz (2001) has accurately described this backward transformation of the model:

> New investments concentrate on internationally competitive sectors and end up undermining the former local manufacturing complex that had developed in some countries, between the two wars and in the twenty years following the Second World War. This has all sorts of consequences. For example, the projects that were emerging to adapt technology to production for the domestic market have ground to a halt. Research and development activities have fallen back. Assembly lines have replaced the previous objective of a complete industrial model, at least in the most advanced countries of Latin America such as Brazil, Mexico, and Argentina.

1994–2003: A new spiral of crises and negative net transfers for Latin America

The crisis that erupted in Mexico in 1994 was followed by a series of crises, sparing none of the main economies of Latin America. Finally, the period during which the continent received more credit input than it was paying out in debt repayments was very short. Since 1996, each year has seen a negative net transfer on debt (see glossary). The total of negative transfers between 1996 and 2002 exceeded $200 billion (see table 15.2). Things began to worsen in 1999. From that year, the net transfer from Latin American countries to their creditors every two years was the equivalent of the Marshall Plan.

Between 1996 and 2002, the Latin American governments alone received $394.17 million in loans and repaid $505.86 million. In other words, they repaid the amount they received in new loans, plus more than $111 billion.

Another way of looking at it is through the net transfer on debt. This is the difference between debt servicing (annual repayments of interest plus principal to creditor countries) and the repatriation of profits by MNCs of the North, on one hand, and on the other, the year's gross payments (loans, donations, and investments from the same creditor countries). The net transfer on debt is considered positive when the country or continent concerned receives more (in loans, donations, and investments) than it pays out in debt payments or repatriated MNC profits. It is negative if the amounts repaid come to more than the amounts coming into the country. From 1982 to 1990, in the case of Latin America, the net transfer was constantly negative. During the same period, more than $200 billion were transferred net from Latin America to the countries of the North. Since 2000, net transfer has become negative again to the detriment of Latin America and the Caribbean.[2]

To conclude this section, a quotation from Oscar Ugarteche (1997, 145–47):

> Virtually all the countries of Latin America have applied structural adjustment policies based on the neoclassical theory of market efficiency and the distortion of those markets due to state intervention. The way in which change has been brought about, from state-managed development to "market-managed" development, is directly attributable to the pressure of the international organizations.... The facts clearly indicate that the opening up policies led to growing balance of trade deficits covered partly by short-term capital investments and loans and stock market investments, and partly by long-term capital attracted by privatization. There is no obvious proof that the real rate of investment increases because of numerous foreign investments.... Criticisms of the neoclassical model applied in the region vary, but the issue of the state is crucial. As long as the role of the state is not restored, and the markets are left to determine the way the economy is conducted, economic results will remain uncertain. A perverse logic reigns.... Deregulation is practiced in a global economy that is not particularly liberal but uniformly capitalist, with the markets constantly under the sway of the MNCs.... The process of internationalizing capital was introduced in Latin America in the 1990s through privatizations and loans to the private sector. As for the public sector, it pays the debt to allow the private sector to get indebted.... A country cannot develop without consolidating the domestic market, which goes hand in hand with a fairer distribution of revenue. That is something that the neoclassical model completely fails to take into account.

Debt in sub-Saharan Africa
at the dawn of the twenty-first century

Throughout the 1990s, reports published by the international financial institutions (IFIs), the OECD, and the media claim that sub-Saharan Africa has got off to a new start thanks to adjustment policies in place there. However, a series of social and economic indicators point in the opposite direction. Living conditions have actually deteriorated and economic indicators are in the red.

According to the 1997 UNDP *Global Human Development Report*, more than 40 percent of sub-Saharan Africa's population of 590 million lives below the threshold of absolute poverty. These people survive on less than one dollar per day. According to the same source, the situation has indeed deteriorated in recent years: "Sub-Saharan Africa has the highest proportion of people in— and the fastest growth in—of human poverty.... Indeed, the sub-Saharan and other least developed countries are poverty stricken—and it is estimated that by 2000 half the people in sub-Saharan Africa will be in income poverty."

Unfortunately, this forecast proved correct. According to the World Bank, the number of people in sub-Saharan Africa who are forced to survive on less than one dollar per day grew from 241 million to 315 million between 1990 and 1999. The UNDP's 2003 report claims that extreme poverty affects half of all Africans and hunger, a third; also, about a sixth of all children die before the age of five.

In 2002, sub-Saharan Africa had about 29 million people with AIDS, i.e., two-thirds of the total number of AIDS victims in the world. The UNDP's 2000 *Poverty Report* tells us that 40 million children in the region will lose their parents to AIDS over the next ten years (UNDP 2000b, 109). Between now and 2010, life expectancy is expected to fall by seventeen years in nine African countries: South Africa, Botswana, Kenya, Malawi, Mozambique, Namibia, Rwanda, Zambia, and Zimbabwe. In 2002, in seven Southern African countries, life expectancy already dropped below forty years of age.

Education is equally disastrous. In its 2003 report, the UNDP writes that the percentage of children receiving primary education is less than 57 percent, while only one child in three completes primary school. High school fees (to cover registration and teachers' salaries) soon dissuade families who cannot possibly devote the equivalent of 20 percent of the per capita income to one child's education, as is the case in Burkina Faso. There, the total rate of registration in primary schools is 36 percent.

The economy in Africa is not doing better than the social indicators of the continent. The debt is at the heart of the tragedy, resulting from geopolitical choices that make it both a powerful instrument of domination over the countries of the South and a formidable mechanism for transferring the wealth of those populations to the creditors of the North, with the local ruling classes helping themselves to a commission on the way.

External debt: A millstone around Africa's neck

In 2002, Africa's external debt came to $204 billion—3.4 times the amount owed in 1980. Sub-Saharan Africa was sucked dry in 2002 to repay the $13.4 billion it owed as debt servicing (capital plus interest). From 1980 to 2002, Africa repaid $250 billion, i.e., four times the debt of 1980. Thus, for one dollar owed in 1980, Africa has repaid four, but still owes another four.

Between 1998 and 2002, the governments of sub-Saharan Africa received

$34.83 billion in fresh loans; they repaid $49.27 billion on previous loans. In short, they transferred more than $15 billion (net negative transfer on the public debt; see glossary) to creditors in the North. Each year, sub-Saharan Africa pays more in debt servicing than the total of all health and education budgets of the entire region.

Trade losses

To repay its external debt, entirely denominated in hard currency, sub-Saharan Africa has to use a considerable share of its export revenues. Therefore, the ratio of the amount of the debt to annual export revenues constitutes a useful indicator of the gravity of the situation. In 2000, the debt represented about 250 percent of the export revenues of the subcontinent, not including South Africa. To repay its debt, the region would have to use all its exports for two and a half years (see table 15.3).

Changes in the region's trade balance are crucial to evaluating its ability to

TABLE 15.3. COUNTRIES WHOSE DEBT REPRESENTED
MORE THAN 300 PERCENT OF EXPORT REVENUES IN 1999

Burkina Faso	379
Burundi	1,792
Cameroon	418
Central African Republic	592
Chad	362
Comoro Islands	420
Ethiopia	588
Guinea	428
Guinea-Bissau	1,604
Madagascar	455
Malawi	457
Mali	430
Mauritania	681
Mozambique	1,115
Niger	539
Rwanda	1,216
Sierra Leone	1,736
Sudan	1,832
Tanzania	637
Uganda	525
Zambia	622

Source: World Bank 2001.

repay its debts. If export revenues are lower than import spending, the debt cannot be repaid without further cuts in social spending, thus increasing poverty.

Now, sub-Saharan Africa has seen the terms of exchange of its export products on the global market against products imported from the industrialized countries deteriorate since the early 1980s. Roughly speaking, since 1980, the value of a basket of goods exported by Africa has lost half of its value compared to products imported from the North. Africa has responded by increasing the volume of its exports on the global market. That has not solved the problem, however, as their prices have been falling faster than the prices of products imported from the North. In fact, in the present system of world trade, the countries of the South are at a disadvantage, especially countries of sub-Saharan Africa, as they export far fewer manufactured products than Latin America, or East or Southeast Asia. Any increase in the volume of their exports tends to bring down their value as demand stagnates or drops in the North. The table 15.4 shows the evolution of world prices for basic commodities between 1996 and April 2000.

Let us examine the evolution of terms of exchange compared to volumes

TABLE 15.4. WORLD PRICES OF BASIC COMMODITIES, 1996–2000
(PERCENT OF VARIATION FROM PRECEDING YEAR)

	1996	1997	1998	1999	2000
All products	−4.2	0.0	−13.0	−14.2	−1.0
Foodstuffs and tropical drinks	2.1	2.8	−14.3	−18.3	−1.0
Coffee	−19.1	54.7	−28.5	−23.2	−24.0
Cocoa	1.2	11.2	3.7	−32.1	−0.8
Tea	...	35.1	4.3	−7.0	9.1
Sugar	−9.9	−4.9	−21.2	−30.0	0.2
Rice	5.0	−10.7	1.3	−18.6	−6.1
Vegetable and grain oils	−4.2	−0.9	7.1	−23.3	0.0
Agricultural produce	−9.9	−10.3	−10.8	−10.3	1.0
Cotton	−14.8	−8.9	−8.3	−22.9	36.7
Tobacco	15.6	15.6	−5.5	−7.0	−3.4
Minerals and metals	−12.1	0.0	−16.0	−1.8	−0.8
copper included	−21.8	−0.8	−27.3	−4.9	−4.9

Source: UNCTAD 2000b.

exported. Here, too, it is quite clear that the situation of sub-Saharan Africa has deteriorated. In 1996–97, it exported 25 percent more in terms of quantity than it had in 1980–81, while the relative value of these exports had fallen by 35 percent (see table 15.5).

TABLE 15.5. TRADING TERMS AND VOLUME OF EXPORTS
FOR SUB-SAHARAN AFRICA

	1980–81	1996–97	
Trade terms	100	64.7	
Volume of exports	100	125	*Source: UNCTAD 2000b.*

Sub-Saharan Africa is bleeding

The two phenomena described above can be summarized in the following way: growing debt burden despite large debt payments; unequal trade creating a growing trade deficit. When all of the negative effects of this state of affairs are considered, it becomes clear that the favorable reports on Africa by the media and the IFIs are little more than abject falsifications.

This evaluation is confirmed in IMF internal documents, where one can occasionally find analyses that stray a long way from the optimistic proclamations of official press statements. For example,

> The debt burden remains extremely high, accumulated overdue payments increase this burden further still. This can be seen in the fact that most countries on the continent owe total debt that is four times annual export earnings.
>
> Only a few countries show signs of being able to service such high debt. For most of the others, however, actual debt servicing accounts for more than twice incoming funds from lenders and donors. The danger is that excessive debt will be an obstacle to direct investment and other private capital flows. (IMF 1995, 44)

The structural adjustment fiasco

The World Bank and the IMF claim that the application of structural adjustment policies (renamed "Poverty Reduction Strategy Papers" in 1999) helps to attract the private capital indispensable to economic liftoff. To attract private capital, African governments are required to radically reduce taxes on profits made by foreign companies and to allow the free transfer (repatriation) of profits back to the mother company (which is, in 95 percent of cases, located in the industrialized countries).

There are other incentives: governments are expected to provide the foreign companies that wish to set up in their country land and communications infrastructures, free of charge. If that is insufficient, they are advised to create free zones, where no taxes are levied and the labor laws or collective contracts in force in the country are not applicable. To get a flow of foreign investments, African states must renounce tax returns, increase expenditure on certain infrastructure costs, give up parts of the national territory, and allow the flouting of their labor legislation.

After at least ten years of application of these policies, what are the results? Is there an influx of foreign private capital (known as foreign direct investment)? No, there is no inflow of such foreign private capital. This has been confirmed by the United Nations Conference on Trade and Development (UNCTAD) in a July 2000 report entitled *Capital Flows and Growth in Africa*. The report makes edifying revelations: not only is there no inflow, but there is a fall (see table 1 of the report). In the period from 1975–82, the input of private capital represented 3.9 percent of gross national product of sub-Saharan African countries. In the period from 1983–98, when adjustment policies became generalized, it represented only 1.8 percent of GNP, a drop of more than 50 percent compared to the period from 1975–82 (i.e., before the debt crisis and the beginning of the adjustment policies). Only one conclusion can be drawn: the IMF, the World Bank, and the African governments that applied their policies failed.

Not only is there no inflow of foreign private capital; national private capital is flowing out of these countries in ever-increasing quantities. The IMF and World Bank have ordered the lifting of controls over the transfer of capital. This enables African capitalists to invest "their" money abroad more easily than before. In the jargon, this is called "the purchase of foreign assets by African residents in Africa." UNCTAD (2000c) says no less in the following passage: "During the last ten years, certain African countries, too, have liberalized the transfer of funds, facilitating the acquisition of assets abroad." Only a few countries have not liberalized or have tightened controls, such as Sudan, Zimbabwe, and the Democratic Republic of the Congo.

In the following excerpt, UNCTAD (2000c), albeit prudently, acknowledges the overall negative impact: "The data on Africa tends to confirm the conclusion arrived at for emerging markets, namely that the liberalization of short-term capital movements not only contributes very little to net capital input, but is a considerable source of instability." In other words, adjustment policies in their role of "liberalizing capital movements" bring no lasting positive results to the countries that apply them.

Rubens Ricupero, secretary-general of UNCTAD, in his introduction to UNCTAD's 1998 *Trade and Development Report* made the same point more emphatically, and challenged the governments of the most industrialized countries over banking codes that allow the dissimulation of capital, which, although transferred legally from countries of the South, is nonetheless the product of theft.

Later, we will see that a correlation exists between external indebtedness and the amount of ill-gotten gains placed safely outside the country. The implications of this underscore the importance of the struggle for the cancellation of the debt and the restitution of ill-gotten gains both as a significant source of funding for development that guarantees the fulfillment of basic human needs and as a means of fighting corruption and private enrichment to the detriment of the community.

Private capital and development

According to the principles of structural adjustment, private capital is the motor of development. Is this true? UNCTAD (2000c) takes the opposite position, explaining that for Africa, "private capital inflows, in particular foreign direct investment (FDI), lag behind rather than lead growth." Since growth never comes unaided, "the task of filling the resource gap inevitably falls on official financing." According to UNCTAD,

> This initial big push could only come from official sources of finance, and it would need to be combined with policies that recognize the need not only for market-based incentives, but also for a greater role for the state and for institution building.

Public capital comes from loans or donations made by the most industrialized countries, the World Bank, the IMF, the regional development banks, and a series of UN institutions. In the period from 1990–98, public contribution of capital represented 7.5 percent of the GNP of sub-Saharan Africa—four times the amount contributed by private capital, which represented 1.8 percent of GNP (see UNCTAD 2000c, table 1). Although much greater than private capital investments, public funding is wholly insufficient and falling rapidly. According to UNCTAD, by the end of the 1990s, the real value of public funding per head of population represented less than half of what it was in the early 1980s!

To conclude, the results of the policies dictated by the World Bank and the IMF are, in practical terms, a reduction in external public funding, a reduction in external private funding, and an increase in the flight of African capital toward the industrialized countries.

Agriculture

The second declared objective of structural adjustment is to improve the situation of small private producers, as an incentive to increase production. Another key stratagem of adjustment is as follows: the radical reduction in the interventionism of public authorities in agriculture is to liberate private initiative and open the way to improved living conditions for small farmers. UNCTAD's research shows that, in reality, far from improving the lot of farmers in general and small farmers in particular, adjustment has led to severe deterioration:

> There are indications that some ingredients of reforms have actually aggravated constraints on the growth of smallholder production.... [A]ccess to inputs and credit has not improved because input subsidies and public agricultural services (input provision, product distribution, credit and extension) have been reduced, and the private sector has not adequately taken over these functions. (UNCTAD 1998b)

The same report argues:

> The findings... show that despite widespread market-oriented agricultural price reforms, the past ten years have not produced significant improvements in relative prices and terms of trade for agriculture or lowered the rates of taxation of farmers.

Impossible growth

The third declared objective of structural adjustment is to achieve sustained economic growth. The IMF and World Bank systematically base on optimistic forecasts of growth the adjustment therapies they impose on the countries of the periphery. With a few rare exceptions, these forecasts are in contradiction with the facts. Not surprisingly, since prices of exotic agricultural products and raw materials are unlikely to rise if all of the countries are competing to increase the quantities exported, while the demand for these products stagnates (or even falls) in the most industrialized economies. How could economic growth persist in countries that have had imposed, on the one hand, high interest rates, and on the other, a reduction in income for small producers and depressed salaries? If the domestic market of a given country is depressed because of IMF and World Bank policies, exports are the only way to achieve a high rate of economic growth. However, this is not usually possible because of the depressed prices of the raw materials exported to the global market.

We claim that the IMF and the World Bank generally make highly optimistic forecasts for tomorrow to justify their shock policies for today. Let us take the example of Tanzania. In 2000, the IMF persuaded the Tanzanian authorities to start another new, long period of adjustment, based on glaringly unrealistic projections. Between 2000 and 2018, export revenues were to progress by 9.9 percent a year! External donations would progress by 2.1 percent a year, and FDI would increase by 8.3 percent a year (IMF document cited in UNCTAD 2000d). Here we are dealing with sensation-seeking prognoses that the future will unfortunately expose as false. Meanwhile, policies will be carried out that force the poor (more than 70 percent of the Tanzanian population live below the absolute poverty level) to pay the price of an adjustment that entails handing over a little more of the country to the interests of the multinationals.

TABLE 15.6. PERCENTAGE OF EXTERNAL DEBT OWED TO THE PRIVATE SEC-
TOR BY AFRICAN COUNTRIES, 2001

0	1	2	3	4
Benin	Guinea	Ethiopia	Gabon	Cape Verde
Burkina Faso	Mauritania	Madagascar	Zambia	Central African Republic
Burundi	Uganda	São Tomé e Principe	Ghana	
Comoro Islands	Chad	Senegal	Niger	
Djibouti	Somalia			
Eritrea	Tanzania			
Gambia				
Guinea-Bissau				
Malawi				
Mali				
Rwanda				
Sierra Leone				
Togo				

Various international organizations (UNCTAD, the IMF, the World Bank) agree on the need for real growth at the rate of 6 percent per year over a period of fifteen years to enable the countries of sub-Saharan Africa to take off economically. Each year, for at least ten years now, the World Bank and IMF have announced that these figures will be achieved the following year. Let us examine what is really happening.

In the 1970s, the average rate of growth for the region was about 3.5 percent; in the 1980s, the average rate of growth fell to 2.5 percent. The decline in growth continued between 1989 and 1998, to reach a mere 2.2 percent (see UNCTAD 2000b). In 2002, it reached 2.6 percent, according to the World Bank (2002c).

Specific features of sub-Saharan Africa's foreign debt in the early 2000s

Unlike most Latin American and Southeast Asian countries, sub-Saharan Africa (excluding South Africa) no longer has access to financial markets. Bank loans have become scarce, accounting for only 2 percent of the region's total debt stock. Public debt bonds issued by those countries to try to raise foreign private capital are not at all popular on foreign financial markets. The bonds only represent 2 percent of sub-Saharan external debt. Furthermore, 90 percent of this tiny investment in bonds goes toward four countries, with South Africa again in the lead.

In recent years, private banks have been reimbursed by the debtor countries in question to the extent that a large number of African countries now owe them nothing or very little. Table 15.6 lists the countries with less than 5 percent of their external debt owed to the private sector in 2001(World Bank 2003a).

As for the governments of the North, they hold almost half of sub-Saharan Africa's debt (not including South Africa, which is still in the banks' good books). The international financial institutions (World Bank, IMF, African Development Bank) hold more than a third of this debt. The poorer an African country is, the more its debt is held by the IFIs. For example, in 2001, the IFIs held 72 percent of Niger's external public debt, 88 percent of Burundi's debt, 87 percent of the Rwanda's debt, 73 percent of the Central African Republic's debt, and 82 percent of Burkina Faso's debt (World Bank 2001).

With a few exceptions, sub-Saharan Africa's debt is held by the IFIs and the governments of the North (especially the former colonial powers). A significant portion of official development assistance provided by the countries of the North is used to pay back the IFIs. Apart from South Africa (given the weight of its economy and the strength of its capitalist class) and Sudan (which has broken away from the IFIs), the region's governments are very much under the thumb of the IMF, the World Bank, and the Paris Club, which brings together the various lender governments of the North.

Is sub-Saharan Africa a creditor or a debtor?

In their fascinating study on capital flight from sub-Saharan Africa to the highly industrialized countries, "Is Africa a net creditor?", James K. Boyce and Léonce Ndikumana (2000) draw very interesting conclusions. They estimate that capital flight from twenty-six sub-Saharan African countries (excluding South Africa),[3] representing 92 percent of the subcontinent's population, 93 percent of its GDP, and 91 percent of its external debt, is as much as $193 billion from 1970 to 1996. This is considerably more than the external debt stock of those countries, which came to $178 billion in 1996. They calculate that if this money had been deposited in a bank at normal rates, $193 billion plus interest would come to $285 billion at the end of that period—that is, 50 percent more than the total debt of the countries concerned. In short, in either hypothesis, the amount of Africa's total assets deposited abroad is greater than its debt. This is why Boyce and Ndikumana are able to answer the question posed by their study in the affirmative. Yes, sub-Saharan Africa is a net creditor.

The authors write:

> [C]apital flight is likely to have pronounced regressive effects on the distribution of wealth. The individuals who engage in capital flight generally are members of the subcontinent's economic and political élites, who take advantage of their privileged positions to acquire and channel funds abroad. Both the acquisition and the transfer of funds often involve legally questionable practices, including the falsification of trade documents (trade misinvoicing), the embezzlement of export revenues, and kickbacks on public and private sector contracts (see, for example, Ndikumana and Boyce, 1998). The negative effects of the resulting shortages of revenue and foreign exchange fall disproportionately on the shoulders of the less wealthy members of the society.

They continue, "Insofar as the proceeds of external borrowing were used not to the benefit of the African public, but rather to finance the accumulation of private external assets by the ruling élites, the moral and legal legitimacy of these debt-service obligations is open to challenge."

Working from various studies by Niels Hermes and Robert Lensink, the authors also consider that capital flight is proportionately greater in sub-Saharan Africa than in Latin America, a continent notorious for its capital flight.

In the case of Zaire (known as the Democratic Republic of the Congo, DRC, since 1997), they claim that capital flight between 1968 and 1990 reached $12 billion, a far higher sum than the country's external debt at the time.

Table 15.7 presents the results of Boyce and Ndikumana's estimations. The authors make the following comments on the table:

> For the 25-country sample as a whole, external assets exceed external debts by $14.5 billion to $106.5 billion, depending on whether we count imputed interest earnings on the asset side. The region's assets are 1.1 to 1.6 times the stock of debts. For some individual countries, the results are even more dramatic: Nigeria's external assets are 2.8 times its external debt by the conservative measure, and 4.1 times higher when we include imputed interest earnings on capital flight.

We completely endorse all of their conclusions, of which some large extracts follow.

> If sub-Saharan Africa is truly a net creditor, why are so many of its people so poor? The answer, of course, is that the subcontinent's private external assets belong to a narrow, relatively wealthy stratum of its population, while public external debts are borne by the populace at large through their governments. This asymmetry is not only regrettable, in that it exacerbates poverty in a region in which many are already desperately poor. It also raises profound questions as to precisely what belongs to whom, that is, how rights to external assets and responsibilities for external liabilities are to be distributed across the population.
>
> Rights to sub-Saharan Africa's "private" external assets are by no means clearly defined or incontestable. The fact that the Nigerian government has been able to obtain a Swiss court order freezing the bank accounts of General Sani Abacha's family is but one indication of the scope for legal, ethical, and political challenges

TABLE 15.7. EXTERNAL DEBT AND NET EXTERNAL ASSETS IN 1996
(MILLIONS OF DOLLARS)

Country	Debt stock 1996	Net external assets Capital flight less debt stock	Capital flight plus interest on same, less debt stock
Angola	11,225.1	5,807.4	9,179.9
Burkina Faso	1,196.1	69.4	700.4
Burundi	1,126.9	−308.0	−146.0
Cameroon	9,541.6	3,557.8	7,364.4
Central African Republic	941.1	−691.0	−482.1
Democratic Republic of Congo	12,826.4	561.4	10,164.1
Congo-Brazzaville	5,240.6	−4,781.4	−3986.6
Ivory Coast	19,523.6	3,847.4	15,221.9
Ethiopia	10,078.6	−4,555.8	−2060.7
Ghana	6,442.2	−6,034.9	−6,152.9
Guinea	3,240.3	−2,897.5	−2,806.1
Kenya	6,931.0	−6,115.9	−4,458.4
Madagascar	4,145.8	−2,496.8	−2,568.3
Malawi	2,146.1	−1,441.0	−971.3
Mali	3,006.0	−4,209.6	−4,533.2
Mauritania	2,404.2	−1,273.4	−572.2
Mozambique	7,566.3	−2,255.0	−1,359.4
Niger	1,623.3	−4,776.3	−6,392.1
Nigeria	31,406.6	55,355.3	98,254.4
Rwanda	1,043.1	1,072.8	2,470.8
Sierra Leone	1,205.1	267.6	1,072.7
Sudan	16,972.0	−9,989.3	−5,358.3
Tanzania	7,361.8	−5,662.7	−1,158.4
Uganda	3,674.4	−1,519.5	−358.3
Zambia	7,639.4	2,984.1	5,491.8
Total	178,507.6	14,515.1	106,556.1

Sources: Calculated by Boyce and Ndikumana (2000) based on IMF, Direction of Trade Statistics Yearbook (various issues); IMF, International Financial Statistics Yearbook (various issues); World Bank, World Development Indicators 2000 (CD-ROM edition); and World Bank, Global Development Finance 2000 (CD-ROM edition).

to the ownership of these assets. Not only did capital flight itself generally violate foreign-exchange controls (hence its omission from the official balance of payments), but in many cases the capital itself was acquired by legally dubious means.

Efforts to recover and repatriate illicit private fortunes are one way in which African peoples and their governments can attempt to repair the disjuncture between public external debts and private external assets. This is a difficult route, however, since it places the burden of proof squarely on the African governments to locate and reclaim the money (see, for example, *The Financial Times*, 1999). As a result, such efforts offer only limited possibilities for easing sub-Saharan Africa's public external debt burden.

An alternative, complementary strategy would apply the same principles to the region's external liabilities. Sub-Saharan African governments could inform their creditors that outstanding debts will be treated as legitimate if, and only if, the real counterparts of the borrowing can be identified. If the creditors can document where the money went, and show when and how it benefited citizens of the borrowing country via investment or consumption, then the debt will be regarded as a *bona fide* external obligation of the government (and hence an external asset of the creditor bank or government). But if the fate of the borrowed money cannot be traced, then the present African governments must infer that it was diverted into private pockets, and possibly into capital flight. In such cases, it can be argued, the liability for the debt lies not with the government, but with the private individuals whose personal fortunes are the real counterpart of the debts.

In adopting such a strategy, Africans could invoke as a precedent the US government's stance toward the creditors of the erstwhile Spanish colonial regime in Cuba after the Spanish-American war, a century ago: the creditors knew, or should have known, the risks they faced when they made the loans to the predecessor regime, and they "took the chances of the investment."

The odious policy of the World Bank and IMF toward the Congolese people

> *The issue of the moral responsibility of the creditors was particularly apparent in the case of cold war loans. When the IMF and the World Bank lent money to Democratic Republic of Congo's notorious ruler Mobutu, they knew (or should have known) that most of the money would not go to help that country's poor people, but rather would be used to enrich Mobutu. It was money paid to ensure that this corrupt leader would keep his country aligned with the West. To many, it doesn't seem fair for ordinary tax-payers in countries with corrupt governments to have to repay loans that were made to leaders who did not represent them.*

—*Joseph Stiglitz*, Globalization and Its Discontents

The external debt of the DRC, officially about $12 billion, was (almost) entirely contracted under Mobutu Sese Seko's despotic regime. It should have been canceled when his regime fell.

The World Bank and the IMF have claimed the $2 billion they had lent to Mobutu from the regime that succeeded the dictatorship.

When Mobutu fell, the *Financial Times* (May 12, 1997) published the results of an investigation it had commissioned. The findings were that in the early years of his "reign," Mobutu was directly financed by the CIA. The *Financial Times* (*FT*) claims that in the 1980s, both the IMF and the US Treasury estimated Mobutu's external assets at $4 billion. In 1982, the directors of the IMF—Jacques de Larosière, of France, was director general at the time—received a detailed report by Erwin Blumenthal, a German banker. It described the extreme level of corruption of Mobutu's regime. However, after receiving Blumenthal's report, the IMF considerably increased its loans. The *FT* reports that it contacted de Larosière (who by then had become president of the EBRD—European Bank for Reconstruction and Development), in May 1997, to ask for his comments. De Larosière declared that he did not wish to discuss his role in Zaire. They also contacted the IMF, which declared that it was not prepared to comment.

For many years, until 1995–96, the IMF and World Bank never stopped financing the Mobutu regime. The regime applied extremely harsh neoliberal policies while Kengo Wa Dondo, known at the time as "Mr. World Bank," was minister. (He is now enjoying a comfortable retirement in Belgium.) Mobutu happily plunged his country into debt to the IMF and World Bank, while placing a good portion of the loans in his private moneybox. The IMF and the World Bank turned a blind eye, as Mobutu applied their structural adjustment plans and remained an ally of the United States.

When Laurent Désiré Kabila overthrew Mobutu, he decided to stop paying off the Bretton Woods institutions. They tried to persuade him to resume payments, but Kabila resisted. He wanted them to make a strong gesture in terms of debt cancellation, and he did not want to further subjugate his country to structural adjustment. Kabila was assassinated in January 2001. The World Bank and the IMF turned on the charm with his successor, Joseph Kabila (Laurent Désiré's son). The Bank announced a donation of $50 million. The two institutions demanded that Belgium, the former colonial power, pay off part of the debt contracted by Mobutu. Belgium did so, using the money normally earmarked for cooperation and development, which should have gone directly to the Congolese people. The World Bank and IMF had a dual objective: to clean up the odious debts contracted by Mobutu and to restart the lending machine, so they could dictate structural adjustment policies to the DRC once more.

In search of an alternative solution, for some years now citizens' movements in the DRC[4] and in Belgium[5] have collaborated on the external debt file of the DRC and are demanding its cancellation. The debt is being audited in both Kinshasa and Belgium. Exchange visits have been organized. Street demonstrations regularly take place in both Belgium and the DRC. The movements for the cancellation of the debt have by no means given up.

South Africa and the odious debt of apartheid

From 1950 to 1990, South Africa was subjected to the apartheid regime. Condemned in 1973 by the UN as a crime against humanity, the country was then the object of an international boycott. Despite the boycott, a series of loans and trade transactions went ahead with the outlawed regime. (For many, it seems, business rights take precedence over human rights.) The debts contracted during this period have all the characteristics of odious debt, i.e., a debt contracted by a despotic regime against the population's interests. International condemnation did not prevent the creditors—states, IFIs, MNCs—from continuing to collect the debt payments. Unfortunately, the new democratic regime took on the debt instead of repudiating it. The descendants of the victims of apartheid are therefore still paying the creditors who were complicit in crimes against humanity.

Nevertheless, things are changing. On November 11, 2002, eighty-five of the thirty-two thousand members of the Khulumani organization, a support group for apartheid victims, lodged a complaint in the Eastern District of New York against twenty-one foreign banks.[6] They are demanding reparations for the damage and injustice directly resulting from the complicity of these banks and companies with the apartheid regime. The complaint is based on an American law entitling US citizens to bring a complaint in the United States against anyone who has violated international public law, provided that the person is present on US territory.

The complaint itself is based on the principle of secondary responsibility, i.e., aiding and abetting in a crime against humanity. This doctrine is rooted in the fight to combat slavery. The first US law of this kind was passed in 1794. Neville Gabriel, spokesperson for Jubilee South Africa (a network of four thousand NGOs, which has as one of its main objectives the cancellation of the debt contracted under apartheid), demanded compensation for apartheid victims, declaring that "the damages come to billions of dollars."

The cost of the crimes of apartheid can never be evaluated, whatever the moral and legal force of the arguments. However, it is a political necessity to demand reparation, though the amount claimed can only be symbolic. These citizens' tactics show the way forward. For others involved must also be judged. The legal responsibility of IFIs such as the IMF and World Bank needs to be investigated.

Certainly, it is urgent for the social movement to indict the banks and multinationals and to demand reparation. It is equally urgent to bring the IMF and World Bank to justice for aiding and abetting despotic regimes responsible for crimes against humanity. Finally, it is equally important to repudiate the odious debts they lay claim to.

---

1   In a very interesting study by Pablo Gonzalez Casanova (1999), carried further by Saxe-Fernández and Núñez Rodríguez (2001), there is a qualitative and quantitative analysis of different forms of transfer from Latin America and the Caribbean to the highly industrialized countries of the center for the period 1976–97.

2   These calculations are based on World Bank 2003a.

3   The twenty-six countries considered are Angola, Burkina Faso, Burundi, Cameroon, Central African Republic, Democratic Republic of the Congo (former Zaire), Congo-Brazzaville, Ivory Coast, Ethiopia, Ghana, Guinea, Kenya, Madagascar, Malawi, Mali, Mauritania, Mozambique, Niger, Nigeria, Rwanda, Sierra Leone, Somalia, Sudan, Tanzania, Uganda and Zambia.

4   The National Council of NGOs in Congo (CNONG), the Forum on External Debt (FORDEX), the group for Reflection and Support to Promote Rural Development (GRAPR), and the Congolese Coalition for Abolition of the Debt and for Development (CCADD).

5   CADTM, CNCD—Operation 11.11.11, and KVNZB—11.11.11.

6   Among others, ExxonMobil, Shell Oil, Caltex, Barclays National Bank, Citigroup, Credit Suisse Group, Deutsche Bank AG, JPMorgan Chase, Ford Motor, and DaimlerChrysler AG.

16
Four case studies

Brazil

The current status of the debt audit and the responsibilities of the Lula government

At the time of the crisis in the 1930s, Brazil, along with thirteen other Latin American countries, suspended the payment of principal for several years. (The suspension was total in 1931, partial between 1932 and 1936, and total between 1937 and 1940.) This worked in their favor; in 1943, as a result of negotiations to settle litigation with the cartel of foreign lenders, Brazil obtained the reduction of approximately 50 percent of its remaining debt. The 1930 debt of $1.29 billion was reduced to $698 million in 1945, and $597 million in 1948. In 1930, the service on the debt represented 30 percent of exports, whereas in 1945 it represented a little more than 7 percent.

At the time, to support the unilateral decision to suspend payment, the Brazilian authorities had recourse to an audit. In 1931, a decree was passed requiring a review of all external public borrowing. In 1932, another decree required detailed analysis of these contracts. This audit revealed the existence of numerous irregularities in the way the contracts had been drawn up. In his review of the audit, Arthur de Souza Costa, then finance minister, stated in 1935: "The history of our loans reveals them to be exaggerated in number, onerous, even ruinous, devoid of any aspiration to favoring the development of our country" (cited by Reinaldo Gonçalves in Fattorelli 2003, 115).

The basis of the debt crisis, which would explode in Brazil as in other Third World countries in 1982, originated in the 1960s and 1970s during the long military dictatorship that began in 1964. At the time of the coup d'état in 1964, the external debt had risen to $2.5 billion; when the last general left the presidency in 1985, the debt was more than $100 billion! It had been multiplied by forty in little more than twenty years of dictatorship.

This dictatorship had benefited from the unfailing support of the US government and the World Bank. It was viewed as a strategic ally on the continent of South America in a context of the proliferation of the Cuban Revolution and the great anticapitalist and anti-imperialist struggles. It is worth noting that before the coup d'état of 1964, the World Bank had refused to loan money to Brazil under the progressive president Joao Goulart (popularly known as "Jango"), who had undertaken agrarian reform.

From 1964 on, the US government, via its export credit agency Ex-Im Bank and the World Bank, granted numerous loans to its allies, the generals in power in Brasília. The mega power-plant projects date from this period: hydroelectric dams, thermodynamic installations, and the creation of major highway infrastructures to penetrate the immense region of the Amazon through the Polonoreste program. All of these projects caused enormous environmental destruction, the extinction of certain groups of indigenous peoples, and major population displacement (colonization of areas where forests were destroyed in order to create grazing land, for example).

The enthusiastic support by the United States for dictatorial regimes was one of the causes of their widespread establishment in the Southern Cone (Chile and Uruguay, 1973; Argentina, 1976). The government in Washington was directly involved in setting up the dictatorships and planning the physical extermination of a significant number of left-wing opponents on a continental scale (the sinister Operation Condor program).

When the United States decided on a radical increase of interest rates at the end of 1979, the Brazilian dictatorship, despite its friendly status, was hit hard, as this measure destabilized it in the face of rising popular opposition at the beginning of the 1980s. Between 1979 and 1985, faced with the debt crisis, Brazil transferred to its creditors (principally banks in the United States) $21 billion more than it received in new loans during the same period.

The cartel of banks lending to Brazil was directed by Citibank, which was directly involved in the ruthless dictatorial maneuvering in Latin America during the 1960s and 1970s. Throughout this period, Citibank was extremely active in the field of financial engineering, transforming the public funds of the Southern countries into private funds for governments—preferably military governments. Citibank was also a formidable money-laundering machine. Its reprehensible and destructive activities were not limited to Latin America; it collaborated actively with Nigerian dictator Sani Abacha in the 1990s, providing security for the colossal sums (several billion dollars) he stole from the public treasury of his nation. Citibank (now part of Citigroup) has since been indicted in various scandals, including the Enron affair. The latter resulted in a judgement by New York Attorney General Eliot Spitzer involving a fine of several hundred million dollars in 2003. Note that at the beginning of this decade, Citigroup added to its directors Robert Rubin, treasury secretary of the United States (1995–99), and Stanley Fischer, number two at the IMF.[1]

The IMF first became an actor in the machinations of the odious Brazilian debt in January 1983. It dictated a letter of intent to the dictatorship, but first criticized the latter's concession of too many wage increases to workers.

The sharp increase in interest rates decreed by the US government from the end of 1979 put a financial stranglehold on public authorities in Brazil as elsewhere in Latin America. José Sarney, the first president (1985–89) of the post-dictatorial period, was obliged to decree a suspension of payments in 1987. During this period, which also saw the birth of the Workers' Party (PT), the Unified Workers' Confederation (CUT, the main trade union), and the Landless Rural Workers' Movement (MST), an increased awareness emerged among progressives regarding the question of the debt. Indeed, from 1985, the campaign launched by Fidel Castro on the theme "the debt cannot be paid" echoed favorably throughout Brazil and across the whole continent.

The idea that public authorities could use the audit to achieve complete renegotiation of the debt met with general approval. The benefits of the audit of the 1930s no doubt remained in the collective memory. A large number of progressive movements saw the audit as a way to deal with the crushing debt burden left over from the dictatorship. The request for an audit became such a sensitive subject that legislators included it in the post-dictatorship constitution of 1988. Article 26 of the Temporary Constitutional Provisions Act conferred on the National Congress responsibility for completing an audit of the debt within one year.

At the beginning of the 1990s, the financial situation of the country improved somewhat when capital began to flow in from abroad in the form of bank loans, investments in stock, and direct investments.

In a way, the Brady Plan, applied to Brazil from 1994 on, under the direction of minister of finance Fernando Henrique Cardoso, had the effect of brushing things under the carpet by legitimizing the debts contracted during the long dictatorial night. A significant part ($49 billion of $145 billion) was transformed into new debt known as "Brady bonds." Throughout this period, the debt continued to mount; it was necessary to borrow in order to repay. The Brady operation applied in Brazil with the collaboration of Cardoso significantly increased the service on the debt. (See the analysis of the economist Paulo Nogueira Batista, Jr., cited by José Dirceu, Project of Legislative Decree 645-A, September 13, 2000.)

The situation severely worsened with the onset of the Mexican crisis in

December 1994. The plan of Cardoso, who became president in 1985, to save the private banks of Brazil (PROER in Portuguese, for Program of Incentives for Restructuring and Strengthening the National Financial System) cost the government $20 billion. Within the framework of these accords with the IMF, Cardoso maintained a high interest policy (in fact, the highest in the world), which, while favoring capital investors, was extremely damaging to the production sector.

Table 16.1 shows the evolution of interest rates in Brazil between September 1997 (period of the Asian crisis) and March 1999 (date of a new agreement with the IMF). The fact that, at the beginning of 1999, the net profit declared by the large Brazilian banks was five to eight times higher than that declared in 1998 is a clear demonstration that this policy favors capital investors.

TABLE 16.1. EVOLUTION OF INTEREST RATES IN BRAZIL (PERCENT)

1997	September	20.7	
	November	42.2	"Package 51"
	December	39.5	
1998	January	37.4	
	March	26.2	
	May	22.6	
	August	19.3	Russian Crisis
	September	33.5	
	October	39.3	
	December	29.3	
1999	January	29.9	
	February	38.8	
	March	43.1	IMF Agreement Revised

Source: Central Bank of Brazil, in Arruda 2000.

In addition, between 1997 and the end of 2001, Brazil fell victim to a negative net transfer on debt (see glossary) to the amount of $78.9 billion. If one takes into account government departments only, this corresponds to $27.3 billion of negative net transfer on the public debt between 1996 and the end of 2001 (World Bank 2003a). In other words, if the Brazilian government had decided in 1997 to suspend payment of the debt and, consequently, the different lenders had decided to cut off all credit, the public treasury would have saved the substantial sum of more than $27 billion. Thus, in the case of Brazil, it is invalid to affirm that continued payment of the external debt is better based on the assumption that new loans entering the country are greater than debt payment flowing out of the country. To give an approximate idea of the amounts reimbursed, in the 1999 state budget, service on the debt was five times larger than the public health budget, nine times larger than the education budget, and sixty-nine times larger than the budget of the Ministry of Agrarian Reform (calculations by the author, based on Gonçalves and Pomar 2000).

The deterioration of the situation brought about a new awareness in the population regarding the question of the debt. A debt tribunal was organized on behalf of the social movements in April 1998, in Rio, followed in September 2000 by a referendum in which more than six million Brazilians participated. The Jubilee 2000 Campaign for a Debt-Free Millennium, the National Conference of Bishops, the MST, and the CUT and other trade unions organized the referendum, and several parties on the left, including the PT, supported it.

At the time of the referendum, José Dirceu (then a member of parliament and president of the PT) introduced a proposed legislative decree for "a referendum to enable the population to decide regarding the external debt and whether or not to maintain international agreements between the government of Brazil and the IMF."[2] Article 1 of the proposed decree declared:

> It has been decided by the National Congress...to carry out audits on the external debt and to hold a referendum asking the following questions: (1) Should the government of Brazil break its agreements with the IMF? (2) Should the government of Brazil carry out an audit of the external debt? (3) Should the government of Brazil maintain its present policy of payment of the debt?

The decree continued thus:

> Should popular vote decide in favor of breaking the agreements with the IMF, this shall take effect within 90 days; should popular vote decide in favor of the audit, this shall be completed within 90 days; should popular vote decide in favor of the terms of payment of the debt, the National Congress undertakes to deliberate on the new conditions within 90 days.

This proposal was introduced on September 13, 2000, with the support and signatures of 191 members of parliament, including that of Antonio Palocci, who became minister of finance in January 2003. The parliamentary majority of Cardoso rejected the proposal (although certain deputies who were members of the majority did support it). It was clear at the time of the 2002 elections that the neoliberal Cardoso might be replaced by Lula, who symbolized more than twenty years of working-class struggle against the dictatorship and against the conservatives. This possibility raised enormous enthusiasm and understandable expectations of finally finding solutions to major social problems, as well as the problem of the debt.

These expectations were dashed in 2003. We shall see why, but first, let it be said that creativity, intelligence, loyal combat, and willingness to fight may well provide the necessary impetus for the citizens' movements and the social movements of Brazil. There is hope that they can salvage their leader's earlier commitments and see them put into practice. Was it not Lula and the PT over the years that made the debt an important campaign theme of the PT? An interview with Lula in July 1991, by the author, in Managua, Nicaragua, is included here. Then, we will look at the first moves made by Luiz Inácio Lula de Silva when he took office as president in January 2003.

> *Any Third World government which takes the decision to carry on refunding the external debt is opting for the road to ruin.*
>
> —*Luiz Inácio Lula da Silva, 1991,*
> *at that time, president of the Brazilian PT*

Interview with Lula by Eric Toussaint, July 1991, Managua[1]

Toussaint: After a year and a half of Collor's presidency, what is the situation now in Brazil?

Lula: It has become quite clear for Brazilians that president Collor's neoliberal policy is a failure. Despite all the promises, nothing has been solved; inflation has decreased, but the social cost in terms of unemployment, agrarian policy, wages, health, and education has been extremely high. This means it is now urgent to make counterproposals geared toward the economic growth of Brazil, the redistribution of wealth to compensate the workers for their losses as a result of the plan.

But all of this must be done in conjunction with a major reorganization of the social movement; otherwise, if it remains confined to the struggle over institutional issues, the PT is going to become highly vulnerable. And, if we are to succeed in standing up to the government, the question of alliances with other progressive forces is also crucial.

Toussaint: Not long ago, the headlines of the weekly magazine *The Economist* were "Latin America is for sale." What is the situation regarding the sale of national companies? And what is the position of the PT?

Lula: The IMF wants the indebted countries to sell their state enterprises to help pay off the foreign debt. Our position is clear on this. We defend the state control of all companies in strategic sectors. On the

Continued, next page ▶

▶ *Continued from previous page*

other hand, there is no objection to the privatization of the companies nationalized under the military regime and the companies of lesser importance, such as textiles. Those companies belonging to the strategic sectors, such as oil, iron and steel, water, the ports, electric power…must be under state control. Our struggle to prevent the privatization of these companies favors their democratization. It is important that these companies should be opened up so that they can be administered by civil society. It is important that there should also be union leaders running them. Groups from civil society must be involved in the administration so that, as a whole, they are transformed into assets belonging to the community. In no way can we consent to the privatization of national assets in order to pay the external debt. In fact, until now, the government hasn't gotten very far with its privatization policy because there have been no buyers. But, if it were only up to the government, everything would already be privatized. Another thing to remember is that this urge to privatize is devoid of any popular support—the Argentine example is there for all to see, and there privatization has brought nothing but calamity.

Toussaint: And where does the PT stand regarding the external debt?

Lula: It is our opinion that no Third World country is in a position to pay the debt. We believe that any Third World government which takes the decision to carry on refunding the external debt is opting for the road to ruin. There is a total incompatibility between Third World development policy and refunding the debt. We maintain that there should be an immediate moratorium on the debt, and we demand that an audit be carried out on its history to find out just where the money came from, to find out if the loan was contracted by the state or some other public administration or whether it was a private initiative, to find out what the money was spent on, and so on. All this must be done so that we can get a reliable picture of just what was going on.

And then, with the economies deriving from the nonpayment of the debt, we will be able to set up a development fund to finance research and technological innovation, teaching, health, land reform: a development policy corresponding to the needs of the whole Third World. This development fund would be managed by the country itself. It would be controlled by an authority, as yet to be created, comprising the National Congress (Parliament), the trade-union movements, the political parties;

they would form a commission which would deal with the administration of the fund. An international political initiative is also required. A united front must be set up by the debtor countries to confront the creditors. And it is also necessary for the Third World countries to unite so that each government understands that its problems are no different from those of the other Third World countries. By itself, no country can possibly resolve the problem of the debt.

It is also important to bear in mind that the discussion of the external debt should not be between governments and bankers but on an intergovernmental level. Another thing that must be done is to transform the question of the debt into a political issue. Merely discussing the problem of the debt is not enough; what has to be done is to think about the necessity of a new international economic order. We cannot go on selling raw materials for next to nothing while we pay a fortune for manufactured products. This series of measures cannot be carried through without political action. Political action is the pressure exerted by social movements. This means that the question of the debt must be transformed into something that the population takes into its own hands.

Toussaint: Six years ago, Fidel Castro launched an international campaign based on the theme "the debt cannot be paid." After a good start, this campaign seems to have become bogged down through lack of interest. Now, one has the impression that Bush[2] is riding high with his "Initiative for the Americas."[3] How do you explain that?

Lula: It is a fact that it was the Cuban government which launched this debate, and there were a number of highly constructive international meetings on the subject. But, what is happening in Latin America is that the economic situation is so bad that the majority of the workers just do not have the time to think of medium-term objectives. Often our struggle is focused on immediate goals. It is a fight for survival. And, under this pressure, left-wing organizations do not devote enough time and energy to medium- and long-term objectives. We are attempting to find solutions for unemployment and problems of hunger without making a sufficient link-up with the foreign debt. As a party, we think it is important to put this issue on the agenda; and the same applies at the level of the trade unions, because, unless we solve the debt problem, we won't solve the problem of income distribution, inflation, or develop-

Continued, next page ▶

▶*Continued from previous page*

ment either. But, just to come back for a moment to the causes of the weakness in the debt campaign, it has to be said that there is a lack of international coordination among the Latin American trade-union organizations, and this is, above all, due to the fact that, in each of the countries concerned, the movement is insufficiently developed.

Toussaint: And for the continent as a whole? What can be said about the organization at that level?

Lula: During the Latin American left-wing forum in São Paulo, in June 1991, the question of the foreign debt was tabled. This is an issue which is sufficiently important to unite the left. The question will be put on the agenda of the second meeting which takes place in Mexico City, in June 1992.

Toussaint: And what about socialism? Is this still a possible option?

Lula: I continue to believe in it. I still believe that the only hope for mankind is a fairer world in which wealth is distributed in a more equitable way. We have a great contribution to make. There are millions of us on the surface of the Earth who want to build socialism. But socialism must not be the reflection of what went on in Eastern Europe. The Workers' Party has always condemned the single-party system, the lack of freedom or the right to strike for the trade-union movement. We think that democracy, a multiparty system, the freedom and autonomy of the trade unions, the right to strike, freedom of speech are all prerequisites of socialism. If these don't exist, then it is not socialism. The failure of socialism in Eastern Europe is not to be blamed on socialists but on the bureaucracy. It also should be added that today, everyone is eager to speak about the collapse of Eastern European "socialism," but few are prepared to discuss the necessary solidarity with Cuba, the people of Panama, or those of Africa. One of our prime acts of solidarity must be the defense of Cuba.

---

1   This interview was first published in *CADTM*, nos. 4 and 5, October–November 1991.

2   The reference is to President George H.W. Bush, father of current president George W. Bush.

3   The "Initiative for the Americas" defended by Bush was subsequently defended by Bill Clinton, then George W. Bush in the form of the FTAA (Free Trade Area of the Americas).

The Lula presidency: Change or neoliberal continuity?

The overwhelming victory of Lula in the presidential elections (more than 60 percent in the second round and nearly 20 million votes ahead of his competitor) occurred in the context of a problematic alliance policy. Indeed, the PT candidate obtained a last-minute agreement from his party to forge an alliance with the right-wing Liberal Party. In the event of victory, the Liberal Party would secure the vice presidency of the republic.

The commitments of Lula as a candidate during the electoral campaign were also questionable, in as much as he proposed to pursue the economic policy that had been carried out by the Cardoso government. This economic policy, dictated entirely by the IMF, ensured the repayment of the external debt and the pursuit of structural adjustment. Clearly, this policy considerably reduces the public income available for the progressive part of Lula's program, which included a significant increase in the lowest incomes (the monthly minimum wage was approximately equivalent to $80 and would have increased by 20 percent), the eradication of hunger (40 million Brazilians suffer from chronic or permanent hunger), agrarian reform, and an increase in the number of people covered by social security.

During the first eight months of his presidential mandate, Luiz Inácio Lula da Silva and Antonio Palocci, minister of economy and finance, pursued a neoliberal type of economic and social policy, in contradiction both with a structural transformation project and with any hope of substantially improving living conditions for the majority of Brazilian citizens.

What are the main features of this program? Henrique de Campos Meirelles, a representative of international capital, was appointed governor of the Central Bank of Brazil. Meirelles had been president of global banking and financial services of Fleet Boston, the seventh largest US bank and second in the hierarchy of Brazil's creditors (after Citibank). The role played by Fleet Boston was particularly damaging to national interests during the Argentine crisis, as demonstrated by the continual speculation against the Brazilian currency in order to increase profits. Appointing Meirelles to head the Central Bank was a sign from the new president of allegiance toward international creditors and, more generally, toward international capital. It is widely known that Meirelles had campaigned for José Serra, the candidate of Cardoso who opposed Lula, during the first and second round of elections. On the day of Meirelles's appointment, his Web site still called for a vote for José Serra!

Lula and his minister of finance have announced legal measures in order to guarantee the independence of the Central Bank, which is exactly what the IMF and financial markets wanted. Several components of the Left within the presidential majority have severely criticized this. The Central Bank was made independent of the government, and, to crown it all, a representative of international capital was appointed at its head. The executive relinquished all power to exert direct control over monetary policy (exchange rates and issuing of currency) and interest rates (traditionally set by the Central Bank)!

During his election campaign, Lula declared, as did all other presidential candidates except that of the PSTU (the Portuguese acronym for the United Socialist Workers' Party), that he would respect the agreements signed by his predecessor and the IMF in August 2002. Among other things, this agreement obliged Brazil to show a primary budget superavit (surplus before payment of the debt) of 3.75 percent. In August 2002, even finance speculator George Soros criticized this agreement, arguing that it put government policy into a straitjacket. To achieve a superavit of 3.75 percent would require severely limiting social expenses. During the first months of Lula's presidency, Palocci went even further in the direction of the orthodoxy of the IMF and the markets: the government pledged to show a superavit of 4.25 percent!

In the same vein, Palocci increased the main interest rate of the Brazilian Central Bank to 26 percent, then brought it back to 25.5 percent in August 2003. The effect of this measure is in total opposition to the progressive part of Lula's program: it increases the yield of international capital in the form of profit on loans. As proof, Brazilian banks have invested 67 percent of their assets in highly lucrative debt bonds (*Financial Times*, July 18, 2003). A financial columnist for the *Gazeta Mercantil*, the main Brazilian financial daily, jokingly remarked January 20, 2003, about this policy of high internal interest rates, "[W]ith the base interest rate at 25 percent, it is a real pleasure to make profits by borrowing abroad (with an interest rate of about 13.25 percent) and then buying public debt bonds with this borrowed money. A real pleasure...for the banks." Moreover, this policy reinforces social inequality and unequal income distribution. The gap in Brazil between the poorest and the richest is the highest in the world. According to the 1999 UNDP report, the wealthiest 20 percent of Brazilians took 63.4 percent of income, leaving only 2.5 percent to the poorest 20 percent. A policy of high interest rates encourages those who live parasitically on their private incomes. It is the continuation of the policy of "one law for the rich, another for the poor," reinforcing the hardships of low earners and increasing the opulence of the wealthiest.

Raising interest rates has two other negative effects. First, it automatically increases the amounts that must be repaid on the colossal internal public debt. Second, it makes access to credit even more difficult for small and medium producers (farmers, craftspeople, small contractors, etc.). For the productive sector across the board, this reduces investment, dragging the Brazilian economy into stagnation or recession.

Since 1995, Brazil's real rates of return have been among the highest in the world. Supporters of IMF policy justify this by the necessity to attract foreign capital and keep it within the country. This, however, has not prevented the eruption of six monetary crises. From that point of view, too, Brazil has beaten all records. The rescue plan of the IMF in August 2002 was presented as a backing for Brazil, when in fact it was a backing by Brazil of two large US banks (Fleet Boston and Citibank), competing for two-thirds of the sum lent.

Other government projects are a cause for concern—for example, reform of social security and the labor code (*reforma trabalhista*). In the area of social security reform, Brazil, like other countries throughout the world, is falling foul of a campaign aimed at justifying the proliferation of private pension funds and the weakening of employees' pension rights. On the pretext of ending privileges that benefit marginal categories of government employees (such as top officials of ministries), the aim is to drastically reduce the pensions of all civil servants, to significantly increase the number of working years required to reach retirement, and finally to favor the development of private pension saving through private pension funds.

This counterreform promoted by Lula, which corresponds exactly to the position defended by the World Bank, was met with a series of demonstrations

---

Brazil's debt

▶ At the end of 2002, Brazil's national public debt reached approximately 850 billion reals, of which 40 percent were exchanged into dollars.

▶ Brazil's external public debt reached approximately $120 billion.

▶ The external debt of private companies in Brazil stands at approximately $110 billion.

▶ The total of the external public and private debt represents four years of exports.

▶ Between 1992 and 2002, the proportion of salaries in the GNP dropped from 45 percent to 27 percent.

▶ While salaries now form only 27 percent of GNP, they contribute up to 55 percent of income tax on earnings.

and strikes by public service employees in June and July 2003. During the same period, employees in France and Austria were struggling en masse against the same type of project backed by right-wing governments. Finally, the Brazilian Congress adopted this reform in August 2003, with a few minor amendments, concessions to the resistance movements of public-sector employees.

How can this contradiction between ongoing compliance with IMF agreements and the progressive part of Lula's program, the basis of his election, be explained? Agreements with the IMF imply an increase in the external and national debt, external because the $30 billion promised by the IMF are added

Wall Street loves Lula

"Why are the Wall Street skeptics becoming frankly optimistic?" This was the title of a long commentary in the *Financial Times* of April 8, 2003. Below are excerpts from the full-page review of the first hundred days of the Lula presidency:

Only six months ago, it was feared that Brazil, South America's largest economy, was drifting inexorably towards the reefs of debt payment default and financial bankruptcy. The opposite has happened. Brazil is greatly appreciated by Wall Street. Those very traders and investors who were keeping their distance last year, are now rushing to buy Brazilian shares and debt bonds.... "They have made an impressive start and they have won the first confidence-gaining battle," admits Maurice Goldstein, an economist at the Institute for International Economics in Washington, "They have proved pessimists and skeptics like me wrong."

How did it happen? A rapid change in the policies of the PT (Workers' Party) in power was one of the main reasons. Having voted in December 2001 to "break away" from the "neo-liberal" or market-driven economic model introduced by former president Fernando Henrique Cardoso, the party moved into the center of the political field with astonishing speed. Even before the electoral campaign of October 2002, the PT's leadership had committed itself to repaying the debt and retaining measures in favor of low inflation....

At the end of last year, Luiz Inacio Lula da Silva, the newly elected president, declared that he would respect the budget objectives agreed with the IMF in August 2002. He has kept his word. In some areas, his government has been even more austere than their predecessors, increasing the objective of the primary budgetary superavit from 3.75% to 4.25% of GDP. Henrique Meirelles, designated president of the Central Bank by Mr Lula da Silva, after having managed the Fleet Boston Bank, has raised interest rates to stave off the inflationist tendency resulting from last year's devaluation. Mr Lula da Silva has adopted most of the reforms planned by his predecessor, Mr Cardoso, and is speeding up reforms of the tax and pension systems. "He learns fast," declared Octavio de Barros, chief economist at the Bilbao Viscaya Argenteria Bank (BBVA—a Spanish bank).

to the debt stock and increase the amounts to be reimbursed. Likewise, the amounts to be repaid on the national debt increase proportionally to the rise in interest rates, and these massive repayments must be drawn from public funds. In other words, even if a tax reform were to create pressure on rich people to

Legal instruments available to the citizens

The Brazilian Constitution and national law offer guarantees concerning access to information held by public organizations such as the National Audit Office, the Central Bank, and the Finance Ministry. The information, data, and documents on the debt of a nation are public by nature; the citizens and institutions of that nation are therefore entitled to access them.

There are several methods and procedures available in Brazil:

Popular actions (Federal Constitution, art. 5, § LXXIII): "Any citizen is legitimately entitled to bring a popular action, with a view to overturning any infringement of the public estate or of any entity to which the State contributes, as well as any infringement of administrative morality, the environment, or the historical and cultural heritage."

The law on popular actions (No. 4.717 of June 29, 1965) states, "Any citizen is legitimately entitled to demand the cancellation, or declaration as null and void, of acts detrimental to the heritage of the Union, the federal district, the States, towns, etc." Information can only be refused in cases where there is a threat to the public interest. Refusal in such cases must be properly justified.

Civil public actions (Law No. 7.347 of July 24, 1985): The law sets out the responsibilities for damage caused to the environment, to consumers, to goods or rights of artistic, aesthetic, historical value, etc. Such a civil public action can be brought by a voluntary organization.

The public prosecutor is the most obvious channel for civil public actions. Among his/her duties we can cite "the promotion of public inquiries and civil public actions in protection of the public and social estate [and] the environment...." The investigative power of the public prosecutor is such that on October 5, 1995, the federal Supreme court ruled that the Banco do Brasil was not entitled to claim the right to banking secrecy when in contention with the federal public prosecutor.

Should access to information be refused, legal means are available to demand it (*habeas data*, in particular).

pay, and thus to increase public revenue, the amounts brought in by this reform would immediately go out again as debt repayment. This would automatically prevent an increase in social spending. Moreover, the IMF has never
accepted a significant increase in levies on the income and assets of the
wealthy. Thus, here also, a clear contradiction exists between IMF agreements
and a potential willingness to carry out progressive tax reforms.

Lula is coming under the joint pressure of the social movements, the left
wing of the PT, and other sectors of civil society such as the National Conference of Bishops. Confronted with the pernicious effects of his commitment to
respect the agreements of his predecessors with the IMF, he could announce at
the next negotiations with the IMF that he is not in a position to satisfy the conditions imposed upon him. He could argue that he wants to carry out his objective of eradicating hunger and other priority measures (the extension of agrarian
reform, an increase in the minimum wage). He would be fully within his rights
in doing this. If he does not choose this option, he faces a major risk that his
credibility will collapse in the eyes of the working class. The disaffection of the
majority of Lula's social base will come more slowly than that of the sectors directly hit by the measures concerning the counterreform of pensions. Nevertheless, if Lula does not change course, the erosion of popular support is inevitable.
It will then be difficult for him to recover the trust of the disappointed majority.

Lula's position will not be made easier by the fact that the concessions he
has made to international capital will not protect Brazil from an increase in
capital flight and speculative attacks against the real. Moreover, as a result of
neoliberal macroeconomic policy, Brazil was hit by recession in 2003. During
2003, unless there is a change in direction, more money will be drained from
public funds through the repayment of the external and national debt than
was in 2002, under Cardoso.

On other issues, Lula's government has sent out contradictory signals. It
stood firm against the United States and the European Union at the interministerial summit of the WTO at Cancún, Mexico, in September 2003, and helped
to delay those who wanted an even greater acceleration of the extension of market logic to every area of human activity. Unfortunately, the proposals put forward do not constitute a real alternative, just robust support for the periphery's
export companies, first and foremost Brazilian exporters who are indignant at
the protectionism of the United States in particular and the Triad in general.

Concerning the protection of the environment and food quality, Lula's government made some terrible decisions in October 2003: the legalization of use
of genetically modified organisms (GMOs) in agriculture (mainly to suit the
big Brazilian exporters of genetically modified soybeans), and the plan to pro-

duce enriched uranium. On the issue of agrarian reform, the ministry responsible did not get enough money to go ahead. The government did not abrogate the decree to make invasion of land a criminal offence, and, with regard to the rights of indigenous peoples, the government is dragging its feet in specifying which territory rightfully belongs to the Indians in the Amazon and other areas.

Auditing the national debt as provided for in the constitution

Performing an external debt audit is an essential part of the general framework of alternative policies. José Dirceu's arguments for proposing legislative decree 645-A (see above) in 2000 remain just as relevant today:

> The various forms of debt, external, national, public, or private, however different in their application or origins, impose a burden of obligations on society with a variety of consequences: ...an increase in the external vulnerability and economic dependence of a nation; ...an increase in the sums to be repaid in foreign currency (both in the present and in the future), compromising the future of the younger generation; ...a loss of sovereignty and submission to the international strategies of financial capital and the hegemony of the superpowers; ...the sacrifice of the poor and vulnerable in the population who, while having received none of the benefits at the time the debts were contracted are nevertheless required to bear the brunt of the repayment.... The aim of the legislation currently being proposed is to establish a democratic mechanism for consulting the population on the action to be taken on issues which, without any doubt, have a direct or indirect bearing on the life of our people.

According to Marcus de Freitas Gouvêa, legal counsel at the finance ministry and administrative director of the national trade union of legal counsels at that ministry, it is possible to require of the National Congress, via the courts, the implementation of article 26 (in Fattorelli 2003).

The example of Brazil's Campaign for a National Debt Audit should encourage citizens' organizations in other countries to bring their own national constitutions and legislation under scrutiny, in search of the legal instruments that might entitle them to obtain information and a quashing order. This is particularly true in those young constitutions established formally to codify democratic rights at the fall of a despotic regime. This is now important in every country, at a time when the WTO and the provisions in its various agreements (including the General Agreement on Trade in Services, or GATS) are threatening to oust national laws in favor of the single law of profit.

Changing direction: an alternative approach

As we have seen above, it is essential that the debt be audited. This should imply the following:

- Annulment (because it is odious) of the debt contracted by the dictatorship (1964–85) and the debts subsequently contracted to refinance it;

- meticulous review of other debts to identify those meriting negotiation with creditors (we should note with Marcos Arruda [2000] that Brazil, together with other indebted countries, was subjected to a real *coup de force* by the United States at the end of 1979, when it unilaterally introduced a dramatic rise in interest rates);

- revocation of Brazil's agreements with the IMF, thus reinvesting its public authorities with freedom of action and full responsibility for their actions;

- creation of a national solidarity fund dedicated to the eradication of hunger, the upholding of human rights, and the protection of the environment, financed by a special tax on the estate of the richest 10 percent of the population (for example, a 10–20 percent tax) and also benefiting from the recuperation of ill-gotten gains invested abroad. The priorities of the fund would be to

  - finance employment measures, land reform, urban change, etc.;

  - renationalize privatized companies;

  - enact redistributive tax reform;

  - control capital movement and exchange controls;

  - refuse the FTAA, and reinforce and extend Mercosur;

  - mobilize a Latin American–Caribbean coalition for the nonpayment of the debt;

  - appeal for a debate on debt at the UN General Assembly.

President Lula's "realpolitik" and the "alterglobalization" movement

An interview with Eric Toussaint of the Committee for the Abolition of the Third World Debt (CADTM) by Frédéric Lévêque, in Geneva, in the context of the "Illegal G8" countersummit, following Toussaint's meeting on June 2, 2003 with President Lula of Brazil.

Context: On the occasion of the annual summit of the G8 countries (United States, Japan, Germany, UK, France, Italy, Canada, Russia) in the French town of Evian on June 1–2, 2003, several heads of state outside the G8 group were invited to attend by French president Jacques Chirac, who was keen to demonstrate to international public opinion that, through this invitation to the nonmember states, the G8, and France in particular, was seeking dialogue with the rest of the world. Among those who attended were President Lula of Brazil and the heads of state or government of China, India, Nigeria, Senegal, South Africa, Egypt, and Mexico. This invitation was essentially intended to further legitimize the G8, the informal club of the world's main powers, at a time when its credibility rating was at an all-time low.

President Chirac's guests met in Evian before the official start of the G8 meeting, at the same time as more than 100,000 people were filling the streets of Geneva (Switzerland) and Annemasse (France) demonstrating against this illegal G8. The main topics included the cancellation of the Third World debt, the rejection of militarism, the battle against the WTO, solidarity with the Palestinian people, access to generic medicines… and a refusal of the neoliberal reform of the French pension and education systems, which was bringing millions of workers onto the streets of France.

Fred Lévêque: Yesterday, with others, you were able to meet one of the heads of state specially invited to the G8, President Lula of Brazil. Could you explain for us the purpose of the meeting and, at the same time, the policies being pursued by President Lula?

Eric Toussaint: Luiz Inácio Lula Da Silva was elected president in October 2002, with an overwhelming majority of votes—more than 65 percent; he was interested in meeting representatives of the "alterglobalization" movement in Europe. Four of us, representatives of these movements, attended this meeting: Jacques Nikonoff, president of ATTAC-France; Rafaella Bolini, of the Italian Social Forum; Helena Tagesson (Sweden), from the campaign against the WTO; and myself from the CADTM. The meeting took place in Geneva at the Brazilian ambassador's residence.

Before going to the meeting we had decided to make clear that we could not act on behalf of the movement and that we had been given no mandate to represent others. We could speak only for ourselves, and had no intention of being coaxed into a press conference, for example, offering the Brazilian president opportunities to associate us with the policies he was conducting. We would have done the same with any other president, but in this case we were faced with the fact that, within months of taking office, Lula's policies were in obvious contradiction with the expectations of the range of social movements with which we were working.

Lévêque: How did the meeting turn out?

Toussaint: Understandably, given the policies I've just outlined, we felt as if we were walking on eggshells, and were anxious not to find ourselves being trapped or used. We decided, in an agreement on the organization of the meeting, that each of us (the four delegates) would take five minutes to present the main demands of our movements for alterna-

Continued, next page ▶

►*Continued from previous page*

tives to the current globalization process, which directly concern Brazil. As for the meeting itself…we were received by President Lula, in the company of his labor minister and the minister for foreign relations, as well as several members of parliament and two of his closest counselors. President Lula spent half an hour outlining his government's policy; he defended the austerity measures adopted (the increase in interest rates; budget slashed by more than $3 billion—14 billion reals) on the grounds that they were necessary to stabilize the very difficult economic situation. He announced his intention of making good, as of now (while admitting that the process would be long) the commitments he had made to the population during his election campaign.

We for our part made the following points: Jacques Nikonoff, president of ATTAC-France, expressed the clear opposition of his organization to private pension funds, and its concern at the current Brazilian government's promotion of these. Second, he reiterated ATTAC's ardent desire to see Brazil declaring its support for the introduction of the Tobin Tax. It should be noted that Lula came to the G8 with a proposal for a tax on the sale of arms, the revenue from which could be used to finance a global drive against hunger. In a press conference, Chirac had remarked that Lula's proposal seemed to present a greater interest than the Tobin Tax, thus taking the opportunity to attack the tax. These were the two main topics raised by Jacques Nikonoff.

For my part, I pointed out the CADTM's concern that Latin America was now faced, as in the eighties, with an enormous outflow of resources, and that these were leaving the region in favor of creditors in the North. Negative net transfers on debt came to more than $200 billion between 1996 and 2002, the equivalent of two Marshall Plans. Brazil alone lost more than $70 billion in net negative transfers on debt between 1997 and 2001, $27 billion of which had come directly from the public coffers. The creditors in question were essentially private banks, the financial markets, the IMF, and the World Bank. I insisted on the fact that Brazil should not wait for a payment crisis, or the point of default, before taking defensive action. Before, that is, carrying out an audit on the origins and exact composition of Brazil's external debt with a view to defining what is legitimate and what illegitimate—as provided for, in fact, by Brazil's 1988 national constitution. In 2000, during a referendum organized by the [MST, the CUT], Brazil's Jubilee South

Campaign, and the National Conference of Bishops (with the support of the Workers' Party—the PT), more than 90 percent of the six million Brazilians voting declared themselves to be in favor of a suspension of debt payments for the duration of the audit period. The PT parliamentarians proposed a bill to this effect. No president has ever taken the step. I said to Lula: "There is now a real opportunity, since you have the power in your hands, to launch an initiative and create the conditions for a suspension of payments; the funds destined to service the debt could be diverted toward social capital, development projects, etc." I then suggested that Brazil appeal to the other Latin American countries to join a coalition of indebted countries for nonpayment of the debt.

Helena Tagesson, the third speaker of our group, from Sweden, raised the need for action at the Cancún summit in September 2003, to block the WTO agreements made at Doha in November 2001. The meeting should be paralyzed in the same way as at Seattle in late November–early December 1999, when, through our mobilization and the contradictions between the United States and Europe, we succeeded in blocking an even stronger trade liberalization offensive. In 2001, the WTO took revenge. It succeeded in setting a highly neoliberal agenda with the General Agreement on Trade in Services, which is to be finally defined and decided at Cancún. She therefore insisted on the fact that we have four months left to try to paralyze Cancún. She proposed that Brazil, in concert with other Third World countries, work to this end, also paying special attention to the question of water privatization being pursued by the WTO. Brazil could provide experimental models, as in Porto Alegre for example, on the exploitation and distribution of water—experiments that would be lost forever if the Doha agenda were approved at Cancún.

The fourth of our group was Rafaella Bolini, of the Italian Social Forum. She is one of the leaders of the antiwar movement, and the Italians were extremely active in the campaign against the war in Iraq. She asked Brazil to call for a meeting of the UN General Assembly, to obtain a vote condemning the occupation of Iraq by the United States and their allies. The UN Security Council had in fact voted a resolution on May 22, legitimizing the military occupation of Iraq by the United States, the UK, and Australia. We have of course no confidence in the Security Council. However, without fostering too many illusions, a ma-

Continued, next page ▶

▶ *Continued from previous page*

jority against the occupation of Iraq might be possible, if there were really to be a debate at the General Assembly, and if the member states had a genuine vote. This was achieved on several occasions in the seventies and eighties. Israel was condemned several times, despite United States opposition, as the United States was in a minority.

Lula's response to this was that there is a great difference between what is desirable and what is feasible. All our proposals in other words were very interesting, but he saw no way of putting them into action. He stood by his policy on private pension funds. He made no commitment on the debt issue. On the question of trade he said that he did indeed wish to curb deregulation and limit the scope of the General Agreement on Trade in Services. Concerning Iraq, he said that as a country he had taken a clear stand against the war in Iraq. But he went no further, and he did not offer to take any initiative with the UN Assembly.

That is a concise summary of our meeting. I can only conclude that the huge expectations, not only of the majority of Brazilians, but of others in Latin America and the world, of a progressive government orienting its policies away from neoliberalism are clearly heading for a major disappointment. And we might as well be clear about it from the start—if not, the more we continue to entertain illusions about the real direction of the Lula government, the harder we will fall. Somehow, what comes out of the last few months in Latin America is that people have voted clearly in several countries for leftist programs. I'm thinking of Evo Morales in Bolivia, who made great electoral progress although not achieving the presidency...or Lucio Gutierrez in Ecuador, who, backed by the indigenous people's movement Pachakutik and the CONAIE, was elected on a progressive program...and Lula.... In the last two cases, Lula and Gutierrez were elected president but lost no time in making concessions to the financial markets and ensuring the continuity of the neoliberal program of the predecessors they had condemned in their election campaigns. And it's even worse with Gutierrez—he has turned out to be Bush's best friend in the region and claims to be a great friend of the Colombian president, and has distinctly kept his distance from President Chávez of Venezuela.

There is a very clear message here for the social movements: they must retain their independence from their governments. The fact that a party comes to power on, in principle, the program of the social movements does not mean that these movements should reduce their expectations, abandon their radicalism, and sit back saying "No need to throw a wrench in the works for our friends in the government." On the contrary, we must increase the pressure on these governments, to ensure that they act in line with the promises that brought them to power.

Argentina

The debt tango

The people of Argentina rose up against the neoliberal policies conducted by the center-left government of Fernando de la Rúa and his minister Domingo Cavallo. The crisis that erupted in December 2001 has shown that action by citizens can change the course of history. In the few weeks from the end of 2001 to early 2002, three presidents of the Republic succeeded one another, and the suspension of external debt repayments was decreed. Hundreds of factories, abandoned by their owners, were occupied by the workers, and their activities resumed. For months, hundreds of thousands of people regularly took part in local assemblies. The unemployed were able to improve their organization and became more active within the framework of the *piqueteros* movements, which, by 2002–03, had several tens of thousands of members.

The national currency underwent drastic devaluation, from one Argentine peso to the dollar, to three pesos to the dollar. The government created local currencies.

One cry was heard repeatedly in the demonstrations: "Que se vayan todos!" ("Down with all politicians!"), expressing the demand for a different approach to politics, with power in the hands of the citizens.

The string of concrete decisions that led up to the riots in the night of December 19–20, 2001, began with the refusal by the IMF to grant a loan to the Argentine government on the agreed date, despite the fact that the latter had readily applied the unpopular measures recommended by the Bretton Woods institutions. The de la Rúa government responded by blocking all savings accounts. That was the last straw. The population spontaneously acted in unison, when the middle class (in fact, the large majority of salaried workers) went into the streets and were joined by the "have-nots" (the unemployed, the slum dwellers, the day laborers, etc.).

The Argentine crisis marks a quantum leap in the rejection of policies dictated by the Bretton Woods institutions. It occurred after more than a quarter of a century of understanding between the IMF and the Argentine authorities, from the sinister dictatorship of Jorge Rafaél Videla in 1976, to the center-left government of de la Rúa. The failure is obvious, and the decision of the president who succeeded de la Rúa to give in to the pressure from the street marks a dramatic about-face in the relationship with the IMF. Rodriguez Saa announced at the end of December 2001 that Argentina was suspending debt repayments until there was full employment. Argentina's default on debt repayment was the biggest in the history of debt crises.

Is Argentina the weak link in the global chain of indebtedness?[3]

In 2001, the situation in Argentina had become dramatic, after three years of recession due to the application of particularly aggressive neoliberal policies.

For nearly twenty years, successive governments have pursued the transformation of the country initiated by the dictators in 1976–83. Contrary to popular belief, no real changes were made when the dictatorship ended. None of the subsequent governments has made any fundamental difference to the downhill course that Argentina was set on by the ruling class over the last decades.

The Argentina of today is fundamentally different from the Argentina of the 1940s, 1950s, and 1960s. Its relative importance as an industrial power of the periphery has diminished and the standard of living is, for the majority of the population, lower now than it was thirty years ago.

Between the start of the dictatorship in March 1976 and the year 2001, the debt was multiplied by nearly twenty, from less than $8 billion to almost $160 billion. Over the same period, Argentina repaid about $200 billion , or about twenty-five times what it owed in March 1976 (see table 16.2).

Argentina exemplifies the worst extremes of the pernicious debt spiral in which the Third World, indeed the periphery in general, is trapped. Because of debt payments, not in spite of them, in 2001, Argentina owed nearly twenty times the amount it had at the beginning of the dictatorship—a large proportion of fresh loans was used to refinance or repay old debts as they fell due. For Argentina, repaying the debt was and is a formidable mechanism for transferring the wealth produced by wage earners to capital holders—whether Argentines or residents of the highly industrialized countries, with the United States and Western Europe in the fore.

The mechanism is simple. The Argentine state devotes an ever-increasing part of its tax revenues (most of which come from the population) to repaying the external debt and to various sorts of handouts to the capitalist sector. Who gets the money repaid by the Argentine state? The big private IFIs that hold more than 80 percent of Argentina's external debt. The ultimate irony, however, is that on the same North American and European financial markets where the loans are issued, Argentine capitalists buy Argentine debt bonds with money taken out of the country, thus collecting part of the debt payments.

The rest of this section will demonstrate how the Argentine capitalists blithely indebted the country during the dictatorship, while at the same time depositing a large part of the money abroad (capital flight). The total amount of capital invested by Argentine capitalists in the highly industrialized countries and tax havens during the dictatorship exceeded the amount borrowed. The technical explanation for this phenomenon can be found in various works: Calcagno 1999, Rapoport 2000, and in the Ballestero ruling in Poder

TABLE 16.2. ARGENTINA'S DEBT AND SERVICING, 1975–99
(BILLIONS OF DOLLARS)

Year	Debt	Service paid (capital + interest)
1975	7.88	
1976	8.28	1.62
1977	9.68	1.85
1978	12.50	3.31
1979	19.03	2.26
1980	27.07	4.18
1981	35.67	5.39
1982	43.63	4.88
1983	45.09	6.80
1984	46.90	6.28
1985	48.31	6.21
1986	52.45	7.32
1987	58.43	6.24
1988	58.83	5.02
1989	65.26	4.36
1990	62.73	6.16
1991	65.41	5.42
1992	68.94	4.88
1993	65.33	5.86
1994	75.76	5.77
1995	99.36	8.89
1996	111.93	13.05
1997	130.83	18.31
1998	144.05	21.57
1999	147.88	25.72

Source: World Bank 2000b.

Judicial de la Nación 2000.

In 1980–82 alone, the World Bank estimated capital flight at more than $21 billion (Rapoport 2000). As a supreme gift to Argentine (and foreign) capitalists, the state assumed their debts when the dictatorship ended. From then on, the state has been burdened with the debts of private companies, as it honored obligations toward the creditors. Meanwhile, Argentine capitalists have kept up their capital flight tactics as though it were a national sport—so much so, that if there were Latin American capital flight championships, the Argentine capitalist class would win hands down, despite some very experienced competitors: Brazilian, Mexican, and Venezuelan capitalists all excelling in this event.

On the other hand, the debts of publicly owned companies, which had also greatly increased during the dictatorship, were not canceled, except when they were to be privatized. Those in power after the fall of the dictatorship used the indebtedness of public companies as a pretext for their privatization, while taking care to shift their debts onto the state before selling them. (See the case of Aerolineas Argentinas below.) This is just one more disgraceful example of a gift handed out to Argentine or foreign capitalists.

A quarter of a century of this has bled the country dry. Wages and social revenues have plummeted, unemployment is at its highest ever, public services have been decimated, and poverty is spreading to more and more sectors of the population—including sectors that used to enjoy a relatively comfortable standard of living. The state's coffers are empty, much of the industrial infrastructure has fallen into utter neglect, and the rest has fallen into foreign hands. There is not much left to privatize. Undercurrents of revolt are becoming increasingly apparent: several general strikes occurred in 2000; roads were blocked by piqueteros; whole neighborhoods and towns, reduced to poverty, have risen in rebellion.

Clearly, Argentina is one of the weak links in the chain of international indebtedness, and it might well be thanks to Argentina that the chain is broken. There is no telling—the crisis could go on for years. The damage done to workers' organizations and the social movement in general by the dictatorship between 1973 and 1983 has had lasting effects. Although the people of Argentina have a hundred reasons to shout "*Ya basta!*" they seem to hesitate, not certain of the outcome. Trade-union leaders are not fully engaged in this crucial battle. Yet, from an international point of view, if Argentina were to change its attitude regarding the debt, the repercussions would be enormous. The amounts it has to pay back to the financial markets of the highly industrialized countries are so huge that if it defaulted, the shock would be so great as to force them into a dialogue. In order for not only Argentina, but also the other indebted countries to benefit, it would be necessary for the pressure of citizens' movements to oblige the Argentine government, unlike Alan Garcia in Peru in

TABLE 16.3: EVOLUTION OF ARGENTINA'S EXTERNAL PUBLIC DEBT, 1975–85

Year	Total debt ($million)	Increase (percent)
1975	7,875	
1976	8,280	5.14
1977	9,679	16.90
1978	12,496	29.10
1979	19,034	52.32
1980	27,072	42.23
1981	35,671	31.76
1982	43,634	22.32
1983	45,087	3.33
1984	46,903	4.02
1985	48,312	3.00

Source: Argentine Central Bank,
quoted in the Ballestero judgement
(Poder Judicial de la Nación 2000).

1985 or the Brazilian regime of 1987, to adopt a long-term, unwavering stance. This would have to be combined with economic reforms that would enable a fairer distribution of national revenue through a redistributive fiscal policy, organize the return to public ownership of privatized companies, favor regional South-South agreements over trade relations with the United States as regimented by the FTAA (Free Trade Area of the Americas).

If external debt payments were to be stopped and a different economic policy implemented, it would mean breaking the agreements between the Argentine government and the IMF. Far from damaging Argentina, the rupture would open new vistas, and there is no doubt that for the Argentine population and its social movements, it would be an opportunity. The question is, will they seize it?

There follows a historical overview of the events that led to the present situation of indebtedness, starting with the dictatorship.

Debt and dictatorship

Argentina's foreign debt skyrocketed under the military dictatorship of General Videla, which lasted from 1976 to 1981 (see table 16.3). From April 2, 1976, on, the economic minister, Martinez de Hoz, pursued a policy that marked the beginning of a process that devastated the country's productive apparatus—and paved the way for a speculative economy that has bled the country dry. Most of the loan money granted to the Argentine dictatorship came from private banks from the North. It is important to note that the US authorities (both the Federal Reserve and the administration) fully supported

Argentina's policy of debt accumulation. The architects of Argentina's policy of debt accumulation were de Hoz and the secretary of economic coordination and planning, Guillermo Walter Klein. In order to secure credit from private banks, the government forced state-owned companies to borrow from international private banks. State-owned companies became the cornerstone of a strategy aimed at denationalizing the state through an accumulation of debt that has forced the country to sacrifice much of its national sovereignty.

Forcing debt on state-owned companies

The main Argentine state-owned company, the Yacimientos Petroliferos Fiscales (YPF) oil firm, was forced to take on foreign debt, though it had sufficient funds for its own development. At the time of the March 24, 1976, military coup, YPF's foreign debt was $372 million. Seven years later, when the dictatorship fell, it owed $6 billion. Its debt had been multiplied by sixteen in seven years. Hardly a cent of the borrowed foreign funds actually went into company coffers; the money lined the regime's pockets. Under the dictatorship, productivity per worker at YPF jumped by 80 percent; the total number of workers at YPF fell from 47,000 to 34,000. In order to boost its own earnings, the dictatorship reduced by 50 percent the subsidy it gave YPF for gasoline sales to the population. Moreover, YPF was obliged to have the oil it extracted refined by private multinationals (Shell and Esso). Given its sound financial health before the dictatorship, it could have had its own refinery. By June 1982, not a penny of company assets was debt-free.

Government debt

The IMF and those in charge of the dictatorship's economic policy argued that massive government debt was justified, since the country needed to boost its hard-currency reserves if it wanted to open up the economy from a position of force. A sound economic policy would have sought increased foreign reserves in the country's international trading activity. Instead, the dictatorship obtained its foreign currency by going into debt.

These foreign reserves were neither managed nor supervised by the Central Bank. In fact, the huge sums borrowed from the North's banks were usually deposited directly into the same banks, or at least into competing institutions. In 1979, 83 percent of these reserves were deposited in foreign banking institutions. The reserves were worth $10.1 billion; deposits in foreign accounts totaled $8.4 billion. That same year, foreign debt rose from $12.5 billion to $19 billion (Olmos 1995). Of course, interest earned on these foreign deposits was lower than interest owed on the borrowed amounts.

The Argentine authorities pursued this line of action for the following reasons: first, individuals in the regime grew rich off the commissions offered by the North's banks; second, increased foreign reserves meant a significantly increased capacity to import—in particular, to import arms; third, the policy of economic liberalization and debt accumulation recommended by the IMF improved the dictatorship's credibility with the main industrialized countries, especially with the United States. The dictatorship could not have sustained the initial years of domestic terror (1976–80) without the blessing of the US administration.

For its part, the US Federal Reserve was all the more favorably inclined to the dictatorship's policies since most of the borrowed money was deposited in US banks. From the point of view of the US administration and the IMF, Argentina's growing debt load was bringing the country back into the US fold, after decades during which Argentina had been something of a nationalist rebel and achieved real economic progress within the framework of the Perónist system.

Private-sector debt

Private Argentine companies and Argentine subsidiaries of foreign MNCs were also encouraged to amass debt. Private debt rose to more than $14 billion.

Conflicts of interest

Walter Klein was secretary of economic coordination and planning from 1976 until March 1981. At the same time, he headed a private research firm that represented the interests of foreign creditors in Buenos Aires. When he joined the military regime, his firm represented the interests of one bank, the Scandinavian Enskilda Bank. A few years later, it represented the interests of twenty-two foreign banks. In March 1981, he left his government job as General Viola was replacing Videla at the head of the dictatorship. A few weeks later—on April 7, 1982, five days after the Argentine armed forces had occupied the Malvinas (Falkland Islands) and Britain had declared war—Klein was made the authorized representative in Buenos Aires of the British-based Barclays Bank Limited, one of the main private holders of Argentine public and private debt. When the dictatorship fell and Raúl Alfonsín rose to power in 1984, his research firm continued in its role as defender of the interests of foreign creditors.

After the military dictatorship: Alfonsín and impunity

The Central Bank announced that it had no record of public foreign debt. Indeed, post-dictatorship government officials have had to rely on the claims of foreign creditors and on contracts signed by officials in the military dictatorship, though such contracts had never been approved by the Central Bank.

Nevertheless, the first post-dictatorship government of President Alfonsín decided to honor the dictatorship-era debt in its entirety, public and private. Just as the military's torturers were amnestied under the 1986 "full stop" and "required obedience" laws, so too were those in charge of the dictatorship's economic policy treated with clemency. Most of the dictatorship's top economic and financial officials retained their jobs in the state apparatus; some were even promoted. Military officials responsible for the repression that claimed at least 30,000 lives also kept their jobs or were granted early retirements. A scandal erupted when one of them, Captain Astiz, finally broke the rule of silence observed by the dictatorship's military officials: "In 1982, a friend asked me if there had indeed been disappearances. I replied, 'Of course, there were 6,500, even more, but no more than 10,000. All of them were eliminated'" (*Le Soir*, January 16, 1998).

When the state honors private debt

Private Argentine businesses were also encouraged to borrow money under the dictatorship. Total private debt came to more than $14 billion. The long list of indebted private companies included the Argentine subsidiaries of MNCs: for example, Renault Argentina, Mercedes-Benz Argentina, Ford Motor Argentina, IBM Argentina, Citibank, First National Bank of Boston, Chase Manhattan Bank, Bank of America, and Deutsche Bank.

The Argentine government paid off the creditors of these private companies: Renault France, Mercedes-Benz, Citibank, Chase Manhattan Bank, Bank of America, First National Bank of Boston, Credit Lyonnais, Deutsche Bank, and Société Générale. In other words, Argentine taxpayers repaid debt contracted by the subsidiaries of MNCs with their head offices, or with international banks. It is reasonable to suspect that the MNCs in question actually created the debt of their Argentine subsidiaries with some creative accounting. Argentine government officials have no way of verifying this information.

A wave of privatization

In 1990–92, the government of Alfonsín's successor, Carlos Saúl Menem, undertook a vast program of privatization, selling off most of the nation's wealth at rock-bottom prices. The country is estimated to have lost $60 billion in the process. Menem argued that Argentina's state-owned companies were deeply in debt in order to justify the sell-off. Yet their poor financial position resulted from the debt load they had been forced to take on by the dictatorship; most of the borrowed funds never made it into company coffers.

Menem asked the US investment bank and brokerage firm Merrill Lynch to determine the value of YPF. Merrill Lynch deliberately underestimated company oil reserves by 30 percent in order to lower YPF's paper value before privatization. Once the privatization had been carried out, the hidden reserves were factored back into the company's assets; financial operators who had bought company stock at a low price made huge profits when YPF share values subsequently rose. The windfall also led many to vaunt the superiority of private over state-owned companies.

It is interesting to note that in 1997, Brazilian president Fernando Henrique Cardoso asked the same US firm, Merrill Lynch, to determine the value of the country's main state-owned concern, the mining company Vale do Rio Doce. A number of Brazilian members of parliament have accused Merrill Lynch of undervaluing the company's mineral reserves by 75 percent (*O Globo*, April 8, 1997).

Apart from YPF (sold to the Spanish multinational oil company Repsol in 1999), another Argentine gem was sold for a song: Aerolineas Argentinas. The airline's Boeing 707s were sold for a token sum—one dollar and fifty-four cents, to be exact! A few years on, these planes continue to work the routes of the now-privatized company. The value of the company's rights over certain routes—$800 million —was estimated to be only $60 million before privatization. The company was sold to Iberia for $130 million in cash; the rest was made up of debt write-offs. Iberia borrowed to buy the firm and placed the entire burden of the loan on the new company, Aerolineas Argentinas, which thus found itself indebted from the start. In 2001, Aerolineas Argentinas, owned by Iberia, was on the verge of bankruptcy through the fault of its owners. The case of Aerolineas Argentinas is exceptional. State-owned companies were normally privatized free of debt, which was instead absorbed by the public purse.

The dictatorship on trial

After the fall of the dictatorship, the debt scandal did not fail to attract public attention. The first civilian government established a parliamentary commission, which was dissolved after a year and a half of deliberations. Its findings were considered too threatening to Alfonsín's economic policy, given that, in the meantime, he had decided to nationalize the debt. Menem had at one time also railed against the debt; once in power, though, he abandoned all talk of revisiting this eminently taboo subject.

In spite of all the delays and compromises, a trial finally reached its conclusion in July 2000. The trial resulted from a complaint raised by an Argentine citizen in October 1982, while the country was still ruled by a dictatorship. Thanks to this courageous and tireless journalist, judicial authorities began to examine the question of who is responsible for the country's debt burden. Many of the dictatorship's economic officials and heads of state-owned companies had to testify at trial hearings. Walter Klein's research firm was searched, and most of the documents from the period in question were seized and placed in safe-keeping at the Central Bank. The judgement pronounced on July 13, 2000, did not give rise to any conviction (mainly because it was covered by the statute of limitations), but revealed the full extent of the Argentine debt scandal. Judge Ballestero's 195-page judgement confirmed a series of grave accusations.

One of the ways in which the IMF actively supported the Argentine dicta-torship was to provide it with one of the IMF's top civil servants, Dante Si-mone (Poder Judicial de la Nación 2000). The Federal Reserve of New York, directly serving as go-between for a series of operations of the Argentine Cen-tral Bank, had previously done the same to get private US banks to lend money to the dictatorship. At the same time, as it was increasing the indebted-ness of the public treasury and national companies, the dictatorship was allow-ing Argentine capitalists to deposit huge quantities of capital abroad. Between 1978 and 1981, more than $38 billion are thought to have left the country in an "excessive or unjustified" manner. The fact that each Argentine resident was entitled to buy $20,000 a day, which could then be deposited abroad, facili-tated this. In other words, the state took on increasing debts, while the capital-ists cheerfully decapitalized.

Approximately 90 percent of resources coming from outside in the form of loans by public and private companies and the government were transferred abroad in speculative financial operations. Large sums borrowed from private banks in the United States and Western Europe were then deposited in those same banks. Public companies such as YPF were systematically put into diffi-culty (Poder Judicial de la Nación 2000).

The regime of "democratic" transition that followed the dictatorship trans-formed the debts of private companies into public debt through wholly illegal means. This means that it should be possible to modify the decision. Among the private companies whose debt was absorbed by the state, twenty-six were financial firms, including numerous foreign banks established in Argentina: Citibank, First National Bank of Boston, Deutsche Bank, Chase Manhattan Bank, Bank of America. In other words, the Argentine state, with debts to-ward these banks, decided to take over the banks' debts (Poder Judicial de la Nación 2000). No comment.

To give a specific example of collusion between a private bank of the North and the Argentine dictatorship, between July and November 1976, the Chase Manhattan Bank received monthly deposits of $22 million (the amounts subsequently increased) and remunerated them at a rate of 5.5 percent. At the same time, and at the same rhythm, the Argentine Central Bank borrowed $30 million from the same Chase Manhattan Bank at a rate of 8.75 percent (Poder Judicial de la Nación 2000).

The judgement and its conclusions are damning for the dictatorship, the regime that followed it, the IMF, and the private creditors. The sentence handed down by the court states:

> "[T]he nation's external debt...was greatly increased from 1976 on, because of a nefarious economic policy which brought the country to its knees. This calamitous policy used methods, already analyzed in the present text, which tended to benefit and support private companies to the detriment of public companies. The latter got daily poorer, resulting in very low value at the time of their privatization.

The judgement should give grounds for a resolute action of nonpayment of Argentina's external public debt and for its cancellation. The debt is both odious and unlawful, and the creditors have no legal right to continue receiving service on it. Their credits are null and void. In addition, as new debts contracted since 1982–83 have mainly served to repay the old ones, they are also largely illegitimate. Argentina can turn to international law to justify a decision not to repay the external debt. Several legal arguments can be invoked here, for example, the notion of odious debt—the Argentine debt was contracted by a despotic regime guilty of crimes against humanity, as the creditors were bound to have known; the case of force majeure—like other indebted countries, Argentina underwent a dramatic change of circumstances due to the unilateral US decision to raise interest rates in 1979; and the state of necessity—Argentina's financial situation prohibits it from repaying the debt, as to do so would prevent the state from fulfilling its obligations to its citizens with respect to their social and economic rights, in line with international pacts it has signed.

Cessation of debt repayment needs to be accompanied by other essential measures. Some proposals follow to fuel the necessary debate. First, there has to be an international inquiry into the assets illegitimately accumulated and deposited abroad by Argentine residents. The deposits of Argentine capitalists in the banks of the highly industrialized countries total roughly $40 billion (see BIS 2001b). The aim is to recover a maximum of funds stolen from the nation. Second, measures to control capital movements and exchange operations need to be set up as a protection against capital flight and speculative attacks. Third, a redistributive tax policy needs to be established, including an exceptional tax on the assets of the richest tenth of the population, taxation of capital revenues, reduction of VAT on basic commodities and services, etc. Fourth, the abrogation of decrees and laws imposing salary and pension cuts (and other welfare benefits) is required. The social security system needs to be defended and reinforced. Revenue for the unemployed should be guaranteed, and salaries and pensions should increase to improve purchasing power. These are the minimal conditions for a real alternative. Fifth, companies that were wrongly privatized should be returned to the public domain, starting with the strategic sectors (energy, oil, communications, etc.).

On the international level, indebted countries should form a common front, and South-South trading and complementarities should be developed. The FTAA has to be resolutely opposed, as does the US military offensive (US military bases, Bush's antimissile shield, the strategic base he intends to create in the Southern Cone, Plan Colombia, etc.). Initiatives in favor of a Tobin-type tax on international financial transactions should be encouraged.

All of these proposals are avenues for an alternative to the neoliberal model. It is not a program to accept or reject as a whole. The idea is to show that solutions exist, if we want to turn our backs on the infernal logic of indebtedness and excessive dependency.[4]

2002-03: Argentine resistance

At the end of 2002, Argentina's external public debt came to $137 billion, distributed as follows: about $87 billion owed in the form of public debt paper, about $37 billion in the form of loans, and about $13 billion in payment arrears. Argentine banks and pension funds (Administradoras de Fondos de Jubilaciones y Pensiones, AFJPs), created in the 1990s as part of the neoliberal reform of the pension system, hold roughly half of the $87 billion in debt paper. Foreigners, individual investors, and banks hold the other half of the bonds. In September 2003, these bonds were selling on the secondary debt market at about 30 percent of their value.

Of the $37 billion owed in the form of loans, $30 billion are owed to the IMF, the World Bank, and the Inter-American Development Bank (IDB). The rest is owed to the Paris Club, other bilateral creditors, and private banks of the North.

The crisis at the end of 2001 followed three years of recession and antisocial policies that brought about a radical deterioration of living conditions for the majority of the population. In 2002–03, more than 50 percent of Argentines were living below the poverty line. After devaluation of Argentina's currency in early 2002, salaries and pensions fell 30 percent in real terms. Unemployment levels exceeded 20 percent. The Argentines were stupefied to discover that a significant percentage of the population was suffering from severe malnutrition. In 2002–03, children even died of malnutrition in the Northern provinces—something Argentines would never have believed possible. Meanwhile, Argentina had continued to export enough food to feed six times its total population. This situation is both absurd and intolerable.

The dramatic degradation of living conditions had been coming for some time. It was due to more than twenty-five years of submission to external creditors and favors to big Argentine capital. The powerful social mobilization that led to the overthrow of de la Rúa in December 2001 gained in size throughout 2002. This led the governments that followed the night of December 19–20, 2001 (presidents Saa, Eduardo Duhalde, and finally Nestor Kirchner, after the elections of April 2003), to make certain concessions to the people's movement. Fear of overthrow by another popular uprising combined with the desire to regain lost legitimacy in the eyes of the population led those in power to depart from neoliberal policies and resist the demands of the IMF and the private creditors.

Here are some examples of measures taken to appease the population:

- Instigation of a minimum subsistence revenue for the unemployed: two million people now receive one hundred and fifty pesos (about fifty dollars) a month. This benefit, called "work plan," is distributed partly by the piqueteros movements, who run 120,000–150,000 "work plans."

- Abrogation of the 12 percent cut in civil servants' salaries and pensions that had been decreed by de la Rúa in the middle of 2001.

- Forbidding of creditors to evict tenants who are having difficulty making mortgage payments (this concerned 150,000–200,000 households).

- Payment of compensation to small savers to limit the extent of their losses due to devaluation.

- Freezing of payment applied to basic services (water, gas, electricity), to the dismay of the MNCs, which have controlled these companies since they were privatized.

- Abrogation of "*punto final*," the law adopted under Raul Alfonsín in the middle of the 1980s that guaranteed almost total impunity to the military, and the beginning of legal actions against torturers (particularly Astiz, mentioned above).

- A partial, more "democratic" change in the composition of the Supreme Court of Justice.

These concessions to the Argentine people made by their rulers are by no means negligible. They show what massive social mobilization can achieve.

In December 2001, when Argentina suspended debt payments to private creditors and expressed doubts about payments due to the IMF and the World Bank, many commentators announced that the reprisals would be harsh. It was not so. In September 2003, when important negotiations were taking place between the Argentine authorities and the IMF, there was a clear demonstration that a firm attitude on the part of an indebted country could enhance its position. The IMF agreed to tone down its demands on Argentina, although it had been inflexible toward Brazil a year earlier. The IMF had insisted that the Brazilian government should produce a budget surplus of 4.25 percent compared to the GDP and use this surplus to repay its debt. Argentina refused such a high rate and reached an agreement with the IMF based on a 2.5 percent budget surplus. It then proposed that private holders of debt bonds should renounce 75 percent of their (face) value. It pays to be firm.

Having said that, it would be illusory to think that Kirchner has any intention of veering to the left. He is maneuvering between the demands of the IMF, the MNCs, and the capitalists of Argentina, on the one hand, and the expectations of the people's movement on the other. He is counting on the demobilization of the movement, which would enable him to return to harsher neoliberal policies than those applied since the overthrow of de la Rúa.

An alternative is needed to Kirchner's commitments to the IMF.

(1) The debt that Argentina owes the IMF, the World Bank, and the IDB must be considered null, as it was contracted to carry out policies harmful to and against the interests of the citizens. Furthermore, the agencies concerned aided and abetted the military dictatorship that prevailed from 1976 to 1983.

(2) The following course of action might be applied to the somewhat more complex question of how to deal satisfactorily with the AFJP: The debts could be canceled, the AFJP abolished, and the distributive pension system restored. Then, after a thorough discussion of terms and conditions, and after reasonable deductions are made, the Argentine state could transfer the equivalent of the debt owed to the AFJP to the state pension fund, which would ensure the viability of the distributive pension scheme.

(3) The debt in the form of bonds held by foreigners must be scrupulously audited. The odious part must be completely canceled. For the rest, it would be possible to devise a procedure adapted to each type of holder in order to avoid penalizing small foreign savers unfairly. The bonds held by rentiers, banks, and other private financial bodies must be canceled or subject to a general abatement of at least 90 percent.

(4) Payment arrears should be canceled.

Iraq

The "odious" Iraqi debt

For twenty years, as long as the governments of the indebted countries did not contest their odious debt, the major powers (who are also the main creditors) have managed to keep the issue of odious debt out of the limelight. Suddenly, on April 10–11, 2003, the notion of odious debt appeared in the speeches of the Bush administration. The demands were that France, Germany, and Russia (who had been against the war on Iraq) should drop their claims on Iraq. The international press seized on the demands. Odious debt was explicitly and correctly mentioned.

After a few days, most of the press were no longer following up the story, apart from the *Financial Times*, and a few other international papers (*International Herald Tribune*, *Wall Street Journal*). The editorial staff of the *Financial Times* firmly opposed the idea of renouncing the debt. For it, the same line would have to be applied to many countries of the developing world and to many former Soviet states. This could give the governments of indebted countries all sorts of ideas—in the end, they would wish to have the same line applied to their debts. Even if they did not, the social movements in their countries might pick up on the idea (e.g., in Brazil or in South Africa, where the debt of the apartheid regime has now reached $24 billion). The *Financial Times* explained that the Bush administration was playing with fire and putting creditors at risk.[5]

What is an "odious" debt?

According to Alexander Sack (1927),

> If a despotic power [e.g., Saddam Hussein's regime] takes out a loan at odds with the needs and interests of the state in order to strengthen its despotic regime or in order to put down the population who fights him, this debt is odious for the whole people of that country. This debt involves no obligation to the nation: it's a debt of the regime, a personal debt of the power that took it ought, and for this reason it expires with the fall of that same power.

The concept of "odious" debt is perfectly applicable to Iraq. The doctrine has its origins in the nineteenth century. It was applied during the Spanish-American War in 1898. Cuba, at the time a Spanish colony, was occupied by the United States (as a "protectorate"), and Spain asked the US to pay back the debt owed to it by Cuba. The US refused and declared the debt to be odious, that is, contracted by a despotic regime in order to finance policies contrary to interests of the people. This declaration, accepted in the end by Spain, was laid down in an international treaty, the Treaty of Paris, and thus provides a legal precedent. Other cases include the debts incurred by Napoleon that were renounced during the Restoration as "odious" and contrary to the interests of the French, and, after the American Civil War, the refusal by the victorious North to take on the South's debt, which had been used for the defense of a system based on slavery.

After the First World War, the Treaty of Versailles declared the debt that the German Kaiser had contracted in order to colonize Poland null and void and not transferable to the newly reestablished Polish state. The dictatorial regime of FedericoTinoco in Costa Rica had run into debt against the British Crown.[6] Chief Justice Taft of the US Supreme Court, who had been called upon to arbitrate in the judicial conflict (*Great Britain vs. Costa Rica*, 1923), ruled that the debt was the personal legacy of the despot. The lending bankers, who had known about the despotic nature of Tinoco's rule, should not turn to the democratic regime that followed Tinoco for reparation, but to themselves. Taft added that the lenders had failed to prove their good faith.

The doctrine of odious debt was first formulated by Alexander Sack (a for-

Landmarks in the history of the war on Iraq

In the 1980s, the United States and its allies supported Saddam Hussein in the war against Iran, in which more than a million died. Iraq incurred debts to the United States and its allies. In 1990, Iraq invaded Kuwait. Several theories exist as to the reasons for this incursion, but it is not impossible that the first Bush administration led Saddam Hussein to believe that such an aggression would not encounter any obstacles, effectively setting him a trap. After the end of the first war, called "Operation Desert Storm" by the victors, Saddam Hussein was deliberately kept in power. The United States feared that the country (and its oil reserves) might otherwise fall into the hands of an uncontrollable revolution in the neighborhood of Iran, itself uncontrollable. The allied troops let Saddam Hussein put down the uprising of Basra. The war was waged while a UN mandate that had frozen all Iraqi foreign assets and proclaimed an embargo was in operation.

Later, the "oil for food" program was launched. Fifty percent of Iraqi oil revenues from this program were used to buy food and medicine. That this figure was wholly inadequate can be seen by the deaths of more than 500,000 children as a consequence of the embargo. The exis-

mer minister of the tsar who emigrated to France after the revolution of October 1917 and later became a professor of law in Paris) in 1927, in his compendium on the transfer of debt in case of regime change.[7] In the following thirty years, no debtor (to our knowledge) made use of the doctrine of odious debt to renounce debt unilaterally or to call for arbitration. Jointly with other authors (in particular, Jean-Claude Willame and Patricia Adams) and movements (Jubilee South Africa, Jubilee South), the CADTM has long been analyzing Third World debt from this legal point of view: The debts incurred by Mobutu in Zaire (now the Democratic Republic of the Congo), Habyarimana in Rwanda, Marcos in the Philippines, or Suharto in Indonesia, by the generals of the Argentine dictatorship, Pinochet in Chile, the Uruguayan dictatorship, or the Brazilian dictatorship, the debts of Nigeria, Togo, South Africa, etc.

This is not past history: the people of these countries are still paying off these odious debts by taking out more debt. The Democratic Republic of the Congo is a case in point: in 2003 the debt amounted to $13 billion, which roughly corresponded to the total debt contracted by Mobutu, since there has

tence of this program was common knowledge to international community, and it was even used for propaganda purposes. However, the fact that 25 percent of the oil revenues were distributed to neighboring countries in the form of reparation payments was little known. The United Nations Compensation Commission (UNCC) had recognized, since 1991, the validity of reparation claims totaling $44 billion (which only covered part of the demands). The claims were filed by individuals, companies, and governments. With a quarter of all revenues at its disposal, the UNCC handed out—until the war in March and April 2003—$17.6 billion to the claimants as reparation, prioritizing individuals and families. So, $26 billion of reparations remained to be paid, and many claims remained to be considered when payment was stalled (*Financial Times*, June 24, 2003). Nevertheless, when oil revenues were made available, absolute priority was not given to the satisfaction of the Iraqi population's needs in terms of food and medicine.

In 2003, a US-led coalition attacked Iraq. Great Britain, Australia, the Netherlands, and Denmark directly took part in military action, while other countries gave support in various other ways. This coalition acted in violation of the UN Charter. According to the charter, it committed an act of aggression.

been virtually no new borrowing since he was ousted in 1997. The entire debt of the DRC should thus be canceled.

Why did the Bush administration raise the subject of odious debt?

On April 10–11, 2003, the finance ministers of the G8 nations assembled in Washington, where the US secretary of the treasury, John Snow, demanded in particular that Russia, France, and Germany should cancel their odious debt owed by Iraq. The United States made this demand not because they were interested in seeing the debt dropped, but as a political bargain, a way of raising the stakes against countries opposed to the war. The idea was to convince France, Germany, and Russia to change their position, thereby legitimizing the war and enabling those who had taken military action to start immediately the reconstruction of Iraq by using the oil revenues without servicing debt payments. The higher the outstanding debt before the war in 2003, the longer the United States and its allies would have to wait for reimbursement for the costs of reconstruction.

Germany announced at the April meeting that dropping the debt was out of the question, but that it would be rescheduled. The United States continued haggling in order to convince France, Russia, and Germany to make an effort over debt cancellation. In exchange for their cooperation, companies from these countries could expect to benefit from contracts linked with reconstruction.

Clearly, the United States achieved concessions from the French and the Russians in the end. In fact, on May 22, 2003, the UN Security Council lifted its sanctions against Iraq and entrusted the US-designated civil administrator in Iraq, Paul Bremer, with handling the exploitation of Iraqi oil.[8] The fifteen-member UN Security Council (which includes countries that had opposed the war, such as France, Russia, and China) recognized the legitimacy of the occupation and granted the United States management of Iraq's oil by a vote of fourteen to none. Syria left when voting took place, to avoid taking a position. The UN named Sergio Vieira de Mello as its representative in Iraq, with much lower status than that accorded to Bremer. In August, Vieira de Mello, along with twenty-three others, was killed in an attack on the UN headquarters in Baghdad.

Lifting the sanctions against Iraq means that companies, above all US companies, can now do business in Iraq. The *Financial Times* headline on May 23, 2003, read, "UN removal of sanctions clears way for business." Also, all of the foreign assets of Saddam Hussein and Iraq as a whole that had been frozen (again, especially in the United States) for more than twelve years are now "freed up." The United States intends to use them to pay for the war effort and reconstruction; the money will not be returned to the Iraqi people. The *Financial Times* writes, "It [the lifting of sanctions by the Security Council] will free up billions of dollars in frozen assets and future oil revenues from UN control and place it at the disposal of coalition forces and interim Iraqi leaders to pay for reconstruction" (May 23, 2003).

The Iraqi debt cannot be paid

How much does Iraq owe? A 2002 study by the US Department of Energy estimated it at $62 billion.[9] According to a joint study by the World Bank and the Bank of International Settlements, it totaled $127 billion—$47 billion in interest arrears.[10] According to a private Washington think tank, the overall level of Iraq's financial obligations (debt, reparations, and contractual obligations) was $383 billion at the beginning of 2003, of which $127 billion was estimated debt.

The creditor countries fall into two categories: members and nonmembers of the Paris Club. The Paris Club includes nineteen creditor states and some invited guests (Brazil, Korea) following the fancy of the nineteen founders. The Paris Club estimates that it can claim $21 billion of debt from Iraq, to which $21 billion of due interest payments must be added, for a total of $42 billion (*Financial Times*, July 12–13, 2003). The second category comprises Arab countries (the United Arab Emirates, Kuwait, Egypt, Jordan, Morocco, Saudi Arabia), Turkey, and some countries from the former Soviet Bloc (Poland, Bulgaria, Hungary), since turned staunch US-allies. These countries have a combined claim of about $55 billion in debt. More than half of this sum ($30 billion) is claimed by the Gulf States (excluding Kuwait), but this debt is subject to a long-running legal challenge by Iraq. Iraq claims that the $30 billion was donated by those countries in order to fight the war against Iran, while the latter maintain that it was a loan. The two above-mentioned categories cover all bilateral debts (in total, $97 billion).

The stakes are not as high for the private banks involved (primarily the Bank of New York and JPMorgan). They claim about $2 billion in debts. As for the World Bank and the IMF, Iraq's debt toward them is less than $200 million.

In short then, the negotiations between Iraq and its creditors concern an initial sum of around $100 billion: $42 billion (Paris Club) plus $55 billion (other bilateral loans) plus $2 billion (banks) plus $0.2 billion (World Bank and IMF). This sum does not include the outstanding compensation claims (around $160 billion for the 1990–91 war), contracts that were concluded just before the outbreak of war ($90 billion), and, above all, the new debts incurred since March–April 2003.

The main negotiations will in fact take place between the creditors themselves and not between the creditors and the US-nominated Iraqi "authorities." The creditors will have to work out among themselves who will set the example in waiving claims to a certain proportion of the debt in order to make repayment of the rest "sustainable." In this case, "sustainable" means that the debt can be paid back by the due date. There is no question of the creditors considering whether the repayment of the debt is manageable with respect to the needs of the Iraqi population. The United States will ask its colleagues in the Paris Club, as well as the Arab countries, Turkey, Poland, Bulgaria, and Hungary, to make a joint effort to reduce their claims by a third to two-thirds. If that happens, the amount of bilateral debt could be reduced to $65 billion (one-third reduction) or even $32 billion (two-thirds reduction), instead of the original $97 billion (see above). The United States is keen to achieve such a reduction so it can add to the already existing debts those arising from reconstruction. Many months of negotiations are therefore to be expected.

In this context, it is worth looking at the sums claimed by the members of the Paris Club, within which two opposing factions formed before the outbreak of war. At the famous meeting of the G7 finance ministers on the April 10–11, 2003, in Washington,[11] the press noted that Russia, France, and Germany were the main creditors of odious debt to Iraq. In reality, the figures are not so clear-cut, as can be seen in table 16.4, where the debt of the belligerents is contrasted to that of the "peace camp." The table illustrates that the belligerents have a greater claim to odious debt than the "peace camp," which was not what the Bush administration implied at the time of its blackmail attempts in April 2003. Furthermore, it should not be forgotten that at the start of the negotiations, the amount of debt had been deliberately exaggerated.

TABLE 16.4. IRAQI DEBT TO THE PARIS CLUB (BILLIONS OF DOLLARS)

"Peace Camp"		Belligerents	
Russia	3.45	Japan	4.10
France	3.00	United States	2.20
Germany	2.40	Italy	1.72
Canada	0.56	Great Britain	0.93
Brazil	0.20	Australia	0.50
Belgium	0.18	Spain	0.32
		Netherlands	0.10
		Denmark	0.03
Sum	9.79	Sum	9.90

Source: Table compiled by the author, based on Financial Times, July 12–13, 2003.

Another thing to remember is that the Paris Club claimed twice the amount it was owed: $42 billion instead of $21 billion. The justification advanced was that the sum corresponded to outstanding interest payments for the period since

1991. This is clearly an absurd demand, since, because of sanctions, the UN was in control of all of the oil revenues, and Iraqi assets abroad had been frozen. Nevertheless, the Paris Club (along with most of the other bilateral creditors) included the interest in the calculation, so the debt is now doubled. If, during the course of the talks, the stipulation of interest payments were to be dropped, the Paris Club could then present to international public opinion and the Iraqis the reduction in debt of $21 billion as a sign of generosity.

Iraq and the debt: The danger of a vicious circle

Whatever the debt—$50 billion, $100 billion, or $200 billion—the Iraqi financial expenses will drag the country into a vicious circle of debt and, consequently, into a position of subordination to the creditors who will plunder the oil reserves, with the United States taking the lion's share.

To verify the value of this claim, let us try to calculate what reimbursing the debt would imply in the future. Imagine the following scenario: creditors agree to reduce their demands, and gauge the total amount of debt inherited from the prewar period of March–April 2003 at around $62 billion, a one-third reduction,[12] to which $50 billion in reparations would be added. Then, several tens of billions of dollars in new debt linked to reconstruction would surely have to be added to that total, let us say $38 billion for 2003–05. Suppose that creditors postponed the beginning of repayment to 2005. In this hypothesis, the total amount of debt and reparations weighing on Iraq would be around $150 billion.

How will the creditors set up the reimbursement plan? One plausible hypothesis is the following: they would demand that the insolvent Iraqi authorities use oil revenues for repayment, and here several other problems arise. First unknown factor: By 2005, will there be Iraqi authorities with enough legitimacy to make commitments in the name of the state of Iraq (i.e., the Iraqi people)? This is far from certain. Second unknown factor: Will oil production capacity have been fully reestablished? In August 2003, production was barely at 300,000 barrels a day, compared with 1,700,000 before the 2003 war, and 2,700,000 before the first Gulf War. The estimated cost to completely restore oil production installations varies from $30 million to $40 million. Who will pay? How will the security of those companies in charge of restoring, then exploiting, the fields be ensured?

According to the *Financial Times* (July 25, 2003), the major oil companies have met with Bush administration representatives several times and conveyed the message that it is out of the question for them to spend anything on restoring the production apparatus or on production itself as long as security cannot be guaranteed. They added, via spokesperson Sir Philip Watts, then president of the oil multinational Royal Dutch/Shell, that they will determine when the future Iraqi regime meets the conditions of legitimacy: "When authorities that are legitimate in the eyes of the Iraqi people are in place, we will meet and recognize them"! In other words, the firms are telling the administration that the Iraqi authorities set up by the occupying troops do not meet the necessary conditions. Another part of the message is that they do indeed plan on having the government pay for the expense of restoring the production apparatus destroyed by the coalition. The message is a severe snub for Bush.

Third unknown factor: What will be the price of a barrel of oil in 2005? Fourth unknown factor: Will the oil industry be publicly owned? If so, much of the revenue will go into the coffers of the state and can be used for debt reimbursement (which would please the creditors). However, this poses a problem regarding the Bush administration's avowed desire to privatize. If the industry is privatized, the state will only make tax revenue from the proceeds; yet, it is the state that will have to pay off $150 billion in debts. According to various sources, in the best (and highly unlikely) scenario, oil revenues will hover from $10–$20 billion in 2005.

How much will the reimbursement of $150 billion cost annually? Let us suppose that creditors will "accept" a reimbursement plan at a preferential fixed interest rate of, say, 7 percent over twenty years.[13] One hundred and fifty billion dollars to be repaid over twenty years at 7 percent represents an annual payment of about $18 billion (repayment on the interest and principal). In short, it is like trying to stick a square peg in a round hole. Based on export revenue of $10–$20 billion, it is asking the impossible.

The US position in mid-2003

A few days after the invasion of Iraq by American, British, and Australian troops had begun on March 20, 2003, George W. Bush estimated before Congress that the costs of the war for the US Treasury would be around $80 billion. On September 7, 2003, Bush declared to Congress that he was asking for $87 billion more. According to the UNDP and UNICEF, $80 billion is exactly the extra sum needed each year, over ten years, to guarantee universal access to clean water, basic education, and health care (including nutrition), and gynecological and obstetric care for all women for the entire planet. This sum that no world summit of the last few years has managed to come up with (at Genoa in 2001, the G7 only raised a little under one billion dollars to fight against AIDS, malaria, and tuberculosis), the U.S. government managed to raise and spend in a few months. The $80 billion that Bush got from Congress (to which another $87 billion was added) is what it cost to destroy a certain amount of infrastructure and human life in Iraq and underwrite territorial occupation through the end of December 2003.

Faced with unforeseen resistance, the United States is confronted with major difficulties. Although they remain the undisputed masters on the international scene and occupy the country, they are nevertheless hated by a large majority of the population. Their troops are under constant harassment. The cost of military occupation has far exceeded expectations and is now running at around $4 billion a month ($48 billion a year) for more than 130,000 soldiers who are currently serving. The British contingent numbers 11,000 troops, but the 30,000 that were supposed to be supplied by other alliance members have yet to show up.[14]

In no way does this prevent companies in the United States and elsewhere from doing business. By spring 2003, Halliburton (from Texas) was already on the scene carrying out emergency repairs to oil production equipment for a $7 billion contract. Dick Cheney, US vice president, was the firm's CEO until August 2000. Competitor Bechtel (responsible for the water conflicts in Cochabamba in Bolivia), which obtained a $680 million contract to repair water and electricity distribution systems and certain communication systems, called a meeting in Washington in May 2003 on the theme "How can US companies participate in reconstruction?" The enthusiasm of the 1,800 small and medium-sized businesses present was somewhat dampened after they were told that they would have to ensure the safety of their employees and equipment themselves. Bechtel held the same kind of meeting in London and Kuwait City.

The big agro-industry corporations, in particular the Anglo-Swiss multinational Syngenta, are also interested in the future of Iraq, as the country has traditionally been a big grain exporter. However, Monsanto has made it known that it is not interested, perhaps due to pressing issues elsewhere.

In Iraq, administrator Paul Bremer is doing his utmost to attract investment; in classic neoliberal style, he has declared that everything must be privatized, subsidies must be eliminated, and private property rights increased. In exchange, he concedes the need for a social security safety net. As an indication of what this means, note that in May 2003, the United States paid 400,000 Iraqi workers and civil servants a monthly salary of $20.00, which adds up to $8 million total—500 times less than what the United States spends each month maintaining its troops in Iraq.

For cancellation of Iraq's odious debt and payment of reparations

It is not because the United States used the notion of odious debt in an opportunistic way that we should refuse to demand its application to guarantee justice and fundamental rights for the Iraqi people. Therefore, we must support the idea of a legitimate power in Iraq that could repudiate this debt. The question of reparation rights must also be broached. The cost must take into account the damages that the United States and other aggressors never take into account—individual suffering, cultural pillage, etc.—for which they are nonetheless responsible since, as an occupying force, they are responsible for the security of people and property.

Applying the odious debt doctrine to Iraq would be of the utmost importance for the future of the Iraqi population and, beyond that, for a majority of the populations of indebted or so-called developing nations. The citizens of these countries are perfectly within their rights to demand that a significant portion of their countries' debt be declared null and void based on the odious

Petition for the abolition of the Iraqi debt and right to reparations

We, citizens of the world, unite in declaring that the Iraqi people cannot be held responsible for debts contracted and expenses incurred by Saddam Hussein and his despotic regime. Under the terms of the doctrine of "odious debt," these debts are contingent on the regime that contracted them. Likewise, the Iraqi people cannot be required to bear the cost of the occupation of Iraq by the troops of the Coalition of the United States, the United Kingdom, and Australia.

We call on all creditors to cancel the odious debt contracted by Saddam Hussein. We declare that the cost of the war and the present occupation cannot be transformed into a further debt. We consider that the destruction and pillage caused by the war entitle the Iraqi people to reparations.

We call upon the United Nations General Assembly to support the Iraqi people in demanding the cancellation of the debt and the provision of reparations for the damage caused by the war waged by the Coalition in violation of the United Nations Charter.

The Iraqi people and their freely elected representatives must be allowed to enter a new stage of their history with full independence. Henceforth, all of Iraq's resources must be made available for use by and for the Iraqi people, so they can reconstruct their country.

We call on all countries, all organizations, and all citizens to support this declaration.

FIRST SIGNATORIES: **Acosta** Alberto (Univ. of Cuenca, Ecuador), **Albala** Nuri (lawyer, Paris), **Badrul** Alam (Secretary-General, Bangladesh Krishok Federation, Bangladesh), **Boudjenah** Yasmine (Member of the European

debt principle.

It is up to the antiglobalization movement to press for the cancellation of Iraq's external public debt along with other demands, such as the withdrawal of the occupying troops; the full exercise of Iraqi sovereignty, including the exploitation of natural resources; and the payment of reparations to Iraqi citizens for the destruction and pillage suffered during the course of the war waged, in violation of the UN Charter, by the American/British/Australian coalition. Moreover, it is imperative that George W. Bush, Tony Blair, and John Howard (the Australian prime minister), along with the heads of the Danish and Dutch governments (these countries participated directly in the invasion),

Parliament GUE/NGL, France), **Briault Manus** Vicki (translator, CADTM-France), **Bugra** Ayse (Univ. Bebek of Istanbul, Turkey), **Chomsky** Noam (United States), **Cirera** Daniel (French Communist Party, International Relations), **Cockroft** James (author, United States), **Comanne** Denise (CADTM-Belgium), **Eliecer Mejia Diaz** Jorge (lawyer, criminal law specialist, France), **Gazi** Carmen (architect, president of CADTM-Switzerland), **Gillardi** Paolo (Anti-War Coalition, Movement for Socialism, Switzerland), **Gottschalk** Janet (Medical Mission Sisters' Alliance for Justice), **Hediger** André (Mayor of Geneva, Switzerland), **Husson** Michel (economist, France), **Khiari** Sadri (Fine Artist, CNLT, Raid Attac, Tunisia), **Kitazawa** Yoko (Japan Network on Debt and Poverty, Peace Studies Association of Japan), **Krivine** Alain (Member of the European Parliament GUE/NGL, France), **Künzi** Daniel (film director, Municipal Council of the City of Geneva, Switzerland), **Lambert** Jean-Marie (international law professor at Cathol. Univ. of Goiás, Brazil), **Magniadas** Jean (Doctor of economic science, honorary member of the Economic and Social Council, France), **Martinez Cruz** José (Independent Human Rights Commissioner, Morelos, Mexico), **Maystre** Nicolas (student, secretary of CADTM-Switzerland), **Mendès France** Mireille (lawyer, Paris), **Millet** Damien (Secretary-General, CADTM-France), **Nieto Pereira** Luis (Asociación Paz con Dignidad, Spain), **Nzuzi Mbembe** Victor (farmer, GRAPR, Democratic Republic of Congo), **Pazmiño Freire** Patricio (lawyer, general coordinator, CDES, Ecuador), **Pérez Casas** Luis Guillermo (José Alvear Restrepo lawyers' collective before the EU and the United Nations, Columbia), **Pérez Vega** Ana (Univ. of Seville, Spain), **Pfefferkorn** Roland (sociologist, France), **Piningre** Denis (film director), **Said Alli** Abd Rahman (Perak Consumers' Association, Malaysia), **Saumon** Alain (president, CADTM-France), **Soueissi** Ahmad (Nord-Sud XXI), **Theodoris** Nassos (lawyer, Greece), **Toussaint** Eric (CADTM, Belgium), **Verschave** François-Xavier (author, France), **Yacouba** Ibrahim (National "debt and development" network, Niger), **Ziegler** Jean (writer, North-South Foundation for Dialogue, Switzerland).

Signatures should be sent to info@cadtm.org. Or, by post, send to CADTM, 345 avenue de l'Observatoire, 4000 Liège, Belgium.

should be prosecuted and condemned for direct responsibility for the crime of aggression, as defined by the UN Charter, and for war crimes.

Concerning proposals for the Iraqi debt, the following points should be stressed:

- the debt contracted under Saddam Hussein's regime is an odious debt, and therefore null and void;

- a subsequent democratic regime should refuse to take responsibility for that debt and would be within its rights to repudiate it;

- new debts due to the costs of war and reconstruction are also odious, and therefore null and void;

- victims of Saddam Hussein, of American aggression, of pillage, and of the current occupation have the right to reparations;

- citizens and civil authorities must participate in general mobilizations and petition drives, such as the one launched by CADTM (below), but we must also demand audits from the authorities—not necessarily wait for them, but organize our own citizens' audits—on the debts that creditors are claiming against Iraq. (What are they? Any creditor claiming reimbursement of a debt from Iraq must answer citizens' questions on the nature of these debts. In what contract are they defined? Who were the contracting parties? What were they for? Arms? Equipment for civilian use? What were the contract terms? What amounts have already been paid? Doing the research work here may contribute to showing that the debts at stake are in fact odious.)

Rwanda

The 1994 genocide

Beginning on April 7, 1994, within a period of three months, more than one million Rwandans—the exact figure has yet to be determined—were exterminated because they were Tutsis or thought to be. Several tens of thousands of Hutus were also killed, political opponents of the regime and people who refused or might have refused to support the genocide. The population of Rwanda before the atrocities is estimated to have been about 7.5 million. Comparisons with the genocide of the Jews and Gypsies are fully justified. Of course, there are differences: the absolute number of victims (the Nazis murdered six million Jews) and the methods used (the Nazis designed and used industrial techniques to implement the final solution). However, what occurred in Rwanda was a genocide, that is, the planned destruction of an entire community through mass murder, with the objective of preventing it from reproducing itself biologically and socially.

Policies of the multilateral financial institutions

It is crucial that we examine the role of international lenders. The policies imposed by the international financial institutions—the Habyarimana regime's main lenders—accelerated the process that led to genocide. In general, the negative repercussions of these policies are not taken into consideration to explain the dramatic conclusion of the Rwandan crisis. Only a handful of scholars highlight the responsibility of the Bretton Woods institutions (such as Chossudovsky 1995). The institutions themselves reject all criticism on this score. More surprising, some authors with links to NGOs have also published studies that seek to tone down criticism of the role of the World Bank and the IMF (Woodward 1996).

At the beginning of the 1980s, when the Third World debt crisis broke out, Rwanda (like its neighbor Burundi) had an extremely low level of indebtedness. Elsewhere, the World Bank and the IMF jettisoned their policy of active lending, preaching austerity instead. In Rwanda, however, they adopted a different approach, and began to lend large sums. Rwanda's foreign debt increased twenty-fold between 1976 and 1994. In 1976, it stood at $49 million; by 1994, it was more than $1 billion. Most of this growth took place after 1982. The country's main lenders were the World Bank, the IMF, and related institutions, with the World Bank and IMF playing the most active role. In 1999, they held 87 percent of Rwanda's foreign debt, which at the time was spread as follows: 87 percent owed to the multilateral institutions, 13 percent owed bilaterally, and 0 percent owed to private creditors (World Bank 2001).

The dictatorial regime in place since 1973 was a guarantee against progressive structural change. For this reason, it received the active backing of Western powers, particularly Belgium, France, and Switzerland. It was a bulwark against those states in the region that sought to protect their independence and effect progressive change (for example, neighboring Tanzania under progressive president Julius Nyerere, one of the African leaders of the Nonaligned Movement).

Between 1980 and 1994, Rwanda received large sums in loan money; the Habyarimana dictatorship channeled a significant share into its own coffers. The loans were meant to help Rwanda integrate into the world economy more fully by developing its coffee, tea, and tin exporting capacities, to the detriment of crops destined for domestic consumption. This model worked until the mid-1980s, when world tin prices collapsed—soon followed by world coffee and tea prices.

When the US broke up the coffee cartel in the early 1990s, the Rwandan economy, for which coffee was the main source of hard currency, was devastated.

International loans used to prepare genocide

A few weeks before the Rwandan Patriotic Front (RPF) launched its October 1990 offensive, the Rwandan authorities signed an agreement with the IMF and the World Bank to implement a structural adjustment program (SAP).

The SAP was implemented in November 1990, and one of the first measures was a 67 percent devaluation of the Rwandan franc. In exchange, the IMF provided credit in the form of quick disbursing loans to enable the country to maintain the flow of imports. As a result, the country was able to redress its balance of payments. There was a meteoric rise in the price of imported goods; gas rose by 79 percent. Earnings from the sale of imported goods on the domestic market enabled the government to pay the salaries of members of the armed forces, whose ranks were growing rapidly in size. The SAP prescribed a drop in public spending; indeed, wage freezes and dismissals occurred in the public sector, but part of the savings were transferred to the armed forces.

While import prices soared, in response to IMF insistence, the price at which coffee was bought from local producers was frozen. As a result, hundreds of thousands of small coffee farmers were ruined (Maton 1994). Alongside the poorest sectors of the urban population, these destitute farmers became a permanent reservoir of recruits for the Interahamwe militia and the army.

The measures imposed by the World Bank and the IMF as part of the SAP included increased taxes on consumption and lower business taxes, increased direct taxes on low-income households through a reduction in tax allowances for large families, and cuts in lending programs for small farmers. To account for the sums loaned by the World Bank and the IMF, Rwanda was authorized to present old invoices for imported goods. Thanks to this system, the regime was able to finance massive arms purchases used in the genocide. Military spending tripled between 1990 and 1992 (Nduhungirehe 1995). The World Bank and the IMF sent several delegations of experts during this period; they highlighted the positive features of Habyarimana's austerity policies, but nonetheless threatened to suspend credit unless military spending stopped increasing. The Rwandan authorities maneuvered their way around these restrictions in order to hide rising military spending: trucks imported for the army were put on the Transport Ministry's account, a significant share of the gas used for militia and army vehicles was put on the Health Ministry's account, and so on.

Finally, the World Bank and the IMF suspended financing at the beginning of 1993—neglecting, however, to freeze the large sums of money held in accounts in foreign banks, which the regime used to buy arms. It can be argued that the Washington-based institutions failed in their duty to monitor the way in which loan money was used. They should have suspended credit in early 1992, when they realized that the money was being used for arms purchases. They should have alerted the United Nations. By continuing to provide financing until early 1993, they helped a regime that was preparing genocide.

Since 1991, human-rights organizations had been reporting and condemning the massacres that paved the way to genocide. The World Bank and the IMF systematically helped the dictatorship, since it was an ally of the United States, France, and Belgium.

Rising social conflict

For the genocide to be perpetrated, more was required than a regime that had merely developed a blueprint and equipped itself with the necessary hardware. It was also necessary to have an impoverished population, a population that had been "lumpenized," prepared to do the irreparable. In Rwanda, 90 percent of the population lives in the countryside, and 20 percent of peasant families own less than half an acre. Between 1982 and 1994, there had been a process of large-scale impoverishment of the majority of the rural population, while, at the same time, a tiny section of the population had grown fabulously rich.

According to Jef Maton (1994), in 1982, the wealthiest 10 percent of the population took in 20 percent of rural revenues; in 1992, they took in 41 percent; in 1993, 45 percent; and by the beginning of 1994, 51 percent. The catastrophic social impact of policies dictated by the IMF and World Bank, and the fall in coffee prices on the global market (a fall linked to the policies of the Bretton Woods institutions and the United States), played a central role in the Rwandan crisis. The massive social discontent was channeled by the Habyarimana regime into implementing its plan for genocide.

The genocide's financiers

Between 1990 and 1994, Rwanda's main arms suppliers were France, Belgium, South Africa, Egypt, and China. China also provided 500,000 machetes. Egypt—whose deputy prime minister of foreign affairs, responsible for relations with the African continent, was none other than Boutros Boutros-Ghali—granted Rwanda a $6 million, interest-free loan in 1991 to purchase arms for its infantry divisions. When the genocide got under way, France and the British firm Miltec provided arms to the rampaging army via the Goma Airport across the border in Zaire, violating the May 11, 1994, UN embargo on arms sales to Rwanda (Toussaint 1996b). Once the Rwandan capital Kigali had been overrun by the opposition RPF, a certain number of the key leaders of the genocide were received by the French president. Rwandan leaders-in-exile set up the head office of the Banque Nationale du Rwanda in Goma, with the help of the French army. Until August 1994, the bank disbursed funds to repay debts for previous arms purchases and to buy new arms. Private banks (Belgolaise, Générale de Banque, BNP, and Dresdner Bank, among others) accepted payment orders from those responsible for the genocide and repaid those who financed the genocide.

Rwanda after the genocide

After the fall of the dictatorship in July 1994, the World Bank and the IMF demanded that the new Rwandan government limit the number of public-sector employees to 50 percent of the number agreed on before the genocide. The new government complied. Initial financial assistance provided by the United States and Belgium in late 1994 went toward repaying the Habyarimana regime's debt arrears with the World Bank. Financial aid from the West has been barely trickling into the country since then, despite the urgent need to rebuild and provide for the more than 800,000 refugees on its soil since November 1996.

According to David Woodward's report for Oxfam, agricultural production did recover somewhat in 1996. However, first harvests were 38 percent lower than usual, and second harvests were 28 percent lower than usual. Industry was taking longer to recover: only fifty-four of eighty-eight industrial concerns in operation before April 1994 had resumed activity; most were operating well below previous levels. At the end of 1995, the total value of industrial production was 47 percent of 1990 levels.

A 20 percent wage increase in the public sector in January 1996 was the first such rise since 1981; official estimates, however, are that 80 percent of public-sector workers live below the poverty line. It comes as no surprise that Rwandans prefer to work in NGOs as drivers and cooks rather than in the public sector. These poverty statistics are not peculiar to the public sector: in 1996, the World Bank estimated that 85–95 percent of Rwandans lived below the threshold of absolute poverty.

It should be noted that the number of households run by women has significantly increased: from 21.7 percent before the genocide, to 29.3 percent now, with peaks of 40 percent in some districts. Their situation is particularly disturbing in view of the profound discrimination against women in such matters as inheritance, access to credit, and property rights. Even before the genocide, 35 percent of women heads of household earned less than five thousand Rwandan francs (seventeen dollars) per month; the corresponding figure for men was 22 percent.

In spite of a high rate of adoption of orphans (from the genocide and AIDS deaths), there are between 95,000 and 150,000 children without families. In the education system, only 65 percent of children are enrolled in primary schools, and no more than 8 percent in secondary schools (Woodward 1996).

In 1994, Rwanda's foreign debt had reached nearly one billion dollars, the totality of which had been contracted by the Habyarimana regime. Five years later, the debt had increased by about 30 percent, and Rwanda repaid $31 million (1999 figures). The debt contracted before 1994 fits the definition of odious debt perfectly; it follows that the new regime should have been totally exonerated from paying it off. The multilateral and bilateral creditors knew very well who they were dealing with when they lent money to Habyarimana's regime. After the change of regime, there was not the slightest justification for transferring their claims onto the new Rwanda. Nevertheless, it was done quite shamelessly.

The new Rwandan government that came into power in 1994 tried to persuade the World Bank and IMF to renounce their loans. The two institutions refused, threatening to cut off funding if Kigali persisted. They put pressure on Kigali to keep quiet about the aid they had provided to the Habyarimana regime, in exchange for new loans and a promise of future debt cancellation as part of the initiative in favor of the heavily indebted poor countries (HIPC) launched in 1996.

One can only deplore that the government should have accepted such blackmail. The consequences are pernicious: continued structural adjustment, with its disastrous social and economic consequences, and an increase in foreign debt. In complying, the government of Kigali has gained "good pupil" status in the eyes of the IMF, the World Bank, and the Paris Club. Worse still, the Rwandan regime has become the accomplice of the United States and Great Britain, whose policy is to weaken the Democratic Republic of the Congo (DRC), by taking part, as of August 1998, in the military occupation of its neighbor, the DRC, and by plundering its natural resources.

---

1   On this, Joseph Stiglitz (2002) writes: "Robert Rubin, the treasury secretary...came from the largest investment bank, Goldman Sachs, and he returned to the firm, Citigroup, that controlled the largest commercial bank, Citibank. The number-two person at the IMF during this period, Stan Fischer, went straight from the IMF to Citigroup. These individuals naturally see the world through the eyes of the financial community." Immediately before this is a passage applicable to the designation of the new president of the Central Bank of Brazil by President Lula in January, 2003: "The finance ministers and central bank governors typically are closely tied to the financial community; they come from financial firms, and after their period of government service, that is where they return."

2   Proposed legislative decree no. 645-A, 2000.

3   This section was written by the author in August 2001, a few months before the debt crisis erupted in December. No changes have been made to this text, entitled "Is Argentina the weak link in the global chain of indebtedness?" The concrete actions of the Argentines have transformed this question into an affirmation. The original text is supplemented by an extra passage covering the period up to 2002–03.

4   Here ends the article written in August 2001 for the second edition of *Your Money or Your Life* in Castillian Spanish, published by three publishers in 2002 (Gakoa in Spain, Abya-Yala in Ecuador, CSAPN and SNTE in Mexico), and for the first Portuguese edition published in Brazil in 2002 by the Perseu Abramo Foundation.

5   Renouncing the odious debt would not, in any case, cause the bankruptcy of large banks, as odious debt represents, on average, less than 5 percent of their turnover. However, the bankers and other creditors tend to believe that they have an inalienable right to lend to whomever they wish. Similarly, they are convinced that they have the right to demand repayment whatever the circumstances of the debtor.

6   See Toussaint and Millet 2004.

7   Alexander Sack was convinced that debts should, in general, be carried on from one regime to the next, except in the case of odious debts.

8   Between 1991 and May 22, 2003, Iraqi oil was controlled by the United Nations.

9   US Department of Energy, Energy Information Administration, Iraq Country Analysis Brief, October 2002, www.eia.doe.gov/emeu/cabs/iraq.html.

10 Cited by David Chance, Regime Change Could Benefit Iraqi Creditors, Reuters News Wire, Sept. 13, 2002.

11 Russia had not yet been invited to the financial summits of the major powers. Thus, it was the G7, not the G8.

12 This corresponds to the Bush administration Energy Department estimate made in October 2002.

13 In August 2003, Brazil was paying an interest rate of 12–14 percent to borrow on the international market; Argentina was paying 37–39 percent; Turkey, 7–9 percent; the Philippines, 6–7 percent; Mexico, 5 percent.

14 The allied commitments for troops in spring 2003 were in principle as follows: Spain, 1,200 soldiers; Poland, 2,000; Ukraine, 2,300; Norway, 140; Italy, 2,800; Romania, 520; Portugal, 130; the Netherlands, 1,100; the Czech Republic, 300; and Denmark, 450.

17

Asian storms: Will those tamed dragons breathe fire once more?

The crisis that shook East and Southeast Asia in 1997–98 had lasting effects regionally and nationally, and considerably weakened the region. Until 1997, "mainstream" economists presented it to the countries of Latin America, Africa, and Eastern Europe as the model to follow. Now the region has joined the other countries of the periphery in the debt crisis and structural adjustment. Encouraged by the IMF and the World Bank, the MNCs of the highly industrialized countries, especially the United States and Europe, took advantage of the crisis to acquire numerous companies in which they imposed harsher working conditions. Furthermore, national industrial projects, such as the construction of a national car or a passenger aircraft carrier in Indonesia, had to be abandoned.

South Korea, hitherto untouched by structural adjustment, agreed to the conditionalities laid down by the IMF. In the whole region, only Malaysia refused them. As Joseph Stiglitz put it after leaving his post at the World Bank, "All the IMF has done is to make the East Asian recession deeper, harsher and longer" (*New Republic*, April 17, 2000). It was a deliberate ploy on the part of the highly industrialized countries to weaken countries that over the years had become dangerous competitors.

The rapid and partly autonomous cycle of development of the newly industrialized countries (NICs) of East and Southeast Asia seems finally over. In 2003, however, certain governments showed clear signs of resistance. China refused to carry out the policies required by the Triad, in particular the United States. The Chinese authorities maintained a firm control on capital movements, the national currency (the renminbi is not convertible), and investments. Malaysia prided itself on standing up to the IMF and the United States. Thailand's prime minister, Thaksin Shinawatra, implemented strong policies of public intervention, to the displeasure of the Bretton Woods institutions. Then, in August 2003, he proudly announced that Thailand was shaking completely free of the IMF, having paid in advance the balance owed on money borrowed during the crisis in 1997–98. For their part, the Indonesian authorities signaled their intention to follow Thailand. All of this is indicative of a wish to regain a certain independence in response to the dramatic effects of the 1999–98 crisis and the policies dictated by Washington.

In the three years from 1998 to 2000, the East and Southeast Asian countries (including China) repaid the astronomical sum of $291 billion to their foreign creditors. Over the same period, the net negative transfer on debt came to $150 billion. Just when those countries needed the money to restart their economies, the governments in power and the Bretton Woods institutions decided to transfer it to international creditors, though the latter were largely responsible for the crisis. In fact, banks and other private financial institutions of the industrialized countries stopped lending and insisted on the reimbursement of previous debts down to the last farthing. The governments of the indebted countries nationalized a substantial part of the debts owned by private companies. So the populations of the region footed the bill of rescuing the private sector, which came to $59 billion in Korea and $90 billion in Indonesia. The way the crisis was managed (i.e., in the interests of international capital and local capitalists) engendered enormous social costs.

Global financial and stock market instability significantly increased with the Asian crisis. What caused the crisis, and how did it spread?

Checkmate for Asia's four "dragons"

In April 1997, a major economic and financial crisis broke out in Southeast Asia. It began in Thailand in February 1997, spreading from July on to Malaysia, Indonesia, and the Philippines. These four countries had not long before been cited by the IMF, the World Bank, and private banks as the models to emulate, due to their high degree of openness to the world market, low rate of inflation, and high rates of growth. They were Asia's four "dragons," engaged in a race to catch up with the region's four "tigers" (South Korea, Taiwan, Hong Kong, and Singapore). Today, the same institutions criticize these countries for giving the state too strong a role; moreover, they accuse the state of allowing private financial and industrial concerns to accumulate exaggerated levels of debt and to speculate.

Between 1990 and 1997, the external indebtedness of the four dragons rocketed (a 50 percent increase for the Philippines and more than 100 percent for the others), as can be seen in table 17.1, which shows the evolution of the external debt of the main indebted developing countries of Asia. (The dragons appear in bold.) External debt also markedly increased for South Korea and China, and more slowly for India, Pakistan, Vietnam, Bangladesh, and Sri Lanka.

TABLE 17.1. EXTERNAL DEBT FOR MAIN INDEBTED
ASIAN DEVELOPING COUNTRIES (BILLIONS OF DOLLARS)

	1970	1980	1990	1995	1997	1999
China	NA*	NA*	55.3	118.1	146.7	154.2
Indonesia	**4.5**	**20.9**	**69.9**	**124.4**	**136.2**	**150.1**
Korea	NA*	NA*	31.7	127.5	159.2	136.4
Thailand	**1.0**	**8.3**	**28.2**	**100.1**	**109.7**	**96.3**
India	8.4	20.7	83.7	94.5	94.3	94.4
Philippines	**2.2**	**17.4**	**30.6**	**37.8**	**45.7**	**52.0**
Malaysia	**0.5**	**6.6**	**15.3**	**34.3**	**47.2**	**45.9**
Pakistan	3.4	9.9	20.7	30.2	30.1	34.3
Vietnam	NA*	NA*	23.3	25.4	21.8	23.3
Bangladesh	NA*	4.2	12.8	16.3	15.1	17.5
Sri Lanka	0.4	1.8	5.9	8.2	7.7	9.5
Subtotal			377.2	716.9	813.7	814.0

*NA = not available   *Source: World Bank 2001.*

The crisis that hit the four dragons head on in 1997 triggered a problem of debt repayment, as the speculative attacks against their currencies resulted in devaluation, and, at the same time, the credit lines opened by international banks suddenly shut down.

Growth in the dragon countries (Thailand, with a population of 60 million; Indonesia, 203 million; the Philippines, 73 million; and Malaysia, 20 million) was driven by an inflow of foreign capital, importation of goods and machinery, and low salaries. This soon led to the appearance of two negative factors: first, the external debt—largely in the form of short-term loans contracted on the financial markets—grew rapidly; second, the trade deficit continued to rise. Indeed, imports were systematically higher than exports. In other words, the productivity of these countries remained structurally lower than that of the industrialized countries with which they were trading.

The four dragons have thus retained the characteristics of Third World economies and suffer from the effects of unequal trade. The relative prices of their exports are lower than the relative prices of the goods they must import in order to reach their growth targets and satisfy the consumer needs of the wealthiest sectors of the population. Only these sections of the population have the necessary purchasing power to buy high-quality consumer goods. A large section of the population did not benefit from the economic growth, which explains why the gap between rich and poor within these countries actually widened, in spite of an overall increase in the national income. Now that the crisis has struck, the richest sectors of the population continue to amass riches, while the majority of the population—including most of the middle class—is seeing their incomes plummet. This will only serve to accentuate the

Chronology of the crisis

January–August 1997: Stock markets continued to climb in the United States, Europe, Hong Kong and Latin America; Japanese markets stagnated, and in August 1997, markets in the four dragons crashed

February 1997: Capital flight from Thailand begins

July 2, 1997: First devaluation of Thai baht

August 1997: IMF announces rescue package for Thailand; package accompanied by harsh austerity measures

October 1997: Stock market crash in Hong Kong and a number of other markets (the term "crash" is usually used to describe a drop in share values of more than 10 percent in a single session)

October 27, 1997: Generalized fall on world stock markets—New York, -7.2 percent (554 points down), trading stopped twice on Wall Street; São Paulo, -14.9 percent; Mexico City, -13.7 percent; Buenos Aires, -13.3 percent; Toronto, -6.1 percent; Hong Kong, -13.7 percent (or -33.4 percent in eight days); Tokyo, -4.3 percent; London, -8.4 percent; Frankfurt, -11 percent; Madrid, -14 percent; Amsterdam, -8.7 percent; Paris, -9.1 percent; Brussels, -1.2 percent; Manila, -6.3 percent; Seoul, -6.6 percent; Taipei, -6.9 percent; Sydney, -7.2 percent; Shanghai, -7.2 percent; Auckland, -12.5 percent; Moscow (October 28), -21.1 percent

December 1997: South Korea accepts IMF conditions

January 15, 1998: Indonesia accepts IMF conditions

July 2, 1997–January 8, 1998: Depreciation of Asian currencies against the dollar—Indonesian rupiah, -80 percent; South Korean won, -96.5 percent; Thai baht, -87.4 percent; Malaysian ringgit, -78.5 percent; Filipino peso, -70.5 percent; Singapore dollar, -21.5 percent; Japanese yen, -15.5 percent; Indian rupee, -11 percent.

characteristic features of an "underdeveloped" economy.

Thailand was the first country to plunge into crisis. Its money was pegged to the dollar, which was not the case for the other three dragons. The Thai baht therefore kept in step with the dollar, which rose sharply. This made Thai exports much less competitive, provoking capital flight. The three other dragons were dragged down by the Thai collapse. Thailand is the seventh most indebted Third World country in absolute terms, just behind Brazil (population 170 million), Mexico (population 90 million), China (population 1.2 billion), Indonesia (population 203 million), Argentina (population 30 million), and South Korea (population 45 million).

The global stock market crisis

The crisis was not limited to the four dragons. In October 1997, it hit Hong Kong hard and began to undermine South Korea, deepening the economic crisis already affecting Japan. By late October and early November, world stock markets were shaken. The big institutional investors—pension and mutual funds, insurance companies, and banks—panicked in the face of the monetary and stock market instability (for which they were largely responsible). They sold off shares, converting them into liquidity or buying government bonds from the major industrialized countries, thus further worsening the crisis. These bonds were seen as safe havens, although their yield immediately dropped in response to the flood of money in their direction.

Capital flight out of Southeast Asia began in early 1997. The scale of this flight forced the dragons progressively to devalue their currencies relative to the dollar from July on. The outward flow of capital eventually affected Hong Kong—the main stock market in the Third World and the sixth biggest in the world. The wealthy classes of Latin America hoped to attract this outflow of investment from Asia into long-term investment in Latin America, but this was not to be. On October 27, the stock markets of Mexico City, São Paulo, and Buenos Aires—the three main financial centers in Latin America—crashed simultaneously. The crisis spun out of control; all of the world's stock markets plummeted on October 27–28. As for the four dragons—under the combined effects of the huge devaluation of their currencies, emergency loans from the IMF, World Bank, other financial institutions, and some governments—the weight of their external debt increased dramatically. Now that the two American credit-rating agencies Moody's and Standard and Poor's have downgraded the country risk rating of the dragons and South Korea, these countries have to pay high short-term interest rates in order to contract loans to pay off past debts.

A failing grade for the IMF

The IMF had sworn that it would never again be caught off guard by a financial crisis characterized in particular by the massive outflow of capital from a given country. Following the Mexican crisis of 1994, the IMF established a surveillance system for each country's national economy, aimed at eliminating the possibility of another Mexico-like crisis. But this system proved to be of no use. The IMF's *Annual Report* (1997b) was written during the summer of 1997, while the Southeast Asian crisis was gathering steam, and published in September. It is a dismaying read for a number of reasons. The report reveals an IMF steeped in illusion about its own ability to pinpoint the beginnings of a crisis in time: "[We] note that consistent progress has been made, especially concerning the IMF's ability to detect the appearance of financial tensions at an early phase." The actual course of events soon showed how baseless these self-satisfied comments had been. The IMF did not foresee the major financial crisis that hit the four dragons. Worse, in its *World Economic Outlook* written during autumn1997, the IMF did not foresee the crisis that would hit South Korea, the world's eleventh strongest economy, in November 1997. The IMF's pronouncements recall a well-known French song from the Depression-era 1930s, "All is well, Madame la Marquise." In it, the maidservant replies to the marquise's question about the state of her castle, "Your castle is burning to the ground, but all is well."

IMF president Michel Camdessus constantly changed his explanation for what was happening. He became a champion of political and diplomatic doublespeak. At a press conference held at IMF headquarters on December 18, 1997, he said that the IMF had underestimated both the danger and scale of the crisis. Yet, in Brussels, on January 21, 1998, he blamed the crisis on the leaders of the countries affected. He accused them of not heeding IMF warnings! He added, "If we had been able to act six months earlier, the crisis in South Korea would never have happened" (*Le Soir*, January 22, 1998). Two years later, although he had resigned before the end of his mandate, Camdessus persisted in his bragging: "The IMF's response to the Asian crisis was a wonderful success, not only in Korea and Thailand, but also in Indonesia" (*Bangkok Post*, September 24, 2000).

The IMF and the Asian dragons

It is worth recalling that beginning in the 1980s, both the IMF and the World Bank had pointed to the four dragons as models to be emulated by all Third World countries, and even by those of Eastern Europe. This position was maintained right up to the outbreak of the crisis.

On the subject of Thailand, the 1997 *Annual Report* includes a summary of a working meeting held between the IMF and Thai officials in 1996. According to the report, the external debt had risen sharply between 1991 and 1995, going from 39 percent to 49.5 percent of GDP. Furthermore, it says, half of this external debt was contracted on a short-term, high-interest basis, and the trade balance was increasingly in the red. The report highlights other reasons for concern. Nevertheless, it draws the following conclusion:

> Directors strongly praised Thailand's remarkable economic performance and the authorities' consistent record of sound macroeconomic policies. They noted that financial policies had been tightened in 1995 in response to the widening of the external current account deficit and the pickup in inflation, and this had begun to bear results, but they cautioned that there was no room for complacency.

Indonesia also earned IMF kudos: "Directors commended the authorities for Indonesia's economic achievements of recent years, especially the sizable reduction in poverty and the improvement in many social indicators." Further on, IMF governors praise Indonesia for prioritizing the free circulation of capital, although a few lines earlier they highlight some of the dangers this entails. "[L]arge capital inflows had raised important policy challenges," according to the report. The analysis continues with praise for the Indonesian authorities, indicating that they would handle the new challenges with comparative ease: "The authorities' flexibility in adapting the policy mix to meet changing circumstances had been an important aspect of their success over the years and would remain essential in addressing those challenges."

As for Malaysia, the report contains the following passage:

> In their discussion, Directors commended the authorities for Malaysia's continued impressive economic performance, which had been marked by robust, outward-oriented growth, low inflation, and remarkable social progress in reducing poverty and improving income distribution. Sustained prudent macroeconomic management and wide-ranging structural reforms underpinned these achievements.

Soon after, once the crisis had begun, these very same Thai, Indonesian, and Malaysian officials became the targets of criticism from the IMF and neoliberal ideologues. Malaysian prime minister Mahathir bin Mohamad was a particular source of irritation to the IMF for a number of reasons: from late July 1997, he denounced the criminal role of big speculating financial institutions; he criticized the IMF and refused its assistance; he visited Fidel Castro in September 1997; and his country hosted the G15 summit in the fall of 1997, bringing together the main countries of the Third World in a (sadly) failed attempt to put pressure on the governments of the industrialized countries.

As previously stated, one of the main causes for the crisis in the dragon countries was a high growth rate based on a massive inflow of foreign capital combined with a level of imports that consistently exceeded the value of exports. This led to an increasing current account deficit, accentuated by the rise in the value of the dollar in 1996 and 1997. These countries pursued a low-wage and high-interest policy aimed at attracting foreign direct investment and speculative capital. This policy created a distorted domestic market in which only a small wealthy minority enjoyed high levels of consumption and speculative investment exploded in sectors such as real estate. Financial and industrial concerns in the dragons all assumed high levels of debt to undertake major development projects and to engage in speculative investment practices. Local banks and brokerage firms granted huge loans without requesting adequate guarantees from their debtors. When the vanguard among international and local financial speculators—with George Soros's Quantum Fund in the lead—determined that governments would be unable to defend their currencies, they unleashed their attack, starting with the Thai baht. The first round of attacks proved to be a success, a wave of panic selling followed; the local capitalists that could were quick to offload their local currencies in exchange for dollars, which they invested in safer markets far away.

The IMF and the South Korean crisis

The crisis thundered into South Korea in November 1997. In its October 1997 quarterly bulletin on economic prospects for the coming two years, the IMF makes absolutely no mention of the crisis that would hit the world's eleventh most powerful economy a few days later.

After the fact, the IMF did exactly the same thing as the army of neoliberal editorialists and economists. Having praised South Korea to the heavens until 1996, it changed its tone overnight. The South Korean system, it now said, was based on too much overlap between state employees and institutions, financial establishments, and industrial houses. These financial and industrial establishments form huge conglomerates—the chaebols—that finance political leaders in exchange for continued economic privileges. The neoliberals also criticized South Korea for upholding a highly protectionist arrangement, an overly strong public sector, and a social welfare system seen as too favorable for workers.

Is it true that the South Korean government opposed liberalization? Definitely not. For proof, one need go no further than a report filed by an IMF mission sent to the country in November 1996, and the minutes of the debate between IMF leaders following that trip. Some excerpts from the 1997 *Annual Report* follow.

On the question of the elimination of tariff barriers and other obstacles to imports:

Since 1994, the authorities have progressively dismantled import barriers and cut tariffs in accordance with the Uruguay Round; except for a small number of products with potentially adverse health or security effects, import licensing is now automatic.

On the question of privatization:

Over the past ten years, the authorities had partially implemented two public enterprise privatization programs; the program introduced in December 1993 envisaged privatization of 58 of 133 public enterprises during 1994–98. As of mid-1996, 16 enterprises had been privatized.

On the liberalization of capital flows:

[Directors] also welcomed the recent acceleration of capital account liberalization; although some Directors agreed with the authorities' gradual approach to capital account liberalization, a number of Directors considered that rapid and complete liberalization offered many benefits at Korea's state of economic development.

The IMF report on South Korea concludes, "The Board welcomed the broadening of structural reforms, including labor market reforms and privatization, that should contribute to productivity gains and ensure the continued competitiveness of the Korean economy." Finally, from early 1997 on, IMF governors backed South Korean government plans to reform the labor code to make it easier to lay off workers.

What were the causes of the South Korean crisis?

South Korea's industrial development is more advanced and began long before that of the four dragons. Some South Korean multinationals had even managed to compete directly with powerful companies from the advanced industrialized countries in a number of sectors (computer semiconductors, automobiles, shipbuilding, industrial goods). South Korea's share of the world market continued to grow until 1996.

The South Korean development model was in many ways the antithesis of the neoliberal model. It involved a radical agrarian reform in the 1950s, industrialization fostered and protected by the state, military dictatorship and repression of the trade-union movement, followed by significant concessions to labor in the face of powerful working-class mobilization. After the Japanese, South Korean workers have the highest wages in Asia.

The causes of the South Korean crisis belong to three distinct categories. First, the country experienced a decline in terms of trade between the relative value of its exports and that of its imports. In 1996–97, the volume of South Korean exports rose by 37 percent, but brought in only 5 percent more revenue. The dollar value of South Korean exports dropped by about 15 percent in 1996, and 12 percent in 1997. The weakening of the Japanese yen made

Japanese exports more competitive. South Korea was also confronted with competition from China and the four dragons, whose competitiveness was linked to a low-wage policy. Finally, South Korea had carved out a specialized niche for itself in the production and export of semiconductors, and therefore was hit hard by the drop in prices.

Second, South Korea had grown increasingly dependent on the recent and massive inflows of foreign capital in its most volatile form—portfolio investment and short-term loans. In order to compensate for export losses, South Korean firms took out huge short-term loans in expectation of an economic recovery that never came.

Third, South Korean employers failed in their attempt to link workers' pay to export losses. They tried to tackle industrial workers (whose wages had risen at an annual rate of 16 percent between 1987 and 1996) by getting the government to hurriedly adopt a reform to the labor code in late December 1996, in the absence of parliamentary opposition. This measure provoked a general strike, which was victorious inasmuch as the workers obtained a two-year moratorium on layoffs.

The world's eleventh most powerful economy was plunged into a major crisis under the combined effects of the Southeast Asian crisis, the continued rise in the value of the dollar and the depreciation of the yen, and the accelerated outflow of volatile capital from the country (which had begun in earnest in spring 1997). This crisis placed it at the mercy of the IMF and the United States. The Seoul stock market plummeted 67 percent between August 11 and December 17, 1997; the South Korean currency lost 96.5 percent of its value against the dollar between July 2, 1997, and January 8, 1998.

China

China has maintained state control over capital movements and external trade. Its currency, the renminbi, has remained nonconvertible, protecting it from speculation. These protection mechanisms combined with the attraction its economy holds for foreign investors have enabled it to avoid the worst effects of the crisis.

All of this does not mean that China provides an alternative. Its antidemocratic political regime and an economic model based on unequal distribution of revenue and wealth cannot possibly be seen by the region's populations as a viable alternative to the methods practiced by its neighbors. The capitalist transformation of China now under way combines overexploitation of workers with lightning wealth for the new capitalists and development of the criminal activities that go with capitalist accumulation.

India and Pakistan spared by their protectionism

In its 1997 *Annual Report*, the IMF celebrated globalization: "Directors agreed that globalization had contributed enormously to global prosperity." Once again, it warned those governments that might seek to control capital flows and partially protect their economies: "Countries resisting globalization faced increased risk of becoming marginalized."

This assertion has been refuted by real life. India and Pakistan, the two giants of South Asia, have not yet been seriously affected by the financial storm in Southeast Asia. Pakistan and India are experiencing serious economic problems (Pakistan devotes 40 percent of public spending to servicing its external debt), but the relative slowness with which they have embraced globalization has protected them from the speculative domino effect. Far from marginalizing them, the maintenance of protective barriers and controls on capital flows, as well as the slow pace of privatization, have shielded them from the constant attempts at destabilization they face.

However, the increasingly neoliberal orientations taken since then by the regimes currently in power, with acceleration of privatization, opening up of the markets, and increased military spending, are gradually reducing India's and Pakistan's ability to resist future crises.

Japan and the United States

The Japanese crisis was so serious that the country's government and capitalists were unable to implement measures that might have stabilized the situation in 1997–98. Rather, the United States—with the IMF in tow—has taken control of the situation. In 1997, with the crisis in full spate, the United States torpedoed the East Asian countries' wish to establish an Asian Monetary Fund, which could have tried to head off the crisis without having recourse to IMF intervention.

Malaysia

The Malaysian government distinguished itself by its response to the crisis. Malaysia was the only country, when the crisis erupted in 1997, to refuse the "rescue plan" cooked up by the IMF. The choice proved to be the right one. It allowed the country to escape the disastrous conditionalities accepted by the three other dragons and Korea. A year after the crisis had erupted, in September 1998, while its currency, the ringgit, was still undergoing speculative attacks, mainly from the *offshore* market of Singapore, Malaysia instigated strict controls of capital movement and exchange.

The decision was thus taken to close the Singapore market by making offshore ringgit transactions illegal....

In a series of measures introduced at the beginning of September 1998, domestic banks were prohibited from lending to non-resident banks and stockbrokers, or from engaging in any swap or repurchase transactions with non-residents, to eliminate non-resident ownership of ringgit balances held abroad. (UNCTAD, 2000b)

This angered the IMF and international finance, which feared that other governments might do the same. The fact is that the Malaysian economy got back on course faster and better than those of the other countries affected by the crisis. It gave rise to discussions as far as the inner circles of the IMF. Traces of these can be found in the 2000 IMF *Annual Report*. The example of Malaysia shows that even a modest-sized country can successfully restore the mechanisms of capital control. This is fundamental.

IMF-imposed structural adjustment in South Korea, Thailand, and Indonesia

A thoroughgoing structural overhaul is under way. A number of financial establishments have been shut down; there have been extensive layoffs; the central bank has been given autonomy of the government (making it easier for the IMF to exercise its influence); interest rates have skyrocketed (sinking local industry and consumer spending into recession); and major investment projects have been abandoned. In South Korea, the big conglomerates (the chaebols) are being dismantled, and the labor code is being reformed to allow for extensive layoffs. Indonesia has abandoned its ambitions in the aviation and automobile sectors. These countries have been plunged into a deep recession, with a fall in GDP of more than 10 percent in 1998.

Governments have agreed to be under the supervision of the IMF, the World Bank—and the G7 countries, particularly the United States. This represents nothing less than a loss of national sovereignty.

The loans provided by the IMF, the World Bank, and private banks include a risk premium tacked on to the market interest rate (except for a small number of World Bank loans, which target the most vulnerable sections of the population). These institutions thus made huge profits when repayments came in. The tens of billions of dollars contracted in loans were immediately used to pay back the banks and other international financial institutions. Every one of the contributors to the so-called rescue package was repaid, thanks to the countries' export revenues and savage cuts in public spending. The public debt of the countries concerned grew considerably due to the state taking on the debts of private companies. Tax revenues will also go toward paying off the external debt. Table 17.2 shows the sharp increase of public debt compared to

GDP. The increase in the public debt served as a pretext to make further savage cuts in social spending and push on with the privatization program.

TABLE 17.2. PUBLIC DEBT AS PERCENTAGE OF GDP

	1977 (before crisis)	2000 (April)
Thailand	15.7	51.9
Indonesia	23	93
South Korea	12	22.2 (late 1999)

Source: Focus on the Global South 2000.

The measures imposed on the newly industrialized countries (NICs) of Asia are intended to keep down the workers of those countries, on the one hand, and to prevent the countries from carrying on with their process of industrialization, on the other.

To take the first of these objectives, in the years leading up to the crisis, industrial workers managed to get significant, even very significant, pay increases through their struggles. The crisis was an opportunity for the bosses to turn the situation around to their advantage (see table 17.3).

TABLE 17.3. EVOLUTION OF SALARIES IN REAL TERMS IN THE MANUFACTURING INDUSTRY (PERCENT)

	Expansion Period	Real salary	Crisis 1998
Indonesia	1990–96	46	-25.1
South Korea	1990 96	67	-4.9
Thailand	1988–96	32	-2.3
Malaysia	1991–96	22	-1.2

Source: UNCTAD 2000b.

Now let us look at the second objective, that of preventing the NICs of Asia from pursuing their original industrialization process. Walden Bello (2000a) reminds us that one of the ingredients of the past successes of NICs such as Korea and Malaysia was their recourse to innovations, such as requiring a high percentage of local components in production. Foreign or national investors had to use large quantities of local inputs in the fabrication of products destined both for the domestic and the export markets.

These rules gave foreign investors less leeway, but finally proved successful, as they enabled the NICs to combine foreign investment and national industrialization. This gave them the opportunity to draw off highly capital-intensive export revenues, develop related industries and import technologies, while protecting local businessmen by offering them preferential access to the national market. In

Malaysia, for example, the strategy of demanding that industrial products should include a high percentage of local components enabled them to produce a national automobile, in cooperation with Mitsubishi. The national automobile is produced with 80 percent of local inputs and represents 70 percent of the Malaysian market.

The measures imposed by the IMF as part of the TRIMS agreement (Trade-Related Investment Measures) outlaw the continuation of policies such as those mentioned above.

One can only agree with Bello when he places the process of brutal subjugation of the Asian NICs to the strategic interests of the main industrialized countries into historical perspective. He begins with the United States, which directed maneuvers. During the Cold War, the fact that South Korea, Malaysia, and Indonesia occupied strategic positions with regard to the socialist "enemy" led the United States to turn a blind eye to the misdemeanors of their regimes, explains Bello. Those regimes were able to set up strong policies of what he calls "state-assisted capitalism."

Similar policies had been adopted previously in other periphery countries— e.g., Argentina in the 1940s and 1950s—but they were abandoned from the 1980s, in the context of the debt crisis exploited by the Reagan administration (see chapters 7 and 14). Unlike Latin America, in the 1980s and early 1990s, the East Asian countries, less affected by the debt crisis and in the front line against the socialist "threat," were allowed to pursue their active policy of industrialization characterized by strong state intervention and protectionism.

The collapse of the Soviet Bloc at the end of the 1980s and the evolution of China modified the international situation. The United States exerted extra pressure on the NICs to make them implement policies more in line with the interests of Washington. They began to change direction gradually in the mid-1990s, but had to speed up dramatically when the crisis erupted in 1997.

Bello quotes Jeff Garten, commerce under-secretary for international trade in the Clinton administration, who said that most of these countries were going through a dark tunnel, but they would emerge at the other end as a completely different Asia, where US firms would have greater market penetration.

For an overall explanation, Bello's perspective would need to be supplemented by an analysis of the behavior of the ruling classes in the NICs, in order to understand why none of them, except Malaysia, resisted US demands in 1997–98.

In the years that followed the crisis, several factors have made certain governments in the region want to distance themselves from the Bretton Woods institutions and the US government.[1] There has been the patent accumulation of negative effects of the policies dictated by the IMF and the World Bank, in both Asia and other areas of the periphery. There is the crisis these institutions are going through. There are the aggressive policies of the United States and the mounting protests they give rise to, especially in countries with a Muslim majority, such as Malaysia and Indonesia.

Yet, no left turn is in sight regarding structural measures and redistribution of wealth. Austerity policies and privatization programs forge ahead. So does the repression of social movements. However, this distancing can only accentuate the crisis of the Washington Consensus, which cannot be a bad thing.

---

1   With the exception of the governments of the Philippines and, to a lesser extent, South Korea, which backed the United States in the war on Iraq.

18

The ups and downs of the World Bank/IMF/WTO trio

The outbreak of the debt crisis in 1982 gave the World Bank and the IMF a chance to develop their combined actions regarding the indebted countries of the periphery. The World Bank and the IMF formed a duo that took upon itself both to impose neoliberal discipline on the indebted countries (via structural adjustment plans—SAPs) and to ensure the continuity of debt repayments. The duo had endless internal rivalries, but from a historical perspective, what counts is the coherence of their involvement within the context of the Washington Consensus.[1]

From the start, the SAPs were intended to open up the economies of the indebted countries to the multinational corporations (MNCs) of the highly industrialized countries and to the strategic interests of the Triad countries. The two usually converge. The close alliance between public creditors (the Bretton Woods institutions and the Paris Club) enabled them to bring the countries of the periphery back into a cycle of increased dependency. The position of the MNCs of the center in the markets of the periphery was strongly reinforced, not only in terms of market shares but also in controlling the strategic levers of economic activity and natural resources.

The creation of the World Trade Organization (WTO) reinforced the control mechanism. From 1995, when the WTO came into action, the directors of the three multilateral institutions coordinated their efforts to push ahead with neoliberal globalization. The World Bank, the IMF, and the WTO had become a trio. Article 3, clause 5, of the Marrakech Accords, from which the WTO emerged, explicitly mentions the collaboration between the three institutions: "With a view to greater coherence in the economic policies applied on a global level, the WTO will cooperate, in appropriate ways, with the IMF and the World Bank."

A fact sheet published by the IMF on its Web site in September 2003, states, "The IMF and the WTO work together on many levels, with the aim of ensuring greater coherence in global economic policymaking." Further on, we learn that the IMF, the World Bank, and the WTO have elaborated for the least developed countries an "Integrated Framework [which] seeks to ensure that trade matters are incorporated into the Poverty Reduction and Strategy Papers (PRSPs) prepared by countries in consultation with the IMF, World Bank, and other development partners."[2]

At a meeting of the WTO General Council in Geneva in May 2003 to prepare the WTO interministerial summit planned at Cancún for September 2003, Supachai Panitchpakdi, director-general of the WTO, Horst Köhler, managing director of the IMF, and James Wolfensohn, president of the World Bank, made a joint declaration calling on the leaders of the G8 countries to take political leadership in the negotiations to ensure the success of Cancún. They added, "The WTO, the IMF and the World Bank are cooperating to support the full engagement of developing countries in global trade negotiations to produce an outcome that favors the expansion of their trade." They reiterated the neoliberal dogma, according to which maximum insertion in international trade increases development possibilities of developing countries:

> Trade is vital not only for the direct benefits it brings, but also for increasing the flows of financial and real investment resources to developing countries which generate the income growth and job opportunities that help raise people out of poverty and make economies more resilient to shocks.

Finally, they added, "[T]he G8 will help maintain the momentum of structural economic reform over the longer term in the developed and developing countries alike."[3]

It is essential to recognize the coherence of the policies recommended by the World Bank/IMF/WTO trio. The IMF and the World Bank use their status as privileged creditors to make loans to the governments of the periphery conditional upon the implementation of economic reforms that open up the markets of the indebted countries to the global market dominated by the highly industrialized countries and the MNCs that are mainly based in those countries. Strengthening the connection between the economies of the countries of the periphery and the global market, with its present stratification, is detrimental to their local producers, their domestic markets, and to the chances of forging stronger intra-periphery (South-South) links.

Contrary to the claims of neoliberal dogma, greater openness and stronger connections with the global market constitute an obstacle to development for the countries of the periphery. The complete insertion of a country of the periphery in the global market generates a structural deficit in the balance of trade, i.e., imports grow faster than exports. The deficit tends to be compensated by external loans, which increase indebtedness.[4] A vicious circle is set in motion. The policies of the World Bank/IMF/WTO trio traps the countries of the periphery in an infernal spiral of indebtedness and dependency.

In chapter 19, we shall look at some alternatives that could be substituted for these policies.

Anne Krueger, the white knight of globalization

In a speech she gave at the Seventh St. Petersburg International Economic Forum on June 18, 2003, Anne Krueger, chief economist of the World Bank during the Reagan presidency, now first deputy managing director of the IMF, summarized remarkably well the arguments put forward by the champions of neoliberal globalization. What she said was clearly in line with the strategies of the World Bank/IMF/WTO trio. Disproving claims that the IMF has become more considerate of human rights, Krueger took up the sheer, unconditional defense of the neoliberal program.

In her introduction, she expresses her pleasure at finding herself in a city founded three centuries ago as an open door between Russia and the West, the global market and modernity: "It would be fair to say that global trade, the drive to open the Russian economy, was one of Peter the Great's principal motives in founding this great city." From the outset, she refers to the antiglobalization protesters, who have always existed because "fear of change has always been with us. There have always been those resistant to new and novel ideas and who wanted to reject the unfamiliar." She adds that innovators have found different ways of dealing with protesters—gentle or harsh, according to the period. She clearly does not condemn harsher ways:

> Sometimes persuasion is the best way of overcoming such prejudice [of the protesters—*author*]. At other times, those who wanted to embrace the new and the different have used the stick rather than the carrot. Peter the Great wanted to use St. Petersburg to modernize Russia. New, Western ideas were in, old traditional ideas were out. I'm told that beards, as symbols of the old order, were taxed.

Krueger proceeds to give an edifying historical overview of trade and globalization. She proclaims her belief in the Ricardian theory of comparative advantage, explaining that it is not merely an attitude of mind, but a true reflection of actual phenomena. Convinced that "international trade has a long and honorable pedigree," she glosses over the sixteenth century, the era of the great voyages of discovery, as "a period of rapid, constant change and, significantly, of contact between people across huge distances" without the slightest reference to the pillage and crimes against humanity that characterized the period. She refers to the nineteenth century with the same enthusiasm, emphasizing that "the export of capital from Britain in particular fueled growth across the British Empire and in the new world," with no hint of a reference to the crimes of colonialism. Again, she sings the praises of the migration of thirty-six million Europeans between 1871 and 1915 mainly to the Americas without any allusion to the Irish famine caused by capitalist development and the victory of free trade.

She next discusses those who oppose globalization, mentioning that they have not grasped that from time immemorial, "[l]arge-scale welfare gains are often accompanied by localized, short-term losses. Technological progress inevitably means some jobs will become redundant." Her intention is to indicate that people who oppose globalization only see the marginal, temporarily negative effects of a powerful, progressive movement.

Twentieth-century globalization

Krueger stresses that growth in the twentieth century was far greater than in the nineteenth century. She presents globalization as a true-life fairy tale, where the latest arrivals benefit from the advantages of the most advanced nations. For example, she attributes the great success of South Korea to the fact that it took total advantage of the opportunities offered by globalization, whereas India, more wary, had much slower growth.

In fact, reality largely contradicts these affirmations, since the success of South Korea was due, above all, to a combination of antiliberal measures (strong state intervention, development of the domestic market, reduction of the income gap, protectionism, pay increases, etc.). It was when it had ended strict control of capital movements and implemented reforms in line with globalization that South Korea hit a crisis in 1997–98. As for India, thanks to its mistrust of totally opening up the economy, it was able to protect itself from the worst effects of the Asian crisis of 1997–98. Indeed, later in her speech, Krueger cites India as an example of poverty reduction, in complete contradiction with the passage mentioned above.

The benefits of growth

Krueger explains that living conditions have greatly improved over the last decades. Infant mortality has fallen, literacy has increased, fewer people are poor, and the gap in life expectancy between rich and poor countries has narrowed. Not once during her speech does she mention that in a large number of countries, populations have undergone a deterioration of living conditions over the last twenty years.

Blind faith in growth and the productivist model

Krueger further explains that there are more and bigger oil reserves today than in 1950 and that no irreparable damage has been caused to the planet's environment. She claims that as time goes by, we shall find more oil reserves and, in the same optimistic vein, that after a normal phase of environmental degradation, the situation will improve in line with the objective laws of economy.

> Take the perennial concern that rapid growth depletes our fuel resources and once that happens growth will come to a complete dead stop. World oil reserves today are higher today than in 1950. Then the world's known reserves of oil were expected to be enough for only 20 more years of consumption. We were expected to run out by 1970. It did not happen. Today, our known reserves are enough to keep us going for another 40 years at our present rate of consumption. There is no doubt that by the time 2040 rolls around research and development will have delivered new breakthroughs in energy production and use.
>
> Nor have we done irreparable harm to the environment. The evidence shows quite convincingly that economic growth brings an initial phase of deterioration in some aspects: but that this is followed by a subsequent phase of improvement. The turning point at which people begin choosing to invest in cleaning up and preventing pollution occurs at a per capita GDP of about $5000.

Krueger warns against condemning sweatshops or child labor out of hand. Faced with protesters who, she says, have no faith in moral relativism, she does not hesitate to warn against condemning out of hand the "so-called 'sweatshop factories.'" She explains that sweatshop workers in Vietnam saw their pay multiplied by five in a short period of time, which "completely transformed for the better the lives of those workers and their families." She adds that giving those workers a "'decent wage' by industrial country standards would completely erode any competitive advantage for businesses using unskilled labor on the international market." In the same way, she says, one should beware of condemning child labor out of hand, for, as she puts it, "the alternatives are so much worse: starvation or malnutrition…." According to Krueger, there is no need to prohibit child labor since, thanks to growth, it will disappear unaided.

She maintains that worries that citizens and governments are losing control to the MNCs and capital flows are misplaced. Her response to the criticism that the benefits of globalization are not fairly distributed to all is that inequality is not the main problem and "there is no evidence that globalization has any systematic impact on a country's income inequality." She declares, "At the global level, the news is actually very encouraging. The evidence, though difficult to piece together, suggests that world inequality is declining."

Note that she attributes the reduction of poverty to the "phenomenal growth of China and India" without mentioning that these two countries, with the planet's largest populations, are among those that hesitate the most to completely open up their economies. Krueger finishes with a long eulogy of the Doha agenda. She says that governments in general are afraid to completely open up their economies because of the job losses it will inevitably cause. Some governments

> find it hard to resist pressure from special interest groups.... It is [almost] always a mistake, though. Interfering with the market inevitably produces distortions. Protecting one group of workers, from foreign competition, say, can have the effect of penalizing others—in the same country. Without exception, such protection, whatever form it takes, puts up the price for consumers.

As her final argument, Krueger declares that if Russia wants to double its per capita revenue in ten years, the only way to do it would be to join the WTO, which would mean totally opening up its economy. With a dazzling demonstration of ignorance and/or bad faith, she adds, "I know of no economy that has achieved income-doubling in a decade that has not been integrating with the international economy as it did so." She concludes, "[O]ur central role is to facilitate the process of globalization. In a very real sense, that is what we exist for."

The trio at work in four very different countries

The rest of this chapter will be devoted to a rapid world tour, beginning with Russia, which has just been referred to indirectly, and continuing with three other countries in three different regions: East Timor in Oceania, Malawi in Southern Africa, and Bolivia in the South American Andes. We examine certain aspects of their present relationships with the World Bank/IMF/WTO trio.

Stage one: Russia in the context of neoliberal globalization

While Krueger was giving her speech, the new Russian capitalists, or oligarchs, as they are known, and their shady dealings had come up against the law, shaking Russia to its very foundations. The Russian judicial system was prosecuting them for murder, theft of public property, conspiracy, corruption, etc. The oligarchs accumulated a colossal fortune in just a few years with the direct support of the IMF, the World Bank, the governments of the Triad (especially the US, British, and German governments), major private banks, and clearing houses such as Clearstream (see Robert and Backes 2001; Robert 2002).

These oligarchs emerged as a result of the implosion of the bureaucratic system of the East and capitalist restoration in the late 1980s and the 1990s. The US government, the IMF, and the World Bank gave their active support to the Russian president, Boris Yeltsin (and partly guided his footsteps), in the rapid and gigantic wave of privatizations that he imposed on Russia. Those privatizations constitute the systematic pillage of Russia's public goods in favor of the oligarchs and a few MNCs of the Triad.

The Russian oligarchs used brutal and criminal methods like those used by the "robber barons" in the United States at the end of the late nineteenth and early twentieth centuries. History repeated itself, as once again primitive capitalist accumulation took place in violence and chaos. But history does not repeat itself—this time, the pillage was carried out under the high protection of international multilateral bodies with multiple missions by economics experts and multilateral loans to facilitate "the transition from a planned economy to a market economy," to use the expression favored by the Bretton Woods institutions.

In chapters 5 and 6 of *Globalization and Its Discontents*, we read Joseph Stiglitz's sharp analysis of the transition in Russia. He denounces the responsibility of the IMF and the US Treasury, which supported, counseled, and guided the Russian bureaucrats' conversion to capitalism, especially Yeltsin. There was nothing democratic about the methods used.

> It is not surprising that many of the market reformers showed a remarkable affinity to the old ways of doing business: in Russia, President Yeltsin, with enormously greater powers than his counterparts in any Western democracy, was encouraged to circumvent the democratically elected Duma (parliament) and to enact market reforms by decree.

Public companies went for a song. "[T]he government, pressured by the United States, the World Bank, and the IMF to privatize rapidly, had turned over its state assets for a pittance."

Privatization was a vast act of pillage that benefited the oligarchs who invested part of their booty in the West so that it was laundered and out of reach of the law.

> Privatization, accompanied by the opening of the capital markets, led not to wealth creation but to asset stripping. It was perfectly logical. An oligarch who has just been able to use political influence to garner assets worth billions, after paying only a pittance, would naturally want to get his money out of the country. Keeping money in Russia meant investing it in a country in deep depression, and risking not only low returns but having the assets seized by the next government, which would inevitably complain, quite rightly, about the "illegitimacy" of the privatization process. Anyone smart enough to be a winner in the privatization sweepstakes would be smart enough to put their money in the booming US stock market, or into the safe haven of secretive offshore bank accounts. It was not even a close call; and not surprisingly, billions poured out of the country. (Stiglitz 2002)

The IMF and the World Bank got Russia into debt. A large part of the money lent has been embezzled and is back in the West. Western bankers, Russian oligarchs, and government officials got rich, while the impoverished Russian citizens have to foot the bill.

When the crisis hit, the IMF led the rescue efforts, but it wanted the World Bank to provide $6 billion of the rescue package. The total rescue package was for $22.6 billion. The IMF would provide $11.2; the World Bank would lend $6 billion; the rest would be provided by the Japanese government.

> This was hotly debated inside the World Bank. There were many of us who had been questioning lending to Russia all along....
>
> In spite of strong opposition from its own staff, the Bank was under enormous political pressure from the Clinton administration to lend money to Russia.... Remarkably, the IMF seemed able to overlook the corruption, and the attendant risks with what would happen with the money....
>
> ...When the IMF was confronted with the facts—the billions of dollars that it had given (loaned) Russia was showing up in Swiss and Cypriot bank accounts just days after the loan was made—it claimed that these weren't *their* dollars....
>
> By lending Russia money for a doomed cause, IMF policies led Russia into deeper debt, with nothing to show for it. The cost of the mistake was not borne by the IMF officials who gave the loan, or America who had pushed for it, or the Western bankers and the oligarchs who benefited from the loan, but by the Russian taxpayer....
>
> ...The US Treasury and the IMF entered into the political life of Russia. By siding so firmly for so long with those at the helm when the huge inequality was created through this corrupt privatization process, the United States, the IMF, and the international community have indelibly associated themselves with policies that, at best, promoted the interests of the wealthy at the expense of the average Russian.

Stiglitz adds that the directors of the World Bank forbade him to meet the inspector general of the Duma when the latter made the trip to Washington to denounce the extent of the corruption. "Within the World Bank, I was urged not to meet with him, lest we give credence to his charges."

The odious debt of Russia and other former Soviet Bloc countries

The case of the Russian debt, like those of other states arising from the implosion of the former Soviet Bloc, is hardly debated on the international scene, even within the progressive movements of the countries concerned; yet, the debt contracted by Russia in the circumstances just described quite obviously fits the category of odious debt. The debt was not contracted to conduct policies in the citizens' interests, quite the contrary. Furthermore, a large part of the loans was embezzled in full view of the creditors. The creditors—the IMF, the World Bank, members of the Paris Club, private lenders—knew of the criminal practices of the borrowers. If the citizens of Russia were to get themselves a new regime, they would be entitled to refuse to pay the debt incurred by the transition to the market economy. They would also be entitled to refuse to pay the debt inherited from the old bureaucratic dictatorial regime. The same probably goes for the other states of the former Soviet Bloc.

Russian oligarchs get good write-ups in the Western press

When the Russian legal system held the oligarchs to account in 2003, the big names of the Western press (and the Western governments, too, but more discreetly) responded by asking for clemency on their behalf—not that the media considered the oligarchs at all innocent. The question hinged on the future of privatizations. The media concerned thought it would be dangerous to go back on them, even if *Le Monde* (July 23, 2003) recognized that "[a]ccording to a poll by the ROMIR institute, 77 percent of Russians are in favor of revising the privatizations." Marie-Pierre Subtil, Moscow correspondent for *Le Monde*, wrote several articles criticizing the actions of the Russian courts ("which open the door to revision of the privatizations," *Le Monde,* July 27–28, 2003) against the oligarchs, even though she did admit that they had made their money by fraud on a grand scale. Of the main oligarch under investigation, Mikhaïl Khodorkovski (born 1963), CEO of Yukos,[5] she wrote that he is "certainly no angel. His fortune—the largest in Russia, estimated at $7.2 billion by the magazine *Fortune*—was made in the 1990s, when the most ambitious and least scrupulous of Russians bought up state assets for next to nothing at the time of privatization." Yet, at the same time, the same journalist gives a list of this new robber baron's good deeds, including the creation of an international philanthropic foundation that counts Henry Kissinger among its administrators.

Another oligarch deserves mention. Roman Abramovich (born 1966). In 2003, he also fell foul of the Russian courts. He is at the head of an empire that includes, among others, the oil company Sibneft, the aluminum producer RUSAL, and the pharmaceutical company ICN Russia. In 2003, he bought the prestigious British football club Chelsea. The holding company that enables him to own this empire is based in the City of London. According to the *Financial Times*, in 2003, he was trying to sell off most of his Russian assets so that he could place the capital somewhere safe.

In an editorial, we read that Russia is once again at a crossroads. It has to choose between consolidating capitalism by granting amnesty to the oligarchs who are guilty of economic crimes, which implies accepting profound inequalities, or having a revolution. The editorialist, tongue in cheek, proposes opting for the first solution:

> At the root of the problem is Russia's flawed privatization process. Because the division of the spoils was so chaotic—and so profoundly unjust—Russia's rulers will always have a powerful weapon to use against its capitalists. Ultimately, there are

only two ways to end this standoff: grant an official amnesty, at least for the oligarchs' economic crimes, or take their property away. It is a choice between accepting gross inequality and imposing yet another revolution. Neither option is appealing. But having tried the latter in 1917, Russia might find it safer this time to find a way to live with its unsavory oligarchs. (*Financial Times*, July 21, 2003)

The IMF, the World Bank, the US Treasury, and the private creditors are all absolutely in favor of the solution proposed by the *Financial Times* and other international newspapers: they would also be affected by an amnesty, as they are directly involved in the economic crimes as accomplices and as beneficiaries. As for the MNCs of the Triad, especially of the United States, they are ready and waiting to acquire large chunks of Yukos, Sibneft, and the rest. Specific offers were publicized in the course of 2003. The oligarchs who own Yukos and Sibneft responded positively: they want *cash* that they can deposit outside Russia. Lastly, the US Treasury,[6] the IMF, and the World Bank, in concert with the directors of the WTO, are preparing Russia's membership of the institution. It is in this light that we should understand the tone and content of Krueger's address on June 18, 2003, in St. Petersburg.

Stage two: The World Bank and IMF lay claim to East Timor[7]

With 800,000 inhabitants, situated 500 kilometers off the Australian coast, East Timor became independent in May 2002, after several decades of liberation struggle. Two in five Timorese live on less than 55 cents a day ($US). Three-quarters of the population have no access to electricity, and half have no drinking water. A Portuguese colony until 1975, East Timor was annexed by Indonesia under the Suharto dictatorship. The struggle for liberation reached a high point in the 1970s at the end of the Portuguese regime. One of the results of the famous Revolution of Carnations in 1974 in Portugal was the independence of the Portuguese colonies: Guinea-Bissau, Cape Verde, Angola, Mozambique, and East Timor.

In 1998–99, after Suharto was overthrown by the Indonesian people, the main liberation movement, FRETILIN, which had been involved in armed struggle for nearly thirty years, today has a comfortable parliamentary majority. The president of the republic, Xanana Gusmao, is a historical figure of FRETILIN. The liberation struggle after the fall of Suharto cost the lives of more than 100,000 Timorese. After the 1999 referendum, when an overwhelming majority of the Timorese population chose independence, the country was placed under UN administration.

The country is very poor, with a weak economy, little diversification, and no industry. Its main activity is agriculture—more than 75 percent of the population is rural. Apart from coffee for export, most of the agricultural production goes toward satisfying the domestic demand, which in my opinion is an advantage. The challenge for any economic policy that aims to improve the living conditions of the population is to take into account the local agriculture. However, oil and gas are going to be the decisive elements in East Timor's future. There are large reserves of oil and gas at sea, where the East Timorese territorial waters meet Australia's. Australia's powerful financial and economic interests managed to get their hands on the biggest share in the days of the Suharto dictatorship. When East Timor finally became independent and wanted to renegotiate the agreements to get part of its rightful share, Australia refused. The Timorese authorities were considering making an appeal at the International Court of Justice at The Hague, but finally renounced it under threat of economic retaliatory measures from Australia.

There is a great risk that East Timor may undergo the same fate as countries such as Angola or Congo-Brazzaville, as the exploitation of their fields of oil and gas will be dominated by a few multinational oil companies. The government has to beware of a situation where the country and the well-being of the majority of its inhabitants are sacrificed to the good fortune of the oil companies and the wealthy minority.

A government that wants to keep its country out of debt

The new state was born debt-free, and the government has made the wise decision to refuse to borrow. How long will it be able to resist the lenders? For the country's reconstruction, it only accepts donations. The World Bank, which had come barging in with a plan for indebtedness, has had to adopt a new strategy to persuade the authorities to apply the Washington Consensus. It has managed to impose itself as the institution that coordinates most of the donations from the international community. It takes advantage of its role as go-between to get the receiving authorities to agree to apply neoliberal policies. This means, for example, the abandonment of tariff barriers, detrimental to local farmers, especially for rice production; the imposition of a cost-recovery program, with high registration fees for secondary and higher education and health-care fees; privatization of the electricity sector and installation of pre-pay electricity meters.

Another serious problem has to be discussed. Only a minor amount of each donation actually reaches the local economy—from 10 percent to 20 percent. The major part of the donations is spent outside Timor, in the form of pay for foreign experts, or on goods and services bought on the international markets. The World Bank succeeded in imposing international consultants—some straight from the World Bank—whose fees come to 15–30 percent of the donations. The World Bank also skims 2 percent of every donation it handles.

Inequality of pay is striking. An international expert earns a salary of $500 per day, plus all expenses paid while he is there. The average Timorese worker, on the other hand, earns from three to five dollars per day. As for the World Bank representative, she earns about $15,000 per month. Her colleague of the IMF, who earns the same, is actively opposed to a law fixing a legal minimum salary that parliament wants to adopt. He did not hesitate to write that a salary of three to five dollars per day was too high.

In the seminars I gave, I compared the World Bank's attitude to that of Christopher Columbus and other conquistadors who, when they wanted to settle on a territory, began by making gifts. The first time I made the comparison, I was expecting to hear protests from the audience. None came. In Timor, many people sincerely committed to the reconstruction of their country are worried at the position of influence taken by the World Bank. They have the impression that their government itself is beginning to succumb to the neoliberal creed and are wondering how to steer clear of it all.

Stage three: Famine in Malawi—the role of the IMF

The June 2000 newsletter of the 50 Years Is Enough network revealed the incompetence of the IMF and its responsibility in the deaths of thousands in Malawi. Since 1998, Malawi, a country of eleven million inhabitants,[8] has joined the list of heavily indebted poor countries (HIPCs). However, between 2000 and 2002, the debt reduction program was suspended for a variety of reasons—lack of transparency in spending, contradictory financial reports, delays in privatization programs, corruption, and poor economic performance. Like other countries subjected to the diktat of Bretton Woods institutions, Malawi was made to apply a rapid and sweeping privatization program. The cardinal point of the program was the privatization of agencies of aid and control of agricultural production (one of these managed the country's food stocks and the other, food marketing and distribution). The start of privatization was accompanied, in the best traditions of structural adjustment, by cutting aid for small farmers, such as access to credit and supplies of fertilizers and seed, cutting subsidies on basic foodstuffs for consumers, and eradicating other forms of intervention to stabilize prices.

As well as the two culprits, the IMF and the World Bank, there was now a third, the WTO. The famine that ravaged Southern Africa, and Malawi in particular, was largely caused by the effects of liberalized trade in agricultural produce, and to dumping due to the agricultural subsidies on exports from the countries of the North.

The first signs of famine in the rural areas appeared in October 2001. There had been a drought in 1991–92, but it did not cause famine. The economic policies imposed by a decade of structural adjustment programs led to catastrophic food shortages in 2001 and 2002.

A series of measures precipitated Malawi into crisis

The IMF and the European Union repeatedly insisted that Malawi should privatize the management of its grain reserves and introduce a system based on cost recovery. In 1999, the National Food Reserve Agency (NFRA) was partly privatized, but neither the government nor international creditors saw fit to provide startup capital. So the agency was obliged to make several loans from private and government banks, which turned out to be suicidal, since some of these loans had annual interest rates of 56 percent.

To free up liquidities, the IMF and the World Bank urged the agency to sell off part of its stock, just when the price of maize was at its lowest, resulting in huge losses. The liquidities raised from these sales were mainly used to pay off the commercial loans.

When food shortages first appeared, the government sought Western food aid. When this proved fruitless, it had to borrow $30 million on the international markets to pay for 130,000 tons of maize, just when prices were rising.

The coup de grâce was given by the international institutions, which, suspecting corruption in the management of the NFRA, suspended aid to the government. An IMF mission in May 2002 ended with its refusal to grant a loan of $47 million and with the suspension of the debt reduction program within the HIPC Initiative.

The United States then took advantage of the emergency caused by the famine and the trade opening imposed by the WTO to flood Malawi with tons of genetically modified maize, which the country would have refused in less drastic circumstances. For Malawi, like other countries, fears the risks of GMOs for human health and biodiversity, but worse still, it fears that once GMOs enter their production, future exports to Europe will be blocked if the EU maintains its restrictions on genetically modified products.

The final report of the IMF's May 2002 mission says, "[T]he para-state sector continues to constitute a risk for good budgetary decision-making in 2002 and 2003." Despite the crisis, the IMF continued to see the NFRA as a hole in the budget. The IMF's priority was that the agency's expenditure be reduced to free up money for the service of the debt. They failed to mention that during the 1991–92 drought, before the swathe of privatizations, the NFRA had managed to distribute food stocks at reasonable prices throughout the country to the furthest rural outposts. In 2002, this capacity had completely disappeared.

The maize market before the reforms was the exclusive preserve of a state body, the Agricultural Development and Marketing Corporation (AD-MARC). This monopoly was removed. In future, ADMARC will no longer be able to take out state-guaranteed loans for price or deficit intervention actions. Despite the fact that few private agents were interested in buying up the unprofitable activities in the remote rural areas of the country, the directors of the IMF and the World Bank nevertheless highly recommended that the objective of total privatization by the end of 2002 be maintained.

Is it not surprising that the IMF, which claims not to have any experience of food-security policies, should lay down the law in an area that directly affects food security? What is the point of pursuing macroeconomic objectives such as total privatization, dogmatic budget austerity, and increased exports if these objectives have only a weak impact on the economy's ability to ensure its own food security?

Fourth stage: Bolivia and the struggle to exercise sovereign rights over natural resources

On two occasions since 2000, the population of Bolivia (about ten million inhabitants) has become mobilized to defend public goods. In February 2000, mobilization was limited to the region of Cochabamba, and the objective was to keep water in public ownership. In September–October 2003, vast numbers of the Bolivian population rose in protest against the sale of a large part of the country's natural gas reserves to a multinational consortium. In a way, the population of Bolivia, of whom the majority are Indians, is setting an example to the rest of humanity by trying to put a stop to the transfer of public goods and natural resources to the private domain. This aspect of the Bolivian people's struggle directly concerns both the populations of the center and those of the periphery, as all are affected by the privatizations steamrollered in by the World Bank/IMF/WTO trio.

For the populations of the periphery, there is an extra concern—to stop the pillage and dilapidation of their natural resources by the MNCs of the countries of the center, aided and abetted by the local governments and ruling classes.

Bolivia is considered the poorest country of Latin America, with a per capita annual income of $882 in 2002, and a third of the population, i.e., about 2.7 million people, living on $200 per year. The per capita income has been systematically and constantly reduced over the last four years, according to the INE (National Statistics Institute). The poor and the vulnerable sections of society are the ones who have been hardest hit by this fall.

Bolivia is one of the four Latin American countries that figure on the list of the forty-two HIPCs. The Bretton Woods institutions consider it a fine example of consultation of civil society whether by the government or by themselves. The US government, for its part, considers Bolivia a faithful friend—at least until the time of writing.[9] It gives the US military the run of its territory and has carried out a vast program of destruction of coca crops, the traditional plant of the native Bolivians. And the WTO can rub its hands, as Bolivia has drastically reduced its customs tariffs and placed its local producers in competition with the North's MNCs.

What Washington sees as a success story is a tragedy for the population, which began in 1985, when partisans of the former dictator Hugo Banzer and of Paz Estenssoro, won the elections and imposed a harsh structural adjustment plan.[10] Over the next fifteen years, the wave of privatizations affected practically all sectors: fossil fuels (petroleum and gas), railways, telecommunications, air transport, the pension system, electricity, mines, forests, etc.

The battle for water resources

In 1999, the government offered a concessional contract to the international consortium Aguas de Tunari for the zone of Cochabamba. Its main stipulations were that water would be invoiced in dollars, with the price adjusted for US inflation, and that all drinking-water systems (often built by the inhabitants, local cooperatives, etc.) would be handed over to the consortium with nothing in exchange. Despite a maximum price increase of 35 percent stipulated in the contract, rates rose by 400 percent from the outset, with no improvement in service.

Water had become a commodity and was no longer a public good. In Cochabamba, the Bolivian people set to work. They created a Coordination; organized peaceful marches, negotiations, mediations; consulted the people; blocked the streets. Under pressure, the government gave in, and the Coordination achieved its main objectives.

As Carmen Julieta Peredo Montaño, a member of the Coordination, explains, this exemplary struggle was based on the fact that

> when rural organizations exploit water resources they see them as public goods lent to them by "Mother Nature." They consider water as synonymous with life. It cannot be considered as a commodity, as the Bolivian government, in complete submission to the "recommendations" of the World Bank and the IMF, would have it. The latter make economic support for clean drinking water and basic sanitation projects conditional upon commercializing and privatizing it through laws and contracts that the citizens of Cochabamba have systematically rejected. (Vía Campesina 2002)

Raúl Zibechi describes the evolution of the social movements:

> The social eruptions of 2000 have profoundly modified the country's sociopolitical profile. The peasant-farmers' movement has emerged as the main social force, organized around the Federation of Coca Growers of Chapare (headed by the parliamentary representative, Evo Morales) and the CSUTCB (United Trade Union

Confederation of Bolivian Peasant-Farmers), headed by Felipe Quispe. The peasant-farmers' organizations themselves have also undergone profound changes. The CSUTCB was founded in 1979 along the same lines as the COB (Bolivian Labor Confederation) and with its full support, and defined itself as a peasant-farmers' organization. Two decades later, taking account of the subjective changes experienced by the country's social majority, it redefined itself as "an indigenous organization bringing together all the indigenous peoples and nations of Bolivia."

Although not dropping social-class discourse, it has taken on the historical and ethnic discourse that lays claim to land and territory, implying participative management of natural resources. This new development reflects how the working class has lost its status due to the neoliberal policies introduced from the mid-eighties on. Nevertheless, the movement has reached broad sections of the Bolivian population, especially in the Altiplano, leading to the emergence of a new heterogeneous social identity, diversified, but hinging on the Aymara identity. This new national identity is manifested by the rainbow flag known as the Wiphala in the Aymara language and is anchored in several zones, such as El Alto, and in the indigenous communities.

In the elections of June 2002, this new Bolivian identity gained significant representation in the state institutions. The two electoral fronts that stood—Morales's Movement Toward Socialism and Quispe's Pachakutik—won a quarter of all votes and almost challenged the US Embassy's candidate, Sanchez de Lozada, for the presidency. (Taken from "Bolivia en la encrucijada" (Bolivia at the Crossroads), ALAI, America Latina en Movimiento, October 16, 2003)

The battle for natural gas resources of September–October 2003

Frida Villareal, Ana María Seifert, and Roxana Paniagua write in "La Bolivie et le gaz naturel" (*L'aut'journal*, October 15, 2003):

> For a full grasp of the issues surrounding the export of natural gas in Bolivia, several outstanding events of recent years need to be mentioned. It all goes back to 1985, when the first structural adjustment program was imposed by the IMF. One of the program's measures aimed to stabilize the country's currency and concerned the state-owned petroleum industry, Yacimientos Petrolíferos Fiscales Bolivianos (YPFB). Seventy-five to eighty-five percent of the company's revenues were transferred to the National Treasury, which severely weakened it, slowing down exploitation and production and paralyzing the construction of gas distribution networks within the country. The measures increased the company's indebtedness and served as a pretext to denounce the "bad management" of state companies.
>
> From 1990, privatization or "capitalization" are put forward as the solution to the crisis—YPFB's monopoly over the different stages of hydrocarbon processing was abolished. In 1996, the Hydrocarbons Law authorized, among other things, the total liberalization of the market for petroleum products and introduced very low taxation of private companies. Since then, foreign petroleum companies control the greater part of petroleum reserves. In fact, 80 percent of gas reserves are controlled by Petrobras (Brazil), Total, Maxus (Ibero-French), and Repsol (Spain).

It is worth noting in passing that the procedures just described are exactly comparable to what happened to the company YPF in Argentina at the same period (see chapter 16).

Since 1997, considerable reserves of natural gas have been discovered in the country. The international firm Goldyer & Mac Naughton estimated the natural gas reserves of Bolivia at 52 trillion cubic feet in 2003. It is the second largest reserve in South America, according to Energy International. Reserves certified for the South American subregion totaled 123.7 trillion cubic feet, of which 42 percent are in Bolivia, 20.8 percent in Argentina, and 16.6 percent in Venezuela. Once the internal demand and export contracts within the subregion have been satisfied, there is enough left to export elsewhere. So gas shortages are not a problem. The problem concerns ownership of the gas reserves, the transformation and distribution of the resource, and the income it would generate for the Bolivian state if it could export the gas without any intermediaries.

The media have not failed to mention the historic roots of the revolt—the gas should have been exported to the United States and Mexico via the Chilean coast, but Bolivia and Chile have been on bad terms since 1879, when Santiago annexed the former Bolivian coast. However, there is another source of discontent that has received far less press coverage: the indigenous peoples' wish to regain control over their natural resources from the MNCs.

In order to make prices competitive—in other words, to make profit levels acceptable to the international consortium that would be responsible for exporting the gas (Pacific LNG)—the Bolivian government has been asked to reduce its monetary demands. As we saw above, these have already been reduced as a result of the Hydrocarbons Law of 1996. Under this project, Bolivia would get $70 million a year in hard currency, while the Pacific LNG would get $1.3 billion. So, for every dollar paid in tax in Bolivia, the petroleum companies would gain twenty dollars.

The Bolivians pay a high price for their gas cylinders, and despite the fact that the country has immense reserves of natural gas, many peasants in the Altiplano are still using dried dung to heat their homes or cooking over wood and straw fires. Not only do the Bolivians see their natural resources being sold off cheaply to multinational petroleum companies, but the latter make huge profits from them. The problem as emphasized by Evo Morales, the founder of the MAS (Movement Toward Socialism), is not to refuse to sell the gas, but to sell it under different conditions more favorable to the Bolivian people:

> The Bolivians have lost the control of this rich resource to the multinationals, and the present project for exporting the gas would not be at all profitable for us. Hydrocarbons are our livelihood, our hope, our heritage. How can it be right that while our ancestral lands are being pillaged and our wealth exported, we get poorer and poorer? (*Le Courrier*, October 4, 2003)

The enormous mobilization of the people that shook the country in September and October 2003 was brutally repressed, with blood shed, by the Gonzalo Sanchez de Lozada regime. More than 150 people died. Instead of intimidating them, this only made the population more determined, and they stood firm against this state terrorism. It was the regime that crumbled, and the president finally resigned on October 17, and fled to Miami.

---

1   Joseph Stiglitz, in *Globalization and Its Discontents*, attempts unconvincingly to separate the respective roles of the World Bank and the IMF. He criticizes the IMF roundly, while treating the bank more kindly.

2   See www.imf.org/external/np/exr/facts/fre/imfwtof.htm.

3   See www.imf.org/external/np/sec/pr/2003/pr0368.htm.

4   Some would use the example of China to refute this argument. China maintains a good positive trade balance. It exports more to Triad countries (with the United States in the lead) and the rest of the world than it imports. Its external debt is relatively modest considering the size of the economy, and all things equal, is not really a serious problem, since the country has a large savings reserve, mainly in dollars. China and Japan are, relatively speaking, the main holders of US Treasury bonds. In other words, the United States is indebted to China. China's external public debt is roughly equivalent to the credits it holds on the United States in the form of Treasury bonds. According to the Union of Swiss Banks and the OECD, in June 2003, China, Japan, Hong Kong, and South Korea together held $696 billion worth of US Treasury bonds. The example of China does not contradict the author's arguments, as China's insertion in the global market is of a particular kind. It maintains considerable protectionist measures with regard to the global market, and its domestic market is enormous. The danger for China would be if its authorities were to give in to the demands of the World Bank/IMF/WTO trio, abandoning control over capital movements, making the currency convertible, liberalizing investment controls, and removing tariff barriers. All of these measures are demanded by the EU, the United States, and Japan, and relayed by the trio. Time will tell if the present process of capitalist restoration in China will go as far as the application of the Washington Consensus. If it does, the negative effects of neoliberal policies—already perceptible—will take on dramatic proportions for the majority of the population.

5   Yukos, the main Russian oil company, has announced its merger with Sibneft, another Russian oil company. The entity resulting from the merger could be the world's fourth largest oil company. *Le Monde* journalist Sophie Shihab gave the following subheading to her article of August 6, 2003: "The Yukos group, one of the most influential and least opaque (sic) in Russian-style capitalism, has been officially targeted with accusations of theft, murder and tax evasion. Populist Vladimir Putin is playing to public demands for revision of the privatizations."

6   Concerning the attitude of the US Treasury toward international trade, Stiglitz (2002) mentions a striking episode from the days when he was one of Clinton's counselors. He denounces Paul O'Neil, who was secretary of the treasury under George W. Bush (O'Neil was replaced by John Snow in December 2002). In 1994, while he was director of the aluminum-producing MNC ALCOA, O'Neil set up with Russia a cartel of aluminum producers to limit the fall in aluminum prices on the global market.

7   These pages were written after a short stay in East Timor. The author went to Dili, the capital, from March 18–23, 2003, at the invitation of the Ministry of Planning and Finance and the National University. He was accompanied by an official from the Bangkok-based Focus on the Global South. The institutions that invited us wanted a critical course on the World Bank and the policies it recommends. A short course was given to top officials of the Ministry of Planning and Finance, and also to students and lecturers of the National University. The visit also provided the opportunity to meet citizens' movements, social organizations, the plenipotentiary representative of the World Bank, and his homologue at the IMF.

8   More than 15 percent of the population is HIV-positive and a loss of seventeen years in life expectancy is forecast by 2010.

9   Written on October 19, 2003, two days after President Gonzalez Sanchez de Lozada's resignation and his flight to Miami by helicopter.

10 At the time the government was taking advice from economist Jeffrey Sachs who, twelve years later, was to become a violent critic of the IMF and the World Bank. In 2003, however, Sachs still defended the program applied in Bolivia in 1985 (see *Financial Times*, April 9, 2003).

19

Ideas for alternatives[1]

T he final part of this book puts forward suggestions and alternative avenues for debate. They do not make up an all-inclusive program, nor
should they be seen as proposals to accept or reject en bloc. At best,
they are a collection of necessary-but-insufficient conditions for charting the
path forward. The starting point for this debate has to be the fulfillment of
basic human rights. The question we have tried to address may be summarized
thus: How does one move from an economy of indebtedness toward financing
sustainable and socially just development?[2]

The Universal Declaration of Human Rights states, "Everyone has the
right to a standard of living adequate for the health and well-being of himself
and of his family, including food, clothing, housing and medical care and necessary social services." It also states that everyone has a right to education,
work, and social security (see articles 22–26).

The UN Declaration on the Right to Development stipulates:

> 3. States have the right and the duty to formulate appropriate national develop-
> ment policies that aim at the constant improvement of the well-being of the entire
> population and of all individuals, on the basis of their active, free and meaningful
> participation in development and in the fair distribution of the benefits resulting
> therefrom. (Source: Declaration on the Right to Development. Adopted by Gen-
> eral Assembly resolution 41/128 of 4 December 1986, http://www.unhchr.ch/
> html/menu3/b/74.htm)

The UN Committee for Economic, Social, and Cultural Rights interprets
the obligations of the International Pact for Economic, Social, and Cultural
Rights, ratified by the majority of UN member states, as follows: "A member
state in which a large number of individuals are deprived of basic foods, primary health care, decent clothing and housing or elementary education, is not
fulfilling its obligations as laid down by this Covenant."

Despite this, and the fact that total world wealth has increased eightfold since 1960, at the present time, one in two human beings lives on less than two dollars per day, one in three has no access to electricity, one in four lives on less than a dollar per day, one in five has no access to clean drinking water, one in six is illiterate, and one in seven adults and one in three children suffer from malnutrition.

Several specialized United Nations institutions co-wrote a document estimating that $80 billion a year for ten years would be enough to guarantee to every person on the planet access to basic education; basic health care; adequate food, drinking water, and sanitation; and, for women, gynecological and obstetric care.[3] In 2003, $80 billion represented about four times less than the sum repaid by the Third World on its external debt, about one-fifth of the US defense budget, 9 percent of world military expenditure, 8 percent of annual spending on publicity worldwide, half the cumulated wealth of the four richest people on the planet,[4] and 0.3 percent of the combined wealth of the richest one-thousandth of the global population.[5] Present-day misery could be transformed with such wealth.

The laws of the market and profit cannot be expected to satisfy essential needs. The 1.3 billion people deprived of clean drinking water and the 2 billion without access to medicines or health care have too little purchasing power to interest the markets. Not enough profit can be made.[6]

Only resolute public policies can ever guarantee the fulfillment of basic human needs for all.[7] This is why the public authorities must have at their disposal the political and financial means of honoring their obligations toward their citizens. The latter must also be able to exercise fully their right to play a central role in the political life of the state. To bring that about, efficient judiciary mechanisms and economic policies must be implemented in a dynamic of participative democracy. The example of a participative budget practiced in Porto Alegre since the early 1990s should be adopted on a worldwide scale, and should inspire original policies of radical democracy.

The application of the Universal Declaration of Human Rights and the International Covenant on Economic, Social, and Cultural Rights has to be backed up by a powerful social and citizens' movement. This can only be an authentic revolutionary project, no more, no less. First, the hemorrhage of wealth represented by debt repayments has to be stemmed. Next, different sources of funding must be found for socially just and ecologically sustainable development. Finally, we must break away from the old logic that leads to the cycle of indebtedness, to embezzlement and large-scale pillage of local wealth, and to dependence on the financial markets and condition-laden loans of the international financial institutions.

1. Breaking the infernal cycle of debt

The champions of neoliberal globalization tell us that the developing countries (in which they include Eastern Europe) must repay their external debt if they wish to benefit from constant flows of funding. In fact, since the debt crisis in 1982, the flows have been going from the periphery to the center, not the other way, as the leaders of the international financial institutions would have us believe. In order to estimate real flows, as shown in chapter 9, the following factors have to be taken into account: repayment of the external debt; capital outflow due to residents of periphery countries; the repatriation of profits by multinational firms (including invisible transfers, especially via such procedures as "over-" or "under-" billing on invoices); the acquisition of privatized businesses in the periphery at extremely low prices by capitalists of the highly industrialized countries; the purchase at low prices of raw materials produced by the populations of the periphery (degradation of the terms of exchange); the "brain drain"; genetic pillage; pillage of natural resources and destruction of the ecosystem, etc. The donors are not who we are led to believe. It is a gross error of language to consider the OECD countries, members of the Development Assistance Committee, and the Bretton Woods institutions to be "donors."

In the last two decades, a massive net transfer of wealth from the periphery to the center has occurred. The added mechanism of debt repayment has become a powerful support to those previously in operation (unfair trading, exploitation of natural and human resources, the brain drain, repatriation of profits to the parent company, etc.). Since 1982, the populations of the periphery countries have sent their creditors the equivalent of several times the Marshall Plan, with the local capitalist elite skimming off their commission on the way (see chapter 9).

It has become urgent to adopt the opposite view from that of official discourse: the Third World's external public debt must be canceled. Scrutiny reveals that the debt owed by the Third World is slight compared to the historic social and ecological debt that the rich Northern countries owe to it. In 2002, the Third World debt (former Eastern Bloc countries included) came to about $2.4 trillion (of which about $1.6 trillion is public debt), merely a small percentage of the world debt, which comes to more than $60 trillion. (The total sum of public and private debt for the United States alone is $30 trillion.) If the South's external public debt were entirely canceled without indemnifying the creditors, they would suffer a paltry loss of barely 5 percent in their portfolios. On the other hand, to the populations liberated at last from the burden of debt, those sums, which could be used to improve health and education, create jobs, etc., would mean a great deal. Indeed, the repayment of the South's external public debt represents, on average, expenditure of about $190 billion to $220 billion a year, that is, about two to three times the amount required to satisfy basic human needs as defined by the United Nations.

Some claim that debt cancellation leads to permanent exclusion from access to international capital. No serious study of the history of debt crises supports this claim. Between the end of the eighteenth century, when the United States canceled its debt toward the British Crown, and the end of the twentieth century, with the cancellation of part of Poland's debt in 1991 (one of the rare examples in which the creditors made a spontaneous effort—obviously strategic interests were at stake), numerous debt-cancellation measures have been taken. For example, Mexico stopped repaying its debt between 1914 and 1946 (Marichal 1989); the Bolshevik government declared unilateral cancellation of the debts of the tsarist empire. In no case did disaster ensue, as predicted by the creditors. On the other hand, there is no shortage of examples of countries that have become weakened and impoverished through debt repayment. Argentina is a case in hand.

Since the end of the 1990s, flows related to international loans have become negative. Indebted countries taken as a whole repay more each year than they receive in the form of loans (whether bank loans, bonds, bilateral loans, or World Bank loans). Every year since 1999, the loans granted by commercial banks have been less than the repayments they have received. The same has been true of bilateral loans since 1996. The flows have been negative for the issue of debt paper since 2000. For World Bank loans, ODA included, flows have been negative since 2000 (World Bank 2003a).[8] Furthermore, the threat of exclusion from access to private external capital means little to most Third World countries, which have had hardly any access to that capital for years. The UNDP (1999) states: "Today only 25 developing countries have access to private markets for bonds, commercial bank loans and portfolio equity." Note that the UNDP includes the East European states in the twenty-five countries mentioned and that the total number of developing countries, as they define them, is 180.

According to the United Nations, in 1999, the forty-eight least developed countries (LDC), with their nearly six hundred million inhabitants, received only 0.5 percent of foreign direct investment (FDI), destined for developing countries (DC). Indeed, the DC's share of FDI has been in constant decline over the last three years—while the rich countries get 80 percent of these flows.

For the handful of Third World countries with access to international capital (four countries—China, Brazil, Mexico, and Thailand—received more than 50 percent of FDI flow in 1998), the acquisition of preexisting businesses taken over by multinationals of the most industrialized countries accounts for 80 percent of foreign investment input. This does not result in job creation—quite the opposite. Furthermore, these acquisitions imply a loss of national control over the productive infrastructure, not to mention the highly volatile and speculative nature of the other capital flows (one of the lessons of the financial crises of the 1990s).

Restricting this type of flow would do no harm to the economies of these countries. We propose replacing these unproductive, even damaging, flows by alternative sources of funding (see the second part of this), to significantly reduce dependence on financial markets and the Bretton Woods institutions.

Judicial basis for debt cancellation

Debt cancellation is made more legitimate because it can be justified by several legal arguments, including the notions of "odious debt," "force majeure," and "state of necessity."

Odious debt

State debts contracted against the interests of local populations are judged unlawful. According to Alexander Sack (1927), who theorized this doctrine,

> If a despotic power incurs a debt not for the needs or in the interest of the State, but to strengthen its despotic regime, to repress the population that fights against it, etc., this debt is odious for the population of all the State.
> This debt is not an obligation for the nation; it is a regime's debt, a personal debt of the power that as incurred it, consequently it falls with the fall of this power.

Thus, debts contracted against the interests of the population of the indebted territory are odious and, in the case of a regime change, the new authorities are not held to repay them.

This notion dates back to the end of the nineteenth century.[9] One of its applications was in 1898, when the United States gained control of Cuba after a war with Spain.[10] The latter demanded that the victor take on the Cuban debt toward the Spanish Crown, in accordance with international law. The US negotiating commission refused to do so on the grounds that the debt was "a burden imposed upon the Cuban people without their consent." The commission argued, "The debt was incurred by the Government of Spain for its own interests and by its own agents. Cuba had no say in the matter." The commission added, "The creditors accepted the risk of their investments." An international treaty between the United States and Spain, signed in Paris in 1898, resolved the dispute. The debt was completely canceled.

Later, in 1923, an international court of arbitration—in which William H. Taft, chief justice of the United States Supreme Court, took part—declared that loans made to Tinoco of Costa Rica by a British bank established in Canada were null and void since they had not served the country's interests but the personal interest of a nondemocratic government. On this occasion, Judge Taft declared:

> The case of the Royal Bank rests not simply upon the form of the transaction, but upon the bank's good faith at the time of the loan for the effective use of the Costa Rican government under Tinoco's regime. The Bank must prove that the money was lent to the government for legitimate purposes. It has not done so. (Cited in Adams 1991)

The legal regimes (recognized lawful governments) that followed the dictatorships of South America in the 1980s (in Argentina, Uruguay, Brazil, etc.) should have drawn upon international law to have their odious debts canceled. They did not, for the very good reason that the dictatorships had benefited from the active support of the United States (when it was not the United States that had helped to get them into power) and the main lenders were none other than US banks.

Other countries, too, had a perfect right to demand the cancellation of their debts. To give a few more flagrant examples: in the Philippines after the overthrow of the dictator Marcos, in 1986; in Rwanda, in 1994, after the genocide perpetrated by its dictatorial regime;[11] in the Republic of South Africa as it emerged from apartheid (1994); in the Democratic Republic of the Congo, in 1997, when Mobutu was overthrown; in Indonesia, in 1998, when Suharto left power. Instead of turning to national and international law, those newly in power prefer to negotiate with the creditors to spread out the repayments or make cosmetic reductions. Once they are sucked into the interminable cycle of external debt, their populations bear the cost.

This system of creating dependency has to end. Full support must be given to the social and citizens' movements in developing countries that call on their governments to repudiate the external public debt and stop repayments. Citizens' movements in favor of debt cancellation have regularly invoked the doctrine of odious debt, but postdictatorship regimes, and of course the lenders, have turned a deaf ear.

The US government took up the issue of odious debt in April 2003. In circumstances not unlike the precedent of the 1898 war between Spain and the US, the US has asked Russia, France, and Germany to cancel the odious debts owed by Iraq. Taking word for word the definition of odious debt as quoted above, the debts contracted by the dictator Saddam Hussein were declared null and void. The United States, along with their British, Australian, Dutch, and Danish allies, attacked Iraq in violation of the UN Charter in March 2003. They then occupied it with more than 100,000 soldiers and were preparing to establish a protectorate, de facto or legally, over the country. They would have liked to persuade some of the main creditors, especially the three powers that opposed the war (France, Russia, and Germany), to renounce what they were owed.

The objective of the United States was, and still is, to get its hands on Iraq's oil revenues generally, and particularly to use them to pay the costs of the military intervention and ensuing destruction, of reconstruction, and of the current occupation. They want to prevent the use of oil revenues to repay debts to the powers that did not support military intervention. The US used the argument of odious debt purely as an opportunistic ploy. Its idea was for Iraq to be relieved of old debts in order to guarantee the repayment of the newly incurred ones to the new main creditors, especially the US, down to the last cent. This has been analyzed in chapter 16. Nevertheless, the United States has shown the

TABLE 19.1. ODIOUS DEBTS.

Country	Dictatorial Regime	Period of Dictatorship	Odious Debt ($billion)	Debt Stock (2001)
Indonesia	Suharto	1965–98	150.0	135.0
Iraq	Saddam Hussein	1979–2003	122.0	122.0
Brazil	Military junta	1964–85	100.0	226.0
Argentina	Military junta	1976–83	45.0	137.0
South Korea	Military	1961–81	30.0	110.0
Nigeria	Buhari–Abacha	1984–98	30.0	31.0
Turkey	Military	1980–89	30.0	115.0
Philippines	Marcos	1965–86	27.0	52.0
South Africa	Apartheid	1948–91	22.0	24.0
Syria	Assad regimes	1971–	21.0	21.0
Thailand	Military	1963–88	21.0	67.0
Morocco	Hassan II	1961–99	19.0	17.0
Zaire/DRC	Mobutu	1965–97	13.0	11.0
Chile	Pinochet	1973–90	12.0	38.0
Tunisia	Ben Ali	1987–	11.0	11.0
Pakistan	Military	1978–88	10.0	32.0
Peru	Fujimori	1990–2000	9.0	27.0
Sudan	Nimeiri	1969–85	9.0	15.0
Ethiopia	Mengistu	1974–91	8.0	5.7
Kenya	Moi	1978–2002	5.8	5.8
Congo	Sassou	1979–	4.5	4.5

world that the doctrine of odious debt is not a thing of the past. The Iraqi people are entitled to recover completely their freedom (which means the departure of the foreign occupying forces) and to see the debts contracted by Saddam Hussein wiped out. Furthermore, they are entitled to reparations on the part of their aggressors. Other populations bearing the burden of odious debts have every right to demand their cancellation.

Citizens' surveys (audits) to investigate the legitimacy of debts that their country is expected to repay are a fundamental tool. Parliaments and governments of indebted countries could carry out debt audits. Some countries have clauses in their constitutions that expressly provide for this (Brazil's 1988 constitution; the 1999 constitution of the Bolivarian republic of Venezuela). Powerful mobilizations of citizens in various countries have clamored for the start of auditing procedures. Brazil in September 2000 is one example, when the Jubilee South Campaign, the National Conference of Bishops, the Landless

Country	Dictatorial Regime	Period of Dictatorship	Odious Debt ($billion)	Debt Stock (2001)
Iran	Shah	1941–79	4.5	7.5
Bolivia	Military junta	1964–82	3.0	4.7
Guatemala	Military	1954–85	2.7	4.5
Mali	Traore	1968–91	2.5	2.9
Somalia	Siad Barre	1969–91	2.3	2.5
Malawi	Banda	1966–94	2.2	2.6
Paraguay	Stroessner	1954–89	2.1	2.8
Nicaragua	Somoza regimes	1937–79	2.0	6.4
Kampuchea	Khmer Rouge	1975–89	1.8	2.7
Togo	Eyadema	1967–2005	1.4	1.4
Liberia	Doe	1980–90	1.2	2.0
Myanmar	Military	1988–	1.2	5.7
Rwanda	Habyarimana	1973–94	1.0	1.3
El Salvador	Military junta	1962–80	1.0	4.7
Haiti	Duvalier regimes	1957–86	0.8	1.2
Uganda	Idi Amin Dada	1971–79	0.6	3.7
Central African Republic	Bokassa	1966–79	0.2	0.8

Source: Table by Damien Millet and the author, based on preliminary work by
Joseph Hanlon in "Dictators and Debt" (1998), Jubilee 2000.
(See http://www.jubileeplus.org/analysis/reports/dictatorsreport.htm)

Rural Workers' Movement, and the CUT (the Portuguese acronym for Brazil's Unified Workers) organized a referendum on the debt. Six million citizens took part and more than 95 percent of those voted in favor of organizing an audit. Numerous Brazilian social movements asked the new president Lula, who came into power in January 2003, to organize the audit as provided for in the Brazilian constitution of 1988. The powerful Confederation of Indigenous Nationalities of Ecuador (CONAIE) put pressure on the new Ecuadorian president Lucio Gutierrez to do an audit. President Chávez of Venezuela announced a similar initiative.

A great deal hangs on doing audits to determine whether all or part of a country's debt is odious. Table 19.1 gives a provisional and nonexhaustive list of the debts of a few countries. The amounts involved in odious debts are considerable. The table is provisional because only a precise and rigorous audit (carried out with citizen participation) can properly determine the size of the odious debt to be declared null and void. The table nevertheless gives food for thought and action.

The amounts given in table 19.1 as odious debt are in most cases lower than the real figures, as they only concern the period of the dictatorships sensu stricto. They do not include debts contracted to repay the odious debts. The point of an audit would be to determine the precise amount of debt that can be rightly considered odious. The list of eligible countries is also incomplete.

Several additions are required to the doctrine of odious debt as formulated by Alexander Sack. The Center for International Sustainable Development Law (CISDL) at McGill University (Canada) has proposed a general definition that seems appropriate: "Odious debts are those contracted against the interests of the population of a state, without its consent and with the full awareness of the creditors" (Khalfan, King, and Thomas 2002). So, the issue of odious debt should not be abandoned on any account, even if creditors of every kind like to consider it closed. Indebted states have not finished repaying odious debts. They can still make a decision grounded in law to repudiate these debts. New debts contracted in the 1990s and early 2000s by legitimate regimes to repay odious debts contracted by previous despotic regimes also should fall into the category of odious debt. This is the opinion of various experts, such as those at the CISDL, as well as Joseph Hanlon (Great Britain), Hugo Ruiz Diaz (Paraguay–Belgium), and Patricio Pazmino (Ecuador).[12]

The definition proposed by the CISDL implies that private creditors who have lent (or lend) money to regimes (legitimate or not) or to companies guaranteed by the state for projects that have not been decided through democratic consultation or that are detrimental to society risk seeing their loans canceled. All the more so in cases where the creditor has also actively or passively colluded with embezzlement. A great number of projects, old and new, come under this category. The great Three Gorges Dam project in China is a case in hand. Once the notion of odious debt is well established, creditors will be forced to make clear their responsibilities and commitments and to respect democratic, social, and environmental rules. If they do not, they may find themselves forced to give up all hope of recovering the money they lent.

The doctrine of odious debt also needs to be extended to cover debts contracted with the Bretton Woods institutions (the IMF, the World Bank, and the regional development banks).

Why? The IMF and the World Bank (multilateral lenders) hold about $450 billion of credits on indebted countries[13] and a large part of those debts fall into the "odious" category.

Several examples of cases where the doctrine of odious debt should be applied, in line with the CISDL's definition, follow.

(1) Multilateral debts contracted by despotic regimes (all of the dictatorships mentioned earlier were supported by the IMF and the World Bank) must be considered odious. The IMF and the World Bank have no right to demand repayment from the democratic regimes that replace dictatorships.*

(2) Multilateral debts contracted by legal and legitimate regimes to repay debts contracted by despotic regimes are themselves odious and must not be repaid. This is the case for about thirty countries mentioned in (nonexhaustive) table 19.1.*

(3) Multilateral debts contracted by legal and legitimate regimes within the framework of structural adjustment policies detrimental to populations are also odious. (Numerous writers and international organizations, especially branches of the UN, have amply demonstrated the detrimental nature of these policies—see below.) For twenty years, the IMF and the World Bank have continued to define and impose, come hell or high water, conditionalities that turned out to have catastrophic consequences for basic human rights. This amounts to *dolus malus*,[14] defrauding the borrowers and their populations. The loan contract concerned is null and void. The letters of intent that the governments of indebted countries are obliged to send to the IMF and the World Bank (which dictates their contents) are invented by these institutions to cover themselves in the eventuality of legal proceedings against them. The procedure is nothing but an artifice and therefore has no legal value.[15] Just as an individual does not have the *right* to agree to be reduced to slavery

(the contract whereby a person renounces his or her liberty has strictly no legal value), a government has no right to renounce the exercise of its country's sovereignty. Insofar as it cancels a state's exercise of its sovereignty, such a letter is null and void. The Bretton Woods institutions cannot use this letter of intent to escape responsibility. They remain fully responsible for the wrongs done to populations through the application of the conditionalities they impose—structural adjustment, which has now been renamed Poverty Reduction Strategy Papers (PRSP) for the HIPC, or Poverty Reduction and Growth Facility (PRGF) for the rest.

(4) The antidemocratic, despotic nature of the Bretton Woods institutions themselves also needs to be recognized. The required majority is 85 percent, giving the United States a veto, as they hold about 17 percent of the votes. There is a clear imbalance in the distribution of voting rights.

(5) At the same time as actions are brought to cancel multilateral loans, the Bretton Woods institutions must also be forced to make reparations to the populations who have suffered the human and environmental damage caused by their policies.*

(6) Lastly, civil and criminal actions must be brought against the officials of those institutions, who should be held responsible for the violations of basic human rights they have perpetrated and still perpetrate by imposing structural adjustment and/or by lending support to despotic regimes.*

All points marked with an asterisk (*) apply equally to bilateral debts and bilateral creditors. To illustrate point number six, in the future, a democratic Togo freed of the dictator Eyadema could bring a court action against France in The Hague (or even the International Criminal Court) for its active support of the dictatorship. Furthermore, in strict application of the doctrine of odious debt, a democratic, post-Eyadema Togo would no longer owe the debts contracted under the dictatorship.

Force majeure

Another means provided by the law of supporting debt cancellation and stopping repayments is to use the argument of force majeure and that of a fundamental change of circumstances.[16] The UN International Law Commission (ILC) defines "force majeure" as follows: "The impossibility to act legally...is the situation that arises when unforeseen circumstances beyond the control of the person or persons concerned absolutely prevent them from respecting their international obligation, by virtue of the principle that one cannot do the impossible."[17]

This principle of international law acknowledges that a change in the conditions of a contract may render it invalid.[18] This means that contracts requiring the fulfillment of a succession of future commitments are subject to the condition that the circumstances should remain unchanged. (In common law, several doctrines are based on a similar principle, including "force majeure" [circumstances beyond one's control], "frustration," "impossibility," and "nonfeasibility.")

Force majeure and a fundamental change of circumstances quite clearly apply to the debt crisis of the 1980s. Indeed, the fundamental causes of the debt crisis from 1982 on were two exogenous factors: the dramatic rise in interest rates imposed worldwide by the United States government from the end of 1979, and the drop in export prices for the periphery countries from 1980 on. Creditor countries instigated both of these factors. They are cases of force majeure that fundamentally modify the situation and prevent the debtors from fulfilling their obligations.[19]

State of necessity

To justify a refusal to pay in law, the argument of a state of necessity can also be used. A state of necessity can be invoked when it would cause unreasonable sacrifice and hardship to the populations concerned to continue making repayments, thus directly affecting the state's fundamental obligations toward its citizens. Regarding this point, the ILC declares:

> A state cannot be expected to close its schools, universities, and law courts and to do away with public services, plunging the community into chaos and anarchy simply to be able to use the money to repay its national or foreign creditors. There are limits to what can reasonably be expected from a state as there are for an individual. (ILC 1980, 164–67)

It is time to break away from old habits of dependency and subjugation. It is time to support the social and citizens' movements in the countries of the periphery that are calling upon their governments to repudiate the external public debt and stop paying it.

2. Extra resources to finance development

2.1. Establish a development fund

For debt cancellation to serve the purpose of human development, obviously the money previously earmarked for debt repayment needs to be used to fulfill basic human rights. This means that a democratically determined portion should be paid into a development fund, under the direct and active control of the local population. The emphasis must be on citizen participation in deciding priorities and working out projects to meet these priorities, and in overseeing how financial and human resources are spent. However, once this first step of debt cancellation has been taken, the present economy based on international indebtedness must be replaced by a model that is both socially just and ecologically sustainable, and independent of the fluctuations of the money markets and of the loan conditionalities imposed by the World Bank and the IMF.

This development fund, already supplied with money saved through debt cancellation,[20] must also be financed by the following measures:

2.1.1. Restitution of stolen property to the citizens of the Global South

The considerable wealth illicitly accumulated by the ruling authorities and local capitalists has been deposited securely in the most industrialized countries with the active collusion of private financial institutions and the tacit agreement of the Northern governments (the practice continues to this day).

Take, for example, Argentina under the military junta (1976–83). This country's debt increased sixfold. Members of the regime deposited a large part of the money borrowed in banks in the United States, Great Britain, and other industrialized countries (see chapter 16). Financial and industrial firms in the industrialized countries, as well as members of successive Argentine governments, thus became rich through illegal means. The Argentine judiciary established the facts in the course of a trial that took place in July 2000.[21] The collusion of the IMF and the New York Federal Reserve was proven. Based on the judgment passed, which should set a legal precedent, the populations thus robbed should be able to receive compensation.

Imagine, for example, what it would mean to the population of Argentina to recover the money deposited by the military junta (1976–1983) in the most industrialized countries. Imagine what the return of a large part of the late Mobutu's fortune (equivalent to ten times the Democratic Republic of the Congo's annual national budget) would mean to the Congolese people, or what it would mean to the population of Nigeria if they could recover the fortune of the dictator Abacha, safely invested in Switzerland and Great Britain with the collusion of the major banks. Remember, too, the colossal fortune deposited mainly in the same two financial centers by Russian oligarchs in the 1990s and early 2000s.

To operate such restitution implies the completion of legal proceedings in the Third World countries and the most industrialized countries. The example of the retrocession to the Philippine government, in 2003, of part of the fortune of the dictator Marcos ($658 million) by the Swiss authorities proves that it can be done.[22] Such investigations would require full international cooperation and the ratification of the Convention of Rome of March 1991, which deems the misappropriation of public property to be a human rights violation. Among other things, they would serve to ensure that people guilty of corruption do not get off scot-free. This is the only hope, if democracy and transparency are one day to triumph over corruption.

2.1.2. Support for the resolutions made at the international meeting held in Dakar, in December 2000, demanding compensation for the pillage that the peoples of the periphery have been subject to over the last five centuries[23]

This includes the restitution of economic and cultural property stolen from the Asian, African, and South American continents and from the Amerindian, Caribbean, and Oceanic peoples.

Ever more numerous and more active movements are stating the case for reparations. Under pressure from African social movements and associations of both North and South America, the subject was officially placed on the agenda of the United Nations World Conference against Racism in Durban in August–September 2001. The US government withdrew from the conference, and the European Union maneuvered to limit the effect of the final resolution. Its delegate was not prepared to go further than recognizing the slave trade as a crime against humanity. He wanted to avoid anything that might open the way to demands for reparations. Although it already has a long history, the battle over this issue is only now beginning. It is a battle that must be won, for moral as well as economic reasons.

The environmental debt, contracted mainly by the multinational corporations of the highly industrialized countries, the governments of the North, and the World Bank, is also an integral part of the demand for reparations.[24] Remember the damage caused and the pillage by oil, mining, and agribusiness multinationals.

2.2. Nationalization/socialization of the domestic assets of dictatorial regimes

Debt cancellation sets the clock back to zero. The expropriation of ill-gotten gains—holdings abroad of dictators (and their entourages)—would provide the ideal basis for a development fund. To this fund should be added the wealth accumulated by these predatory regimes within their own borders. A proper register of these holdings must be established. The regime's physical wealth (not just financial) should also be placed at the disposal of the development fund. This fund is essential for undertaking constructive projects aimed at satisfying the real needs of the population, and for setting up a host of social and environmental programs.

2.3. Making fraudulent capitalists pay their fair share

Holders of capital from the South have large sums of money in foreign accounts. They have enriched themselves on the backs of their people, through out-and-out theft and/or organized capital flight. A proper register of domestic and foreign-held wealth must be established. This means that officials in each country, under the pressure of the social movements, must take legal steps to demand that banking secrecy be lifted at both national and international levels.

These same officials must determine how much wealth is involved and who controls it. One way of doing this would be to send commissions of inquiry to private foreign banks. With this information in hand, governments could establish what tax penalty should be imposed to ensure that state coffers receive all taxes due.

Since those with assets abroad also hold domestic assets, their domestic wealth could be frozen as long as the tax penalty is not paid. If the penalty is never paid, a part of the person's domestic assets could be confiscated and transferred into the public domain.

2.4. Monetary reform by redistribution

A redistribution of wealth can also be achieved by means of appropriate monetary reforms. Without going into too much detail, one model is the kind of monetary reform carried out after the Second World War by the Belgian government or, on the other side of the planet and in more recent times, by the Nicaraguan government in 1985. The idea is to tap into the wealth of those who got rich at the expense of others. The principle is straightforward: at the time of a change of legal tender, automatic parity between the old money and the new is only guaranteed up to a certain limit. Beyond this ceiling, any remaining monies must be placed in a blocked account and its origin justified and authenticated. As a rule, the remainder above the fixed limit is exchanged at a less favorable rate (e.g., two old francs for one new). In cases where it is clear that the money has criminal origins, it can be seized.[25]

Such monetary reform enables part of the wealth to be distributed in a socially fairer manner. Another objective of the reform is to reduce the total amount of money in circulation, diminishing inflationary tendencies. For the reform to succeed, capital movements and exchanges would need to be subjected to strict controls.

2.5. On the international level, set up global taxation

2.5.1. Tax financial transactions

Initially proposed by the 1981 winner of the Nobel Prize for economics, James Tobin, other economists, then the international network ATTAC (Association for the Taxation of Financial Transactions for Aid to Citizens), took up the idea. Such a tax would liberate considerable sums of money for development.

United Nations Conference on Trade and Development (UNCTAD) calculates that $1 trillion a day taxed at 1 percent would produce $720 billion a year. As a working hypothesis, they propose splitting it in two: $360 billion for a social and ecological fund in the countries where the transactions took place, and $360 billion for a redistribution fund for the countries of the South (for health, education, etc.). Mixed boards of directors representing civil society and governments would manage the two funds. ATTAC's international platform suggests a tax of 0.1 percent, bringing in some $100 billion annually, which could be used to combat inequality and to provide public health and education services, food security, and sustainable development. Obviously, it is impossible to calculate exactly how much such a tax would raise, since it depends on the rate of the tax and the volume of financial flows.[26] ATTAC, with the support of other movements (including the CADTM), considers that the EU (or the Euro Zone within it) is large enough to apply a Tobin-type tax without waiting for an international consensus.

Furthermore, in view of the globalization of markets that has been taking place since Tobin's initial proposal (and especially the development of derivative products bridging all the gaps between markets), it would seem necessary to tax all financial transactions (shares, bonds, hard currency, and derivatives), so that operators cannot dodge this solidarity tax by turning to other markets. Centralized computerization of clearing operations, through clearing houses such as SWIFT for the exchange market, and Clearstream and Euroclear for international transferable securities transactions, makes the application of such a tax perfectly feasible, since all international financial transactions are traceable and carried out only in these places.

2.5.2. Taxes on FDI and the profits of MNCs, and other global taxes

ATTAC also proposes to tax foreign direct investment (FDI). ATTAC France envisions this as fluctuating between a rate of 20 percent and 10 percent, according to a classification worked out by the International Labor Organization (ILO), based on the degree to which workers' basic rights are respected, with a specific scale for different categories of countries. ATTAC also proposes a tax on the profits of multinational corporations (MNCs). The idea is that the Tobin-type tax, the FDI taxes, and those on MNC profits should be pooled in a global fund for the guarantee of human rights and the protection of the environment (which is in line with the proposal made in this chapter).

On the matter of global taxes, apart from the wealth tax suggested in 2.7 (below), certain movements are also discussing the idea of a tax on the kerosene used by airline companies. Aviation kerosene is the only fossil fuel that is not taxed. Its combustion damages the environment and contributes to the exhaustion of nonrenewable sources of energy. Considering that the ill effects are global, it is logical to think in terms of a global tax, which airline companies would have to pay into a global fund for the guarantee of human rights and the protection of the environment. The idea of taxing CO_2 emissions (with negative effects as global as those of kerosene) is also under discussion.

2.6. Raise ODA to at least 0.7 percent of GDP.
Instead, let's talk about reparation funds.

The present level of official development assistance (ODA) does not balance out the negative effect of debt repayment (see chapter 9). First, loans to be repaid make up a significant part of ODA. Next, in 2002, the grand total of ODA did not exceed $57 billion, i.e., about six times less than the amount repaid by the Third World in external debt servicing.

In 2002, ODA represented a mere 0.23 percent of the gross domestic product of the most industrialized countries, despite their commitment, frequently reiterated within the framework of the United Nations, to reach the objective of 0.7 percent. In fact, ODA fell by more than 30 percent between 1992 and 2002, in scandalous contradiction to promises made in Rio (1992) by the heads of state of the industrialized countries.

Taking the present average of 0.23 percent, ODA must be multiplied threefold to fulfill the commitments made. Considering that ODA represents a little less than $50 billion, if it is multiplied by three, it should reach $150 billion a year, which should be entirely paid out as donations (as compensation and no longer, as is too often the case, in the form of loans).

Finally, rather than speak of "aid," henceforth it would be more appropriate to use the term "reparation." The idea would be to make reparation for all the damage caused by centuries of pillage and unfair trade. Part of the sum of $150 billion of donations should be paid into a global fund guaranteeing human rights and the protection of the environment, managed by the DC (within the framework of the UN), and part into national development funds run by the populations concerned and their representatives.

2.7. Levy an exceptional tax on the estate of the very wealthy

In its 1995 report, UNCTAD suggests levying a single, exceptional tax on the estates of the very wealthy. Such a tax levied throughout the world would mobilize considerable funds. This exceptional tax (different from recurrent property taxes such as exist in several countries around the planet) could also be levied at a national level without waiting for a global decision. UNCTAD does not suggest a particular rate or a particular target among the large fortunes.

It is time to take the plunge. An exceptional solidarity tax such as this, once in a lifetime, of say 10 percent of the fortune of the wealthiest tenth of the population in each country could generate considerable internal resources. In most countries, taxpayers pay tax at both national and federal levels, in addition to local taxes at municipal or regional level. All it means is that extra rich taxpayers would be subject to the same type of rules, extended to the entire planet. On top of their national taxes, they will have to pay once an exceptional world tax on their fortune, levied where their fortune is, and paid into a global fund for the guarantee of human rights and the protection of the environment.

The concentration of wealth in the hands of a tiny minority has reached a point never previously known in the history of humankind. This is the case in all of the countries on the planet, with only a handful of exceptions. The accumulated wealth comes to such absurd amounts as to be an insult to the human conscience and to the peoples of the world. The 2003 edition of the *World Wealth Report*, produced by the wealth management consultants Cap Gemini Ernst & Young and the investment bank Merrill Lynch, indicates that, in 2002, there were about 7.3 million millionaires in dollars (i.e., about one-thousandth of the world's population), with about $27.2 trillion between them, not including their principal places of residence (see footnote 6).

An exceptional global tax of 20 percent on the fortunes of the richest thousandth of the planet would bring in roughly $5.5 trillion (27.2 divided by 5 = $5), which would go into the global fund to guarantee human rights and the protection of the environment, already permanently financed by a Tobin-type tax and other global taxes. Part would be spent in the form of donations; another part would be lent at low interest rates or none at all, so that the fund would be permanently resupplied.

Many questions remain. What rate to apply? A single rate? Of how much? Or a progressive rate? What percentage of the fund's resources would be distributed as donations? What percentage as loans? At what rate of interest? On what terms? What percentage of the fund would go toward global projects? Toward continental projects? Toward a reforestation fund? Toward a fund for complete denuclearization? What priorities, what projects? Who decides? The UN General Assembly preceded by national referenda? Continental referenda? What percentage would go to local projects?

More generally, the idea is to work toward a truly redistributive system of taxation, giving governments the means to fulfill their obligations toward their citizens with regard to their economic, social, and cultural rights.

3. A new development strategy

Instead of the present development strategy, which consists of the creditors forcing Southern countries to adopt neoliberal-type adjustment programs, an endogenous and integrated development strategy should be embraced. The change would be implemented in the following stages:

3.1. End structural adjustment programs

Structural adjustment programs (SAPs) result in the weakening of states by making them more dependent on external fluctuations (world market movements, speculative attacks, etc.) and by subjecting them to conditionalities imposed by the IMF–World Bank duo, backed up by the governments of the creditor countries grouped within the Paris Club.

SAPs deliver up the economies of the Third World to the appetites of the great multinational firms. Far from solving the problem of indebtedness (the Third World debt has quadrupled since the first SAPs were set up, though it has been repaid six times during the same period), they entail massive layoffs and drastic cuts in social budgets. They prevent any real human development.

The UN Commission on Human Rights has repeatedly adopted resolutions concerning the debt problem and structural adjustment.[27] In a resolution adopted in 1999, the commission states:

> For the population of an indebted country, the exercise of their basic rights to food, housing, clothing, work, education, medical care, and a healthy environment may not be subordinated to the application of structural adjustment programs and economic reforms generated by the debt.

A report of the UN secretary-general in 1995 states:

> The Special Rapporteur [on the realization of economic, social, and cultural rights] underlined that the structural adjustment measures and accompanying conditionalities advocated by the international financial institutions have a decidedly negative influence, both directly and indirectly, on the attainment of economic, social and cultural rights and are incompatible with the realization of these rights. (UN Economic and Social Council, E/CN.4/Sub.2/1995/10)

Furthermore, according to the same UN report, certain conditions fixed by the creditors and the funding agencies constitute a violation of the right to self-determination of the populations concerned:

> Every country has the sovereign right freely to dispose of its natural resources in the interest of the economic development and well-being of its own people; any external, political or economic measures or pressures brought to bear on the exercise of this right is a flagrant violation of the principles of self-determination of peoples and non-intervention, as set forth in the Charter of the United Nations....
>
> ...Such measures include economic pressure designed to influence the policy of another country or to obtain control of essential sectors of its national economy....
>
> The provision of economic and technical assistance, loans and increased foreign investment must not be subject to conditions which conflict with the interests of the recipient State.

Fantu Cheru, the UN's special reporter on the effects of SAPs and the external debt on the effective enjoyment of all human rights, especially economic, social, and cultural rights [sic.], declares:

> Increasing malnutrition, falling school enrollments and rising unemployment have been attributed to the policies of structural adjustment. Yet these same institutions [the international financial institutions] continue to prescribe the same medicine as a condition for debt relief, dismissing the overwhelming evidence that SAPs have increased poverty. (UN Economic and Social Council, E/CN.4/2001/56)

The human consequences of structural adjustment programs are incontestably negative. The latter must therefore be canceled and replaced with policies aimed at satisfying basic human needs, giving priority to domestic markets, food security, and complementary exchanges on a regional or continental basis.

3.2. Ensure the return of privatized strategic sectors to the public domain

Water reserves and distribution, electricity production and distribution, telecommunications, postal services, railways, companies that extract and transform raw materials, the credit system, certain education and health sectors, etc., have been systematically privatized or are in the process of being privatized. These companies must be returned to the public domain.

3.3. Adopt a partly self-based development model

Such models entail constructing sufficiently solid internal economic foundations to allow the country to open up to international trading. This type of development involves creating politically and economically integrated zones, bringing to bear endogenous development models, strengthening internal markets, creating local savings funds for local financing, developing education and health, setting up progressive taxation and other mechanisms to ensure the redistribution of wealth, diversifying exports, introducing agrarian reform to guarantee universal access to land for small farmers and urban reform to guarantee universal access to housing, etc.

Today's global architecture, structured on the idea of a "periphery" that is forced to provide raw materials and cheap labor to a "center" that has all of the technology and capital, must be replaced by regional economic groupings. Only such self-based development would allow South-South relations to emerge, which is the condition sine qua non for the economic development of the Third World (therefore, by extension, of the world). These integrated zones could establish regional authorities with powers of economic and social regulation.

3.4. Act upon trading practice

The existence of unfair exchange between the most industrialized countries and those of the periphery is one of the fundamental causes of the latter's indebtedness. In fact, unequal exchange creates a structural deficit in the balance of payments: imports grow faster than exports, leading to indebtedness.

The historical tendency to downgrade the terms of exchange must be brought to an end. To do this, mechanisms guaranteeing a better price for the basket of products exported on the world market by developing countries (DC) must be introduced. (These might include stabilizing the prices of raw materials, building up regulatory stocks—which means doing away with zero stocks—etc.)

To set up such concerted mechanisms, the DC's efforts to establish cartels of producer countries must be actively encouraged. OPEC is too often decried, while in several respects it plays a positive role.[28] The creation of such cartels could simultaneously result in a reduction of the quantities exported (which, on the one hand, would limit the exhaustion of natural resources, and, on the other, would free up areas for cultivation of food crops) and an increase in export revenues that the beneficiary countries could reinvest in development. Why not a cartel of copper producers? (Not long ago, Chile alone accounted for 30 percent of global exports.) A coffee cartel? A tea cartel? The countries of the periphery must have recourse to protection measures for their local production.

As for agriculture, as demanded by Vía Campesina, the right of each country, or group of countries, to nutritional sovereignty, and especially to self-sufficiency in staple foodstuffs, must be recognized. Import protection is the logical corollary, in total opposition to the minimum agricultural import quota of 5 percent now imposed on all member countries by WTO rules. In the words of Vía Campesina:

> To guarantee the independence and food sovereignty of all the peoples of the world, food has to be produced within small-holder based systems of diversified

production. Food sovereignty means a population's unalienable right to define its own agricultural policies and, concerning food, to protect and regulate national agricultural production and the domestic market so that sustainable objectives can be met. It means deciding on ways of reaching self-sufficiency without getting rid of their overproduction by dumping it on other countries....

International trade must not be given priority over social, cultural, environmental or development criteria.

Furthermore, Vía Campesina favors "the abolition of all backing or subsidies, direct or indirect, of exports," "the prohibition of the production and marketing of seed and genetically modified organisms," and "the prohibition of patents on life and the private appropriation of knowledge related to agriculture and food" (quoted in Díaz-Salazar 2002, 87, 90).

The rules of global trading must be subordinate to strict environmental, social, and cultural criteria. Health, education, water, and culture can have no place in the field of world commerce. Public services in the general interest are the guarantee of basic rights and must therefore be excluded from the General Agreement on Trade in Services (GATS). Furthermore, the Trade-Related Aspects of Intellectual Property Rights (TRIPs) agreement needs to be abolished, aspects of which allow the North to appropriate the rich natural resources of the South and prevent the Southern countries from freely producing goods (such as medicines) to satisfy the needs of their populations.

3.5. Guarantee people's right to circulate and to settle

Apart from the fact that the freedom to circulate and to settle constitutes a basic human right, it should be remembered that migrant workers' remittances to their families living in the DC represent an important resource for tens of millions of families. In 2002 alone, migrants' remittances represented $80 billion (see details in chapter 9), i.e., twice as much as the "donation" part of all ODA. The free circulation of capital and merchandise needs to be combated, and, in the struggle against selfish, neoliberal policies, people's right to circulate freely and settle needs to be firmly upheld. Obviously, based on the real improvement in living conditions that would result from the application of the measures outlined above, the reasons for migrating would disappear. That is the way to deal with the problem, not by closing borders to human beings.

4. New rules of good financial practice

The repeated financial crises of the 1990s proved by their absurdity that there can be no sustainable development without strict controls of capital movements and tax evasion. Several strategies are therefore required to subordinate the money markets to the fulfillment of basic human needs.

4.1. Re-regulate the financial markets

The deregulation of the money markets has led to the inordinate development of financial speculation. It is time to regulate the money markets once again, beginning by establishing a means of tracing all financial operations (to determine who does what and for what purpose).

4.2. Control capital movements to avoid the devastating effects of the remorseless ebb and flow of international capital

Article VI of the IMF Articles of Agreement explicitly recognizes the merits of the adoption of measures by governments to control capital movements. The article permits a member country of the IMF to "exercise such controls as are necessary to regulate international capital movements."

An appropriate measure would be to establish a temporary obligatory deposit, whereby every capital entry would be conditional upon an accompanying deposit for one year of 30 percent of the sum invested. After a year, the deposit would be returned to the investor (encouraged to invest only in the long term). The deposit would not earn any interest.

Numerous other control measures exist, for example, the obligation to hold shares and bonds for a minimum of one year before selling them, the limitation of currency exchange to commercial transactions (excluding financial operations), and heavy taxation in the case of excessive fluctuation (as proposed by the economist Bernd Spahn).

4.3. Eliminate tax havens

Tax havens contribute to inflating the financial bubble and weakening the legitimate economies (between $500 billion and $1.5 trillion are laundered each year). To eliminate them, each state must identify through the clearinghouses which transactions come from tax havens and tax them heavily to cancel out the benefit of unfair fiscal policy. At the same time, they must remove the bankers' rule of secrecy to combat more efficiently tax evasion, embezzlement of public funds, and corruption.

4.4. Adopt rules to ensure the protection of countries that have recourse to external indebtedness

External indebtedness may be justified if decided democratically by the countries concerned. However, the manner in which the borrowed money will be used must be organized according to principles radically different from those that have hitherto prevailed. Two new principles must be adhered to.

First, a "reverse" conditionality: the obligation to repay and pay interest on these loans, made at low rates of interest and below market conditions, will only be valid if the debt is proven to have enabled sufficient creation of wealth in the countries concerned. Second, the lender countries should organize strong and efficient protection for the DC on an international scale, to enable the latter to defend themselves against all forms of abuse and despoilment by banks, private international investors, or the international financial institutions.

Furthermore, as Carlos Marichal (2002) suggests, private companies that contract debts must be made to take the risks on themselves. Any company that borrows from outside will have to take out insurance with a big international insurance company. This should prevent the state—and thus the taxpayers—from having to bail out the company in case of bankruptcy, as happens regularly now. For example, in the crises of the 1990s, the governments of the indebted countries of East Asia and Latin America took over the private debts.

Lastly, every loan contract should stipulate that the courts of the borrowing countries will deal with any litigation that might arise between borrower and lender. This would reverse the present situation in which systematically the courts of the creditor countries deal with cases of litigation. Perusal of the sentences handed down make clear that the courts of the creditor countries tend to find in favor of the lender. It would be far preferable for the courts of the borrowing countries to deal with such cases, so that borrowers would be better protected and lenders made to assume their responsibilities.

4.5. Democratic control of political indebtedness

The decision by a state to contract debts and the terms under which they are contracted must be submitted to popular approval (by debate and vote in parliament, and citizens' control).

5. Further indispensable measures

Canceling the external public debts of the periphery, abandoning structural adjustment policies, and other measures proposed above are necessary conditions, but insufficient as such to guarantee the authentic human development of the peoples of the world. Further measures are indispensable, beginning with equality between women and men and the right to self-determination for indigenous peoples.

On a global level, the following must be guaranteed for all: freedom to circulate and freedom to settle; the universal right to employment by a radical reduction of working hours, contrary to the present line of reasoning, which results in the unemployed coexisting alongside overworked and stressed wage earners;[29] the universal right to a citizen's income (Passet 2000; ATTAC 2001a); the discontinuance by the North of the public debt mechanism that engenders austerity policies and the massive transfer of citizens' income to capital holders;[30] the defense of the pension system by distribution, as opposed to the system by capitalization—and the introduction of the distribution pension system where it does not exist (Khalfa in ATTAC 2001b); free education and health; prohibition of GMOs in agriculture, as demanded by Vía Campesina; vast socially useful and environmentally friendly public works programs (for example, building accommodation and urban facilities, renovation of existing accommodations, and railway infrastructure for public transport); literacy campaigns; vaccination campaigns; primary health care of the sort seen in Nicaragua between 1980 and 1983 and in Cuba in the first phase of the revolution, with spectacular results; etc.

Arms expenditure

Particular attention must be brought to the drastic reduction of arms expenditure, which represents about $800 billion per year. The vast majority of arms are produced by G8 countries (see chapter 8). These countries, using export credits, push the periphery countries to buy arms, despite hypocritical speeches to the contrary. The most highly industrialized countries, starting with the United States (about $400 billion), spend outrageous sums on producing tools of destruction and death. A drastic reduction in arms spending and a move toward total disarmament would free up the enormous peace dividends, to be shared to the benefit of all.

Multinational corporations

They must be made to take legal responsibility with regard to both national and international jurisdiction, including in countries where they have subsidiaries. What about the families of the more than 100,000 Bhopal inhabitants who died in atrocious circumstances due to the negligence of the MNC Union Carbide in India in December 1984? The directors of Union Carbide got off scot-free.

However, the wind of change is blowing. In 2002, a group of victims of apartheid brought an action against twenty-one MNCs in a New York court. The MNCs are accused of aiding and abetting a regime responsible for crimes against humanity. Governments must use their power to hold MNCs to respecting international and national treaties and conventions on human rights and protection of the environment. The Bilateral Agreements on Investment

(BAI) should also be done away with; they are simply the MAI (Multilateral Agreement on Investment) in sheep's clothing. They confer exorbitant powers on the MNCs and lead governments to give up their national sovereignty. States should implement their right to nationalize MNC subsidiaries so that their own citizens can dispose of their own natural resources.

Political democracy

The question of political democracy is obviously central. Without the active intervention of citizens at all levels of political decision-making, none of the proposals made here would make much sense.

Global public goods

One of the issues dear to the heart of antiglobalization is global public goods. A variety of terms are used—common goods, human heritage, the common inheritance of humankind—and the field they cover is broadening all the time. Indeed, "The fundamental rights and needs of the human person and ecological necessity are the decisive factors in identifying something as a global public good" (Lille and Verschave 2003). To draw up a complete list of public goods would require a vast democratic consultation, reflecting different histories and cultures.

The notion of "public good" intersects the notion of "right" at many points. The protection of public goods means guaranteeing the universal right and access to water, clean air, energy, food, transport, basic education, and also to knowledge in the wider sense, to development, to equality, freedom, pleasure...in other words, the right to life. All of these rights have been magnificently expressed in the pacts and charters of the United Nations.

Compared to these historical antecedents, the millennium objectives are minimalist. By fighting for public goods, the antiglobalization movement is a spur, urging a return to the founding texts to bring them up to date. Access to public goods for all, now and in the future, and their conservation, for things like water, air, and energy for example, mean that we need proper global ecological legislation, which now barely exists. The right to development would also require economic legislation that would make it possible to argue in court for the criminal nature of usurious indebtedness.

From this it follows, still in the context of rights and law, that justice itself must be considered a public good—criminal justice, and economic and social justice. For justice intersects with all other global public goods. It is both a condition and a component of the most fundamental public goods: equality, liberty, and solidarity.

6. What future for the IMF, the World Bank, and the WTO?

Can the IMF and the World Bank be reformed? There is every reason to doubt it. In my opinion, these institutions should be abolished and replaced by other global institutions.[31] They should be abolished because their property-based constitutions, their allegiance to a very limited number of countries (of which only one, the United States, has the veto on any decision it may wish to block, even if all 183 other members want it to go forward), and the distribution of power within their ranks are incompatible with any truly democratic reform (see chapters 10 and 11).

Other multilateral institutions should be set up in their stead (whether with the same or different names does not matter) based on the democratic principle contained in the UN Charter (one state, one vote), and with the mission of ensuring monetary stability internationally, controlling capital movements, offering low-interest loans not tied to neoliberal monetarist conditionalities, and returning to the countries of the periphery what was stolen from them. Humankind should be endowed with international institutions where every people of the world can really find their place. Institutions where the national delegates could debate questions central to humanity in public (broadcast on television and radio). Institutions where the GDP or the military force of certain countries—or of one country—would have no weight in the decision-making process.

For years now, the possibility of reforming a whole series of international institutions, in particular the WTO, the IMF, the World Bank, and the related regional development banks, has been a subject of open debate. Certain points are not even worth debating: do we need global public institutions in such crucial areas as trade, money, and credit? The answer is affirmative; we will never be able to resolve international problems without permanent, internationally recognized institutions that have democratic legitimacy.

The second point of debate could be the object of a consensus: do we only need institutions of global scope, or would it be a good idea to delegate certain tasks to regional bodies, to avoid too much centralization, with institutions too far removed from the day-to-day reality of peoples around the world? It might be agreed that within the global organizations, regional structures should be given considerable autonomy.

As an example, during the Asian crisis of 1997–98, the US government and the directors of the IMF opposed the creation of an Asian monetary fund, which had it existed, would have permitted a concerted and far more efficacious response to the speculative attacks than a global organization could provide. It is perfectly conceivable that the IMF coexist with regional monetary funds.

Another example: a Latin American and Caribbean monetary fund could give rise to a single currency for the nations of Latin America and the Caribbean. One would hardly expect a global organization to encourage the creation of a regional currency. Of course, if it were possible to get to the point where the whole planet adopted a single currency, that would be real progress, but there are obviously several stages ahead before that point is reached. One is that the periphery countries should band together to equip themselves with a common currency so that they can do without the dollar, the euro, and the yen as much as possible, connecting among themselves and becoming less dependent on the fluctuations of those three hard currencies.

The most burning question of the debate is, Can we concentrate on reforming the institutions (in particular the above-mentioned trio), or should we be taking action to replace them with new ones? Whether the IMF, the World Bank, and the WTO should be reformed or replaced is the object of ongoing debate within the different social movements and networks belonging to the movement for a different type of globalization. There is general agreement both on the need for global institutions for exchange, credit, and trade, and on the rejection of the policies upheld by the IMF, the World Bank, and the WTO.[32] This was what Gus Massiah, president of the CRID (the French Center for Research and Information on Development) and vice president of ATTAC France, explained in his closing speech at the seminar on the future of the international financial institutions held at the National Assembly in Paris on June 22–23, 2001:

> High on today's agenda is the discussion between those who feel that the time has come to demand that [the IFIs] should be dismantled or set aside while new institutions are put in their place, and those who think that their present crisis provides an opportunity to make them advance by imposing structural reforms. It is not a dogmatic or theological issue, but an analysis of the situation and inherent political opportunities. The debate is open, each movement must decide what steps to take regarding common objectives.

Let us continue the debate, while at the same time reinforcing the unity between partisans of radical reform of the institutions and partisans of their replacement.

It would first be helpful to define the kind of institutions that might replace the present ones. We should opt for proposals that radically redefine the basis of the international architecture (missions, modes of operation, etc.). Let us reconsider the case of those specialized global institutions, the WTO, the IMF, and the World Bank. Concerning the World Trade Organization, we share the abolitionist point of view of Walden Bello and Nicola Bullard of the Focus on the Global South network (Bello 2000a), and that of François

Houtart and Samir Amin of the World Forum for Alternatives (2000). Michel Husson (2000) summarizes the arguments as follows:

> The treaty which instituted the WTO is a contract with advantages for only a few, in the imperial style. It cannot serve as a basis for a world economic order favoring development. This is why we are fighting to have the WTO dismantled, and its functions devolved upon other institutions. UNCTAD could provide the framework within which agreements could be made with the aim of true co-development. The function of such an institution would be to guarantee and organize the right of the countries of the South to take the protection measures necessary for their integration into the world market, whereas the entire logic of the WTO is founded on the negation of that right. It would also ensure the transfer of technology, unlike the WTO mainly preoccupied by the protection of property rights and the patenting of anything that can be patented. Finally, instead of giving the WTO the role of judge in questions of labor legislation, the powers and competence of the International Labor Organization should be broadened, by giving it possibilities of recourse. It is within this context that the debate over "social clauses" should be held, and that the NGOs and trade unions should constitute a common front for universal advances in social rights.

In the domain of trade, the new WTO or the organization that replaces it should aim to guarantee the fulfillment of a series of international pacts and treaties, starting with the Universal Declaration of Human Rights and all of the fundamental treaties on human rights (individual and collective) and the environment. Its main function would be to supervise and regulate trade so that it conforms strictly to social (the conventions of the ILO) and environmental norms. This definition is in direct opposition to the WTO's present objectives, which are to impose free trade, commercialize every aspect of human activity and all natural resources, and generalize new rules uniquely and systematically in the interests of the MNCs (and usually of their making). Of course, this necessitates a strict separation of powers. There is no question of allowing the WTO, or any other organization, for that matter, to have its own court. Therefore, the Dispute Settlement Body will have to go.

The World Bank, or whatever stands in for it, would regain its legitimacy if it were largely regionalized and had as its function to make loans at low or zero interest rates and donations, conditional upon express guarantees that they are used only in strict observance of social and environmental norms and, more generally, basic human rights. Unlike today's World Bank, the new one, the one the world needs, would not seek to defend the interests of the creditors and force the borrowers into submission to the market king. This new bank would have as its principal mission to defend the interests of the populations who receive loans and donations.

As for the IMF in its new form, which in some respects would resemble its original mandate, it should guarantee the stability of currencies, fight speculation, control capital movements, and take measures to prohibit tax havens and fiscal fraud. To attain this last objective, it could contribute, along with governments and regional monetary funds, to the pool of different taxes (Tobin-type taxes, Spahn-type taxes, taxes on foreign direct investment...).

All of these avenues require a new, coherent, global architecture, with its own hierarchy and division of powers. The cornerstone should be the United Nations, provided that its General Assembly becomes the true decision-making hub. This implies eradicating the status of permanent member of the Security Council, and the veto that goes with it. The General Assembly could delegate specific missions to ad hoc committees.

The UN could also be reformed, as Gilbert Achcar (2002) proposes, by giving it a double-chamber system along the lines of the US Constitution or that of the USSR in 1923. There would be the Chamber of States, rather like the present General Assembly, and the Chamber of Peoples, elected by direct suffrage with proportional representation of the populations. As a permanent body, alongside the Security Council, which could only act on a General Assembly mandate, there could be an Economic and Social Council like the present ECOSOC, but with real powers issuing from a clear General Assembly mandate. As a useful comparison, the Security Council and the Economic and Social Council should not be given sweeping and undemocratic powers comparable to those of the European Commission. The Security Council and the Economic and Social Council should be subordinate to the UN General Assembly.

Another thing: Today, the UN usually plays the role of an international fire brigade or ambulance. In some cases, it simply serves as an alibi or cover for military aggression waged by the world's most powerful countries, as was the case in the intervention of the United States and its allies in the first Gulf War in 1991, and in Somalia in 1992. Increasingly, it promotes the interests of the most powerful MNCs—as in the case of the Global Compact initiative taken by secretary-general Kofi Annan in 2000. The UN must turn its back on these practices, unworthy of its initial mandate, and become (once more) the champion of a new global economic and social order based on the Universal Declaration of Human Rights and other international pacts and treaties on human rights (individual and collective) and the environment.

We believe that it is necessary and possible to reform the UN for three fundamental reasons: its charter is globally progressive and democratic; the principle underlying its composition is democratic (one state, one vote)—even if it needs to be completed by a system of direct proportional representation, as suggested above; and during part of its past, in the 1960s and 1970s, the General Assembly adopted resolutions and made declarations that were distinctly progressive (and which remain applicable, in principle) and set up several useful institutions (the ILO, UNCTAD, the WHO).

The situation of the World Bank and the IMF is quite different. Their constitutions are antidemocratic, indeed frankly despotic, and the US government's veto makes any significant change impossible in the near future. The World Bank has never hesitated to violate UN resolutions (particularly those of 1964 condemning South Africa and apartheid, and Portugal for maintaining its colonial empire). As for the WTO, even if, in principle, its mode of representation is democratic (one state, one vote), the fairy godmothers that presided over its cradle sent it shooting off into an orbit diametrically opposed to that of the interests of humankind. It has to be prevented from doing any (further) harm as soon as possible.

One other question that has not yet been taken far enough is that of an international legal system, an international judiciary, independent of the other international instances of power, which would complete the present system, mainly composed of the International Court at The Hague and the young International Criminal Court. With the neoliberal offensive of the last twenty years, the laws of commerce have progressively taken over public law. Undemocratic international institutions such as the WTO and the World Bank function with their own legal structures: the Dispute Settlement Body, part of the WTO, and the ICSID (International Center for Settlement of Investment Disputes), which has taken on a disproportionate importance since the multiplication of BAI. The UN Charter is (regularly) violated by permanent members of its Security Council, the United States, and the UK in particular. New places where the rule of law does not apply have been created. Prisoners deprived of all rights are held in Guantánamo by the United States. After impugning the International Court of The Hague, where it was condemned in 1985 for attacking Nicaragua, the United States now refuses to recognize the International Criminal Court.

All of that is extremely worrying and requires urgent initiatives to be taken to complete the international legal system. This means elaborating or adopting international law on matters where there is an absence of, or inadequate, legal definition. One example would be the International Arbitration Tribunal for the debt, proposed by certain movements. The idea is attractive, but the question is, what law would apply there? International trade law? That is, the trade laws of the creditor states? (Almost 80 percent of loan contracts stipulate that the competent legal authority is that of the United States or the UK.) If that were the case, the borrowers would be almost certain to lose. Should there not first (or at least, at the same time) be a redefinition of the law regulating relations between borrowers and lenders? The question contains its own answer.

At the beginning of this chapter, the limits of the proposals were emphasized. The question that we have tried to answer was summarized as follows: How does one move from an economy of indebtedness toward financing sustainable and socially just development? To answer it, we have scanned a broad range of ideas, yet without claiming to lay down a complete coherent set of proposals. Some fundamental issues could not be addressed in the chapter, though they constitute a necessary part of any alternative on both a national and a global scale. Some of these issues will require specific elaboration: how to weave the gender dimension into the proposals, so that they promote real advances toward equality between men and women? Is the proposal to include social clauses central to the quest to improve workers' rights internationally? What about environmental clauses? What strategy should be adopted with regard to multinationals?

Complementary measures are dealt with in other documents prepared by different international networks and movements—such as ATTAC, the CADTM, Vía Campesina, Focus on the Global South, the World Forum for Alternatives, the World March of Women, and Jubilee South—or adopted at large international meetings such as those of Saint-Denis, Paris (June 1999), Bangkok (February 2000), Geneva (June 2000), Dakar (December 2000), and Porto Alegre (the social movements' declaration at the World Social Forum in Porto Alegre in 2001, 2002, and 2003, and in Mumbai in 2004). For a broader alternative view, these documents are well worth consulting.

---

1   This chapter is an entirely reworked and augmented version of a text written in collaboration with Arnaud Zacharie, "Guarantee the Satisfaction of Basic Human Needs for All." It was the CADTM's contribution to the second World Social Forum held in Porto Alegre, in January 2002. The new additions are the sole responsibility of the author.

2   "Sustainable development" is defined as development that "enables fulfillment of present needs without compromising the ability of future generations to fulfill theirs," cited in Passet 2000. The concept of sustainable development is criticized, as it is usually associated with the idea of continued growth. The issues raised by sustainable development are beyond the scope of this work.

3   See *Implementing the 20/20 Initiative: Achieving Universal Access to Basic Social Services*, a joint publication of UNDP, UNESCO, UNFPA, UNICEF, WHO, and the World Bank (1998), available online at www.unicef.org/publications/files/pub_implement2020_en.pdf. The above-mentioned organizations estimate that it would cost an extra $80 billion per year over the $136 billion already spent (1995 dollars) to reach the amount required for basic social services.

4   According to *Forbes* magazine, in 2000, the combined assets of Bill Gates, Larry Ellison, Paul Allen, and Warren Buffett came to $160.6 billion.

5   According to the 2003 edition of the *World Wealth Report*, produced by wealth management consultants Cap Gemini Ernst & Young and the investment bank Merrill Lynch, in 2002, there were about 7.3 million millionaires (in dollars)—i.e., about one-thousandth of the world's population—with about $27.2 trillion between them (not including their main place of residence).

6   See Medecins sans Frontieres (MSF, Doctors without Borders 2002), "Acces aux medicaments et sante publique universelle" (Access to medicines and universal public health), on the Web site of the World Social Forum. They report: "Of the 1,223 new medicines to have been marketed between 1975 and 1997, only thirteen were designed to treat tropical infectious diseases and half of those derived from veterinary research. Only 0.2 percent of the global budget for pharmaceutical research, which fluctuates between $50 billion and $60 billion, is devoted to acute respiratory diseases, tuberculosis, and diarrhea-type diseases, which together account for 18 percent of global mortality." In the same document, MSF explains that the pharmaceutical company Aventis abandoned production of the only efficient drug to treat sleeping sickness in 1994. The reason given was insufficient profits.

7   It is not enough for governments to guarantee basic needs, with the rest depending on private initiative. For example, governments must ensure universal access not only to primary, but also to secondary and higher education.

8   This is up to and including 2003 (at time of writing). It is unlikely that the flows will become positive in 2004–05.

9   See Hugo Ruiz Diaz's concise introduction in "La dette odieuse ou la nullite de la dette" (Odious or invalid debt), his contribution at the Second Seminar on International Law and the Debt organized by the CADTM in Amsterdam in December 2002. Text available on the CADTM web-site http://www.cadtm.org/article.php3?id_article=190.

10 Cuba, 1895–98: In 1895, the poet José Martí, a Jacobite with ideas close to those of socialism, started off an independence war. The whole country was at war. Martí organized the Liberation Army (more than fifty thousand fighters) and founded the Republic in Arms. More than 150,000 people came to live in the rebel-held areas. Spain waged total war in 1896–97, with concentration camps; some 400,000 people died there. However, Spain lost, despite her 250,000 soldiers, and had to grant autonomy in January 1898. The revolutionaries did not accept and continued fighting. The United States declared war on Spain. After a brief campaign, when it got the support of the Cuban revolutionaries, the US Army took over the island. Without recognizing the Cuban republic, the United States signed a pact with Spain whereby Spain renounced all claim to Cuba (Treaty of Paris, December 10, 1898). Cuba, 1898–1902: The United States occupied the island for almost four years and obliged the members of the Constitutive Assembly of 1901 to adopt the Platt Amendment (1902). Cuba had to grant the United States the right to intervene in the island to "preserve Cuban independence" and to have a government that would "protect life, property and intellectual liberty." Washington obtained the Guantánamo base for an indefinite period. The Republic of Cuba was founded on May 20, 1902. Until the revolutionary victory of January 1, 1959, Cuba was under the neocolonial domination of the United States. (See Yannick Bovy and Eric Toussaint, *Cuba: Le pas suspendu de la revolution* [The suspended step of the revolution], Belgium: Cuesmes, 2001: 36–37).

11 In the case of Rwanda, the International Development Committee of the British parliament explicitly evoked the notion of "odious debt" in pleading for its cancellation: "The bulk of Rwanda's external debt was incurred by the genocidal regime.... Some argue that loans were used by the genocidal regime to purchase weapons, and that the current administration, and ultimately the people of Rwanda, should not have to repay these 'odious' debts.... We recommend that the Government urge all bilateral creditors, in particular France, to cancel debt incurred by the previous regime" (cited in Jochnick, Pazmino, and Teran 2000).

12 See Pazmino's contribution at the Second Seminar on International Law and the Debt organized by the CADTM in Amsterdam, in December 2002.

13 In general, the poorer a country of the South, the higher the share of its debt due to the IMF and the World Bank. In the case of many African countries without strategic natural resources, more than 70 percent of their debts are due to the Bretton Woods institutions.

14 *Dolus malus* is a legal term that means "willful misrepresentation."

15 In *Globalization and Its Discontents*, Stiglitz describes a situation that goes back to the time when he was vice president of the World Bank: "A picture can be worth a thousand words, and a single picture snapped in 1998, shown throughout the world, has engraved itself in the minds of millions, particularly those in the former colonies. The IMF's managing director, Michel

Camdessus…, a short, neatly dressed former French Treasury bureaucrat…, is standing with a stern face and crossed arms over the seated and humiliated president of Indonesia. The hapless president was being forced, in effect, to turn over the economic sovereignty of his country to the IMF in return for the aid his country needed. In the end, ironically, much of the money went not to help Indonesia but to bail out the "colonial power's" private sector creditors. (Officially, the "ceremony" was the signing of a letter of agreement, an agreement effectively dictated by the IMF, though it often still keeps up the pretense that the letter of intent comes from the country's government!)"

16 For an analysis of the force majeure argument in the case of debt cancellation, see Hugo Ruiz Diaz's paper: "La dette extérieure: mécanismes juridiques de non paiement, moratoire ou suspension de paiement" (External debt: The legal mechanisms of nonpayment, moratorium, or suspension of payment), presented at the First Seminar on International Law and the Debt, organized by the CADTM in Brussels, in December 2001.

17 ILC, Draft article 31, A/CN, 4/315, *ACDI* 1978, II, vol. 1, p. 58

18 Originally formulated thus: Contractus qui habent tractum successivum et dependetiam de futurum, rebus sic stan, tibus intelligentur.

19 Charles Fenwick, *International Law* (third edition, 1948); similarly, one of the definitive texts on common law explains that "a tacit condition, binding all contracts, is that they cease to be obligatory when substantial changes arise in the state of affairs or conditions upon which they were drawn up" (*Black's Law Dictionary*, sixth edition, 1990, 1267). See also, in international jurisprudence, the sentence pronounced by arbitration on November 11, 1912, in the affair of the state loan between Turkey and Russia: "…the exception of force majeure…may be contested in international law" (Sentence by arbitration, *Recueil des Arbitrages internationaux*, T.II, 1928, 545ff.). Furthermore, the Argentine Civil Code stipulates that the debtor's obligation ceases "when the benefit which constitutes the object of the debt becomes physically or legally impossible, through no fault of the debtor's" (articles 724 and 888).

20 In 2000, the countries of the periphery repaid approximately $343 billion ($240 billion in repayment of the principal and $103 billion of interest), while at the same time receiving fresh loans worth about $248 billion. If they had refused to service the debt and had taken out no fresh loans, they would have economized: $343 billion - $248 billion = $95 billion, i.e., more than the $80 billion needed to begin fulfilling basic human needs (*source*: World Bank 2001).

21 The complete Spanish text of the sentence is available on the CADTM Web site at www.cadtm.org/pages/espanol/olmos.pdf.

22 According to the *Financial Times* (July 16, 2003), the amount recovered by the Philippine government was $658 million, while Marcos is estimated to have accumulated at least $5 billion, even $10 billion. The procedure was complicated by the fact that the Swiss Supreme Court demanded that a Philippine court pronounce judgment on the sum transferred by Switzerland to a Philippine bank account. The late Marcos's entourage was trying to claim the money. In July 2003, the Philippine Supreme Court finally decided, by 12 votes to 0 and one abstention, that Marcos had acquired the money at issue by illegal means and it should therefore be handed over to the Philippine government.

23 *From Resistance to Alternatives*, complete text available on the CADTM Web site. URL of the text in French: http://www.cadtm.org/article.php3?id_article=518

24 On this subject, see the Southern Peoples' Ecological Debt Creditors Alliance of the environmental debt, work by Joan Martinez—University of Barcelona, and Aurora Donoso—Accion Ecologica, Ecuador.

25 Such a proposal is bound to raise howls of protest from neoliberals, in the name of freedom and justice. However, they had no scruples about the high-handed devaluation of the CFA franc in January 1994, and many other devaluations that enable the rich to get richer. The rich only need to have part of their holdings in hard currency for that part of their wealth to increase to a value inversely proportional to the devaluation. The Franc Zone capitalists, knowing that devaluation was in the offing, bought hard currency with "their" CFA francs. Once the CFA franc had been devalued by 50 percent in January 1994, they had only to buy them back with their hard cur-

rency to double their initial outlay. This occurred on a large scale, and none of the leading figures of the IMF or the World Bank were heard to complain.

26 In 2002, French economist Bruno Jetin published a very useful and readable book on the feasibility and finalities of the Tobin Tax. On the question of how much might be raised using a Tobin-type tax (TTT), "One hundred billion dollars would seem a reasonable estimate of the minimum revenue that might be levied by the TTT, without excluding the possibility that it might be three times higher." As to how to use the revenues thus procured, Jetin writes, "In our opinion, all the TTT revenues should be used for international programs of general interest in areas such as health or the environment, on the one hand, and for national development programs in the countries of the South, on the other." (Bruno Jetin, *La taxe Tobin et la Solidarité entre les Nations* [The Tobin Tax and Solidarity between Nations]. Paris: Edition Descartes et Cie, 2002).

27 With reference to the investigations of special reporters, expert working groups, and the UN secretary-general.

28 For example, Venezuela, an OPEC member, has signed agreements with about a dozen Caribbean and Latin American countries, including Cuba, whereby it sells them oil at "friendly" prices, much lower than the price it charges the United States, for which it is one of the main suppliers.

29 "An explicit objective must be that of abolishing unemployment, which is the main mechanism for social discrimination of the worst sort. All the debates about the end of waged labor, and the wonders of free time and a well-rounded lifestyle, are no obstacle to this objective. Indeed, these matters cannot be properly addressed as long as so many are excluded from the terms of the debate. This is why a generalized reduction of working time is pivotal for finding an egalitarian solution to the social crisis" (Husson 1996). Such a project implies workers' control to guarantee the full application of these measures, and the rhythm and organization of work (no overtime allowed, no night shifts where not socially necessary, no piecework).

30 As François Chesnais (1998) observes, "In simple terms, this is precisely the most solid mechanism set up by financial liberalization for the transfer of the wealth of certain social groups and certain countries to others. Any attack on the foundations of finance means dismantling these mechanisms and therefore canceling public debts, not only those of the poorest countries, but also those of any country where the living, breathing social forces refuse to see their government subject its citizens to austerity budgets on the pretext of repaying the public debt."

31 Michel Husson, in a text destined for the editorial committee of ATTAC France, advances a similar point of view: "The IMF and the World Bank have lost all credibility; they are universally denounced, criticized, and opposed. They have been widely discredited, which is why they must be abandoned or dismantled. Walden Bello, of Focus on the Global South, talks of decommissioning them, the term used for nuclear power stations. In other words, the Bretton Woods institutions must be left behind and replaced by new ones, better suited to a new conception of globalization. No one denies the need to dispose of institutions, and there is no question of rallying to the ultraliberal logic of the Meltzer report, which seeks, from a narrow viewpoint, to uphold the logic of the present way of running the IFIs. Neither does this position imply a lack of concern about the institutional terrain. The growing success of our demonstrations makes it all the more relevant and necessary to build there. If indeed there is to be a debate between the "abolitionists," who want to replace the existing financial institutions with new ones, and the "reformists," who propose to transform the present institutions into new ones, then let it go ahead without delaying the process. All are agreed upon the objective, which is to set up more democratic institutions, centered on the interests of the citizens of the world" (June 2001).

32 "We therefore consider that international financial institutions are necessary for long-term action, but we do not trust the orientations and functioning of those in place. What we expect from these institutions is, very specifically, stability of the monetary system, the prevention of financial crises, and a finance system which promotes development respectful of human rights, which we will call, to keep it simple, sustainable development. Moreover, we expect these institutions to function democratically" (Gus Massiah, June 2001).

20
Another world is possible after all!

Those who say that globalization is unavoidable should realize that they can be bypassed or overthrown.

Neoliberal thought nurtures the idea of inevitability. The system that exists must exist because it exists. Globalization in its current form cannot be avoided; everyone must fall into line. This is a recipe for mysticism and fatalism. Any serious study of history reveals that nothing is "irreversible."

Take finance, for example. At the beginning of the twentieth century, the free flow of capital made possible by the gold standard and free trade guaranteed by treaties on trade and investment seemed irreversible. The First World War put an end to that. In the 1920s, the omnipotence of financial markets seemed just as irreversible then as it does now. The 1929 crash and the long crisis that followed forced governments to monitor closely banking and financial activities. At the end of the Second World War, the governments of the main victorious capitalist countries agreed to set up bodies to regulate global finance. The IMF, for example, was established primarily to ensure that this regulation would be carried out (article 4 of its Articles of Agreement is very clear in this respect). Beginning in 1945, a number of Western European governments carried out extensive nationalization, including in the banking sector, in the face of pressure from organized labor.

Neoliberal theoretical "certainties" held forth in recent years are no more valid than those of the conservatives that held power in the 1920s on the eve of the financial meltdown. The economic failure and social disaster created by today's neoliberals might well lead to a round of major political and social changes. Globalization is not a steamroller that crushes everything in its path. Resistance is alive and well in many places. Globalization is a long way from the creation of a coherent and harmonious economic order. There are many contradictions within the Triad—contradictions between imperialist powers, contradictions between companies, social discontent, a crisis of legitimacy of the existing political system and growing criminality in the behavior of the main economic players (Enron, Andersen, Merrill Lynch, Citigroup), and a crisis of legitimacy of the World Bank, the IMF, and the WTO.

Furthermore, there are growing contradictions between the center and the periphery, due to the excluding effect of globalization in its present form. Yet, the countries of the periphery account for 85 percent of total world population. Those who believe that these populations will quietly allow themselves to be marginalized are utterly wrong—as wrong as those governments in the 1940s and 1950s that believed their colonial rule in Africa and large parts of Asia would last forever.

Within the periphery, governments that have chosen a neoliberal path are experiencing a growing crisis of legitimacy inside their respective countries. The ruling classes in these countries are, for the most part, incapable of offering credible prospects for progress to the great majority of their citizens.

Is it unrealistic to expect that the inevitable social discontent will reassert itself through broad-based projects for emancipation? Nowhere is it written that discontent must be expressed in an inward-looking "ethnic" or religious manner. Action by living, breathing social forces can transform even the most seemingly inextricable economic and political situation.

More than ever before, any alternative must take into account a number of different dimensions:

- *The political dimension.* While governments have deliberately cast aside a part of their regulatory functions to allow for the deregulation of capital flows, they can be pressured into reinstating these functions. It is a question of political will; if those in power cannot rise to the task, they either can step aside or be ousted.

- *The dimensions of citizenship and class.* Those "from below" and their organizations—whether from the labor movement born in the nineteenth century (parties, unions), from other grassroots movements, or from new social movements born in the latter half of the twentieth century— must reclaim their right to intervene in society and exercise control over certain aspects of public life, to exert pressure on other political and economic players, and to raise in concrete terms the question of hands-on political power.

- *The economic dimension.* Economic decisions lie at the junction of all the other dimensions. Such decisions should be directed at placing restrictions on capital flows and on those who control them, the holders of capital.[1]

The inviolable nature of the private property of capital holders will also be at the center of forthcoming debates. In defending the common good and universal access to basic services, certain issues will have to be discussed, such as the need to transfer private companies that monopolize the world's resources and prevent the fulfillment of basic human needs to the public domain. Common property must be excluded from both the dominion of such bodies as the WTO and the activities of private enterprise.

The recent evolution of capitalism has given renewed urgency to the debate on new forms of radicalism. Indeed, forms of consensus and compromise inherited from the past have been swept aside by the economic crisis and the neoliberal onslaught.

Although the Fordist social consensus in the North, the developmentalist consensus in the South, and bureaucratic control in the East did not do away with the use of force by those in positions of power—far from it—each of the three paths gave rise to genuine social progress in a number of fields. In fact, compromise was only possible thanks to this social progress. Yet, these compromises have now been split apart by the current logic of capital and the paths chosen by the different governments. In response, a new approach is needed that is antisystemic and seeks to make a clean break with the current order.

This means that those "at the bottom" have to become central players in the fight for change and in the administration of this change once it begins to take place. Equally important, this means that social movements have to remain loyal to the interests of those they represent and remain scrupulously independent of the institutions of political power. This can only be obtained by fostering real forms of internal democracy that give voice to those engaged in the daily grind of politics, allow for choices to be made from a variety of contending approaches, and stimulate the debate on concrete strategies for attaining a movement's objectives.

Concerted action by workers and social movements

The neoliberal offensive is so relentless and wide-ranging that it calls for a concerted response from workers and the oppressed the world over. Such a response is mandatory for eliminating unemployment. Such an objective can only be attained through a generalized reduction of working time, with no loss in wages and with compensatory job creation. The reduction of working hours is required to oppose job dismissals and the transfer of workplaces to other regions and countries. Workers in the South need support from workers in the North if they are to obtain wage increases and the trade-union rights that can pave the way for an overall improvement of their living conditions to levels similar to those that exist in the North.

At present, the labor movement remains the most powerful springboard for direct involvement in political struggles. It is essential, though, that those on the margins of the productive process be closely linked to the labor movement and its activities. All social movements fighting against oppression, whatever form this oppression takes, must also be intimately involved in a concerted effort of resistance.

Pessimism of the intellect, optimism of the will

"Pessimism of the intellect" is essential for taking stock of the scale of the neoliberal offensive and the powerful organization of its proponents. At the same time, it would be wrong to overlook the "optimism of the will" that spurs on whole sections of the global population. Had this determined and courageous resistance not existed in the four corners of the planet, the ideologues and driving forces behind globalization would have gone much further than they have been able to thus far. This is an achievement in itself, although far from sufficient.

Breaking down the walls of isolation

It is no secret that the capitalist class keeps the media, especially television, on a tight leash. It is not in its interest to broadcast images of struggles in which the oppressed demonstrate their creativity and courage. While we may be shown confrontations with the police and army often enough, seldom are we given any insight into the struggle in question, the inventiveness of workers, the resourcefulness of demonstrators, and details of the initiatives that attained their objectives. To do so would give ideas to other movements elsewhere; that element of the "news" represents a danger for the capitalist class. On those rare occasions, however, that the media do honestly relate the intelligence and scale of a movement, there is a tremendous accelerating effect on the mobilization itself.

Struggles have not declined in number; there has even been an overall increase in proportion to the growing number of attacks. Yet, a persistent sense of isolation is one of the most cumbersome problems encountered by movements of resistance. One of the most pressing tasks for progressives is to break down these walls of isolation and work toward a convergence of struggles.

Given the small number of decision makers on a world level and the generalized drop in living conditions that they are imposing around the globe, the struggle of landless peasants in Brazil is at one with the struggle of Volkswagen workers against their multinational company. The struggle by Zapatista indigenous peoples for dignity in the rural areas of Mexico is at one with the strike of

American UPS workers. The struggle of hundreds of thousands of Indian farmers against the WTO is at one with the *sans papiers* (undocumented immigrants) movement in France and Spain. The struggle by South Korean trade unions to defend their social gains is at one with the campaign by grassroots African communities for the cancellation of the debt. The struggle of the population of Honduras against the privatization of the health sector ties in with that of workers in France, Austria, and Brazil, as does the combat against the undermining of earned pension rights and the promotion of private pension funds. The struggle of Algerian women is at one with the people's tribunals in Argentina that denounce the country's illegitimate debt. The struggle of students in Nicaragua, Burkina Faso, Niger, and the United States against increases in tuition is at one with the campaigns of teachers in France and Peru. Citizens in Bolivia (Cochabamba), South Africa (Soweto), and India fight water privatization just as those of Peru (Arequipa) and trade unionists in Senegal (at SENELEC) fight privatization of electricity. The list goes on.

The tremors of rebellion can be felt around the world. Wherever one goes, there are murmurs of discontent; people resent the indignities forced upon them. They aspire toward a better life and are revolted by the injustice and violence of a system portrayed as the be-all and end-all celebration of the "end of history." It is important to realize that in many places around the world, the warlords of neoliberalism have not gone unchallenged.

Present state of struggles against capitalist globalization

The present phase of neoliberal globalization began in the 1970s and 1980s. The electoral victories of Thatcher in Great Britain and Reagan in the United States signaled an all-out offensive of capital against labor and of the main developed capitalist powers against the dependent capitalist countries whose populations were the first victims.

The offensive took the form of attempts to destroy trade unions (the Professional Air Traffic Controllers Organization, PATCO, in the United States under Reagan, and the National Union of Mineworkers, NUM, in Great Britain under Thatcher), massive privatization, raised interest rates, frozen salaries, more taxation of labor and less of capital. There were the start of the debt crisis in the Third World and several countries of the former Soviet Bloc, structural adjustment policies in the countries of the periphery, and wars waged on humanitarian pretexts by military alliances of the industrialized countries against the countries of the periphery. These policies were accompanied by closure of the borders of the industrialized countries; reinforcement of the powers of intervention of multilateral institutions controlled by the industrialized countries, especially the United States (IMF, World Bank, WTO); domination of the UN by these same powers; and reinforcement of the powers of multinational corporations. On the social level, changes have included flexible working hours and weakening of statutes, increased female poverty, attacks on social welfare, extension of GMO plantations, and commercialization of a series of human activities hitherto relatively protected from multinational activities. Such are the main signs of an offensive still running rife.

The global dimension of this offensive and the imposition of the same type of neoliberal policies in all corners of the world give an effect of synchronization resembling that of other historical crossroads over the last two centuries. Previous examples are the revolution in Europe in 1848, the First World War and the victory of fascism leading to the Second World War, the wave of independence in the 1950s and 1960s, and May 1968.

Certainly there are major differences. So far, we have synchronized offensives and the promising beginnings of synchronized resistance and counteroffensives. The growth and expansion of the antiglobalization movement can be seen around the world, with a few exceptions. (China, in particular, remains aloof—but for how much longer?) The different elements of the offensive described above are, perhaps for the first time ever, being experienced simultaneously by the great majority of the populations of the planet. And more than at any other time in the history of capitalism, certain international institutions have come to symbolize the hardships experienced by large sections of the world's population: the IMF, the World Bank, the WTO, the big multinational corporations, the main financial centers, and the G8.

Many forms of resistance to this vast offensive have developed over the last twenty years or more. Some ended in defeat (for example, PATCO in 1982, and the NUM strike in 1984–85); others with victory. In Latin America, from 2000 onward, there have been several successful campaigns against privatization. Emblematic of these is the campaign led by the population of Arequipa in Peru against the privatization of electricity, or the victorious struggle of the Bolivian people of Cochabamba against privatization of water in April 2000 and against exportation of their natural gas in September–October 2003. Since the Battle of Seattle in November 1999, it is generally agreed that the resistance movement against globalization has become international. The victory of the Bolivian people in 2003 has opened a new cycle of struggles to recover public and collective control of natural resources.

If any year were to symbolize the turning point when this internationalization came about, it would be 1994. First of all, in January, the Zapatista rebellion in the Chiapas region found ways of talking about oppression, until then perceived as a localized problem, in a universal language that was heard across the generations. Second, 1994 marked the fiftieth anniversary of the IMF and the World Bank, commemorated in Madrid in September. The huge international protest demonstration this gave rise to was particularly well supported by young people. Third, the Mexican crisis broke out in December, for the first time pulverizing the myth of the neoliberal development model for countries of the periphery.

Before that, there had been significant international mobilization. In 1988, there was an enormous demonstration against the IMF in Berlin; in 1989, another took place in Paris on the occasion of the G7 summit. However, these did not have the same international impact, as the myths of the "definitive victory" of capitalism and the "end of history" were still in full spate.

After 1994, the accumulation of experience and forces led to a counteroffensive. It was an unequal, nonlinear process, fairly marginal, which has nevertheless continued to grow. Several dates stand out as milestones throughout the period from 1994–2000:

- the powerful social movement in France of autumn 1995, which had no direct link with the antiglobalization movement, yet had significant repercussions for that movement within France;
- the "Other Voices of the Planet" countersummit during the G7 summit in June 1996, in Lyon, which led to a demonstration 30,000 strong called by all of the trade unions;
- the intercontinental meeting convened by the Zapatistas in the Chiapas in summer 1996;
- the victorious strike by UPS workers in the United States;
- the Korean workers' strike in winter 1996–97;
- the Indian small-farmers' movement against the WTO in 1996–97;
- the citizens' campaign against the Multilateral Agreement on Investment (MAI), which led to victory in October 1998;
- the mobilization of Jubilee 2000 in May 1998, in Birmingham, and June 1999, in Cologne;
- the European Marches in May 1997, in Amsterdam, and May 1999, in Cologne;
- the Battle of Seattle in November 1999.

Since then, there have been more and more rallies. There were rallies throughout 2000, whenever the international institutions held their meetings: February 2000, in Bangkok; April 2000, in Washington; June 2000, in

Geneva; July 2000, in Okinawa; September 2000, in Melbourne and Prague; October 2000, in Seoul; the World March of Women in October 2000, in Brussels, New York, and Washington; and December 2000, in Nice. There have been international conferences and meetings to seek and define alternatives, such as "Africa: From Resistance to Alternatives," in Dakar, in December 2000, and the World Social Forum, in Porto Alegre, in January 2001. There were mobilizations against the Summit of the Americas in Buenos Aires and Quebec in April 2001, Barcelona in June 2001 (100,000 demonstrators against the World Bank), and Genoa in July 2001 (nearly 300,000 demonstrators protesting against the G8). Every one of these rallies mobilized between several thousand and several hundred thousand demonstrators or strikers. Most of the rallies were directed at globalization-related issues. In every case, there were talks, debates, and workshops organized on the sidelines.

The attacks against New York and Washington on September 11, 2001, and the war subsequently launched by the United States and its allies have profoundly modified the international situation. The economic crisis that began in early 2001 was accompanied by a massive wave of layoffs on a global scale. A new debt crisis broke out in the countries of the periphery. The champions of neoliberal globalization have launched an offensive aimed at putting the movement against neoliberal globalization on its guard, or even paralyzing it. They have failed.

From September 2001, the movement has added to its platform war and the new arms race. Its potential for mobilization has continued to grow. Furthermore, the year 2001 ended with an impressive popular revolt throughout Argentina. The center-left government, which had been enforcing IMF policies, was thrown out after massive street protests.

Huge antiwar protests punctuated 2002: 250,000 people in Barcelona on March 16; 60,000 in Washington on April 16; 250,000 in London on September 26; nearly a million in Florence on November 9, 2002. Resistance to privatization grew in different places around the world. Peru won the battle against privatization of electricity in Arequipa, and there were campaigns in Mexico and France. In 2002, there were also mass demonstrations in Venezuela that managed to prevent the overthrow of the president, Hugo Chávez. Then there were the electoral victories of Luiz Inácio "Lula" da Silva in Brazil and Lucio Gutierrez in Ecuador.

At the third World Social Forum, held in Porto Alegre in January 2003, about 100,000 participants from around the globe gathered to discuss alternatives. There were also international demonstrations against the war in Iraq on February 15, 2003 (more than twelve million), and March 22, 2003 (several million strong), as well as against the G8 in Geneva-Evian (100,000). In May and June 2003, there was also massive social mobilization against neoliberal plans for pension reform (France, Austria, Brazil). The meeting in the Larzac region of Southern France in mid-August 2003 was a roaring success, with more than 200,000 participants over three days, when 50,000–80,000 were expected. Issues dealt with in Larzac were opposition to the Doha agenda that had been relegated to the interministerial summit in Cancún (Mexico) of mid-September 2003; support for the campaign of civil disobedience in protest against GMO experimentation; solidarity with Palestine; and convergence between the various French campaigns (such as the defense of the distributive pension scheme and the struggles waged by schoolteachers and casual workers in the entertainment industry).

From the defeat of the MAI (1998) to that of Cancún (2003) via Seattle, Genoa, Doha, Buenos Aires, and Baghdad

Elements of crisis within the instruments of domination

▶ **1.** The IMF, the World Bank, and the WTO are key instruments in the offensive of capital against labor and of the countries of the center against those of the periphery. Since 1998, these institutions have been undergoing a profound crisis of legitimacy. The economic, social, and environmental disasters caused by policies imposed on periphery countries by the IMF and the World Bank have obviously cost these institutions their credibility on a massive scale within the countries concerned. Trade regulation policies conducted by the multinational corporations and attacks on state sovereignty have also made public opinion in both the center and the periphery wary of the WTO. The structural adjustment policies dictated by the IMF and the World Bank are detested by the vast majority of countries where they are enforced.

▶ **2.** This crisis of legitimacy is heightened by debates and battles within the US administration. The crisis of the IMF and the World Bank is exacerbated by the fact that there is no consensus position within the one government with undisputed ascendancy. The Republican-dominated Congress has refused to pay the US share for certain IMF initiatives (in 1997–98). The bipartisan Meltzer commission of the US Congress proposed a drastically reduced role for the IMF and the World Bank (February 2000); in March and April 2003, the US Treasury scuttled the mechanism for restructuring sovereign state debt that had been proposed by Anne Krueger, first deputy managing director of the IMF.

▶ **3.** The third level of the crisis is the internal crisis of the IMF and the World Bank (especially the latter). This was evident from, among other things, the thunderous departure, in November 1999, of Joseph Stiglitz, chief economist and senior vice president of the World Bank, and, in June 2000, by the shattering resignation of Ravi Kanbur, director of the World Bank's annual *World Development Report*. In 1998–99, the bitter struggle between Michel Camdessus and Stanley Fischer, numbers one and two in the IMF, ended with Camdessus resigning before the end of his mandate and the precipitate departure in 2003 of the director of the research department, the highly neoliberal Kenneth Rogoff.

▶ **4.** Further elements of crisis lie in the conflicts between the major powers: the trade wars between the Triad countries (bananas, beef with hormones, subsidies on agricultural and industrial products, GMOs, etc.); the struggles for influence (e.g., the war of succession over the replacement of Michel Camdessus in February–March 2000); and the disagreements that arose over the war on Iraq. All of these divergences undermine the industrialized countries' capacity to impose their strategy in each set of circumstances. France's withdrawal from the MAI negotiations, putting the whole project on hold, is a good illustration. French prime minister Lionel Jospin announced that France was withdrawing, not only because of the citizens' campaign, but also because of the trade wars between France, the United States, and other rogues. Conflicts between powers were ratcheted up a notch in 2002–03. In terms of competition in trade and industry, there was a rise in protectionism; in terms of international politics, the war on Iraq opened new rifts. To a lesser degree, events in the Middle East concerning the Palestinian people's liberation struggle continued to be a source of disagreement. All attempts to "cobble together" agreements came up against major obstacles.

▶ **5.** Then there are the conflicts between the Triad and the countries of the periphery. The failure of the Millennium Round of trade talks in Seattle in 1999 was the result of a combination of the different elements of the crises mentioned above. The legitimacy crisis is giving rise to powerful mass mobilization, contradictions within the Triad, and the discontent of the countries of the periphery regarding the pretensions of the major industrial powers. Starting with the war in Afghanistan (2001), then the war on Iraq (2003), there were particularly strong disagreements between the United States and its allies, on the one hand, and the United States and many of the countries of the periphery, on the other. This was particularly evident with the Arab world and, subsequently, with the Muslim world as a whole. However, these are not the only disgruntled countries. Brazil, China, Mexico, India, South Africa, and Russia have all expressed more or less vehemently their opposition to the war on Iraq.

The failure of the interministerial WTO summit in Cancún (Mexico) in September 2003 was due to the combined action of several periphery countries, led by Brazil, India, and China. The Bush administration, already entangled in the hornets' nest of Iraq, faced with a continuing economic crisis on the domestic front, and losing ground in the polls for the presidential elections in 2004, did not want to make the concessions demanded by certain major countries of the periphery, such as Brazil. The administration preferred to maintain a highly protectionist stance to win (back) its electorate.

▶ **6.** The war against Iraq and the Palestinian crisis undermine the credibility of the United States. The occupying forces in Iraq have proved unable to guarantee the security of their troops and to fully relaunch the oil industry. The revelations concerning the lies of the Bush administration, Tony Blair, and the Australian government about the presence of weapons of mass destruction in Iraq have shaken public opinion. There is a chronic inability (or lack of will) to oblige the Israeli government to make concessions regarding the Palestinians' struggle. All of these factors have led to a vast political awakening and have brought about the legitimacy crisis of the US world leadership.

▶ **7.** There is growing disenchantment in the face of the lack of legitimacy of US world leadership. The behavior of the US government during the 1990s and early 2000s is making it increasingly unpopular: military aggression; the sabotage of the International Criminal Court; the contempt displayed toward the UN and UN organizations such as UNESCO; the rejection of the Kyoto agreements on the grounds that the North Americans have the right to maintain their present extravagant lifestyle; protectionism for the rich; blatant recourse to lies to justify military operations; restriction of human rights (650 prisoners have been detained at Guantánamo without respect for their rights); the abuse of the presidency, whether under Clinton or either of the Bushes; blackmail of small countries by a major power; vote buying from other countries within the WTO, the UN, and the Bretton Woods institutions; retention of the death penalty, etc. Ever fewer citizens around the world (including in the United States) are convinced by the pretexts of the war on terror and the "axis of evil" campaign where Good declares war on Evil. Polls show a sharp fall in popularity for the United States in a large number of countries, starting with the Arab world, of course, and the rest of the Muslim countries.

▶ **8.** The World Bank and the IMF, although wielding such power when it comes to imposing structural adjustment policies on periphery countries or making them repay their debts, are helpless when it comes to preventing crises. They failed to prevent or even predict those of 1997 in Southeast Asia, 1998 in Russia, 1999 in Brazil, 2000–02 in Argentina and Turkey, and 2002–03 in Brazil. What of their inability to prevent an international stock exchange crash...or to relaunch the ailing world economy of 2001–03? Some governments that have so far toed the line are beginning to show signs of resistance to the edicts of the Bretton Woods institutions. In 2003, Argentine president Néstor Kirchner refused to meet all of the IMF's demands, and Thailand and Indonesia decided not to extend their agreements with the IMF.

▶ **9.** A multiplicity of scandals from Enron's bankruptcy to the Russian oligarchs; the patent failure of neoliberalism revealed by the Argentine crisis; the absence of any serious measures to cope with the AIDS pandemic mainly in Africa; increased restriction of democratic rights and freedom since September 11, 2001; the UN alternately ignored or instrumentalized by the major powers; moral duplicity and "one law for the rich, another for the poor"—all add an ethical and democratic dimension to the crisis of the neoliberal model in the minds of increasing numbers of people around the world, especially young people.

▶ **10.** Multinational corporations are also affected by a crisis in confidence. The frenzied pursuit of profit with no concern for human rights or the environment, widespread evidence of corruption and the extraordinary sums of money granted to company directors, systematic recourse to tax evasion and fraud, stock exchange–driven redundancies—all of these have generated a growing spirit of defiance toward multinationals and serious doubts about globalization as it is conducted by them.

One characteristic of the situation opened up by the failure of the MAI is the way that the citizens' movement has appeared on the scene at all of the negotiations of the major institutions and the major powers. Over the last few years, every single meeting of the powermongers of the world has been attended by mass demonstrations, and the more recent ones have been disrupted, even paralyzed, by the demonstrators. The neoliberal offensive has only managed to carry on in fits and starts, with delays in the implementation of its new plans, to the consternation of the system's defenders.

The crisis of legitimacy of the G8, the IMF, the World Bank, and the WTO has reached the point where they no longer dare to meet with trumpets blaring. They call much smaller meetings in the most inaccessible places for protest. The WTO met in Doha, Qatar, in November 2001; the G8 of 2002 was held in a remote village in the Canadian Rockies; that of 2003 in Evian, a small town of 15,000 inhabitants sandwiched between a lake on one side and mountains on the other; and that of 2004 was held in Sea Island, Georgia. The 2003 interministerial meeting of the WTO was held in Cancún, another seaside resort, cut off from the rest of Mexico on the Yucatan Peninsula. The World Bank had to cancel the meeting it was planning in Barcelona in June 2001, which did not prevent 100,000 young Catalans from demonstrating against its policies. Gone are the good old days for the World Bank and IMF, when the two institutions met every three years with great pomp in a prestigious capital, with up to 15,000 international guests. There was Berlin in 1988; Bangkok, 1991; Madrid, 1994; Hong Kong, 1997; and Prague, 2000. In September 2003, they had to meet in Dubai (in the United Arab Emirates), out of reach of mass protests, showing how vulnerable they now feel. The antiglobalization movement deserves to savor this victory, however partial.

The self-styled leaders of the world have no intention of giving in to the ever more numerous protests. They now have a combination of two tactics to try to stifle the movement. One is to discourage it by increasingly vigorous repression and a mudslinging campaign aimed at sullying the image of the protesters. This includes querying how representative they are and their ability to come up with alternatives, and depicting the whole movement as criminal by deliberately presenting small violent groups as typical of the great majority. The other tactic is to attempt to co-opt part of the movement, especially NGOs, by appealing to a sort of spirit of collaboration.

As Napoleon Bonaparte, the dictator, used to say, "You can do anything with bayonets except sit on them." Antonio Gramsci said the same thing in a less trivial manner; speaking of hegemony, he saw the need for a consensus to ensure the stability of the system. The crisis of legitimacy and the lack of a consensus encourage the search for alternative solutions and lead to ever-greater mobilization. Repeated use of police violence with its inevitable victims (including the ones that get shot) can only further reduce the legitimacy of the institutions that claim to be running neoliberal globalization.

As far as the protest movement is concerned, several positive factors can be identified at present:

▶ *First,* the birth of the of the World Social Forum (WSF), which took place for the first time in 2001, in Porto Alegre (Brazil), and the growing success of this annual event (12,000 participants in 2001; 30,000 in 2002; and 100,000 in 2003). The idea has been extended to a continental level, with the Asian Social Forum, the European Social Forum, the African Social Forum, soon to be followed by the North American Social Forum. The idea of the Social Forum has also taken root on a local level in a large number of countries. The WSF was launched as a result of the convergence of different initiatives, some from the North and some from the South. It has an International Council. The WSF has succeeded in appearing as a legitimate alternative to the World Economic Forum in Davos, where the bosses of the multinational corporations, world rulers, and the directors of the WTO, the IMF, and the World Bank all meet up.

▶ *Second,* the convergence of social movements and other types of organization, such as Vía Campesina, ATTAC, the World March of Women, various trade unions, think tanks such as the World Forum for Alternatives, International Forum on Globalization, Focus on the Global South, movements against the debt such as Jubilee South and the CADTM, educational movements, and a variety of NGOs. A glimpse of the calendar of activities and shared objectives resulting from this convergence can be found in the declaration of the Assembly of Social Movements at the World Social Forum of Porto Alegre in January 2001 (see box 20.1), followed by other declarations made at the later WSFs, and the Asian and European Social Forums. A provisional international secretariat has been set up by the Landless Rural Workers' Movement in Brazil.

▶ *Third,* the establishment of worldwide networks in line with the movement, even if there is some imbalance (more people involved in Western Europe, the Americas, and Asia; fewer in Africa and Eastern Europe; none in China).

▶ *Fourth,* the beginning of a cycle of radicalization of a significant number of young people, with the same imbalance across the planet. The regions where this is most in evidence are North America, Southern Europe, Great Britain, and Scandinavia. The phenomenon is clearly spreading. Youth movements are active in Algeria (especially the province of Kabylia), in South Korea, Peru, Mexico, and numerous countries in sub-Saharan Africa.

▶ *Fifth,* the birth of a strong international antiwar movement in 2001, during the war in Afghanistan. This movement has been reinforced in the course of 2003.

In the future, it is important to maintain the movement's plurality, its independence with regard to governments in power, and its ability to develop convergence between different campaigns, such as the ones against the WTO or for the cancellation of the debt. The antiwar movement needs be kept alive and new vigor breathed into international solidarity with populations struggling for their liberation (especially the Palestinian people).

A tale of subversion grounded in day-to-day life

This broad antiglobalization movement, created in response to defining moments in recent times, is also grounded in real everyday life. Those involved have met and discussed their experiences, visited one another. This has fostered a wonderfully human culture of subversion. Our values are defined in pluralistic terms, for happily the oppressed do not speak with one voice. This is why it is essential to bring out "the planet's other voices." Yet, our ideas are not those of the oppressors; our pluralism does not brook submission to the dictates of those who seek immediate profit and gain. Why on earth should we submit to their dictates?

Resistance is also boosted by struggles on a national level. Blows must be

Summary of the points of agreement between social movements at the World Social Forum in Porto Alegre, January 2001

- The need for a democratic and internationalist alternative to neoliberal capitalist globalization;

- the supremacy of human rights, social rights, and the rights of the environment over the demands of capital;

- the need to bring about equality between women and men;

- the need to expose the deepening crisis of legitimacy of the World Bank, the IMF, the WTO, the Davos Forum, the G8, and the big multinationals;

- the demand for unconditional cancellation of the Third World debt and the abandonment of structural adjustment policies;

- the demand for a halt to trade deregulation and rejection of the present definition of trade-related intellectual property rights;

- the demand for protection of natural resources and public property by preventing their privatization;

- the demand for a ban on the use of genetically modified plants and patents on life;

- the obstruction of arms trade and militarist policies (such as the US Plan Colombia);

- the assertion of the right of populations to endogenous development;

- the need to find sources of funding based on the taxation of capital (beginning with a Tobin-type tax), which entails the abolition of tax havens;

- the assertion of the rights of indigenous peoples;

- the need for agrarian reform and a generalized reduction of working hours;

- the need for a common struggle linking North and South, East and West;

- the promotion of democratic experiments such as the participatory budget of Porto Alegre.

dealt to one's own capitalist class in order to weaken the whole. The French strikes of late 1995 sparked a political sea change whose first upshot, however inadequate, was the defeat of the Right in the 1997 parliamentary elections.

The organized labor movement is struggling for the generalized reduction of working hours and for the protection of hard-won social welfare programs in industrialized countries and in those countries of the periphery (in the South and East) where such programs were fought for and won.

Instead of going clandestine, the *sans papiers* in France, Spain, and Belgium have come out openly to demand that the government legalize their situation with the proper documents.

Globalization has had the positive side effect of forcing organizations genuinely committed to defending the interests of the oppressed to link up with other like-minded organizations. Indeed, how can anyone hope to defend effectively the right to asylum without an overall view of the situation in the Third World? Or, in the current situation, how can workers resist the temptation to back "their" employer to save a job in "their" workplace, to the detriment of workers in neighboring countries? How can an NGO ensure that it remains independent short of linking up with others in its own country to promote the same demands for social justice that it raises in faraway lands? How can any progress be made in the fight against exclusion and unemployment without an ongoing dialogue with the trade-union movement?

One often hears the complaint that it is increasingly difficult to determine exactly who is "in charge." The target is no longer the local boss, but rather the board of directors of a multinational company. It is useless to take on national governments, since the European Union Council of Ministers or the G8 calls the shots. To be sure, it is necessary to adapt strategy to the changing landscape. However, the new forces that can be harnessed to overcome what is said to be insurmountable are potentially many times more powerful than before. The key thing is to be aware of the current situation and to spare no effort in seeking to harness this potential. It is important to stress that the need for determined political will does not imply the stifling of internal debate within movements. On the contrary, the wealth of social movements is rooted in their diversity and pluralism. These inner strengths must be fully protected by ensuring the fullest democracy in relations between the various component parts of social movements.

Obstacles and new forms of organization

The world over, the labor movement is experiencing a crisis of representation. The trade-union movement and left-wing parties are no longer seen as the legitimate representatives of their theoretically natural constituents. The trade-union movement is increasingly unable to defend the interests of workers and their families. Nor has its approach to the problems at hand succeeded at drawing in the other social movements.

NGOs, of which a significant number radicalized during the 1970s, are also clearly in crisis. Many of them have fallen into line with their national governments or with the international organizations (World Bank, UN, UNDP).

This crisis of representation has created deep-seated skepticism about projects for radical change. Socialism, to take the most clear-cut example, has been hugely discredited by the bureaucratic experience in the so-called socialist camp in the East and by the capitulation of Western socialists to the capitalist classes of their own countries.

Nevertheless, social struggle continues and in some cases has grown more radical. New forms of organization and consciousness appear fleetingly, thus far unable to give rise to a new and coherent program. Let us not, however, make the mistake of underestimating their radicalism.

Doubtless, social movements have chalked up a long list of failures in recent years, but the history of struggles for emancipation is not a matter of adding and subtracting victories and defeats.

Can the crises of all of the various social movements give way to a new upward cycle of positive experiences and rising consciousness? The events of recent years provide cause for cautious optimism. The case for standing on the sidelines is less convincing than ever.

A tiny minority of decision makers spare no effort to strip the human individual of his or her fundamental rights; to reduce human beings to the status of one "resource" among others; to replace the idea of society by that of the market; to reduce the creativity and wealth of labor to one commodity among many; to destroy social awareness and leave individualism in its stead; to empty politics of all meaning except that of giving capital and its thirst for immediate profits control over all key decisions; and to smother culture in the quest for a "normal" way of life.

The time is ripe for the millions of people and tens of thousands of organizations in the struggle to learn to live together through recognition of the complementarity and interdependence of their projects, to organize and promote the globalization of forces for the (re)building of our common future, and to broadcast far and wide a worldview rooted in solidarity.

The time is ripe.

---

1   François Chesnais (1994) rightly claimed: "It is difficult to see how mankind can avoid taking measures to expropriate capital. Their precise form will have to be worked out in the light of the experience of the last century. Of course, it is possible that we are once again underestimating the flexibility of the dominant mode and the capability of those

who rule it. Perhaps we will be proved wrong by events, but we doubt, to take some obvious examples, whether the G7 states will manage to regain control of the finance markets by regulating them, whether they will pronounce the cancellation of the Third World and Forth World debts, or whether companies in the great majority of OECD countries will be persuaded by straightforward intellectual arguments to adopt the 30- or 35-hour week. So, this book aims to contribute to discussions among the working classes and those who identify with them."

An example of convergence: The Belgian-based Committee for the Abolition of the Third World Debt

Impressed by the initiative taken by French activists to counter the 1989 G7 summit, a number of people called on the French writer Gilles Perrault—one of the spokespeople of the "Enough is Enough" movement—to explain the Bastille Appeal (see below) and the French campaign for the immediate and unconditional cancellation of the Third World debt. At the time, Belgian activists were very much in the doldrums. Solidarity committees were stagnating and trade-union mobilization floundering, subsequent to a number of partial defeats in various sectors. In such a climate, the February 1990 conference with Perrault was an undeniable success. It provided an occasion to take stock of wide-ranging enthusiasm for work around the debt issue, however removed this may have seemed at first glance from the daily concerns of those present.

The Belgian-based Committee for the Abolition of the Third World Debt (known by its French acronym "CADTM") has been pluralist from the start, not only in political outlook (socialist, Christian, ecological, revolutionary), but also in its composition (individuals, trade-union sections, NGOs, political parties, various associations). This is definitely one of the reasons for the CADTM's dynamism and success.

The CADTM's pluralist character has been the keystone for setting up a unitary framework for every initiative, whether for contacting and cooperating with other associations, drawing up statements and petitions, putting together publications and dossiers, or organizing public events.

From the beginning, discussion and debate around the debt issue has gone hand in hand with public activities aimed at jump-starting "mobilization." CADTM participants never viewed the organization as a mere think tank or study circle. Other groups of this sort already exist, and the CADTM cooperates with them on an ongoing basis. Since 1990, CADTM campaigns have attracted an increasingly wider spectrum of people. The names of past CADTM campaigns speak for themselves: "The Third World Debt Time Bomb" (1990); "Third World Debt in a

Time of Cholera" (1991); "While 40,000 Children Die Each Day, Every Minute Counts" (1992–93); "Third World Debt: Necessary Solidarity Among Peoples" (1994–97); "From North to South, Up to Our Ears in Debt" (1997–98); "Resources for Alternatives in Favor of Citizens and Development" (1999–2000); and the current campaign, "Abolish the Debt to Free the Development" (2000–04).

The CADTM also functions as an editorial collective. It has helped to draw up a number of platforms and declarations. Some examples of key events where the CADTM was able to help enrich analytical efforts carried out in various places around the world are Madrid, 1994; Copenhagen, 1995; Brussels, 1995; Chiapas, 1996; Manila, 1996; Mauritius and Caracas, 1997; Saint-Denis, 1999; Bangkok, Geneva, and Dakar, 2000; Porto Alegre, 2001, 2002, and 2003; and Geneva, 2003. These democratic and organizational enterprises are vital for overcoming a sense of isolation and for working together on a given project with others.

The association has always taken pride in its international and internationalist identity. There is nothing surprising about being "international" when dealing with such issues. Beyond this, however, the CADTM has always seen itself as part of a broader anti-imperialist movement, as a partisan of a renewed form of internationalism. Internationalism has taken some hard blows in recent times, yet it is more urgent than ever before to set it back on its feet.

While the CADTM has been building itself patiently in Belgium, it has, at the same time, directly linked with movements in other countries, such as ATTAC (France) and Jubilee South, which were forming in 1998–99. Whenever possible, the CADTM has invited activists from other parts of the world to its events; the CADTM has accepted invitations elsewhere from those who have traveled to Belgium. Over time, it has gradually become an international network with individual members and local committees in several countries in Europe, Africa, Latin America, and Asia. The CADTM has opened up to countries of the former Soviet Bloc, which are also directly confronted with the debt issue and structural adjustment, and where quite a few movements are looking for original alternatives.

This kind of exchange has actually boosted serious grassroots activity on the home front. The CADTM has always been at the ready to respond to calls for action, whether from a university professor, a local parish, a

Continued, next page ▶

▶ *Continued from previous page*

mosque, a group of unemployed workers, or a long-established solidarity committee. The CADTM always focuses its attention on the need to develop awareness, understanding of the issues at hand, and mobilization.

Starting in 1997–98, a vast international campaign grew up on the theme of Jubilee 2000. A great many demonstrations took place. In Birmingham, England, in May 1998, during the G8 summit, 70,000 people formed a human chain; in Cologne, in June 1999, for another G8 summit, 35,000 people brought 17 million signatures for the cancellation of the debt of the poor countries. A coordination of movements in the South fighting for debt cancellation was set up in 1999, called Jubilee South, in which members of the CADTM in the South took part. The campaign for the cancellation of the debt gradually became more of a mass movement. This was seen in Spain after the *consulta* carried out in March 2000 by RCADE (the Spanish acronym for the Citizens' Network for the Abolition of the External Debt), with more than a million participants, and in Brazil with the September 2000 referendum carried out by the social movements, with six million votes. Continental and worldwide initiatives have been "Africa: From Resistance to Alternatives," and "The First North-South Consultation." The ball is rolling.

Through its work analyzing the mechanisms of the Third World debt, based on an ongoing study of the different players and the policies they pursue, the CADTM has had to broaden the scope of its work. Talking about frontal attacks against the education and health-care systems, about privatization, about unemployment, and so on, in the Third World might ring hollow if we are not also able to point to the results of similar policies implemented at home, and if we are unable to fight these policies with the same determination, even if their results are not (yet) as destructive as in other parts of the world.

The CADTM also intervenes in the struggle now being waged on the terrain of justice and law. The possibility of criminal proceedings against the IMF and the World Bank for aiding and abetting dictatorial regimes and imposing policies that infringe human rights is being investigated. In addition, the CADTM has opened another area of intervention through its commitment to referendum-style consultations, such as the *consulta*, and to preparing citizens' audits on the debt. Furthermore, it has included the environmental debt among the issues it covers.

In order to explain the need for a tax on speculative investment on a world level, for example, we have to raise the question of taxing wealthy estates in our own countries.

Last, but not least, anyone intelligent enough to recognize the injustice of the Third World debt also has the moral duty to condemn the public debt in industrialized countries. Indeed, this public debt is responsible for a similar transfer of wealth from workers and small producers to the capitalist class.

The CADTM does not seek to take the place of other initiatives. It supports movements such as ATTAC, Vía Campesina, the World March of Women, Jubilee South, the *sans papiers* movements (and the collectives that support them or combat exclusion policies and closed borders), the European Marches, the World Forum for Alternatives, etc. It is always prepared to participate in coalitions formed in response to key events or developments. It was in this spirit, for example, that the CADTM got involved in the European Marches on Amsterdam in June 1997.

Certainly, the CADTM's activities fall far short of the current challenge. However, the CADTM has provided proof, however modest, that it is indeed possible to build an international movement that is able to analyze the major global changes currently under way, while at the same time acting in response to new problems.

For further information or contacts, visit the CADTM Web site (in three languages: French, English, and Spanish) at www.cadtm.org.

The Bastille Appeal for Cancellation of the Third World Debt

On the eve of the twenty-first century, happiness is still a new idea.

We live in a world where all the conditions for happiness are present, but where the highest growth rate is that of poverty.

A world where hunger kills tens of thousands of children every day, leads to riots on three continents, and kills hope.

A world that mutilates the existence of women, always the first victims when the simple struggle to survive aggravates traditional forms of oppression.

Who is responsible for these tragedies? An economic imperialism that bleeds the Third World dry and crushes it beneath the weight of the debt. It may have its internal rivalries, but when it comes to ensuring

Continued, next page ▶

▶*Continued from previous page*

domination, it is perfectly at one. Only solidarity among the peoples can break its power.

Solidarity does not mean support of regimes that perpetuate the poverty of their countries, stifling the voices and the rights of the population.

After the demonstrations of July 1989 in Paris during the G7 summit and against the debt, we appeal for the union of all the progressive forces in the world.

Cancellation of the debt will not solve all the problems, but is an indispensable prerequisite to any far-reaching solution. To refuse would be to refuse assistance to peoples in danger.

Together, we can and we must revive hope, and do what is needed to make justice and equality our common destiny.

The World Bank, the IMF, and the Third World

A political and environmental chronology from 1944 to the present day.

1944

United States. The World Bank and the International Monetary Fund are founded at Bretton Woods, in the presence of delegations from forty-four countries.

1947

Indonesia. The Netherlands receives loans from the World Bank, while simultaneously putting down the Indonesian independence struggle with 100,000 troops.

1956

Washington DC. The World Bank creates the International Finance Corporation (IFC), which uses government funds for joint investments with private companies.

1960

Washington DC. The International Development Association is created as part of the World Bank Group to obtain low-interest loans for the poorest countries—against the objections of Third World governments that want a separate institution for this purpose.

1964

Thailand. The World Bank finances the Bhumibol hydroelectric dam, whose construction leads to the forced displacement of more than three thousand people. These people have yet to receive appropriate compensation.

Brazil. Though it had refused to provide loans to the democratically elected Goulart government, the World Bank now offers significant financing in the wake of a military coup. These loans grow by leaps and bounds until the mid-1970s, by which time they total some $500 million per year.

1965

The World Bank launches the "Green Revolution." Following its request for limited food aid to deal with a drought, India is obliged to overhaul its agricultural policy, devalue its currency, and implement a series of measures that include the use of ecologically unsustainable agricultural techniques, mandatory export of farm products, and the importation of pesticides and chemical fertilizers. Only after it implements these measures does India receive the requested aid, which it needs for only one season. The major transformation of agriculture that results from the Green Revolution has continuing negative effects (Shiva 1993).

South Africa. The Apartheid regime receives loans from the World Bank, in spite of UN resolutions against such aid. The World Bank persists after an open reprimand from UN secretary-general U Thant.

1968

Indonesia. The World Bank begins loans to the Suharto military regime, which came to power through a bloody coup d'état in 1965 that overthrew the civilian government and killed more than 500,000 people.

1969

Indonesia. The World Bank provides financing for the Transmigration Program. The program uses more than $500 million to shift millions of people to remote and sparsely populated islands. The program has a devastating effect on the country's forests. It profoundly negatively affects the lifestyle of numerous indigenous communities and causes serious environmental damage.

1970

Washington DC. For the first time, the World Bank takes in more money in debt payments than it gives out in new loans.

1973

Chile. The Pinochet dictatorship receives substantial backing from the World Bank in the wake of the overthrow of the Allende government, which had been unable to obtain World Bank funding.

1974

Washington DC. Under pressure from the US Congress, the World Bank sets up the Operations Evaluation Department (OED) to analyze the performance of past projects. On several occasions, the first head of the OED threatens to resign in protest against interference from World Bank executives in the independent evaluation of projects.

1976

Pakistan. The World Bank finances the building of the Tarbela Dam, which leads to the forced removal of 300,000 people, who become homeless.

1978

India. The World Bank provides $451 million in financing for the Upper Krishna dam, which involves the forced removal of nearly 220,000 people in one of the country's poorest regions. According to some estimates, the first 100,000 displaced people see their earnings drop by 50 percent.

1979

Turkey. The World Bank makes its first loan within the framework of a structural adjustment program (SAP).

Argentina. The World Bank makes the first of three loans, totaling more than $1 billion, for the building of the Yacyreta hydroelectric dam on the Parana River between Argentina and Paraguay. Both countries are controlled by dictatorships at the time of the first loan, which is spent before building even begins. Construction lasts more than fifteen years; more than 50,000 people are forcibly removed. Corruption is so extensive that President Menem called Yacyreta "a monument to corruption."

Philippines. The World Bank discreetly withdraws from a project to build four hydroelectric dams on the Chico River, which would have involved the forced removal of 100,000 members of the Bontoc and Kalinga tribes. Ambushes of surveying teams and mass protests and civil disobedience by the local population—including lying down in front of bulldozers—lead Prime Minister Virata to declare in 1981: "One of the four planned dams...will not be built because the people are opposed to it." The experience leads the World Bank to carry out an internal review of policy on minorities threatened by development.

Nicaragua. The World Bank suspends all loans to Nicaragua in the wake of the overthrow of the Somoza dictatorship, in place for nearly fifty years. The World Bank only resumes loans to Nicaragua in 1992, two years after the electoral defeat of the Sandinistas.

1980

Washington DC. The World Bank establishes its first set of policies on forced relocation. It requires borrower countries to provide relocation programs that ensure adequate compensation for displaced people.

1981

Brazil. World Bank loans for the Polonoreste project in the Amazon finance the building of inland roads, which pave the way to massive deforestation and the extinction of indigenous communities.

Brazil. The IFC invests $8 million in COBRAPE, a company in which it is a shareholder, for a rice-field irrigation project. From 1984, more than one hundred families of small farmers resist legal and physical attempts to remove them from their land. In 1987, they persuade a state prosecutor to lodge a complaint against COBRAPE for sending men to assault the farmers, destroy fields and property, and force the farmers to sign away their property rights. In 1986, the NGO Commissão Pastoral da Terra draws the IFC's attention to human-rights violations. Yet, the IFC never contacts the prosecutor or the affected parties. In 1992, the IFC discreetly withdraws from the project, after making investments totaling $4 million.

1982

Mexico. The debt crisis begins, the effects of which continue to affect the Mexican people today. The crisis turns the World Bank and IMF into collection agencies for Western governments and private banks.

Ecuador. A series of draconian antisocial measures are taken in response to World Bank pressure. Gas prices are increased by 120 percent; flour subsidies are eliminated; cigarette, beer, and automobile taxes are increased; and public transport fares are boosted by 25 percent. Reaction is swift and violent. Ministers are kidnapped; there are strikes in transport, education, and other sectors; riots break out. The government is forced to back down on a number of fronts, wage increases are granted to compensate for the rise in prices, and gas prices are decreased.

Burkina Faso. A 15 percent salary reduction provokes a strike of government workers.

1983

United States. The NGO campaign on the World Bank's obligation to reveal the social and environmental impact of its activities begins with two days of hearings at the US Congress. Since 1990, NGOs in most donor countries work with partners in borrower countries to lobby their governments and the World Bank for real reforms.

1984

Zambia. Riots break out in response to a doubling in the price of flour and corn, caused by the elimination of subsidies. Government repression causes fifteen deaths. The government is forced to reinstate subsidies.

Burkina Faso. The government cuts teachers' salaries by 25 percent. Teachers go on strike.

Tunisia. Riots break out in the south in response to a doubling in the price of bread and semolina. Dozens of people die as a result of the ensuing government repression. The minister of the interior is forced to resign, the state of emergency is lifted, bread and semolina subsidies are reinstated, and rent control remains in place.

1985

Latin America. Castro calls for the nonpayment of the debt and for the establishment of a continental common front between the countries of Latin America and the Caribbean.

Ecuador. The government increases the price of gas by 67 percent and bus fares by 50 percent to reduce the budget deficit. The main trade union calls for a two-day general strike; seven people die in the resulting clashes. Two months later, there is another wave of strikes and demonstrations. President Cordero stays in power thanks to military backing.

India. The World Bank provides financing for the Sardar Sarovar dam in the Narmada valley, which threatens to displace some 200,000 people. Mass demonstrations and court challenges drag on for years, finally leading to the first independent evaluation of a World Bank project. The Morse Commission condemns nearly every aspect of the World Bank's involvement in the Narmada project.

Bolivia. Huge price increases in food and gas prices lead to fifteen days of strikes and riots. The increases are carried out in line with the SAP drawn up and financed by the World Bank and the IMF.

1986

Zambia. Hunger riots break out in the copper-belt towns, in response to a 120 percent increase in the price of basic goods. President Kaunda declares that the conditions placed on structural adjustment loans are intolerable.

Brazil. A $500 million loan for an electricity project is used to complete a dam that damages the Amazonian rainforest and its inhabitants.

1988

Nigeria. The government eliminates subsidies for kerosene, used mostly by poor households. The increase provokes riots, during which six people are killed.

1989

Venezuela. More than three hundred people (some place the figure as high as two thousand) are killed during riots against a 100 percent increase in the price of gas and fares for public transport. These increases are part of a package of restructuring measures

adopted to satisfy conditions for IMF and World Bank structural adjustment loans.

Ecuador. Further increases in the price of gas and motor-vehicle taxes lead to a general strike of bus and truck drivers. The president calls out the army to operate public transport. In November, there are violent student demonstrations in response to an increase in bus fares.

1990

Worldwide. Despite numerous internal studies showing that the least expansive techniques are the best for ensuring energy availability, less than 1 percent of World Bank loans between 1980 and 1990 go toward improving energy efficiency and conservation. Of more than $35 billion invested by the World Bank in hydraulic projects between 1981 and 1990, only 0.4 percent went into small-scale irrigation projects, 0.6 percent into water distribution, and 2.3 percent into conservation. It is universally recognized that small-scale projects meet the population's needs at the lowest price. A study from the Ford Foundation says that the World Bank is "wedded to giant-sized projects."

Brussels. The Comité pour l'annulation de la dette du tiers monde (Committee for the Abolition of the Third World Debt—CADTM) is founded.

China. The World Bank resumes its loans after an eight-month suspension in the wake of the Tiananmen Square massacre.

Ivory Coast. The government cuts private-sector salaries by 10 percent and public-sector salaries by 15–40 percent. The measures are met with student demonstrations and riots, then strikes by teachers, health professionals, and bank workers. The government is forced to relent. Still, a general strike is organized with army and police participation, threatening the stability of the regime.

Gabon. In January, major riots erupt following public-sector strikes against salary and job cuts. Fifty people are injured and

250 arrested as a result of government repression.

Morocco. Violent demonstrations take place in Fez against the implementation of the SAP; government forces kill one hundred students. Hunger riots have already taken place in Morocco, especially in Casablanca in 1981.

Congo. The government cuts jobs and salaries in the public sector. A wave of strikes forces the government to withdraw its measures.

1990–93

Rwanda. The World Bank and IMF finance the Habyarimana dictatorship, which is preparing genocide. The massacres are perpetrated during a three-month period beginning in April 1994.

1991

Thailand. Despite strong opposition from the population, the World Bank begins funding the Pak Mun Dam project, which endangers the Mekong ecosystem.

Lesotho. The World Bank provides $110 million for the Highlands hydraulic project, though it will flood major archaeological sites, displace shepherds and poor farmers, and threaten endangered species. Local groups organize opposition to the project, whose objective is to redirect water to South Africa.

Honduras. The national electricity workers' union goes on strike against government plans to privatize the state-owned company and cut staff in line with World Bank and IMF structural adjustment prescriptions. More than seven hundred workers are dismissed over three months; the trade union disappears.

India. The World Bank and IMF provide more than $200 million for an Indian company to construct a 500 megawatt thermal power station on territory belonging to an aboriginal community to provide electricity to Bombay. Local groups take the company to the Bombay High Court and the Indian Supreme Court.

Peru. As part of the "Fujishock," prices on fuel and other basic products are massively increased. According to many observers, the poorest sectors of the population of Lima are no longer able to boil their water, leading to new outbreaks of cholera.

Washington DC. The World Bank's chief economist, Larry Summers, writes an internal memo in which he calls for exporting the North,s polluting industries to the South, which he describes as "vastly UNDER-polluted." He concludes, "In my view, the economic logic of disposing of toxic waste in low-income countries is impeccable." Summer sees this as a rational way to further industrial development while reducing pollution in the North. Among other things, the future secretary of the treasury for the Clinton administration writes: "There are no...limits to the carrying capacity of the earth that are likely to bind at any time in the foreseeable future. There isn't a risk of an apocalypse due to global warming or anything else. The idea that the world is headed over an abyss is profoundly wrong. The idea that we should put limits on growth because of some natural limit is a profound error and one that, were it ever to prove influential, would have staggering social costs." (Better for sickness and death to occur in places where the loss of earnings is the lowest!) His conclusion is typical of the World Bank's approach to such matters: "The environment is a critical global problem. Environmental problems are serious the world over, but it is only in the poor countries that they maim and kill millions of people every year, by aggravating all the other terrible effects of poverty. Any strategy on environmental problems that slows the growth of poor countries, either by direct regulation or by market limitation, is perfectly immoral." (quoted in George and Sabelli 1994).

1992

Chile. The IFC approves a financial package worth $124.9 million for the Pangue

Dam on the Bío-Bío River, disregarding two years of opposition on the local and international levels. In 1993, more than two thousand opponents of the dam attend a meeting of seven Pehuenche communities, billed as "a symbolic act for the defense of the cultural identity and lands of Chilean indigenous peoples." In 1995, the Inspection Panel of the World Bank rejects a request to inspect the project, arguing that IFC projects are outside its jurisdiction.

Rio de Janeiro. The World Bank is handed the job of managing the Global Environment Fund (GEF).

1993

Worldwide. An internal review at the World Bank finds that 37 percent of the Bank's projects do not fulfill its own financial criteria, and 78 percent of conditions for loans are not met. Other internal reports concede that more than two million people have been removed by force to make way for World Bank–financed projects.

China. With human-rights violations continuing apace, China receives a total of $317 billion, becoming the World Bank's biggest borrower.

Washington DC. The World Bank finally agrees to set up an independent Inspection Panel, empowered to investigate the complaints of communities severely affected by projects where the World Bank has not respected its own procedures and policies.

1994

Mexico. The Zapatista rebellion emerges on January 1, in response to NAFTA's coming into effect (the free trade agreement between Mexico, Canada, and the United States). At the end of the year, a financial crisis erupts. The national currency is devalued by 40 percent; 850,000 jobs are eliminated over six months.

India. After persistent local and international protest, the World Bank abandons the Sardar Sarovar dam in the Narmada valley at India's request, confirming the conclusions of the Morse Commission. It is recognized that incontestable human-rights violations have taken place through the contravention of planned rehousing measures. The Indian federal government and the local state government continue to breach rehousing policies stipulated in the loan agreement.

Worldwide. Of more than six thousand loans proposed by the World Bank administration since 1947, not one has been rejected by the World Bank's executive directors.

1995

Papua New Guinea. The SAPs of the World Bank and the IMF are the cause of riots, with the police opening fire, resulting in three deaths. The SAPs aim to open up the economy to exploitation at the hands of multinational corporations.

Washington DC. The IMF finally sets up an independent review unit to oversee its evaluations of the economic conditions in member countries. It does so in response to criticism in the Whittome Report that it had not foreseen the crisis of the Mexican peso in its 1994 economic report on the country. The original analysis contains warnings concerning a situation of "quasi-crisis," but the government persuades IMF officials to water down the report. Since then, the World Bank and the Inter-American Development Bank have spent more than $2 billion to get Mexico's private banks back on their feet.

Nepal. The World Bank agrees to withdraw financing from the Arun Dam after Nepalese citizens' groups take their case to the independent Inspection Panel. The Bank president recognizes that the Arun Dam is not the kind of project that Nepal most needs, and promises to work on obtaining financing for alternative projects drawn up by NGOs.

1996

Jordan. Riots erupt in response to the 200 percent increase in the prices of basic goods that follows SAP-inspired subsidy cuts.

France. In Lyons, on the occasion of the annual G7 Summit, ten thousand people demonstrate for the abolition of the debt and against neoliberalism.

Washington DC. The World Bank and IMF launch an initiative for the Heavily Indebted Poor Countries (HIPC), to make debt repayment more "bearable" (Toussaint 1997c). The initiative does not seek to serve the needs of the populations of the countries in question, but rather to ensure the smooth flow of debt-servicing payments.

1997

Washington DC. The World Bank creates the Structural Adjustment Participatory Review Initiative (SAPRI) to involve NGOs in its SAP-review process, thereby taking the sting out of their criticisms. According to the World Bank's 1997 annual report, 47 percent of its projects have NGO participation, while seventy-two World Bank missions maintain regular contact with local NGOs. Unfortunately, this does not lead to a change in the World Bank's macroeconomic orientations. The Bank says that 29 percent of its loans targeted the poor in 1997, as opposed to 32 percent in 1996. This is a drop of nearly 10 percent in the share of loans going to the poor.

Uganda. The first country to be targeted by the HIPC Initiative, Uganda's debt reduction is postponed to April 1998.

East and Southeast Asia. On several occasions, the World Bank and IMF declare in official documents that there is no threat of a serious crisis in Southeast Asia. This does not prevent a crisis from erupting in the summer. The IMF imposes severe austerity packages involving the elimination of millions of jobs and of subsidies to basic goods. In October, the IMF announces there is no threat of the crisis spreading to South

Korea. In November, South Korea is hit hard by the unfolding crisis. IMF president, Michel Camdessus, declares the crisis to be a "blessing in disguise" (*Libération*, December 1, 1997).

1998

Rwanda. Rwanda is obliged to repay IMF and World Bank loans made to the former Habyarimana regime (1973–94) to buy arms used in the 1994 genocide.

Zimbabwe. Food riots erupt in January against the increase in the price of basic staples.

Mozambique. In January, the Paris Club announces an 80 percent reduction in debt from 1999 or the year 2000 on—in line with IMF and World Bank promises to make a positive gesture in the country's direction. If the reductions are indeed granted, the ratio of total debt to export revenues will, at 200 percent, remain unbearable. This is no solution for one of the planet's poorest countries.

East and Southeast Asia. The "Asian miracle" is over, yet it has been the IMF and World Bank model for twenty years. The social balance sheet is catastrophic. The IMF and local governments impose policies implying nothing less than a sell-off of the countries' national wealth. Who will the next victims be?

Great Britain. In May, at the annual meeting of the G7+1 in Birmingham, seventy thousand British people form a human chain to demand the abolition of the poor countries' debt. The campaign launched by Jubilee Great Britain is in full spate.

Russia. Debt crisis begins in August. Russia suspends unilaterally its debt repayments for six weeks. It renegotiates the debt owed to private creditors (within the London Club) and obtains a significant reduction. It obtains similar concessions from the Paris Club.

United States. Long-Term Capital Management (LTCM), a hedge fund, is on the edge of bankruptcy after the Russian crisis and its consequences on contracts derived in European currencies. The Federal Reserve calls an urgent meeting of several international banks (Union des Banques Suisses, Deutsche Bank, Bankers Trust, Chase Bank, Barclays, Merrill Lynch, Société Générale) to put together the $3.5 billion needed to save LTCM and avoid a chain effect.

Brazil. In September–October, $30 billion leave Brazil.

1999

Brazil. In January, the Brazilian currency undergoes devaluation. An agreement is reached between the IMF and the Brazilian government.

1999. Germany. In June, at the annual G7+1 Summit, seventeen million signatures are presented to the heads of state and governments by the Jubilee 2000 Campaign. (The total number of signatories reaches twenty-three million.) The signatories demand the cancellation of the poor countries' debt. The mobilization is international, with a strong British presence. A human chain of thirty-five thousand people surrounds Cologne, where the summit is held. Jubilee South, a tricontinental network (Asia, Latin America, Africa), is founded to coordinate debt cancellation campaigns.

South Africa. Jubilee South, a movement to unite campaigns in the South for the cancellation of illegitimate debt, is officially founded.

United States. The World Bank and IMF rename SAPs to "Poverty Reduction Strategy Papers" and replace the enhanced structural adjustment facilities with "Poverty Reduction and Growth Facility." They announce their intention thus to accelerate debt-reduction procedures. In fact, the debt of the poorest countries increases from 1996 to 1999. Bill Clinton announces 100 percent cancellation of the debt to the United States of the poorest countries. A huge lie (another one).

United States. In November, Joseph Stiglitz, chief economist and senior vice president of the World Bank, announces that he will be leaving in January 2000. Thus, a "reformist" leaves under pressure from the US Treasury.

2000

Bolivia. A victorious struggle in Cochabamba against water privatization.

Ecuador. In January, the Indians lead a popular uprising. The president is overthrown. Demands include the renunciation of external debt payments and rejection of a US military base.

United States. In February, the report of the US Congress bipartisan commission known as the Meltzer Commission is published. It proposes limiting World Bank intervention to the poorest countries that have no access to the financial markets. The IMF would limit its sphere of influence to the markets of the emerging countries that do have such access.

Spain. For the March elections, the Red Ciudadana por la Abolición de la Deuda Externa (Citizens' Network for the Cancellation of the External Debt) organizes a consultation (referendum) of the people. More than a million Spaniards take part, and of those, more than 95 percent favor abolition of the Third World debt toward Spain.

United States. In March, Michel Camdessus (France) is replaced by Horst Köhler (Germany) at the head of the IMF. Stiglitz, for his part, makes public his deep disagreement with the Washington Consensus. In April, in Washington DC, twenty thousand protesters partly disorganize the spring meeting of the IMF and the World Bank. In June, Ravi Kanbur, director of the World Bank's annual *World Development Report*, resigns. He explains that he disagrees with the conservative orientations of the World Bank and its mentor, the US Treasury.

Japan. In July, in Okinawa, the G7+1 is the occasion for a demonstration thirty thousand strong against the US military bases in Japan. The campaigners for the abolition of the debt also demonstrate.

Brazil. In September, a plebiscite on the theme of the debt is organized by the MST (landless movement), the CUT (trade-union federation), the CNBB (National Conference of Bishops), and Jubilee South, with six million participants. Nearly 90 percent favor stopping debt repayments until the audit of the 1988 constitution has been carried out.

Prague. In September, at the autumn meeting of the IMF and the World Bank, twenty thousand to thirty thousand demonstrators (of highly international composition) manage to disorganize and cut short the institutions' work.

Chad. In December, the controversial Chad-Cameroon oil pipeline, backed by the World Bank, the local dictators, and the oil multinational corporations, turns to scandal. The Chad dictatorship has used a large part of the World Bank loans destined for the pipeline to buy arms.

Senegal. In December, a Pan-African and worldwide meeting on the Third World debt is co-organized by the CADTM, Belgian NGO the CNCD, the CONGAD (a coalition of Senegalese NGOs), and Jubilee South. Five thousand participate in a street demonstration.

2001

Argentina-Turkey. In January and February, a debt crisis erupts.

Spain. In June, the World Bank cancels a meeting planned in Barcelona because of the announced demonstrations. Still, fifty thousand people meet and demonstrate against the institution's policies.

Italy. In July, in Genoa, 300,000 demonstrators demand, among other things, the cancellation of the debt on the occasion of the G7+1 Summit. (Carlo Giuliani, an Italian protester, is killed by the police.)

United States. In September, the annual meeting of the IMF and the World Bank, which was scheduled to last a week, is postponed following the September 11 attacks. It is held in Ottawa, in November.

Mali. The People's Village in Siby. For the first time, in June, an alternative G8 summit is convened by the African social movements. These vigorously oppose the four African heads of state who are presenting the New Partnership for Africa's Development (NEPAD), a structural adjustment plan with an African flavor, at the official G8.

South Africa. On the occasion of the UN World Conference against Racism in Durban, the African social movements put forward the demand for reparations regarding slavery and the transatlantic slave trade.

Qatar. The WTO meeting in November manages to launch a new round of negotiations on how to push forward trade deregulation to the advantage of the multinational corporations of the highly industrialized countries. This is an important success for the highly industrialized countries and the forces that support the neoliberal offensive. It means a temporary halt to the WTO's the glaring failure at Seattle in November 1999. The meeting takes place right in the middle of the military offensive of the United States and its allies in the same region (massive bombardments in Afghanistan). China joins the WTO, bringing the number of members to 143 (Russia is—still—not a member).

United States. The spectacular bankruptcy of the firm ENRON, the world's main broker in petroleum products and a pillar of President George W. Bush's election campaigns, occurs. In a climate of global economic crisis and great financial instability, the destabilizing effects on the international capitalist system are considerable. Anne Krueger, first deputy managing director of the IMF, announces that the latter has begun internal discussions on the implementation of a restructuring mechanism for the sovereign debt of middle-income states. This would affect countries such as Argentina, Brazil, Thailand, Mexico, Turkey, and Russia.

2001–02

Argentina. In December, throughout the country, there is a popular uprising against the government and the IMF. The repression is brutal: thirty-two demonstrators are killed. The debt question is a central preoccupation. President de la Rúa and his government are forced to resign. Several presidents and governments succeed one another in a few weeks. A moratorium on the repayment of the external debt is decreed. Popular demonstrations carry on throughout the year 2002.

2002

East Timor. A new independent state is officially born. The Timorese government decides not to have recourse to indebtedness. The World Bank and the IMF, who have rushed in to offer loans, restrict themselves to donations. The World Bank coordinates the donations from the international community and gets the island's authorities to sign contracts that include the classic recipes for structural adjustment.

Nigeria. Mid-year, Nigeria suspends repayments of its external debt.

Peru. There is a victorious struggle by the inhabitants of Arequipa against the privatization of electricity.

South Africa. There are numerous campaigns against water and electricity privatization. A complaint is brought in the United States against twenty-one multinational corporations for aiding and abetting the Apartheid regime, with a view to demanding reparation for the victims.

Chad-Cameroon. The construction of the pipeline sponsored by the World Bank goes ahead.

Bolivia. In February, massive demonstrations take place against an extra tax on salaries of 12.5 percent imposed by the IMF. The police join in the protests. Twenty-nine are killed in confrontations between the police and the army. In October, there is an uprising to demand that national and public control be maintained over natural resources.

2003

United States. At the April meeting of the World Bank and the IMF, a decision is taken to abandon the project of a restructuring mechanism for the sovereign debt of middle-income states.

Argentina. In September, Argentina threatens not to repay $2.9 billion to the IMF at the arranged date. Finally, agreement is reached. The conditions imposed on Argentina are less harsh than those imposed on Brazil. Argentina's resistance pays off. Later, the Argentine government proposes that the private creditors should cancel 75 percent of the debt.

Mexico. In Cancún, in September, the interministerial meeting of the WTO falls through.

Dubai, United Arab Emirates. Annual meeting of the World Bank and the IMF in a climate of crisis after the failure of the WTO talks in Cancún.

Thailand. The Thai government does not renew its agreement with the IMF and applies different policies from those recommended by the IMF.

Indonesia. The Indonesian authorities threaten to follow Thailand's suit.

Bolivia. In October, President Gonzalo Sanchez de Lozada resigns after a vast popular uprising. The cause for the protests is the people's wish to regain public control of natural gas reserves.

Glossary

Author's note:

In this book, the following terms are used interchangeably: "Third World," "the countries of the South," "the South," "the periphery," and "the developing countries" (DC). These terms are generally used in contrast to "the Triad," "the highly industrialized countries," "the countries of the North," "the center," and "the imperialist countries," which are also considered synonymous. The countries of the former Soviet Bloc are considered part of the periphery.

Balance of payments

A country's balance of current payments is the result of its commercial transactions (i.e., imported and exported goods and services) and financial exchanges with foreign countries. The balance of payments is a measure of the financial position of a country with regard to the rest of the world. A country with a surplus in its current payments is a lending country for the rest of the world. On the other hand, if a country's balance is in the red, that country will have to turn to the international lenders to borrow needed funding. The balance of capital transactions, the opposite of the balance of current payments, completes the balance of payments, which is, by definition, balanced.

Bank for International Settlements (BIS)

Founded at Basel as a public company in 1930 to handle German reparations after the First World War. It manages part of the foreign currency reserves of the central banks. Its capital of 1.5 billion gold francs is divided into 600,000 shares, mainly underwritten by European central banks, with the remainder held by private investors who are entitled to dividends but not votes. The governors of the affiliated central banks, mainly those of the Group of Ten, meet regularly to promote good communication and close cooperation. The federal banks of New York, Canada, and Japan regularly send observers. The BIS plays an important role in gathering data on international banking transactions, published in a quarterly report since the early 1980s. It is responsible for handling financial risks associated with the liberalization of money markets. It also carries out banking transactions, receiving gold and currency deposits mainly from the central banks, selling the currency on the markets, and granting loans to certain central banks.

Bonds

Certificate issued by a borrower raising funds for a period of at least five years and stipulating the conditions of remuneration (interest rate, terms and conditions of payment, existence of a lottery bonus where relevant) and repayment (due date, terms and conditions of repayment, etc.).

Central bank

A country's central bank runs its monetary policy and holds the monopoly on issuing the national currency. Commercial banks must get their currency from it, at a supply price fixed according to the main rates of the central bank.

445

Convertibility

Designates the legal possibility of changing from one currency to another or from currency to the standard (traditionally gold) by which it is officially backed. In the present system of liberalized exchange rates, where supply and demand of currencies determine their respective exchange rates—floating rates—currencies float with respect to the dollar (dollar standard).

Currency market or money market

Market where currencies are exchanged and valued.

Debt

Debt rescheduling

Modification of the terms of a debt, for example, changing due dates or postponing repayment of the capital sum and/or interest. The aim is generally to give a bit of breathing space to a country in difficulty by extending the period of repayments so the amounts can be reduced or by granting a reprieve period when payments are not made.

Debt servicing

Repayment of interest plus amortization of the capital sum.

Multilateral debt

Debts due to the World Bank, IMF, regional development banks such as the African Development Bank, and other multilateral institutions such as the European Development Fund.

Net transfer on debt

Refers to the subtraction of debt servicing (yearly payments—interest plus capital sum—to the industrialized countries) from the year's gross payments (loans) made by the creditors. The net transfer on debt is said to be positive when the country or continent concerned receives more (in loans) than it pays out. It is negative if the sums repaid are greater than the sums lent. Since the mid-1980s, the IMF earns more from sub-Saharan Africa than it sends to it. The net transfer on debt is thus negative in this region of the world.

Private debt

Loans contracted by private borrowers, regardless of the lender.

Public debt

All loans contracted by public borrowers.

Derivatives

A derivative is a futures transaction deriving from "underlying" assets (which might be hard currency, a share, a raw material, or any financial asset). An example of a derivative is the option to buy or call: a bank sells the option to buy Monsanto shares (the underlying share from which the option derives) at the price of $100 in ten months. At the end of that period, either the share is worth more than $100 and the investor can make a profit or, if it is worth less after the ten months, the investor abandons his or her option and the banker pockets the premium. These products were originally created as a response to fluctuations—a sort of insurance offered by an operator who accepts the risk—but in the end, they cause more fluctuation by triggering waves of speculation. The issuer of the option and the buyer will both be speculating on the underlying asset for the ten-month period. A multitude of derivatives of great and varying complexity exist. Some are negotiated on organized and supervised markets, but most are arranged by mutual agreement, i.e., unsupervised and in total opacity.

Devaluation

A lowering of the exchange rate of one currency relative to others.

Eurodollars

Dollars held outside the United States. The eurodollar market is said to have arisen during the Cold War of the 1950s from the Soviet authorities' wish to capitalize their dollar reserves without having to sell them on the American money market. Nevertheless, in structural terms, it was the amount of American capital outflow that caused the market's spectacular boom in the second half of the 1960s. The growing deficit of the balance of American capital during this period resulted from the combination of three elements: massive investment in American firms abroad, especially in Europe; the ceiling imposed on interest rates by Q regulations, which encouraged foreign loans on the American market and discouraged deposits in the United States; and the cost of the Vietnam War. In 1963, US authorities introduced a tax on nonresident borrowing, to slow capital outflow. The result was a shift in the demand for financial backing in dollars from the US market to the European markets, where American bank subsidiaries could operate more freely. The supply of dollars on these markets came partly from American institutions and companies discouraged by the low interest rates in the United States, and partly from the central banks of the rest of the world holding their exchange reserves in dollars. The term "eurobanks" refers to banks dealing in dollars on European soil and, by extension, to the "xenobanks" dealing in any currency outside its country of origin. Free of state control and the obligation to hold reserves, they could offer high returns to their depositors and competitive rates to their clients without reducing their profit margins (Adda 2001).

Export credit agency

When private businesses of the North obtain a market in a developing country, there is a risk that economic or political problems may prevent payment of bills. To protect themselves, they can take out insurance with an export credit agency such as Coface in France or Ducroire in Belgium. If there is a problem, the agency pays instead of the insolvent client, and the Northern business is sure to get what is owed. According to the Jakarta Agreement for the reform of public export credit and credit-insurance agencies, they are "now the greatest source of public funding in the world, underwriting 8 percent of global exports in 1998, i.e., $391 billion of investment, mainly for big civil and military projects in the DC. It is far more than the annual average of official development assistance…which approaches $50 billion. The outstanding debt of the export credit agencies represents 24 percent of the debt of the DC, and 56 percent of public credits held on these countries." One of the main criticisms lodged against export credit agencies is that they are not very fussy about the nature of the contracts insured (arms, infrastructure, and huge energy projects such as the gigantic Three Gorges Dam project in China), or about their social or environmental consequences. They often give their support to repressive and corrupt regimes (e.g., Myanmar, formerly Burma, where Total had a project), which means implicit support for fundamental human-rights violations.

Financialization of a nation or firm

The degree of financialization of a nation or firm is measured by a simple indicator in which the numerator is the financial assets and the denominator is the financial assets plus the real assets. More precisely, it may be said that financialization exists when industrial firms devote an increasing portion of their resources to strictly financial activities, often to the detriment of the principal activity (Chesnais 1996).

Food crops

Crops destined to feed local populations (millet, manioc, etc.), as opposed to cash crops, destined for export (coffee, cocoa, tea, groundnuts, sugar, etc.)

Foreign direct investment
(FDI, taken from Chesnais 1997c)

Foreign investment can take the form of direct investment or portfolio investments. Though it is sometimes difficult to distinguish between the two, for reasons of accountancy, jurisdiction, or statistics, a foreign investment is considered a direct investment if the foreign investor holds 10 percent or more of ordinary shares or voting rights in a company. This criterion, though somewhat arbitrary, is based on the idea that such a holding corresponds to a long-term investment whose holder has some influence on the firm's management decisions. On the other hand, a foreign investment of less than 10 percent is classified as a portfolio investment. Portfolio investors are not considered to have any influence on the management of companies in which they hold shares. Portfolio investments cover all bank deposits and financial investments in the form of public or private securities. The flow of direct investments, to whatever destination, represents the sum of the following elements:

- net capital contributions made by the direct investor in the form of share buying, capital increase, or the founding of a new company;

- net loans, including short-term loans and advances made by a parent company to a subsidiary, and distributed profits (reinvested).

G5 (Group of Five)

The G5 came about in 1967, when the United States and the UK called a meeting of the ministers of finance of the top five industrial countries (Germany, United States, France, UK, and Japan). The G5 nations still carry the most weight in the G7.

G7 (Group of Seven)

Germany, United States, France, UK, Japan, Italy, and Canada. The seven heads of state generally meet annually in late June or early July. The first G7 summit was held in 1975 on the initiative of French president Valéry Giscard d'Estaing.

G8 (Group of Eight)

Composed of the G7 plus the Russian Federation (since 1995).

G10 (Group of Ten)

Composed of the G7 plus Belgium/Luxembourg, the Netherlands, and Sweden, the ten countries that signed the General Agreement to Borrow in 1962, which has been renewed ever since. Switzerland became an associate member in 1976, and is now a full member.

G77 (Group of Seventy-seven)

The G77 arose from the group of DC that met to prepare the first UN Conference on Trade and Development (UNCTAD) in Geneva, in 1964. The group provides a forum for the DC to discuss international economic and monetary issues.

General Agreement on Tariffs and Trade (GATT)

A permanent negotiating forum in which states only had the status of "contractual parties." It was replaced by the WTO on January 1, 1995.

Globalization
(taken from Chesnais 1997c)

The term "globalization" was coined in American business schools to refer to the scope for strategic action that had become relevant to large industrial groups. These major firms are able to adopt a "global" approach—to markets where there is effective demand, to their sources of supply, to the strategies of their rival oligopolies. In this sense, they operate and construct their portfolios, just like financial investors. Because of the connotations that the term "global" has for large industrial groups or large financial investors, the expression "globalization of capital" rather than "globalization of the economy" has always seemed…the more appropriate. In a public debate, the president of one of the biggest European groups explained that "globalization" represented "freedom for his group to set itself up wherever it wanted, for as long as it wanted, to produce whatever it wanted, buying and selling with the least possible number of restrictions as far as labor laws and social conventions were concerned." Until recently, it seemed possible to analyze globalization as the latest stage in the process of internationalization of capital, as exemplified by the large multinational industrial groups. Today this is clearly no longer sufficient. The "globalization of the economy" (Adda 2001) or, more precisely, "the globalization of capital" (Chesnais 1997c) must now be seen as more than just another phase in the process of the internationalization of capital begun over a century ago—or even as something quite different. We are dealing here with specific and important new modes of behavior in world capitalism, and to reach a better understanding of what is taking place, we must examine the underlying mechanisms and trends. Points of departure from the functioning of the main economies, inside or outside the OECD, need to be considered as a whole, on the hypothesis that they are probably part of a single system. My own opinion is that they reflect the passage into a new phase of imperialism (in the terms of the theory of imperialism developed by the left wing of the Second International almost a century ago), which differs greatly from the one in force between the end of the Second World War and the beginning of the 1980s. In the hope that a better description will soon be found through discussion and, if necessary, heated debate, I refer rather awkwardly to this new phase as "the global regime of accumulation mainly through finance." The differentiation and stratification of the contemporary world economy on a planetary scale is as much the result of concentrated capital operations as of the political relationships of dominance and dependency

between states, whose role is by no means diminished, however much the configuration and mechanisms of that dominance have been modified. The origin of "the global regime of accumulation mainly through finance" is both political and economic. It is only in the neoliberal jargon that the state is "outside" the "market." The present triumph of the "market" would have been impossible without the repeated political interventions of the political institutions of the strongest capitalist states (starting with the members of the G7). This freedom has enabled industrial capital, and even more, financial capital, both made respectable as "money," to spread their wings as never before since 1914. Of course, this freedom is also founded on the strength regained after the long period of uninterrupted accumulation of the "boom years" (1950s, 1960s, 1970s)—probably the longest of the entire history of capitalism. But capital could never have achieved its ends without the success of the "conservative revolution" at the end of the 1970s.

Gross domestic product (GDP)

The GDP represents the total wealth produced in a given territory, calculated as the sum of added values.

Gross national product (GNP)

The GNP represents the wealth produced by a nation, as opposed to a given territory. It includes the revenues of citizens of the nation abroad.

Heavily indebted poor countries (HIPC)

The HIPC initiative, launched in 1996 and consolidated in September 1999, is supposed to reduce the debts of poor, heavily indebted poor countries, with the modest aim of making the debts sustainable. It involves four demanding and complex stages that take an inordinately long time. First, countries that hope to qualify must submissively carry out an economic policy approved by the IMF and the World Bank, in the form of adjustment programs. They continue to receive aid money from all of the creditors concerned. Meanwhile, they must adopt a Poverty Reduction Strategy Paper (PRSP), sometimes just in the interim, and obtain results from applying this strategy for at least a year. At the end of the three-year period comes the decision point: the IMF analyzes whether the candidate country's indebtedness is sustainable. If the net value of the ratio between external debt stock and export revenue exceeds 150 percent, after traditional debt-reduction mechanisms have been applied, the country may be declared eligible. However, countries with high export levels (exports/GDP ratio of more than 30 percent) are penalized by this criterion, and their budgetary receipts are looked at rather than their exports. If their indebtedness is clearly high despite good tax recovery (budgetary receipts of more than 15 percent of the GDP, to avoid any laxity in this area), the objective retained is a ratio of net value of debt stock/budgetary receipts of more than 250 percent. In the third stage, if the country is declared eligible, it then benefits from some preliminary reductions on the part of creditor states and private banks, and must pursue its implementation of policies approved by the IMF and the World Bank. The time this stage takes is determined by the satisfactory setup of the key reforms agreed at the decision point, with a view to maintaining macroeconomic stability. Last comes the completion point. The rest of the debt reduction is then applied, so that the country can get back to a situation of sustainable overall debt (in the terms described above) that is judged satisfactory. The cost of the initiative is estimated at about $54 billion, i.e., about 2.6 percent of the Third World's total external debt. Altogether, there are only forty-two HIPC, of which thirty-four are in sub-Saharan Africa, to which should be added Honduras, Nicaragua, Bolivia, Guyana, Laos, Vietnam, and Myanmar. By September 30, 2003, twenty-seven countries had reached the decision point; only

eight had reached completion point: Benin, Bolivia, Burkina Faso, Mali, Mauritania, Mozambique, Tanzania, and Uganda.

Hedge funds

A hedge fund is an investment vehicle that borrows in order to speculate on the world's financial markets. The more a fund has the trust of the financial world, the more it will be able to take temporary control of assets worth far more than its owners' wealth. A hedge-fund investor's revenues depend on results, which incites him or her to take greater risks. Hedge funds played the role of scout in the recent financial crises: speculating on the fall, they impressed the main battalions (institutional investors, pension funds, insurance companies, etc.) with their clairvoyance, thus creating self-fulfilling speculative forecasts.

Human development rating (HDR)

This instrument is used by the UN to estimate a country's degree of development, based on per capita income, the level of education, and the average life expectancy of the population.

Human poverty index (HPI)

Since 1997, the annual UNDP *Global Human Development Report* tries to measure poverty in the Third World using a human poverty index that considers criteria other than monetary income:

- the probability at birth of death before age forty;

- the percentage of illiterate adults;

- services procured by the economy overall. (The quality of these is determined using two elements: the percentage of individuals without access to piped drinking water, and the percentage of children under five who are underweight.)

Despite undeniable monetary poverty, some countries manage to attenuate the impact of that poverty by access to services made available to the population. At the top of the list of such countries in 2002 were Uruguay, Costa Rica, Chile, and Cuba. These countries had managed to reduce human poverty to an HPI below 5 percent.

Import substitution industrialization (ISI)

This strategy mainly concerns a historic experiment in Latin America in the 1930s and 1940s, and the school of thought known as CEPAL (the UN Latin American Economic Commission), and especially work published by Argentine Raúl Prebisch. The starting point is the observation that when faced with a drastic reduction in foreign exchange, the main countries of Latin America had managed to respond to domestic demand by replacing imported products through the development of local production. The CEPAL theory holds that this process can be fruitfully extended to all sectors of industry, one after the other, thus enabling the country to "disconnect" from the center. A good dose of protectionism and coordinated state intervention are expected to promote the expansion of budding industries. It is a sort of reformist version of the dependence theory, which relies on dynamic local entrepreneurs (Coutrot and Husson 1993; Prebisch 1984; Clairmont 1987; Ugarteche 1997).

Industrial free zone

Geographical area where industrial firms producing for export are exempt from paying duty on the production factors they import and to which certain elements of other national regulations are often not applicable. (*Source*: World Bank)

Inflation

The cumulative increase of prices as a whole (e.g., an increase in the price of oil, eventually leading to an increase in salaries, then to an increase in other prices, etc.).

Inflation implies a fall in the value of money since, as time passes, larger sums are required to purchase particular items. This is the reason why corporate-driven policies seek to keep inflation down.

Institutional investors

The name given to the corporate bodies that manage the collective funds that have reached paroxysmal financial proportions on the financial markets, such as pension funds, insurance companies, and other organizations that make collective investments.

Interest rates

When A lends money to B, B repays the amount lent by A (the capital) as well as a supplementary sum known as interest, so that A has an interest in agreeing to this financial operation. The interest is determined by the interest rate, which may be high or low. To take a simple example: if B borrows $100 million for ten years at a fixed interest rate of 5 percent, the first year B will repay a tenth of the capital initially borrowed ($10 million) plus 5 percent of the capital owed, i.e., $5 million, that is, a total of $15 million. In the second year, B will again repay 10 percent of the capital borrowed, but the 5 percent now only applies to the remaining $90 million still due, i.e., $4.5 million, or a total of $14.5 million. And so on, until the tenth year, when B will repay the last $10 million, plus 5 percent of that remaining $10 million, i.e., $0.5 million, for a total of $10.5 million. Over ten years, the total amount repaid will come to $127.5 million. The repayment of the capital is not usually made in equal installments. In the initial years, the repayment concerns mainly the interest, and the proportion of capital repaid increases over the years. In this case, if repayments are stopped, the capital still due is higher. The nominal interest rate is the rate at which the loan is contracted. The real interest rate is the nominal rate reduced by the rate of inflation.

International Labor Organization (ILO)

Founded in 1919 by the Treaty of Versailles and based in Geneva, in 1946, the ILO became the first specialized institution of the United Nations. It includes representatives of governments, employers, and workers with the aim of setting minimal international norms and writing international conventions in the field of work. The ILO is composed of the International Labor Conference, which meets annually; the Governing Body, which is its executive council of fifty-six members (twenty-eight representing governments, fourteen representing employers, and fourteen representing workers), and the International Labor Office, which takes care of administration and policy making. The International Labor Office, composed mainly of statisticians and economists, has limited powers, consisting of publishing a yearly report. In recent years, their reports promote the idea that unemployment results from a lack of growth (from 5 percent in the 1960s, to 2 percent today), in turn caused by a lack of demand. Their remedy is a global consensus for a "virtuous circle" of economic growth and for strategy planning at a national level (of the Dutch type, for example). The ILO claims that it would be naive to explain unemployment by a lack of flexibility, and that technological developments do not necessarily entail automatic downgrading of wages and social welfare.

International Monetary Fund (IMF)

The IMF's capital consists of contributions in strong currencies (and in local currencies) by member countries. According to the size of its contribution, each member state is entitled to special drawing rights (SDRs), which are monetary assets freely and immediately negotiable against the currency of a third state. SDRs are designed to work in what is known as a short-term economic stabilization policy, in order to reduce the country's budget deficit and limit the total amount of money in circulation. This stabilization is usually the first phase of IMF intervention in debtor countries. However, the IMF has taken upon itself (since the first wave of the oil crisis, 1974–75) to bring its influence to bear on the productive base of Third World economies by restructuring whole sectors: this amounts to a longer-term adjustment policy. It does the same thing with the countries said to be in transition toward a market economy (Norel and Saint-Alary 1992).

DISTRIBUTION OF THE TWENTY-FOUR EXECUTIVE DIRECTORS' VOTES (PERCENT)

United States	17.14
Japan	6.15
Germany	6.01
Belgium	5.15
United Kingdom	4.96
France	4.96
Netherlands	4.86
Spain	4.29
Italy	4.19
Canada	3.72

i.e., ten industrialized countries 61.43%.

International Monetary System (IMS)

The IMS is a system of rules and mechanisms set up by states and international organizations to promote international exchanges and coordinate national monetary policies. The present system was set up under the Jamaica Agreement (1976), which overhauled the preceding one, dating from the Bretton Woods Agreement of 1944 (United States).

Least developed countries (LDC)

A notion defined by the UN on the following criteria: low per capita income, poor human resources, and little diversification in the economy. The list includes forty-nine countries at present, with the most recent addition of Senegal in July 2000. Thirty years ago, there were only twenty-five LDC.

LIBOR (London Interbank Offered Rate)

The rate of interest at which banks borrow funds from other banks in the City of London (similar to the American "prime rate," also a basic rate for international loans).

London Club

The private banks that lend to Third World states and companies. During the 1970s, deposit banks had become the main source of credit for countries in difficulty. By the end of the decade, these countries were receiving more than 50 percent of total credit allocated, from all lenders combined. At the time of the debt crisis in 1982, the London Club had an interest in working with the IMF to manage the crises. The groups of deposit banks meet to coordinate debt rescheduling for borrower countries. Such groups are known as advisory commissions. The meetings, unlike those of the Paris Club, are held in New York, London, Paris, Frankfurt, or elsewhere at the convenience of the country concerned and the banks. The advisory commissions, which started in the 1980s, have always advised debtor countries immediately to adopt a policy of stabilization and to ask for IMF support before applying for rescheduling or fresh loans from the deposit banks. Only on rare occasions do commissions pass a project without IMF approval, if the banks are convinced that the country's policies are adequate.

Long waves of capitalist development

Capitalist economies have a cyclic character, with periodic alternation between phases of growth and phases of recession or depression. Usually, two main categories of cycle are studied: short cycles, also known as "Juglar cycles," after Clement Juglar, the economist who first studied them; and long cycles better known as "long waves" or "Kondratieff cycles," after the economist, Nicolai Kondratieff. Short cycles occur over six- to ten-year periods, and long waves over fifty to sixty years. Long waves include short cycles. In the ascending phase, years of growth predominate and, more significantly, the crises that characterize short cycles are less acute and of shorter duration. During the descending or depressive phase, more modest growth is recorded for the best years of the short cycles, while the bad years show poor growth, stagnation, or recession. The question of economic cycles, long or short, is one of the most controversial among economists. One of the most interesting analysts of long waves is Ernest Mandel (1923–95), who analyzed the complex interaction between economic and sociopolitical factors in the long-wave mechanism. Mandel made an important contribution to understanding the political factors involved in triggering expansive long waves and how they develop, which needs to be further explored (Mandel 1975, 1978).

Market tyranny

"This means nothing less than the right of those among whom the money-capital is concentrated, after having made it and greatly increased it, to take for themselves a disproportionate share of the wealth created through the production process" (Serfati 1996).

The Marshall Plan

A program of economic reconstruction proposed in 1947 by US secretary of state George C. Marshall. With a budget of $12.5 billion (about $90 billion in 2003 terms), composed of donations and long-term loans, the Marshall Plan enabled sixteen countries (especially France, the UK, Italy, and the Scandinavian countries) to finance their reconstruction after the Second World War.

Moral hazard

An often used by opponents of debt cancellation, it is based on the liberal theory that considers a situation where there is a borrower and a lender a case of asymmetrical information. Only the borrower knows whether he really intends to repay the lender. By canceling the debt today, there would be a risk that the same facility might be extended to other debtors in future, which would increase the reluctance of creditors to commit capital. They would have no other solution than to demand a higher interest rate including a risk premium. Clearly, the term "moral," here is applied only to the creditors; the debtors are automatically suspected of "amorality." Yet, it is easily demonstrated that this moral hazard is a direct result of the total liberty of capital flows. It is proportionate to the opening of financial markets, as this is what multiplies the potentiality of the market contracts that are supposed to increase the welfare of humankind, but actually bring an increase in risky contracts. So, financiers would like to multiply the opportunities to make money without risk in a society that, we are unceasingly told, is and has to be a high-risk society—a fine contradiction.

Moratorium

A situation where a debt is frozen by the creditor, who foregoes payment until an agreed time. However, during the period of the moratorium, interest continues to accumulate. A moratorium can also be decided by the borrower, as was the case of Russia in 1998, and Ecuador in 1999.

Mutual fund

Collective investment fund in the United States, also known as a unit trust in the UK, and similar to SICAV in France. A more recent innovation, the OEIC (open-ended investment company) is exactly equivalent to a SICAV, but for practical purposes works like a mutual fund/unit trust. The fund buys a lot of shares (or bonds or other financial instruments), so each individual investor has a little piece of the entire portfolio. The main distinction between a SICAV/OEIC and a mutual fund/unit trust is that the former are companies rather than pools of assets. Buying into a SICAV involves purchasing shares in a company (whose sole business is to invest); buying into a mutual fund means that you take a small part of a big investment pool.

NASDAQ

The National Association of Securities Dealers Automated Quotation, existing since 1971, is the electronic stock market of high-yield American securities—part of the Internet-linked "new economy."

NATO (North Atlantic Treaty Organization)

NATO ensures US military protection for the Europeans in case of aggression, but, above all, it gives the United States supremacy over the Western Bloc. Western European countries agreed to place their armed forces within a defense system under US command, and thus recognize the dominance of the United States. NATO was founded in 1949, in Washington, but became less prominent after the end of the Cold War. In 2002, it had nineteen members: Belgium, Canada, Denmark, France, Iceland, Italy, Luxembourg, the Netherlands, Norway, Portugal, the UK, the United States, to which were added Greece and Turkey in 1952; the Federal Republic of Germany in 1955 (replaced by unified Germany in 1990); Spain in 1982; and Hungary, Poland and the Czech Republic in 1999.

Net transfers on debt

Refers to the subtraction of debt servicing (yearly payments—interest plus capital sum—to the industrialized countries) from the year's gross payments (new loans and investments) made by the creditor countries. The net transfer on debt is said to be positive when the country or continent concerned receives more (in loans, donations, or investments) than it repays, including what it pays out in the form of repatriated profits from multinationals. It is negative if the sums repaid are greater than the sums lent to the country or continent concerned. From 1982 to 1990, the net transfer on debt for Latin America was negative every year. Over the same period, net transfers from Latin America to the countries of the North came to more than $200 billion (Ugarteche 1997).

New Deal

This term appeared for the first time at the Democratic Party convention in Chicago, in July 1932. It refers to the experiment attempted in 1933 by President Franklin D. Roosevelt to end the deep economic crisis that the United States had been going through since 1929. The expression "New Deal" covered a series of measures, from aid to the worst hit economic sectors to social reforms. From 1938 on, a new recession occurred and showed the limits of the New Deal. The Second World War finally brought about economic revival. Roosevelt did not draw up a consistent plan, such as the one implemented by the British Labor government of 1945.

Official development assistance (ODA)

The name given to loans granted in financially favorable conditions by the public bodies of the industrialized countries. A loan has only to be agreed at a lower rate of interest than going market rates (a concessionary loan) to be considered aid, even if it is then repaid to the last cent by the borrowing country. Tied bilateral loans (which oblige the borrowing country to buy products or services from the lending country) and debt cancellation are also counted as part of ODA. Apart from food aid, there are three main ways of using these funds: rural development, infrastructures, and nonproject aid (financing budget deficits or the balance of payments). The latter increases continually. This aid is made "conditional" upon reduction of the public deficit, privatization, environmental "good behavior," care of the very poor, democratization, etc. These conditions are laid down by the main governments of the North, the

World Bank, and the IMF. The aid goes through three channels: multilateral aid, bilateral aid, and the NGOs.

Oligopoly

"A state of limited competition when a market is shared by a small number of producers or sellers" (*Shorter Oxford Dictionary*, 1983). The condition of oligopoly arises from the interdependence between the firms that make it up: firms which no longer react to impersonal forces coming from the market, but to their rivals, personally and directly. The global oligopoly is an "area of rivalry," defined by mutual market-dependent relations between the small number of large groups that manage to acquire and keep the status of effective competitor within an industry (or within a complex of industries with a common generic technology) on a world scale. The oligopoly is the focus of both ferocious competition and collaboration between groups (Chesnais 1996).

Organization for Economic Cooperation and Development (OECD)

Founded in 1960 and housed in the Château de la Muette in Paris, in 2002, the OECD included the fifteen members of the European Union plus Switzerland, Norway, and Iceland; in North America, the United States and Canada; and in Asia and the Pacific, Japan, Australia, and New Zealand. The only Third World country that has been a member from the start for geostrategic reasons is Turkey. Between 1994 and 1996, two other Third World countries entered the OECD: Mexico, also part of NAFTA with its two North American neighbors, and South Korea. Since 1995, three countries of the former Eastern Bloc have joined: the Czech Republic, Poland, and Hungary. In 2000, Slovakia became the thirtieth member. Recent additions to the OECD faithfully reflect the configuration of the Triad as described in this book, i.e., the three central axes of the United States (plus Canada), Western Europe, and Japan (plus Australia), and their respective peripheries. The OECD member countries in alphabetical order are Australia, Austria, Belgium, Canada, Czech Republic, Denmark, Finland, France, Germany, Greece, Hungary, Iceland, Ireland, Italy, Japan, Luxembourg, Mexico, Netherlands, New Zealand, Norway, Poland, Portugal, Slovakia, South Korea, Spain, Sweden, Switzerland, Turkey, UK, United States.

Organization of the Petroleum Exporting Countries (OPEC)

OPEC is a group of eleven DC that produce oil: Algeria, Indonesia, Iran, Iraq, Kuwait, Libya, Nigeria, Qatar, Saudi Arabia, United Arab Emirates, and Venezuela. These eleven countries represent 41 percent of oil production in the world and own more than 75 percent of known reserves. Founded in September 1960, and based in Vienna (Austria), OPEC is in charge of coordinating and unifying the petroleum-related policies of its members, with the aim of guaranteeing stable revenues. To this end, production is organized on a quota system. Each country, represented by its minister of energy and oil, takes a turn in running the organization. On July 1, 2002, Venezuelan Alvaro Silva-Calderón became the secretary general of OPEC.

Paris Club

Group of lender states founded in 1956 that specializes in dealing with nonpayment by developing countries (DC). From its beginnings, the president has traditionally been French: in 2003, the director of the French Treasury, Jean-Pierre Jouyet, was the incumbent. The member states of the Paris Club have rescheduled the debts of some eighty DC. Club members own nearly 30 percent of Third World debt stock. Links between the Paris Club and the IMF are extremely close, as witnessed by the observer status enjoyed by the IMF in the Paris Club's otherwise confidential meetings. The IMF plays a key role in the Paris Club's debt strategy, and the club relies on IMF expertise and macroeconomic judgments in instigating one of its basic principles: conditionality. In return, the IMF's status as privileged creditor and the implementation of its adjustment strategies in the DC are bolstered by the Paris Club's actions.

Pension funds

Pension funds collect part of their clients' monthly salaries and speculate on the financial markets to use this capital to advantage. There is a dual objective: first, to provide a pension for their clients when they retire at the end of their working lives; second, to make extra profits for themselves. Both objectives depend on contingencies, and their fulfillment is uncertain. On many occasions, workers have found themselves with neither savings nor a pension after crashing bankruptcies, such as that of the Robert Maxwell business empire in the United Kingdom. The system of pensions by capitalization has become generalized in the Anglo-Saxon world. In 2002, some countries in continental Europe, such as France, still retained a distributive pension system based on transfers between generations.

Poverty Reduction Strategy Paper (PRSP)

Set up by the World Bank and the IMF in 1999, the PRSP was officially designed to fight poverty. In fact, it turns out to be an even more virulent version of the structural adjustment policies in disguise, to try to win the approval and legitimization of the social participants.

Private loans

Loans granted by commercial banks, whoever the borrower.

Public loans

Loans granted by public lending institutions, whoever the borrower.

Real rate of return

Nominal interest rate less the forecast rate of inflation.

Recession

Negative growth of economic activity in a country or an area for at least two successive quarters.

Risk premium

When loans are granted, the creditors take account of the economic situation of the debtor country in fixing the interest rate. If there seems to be a risk that the debtor country may not be able to honor its repayments, then that will lead to an increase in the rates it will be charged. Thus, the creditors receive more interest, which is supposed to compensate for the risk taken in granting the loan. This means that the cost to the borrower country is much higher, accentuating the financial pressure it has to bear. For example, in 2002, Argentina was faced with risk premiums of more than 4,000 points, which means that for a hypothetical market interest rate of 5 percent, Argentina would have to borrow at a rate of 45 percent. This cuts it off de facto from access to credit, forcing it even deeper into crisis. For Brazil, in August 2002, the risk premium was at 2,500 points.

Securitization
(taken from Adda 2001)

Describes the proliferation of new types of securities (e.g., traditional international bonds issued on behalf of a foreign borrower in the financial location and in the currency of the lender country; eurobonds drawn on a different currency from that of the place of issue; international shares). To this should be added the technique of transforming former bank credits into negotiable securities, which enabled banks to disengage from developing countries faster after the debt crisis. The main logic behind this securitization is that it spreads the risk. First, it spreads it numerically, since the risk of defaulting by borrowers is no longer concen-

trated on a small number of closely related multinational banks. Then there is the qualitative spread of the risk, since each component of risk carried by any particular security may lead to the invention of specific negotiable instruments of protection. Examples of these are fixed-term contracts to protect against the exchange risk, fixed-interest contracts to protect against variation in interest rates, negotiable option markets, etc. This proliferation of financial instruments and derivative markets gives the international markets a casino-like air.

Separate funds or shareholders' equity

Assets that are not matched by liabilities, particularly share capital and reserves. A business is started by shareholders who put up a certain amount of capital. The company can use that money, and also borrow, to acquire things—equipment, materials, etc. It hopes to make a profit. Accumulated profit (reserves) and the amount by which the value of the assets exceeds the liabilities (such as debt) will determine the net worth of the company, i.e., the owners' equity. With your house, the idea is the same: your equity is the amount by which the value of the property exceeds the amount you owe on it.

Speculation

Activity destined to make a profit in the form of surplus value by betting on the future value of goods and financial or monetary assets. Speculation generates a divorce between the financial and the productive spheres. Currency markets are where most speculation takes place.

Stock exchange

The place where bonds and shares are issued and traded. A bond is loan paper—to be redeemed at a prearranged rate and date—while a share gives part ownership in a company. New securities are issued for the first time on the primary market. Bonds and shares can then be bought and sold freely on the secondary market.

Structural Adjustment Facility (SAF) and Enhanced Structural Adjustment Facility (ESAF)

These facilities are IMF instruments that emphasize growth, the fight against poverty, structural reforms, and foreign funding reckoned over a period of three years. ESAF loans are greater in amount but demand considerable structural efforts and entail stringent conditionality. Countries have to be very poor to qualify for them. Created in 1987, the ESAF was extended and broadened in scope in February 1994. ESAF loans are repaid in ten six-month installments, ending ten years after the date of initial outlay, held over for five and a half years. Their interest rate is lower than market rates. ESAF funding is allocated to support stringent medium-term structural adjustment plans. It is financed by more than forty member-states of the IMF, about half of which are developing countries. These Adjustment Facilities were renamed Poverty Reduction and Growth Facility in September 1999.

Surplus value

Surplus value is the difference between the value newly produced by labor power and that labor power's own value, that is, the difference between the value newly produced by a worker and the costs of reproducing his or her labor power. Surplus value, that is the sum total of the incomes of the propertied classes (profits plus interest plus ground rent), is thus a deduction from the social product: it is what remains of the social product once the reproduction of the workforce is assured and its maintenance costs covered. It is therefore nothing other than the monetary form of the social surplus product, which is the propertied classes' share in the distribution of the social product in all class-structured societies: slave-owners' income in a slave society; feudal ground rent in a feudal society; tribute in the tributary mode of production, etc. The wage earner, the proletarian, does not sell "labor" but his or her labor power,

his or her production capacity. It is this labor power that bourgeois society transforms into a marketable commodity. It has its own value, which is an objective fact like that of any commodity: its own production costs, its reproduction overheads. Like any commodity, it has its use (use value) for the buyer, which is a precondition for its sale, but which by no means determines its sale price. Yet, the use, or use value, of labor power for its buyer, the capitalist, is precisely that of producing value, since, by definition, all labor in a market economy adds value to the value of the machines and the raw materials it is applied to. Thus, every wage earner produces "value added." However, since the capitalist pays the worker a wage—which represents the cost of reproduction of labor power—he will only buy this labor power if the value "added" by the worker exceeds the value of the labor power itself. This fraction of value newly produced by the wage earner Marx calls "surplus value." The discovery of surplus value as a fundamental category of bourgeois society and its mode of production, along with the explanation of its nature (a result of the surplus labor, of the unpaid, unrewarded work supplied by the wage earner) and of its origins (the economic necessity for the proletarian to sell his or her labor power to the capitalist as a commodity), represents Marx's main contribution to economics and the social sciences in general. This is, in itself, the application of the perfected labor theory of value to the specific context of a specific commodity, labor power (taken from Mandel 1986).

Tobin Tax

A tax on exchange transactions (all transactions involving conversion of currency), originally proposed in 1972 by US economist James Tobin as a means of stabilizing the international financial system. The idea was taken up by the association ATTAC and other movements for an alternative globalization, including the CADTM. Their aim is to reduce financial speculation (which was of the order of $1.5 trillion a day in 2002) and redistribute the money raised by this tax to those who need it most. International speculators who spend their time changing dollars for yen, then for euros, then dollars again, etc., as they calculate which currency will appreciate and which depreciate, will have to pay a small tax, somewhere between 0.1 percent and 1 percent, on each transaction. According to ATTAC, this could raise $100 billion on a global scale. Considered unrealistic by the ruling classes in order to justify their refusal to adopt it, the meticulous analyses of globalized finance carried out by ATTAC and others have, on the contrary, demonstrated how simple and appropriate such a tax would be.

Trade balance and balance of goods and services

The trade balance of a country is the difference between merchandise sold (exports) and merchandise bought (imports). The resulting trade balance either shows a deficit or is in credit. The balance of goods and services includes transactions for services such as transport costs, banking commissions, insurance costs, buying and selling patents, or debt payments. It also includes tourist spending and the payment of salaries, interest, and dividends to non-nationals or on behalf of non nationals.

Trade-Related Aspects of Intellectual Property Rights (TRIPS)

This agreement came into effect in 1995 within the framework of the World Trade Organization (WTO). According to the UNDP's 1999 *Global Human Development Report*, "It affects such diverse areas as computer programming and circuit design, pharmaceuticals and transgenic crops…. [It] imposes minimum standards on patents, copyright, trademarks, and trade secrets. These standards are derived from the legislation of industrial countries, applying the form and level of protection of the industrial world to all WTO members. This is far tighter than existing legislation in most developing countries and often conflicts with

their national interests and needs…. The WTO's TRIPS agreement can be enforced through the integrated dispute settlement system. This effectively means that if a country does not fulfill its intellectual property rights obligations, trade sanctions can be applied against it—a serious threat."

Treasury bonds

Bonds issued by public treasuries to fund government borrowing. They may be issued for periods from a few months to thirty years.

Triad

The expressions "Triad" and "Triadic" come from Kenichi Ohmae (1985). They were first used in business schools and economic journalism before entering common usage. The three axes of the Triad are the United States, the European Union, and Japan, but larger groups have formed around each of these axes. According to Ohmae, the only hope for a developing country—to which must now be added the former so-called socialist countries—is to reach for the status of associate, or even peripheral, member, of one of these axes. This also holds for the newly industrialized countries (NIC) of Asia, which have been gradually integrated into the axis led by Japan, though with marked differences from one country to another (Chesnais 1997c).

United Nations Conference on Trade and Development (UNCTAD)

Established in 1964, after pressure from the DC, to offset the effects of GATT.

United Nations Development Program (UNDP)_

Founded in 1965 and based in New York, the UNDP is the UN's main agency of technical assistance. It helps the DC, without any political restrictions, to set up basic administrative and technical services, trains managerial staff, tries to respond to some of the essential needs of populations, takes the initiative in regional cooperation programs and coordinates, theoretically at least, the local activities of all the UN operations. The UNDP generally relies on Western expertise and techniques, but a third of its contingent of experts comes from the Third World. The UNDP publishes an annual *Human Development Report*, which, among other things, classifies countries by their human development rating (HDR).

Warsaw Pact

A military pact between the countries of the former Soviet Bloc (USSR, Albania, Bulgaria, Hungary, Poland, the German Democratic Republic, Romania, Czechoslovakia). It was signed in Warsaw, in May 1955, as a reaction to the Federal German Republic joining NATO. Albania withdrew in 1968, after Soviet intervention in Czechoslovakia. After the political transformation of the USSR, the pact's military organization was dissolved in April 1991.

Welfare state

Term dates from 1942. It was a pun on "warfare state." Sir William Beveridge wrote two reports for the Conservative government, the second of which, published in 1944, was entitled *Full Employment in a Free Society*. In it, he discusses the ideas of the economist John Maynard Keynes for combating poverty, unemployment, etc. Immediately after the war, with the rise to power of the Labour Party, the expression "welfare state" was applied to cover a series of social reforms. During the 1950s, the term became associated only with the strictly social aspects. The English term "welfare state" has been translated into French as *l'état-providence*, implying that social rights "fall from heaven" onto "passive" and "irresponsible" citizens. It is important not to confuse the British and European sense of "welfare state" with the meaning in the United States, where it refers to handouts only.

World Bank

Founded in 1944 at Bretton Woods in the context of the new international monetary system, the World Bank's capital is provided by member countries and especially borrowed on the international capital markets. The World Bank finances public- or private-sector projects in the Third World and former so-called socialist countries. It is composed of the following five subsidiaries: the International Bank for Reconstruction and Development (IBRD, 184 members in 2003) makes loans for major sectors of activity (agriculture, energy); the International Development Association (IDA, 164 members in 2003) specializes in very long-term loans (thirty–forty years, with the first ten interest free) at zero or very low interest rates to the Least Developed Countries (LDC); the International Finance Corporation (IFC) is the World Bank subsidiary responsible for financing private firms and institutions in the Third World; finally, the International Center for the Settlement of Investment Disputes (ICSID) deals with financial disagreements, while the Multilateral Investment Guarantee Agency (MIGA) seeks to encourage investment in the DC. With the increase in indebtedness, the World Bank and the IMF have adopted a macroeconomic perspective in their dealings. For example, the World Bank increasingly imposes adjustment plans designed to improve the balance of payments of heavily indebted countries. It never hesitates to dispense "advice" to countries undergoing IMF "therapy" on the best ways to reduce budget deficits, mobilize domestic savings, encourage foreign investors to move in, and liberalize currency exchange and prices. Finally, since 1982, the World Bank has made structural adjustment loans in support of these programs to countries that follow its policies. Types of loans granted by the World Bank:

- Project loans, which are traditional-style loans for power stations, oil and petroleum, forestry industry, and agricultural projects, dams, roads, water distribution and purification projects, etc.

- Sectorial adjustment loans aimed at an entire sector of the national economy: energy, agriculture, industry, etc.

- Loans to agencies whose role it is to direct the policies of institutions toward foreign trade and to open the way for multinational corporations. Such loans also finance the privatization of public services and public enterprises.

- Structural adjustment loans, ostensibly designed to mitigate the debt crisis, which invariably encourage neoliberal policies.

- Loans to combat poverty.

World Trade Organization (WTO)

The WTO, founded on January 1, 1995, replaced the General Agreement on Tariffs and Trade (GATT), where states had only had the status of "contractual parties," as a permanent negotiating forum. One of the WTO's objectives is to dismantle state monopolies resulting from a public decision, where such monopolies still exist. This is what happened for telecommunications, for which the decision was made by the WTO in February 1997. But others still remain, such as the railways, and are coveted by the financial groups. Another objective is the liberalization of investments. The projected instrument to achieve this is the Multilateral Agreement on Investment (MAI), which the OECD was set to approve when France withdrew from discussions in October 1998. The MAI, which was originally decided upon at the ministerial meeting of the OECD in May 1995, targets all investments—direct (industry, services, natural resources) and portfolio. It provides protection mechanisms, especially for the total repatriation of profits. The MAI as such was abandoned in 1998 only to reappear in the sheep's clothing of a multitude of Bilateral Agreements on Investment. The WTO functions in "one country–one vote" mode but the delegates from the countries of the South are overwhelmed by the tons of documents to study, the army of staff, lawyers, etc., of the countries of the North. Decisions are made by the powerful in the green rooms. Nevertheless, following the Seattle episode in November 1999, the Cancún (Mexico) conference in September 2003 was marked by the resistance of a group of twenty-two emerging countries from the South, who joined together for the occasion to make the conference fail in the face of the intransigent Northern countries.

Bibliography

ACHCAR, Gilbert. 1999. *La nouvelle guerre froide: Le monde après le Kosovo.* 1st rev. ed. Paris: Presses universitaires de France. Translated into English as "The strategic triad: The US, China, Russia," and "Rasputin plays at chess: How the West blundered into a new cold war." In *Masters of the universe?: NATO's Balkan crusade.* Tariq Ali, ed. London and New York: Verso, 2000.

———. 2002. *The clash of barbarisms: September 11 and the making of the new world disorder* (Choc des barbaries). New York: Monthly Review Press.

ACOSTA, Alberto. 1994. *La deuda externa* (1990). Quito: Libresa, Collection Ensayo.

ACOSTA, Alberto, and Jürgen Schuldt. 1995. *Inflación: Enfoques y políticas alternativos para América Latina y el Ecuador.* 1st. ed. Quito: Libresa, ILDIS.

ADAMS, Chris. 2000. Punishing the poor: Debt, corporate subsidies, and the ADB. In *The transfer of wealth: Debt and the making of a Global South.* Bangkok: Focus on the Global South.

ADAMS, Patricia. 1991. *Odious debts.* Toronto: Probe International.

ADDA, Jacques. 2001. *La mondialisation de l'économie, 1 et 2* (1996). Paris: La Découverte, Collection Repères.

AGARWAL, Anil, and Sunita Narain. 1997. Dying wisdom: The decline and revival of traditional water harvesting systems in India. *The Ecologist* 27(3): 112–16.

AGLIETTA, Michel. 1976. Régulation et crises du capitalisme: L'expérience des États-Unis. Paris: Calmann-Lévy.

———. 1995a. Ordre et désordre: L'expression universelle du capital argent. *Futur Antérieur* 27: 55–85.

———. 1995b. *Macroéconomie financière.* Paris: La Découverte, Collection Repères.

AGLIETTA, Michel, Anton Brender, and Virginie Coudert. 1990. *Globalisation financière: L'aventure obligée.* With the collaboration of Françoise Hyafil; preface by Michel Albert. Paris: Economica, Diffusion, Documentation française.

AGLIETTA, Michel, and Sandra Moatti. 2000. *Le FMI: De l'ordre monétaire aux désordres financiers.* Paris: Economica.

AITEC. 2000. Mondialisation, institutions financières internationales et développement durable. *Carnets de l'AITEC*, no. 14.

———. 2002. Le financement du développement durable. *Carnets de l'AITEC*, no. 16.

ALIBERT, Jacques. 1996. La dette extérieure de l'Afrique. *Problèmes Economiques* 2480: 4–8.

———. 1997. Un accent particulier mis sur le développement du secteur privé. *Marchés Tropicaux* (July 11).

AMIN, Samir. 1971. *L'Accumulation à l'échelle mondiale: Critique de la théorie du sous-développement.* Paris: Anthropos.

———, ed. 1993. *Mondialisation et accumulation.* Preface by Samir Amin and Pablo Gonzalez Casanova. Université des Nations Unies—Tokyo, Forum du Tiers-Monde. Paris: L'Harmattan.

———. 1995. *La gestion capitaliste de la crise: Le cinquantième anniversaire des institutions de Bretton-Woods.* Paris: L'Harmattan.

AMIN, Samir, Hakim Ben Hammouda, and Bernard Founou-Tchuigoua. 1995. *Afrique et monde arabe: Échec de l'insertion internationale; Le sommet social des Nations Unies; Enlisement de l'Afrique et du monde arabe ou départ d'un développement humain?* Paris: L'Harmattan.

AMIN, Samir and François Houtart. 2000. *Mondialisation et alternatives,* Geneva: CETIM/AAJ/LIDLIP/WILPF.

ANDERSON, Perry. 1996. Histoire et leçons du néo-libéralisme: La construction d'une voie unique. *Page Deux* (October).

ANDREFF, Wladimir. 1982. *Les multinationales hors la crise.* Paris: Le Sycomore, 1982.

———. 1996. *Les multinationales globales.* Paris: La Découverte, Collection Repères.

———. 1997. Les effets de la mondialisation du capital sur les pays de l'Est. *La Pensée* 309: 41–61.

ARRUDA, Marcos. 2000. *External debt: Brazil and the international financial crisis* (1999). Peter Lenny, trans. Sterling, Va.: Pluto Press, in association with Christian Aid.

ASIAN DEVELOPMENT BANK and the World Bank. 2000. *The new social policy agenda in Asia: Proceedings of the Manila Social Forum.* Manila: Asian Development Bank and the World Bank.

ATTAC. 1999. *Contre la dictature des marches.* Bernard Cassen, Liêm Hoang-Ngoc, Pierre-André Imbert, eds. Paris: La dispute.

———. 2000a. *Tout sur Attac.* Paris: Mille et une nuits, Collection Les Petits Libres.

———. 2000b. *Les Paradis fiscaux.* Paris: Mille et une nuits, Collection Les Petits Libres.

———. 2001a. *Avenue du plein emploi.* Paris: Mille et une nuits, Collection Les Petits Libres.

———. 2001b. *Une Économie au service de l'homme.* Paris: Mille et une nuits.

———. 2001c. *Enquête au cœur des multinationales.* Georges Menahem, ed. Paris: Mille et une nuits.

———. 2003. *Inégalités, crises, guerres: Sortir de l'impasse.* Paris: Mille et une nuits, Collection Essais.

AVERMAETE, Jean-Pierre, and Arnaud Zacharie. 2002. *Mise à nu des marchés financiers: Les dessous de la globalisation.* Brussels: Syllepse/Visata/ATTAC.

BALASUBRAMANIAM, K. 1996. SAPs and the privatization of health care. *Third World Resurgence,* no. 68.

BARAN, Paul A., and Paul M. Sweezy. 1970. *Le Capitalisme monopoliste, un essai sur la société industrielle américaine* (1966). Paris: François Maspero. Available in English as *Monopoly capital; An essay on the American economic and social order.* New York: Monthly Review Press, 1968.

BARNES, Jim. 1995. Bretton Woods legacy: 1944–95. New York: Friends of Earth.

BEAUD, Michel. 1997. *Le Basculement du monde: De la terre, des hommes et du capitalisme.* Paris: La Découverte.

————. 2000. *Histoire du capitalisme de 1500 à 2000* (1980). Paris: Seuil. Available in English as *A history of capitalism, 1500–2000.* Tom Dickman and Anny Lefebvre, trans. New York: Monthly Review Press, 2001.

BEAUD, Michel, and Gilles Dostaler. 1995. *La Pensée économique depuis Keynes.* Paris: Seuil. Available in English as *Economic thought since Keynes: A history and dictionary of major economists.* Valérie Cauchemez, trans. (with the participation of Eric Litwack). London and New York: Routledge, 1997.

BECKER, Gary. 1976. *The Economic approach to human behavior.* Chicago: University of Chicago Press.

BEINSTEIN, Jorge. 1999. *La larga crisis de la economía global.* Buenos Aires: Corregidor.

BELLO, Walden. 1997. Addicted to capital: The ten-year high and present-day withdrawal trauma of Southeast Asia's economies. *Issues and Letters* (September–December).

————. 2000a. *Why reform of the WTO is the wrong agenda: Four essays on four institutions: WTO, UNCTAD, IMF and the World Bank.* Bangkok: Focus on the Global South.

————. 2000b. The Prague castle debate: Hard answers, please, gentlemen. In *The transfer of wealth: Debt and the making of a Global South.* Bangkok: Focus on the Global South.

————. 2002. *Deglobalization: Ideas for a new world economy.* London and New York: Zed Books.

BEN HAMMOUDA, Hakim. 1999. *L'économie politique du post-ajustement.* Paris: Karthala.

BENIES, Nicolas. 1995. La dérive des marchés dérivés. *Histoire et Anthropologie,* no. 11.

BENSAÏD, Daniel. 1995a. *Marx l'intempestif: Grandeurs et misères d'une aventure critique (XIXe–XXe siècles).* Paris: Fayard.

————. 1995b. *La discordance des temps: Essais sur les crises, les classes, l'histoire.* Paris: Editions de la Passon.

BERTHELOT, Jacques. 2000. Agriculture, le vrai débat Nord-Sud. *Le Monde diplomatique* (March).

————. 2001. Un Autre modèle pour l'agriculture. *Le Monde diplomatique* (April).

BIHR, Alain. 1997. Les médias comme appareils de dépolitisation. *Raison Présente.*

BIHR, Alain and Roland Pfefferkorn. 1995. *Déchiffrer les inégalités.* Paris: Syros.

————. 1996. *Hommes-Femmes: L'Introuvable égalité.* Paris: Les Editions de l'Atelier; Editions Ouvrières.

BIONDI, Aloysio. 2001. *O Brasil privatizado.* 1st ed. São Paulo, SP, Brazil: Editora Fundação Perseu Abramo.

BIS (BANK FOR INTERNATIONAL SETTLEMENTS). 1995, 2000, 2001a, 2002, 2003. *Annual report.* Basel, Switzerland: Bank for International Settlements.

————2001b. *Quarterly review: International banking and financial market developments* (June). Basel, Switzerland: Bank for International Settlements.

BOND, Patrick. 2000. *Elite transition: From apartheid to neoliberalism in South Africa.* London and Sterling, Va.: Pluto Press.

————. 2001. *Against global apartheid: South Africa meets the World Bank, IMF, and international finance.* Lansdowne: University of Cape Town Press.

BONNET, Michael. 1996. Child labour in the light of bonded labour. In *The Exploited Child.* Bernard Schlemmer, ed. London: Zed Books.

BORÓN, Atilio A. 2002. *Imperio & imperialismo: Una lectura crítica de Michael Hardt y Antonio Negri.* 1st. ed. Buenos Aires: CLACSO-Consejo Latinoamericano de Ciencias Sociales, Secretaría Ejecutiva.

BOURDIEU, Pierre. 1996. Analyse d'un passage à l'antenne. *Le Monde diplomatique* (April).

BOURGUINAT, Henri. 1995. *La tyrannie des marchés: Essai sur l'économie virtuelle.* Paris: Economica

———. 1996. Les Capitaux flottants qui favorisent la spéculation menacent-ils les Etats et les entreprises? In *Bilan du Monde: l'Année économique et sociale 1995.* Jacques-François Simon, ed. Paris: Le Monde.

BOVÉ, José. 1999. Pour une agriculture paysanne. *Le Monde diplomatique* (October).

BOVÉ, José, and François Dufour. 2000. *Le monde n'est pas une marchandise: Des paysans contre la malbouffe.* Paris: Découverte.

BOYCE, James K., and Léonce Ndikumana. 2000. Is Africa a net creditor? New estimates of capital flight from severely indebted sub-Saharan African countries, 1970–1996. University of Massachusetts Amherst, Department of Economics, Working Papers 2000–01.

BRAECKMAN, Colette. 1992. *Le dinosaure: Le Zaïre de Mobutu.* Paris: Fayard.

———. 1994. *Rwanda. Histoire d'un génocide.* Paris: Fayard.

BRAINARD, S. Lael, and David A. Riker. 1997a. Are US multinationals exporting US jobs? Working Paper No. W5958. Cambridge, Mass.: National Bureau of Economic Research.

———. 1997b. US multinationals and competition from low wage countries. Working Paper No. W5959. Cambridge, Mass.: National Bureau of Economic Research.

BRAUDEL, Fernand. 1993. *La dynamique du capitalisme.* Paris: Flammarion, Collection Champs.

BRENNER, Robert. 2002. *The boom and the bubble: The U.S. in the world economy.* London and New York: Verso.

BROOKS, Ray, et al. 1998. External debt histories of ten low-income developing countries: Lessons from their experience. Working Paper No. 98/72. Washington DC: IMF.

BROWN, Lester R., et al. *L'État de la planète 1992.* Paris: Economica. Available in English as *State of the world 1992: A Worldwatch Institute report on progress toward a sustainable society.* New York and London: W.W. Norton & Co.

———. *L'État de la planète 1993.* Paris: Economica. Available in English as *State of the world 1993: A Worldwatch Institute report on progress toward a sustainable society.* New York and London: W.W. Norton & Co.

———. *L'État de la planète 1995/1996.* Paris: La Découverte. Available in English as *State of the world 1995: A Worldwatch Institute report on progress toward a sustainable society,* and *State of the world 1996.* New York and London: W.W. Norton & Co.

BRUNHOFF, Suzanne (DE). 1996. L'Instabilité monétaire internationale. In *La mondialisation financière: Genèse, coût et enjeux.* F. Chesnais, ed. Paris: Syros, Alternatives économiques.

BULLARD, Nicola, Walden Bello, and Kamal Malhotra. 1998. Taming the tigers: The IMF and the Asian crisis. *Focus on Trade,* no. 23 (March).

BUSTER, G. 2001. Union européenne: Lamy vend la carotte néolibérale aux pays pauvres. *Inprecor* 457.

CADTM. 1998. *Du Nord au Sud: L'endettement dans tous ses états.* Brussels: 1998 (1st quarter).

CALCAGNO, Alfredo Eric. 1999. *La deuda externa explicada a todos: Los que tienen que pagarla.* Buenos Aires: Catálogos.

CAPUTO, Orlando. 2001. *La economía de EE.UU. y de América latina en las últimas décadas.* Chile: Centro de Investigaciones Sociales (CIS).

CARDOSO, Fernando Henrique, and Enzo Faletto. 1970. *Dependencia y desarrollo en América Latina* (1969). Mexico City: Siglo XXI.

CARTAPANIS, André, ed. 1996. *Turbulences et spéculations dans l'économie mondiale.* Paris: Economica.

CASSEN, Bernard. 2000. Inventer ensemble un "protectionnisme altruiste." *Le Monde diplomatique* (February).

———. 2003. *Tout a commencé à Porto Alegre.* Paris: Mille et une nuits.

CASTEL, Odile. 2002. *Le sud dans la mondialisation, quelles alternatives?* Paris: La Découverte.

CASTRO, Fidel. 1985a. *La cancelación de la deuda externa y el nuevo orden económico internacional como unica alternativa verdadera, otros asuntos de interes político e historico: Texto completo de la entrevista concedida al periodico Excelsior de México.* Havana: Editora Política.

———. 1985b. *Encuentro sobre la deuda externa de América Latina y el Caribe: Discurso, Ciudad de La Habana, 3 de agosto de 1985, sesión de clausura.* Havana: Editora Política.

———. 1985c. *La impagable deuda externa de América Latina y del Tercer Mundo, como puede y debe ser cancelada y la urgente necesidad del nuevo orden económico internacional: Entrevista concedida al periódico Excélsior de México.* Havana: Editora Política.

———. 1985d. *No hay otra alternativa: La cancelación de la deuda.* Havana: Editora Política.

———. 1985e. *Pagar tributo al imperio o pagar tributo a la patria.* Havana: Editora Política.

———. 1997. *Carta a los participantes en el Encuentro Continental "La deuda externa y el Fin del Milenio."* Havana (July 9).

CENTRE TRICONTINENTAL. 1994. Les effets sociaux des programmes d'ajuste-ment structurel dans les sociétés du Sud. *Alternatives Sud* 1:2. Paris: L'Harmattan.

———. 1995. Emploi, croissance et précarité. *Alternatives Sud* 2:1. Paris: L'Harmattan.

———. 1998. Les Tigres du Sud: Crise d'un modèle ou contradictions de l'économie capitaliste. *Alternatives Sud* 5:3. Paris: L'Harmattan.

———. 1998. Rapports de genre et mondialisation des marchés. *Alternatives Sud* 5:4. Paris: L'Harmattan.

———. 1999. Les Organismes financiers internationaux, instruments de l'économie politique libérale. *Alternatives Sud* 6:2. Paris: L'Harmattan.

———. 1999. Démocratie et marché. *Alternatives Sud* 6:3. Paris: L'Harmattan.

———. 2002. Raisons et déraisons de la dette: Le point de vue du Sud. *Alternatives Sud* 10:2–3. Paris: L'Harmattan.

CENTRE D'ETUDES PROSPECTIVES ET D'INFORMATIONS INTERNATIONALES (CEPII). 2000. *L'économie mondiale 2001.* Paris: La Découverte.

CHAUVIER, Jean-Marie. 1995. *L'ajustement dans la CEI.* Unpublished.

CHEMILLIER-GENDREAU, Monique. 1998. *L'Injustifiable: Les politiques françaises de l'immigration,* Paris: Fayard.

CHESNAIS, Francois. 1994. *La mondialisation du capital.* Paris: syros, Alternatives économiques.

———. 1995. Graves secousses dans le système financier mondial. *Le Monde diplomatique* (May).

———, ed. 1996. *La mondialisation financière: Genèse, coût et enjeux.* Paris: Syros, Alternatives économiques.

———. 1997a. Demain, les retraites à la merci des marchés. *Le Monde diplomatique* (April).

———. 1997b. L'émergence d'un régime d'accumulation mondial à dominante financière. *La Pensée* 309.

———. 1997c. *La mondialisation du capital* (1994). Paris: Syros, Alternatives économiques.

———. 1998. *Tobin or not Tobin?* Paris: L'Esprit Frappeur.

CHESNAIS, François, and Jean-Philippe Divès. 2002. *Que se vayan todos!: Le peuple d'Argentine se soulève*. Paris: Nautilus.

CHESNAIS, François, Gérard Duménil, Dominique Lévy, and Immanuel Wallerstein. 2001. *Une Nouvelle phase du capitalisme?* Paris: Syllepse.

CHOMSKY, Noam. 1999. *The new military humanism: Lessons from Kosovo*. Monroe, Maine: Common Courage Press. Available in French as *Le Nouvel humanisme militaire*. Lausanne: Page deux, 1999.

CHOSSUDOVSKY, Michel. 1993. Risques de famine aggravés dans le Sud. *Le Monde diplomatique* (September).

———. 1994. La pauvreté des nations. *CADTM*, No. 12.

———. 1995a. *The global economic crisis.* Department of Economics, University of Ottawa and CADTM.

———. 1995b. Rwanda, Somalie, ex Yougoslavie: Conflits armés, génocide économique et responsabilités des institutions de Bretton Woods. In *Banque, FMI, OMC: ça suffit!* Brussels: CADTM.

———. 1997. *The globalization of poverty: Impacts of IMF and World Bank reforms.* London and Atlantic Highlands, N.J.: Zed Books; Penang, Malaysia: Third World Network.

CHRISTIN, Ivan. 1995. *La Banque Mondiale.* Paris: Que sais-je?, PUF.

CLACSO. 2002. *Observatorio Social de América Latina*, No. 7. Buenos Aires: CLASCO.

CLACSO. 2003. *Observatorio Social de América Latina*, No. 10. Buenos Aires: CLASCO.

CLAIRMONT, Frédéric F. 1987. Prebisch and UNCTAD: The unravelled myths. *Raw Materials Report* 5:2.

———. 1994. L'Holocauste du travail dans les pays industrialisés. In *Banque mondial/FMI: ça suffit!* (I). Brussels: CADTM.

———. 1996. *The rise and fall of economic liberalism.* Penang: Southbound and Third World Network.

———. 1997. Ces deux cents sociétés qui contrôlent le monde. *Le Monde diplomatique* (April).

CLAIRMONT, F.-F., and Cavanagh, J. 1994. Sous les ailes du capitalisme planétaire. *Le Monde diplomatique* (March).

COLLINS, Chuck, and Felice Yeskel, with United for a Fair Economy. 2000. *Economic apartheid in America: A primer on economic inequality & insecurity.* New York: New Press.

COMANNE, Denise, and Eric Toussaint. 1994. Transferts Sud-Nord: ça suffit! In *Banque mondiale/FMI: ça suffit!* (I), Brussels: CADTM.

———. 1995a. Dette, ce nouvel esclavage de l'Afrique: Analyse et propositions. In *Banque mondiale/FMI/Organisation Mondiale du Commerce: ça suffit!* (II), Brussels: CADTM.

———. 1995b. Globalization and debt. In *IMF/World Bank/WTO: The Free Market Fiasco.* Eric Toussaint and Peter Drucker, eds. Notebooks for Study and Research, No. 24/25. Amersterdam: International Institute for Research and Education (IIRE).

COMBEMALE, Pascal. 2003. *Introduction à Keynes* (1999). Paris: La Découverte, Collection Repères.

COMMITTEE FOR ASIAN WOMEN (CAW). 2000. *Dolls & dust: Voices of Asian women workers resisting globalization.* Bangkok: Committee for Asian Women: WAYANG.

CONFERENCE OF NON-GOVERNMENTAL ORGANIZATIONS. 1988. *The external debt, development and international co-operation.* Paris: L'Harmattan.

COUTROT, Thomas. 1991. Les théories de la dépendance à l'épreuve des faits. *Critique Communiste.*

COUTROT, Thomas, and Michel Husson. 1993. *Les destins du Tiers Monde.* Paris: Nathan.

DECORNOY, Jacques. 1993. Hors des multinationales: Point de salut! *Le Monde diplomatique* (September).

———. 1995. Travail, capital: Pour qui chantent les lendemains? *Le Monde diplomatique* (September).

DÍAZ-SALAZAR, Rafael, ed. 2002. *Justicia global: Las alternativas de los movimientos del Foro de Porto Alegre.* 1st ed. Barcelona: Intermón.

DIBLING, Sébastien. 2003. *Le Problème du transfert des pays en développement: Estimations, causes, conséquences. Etude de cas: Argentine, Inde, Tanzanie et Thaïlande.* Free University of Brussels, Solvay Business School, academic year 2002–03.

DUGGAN, Penny, and Heather Dashner, eds. 1994. Les femmes dans la nouvelle économie mondiale. *Cahiers d'étude et de recherche* 22. Amsterdam: IIRE.

DUMÉNIL, Gérard, and Dominique Lévy, eds. 1999. *Le triangle infernal: Crise, mondialisation, financiarisation; Actes du Congrès Marx international II.* 1st rev. ed. Paris: Presses Universitaires de France.

———. 2000. *Crise et sortie de crise: Ordre et désordres néolibéraux.* Paris: Presses Universitaires de France.

EDWARDS, Sebastian. 1997. *Crisis y reforma en América Latina* (1995). Buenos Aires: Emece? Editores. Available in English as *Crisis and reform in Latin America: From despair to hope.* Oxford and New York: Published for the World Bank [by] Oxford University Press, 1995.

EMMANUEL, Arghiri. 1972. *El intercambio desigual* (1969). Mexico City: Siglo XXI. Available in English as *Unequal exchange: A study of the imperialism of trade.* London: New Left Books, 1972.

EURODAD. 1995. *World credit tables: Creditor-debtor relations from another perspective; Analysis creditor profiles tables and matrices, 1994–1995.* Brussels: EURODAD.

———. 1996. *World credit tables, 1996.* Brussels: EURODAD.

———. 1997. *La dette du Tiers Monde dans les années 90.* Brussels: EURODAD.

FATTORELLI CARNEIRO, Maria Lucia, ed. 2003. *Auditoria da divida externa: Questao de soberania.* Rio de Janeiro: Contraponto.

FEB. 1986. Le FMI et la Banque Mondiale, in *Bulletin de la FEB,* March 15–31: 496-97.

FÉLIX, David. 1987. Alternative outcomes of the Latin American debt crisis: Lessons from the past. *Latin American Research Review* 22(2): 3–46.

FERRIÉ, Christian. 1994. Est-il possible de réformer la Banque mondiale? *Le Monde diplomatique* (June).

FISHLOW, Albert. 1985. Lessons from the past: Capital markets during the 19th century and the interwar period. *International Organization* 39(3): 383–439.

FOCUS ON THE GLOBAL SOUTH. 2000. *The transfer of wealth: Debt and the making of a Global South.* Bangkok: Focus on the Global South.

———. 2001. *Porto Alegre 2001: Rumo a um mundo desglobalizado Hacia a un mundo deglobalizado.* Bangkok: Focus on the Global South.

FOOD AND AGRICULTURE ORGANIZATION OF THE UNITED NATIONS. 2002. *The state of food insecurity in the world.* Rome: FAO.

FOURTH INTERNATIONAL. 1996. Confronting capitalist globalization—Resolution of the XIVth World Congress. *International Viewpoint* (February).

FOXLEY, Alejandro. 1988. *Experimentos neoliberales en América latina*. Mexico City: Fondo de Cultura Económica.

FRIEDMAN, Milton. 1970. *The counter-revolution in monetary theory: First Wincott memorial lecture, delivered at the Senate House, University of London, 16 September 1970*. London: Published for the Wincott Foundation by the Institute of Economic Affairs.

GALAND, Pierre, and Gabrielle Lefèvre. 1996. *Coopération au développement: Aide ou business*. Brussels: EVO.

GALEANO, Eduardo. 1993. *Las venas abiertas de América latina* (1970). Mexico City: Siglo XXI. Available in English as *Open veins of Latin America: Five centuries of the pillage of a continent*. Cedric Belfrage, trans. 25th anniversary ed. Foreword by Isabel Allende. New York: Monthly Review Press, 1997.

GEORGE, Susan. 1989. *Jusqu'au cou*. Paris: La Découverte.

———. 1992. *L'effet Boomerang*. Paris: La Découverte, Collection Essais. Available in English as *The debt boomerang: How Third World debt harms us all*. Boulder, Colo.: Westview Press, 1992.

———. 1996. Comment la pensée devient unique. *Le Monde diplomatique* (August).

———. 1999. A l'OMC, trois ans pour achever la mondialisation. *Le Monde diplomatique* (July).

———. 2000. *Le rapport Lugano*. Paris: Fayard. Available in English as *The Lugano report: On preserving capitalism in the twenty-first century*. London and Sterling, Va.: Pluto Press, 1999.

GEORGE, Susan, and Fabrizio Sabelli. 1994. *Crédits sans frontières*. Paris: La Découverte, Collection Essais.

GILDER, George. 1981. *Richesse et Pauvreté*. Paris: Fayard, Albin Michel.

GONÇALVES, Reinaldo, and Valter Pomar. 2000. *O Brazil endividado*. São Paulo: Fundaçao Perseu Abramo.

GONZÁLEZ CASANOVA, Pablo. 1999. *La explotación global*. Mexico: CEIICH-UNAM.

GRESEA. 1996a. *Déclarations officielles du G7 depuis son origine (1975–1995)*. Brussels: GRESEA (May).

———. 1996b. *G7, Mythes et réalités*. Brussels: GRESEA (April).

GUILLÉN ROMO, Arturo. 2000. *México hacia el siglo XXI: Crisis y modelo económico alternativo*. 1st ed. México: Plaza y Valdés Editores.

GUNDER FRANK, André. 1971. *Lumpen-bourgeoisie et lumpen-développement*. Paris: Maspero. Available in English as *Lumpenbourgeoisie: Lumpendevelopment*. New York: Monthly Review Press, 1972.

———. 1977. *L'Accumulation mondiale, 1500–1800*. Paris: Calmann-Lévy.

GUTTMANN, Robert. 1996. Les mutations du capital financier. In *La mondialisation financiere: Genese, cout et enjeux*. F. Chesnais, ed. Paris: Syros, Alternatives économiques.

HARRIBEY, Jean-Marie. 2002. *La Démence sénile du capital*. Bègles: Editions du Passant, Collection Poches de résistance.

HAYEK, Friedrich August (VON). August. 1944. *The road to serfdom*. Chicago: University of Chicago Press.

HENWOOD, Doug. 1998. *Wall Street: How it works and for whom*. London and New York: Verso.

HOBSBAWN, Eric J. 1999. *L'Âge des extrêmes. Le Court Vingtième Siècle* (1994). Brussels: Complexe.

HOCHRAICH, Diana. 2002. *Mondialisation contre développement: Le cas des pays asiatiques*. Paris: Syllepse.

HOLZMANN, Robert. 1999. The World Bank approach to pension reform. Social

Protection Discussion Paper Series, No. 9807.

HORMAN, Denis. 1996. *Commerce mondial: Une clause sociale pour l'emploi et les droits fondamentaux?* Brussels: Luc Pire.

———. 1998. *Stratégies des multinationales: Résistances sociales.* Brussels: GRESEA.

———. 2001. *Mondialisation excluante, nouvelles solidarités: Soumettre ou démettre l'OMC!* Paris: L'Harmattan.

HUERTA GONZÁLEZ, Arturo. 2000. *La dolarización, inestabilidad financiera y alternativa, en el fin del sexenio.* 1st ed. México: Editorial Diana.

HUGON, Philippe. 1999. *L'Économie de l'Afrique* (1993). Paris: La Découverte, Collection Repères.

HUSSON, Michel. 1994. Les fausses évidences du marché: Le cas de l'accord de libre-échange nord-américain. *Cahiers des Sciences Humaines* 30(1–2): 91–109.

———. 1995. Mexico City: La dévaluation du modèle néolibéral. *Critique communiste* 142.

———. 1996. *Misère du capital: Une critique du néo-libéralisme.* Paris: Syros, Collection Pour Débattre.

———. 2000. *Six milliards sur la planète: Sommes-nous trop?* Paris: Textuel.

ILO (INTERNATIONAL LABOR ORGANIZATION). 1995. World Employment 1995. Geneva: ILO.

IMF (INTERNATIONAL MONETARY FUND). 1995, 1997a, 2000a. *World Economic Outlook.* Washington DC: IMF.

———. 1997b, 2000b. *Annual Report.* Washington DC: IMF.

———. 1997c. Debt relief for low-income countries: The HIPC Initiative. In *Pamphlet Series* 51. Washington DC: IMF.

———. 1997d. Press conference with Michel Camdessus. December 18.

INSEE (INSTITUT NATIONAL DE LA STATISTIQUE ET DES ÉTUDES ÉCONOMIQUES).

JACQUARD, Albert. 1996. *J'Accuse l'économie triomphante.* Paris: Calmann-Lévy.

JETIN, Bruno. 2002. *La Taxe Tobin et la solidarité entre les nations.* Paris: Descartes.

JOCHNICK, Chris, Patricio Pazmino, and Juan Fernando Teran. 2000. *Un continente contra la deuda: perspectivas y enfoques para la accion,* Quito: Centro de Derechos Económicos y Sociales.

JUBILÉ SUD. *Déclaration du Sommet Sud-Sud.* Quezon City: Jubilee South International Coordinating Committee.

KAHLER, Miles, ed. 1986. *The politics of international debt.* Ithaca: Cornell University Press.

KATZ, Claudio. 2001. Les nouvelles turbulences d'une économie malmenée par l'impérialisme. *Inprecor* 457 (April).

KETKAR, Suhas, and Dilip Ratha. 2001. Development finance during a crisis: Securitization of future receivables. Policy research working paper (WPS2582). Washington DC: World Bank.

KEYNES, John. M. 1945. *Teoría general de la ocupación, el interés y el dinero* (1936). Mexico City: Fondo de Cultura Económica. Available in English as *The general theory of employment, interest and money.* New York: Harcourt, Brace, 1936.

———. M. 1964. *The general theory of employment, interest and money* (1936). London: Macmillan

KHALFAN, Ashfaq, Jeff King, and Bryan Thomas. 2002. *Advancing the odious debt doctrine.* Working Paper for KAIROS: Canadian Ecumenical Jubilee Initiatives 28 February 2002. Centre for International Sustainable Development Law Document No. COM/RES/ESJ/2001-07.

KHOR, Martin, 1994. South-North resource flows and their implications for sustainable development. *Third World Resurgence* 46.

KILLICK, Tony. 1995. *Solving the multilateral debt problem: Reconciling relief with acceptability*. Report prepared for the Commonwealth Secretariat, for the Commonwealth Finance Ministers Meeting in Jamaica.

KRUEGER, Anne O. 1998. Whither the World Bank and the IMF? *Journal of Economic Literature* 36(4): 1983–2020.

KROLL, Jean-Christophe. 2001. Les limites du cadre de négociation à l'OMC: Pour une régulation institutionnelle efficace des marchés agricoles. Seminar "France-Japon. Quelle agriculture? Quelles politiques agricole et alimentaire pour demain?" Paris, February 19–20. INAPG, Institut National Agronomique Paris-Grignon; Université de Tokyo, Faculté d'Agronomie.

LABARDE, Philippe, and Bernard Maris. 2000. *La Bourse ou la vie: La grande manipulation des petits actionnaires*. Paris: Albin Michel.

LABICA, Georges, and Gérard Bensussan, eds. 1985. *Dictionnaire critique du marxisme* (1982). 2nd ed. Paris: Presses Universitaires de France.

LAFAY, Gérard. 1996. *Comprendre la mondialisation*. Paris: Economica.

LANCASTER, Carol. 1993. Governance and development: The views from Washington. *IDS Bulletin* 24(1).

LEBARON, Frédéric. 2000. *La Croyance économique: Les économistes entre science et politique*. Paris: Seuil.

LECA, Jean, and Roberto Papeni, eds. 1985. *Les Démocraties sont-elles gouvernables?* Paris: Economica.

LEMOINE, Maurice. 2001. *La Dette: Roman de la paysannerie brésilienne*. Nantes: L'Atalante.

LENAIN, Patrick. 1993. *Le FMI*. Paris: La Découverte, Collection Repères.

LEWIS, Paul. 1992. *The crisis of Argentine capitalism* (1990). Chapel Hill: University of North Carolina Press.

LILLE, François, and François-Xavier Verschave. 2003. *On peut changer le monde: À la recherche des biens publics mondiaux*. Paris: La Découverte.

LOSSON, Christian, and Paul Quinio. 2002. *Génération Seattle: Les rebelles de la mondialisation*. Paris: Bernard Grasset.

LÖWY, Michael, ed. 1987. Le Populisme en Amérique latine. *Cahiers d'étude et de recherche* 6. Amsterdam: IIRE.

MACHADO, João, and Paul Singer. 2000. *Economía socialista*. São Paulo: Fundação Perseu Abramo.

MAGDOFF, Harry, and Paul M. Sweezy. 1987. *Stagnation and the financial explosion*. New York: Monthly Review Press.

MAILLARD, Jean de. 1998. *Un Monde sans loi*. Paris: Stock.

MAIZELS, Alfred. 2000. Economic dependence on commodities. Paper presented at UNCTAD X: High-Level Round Table on Trade and Development: Directions for the Twenty-first Century (Bangkok).

MALTHUS, Thomas Robert. 1980. *Essai sur le principe de population* (1798). Paris: PUF.

MANDEL, Ernest. 1968a. L'accumulation primitive et l'industrialisation du tiers monde. In Victor Fay, ed. *En partant du "capital."* Paris: Anthropos.

———. 1968b. *Marxist economic theory*, 2 vols. (1962). Brian Pearce, trans. London: Merlin Press.

———. 1971. *The formation of the economic thought of Karl Marx: 1843 to* Capital. Brian Pearce, trans. New York: Monthly Review Press.

———. 1975a. La hausse du prix du pétrole n'a pas provoqué la 20ème crise de surproduction depuis la formation du marché mondial du capitalisme industriel. *Inprecor* (January 16).

———. 1975b. *Late capitalism*. Rev. ed. Joris De Bres, trans. (from German). London: NLB; Atlantic Highlands, N.J.: Humanities Press.

———. 1982. *La crise, 1974–1982: Les faits, leur interprétation marxiste.* Paris: Flammarion, Collection Champs.

———. 1986. La place du marxisme dans l'histoire. *Cahiers d'étude et de recherche* 1. Amsterdam: IIRE.

———. 1989. L'annulation de la dette du tiers monde. *Dossier Rouge* 29.

———. 1994. La dette du tiers monde, les privatisations, la crise mondiale. *CADTM* 12.

———. 1995. *Long waves of capitalist development: The Marxist interpretation; Based on the Marshall lectures given at the University of Cambridge, 1978* (1980). 2nd rev. ed. London: Verso.

MARICHAL, Carlos. 1989. *A century of debt crises in Latin America: From independence to the Great Depression, 1820–1930.* Princeton, N.J.: Princeton University Press.

———. 1997. The vicious cycles of Mexican debt. *NACLA Report on the Americas* 31(3): 25–31.

———. 2002. *Historia de la deuda externa de America latina* (1988). Madrid: Alianza.

MARIS, Bernard. 1999. *Keynes, ou, L'économiste citoyen.* Paris: Presses de Sciences po, La bibliothèque du citoyen.

MARX, Karl. 1963. *Le Capital*, vol. 1 (1867). Paris: Gallimard, Collection Bibliothèque de la Pléiade.

———. 1968. *Le Capital*, vol. 2 (1869–79). Paris: Gallimard, Collection Bibliothèque de la Pléiade.

———. 1972. *Grundrisse der Kritik der politischen ökonomie* (1857–58), 6 vols. Paris: Union générale d'éditions, Collection 10/18.

———. 1976. *Capital*, vol. 1 (1867). Middlesex: Penguin.

———. 1982. *Le Capital*, vol. 3. Paris: Gallimard, Collection Bibliothèque de la Pléiade.

MARX, Karl, and Friedrich Engels. 1978. *La Crise.* Paris: Union générale d'éditions, Collection 10/18.

MASON, Edward S., and Robert E. Asher. 1973. *The World Bank at quarter century; Highlights of the World Bank since Bretton Woods.* Washington DC: Brookings Institution.

MASSIAH, Gus. 1996. Le G7 en 1996, la montée des resistances. *Inprecor* (June).

MATHIAS, Gilberto, and Pierre Salama. 1983. *L'Etat surdéveloppé: Des métropoles au Tiers monde.* Paris: La Découverte/Maspero.

MATON, Jef. 1994. *Développement économique et social au Rwanda entre 1980 et 1993: Le dixième décile en face de l'apocalypse.* Université de Gand, Faculté de Sciences économiques.

M'BOKOLO, Elikia. 1985. *L'Afrique au XXe siècle* (1980). Paris: Seuil.

McNAMARA, Robert S. 1968. *The essence of security: Reflections in office.* London: Hodder and Stoughton.

———. 1973. *One hundred countries, two billion people.* London: Pall Mall Press.

McNAMARA, Robert S., with Brian Van-DeMark. 1995. *In retrospect: The tragedy and lessons of Vietnam.* New York: Times Books.

MICHALET, Charles Albert. 2002. *Qu'est-ce que la mondialisation? : Petit traité à l'usage de ceux et celles qui ne savent pas encore s'il faut être pour ou contre.* Paris: La Découverte.

MILLET, Damien, and Eric Toussaint. 2004. *Who owes who?* Vicki Briault Manus, trans. London: Zed Books.

———. 2002. *50 Questions/50 réponses sur la dette, le FMI et la Banque mondiale.* Brussels: CADTM; Paris: Syllepse.

MOISSERON, Jean-Yves, and Marc Raffinot, eds. 1999. *Dette and pauvreté: Solvabilité et allègement de la dette des pays à faible revenu.* Paris: DIAL/Economica.

MONTES, Pedro. 1996. *El desorden neoliberal*. Madrid: Editorial Trotta.

MONTLIBERT, Christian de. 2001. *La Violence du chômage*. Strasbourg: Presses Universitaires de Strasbourg.

MORRISSON, Christian. 1996. The political feasibility of adjustment (English translation). Development Center Policy Brief, No. 13. Paris: OECD.

NARAYAN, Deepa, et al. 2000. *Can anyone hear us?* New York: Oxford University Press for the World Bank.

NDIAYE, Badara. 1994. *L'École de la dette: Le cas du Sénégal*. Brussels: CADTM-GRESEA.

NDUHUNGIREHE, Marie-Chantal. 1995. *Les Programmes d'ajustement structurel: Spécificité et application au cas du Rwanda*. B.A. dissertation, Catholic University of Leuwen, Faculty of Economics.

NOREL, Philippe, and Eric Saint-Alary. 1992. *L'Endettement du tiers-monde* (1988). Paris: Syros, Alternatives économiques.

OECD (ORGANIZATION FOR ECONOMIC COOPERATION AND DEVELOPMENT). 1996. *Quelques aspects de la dette extérieure à fin 1995*. Paris: OECD.

———. 2000. *OECD in figures: Statistics on the member countries*. Paris: OECD.

———. 2001. *Statistiques de la dette extérieure: Principaux agrégats, 1998–1999*. Paris: OECD.

OHMAE, Kenichi. 1985. *Triad power: The coming shape of global competition*. New York: Free Press.

———. 1990. *The borderless world: Power and strategy in the interlinked economy*. New York: HarperBusiness.

OLMOS, Alejandro. 1995. *Todo lo que usted quiso saber sobre la deuda externa y siempre le ocultaron* (1990). 3rd ed. Buenos Aires: Editorial de los Argentinos.

OMINAMI, Carlos. 1996. La experiencia chilena y los desafíos regionales. In *Economía latinoamericana: La globalización de los desajustes*. Rafael Urriola, ed. Caracas: Nueva Sociedad; Quito: ILDIS.

OVERBEEK, H. 1994. Mondialisering en regionalisering: De wording van een Europeese migratiepolitiek. *Migrantenstudies* 10(2): 66–84.

OXFAM INTERNATIONAL. 1995. *Multilateral debt: An end to the crisis*. OXFAM International Position Paper (September).

———. 1996. *Multilteral debt: The human costs*. OXFAM International Position Paper (February).

PASSET, René. 2000. *L'Illusion néo-libérale*. Paris: Fayard.

PASTOR, Jaime. 2002. *Qué son los movimientos antiglobalizacion*. Barcelona: RBA Integral.

PAYER, Cheryl. 1975. *The debt trap: The International Monetary Fund and the Third World* (1974). New York and London: Monthly Review Press.

———. 1991. *Lent and lost: Foreign credit and Third World Development*. London and Atlantic Highlands, N.J.: Zed Books.

PETRELLA, Riccardo, ed. 1995. *Limites à la compétitivité: Vers un nouveau contrat mondial*. Brussels: Editions Labor.

———. 2001. *The water manifesto: Arguments for a world water contract*. Patrick Camiller, trans. London and New York: Zed Books.

PIOT, Olivier. 1995. *Finance et économie, la fracture*. Paris: Le Monde.

PLIHON, Dominique. 1991. *Les Taux de change*. Paris: La Découverte, Collection Repères.

———. 1996. Déséquilibres mondiaux et instabilité financière: la responsabilité des politiques liberals. In *La mondialisation financière: Genèse, coût et enjeux*. F. Chesnais, ed. Paris: Syros, Alternatives économiques.

———. 2001. *Le Nouveau capitalisme*. Paris: Dominos Flammarion.

PODER JUDICIAL DE LA NACIÓN. Fallo/causa No. 14.467 caratulada Olmos Alejandro S/dcia, expte No. 7.723/98. Buenos Aires, July 13, 2000.

POLANYI, Karl. 1985. *The great transformation* (1944). Boston: Beacon Press.

PONT, Raul. 2000. *Democracia, participação, ciudadania: Uma visão de esquerda*. Porto Alegre: Palmarenca.

PREBISCH, Raúl. 1984. *Capitalismo periférico: Crisis y transformación* (1981). Mexico City: Fondo de Cultura Económica.

PUBLIC CITIZEN. 2001. *Blind faith: How deregulation and Enron's influence over government looted billions from Americans*. Washington DC: Public Citizen.

RAFFINOT, Marc. 1993. *La Dette des tiers mondes*. Paris: La Découverte.

RAGHAVAN, Chakravarthi. 1990. *Recolonisation, L'avenir du Tiers-Monde and les négociations commerciales du GATT*. Paris: Artel, L'Harmattan, Les Magasins du Monde–Oxfam.

RAINELLI, Michel. 1993. *Le Gatt*. Paris: La Découverte, Collection Repères.

RAPOPORT, Mario, et al. 2000. *Historia Económica, política y social de Argentina 1880–2000*. Buenos Aires, Bogota, Caracas, and Mexico City: Ediciones Macchi.

RICARDO, David. 1977. *Des Principes de l'économie politique et de l'impôt* (On the principles of political economy, and taxation) (1817). Paris: Flammarion.

RICH, Bruce. 1994. *Mortgaging the earth*. Boston: Beacon Press.

ROBERT, Denis. 2002. *La Boîte noire*. Paris: Editions des arènes.

ROBERT, Denis, and Ernest Backes. 2001. *Révélation$*. Paris: Editions des arènes.

ROBINSON, Joan. 1960. *La Acumulación de capital* (Accumulation of capital) (1956).

Mexico City and Buenos Aires: Fondo de Cultura Económica.

———. 1970. *Libertad y necesidad* (Freedom and necessity). Mexico City: Siglo XXI.

SACK, Alexander Nahum. 1927. *Les Effets des transformations des etats sur leurs dettes publiques et autres obligations financières* (The effects of changes of government on states' public debt and other financial obligations). Paris: Recueil Sirey.

SADER, Emir. 2000. *Seculo XX: Uma biografia não-autorizada*. São Paulo: Fundação Perseu Abramo.

SALAMA, Pierre. 1989. *La Dollarisation: Essai sur la monnaie, l'industrialisation et l'endettement des pays sous-développés*. Paris: La Découverte, Agelma.

———. 1996. La Financiarisation excluante: Les leçons des économies latino-américaines. In *La mondialisation financière: Genèse, coût et enjeux*, F. Chesnais, ed. Paris: Syros, Alternatives économiques.

SALAMA, Pierre, and Patrick Tissier. 1982. *L'Industrialisation dans le sous-développement*. Paris: Maspero, Collection Petite.

SALAMA, Pierre, and Jacques Valier. 1994. *Pauvreté et inégalités dans le tiers monde*. Paris: La Découverte.

SALVERDA, Menno. 2000. Balancing the power of money. In *The transfer of wealth: Debt and the making of a Global South*. Bangkok: Focus on the Global South, 59–67.

SAMIZDAT.NET. 2002. *Gênes 19-20-21 juillet 2001: Multitudes en marche contre l'Empire*. Paris: Editions Reflex.

SANTOS, Theotonio (DOS). 1982. *Imperialismo y dependencia* (1978). Mexico City: Era.

SAXE-FERNÁNDEZ, John, and Omar Núñez Rodríguez. 2001. Globalización e imperialismo: A transferencia de excedentes de América Latina. In *Globalización, imperi-*

alismo y clase social. John Saxe-Fernández et al., eds. Mexico: Lumen SRL.

SCHNEIDERMANN, Daniel. 1996. Réponse à Pierre Bourdieu. *Le Monde diplomatique* (May).

SEN, Amartya. 1999. *L'Économie est une science morale.* Paris: La Découverte.

SERFATI, Claude. 1995. *Production d'armes: Croissance et innovation.* Paris: Economica.

———. 1996. Le Rôle actif des groupes à dominante industrielle dans la financiarisation de l'économie. In *La mondialisation financière: Genèse, coût et enjeux,* F. Chesnais, ed. Paris: Syros, Alternatives économiques.

———. 2001. *La Mondialisation armée: Le déséquilibre de la terreur.* Paris: Textuel.

SHAPLEY, Deborah. 1993. *Promise and power: The life and times of Robert McNamara.* Boston: Little, Brown.

SHIVA, Vandana. 1993. *The violence of the Green Revolution.* Malaysia: Third World Network.

———. 1995a. Une autre voix du Sud. In *Banque mondiale/FMI/Organisation Mondiale du Commerce: ça suffit!* (I). Brussels: CADTM.

———. 1995b. Inde: Paysans contre GATT. In *Banque mondiale/FMI/Organisation Mondiale du Commerce: ça suffit!* (I). Brussels: CADTM.

SHIVA, Vandana, et al. 1994. *La Nature sous licence, ou, Le processus d'un pillage.* Geneva: CETIM.

SIMONS, E., B. Verhaegen, and J.C. Willame. 1981. *Endettement, technologies, et industrialisation au Zaïre (1970–1981).* Brussels: CEDAF.

SMITH, ADAM. 1979. *Investigación sobre la naturaleza y causas de la riqueza de las naciones* (An inquiry into the nature and causes of the wealth of nations). Mexico City: Fondo de Cultura Económica.

———. 1983. *An enquiry into the nature and causes of the wealth of nations* (1776). Oxford: Clarendon Press, 2 t.

SMITH, Tony. 1996. La Production flexible: Une utopie capitaliste? *Cahiers d'étude et de recherche* 23. Amsterdam: IIRE.

SOGGE, David. 2002. *Give and take: What's the matter with foreign aid?* New York: Zed Books.

SOROS, George. 1995. *Soros on Soros: Staying ahead of the curve.* New York: John Wiley & Sons.

———. 1998. *The crisis of global capitalism: open society endangered.* New York: PublicAffairs.

STIGLITZ, Joseph E. 2002. *Globalization and its discontents.* New York: W.W. Norton.

SWEEZY, Paul M. 1970. *Teoría del desarrollo capitalista* (1942). Mexico City: Fondo de Cultura Económica.

TAVERNIER, Yves. *Rapport d'information déposé par la Commission des finances, de l'économie générale et du plan, sur les activités et le contrôle du Fonds monétaire international et de la Banque mondiale.* Paris, Assemblée nationale, Commission des finances, de l'économie générale et du plan (Documents d'information de l'Assemblée nationale, No. 2801).

TEMPS MODERNES, LES. 2000. Le Théâtre de la mondialisation: Acteurs, victimes, laissés-pour-compte. Les Temps Modernes 607 (January–February).

THÉRIEN, Jean-Philippe. 1990. *Une voix du Sud: Le discours de la CNUCED.* Paris: L'Harmattan.

TOBIN, James. 1978. A proposal for international monetary reform. *Eastern Economic Journal* 4 (July–October): 153–59.

TOBIN, James, et al. 1995. Two cases for sand in the wheels of international finance. *Economic Journal* 105: 162–72.

TONDEUR, Alain. 1997. *La Crise blanche.* Brussels: Luc Pire and Fondation Léon Lesoil.

TOUSSAINT, Eric. 1983. *Les Multinationales et la crise.* Liège: Fondation André Renard, Ecole de formation de la Fédération Générale du Travail de Belgique.

————. 1994. Mexico City: Le poids des dettes dans les transformations économiques. In *Banque mondiale/FMI/Organisation Mondiale du Commerce: ça suffit!* (I). Brussels: CADTM.

————. 1995. La mondialisation excluante. In *Banque mondiale/FMI/Organisation Mondiale du Commerce: ça suffit!* (I). Brussels: CADTM.

————. 1996a. Le Mexique s'installe dans une crise sociale et politique prolongée. *CADTM* 19. Brussels: CADTM.

————. 1996b. Nouvelles révélations sur les ventes d'armes. *CADTM* 19. Brussels: CADTM.

————. 1996c. Mexique, une crise sociale et politique prolongée. *Inprecor* 405.

————. 1997a. Rwanda: Les créanciers du génocide . *Politique La Revue* (April 1997). Brussels: CADTM; Paris: Syllepse.

————. 1997b. *La décolonisation africaine sous la Vème République* (unpublished).

————. 1997c. *Les médias et la religion du marché. Médias: Le village planétaire* (unpublished).

————. 1999a. Briser la spirale infernale de la dette. *Le Monde diplomatique* (September).

————. 1999b. Enrayer la spirale infernale de la dette. In *ATTAC contre la dictature des marchés.* Paris: Syllepse/La Dispute/Vie Ouvrière.

————. 1999c. *Your money or your life! The tyranny of global finance.* Raghu Krishnan and Vicki Briault Manus, trans. London and Sterling, Va.: Pluto Press.

————. 2000. Du Sud au Nord: Crise de la dette et programmes d'ajustement. In ATTAC, *FMI: Les peuples entrent en résistance.* Brussels: CADTM; Paris: Syllepse; Geneva: CETIM.

————. 2001a. Le faux allégement de la dette. In *Les Autres Voix de la Planète.* Brussels: CADTM.

————. 2001b. Libérer le développement. In ATTAC, *Une économie au service de l'homme.* Paris: Mille et une nuits.

————. 2004. *Globalisation: Reality, resistance and alternatives.* Vicki Briault Manus, trans. Mumbai: Vikas Adhyayan Kendra.

TOUSSAINT, Eric, and Arnaud Zacharie. 2000. *Le bateau ivre de la mondialisation: Escales au sein du village planétaire.* Brussels: CADTM; Paris: Syllepse.

————. 2001. *Afrique: Abolir la dette pour libérer le développement.* Brussels: CADTM; Paris: Syllepse.

————. 2002. *Sortir de l'impasse: Dette et ajustement.* Brussels: CADTM; Paris: Syllepse.

TOUSSAINT, Eric, and Damien Millet. 2003. *The debt scam.* Vicki Briault Manus, trans. Mumbai: Vikas Adhyayan Kendra.

TRAORÉ, Aminata D. 1999. *L'étau: L'Afrique dans un monde sans frontiers.* 1st ed. Arles: Actes sud.

TREILLET, Stéphanie. 2002. *L'Économie du développement.* Paris: Nathan.

UDRY, Charles-André. 1997. Los Origenes del neoliberalismo: F von Hayek; El apostol del neoliberalismo. *Desde los Cuatro Puntos* 1.

UGARTECHE, Oscar. 1997. *El falso dilema.* Caracas: Nueva Sociedad.

UNAIDS, and WHO. 2002. *AIDS epidemic update.* Geneva: UNAIDS/WHO.

UNCTAD (UNITED NATIONS CONFERENCE ON TRADE AND DEVELOPMENT). 1994, 1997a, 1998a, 2000a, 2002. *World investment report.* New York and Geneva: UNCTAD.

————. 1995. *Secretary General's report.* Geneva: UNCTAD.

————. 1996. *Development in a context of globalisation and liberalisation* (Secretary

General's report, 9th session). Geneva: UNCTAD.

———. 1997b. *Approaches to debt sustainability analysis.* Geneva: UNCTAD.

———. 1997c, 1998b,1999, 2000b, 2001. *Trade and development report.* Geneva: UNCTAD.

———. 1997d. *World investment report: Overview.* New York and Geneva: UNCTAD.

———. 2000c. *Capital flows and growth in Africa.* New York and Geneva: UNCTAD.

———. 2000d. *The least developed countries report: Overview.* New York and Geneva: UNCTAD.

UNCTAD, and UNDP. 1997. *Debt sustainability, social and human development, and the experiences of the HIPCS.* Geneva: UNCTAD.

UNDP (UNITED NATIONS DEVELOPMENT PROGRAM). 1990, 1991, 1992, 1993, 1994, 1995, 1996, 1997, 1998, 1999, 2000a, 2001, 2002, 2003. *Global human development report.* New York: UNDP.

———. 2000b. *Overcoming human poverty.* New York: UNDP.

UNEP. 1999. *Global environment outlook 2000* (GEO-2). London: UNEP.

UNEP. 2002. *Global environment outlook 3* (GEO-3). London: UNEP.

UNICEF. 2001. *The state of the world's children.* New York: UNICEF.

URRIOLA, Rafael, ed. 1996. *Economía latinoamerican: La globalización de los desajustes.* Caracas: Nueva Sociedad; Quito: ILDIS.

US BUREAU OF THE CENSUS. 1996. *Poverty in the United States.* Washington DC: Bureau of the Census.

VALIER, Jacques. 1975. *Sur l'impérialisme.* Paris: Maspero.

———. 1996. *Du Nouveau sur les politiques sociales?* (unpublished).

VAN DE LAAR, Aart. 1980. *The World Bank and the poor.* Boston: Martinus Nijhoff.

VERSCHAVE, François-Xavier. 2001. *L'Envers de la dette: Criminalité politique et économique au Congo-Brazza et en Angola.* Marseilles: Editions Agone.

VÍA CAMPESINA. 1998. *Soberanía alimentaria: Un futuro sin hambre.* Guaymuras: Tegucigalpa.

VÍA CAMPESINA. 2002. *Une Alternative paysanne.* Geneva: CETIM.

VIDAL, Gregorio, ed. 2001a. *Mundialización, transnacionalización y subdesarrollo: Segunda conferencia internacional red de estudios sobre el Desarrollo Celso Furtado.* 1st ed. México DF: Universidad Autónoma Metropolitana/Universidad Nacional Autónoma de México/Universidad Autónoma de Zacatecas.

———. 2001b. *Privatizaciones, fusiones y adquisiciones: Las grandes empresas en América latina.* 1st ed. Rubí, Barcelona: Anthropos; México DF: Universidad Autónoma Metropolitana.

VILAS, Carlos. 1987. Le Populisme comme stratégie d'accumulation: L'Amérique latine. *Cahiers d'étude et de recherche* 6. Amsterdam: IIRE.

———. 1989. *Transición desde el subdesarrollo: Revolución y reforma en la periferia.* Caracas: Nueva Sociedad.

———. 1993. *Crisis de la deuda de América latina* (unpublished).

———. 1994. Entre Adam Smith et Thomas Hobbes: Dette, restructuration capitaliste, réforme de l'Etat et classe ouvrière en Amérique latine. *CADTM-GRESEA* 12.

———, ed. 1995. *Estado y politicas sociales despues del ajuste: Debates y alternativas.* Venezuela: Nueva Sociedad; Mexico: Universidad Nacional Autónoma de México.

WALLERSTEIN, Immanuel. 1996. *Le Capitalisme historique* (Historical capitalism)

(1983). Paris: La Découverte, Collection Repères.

WALRAFEN, Thierry, et al. 1994. *Bretton Woods: Mélanges pour un cinquantenaire.* Paris: Association d'économie financière, Le Monde éditions [distributor].

WATKINS, Kevin. 1994. La Banque mondiale et le FMI responsables de la misère africaine. *CADTM-GRESEA* 12.

WENT, Robert. 1996. *Grenzen aan de globalisering?* Amsterdam: Het Spinhuis.

WILLAME, Jean-Claude. 1986. *Zaïre. L'épopée d'Inga: Chronique d'une prédation industrielle.* Paris: L'Harmattan.

WOOD, Angela, and Alex Wilks. 1996. *Recent World Bank assessment of structural adjustment's social impacts.* London.

WOODWARD, David. 1996. *The IMF, the World Bank and economic policy in Rwanda: Economic, social and political implications.* Oxford: OXFAM.

WORLD BANK. 1981, 1982, 1983, 1990, 1991a, 1992a, 1993a, 1994, 1995a, 1996, 1997a, 1998a, 2000a. *World development report.* Washington DC: World Bank.

———. 1991b. El Banco Mundial y el medio ambiente. *Informe sobre la marcha de las actividades, Ejercicio 1991.* Washington DC: World Bank.

———. 1992b. *Governance and development.* Washington DC: World Bank.

———. 1993b. *The East Asian miracle.* New York: Oxford University Press.

———. 1995b. *Advancing social development: A World Bank contribution to the Social Summit.* Washington DC: World Bank.

———. 1997b, 1998b, 1999, 2000b, 2001, 2002a, 2003a. *Global development finance.* Washington DC: World Bank.

———. 1998c. *Global economic prospects and the developing countries 1998/99: Beyond financial crisis.* Washington, DC: World Bank.

———. 2002b, 2003b. *World development indicators,* Washington DC.

WORLD BANK, and International Monetary Fund. 1996a. *Estimated Potential Cost of the HIPC Debt Initiative under Alternative Options.*

———. 1996b. *The HIPC Debt Initiative: Elaboration of Key Features and Proposed Procedures* (unpublished confidential document).

WORLD BANK, and International Monetary Fund. A. Boote, K. Thugge, F. Kilby, and A. Van Trosenburg. 1997. *Debt relief for low-income countries and the HIPC debt initiative.*

ZACHARIE, Arnaud. 2001. Deux ans après le G7 de Cologne, la dette tenace des pays pauvres. *Les Autres Voix de la Planète,* No. 14. Brussels: CADTM.

ZACHARIE, Arnaud, and Olivier Malvoisin. 2003. *FMI: La main visible.* Brussels: Labor.

ZIEGLER, Jean. 1990. *La Suisse lave plus blanc.* Paris: Seuil.

———. 1999. *La Faim dans le monde expliquée à mon fils.* Paris: Seuil.

———. 2002. *Les Nouveaux maîtres du monde et ceux qui leur résistent.* Paris: Fayard.

Index

Page numbers in bold refer to figures and tables.